Lives and Legacies:
An Encyclopedia of People Who Changed the World

Philosophers and Religious Leaders

Edited by Christian D. von Dehsen

Writers

Scott L. Harris

Alexandra Honigsberg

Daniel Jurkovic

Daniel Magurshak

Oliver K. Olson

Rev. G. Thomas Osterfield

Christine Renaud

Philipp Saltz

Matthew Smith

Christian D. von Dehsen

Frederick W. Weidmann

K. Timothy Weidmann

Mimi Yang

ORYX PRESS
1999

The rare Arabian Oryx is believed to have inspired the myth of the unicorn. This desert antelope became virtually extinct in the early 1960s. At that time, several groups of international conservationists arranged to have nine animals sent to the Phoenix Zoo to be the nucleus of a captive breeding herd. Today, the Oryx population is over 1,000, and over 500 have been returned to the Middle East.

© 1999 by The Oryx Press
4041 North Central at Indian School Road, Phoenix, Arizona 85012-3397
http://www.oryxpress.com

Produced by The Moschovitis Group, Inc.
95 Madison Avenue, New York, New York 10016
http://www.MosGroup.com

Executive Editor: Valerie Tomaselli
Design and Layout: Annemarie Redmond
Original Illustrations: TurnStyle Imaging
Editorial Coordinator: Stephanie Schreiber
Editorial Associate: Renée Miller
Copyediting and Proofreading: Carole Campbell, Amy Kaiman,
Kenya McCullum, Joseph Reilly, Paul Scaramazza, Robert Wolfe
Productions Assistant: Yolanda Pluguez
Index: AEIOU, Inc.

Published simultaneously in Canada
Printed and Bound in the United States of America

ISBN 1-57356-152-5

Library of Congress Cataloging-in-Publication Data

Philosophers and religious leaders / edited by Christian D. von Dehsen.
    p. cm. — (Lives and legacies)
    Includes bibliographical references and index.
    ISBN 1-57356-152-5 (alk. paper)
    1. Philosophers—Biography—Encyclopedias. 2. Religious biography—Encyclopedias. I. Von Dehsen, Christian D. II. Series.
B104.P48 1999
109'2—dc21
[B]
                                                                99-045394
                                                                    CIP

∞ The paper used in this publication meets the minimum requirements of American National Standard for Information Science—Permanence of Paper for Printed Library Materials, ANSI Z39.48, 1984.

Table of Contents

Listing of Biographies

'Abduh, Muhammad
Abelard, Peter
Abraham
Afghani, Jamal ad-Din, al-
Akhenaton
Akiba ben Joseph
Anaximander
Anselm of Canterbury, Saint
'Arabi, Ibn al-
Arendt, Hanna
Aristotle
Arjun
Athanasius, Saint
Augustine of Hippo, Saint
Aurobindo Ghose
Averroës
Avicenna
Bacon, Francis
Baha' Allah
Bakunin, Mikhail
Barth, Karl
Benedict of Nursia, Saint
Bentham, Jeremy
Berkeley, George
Bernadette of Lourdes, Saint
Bernard of Clairvaux, Saint
Bihbihani, Aka Sayyid
    Muhammad Bakir
Blavatsky, Helena Petrovna
Boethius, Anicius Manlius
    Severinus
Boff, Leonardo
Bonhoeffer, Dietrich
Buber, Martin
Buddha
Burke, Edmund
Bushnell, Horace
Calvin, John
Camus, Albert
Channing, William Ellery
Columba, Saint
Comte, Auguste
Cone, James Hal
Confucius
Cranmer, Thomas
Cyril of Alexandria, Saint
Dalai Lama
Daly, Mary
David
Derrida, Jacques
Descartes, René

Dewey, John
Diderot, Denis
Du Bois, W. E. B.
Durkheim, Émile
Eddy, Mary Baker
Einhorn, David
Elijah
Emerson, Ralph Waldo
Epictetus
Epicurus
Erasmus, Desiderius
Farabi, al-
Fatimah Bint Muhammad
Fa-tsang
Fichte, Johann Gottlieb
Fortune, Dion
Foucault, Michel
Fox, George
Francis of Assisi, Saint
Gadamer, Hans-Georg
Gandhi, Mohandas Karamchand
Garrison, William Lloyd
Garvey, Marcus
Ghazali, al-
Gladden, Solomon Washington
Gobind Singh
Gregory I, Pope
Gutiérrez, Gustavo
Hallaj, al-
Han-fei-tzu
Hegel, Georg Wilhelm Friedrich
Heidegger, Martin
Herodotus
Heschel, Abraham Joshua
Hildegard von Bingen, Saint
Hillel
Hobbes, Thomas
Hsün-tzu
Hubbard, L. Ron
Hume, David
Hus, Jan
Husserl, Edmund
Ignatius of Loyola, Saint
Israel ben Eliezer
James, William
Jefferson, Thomas
Jeremiah
Jerome, Saint
Jesus
Joan of Arc, Saint
John XXIII, Pope

John Paul II, Pope
Junayd, Abu al-Qasim, al-
Kant, Immanuel
Kaplan, Mordecai Menahem
Keynes, John Maynard
Khaldun, Ibn
Khomeini, Ruhollah
Kierkegaard, Søren Aabye
Kindi, Yaqub ibn Ishaq
    as-Sabah, al-
King, Martin Luther, Jr.
Lao-tzu
Lee, Ann
Locke, John
Luther, Martin
Machiavelli, Niccolò
Madhva
Madison, James
Maharishi Mahesh Yogi
Mahavira
Malcolm X
Mani
Mann, Horace
Marcion
Marcus Aurelius
Marx, Karl
Mary
Matta ibn Yunus
Melanchthon, Philipp
Mencius
Mill, John Stuart
Montaigne, Michel Eyquem de
Montesquieu, Baron de la Brède
    et de
Montessori, Maria
Moon, Sun Myung
More, Sir Thomas, Saint
Moses
Moses ben Maimon
Muhammad
Muhammad, Elijah
Nanak
Niebuhr, Reinhold
Nietzsche, Friedrich Wilhelm
Origen
Palmer, Phoebe Worrall
Parham, Charles Fox
Pascal, Blaise
Patañjali
Patrick, Saint
Paul

Peirce, Charles Sanders
Pestalozzi, Johann Heinrich
Philo Judaeus
Piaget, Jean
Plato
Pythagoras
Rabi'ah al'Adawiyah
Ramakrishna
Ramanuja
Rauschenbusch, Walter
Reid, Thomas
Rousseau, Jean-Jacques
Roy, Ram Mohun
Russell, Bertrand
Russell, Charles Taze
Sa'adia ben Joseph
Sartre, Jean-Paul
Savonarola, Girolamo
Schneerson, Menachem Mendel
Schopenhauer, Arthur
Seton, Elizabeth Ann, Saint
Shafi'i, Abu 'Abd Allah, ash-
Shang Yang
Shankara
Smith, Adam
Smith, Joseph
Socrates of Athens
Spinoza, Benedict de
Stowe, Harriet Beecher
Strong, Josiah
Teresa, Mother
Teresa of Ávila, Saint
Thales of Miletus
Thomas Aquinas, Saint
Thoreau, Henry David
Tillich, Paul
Torquemada, Tomás de
Tutu, Desmond
Urban II, Pope
Vivekananda
Voltaire
Washington, Booker Taliaferro
Wesley, John
White, Ellen Gould
Wise, Isaac Mayer
Wittgenstein, Ludwig
Wovoka
Wycliffe, John
Young, Brigham
Zeno of Citium
Zoroaster

Introduction

This volume provides a synopsis of the lives and legacies of 200 men and women from the areas of religion and philosophy who have "changed the world." These individuals have developed, extended, or exemplified ideas fundamental to the way human beings perceive the meaning and purpose of their own lives and of their societies. Some have challenged prevailing convictions and worked for immediate change during their lifetimes; others have proposed new modes of thinking that have flourished only after their passing.

In the following pages we not only summarize the lives of these people, we also explore each person's enduring impact—their legacy. Each has, in some notable way, contributed to the common understanding of fundamental themes of human existence. Some are best remembered as contributors to a specific discipline, all have had a lasting impact on the way people perceive their world. They have shaped the way we understand our reality and provided methodologies for analyzing it.

It was not easy to decide whom to include in our 200. We have tried to span the breadth of history and civilizations to identify 200 men and women from various cultures and perspectives who influenced the shape of our present world. Obviously, we have left out some individuals of note, but we hope the reader will forgive such omissions. By consulting other volumes in this series, the reader can supplement our list and find such personages as Sigmund Freud (*Scientists, Mathematicians, and Inventors*) and Susan B. Anthony (*Government Leaders, Military Rulers, and Political Activists*). A final note on locating individuals: given the complexity of transliterating some names into English and the need for alphabetizing those names in a larger list for the book, we have tried to identify individuals from non-Western cultures according to the name most likely used when researching that person in other academic resources. We have also provided common alternative names when applicable. When there were serious discrepancies in transliterations and spelling, we used *Merriam-Webster's Biographical Dictionary* as our final authority.

The Quest for Truth

Whenever human beings consider the nature of reality, including what composes it (e.g., matter, spirit, abstract forms) and how it came to be (e.g., divine creation, the mere chance combination of atoms and energy), they frequently turn to philosophers and theologians for insight. Philosophers and theologians have constructed paradigms (patterns of thought) to help find the answers to such questions. In addition, whenever human beings ponder the nature of their own existence, their own meaning and purpose within the larger universe, they often turn to the same thinkers for guidance and inspiration.

One might quickly surmise that philosophers and theologians are useful only in exceptional circumstances, such as those of personal seeking or crisis, or for the sake of academic argument. They would rarely seem relevant to an individual's lifestyle or everyday decisions. In the era of the isolated individual, we live under the illusion that our choices are self-generated and free from external influence. Consequently, many who are highlighted in this book could be viewed as ancient worthies, ivory-tower intellectuals, or religious extremists, whose ideas have seen their day and whose messages are too complicated for or irrelevant to modern life. How can those who lived so long ago offer anything of value to modern circumstances? When we begin to examine the lives and insights of these philosophers and theologians, however, we recognize that they have shaped the way we construct our reality and the way we see ourselves in it. Some ideas that we now take for granted were at one time rejected outright or subordinated to other ideas. By reviewing the lives and thoughts of these individuals, as we do in the following biographies, we may recognize our connections to these ideas and the way these ideas have shaped our own.

Our Inheritance

Some paradigms of our own perspectives are so deeply ingrained that we consider them to be self-evident and beyond dispute. Yet when we pause to consider these perspectives, we quickly come to the recognition that we have not only inherited a set of basic concepts about our world, but that these concepts stand in contrast to others that are similarly claimed by those from different cultures to be self-evident.

For example, the most basic question one can ask is: "What is reality?" Some thinkers, such as Mani and Marcion, contend that the real world is one of spirits and immaterial essences. Our earthly mode of being, they maintain, is only temporary and limited by the exigencies of time, matter, and space. Our bodies, and everything around us, will eventually decay and turn into fodder for other life-forms. A grim picture indeed. Nevertheless, they hold, this world of decay is not the real world, but either a reflection of, or a preliminary stage to, a more glorious, purer world not limited by the constraints of material existence. This nonmaterial world is eternal and free from struggle and erosion. Thus, the real world is not the sensible world, the one people experience with their physiological senses, but a hidden world, glimpsed only through the world of tangible objects.

Others completely reject this concept as a fantasy and as unrealistic. They contend that the only real world is the one we experience day-to-day. Of course, human beings have imagination and insight, and of course humans can think of ideal and utopian situations that transcend the present. (Thomas More wrote *Utopia*, literally "No-Place," as a critique of English society in the sixteenth century!) However, according to this way of thinking, such dreamers actually lose touch with reality; their "heads are in the clouds." It is far better for them to have their "feet on the ground," and engage with the world as it immediately confronts them. Such philosophers as Edmund Husserl and Martin Heidegger became known as phenomenologists because they focused on how human beings interpret the phenomena of this world. More strictly, philosophers of logical positivism, such as Auguste Comte, asserted that all knowledge comes from observation—what cannot be observed cannot be known.

This tension over the way to interpret reality, based on conceptual presuppositions often not consciously articulated, is the contemporary version of a debate originally articulated in fourth-century B.C.E. Greece between Plato and his most prominent pupil, Aristotle.

Plato contended that the real world was the world of immaterial forms. He held that these forms are the essence of things. All physical, material objects are reflections, or shadows, of those forms. Therefore, for example, a person can distinguish chairs from benches, no matter what their shape or color, because chairs reflect the form of "chairness." The essence of the object is not to be found in the material substance, but in the form it reflects. (If the chair were hacked to pieces, the pile of junk would be composed of the same molecules of wood or metal, but it would no longer be recognized as a chair.) Plato's theory of forms promotes a duality of the material and spiritual worlds.

Aristotle became his teacher's staunchest critic. Although he agreed that forms may exist in theory, he held that they do not exist in reality apart from objects within the world. Thus, there is little reason to look for abstract forms; one has to deal with the world as it exists.

Both of these philosophers' legacies are still felt, offering answers to the question: "What is reality?" Both of them have given the world theories that, while contradictory, are still prevalent today. In fact, many people adopt aspects of both perspectives.

Our intention, therefore, is to have the legacies explored throughout the book provoke readers to recognize how ancient debates have influenced present-day life. One can be a Platonist, an Aristotelian, or some combination of both. In any case, the coupling of life with legacy in each biography not only provides historical perspective, but also asks the reader to consider how, and to what extent, those legacies extend into the current time.

To provide a broad spectrum of influential people and ideas, this volume also presents non-Westerners whose ideas have had a significant impact. If the question of reality were posed to Siddhartha Gautama, the Buddha, the answer received would be entirely different from that of a Greek philosopher. The Buddha's enlightenment consisted of the insight that all life was suffering. Such suffering could be overcome only through personal discipline learned over many lifetimes. The goal was to break all attachment with the present world and to blend into the Eternal Absolute so as to lose one's identity entirely in Nirvana. In Nirvana there is no dualism, no "self" as an individual, only a collective whole. (The self joining Nirvana is thought to be like casting a drop of water into the ocean. Once the drop combines with the rest of the water, it is no longer distinguishable as a distinct entity.) Thus, by considering the life and work of Buddha, one becomes exposed to an entirely new, and possibly unsettling, understanding of reality in which the individual ceases to exist. Moreover, insights into the legacy of Buddha provide insights into the understanding of reality held by people in other parts of the world. Therefore, his life *and* legacy are important to consider.

Philosophers and Religious Leaders

The majority of individuals discussed in this book are philosophers or religious thinkers. As we shall see from the example below, both kinds of thinkers address such fundamental questions as "What is the meaning of life?" "What is the purpose of my life in relation to other living beings in creation?" and "Does God exist?" "If so, what effect does God have on the world?" In addition, many people discussed in this volume, such as Avicenna, Averroës, Thomas Aquinas, and Paul Tillich, sought to find connections between faith and reason to address (and answer) such questions.

When we consider, for example, the thought of Anselm and of Jean-Paul Sartre, we would think that they had little in common. Yet both scholars address the question of the existence of God and the importance of God for human beings. Anselm, an eleventh-century Christian theologian, attempted to use philosophical reasoning to construct an ontological proof of the existence of God (one focused on God's being or essence). If one accepts Anselm's proof that God must exist, then it follows that humans are valued as God's creatures, that they hold a special place in creation, and that they are expected to live lives in conformity to God's will. Anselm's argument was addressed by others, both to defend and to refute it. Sartre, in contrast, was a twentieth-century existentialist philosopher who denied the importance of the existence of God and focused exclusively on human existence. If God does not exist, then human life is all there is, he argued. Humans hold no special place in the cosmos; nevertheless, they must live lives responsible to others despite the apparent meaninglessness of existence, often called existential *angst*. Both men address the same questions and leave a legacy to others who advanced their ideas; yet, they are as opposite in perspective as any influential thinkers could be.

This volume, in addition to noting that some thinkers address the same questions from different perspectives, also acknowledges that some individuals draw simultaneously upon philosophical insights and religious teachings, intertwining the insights of faith and reason. Thomas Aquinas, a Christian theologian of the thirteenth century, is remembered for his application of Aristotelian concepts to Christian theology. Like Anselm, he sought to devise a rational proof for the existence of God by drawing, in part, upon Aristotle's conjecture that there must be a first cause, a prime mover for creation. Curiously, Aquinas came into contact with the writings of Aristotle through the commentaries of Avicenna, a tenth-century Islamic philosopher–theologian who, like Aquinas, sought to reconcile some of the tensions between faith and reason. In short, Aquinas himself is part of the legacy of an ancient Greek philosopher and an Islamic religious scholar.

Others combined in their own lives the connections between religious and secular concerns. Some even defy strict categorization. K'ung Ch'iu, commonly known as Confucius, hoped to develop a structure for society that would benefit all. He did so by advocating a social organization along the lines of five fundamental, asymmetrical personal relationships (e.g., husband/wife, older sibling/younger sibling) and by identifying the reciprocal duties and obligations inherent in each relationship. His principles have become the foundation of East Asian culture and function both as religious and societal guidelines for many in such countries as China and Japan. Another individual we profile, Reinhold Niebuhr, a twentieth-century American theologian, became a respected political thinker and an advisor to presidents. He hoped to realize the Christian principles of peace and justice through politically sophisticated engagement with the world. His writings bear the mark of one who addresses the events of his own age—the Great Depression, World War II and Nazism, communism, nuclear warfare—without necessarily providing a systematic theology of his own. Yet he was a theologian, whose grounding was the Christian church in the Midwest and whose pulpit was the pages of his own politically oriented periodical, *The Christian Century*.

There is also Malcolm X. Originally named Malcolm Little, he gave up his slave name and took on "X" to symbolize his unrecoverable African name. As a young man, Malcolm became a Muslim and an influential leader in the Nation of Islam, a black Muslim religious community. Initially, his Islamic beliefs moved him to social action for the sake of promoting the betterment of black people. Ultimately, the universal message of Islam moved him to reject racial separatism and to work for racial equality. Finally, we have Leonardo Boff, a twentieth-century Latin American priest, whose understanding of the Christian gospel compelled him to cast his lot with the poor and oppressed to fight for their spiritual and temporal liberation from the forces of systemic evil. His protests led to conflict not only with political and economic leaders, but also with the hierarchy of the Roman Catholic church, which suspended him from the priesthood for almost a year.

For these people, the insights of their faith and their engagement with the world were seamlessly connected. Their religious and philosophical beliefs complemented one another to provide a basis for social and political action.

Built on the Legacies of Others

From the previous discussion, it should be already clear that these individuals and their ideas cannot easily be viewed in isolation from one another. Not only do the lives and legacies of each individual intertwine, but frequently their legacies shape the lives of those who follow. Thus, the legacy of one person is often an extension of a series of other individuals' legacies.

For example, when examining the life of the Rev. Dr. Martin Luther King, Jr., one sees both how his life has shaped ours, and how his life and work built on those of others. King led an influential movement to assert and to realize the truth of the idea that all people are of equal value under the law. Of course, these ideas had already been established as law by the Civil War Amendments (XIII, XIV, XV) to the Constitution and the decisions of the Supreme Court. Yet some people still suffered from the bias that one race is superior to others. What King lived and, ultimately, died for was the realization of the idea of human equality in American society. Thus, King's life embodied the struggle for an idea central to human society. (It is not coincidental that King was a preacher who motivated people by words and ideas!) Although King's struggles occurred largely in the South in the 1950s and 1960s, they affected the whole fabric of American society. It is not an exaggeration to say that, with the help of King, an idea that was once contrary to the judgment of everyday people has become common and widely accepted.

King himself would admit that he was influenced by those who came before him. Of particular importance to him was Mohandas Gandhi, a Hindu. Although he studied law, Gandhi is best known as a civil rights leader whose nonviolent tactics spearheaded resistance movements for racial justice in South Africa, and later laid the foundation for an independence movement in his native India. Although Gandhi was assassinated in 1948 when King was a teenager, King's later study of Gandhi's efforts led him to adopt the techniques of nonviolence as a method of resistance compatible with his own understanding of Christian social responsibility.

King's inspiration goes back further, however, than the twentieth century. Both he and his father originally bore the name Michael Luther King. When King was a boy, he and his father decided together to change their names to honor the sixteenth-century German church reformer, Martin Luther. A Catholic priest, Luther attacked what he considered abuses of the Roman Catholic church in Germany and was willing to sacrifice his safety for the sake of the Christian gospel. Those who followed Luther eventually broke away from the Roman Catholic church and founded what we now recognize as the churches of Protestantism. Luther's willingness to take on the overwhelming power of the Catholic church inspired King to a similar mission. King fought against entrenched legal tradition and outright bigotry to stand up for the justice required for all people by the Christian gospel. So, across the tides of both time and the Atlantic Ocean, Martin Luther became an inspiration for a young twentieth-century African American in Atlanta, Georgia.

King's personal history, then, exemplifies a major objective of this volume. For him, the idea of racial equality, derived from his own insights into the Christian gospel, inspired by a Hindu leader and a German priest, was one that should rise above any opposition. Indeed, in the last decades of the twentieth century in the United States, few remain who would support the subordination of some people on the basis of race or gender. Thus, King's impact is grounded in the ideas he held as central to human community.

The Clash of Ideas

King also provides an example of another intent of this book. We hope to underscore the premise that ideas are what ground society by giving it an identity and ideas that motivate change. And sometimes the clash of ideas is what alters the character of a society and calls for a new understanding of reality.

Ideas are so central to the way people view and live life that a clash of ideas can often bring about personal and political change. Sometimes, unfortunately, such change is imposed upon a society by force. Other times, ideas take such a hold of people that even military might must give way to the strength of them. Accordingly, we have included people whose lives and thought have had a revolutionary or radical impact on society.

In the last third of the twentieth century, the most significant political change has been the collapse of communism in the Soviet Union and in Eastern Europe. Beginning in 1989, the communist regimes in those countries suffered economic and political collapse, causing thousands to flee. Those who left for Western Europe sought personal political freedom and economic opportunity based on an alternate view of the rights and liberties of the individual vis-à-vis governmental control. In effect, they preferred to live under a view of society contrary to the one dominant in their homeland. They sought to live in states controlled by the governed (democracy) rather than in one managed by a select few, presumably for the benefit of the collective (communism).

Ironically, this "revolution" grew out of several others. Most directly, it overturned the revolutionary conquest of the Bolsheviks under Vladimir Lenin, who appropriated the political philosophy of Karl Marx for the transformation of Czarist Russia into the Soviet Union in 1917. Marx, whose ideas came to light at the end of the nineteenth century, viewed history in terms of class conflict and confronted the European class structure created by the capitalist division of society into the bourgeoisie (owners of land and the means of production) and the proletariat (workers). He contended that the equality of all people required the elimination of private property, allowing all property to be owned communally and to be used for the benefit of the masses. Consequently, the emphasis in communist countries was not on the well-being of the individual, but on how the individual could best contribute to the society as a whole. By 1989, however, this concept of society and economic life had been rejected in many places and capitalism and liberal democracy had won the day.

In addition, the "revolution" of 1989 also relied on the ideas advanced by the American Declaration of Independence (1776) and the French Revolution of 1789. In the Declaration Thomas Jefferson supports the right of the colonists to revolt against the oppressive English throne by asserting the inherent rights of people (life, liberty, the pursuit of happiness) and the rights of the governed to legitimate the government. These ideas were inspired by the writings of John Locke, who lived a century earlier. Locke contended that human beings have natural rights to life, liberty, and property, and that people assign some rights to the government for the sake of peace and the common welfare. Moreover, the assertions of Jefferson and Locke attack the concept of the divine right of kings, the presupposition that God has designated certain "royal" families to rule over the masses. Thus, all of these revolutions, from 1776 through 1989, were grounded in the clash of ideas about who human beings are and how they ought to relate to each other. The victorious ideas shaped the perspectives of those who followed, either to embrace them or to reject them.

Those Who Opened New Doors

Many of the individuals mentioned here have provided entirely new ways to interpret the world. They have been prophetic leaders whose messages provided basic ideas for new religions or completely reformed existing ones. One only has to think of such notable figures as Abraham, Moses, and Baal Shem Tov in Judaism; Jesus, Paul, and John Calvin in Christianity; Muhammad in Islam; or Joseph Smith in Mormonism, to recognize that such people inaugurate a new beginning. Even Marcion's Gnostic attempt to purge Christianity of its evil, material aspects led, in response, to the formation of the canon (list of books) of the Bible. Such individuals have changed the course of human history. Similar affirmations could be made about Confucius and Buddha, whom we have already mentioned. (We have included such ancient figures in the book even though little or no biographical information exists for them outside of that contained in religious sources. Nevertheless, these personages are viewed as being so fundamental to their later religious traditions that—despite the scientifically questionable nature of the biographical material—we have profiled them.)

Others have opened new doors by expanding the parameters of established thought through the application of new insights and methodologies. Often such individuals have provided philosophical grounding for the emergence of entirely new academic disciplines. Herodotus transformed the way history was perceived, from a religious discourse on the events of the gods to a description of human events. Charles Montesquieu conceived of government having limited powers and being restricted by an internal series of checks and balances. Auguste Comte and Émile Durkheim developed the principles of sociology. John Maynard Keynes refocused economic study from attention on the uncontrollable cycles of prosperity and recession to a real-world discipline in which an economy can be managed by attention to the effects of supply and demand. Mary Daly, a radical feminist, devoted her life to unmasking the patriarchal presuppositions she found dominant in the Christian church and in Western culture.

Several of the people discussed are educational philosophers who, in analyzing how individuals relate to the world around them, have developed educational theories that have profoundly altered the way children are taught. John Dewey showed how the teaching of abstract ideas could be connected with instruction to solve practical, everyday problems. Maria Montessori believed that all children learn best by providing them opportunity to progress at their own individual pace. Jean Piaget uncovered new ways of understanding the intellectual development of children and used those insights to rethink the ways curricula are constructed. Each of these people left the world with something new that altered people's lives.

Lives of Exemplary Character

Others in this book are not scholars or thinkers in the strict sense, but their lives have so exemplified principles that they have had a lasting impact on succeeding generations. For example, Mary, the mother of Jesus, was an ordinary woman whom Christians believe God chose to bear God's son. Over time, stories of her faithfulness and devotion to Jesus became an inspiration to later Christians. Devotion to Mary became so important to Roman Catholic teaching that cathedrals, such as Chartres and Notre Dame, were dedicated to her. There is even a movement at present to have the Pope issue an infallible teaching to declare Mary co-redemptrix with Christ. Joan of Arc suffered a cruel death rather than recant her faith. Similarly, Elizabeth Ann Seton and

Mother Teresa of Calcutta have become models of faithfulness and selfless service to others. Their legacies consist not in a body of teaching or writing, but in a model of life for others to emulate.

One can also look to such people as Ramakrishna and his disciple, Vivekanada, whose devotion to the Divine Mother and whose mastery of spiritual meditative techniques both revitalized Hinduism in India and introduced Hinduism to the West through its presentation at the 1898 Chicago Conference of World Religions. Bishop Desmond Tutu has become the central religious figure in the struggle against apartheid in South Africa. His commitment to justice based on his understanding of the Christian faith led him to action that brought social and political liberty to the victims of racial oppression.

The Structure of the Entries

The above discussion has shown that the people chosen for this volume have led lives and have left legacies that have changed the way we look at, think about, and act in the world around us. Because of their enduring significance, we have arranged each entry to enable the reader quickly to appreciate the import of each individual.

Each entry contains four major components. In the section labeled "Life and Work," the reader will find material about the person's life, including biographical information, significant accomplishments, and literary output. The following section, "Legacy," contains a synopsis of the enduring impact of the person in succeeding generations. This section points most directly to the ways each subject changed the world. Next, we supply a timeline of the significant events of that person's life and, simultaneously, place those events within the context of the larger world. Finally, we include a brief bibliography of recent works available in English about that person. These references are intended both to supplement the material presented here and to offer a gateway into the larger scholarly discussion of this person. Many entries are then graced with a sketch of the individual based on a photograph or painting.

We hope that this volume will help introduce the people we have selected, describe their significance to our contemporary world, and motivate its readers to continue to pursue interests in those we present.

Christian D. von Dehsen

The
Biographies

'Abduh, Muhammad

Architect of Islamic Modernism
1849–1905

Life and Work

Muhammad 'Abduh was an Egyptian jurist known as the founder of Islamic modernism.

The son of a well-to-do family, 'Abduh was born in 1849 somewhere in the Nile Delta of Egypt. He studied logic, philosophy, and mysticism at the al-Azhar University in Cairo, receiving the degree of 'alim (scholar) in 1877.

While in Cairo, 'Abduh came under the influence of the Pan-Islamic reformer JAMAL AD-DIN AL-AFGHANI, who inspired 'Abduh's interest in politics. In 1880 'Abduh became the editor of the government's official journal, using it as a platform to denounce Anglo-French rule and call for religious and social reform. For his participation in the 'Urabi Pasha'a revolt of 1881–1882, he was exiled for six years. 'Abduh spent several years in Lebanon, helping establish an Islamic educational system, and, in 1884, he joined al-Afghani in Paris to edit *The Firmest Bond*, a revolutionary journal that promoted anti-British views. By 1888, 'Abduh had returned to Egypt, where he embarked on a legal career. In 1889, he was appointed a judge in the National Courts of First Instance and, in 1891, to the Court of Appeals. He was appointed to the exalted post of *mufti* (Islamic legal counselor) of Egypt in 1899.

'Abduh used his various positions to work for the modernization of Islam to meet contemporary challenges. Instead of relying on a literal and wooden interpretation of the Koran and on the repetition of ancient rituals, he sought the harmony of reason and faith as determined by individuals. He believed that reason and revelation are not opposites, and that individuals can exercise reason through free will to distinguish the essential teachings of Islam from the unessential. The ability to make such distinctions would allow Islam to retain its vibrancy as a meaningful religion in the twentieth century while, at the same time, show how the faith could be compatible with new scientific ideas.

Similarly, 'Abduh believed that such a modernizing approach to Islam would foster social reform, for example, opening schools for the poor, by allowing laws to address changing social circumstances. Most especially, 'Abduh acknowledged cultural changes in social relationships, advocating equality even when this endorsement contradicted the teachings of the Koran. His most important writings were *The Theology of Unity* and various commentaries on the Koran.

'Abduh died just outside of Alexandria, Egypt, on July 11, 1905.

Legacy

'Abduh's thrust toward reforming Islam to make it compatible with the modern world marked a split that shaped the development of Islam in the twentieth century.

In Egypt, modernization affected the political and social arena, taking the form of revitalizing the army and strengthening the government. In 1923, Egypt adopted a constitution asserting the sovereignty of the people rather than that of Allah. In 1925, the educational system was reformed. In the 1920s and 1930s the Muslim Brethren, an Islamic militant opposition group led by Hasan al-Banna (1906–1949), gained momentum. Over the next decades, Egypt remained a deeply divided country, never fully accepting the culture of Western secularism. For example, Anwar Sadat's (Egyptian leader, 1970–1981) attempts to balance concessions to Islamic groups with efforts to construct a peace treaty with Israel in 1978 and 1979 were rejected by extremist Muslim groups and led to Sadat's assassination in 1981.

Turkey became another arena for the struggle of Islamic modernists and fundamentalists. After the Allies recognized Turkey as a nation

in 1923, Mustafa Kemal (1881–1938) attempted to complete the secularization of his country. Over the next few years Kemal replaced the Islamic governing offices with secular ones and exiled the ruler of the house of Osman to Paris. The Swiss legal code replaced the *Shariah* (Islamic law) and people were encouraged to adopt European styles of dress.

Perhaps the most dramatic clash came in Iran, in response to the vigorous westernizing program of Riza Shah Palhavi (1878–1942) and his son, Mohammad Riza Shah (1919–1980). In 1923, Riza Shah began a program of radical reform that was seen as a threat by Islamic conservatives. Continued by his son, these reforms generated heated opposition. By the early 1960s there was direct opposition by *ulama* (Islamic religious scholars) such as RUHOLLAH KHOMEINI (c. 1900–1989), who was exiled to Paris in 1963. Even the efforts of such respected scholars, as Dr. Ali Sharati (1933–1977) were thwarted. Like 'Abduh, he tried to modernize Islam. However, he died mysteriously in 1977. By the end of 1978, religious forces gained power and overthrew the shah, creating a government headed by Khomeini, who quickly reversed all Westernization and reinstituted the *Shariah* as the dominant legal code.

At the end of the twentieth century, it is hard to evaluate the effect of 'Abduh's work. While early in the century there seemed to be much dedication to modernization efforts and attraction to Western culture, the end of the century brought religious resurgence in such countries as Egypt, Iran, Iraq, and Libya.

von Dehsen

World Events		'Abduh's Life
	1849	Muhammad 'Abduh is born
United States Civil War	1861–65	
Germany is united	1871	
	1877	'Abduh graduates from al-Azhar University
	1881–82	'Abduh participates in 'Urabi Pasha'a revolt
	1891	'Abduh is named judge of Court of Appeals
Spanish American War	1898	
	1899	'Abduh becomes *mufti* of Egypt
	1905	'Abduh dies
World War I	1914–18	

For Further Reading:
Badawi, M. A. Zaki. *The Reformers of Egypt*. London: Croom Helm, 1978.
Rahnema, Ali, ed. *Pioneers of Islamic Revival*. Atlantic Highlands, N.J.: Zed Books, 1994.

Abelard, Peter

Theologian and Philosopher;
Proponent of the Modern University
1079–1142

Life and Work

One of the most celebrated figures of the twelfth century, Peter Abelard was a distinguished teacher, philosopher, and theologian who played an important role in the development of the university and in establishing a new intellectual climate in Europe.

The son of a knight, Abelard was born at Le Pallet, near Nantes, in the northern part of present-day France. As the eldest son he was to inherit his father's lands, but he gave up his inheritance to become a scholar. He studied philosophy and theology with several of the most influential scholars of the day, including Anselm of Laon (1113–1117), and then opened his own schools of philosophy first in Melun and then in Corbeil, both in present-day France. From 1117 to 1121 he taught philosophy in Paris.

Early in his career, Abelard became involved in the medieval dispute over whether universals (e.g., courage or kindness) were actual entities or just names. Taking a position between the two extremes, Abelard taught that a universal has no independent existence outside the mind. It is a word that expresses the combined image of that word's common associations within the mind. Universals exist in the mind of God.

In 1115 Abelard was appointed to the prestigious post of lecturer at the cathedral school of Notre Dame in Paris. There he gained a reputation as a brilliant scholar whose lectures attracted vast audiences. Around 1118 he became tutor of Héloise, niece of Fulbert, a canon of the cathedral, and fell in love with her. After the couple had a child, he married her secretly, and then convinced her to enter a convent. Fulbert, thinking Abelard had abandoned her, had him castrated. Abelard later recorded these events in *The Story of My Misfortune*.

Disgraced, Abelard took monastic vows at the Abbey of St. Denis, where he produced his first work, *On the Unity and Trinity of God*, which attempted to explain the Trinity (God as Father, Son, and Holy Spirit) by logic and reason. The book created an uproar and was condemned as heretical and burned at the Council of Soissons in 1121.

Despite the condemnation, Abelard still attracted thousands of students from all over Europe. In his teachings, Abelard emphasized the role of reason in reaffirming authority. His method of logic was a bold attempt to combine faith and free scholarship. He argued that the Christian faith be limited by "rational principles." Reason and faith, he maintained, cannot contradict each other; both come from the same divine source. Dogma, therefore, is subordinate to reason. In *Sic et Non* (*Yes and No*, c. 1140), the work for which he is best known, he contrasted Bible passages and statements of Church fathers that seemed to disagree, leaving judgment to the reader. "By doubting," he wrote, "we come to questioning, and by questioning we learn truth."

In 1125 Abelard became abbot of St. Gildas in Brittany but later resumed his teaching in Paris. Alarmed by the influence of Abelard's teaching, BERNARD OF CLAIRVAUX, a theologian who advocated a mystical approach to reaching God and the renunciation of all intellectual pretension, secured his condemnation for a second time by the Council of Sens, 1140.

Abelard died on April 21, 1142 at the priory at Chalon-sur Saone. According to commonly

understood tradition, he is buried with Héloise in the cemetery of Père Lachaise in Paris.

Legacy

Abelard's legacy lies not only in his works but also in the example of his life, both of which became models of intellectual rigor throughout Europe.

In an era that emphasized the importance of traditional authority, Abelard stressed inquiry and doubt. As a scholar and teacher he was not content merely to transmit received authoritative opinion as was the prevailing monastic tradition; instead he emphasized the importance of evidence in determining truth. Rather than hide his gifts, Abelard reveled in his intellectual achievements and continued to pursue his ideas despite disgrace and condemnation.

Abelard had a profound influence on his pupils, including philosopher and humanist John of Salisbury and Roland Bandinelli, who would become Pope Alexander III. Abelard's brilliant teaching created the reputation of Paris as an intellectual center, and he is given credit for being the true founder of the University of Paris, one of the first universities to establish a fixed course of study and to grant academic degrees. Because of his work on the nature of "universals," he set the course of medieval philosophy for two centuries, influencing THOMAS AQUINAS to explore ways to use philosophical insights for theology.

After his death, Abelard was known chiefly for his love of Héloise, which became a celebrated theme in European literature, inspiring Petrarch, Alexander Pope, and JEAN-JACQUES ROUSSEAU.

Olson

WORLD EVENTS		ABELARD'S LIFE
Schism between Roman Catholic and Orthodox Church	1054	
	1079	Peter Abelard is born
First Crusade	1095	
Settling of Timbuktu, present-day Mali	c 1100	
	1113–17	Abelard studies theology under Anselm of Laon
	1117–21	Abelard teaches philosophy in Paris
	c. 1118	Abelard tutors and falls in love with Héloise
	1121	Abelard is convicted of heresy for *On the Unity and Trinity of God* at Council of Soissons
	1140	Abelard is condemned second time by Council of Sens
	1142	Abelard dies
Islamic ruler of Egypt, Saladin, captures Jerusalem	1187	

For Further Reading:

Clanchy, M. T. *Abelard, A Medieval Life*. Oxford: Blackwell, 1997.

Gilson, Etienne. *Héloise and Abelard*. Ann Arbor: University of Michigan Press, 1960.

Waddell, Helen. *Peter Abelard, a Novel*. New York: Barnes & Noble, 1971.

Abraham

First Biblical Patriarch

c. 2000–1500 B.C.E.

Life and Work

First in the line of ancient biblical patriarchs, Abraham is considered to be the ancestor of both the Hebrew and Arab peoples. He is revered by Christians, Muslims, and Jews as a model of unswerving faith. Most important, the covenant (pact) that to this day still binds Jews to Yahweh was first made with Abraham.

What is known of Abraham is found only in the Old Testament. Originally called Abram, he was born in Ur of the Chaldeans. He later married his half-sister Sarai. Led by a call from the Hebrew god Yahweh, the 75-year-old Abram and his family wandered from Ur to Canaan (modern Israel–Palestine), where he lived as a nomad. During this period the childless Abram received God's covenant that he would become the father of a great nation and that he and his descendants would be given the land of Canaan forever. Yahweh renewed this covenant several times during Abram's life. It was during one of these renewals that the rite of circumcision was established and Abram's name was changed to Abraham and Sarai's to Sarah.

Abraham was 86 when his first son, Ishmael, was born. Ishmael, whose mother was an Egyptian slave, came to be considered the father of the Arab people. When Abraham was 100, he became the father, by Sarah, of Isaac. Jews view Isaac as their ancestor and heir to Yahweh's promise. In a dramatic test of faith, Yahweh later demanded that Abraham sacrifice Isaac. When Abraham prepared to carry out the command without question, God spared Isaac and renewed his covenant.

The Bible records that Abraham died at the age of 175 and was buried beside Sarah in a cave at a place called Machpelah, near what is now Hebron, south of Jerusalem.

Legacy

Abraham's call is central to not only Judaism but also to Christianity and Islam.

The two components of the covenant with Abraham are 1) he would have a multitude of descendants, and 2) his descendants will occupy the land God gave him. These components provide for Jews a self-understanding as God's chosen people to whom God has given the land, Israel. Christians view themselves as those for whom faith in Christ fulfills God's promise to Abraham. Muslims look to Abraham as the spiritual founder of their faith and the faith of their traditional ancestor Ishmael.

Tensions remain to this day between Jews, who trace their lineage through Isaac, and Muslims, who trace their lineage through Ishmael. Moreover, the land promised to Abraham's descendants continues to be fought over by Jews, Muslims, and—to a lesser extent—Christians. Each of these groups considers the land of Israel–Palestine to be their Holy Land. Despite the trials and tribulations of Abraham's life—and how these same tribulations continue to be played out in the present day—he is revered as "Father Abraham," honored by Jews, Christians, and Muslims for his faithfulness to God and the covenant God made with him.

Harris

WORLD EVENTS	ABRAHAM'S LIFE*
	B.C.E.
Pyramids at Giza c. 2500 are built	
	c. 2000 Call of Abraham –1500 and journey to the land of Canaan
	Famine in Canaan and journey to Egypt
	Covenant with Abraham
	Birth of Ishmael
	Birth of Isaac
	Forestalled sacrifice of Isaac
	Death of Abraham
Moses leads Exodus c. 1250 out of Egypt	

* Scholars cannot date the specific events in Abraham's life with accuracy. This chronology is based on the biblical account.

For Further Reading:

Abramovitch, Henry Hanoch. *The First Father: Abraham: The Psychology and Culture of a Spiritual Revolutionary.* Laham, Md.: University Press of America, 1994.

Boice, James Montgomery. *Ordinary Men Called by God: A Study of Abraham, Moses, and David.* Grand Rapids, Mich.: Kregel, 1998.

von Rad, Gerhard. *Genesis: A Commentary.* Philadelphia: Westminster Press, 1976.

Afghani, Jamal ad-Din, al-

Influential Twentieth-Century
Pan-Islamist

c. 1838–1897

Life and Work

Jamal ad-Din al-Asadabadi, better known as al-Afghani, was a political activist and thinker whose support of Pan-Islamism (unification of all Muslims against Western European influences) made him one of the most influential Muslim thinkers in the twentieth century.

Little is known about al-Afghani's early life. Despite his claim to have been born in Afghanistan (hence the name *al-Afghani*), the evidence suggests that he was born in about 1838 to a Shiite family in Iran. As a student he showed great interest in the writings of AVICENNA (980–1037), an Islamic philosopher who attempted to correlate reason and faith.

In the mid-1850s, al-Afghani traveled to India, where he probably witnessed the Indian Mutiny of 1857. It was here that he developed his life-long hatred of the British imperialist rule. For the rest of his life he moved around countries in South Asia, the Middle East, and Europe. Wherever he went he gathered disciples, gave speeches, and wrote articles denouncing European, particularly British, imperialism and urging a revival of Islamic nationalism and pan-nationalism. He was expelled from Afghanistan,

the Ottoman Empire, and Egypt for his religious and political views.

After his expulsion from Egypt in 1879, he returned to India where he published *The Refutation of the Materialists,* which denounced supporters of British rule in the subcontinent. Around 1881 he settled briefly in Paris. There he and his disciple MUHAMMAD 'ABDUH (1849–1905) established the periodical, *The Strongest Link* (i.e., the Koran). Although published for only about a year, it was disseminated free throughout the Muslim world and had a tremendous influence in promoting Pan-Islamic ideas.

Al-Afghani was deeply disturbed at seeing Muslims subjected by foreign powers and sought to promote independence from European political and cultural domination through a new understanding of and obedience to Islam. Influenced by Avicenna as well as Western thinkers, he believed that the Koran, reinterpreted as human knowledge increases, was the embodiment of truth. Rightly understood, it teaches Muslims to act virtuously and in a spirit of solidarity that would enable them to liberate themselves from European control. In order to maintain independence, he urged Muslim states to promote programs of reform and education. Although he stressed independence, his agenda did not include popular rule; he believed that the Muslim masses were incapable of self-government.

Al-Afghani died of cancer in Istanbul in 1897.

Legacy

Al-Afghani ushered in a renaissance in Islamic political philosophy and gave life to the Pan-Islamic movement of the late nineteenth and twentieth centuries.

Al-Afghani and his disciples reinvigorated Islamic political thought, which had languished since the death of AVERROËS just before the beginning of the thirteenth century. Although his chief disciple, Muhammad 'Abduh, renounced al-Afghani's activism, he continued to urge the modernization of Islam to maintain its vibrancy as a meaningful religion and to meet contemporary political challenges. Other thinkers emphasized personal rather than political change to fight the destructive ills of Western society. Hasan al-Banna (1906–1949) urged his followers to fully embrace their faith

and become self-reliant. Abu al A'la al-Mawdudi (1903–1980) attempted to show how Islam could be applied to the problems of modern daily life and viewed Islam rather than nationalism as the best way to overcome Western domination. Even those thinkers stressing spiritual renewal promoted a Muslim political regime.

The Pan-Islamic movement that al-Afghani championed continued in the years after his death. Pan-Islamism became state policy under Ottoman Sultan Abdülhamid II (r. 1876–1909), who utilized it to offset the Ottoman Empire's growing weakness and forestall European incursion. He proclaimed himself the temporal and spiritual leader to whom all Muslims owed allegiance. During World War I the Ottomans, allied with the Germans, tried to use Pan-Islamic themes in an unsuccessful attempt to encourage Muslims among the Allies to revolt.

Pan-Islamic ideas largely disappeared following World War I. In the 1920s and 1930s proponents found themselves competing with other ideologies—communism, secularism, nationalism—and the growing Pan-Arab movement. After World War II support for Pan-Islamic themes resurfaced. Newly independent states such as Saudi Arabia endorsed Muslim solidarity. In 1962 the Muslim World League was founded; in 1969 the Organization of the Islamic Conference, an association of Muslim governments, was established. Even attempts by Saddam Hussein in Iraq (1990–1991) and Muammar al-Qaddafi (1992) to gather Muslims to repel foreign aggression reflected the Pan-Islamic themes promoted a century earlier by al-Afghani.

von Dehsen

WORLD EVENTS	AL-AFGHANI'S LIFE
Greek War of 1821–29 Independence against Turkey	
	c. 1838 Jamal ad-Din al-Afghani is born
Revolutions in 1848 Austria, France, Germany, and Italy	
United States 1861–65 Civil War	
Germany is united 1871	
	1871–79 Al-Afghani is expelled from Egypt and goes to India
	1881 Al-Afghani publishes *The Strongest Link*
	1897 Al-Afghani dies
Spanish American 1898 War	

For Further Reading:

Moazzam, Anwar. *Jamal al-Din al Afghani, A Muslim Intellectual.* New Delhi: Concepts, 1983.

Rejwan, Nissim. *Arabs Face the Modern World: Religious, Cultural, and Political Responses to the West.* Gainesville: University of Florida Press, 1998.

Akhenaton

(Amenhotep IV)

Egyptian Pharaoh;
Advocate of Monolatry
Reigned c. 1367–1350 B.C.E.

Life and Work

Akhenaton was an Egyptian pharaoh who established a state religion based on the worship of one god.

Born to Amenhotep III and Queen Tiy (a commoner), Amenhotep IV (as he was known before he changed his name) married his cousin Nefertiti. His reign began during the peak of Egypt's power. At the time of his elevation, Egyptian religion was dominated by the cult of the sun god Amun-Re, whose priesthood was rich and politically powerful.

In the second year of his rule, Amenhotep replaced Amun-Re as the chief god in favor of Aten, a pre-existing god in the pantheon. Amenhotep hastily built a temple to Aten at Karnak, the most important site of Amun-Re. Two years later, he suspended worship of Amun-Re and had the god's name eradicated. He moved the capital, Thebes, to a new site in central Egypt that he named Akhetaton (Horizon of the Sun Disc). Today the site is known as Tell el-Amarna. At Amarna he built a completely new city around his palace and temple to Aten. He also changed his name to Akhenaton to reflect his allegiance to Aten.

While Akhenaton was not a monotheist, he did promote the worship of one god to the exclusion of others, a practice called "monolatry." He chose to worship the visible aspect of the sun, the sun disk, which he considered a universal, omnipresent spirit and only creator of the world. In fact, both Aten and Akhenaton were considered to be divine, and he served as the essential intercessor to Aten; Akhenaton and Nefertiti worshipped only Aten, but the people prayed to the pharaoh and his wife as well as to Aten. Akhenaton's

motives for the worship of Aten are unclear. He may have wanted to curb the growing political power of the elite Amun priesthood and/or to establish the pharaoh's independent authority and/or to reinforce theocratic absolutism.

Scholars refer to Akhenaton's reign as the "Amarna Revolution." The new religion liberated artists from traditions supported by Amun's priests, and they turned from ritualistic to natural forms. It also generated greater freedom in contemporary literature.

Upon Akhenaton's death in 1350 B.C.E., his movement was repudiated, his name and image removed from all public monuments, and the Amarna Revolution abandoned. His successors moved the capital back to Memphis and reasserted the power of the Amun priesthood.

Legacy

Akhenaton was the first person in history to establish a religion based on the worship of one god.

His elevation of Aten to the status of sole god foreshadowed the concept of monotheism. In ancient Egypt, gods traditionally were thought to have human characteristics and were closely associated with particular geographical areas or aspects of life. Akhenaton divorced Aten from anthropological associations and viewed him chiefly as a creative force. Aten was a universal, omnipotent spirit and the sole creator of the world. Akhenaton's "Hymn to Aten" has survived and shares many ideas found in Psalm 104. In the hymn, Aten is the creator of all. Akhenaton gives thanks to Aten for the benefits of life, which the god gives not only to Egypt but to all nations. Psalm 104, too, is a hymn to God, the creator, who richly gives blessings to the world.

The cult of Aten was never popular, and after the pharaoh's death, Akhenaton was considered a heretic. Nevertheless, he remains an important figure in ancient history. His monolatry was an early element in the long evolutionary process that led to the ethical monotheism of the Hebrew prophets.

Renaud

WORLD EVENTS	AKHENATON'S LIFE*
B.C.E.	
Pyramids at Giza c. 2500 are built	
	c. 1367 Amenhotep IV becomes king of Egypt
	Amenhotep begins to build new capital
	Amenhotep changes name to Akhenaton
	c. 1350 Akhenaton dies
Moses leads Exodus c. 1250 out of Egypt	

* Scholars cannot date the specific events in Akhenaton's life with accuracy.

For Further Reading:

Grimal, Nicholas. *A History of Ancient Egypt.* Oxford: Blackwell, 1992.

Knapp, A. Bernard. *The History and Culture of Ancient Western Asia and Egypt.* Belmont, Calif.: Wadsworth Publishing, 1988.

Akiba ben Joseph

Early Interpreter of Jewish Law
c. 40–c. 135

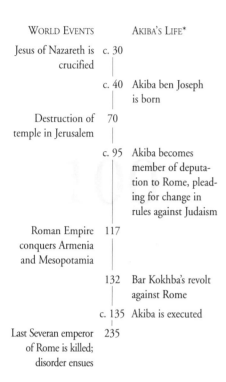

WORLD EVENTS		AKIBA'S LIFE*
Jesus of Nazareth is crucified	c. 30	
	c. 40	Akiba ben Joseph is born
Destruction of temple in Jerusalem	70	
	c. 95	Akiba becomes member of deputation to Rome, pleading for change in rules against Judaism
Roman Empire conquers Armenia and Mesopotamia	117	
	132	Bar Kokhba's revolt against Rome
	c. 135	Akiba is executed
Last Severan emperor of Rome is killed; disorder ensues	235	

* *Scholars cannot date the specific events in Akiba's life with accuracy.*

Life and Work

Akiba ben Joseph was a rabbi whose organization of Jewish oral law and methods of interpreting the Torah (Jewish law) had a profound impact on Jewish history.

Little is known of Akiba's life. He was born in southwestern Judah, near the Dead Sea, to a poor family and remained uneducated until his wife convinced him to devote his life to the study of the Torah. Tradition has it that he began his studies with his son at the age of 40. He later studied with the leading scholars of his day and eventually formed his own academy.

Akiba developed his own method of biblical interpretation (exegesis) that stressed the importance not only of every word but even the shapes of the letters in the Torah. His method was based on his belief that the Torah emanated from God and that every element in it had a definite purpose. He also collected the entire oral law and organized it by subject.

By c. 95–96 Akiba had become known as the greatest scholar of the age and was one of the leaders of the Jewish community. While he never held an official position, he was sent on deputations to Roman authorities to plead for relief from oppressive legislation and to Babylon to determine the correct dates for the Jewish calendar. Because of his concern for the downtrodden, he became overseer of the poor, making numerous journeys to collect funds for them.

According to tradition, Akiba supported the anti-Roman uprising of Bar Kokhba in 132. Akiba publicly recognized him as the promised Messiah, applying to him the biblical name "Bar Kokhba." Bar Kokhba's unsuccessful rebellion was the last military uprising of Jews in ancient times in the Holy Land.

The Romans eventually executed Akiba (c. 135) as a rebel for ignoring the prohibition against studying the Jewish law. As he died, he recited the prayer, the Shema, "Hear O Israel; the Lord our God, the Lord is one." Thus was set precedent for generations of Jews to die with the oneness of God on their lips.

Legacy

Akiba's methods of analyzing scripture and his scholarship influenced every aspect of rabbinic Judaism. His work enabled Judaism to move from a focus on worship at the temple in Jerusalem (which the Romans had destroyed in 70) to an emphasis on the study of Torah.

Akiba had a significant impact on the interpretation and the scope of scripture. His exegetical method, in which every aspect of the text had meaning, established a major trend in biblical commentary, which was carried on by the many who flocked to study under him. Although we do not know the precise steps by which the Jewish community recognized specific writings to be part of scripture, evidence indicates that Akiba's allegorical method of interpretation may have been used to justify the inclusion of both Esther and Song of Songs in the Hebrew scriptures; the scriptural authority of both was in dispute.

Akiba's organization of the oral legal traditions eventually resulted in the development of the Mishnah of Judah the Patriarch around the year 200. In rabbinic Judaism, the Mishnah is seen as having the same legal authority as the Torah itself.

Finally, Akiba's death has served as example for generations of faithful Jews. His faithfulness to the Torah in the face of oppression has strengthened many who have also been called to martyrdom for the Jewish faith. The story of Akiba's dying with the oneness of God upon his lips (recounted in the liturgy for Yom Kippur) also set the example for ordinary Jews to end their lives in the praise of God through the Shema.

Osterfield

For Further Reading:
Finkelstein, Louis. *Akiba: Scholar, Saint and Martyr.* Philadelphia: Jewish Publication Society of America, 1936, 1962.
Nadich, Judah. *Rabbi Akiba and His Contemporaries.* Northvale, N.J.: Jason Aronson, 1997.

Anaximander

Philosopher–Scientist; Early
Developer of Cosmological Theory
c. 611–c. 547 B.C.E.

Life and Work

Anaximander is the first known philosopher to produce a theory of the origin of the universe, commonly known as cosmology.

Although little is known of Anaximander's early years, he was from Miletus on the western coast of Asia Minor (present-day Turkey), the birthplace of Greek natural philosophy. Anaximander was either an associate or disciple of THALES OF MILETUS (died c. 546 B.C.E.), the acknowledged founder of Greek philosophy and the first to propose that creation was not accomplished by the gods.

Anaximander wrote the first prose philosophical work, a treatise called *On the Nature of Things,* where he proposed the first systematic philosophical understanding of the world and the origins of human life. He was also the first to make a map of the inhabited world.

Although only one line of his work survives, the major tenets of Anaximander's world view survive in later texts. For Anaximander the origin of things is in the aperion, the boundless or infinite. The *aperion* surrounds the world and steers or governs the functioning of the world. In the state of the boundless (that which cannot be perceived), all elements of the universe were unified. This state preceded the process of separation, in which the opposites are separated out to generate hot and cold, dry and wet. These processes are biological and cyclical, as well as mechanical.

Anaximander believed that the Earth began with a series of separations from the *aperion.* Ultimately, the Earth became the center of a series of increasingly larger concentric rings made of fire, separated by air. The air had holes, allowing the fire to pass through to create the Sun, Moon, and stars. In addition, there was a cycle of hot and cold, wet and dry, producing the seasons. To complete the cycle of the universe, the cosmos would one day perish into the source from which it arose, the deathless *aperion.*

According to Anaximander, the first human beings were generated from a sort of embryo floating in the sea, an early version of the theory that all life began in the oceans.

Anaximander is thought to have died in Asia Minor in about 547 B.C.E.

Legacy

Anaximander's writings set the tone for future scientific theories of the universe, and he was the first to consider the heavenly bodies not as gods but as circles of fire. So revolutionary are his ideas that they seem modern. He also made Greek prose a suitable language for philosophy. Earlier literature was poetic, consisting largely of mythological tales about the activities of the gods.

Although Anaximander came from the same "school" of Ionian philosophers as Thales, scholars called the Pre-Socratrics (before SOCRATES), he differed markedly from his teachers and contemporaries in that he did not attribute the composition of the world to one element or elements. Thales, for instance, thought that all things are composed of water.

Unlike his predecessors, Anaximander produced a systematic explanation for the cosmos. His theory is remarkable for its speculative nature and for its reliance on rational principles and natural processes for an explanation of the world. In fact, his ideas are the first recorded mechanical model of the universe, and, therefore, his approach to understanding the universe dominated all following physical theories of the universe.

Those Greek scholars who followed Anaximander vigorously debated the nature of the *aperion.* Anaximenes (c. 545 B.C.E.) considered the air boundless, while Xenophanes (c. 570–c. 475 B.C.E.) applied this concept to the flat expanse of the Earth. Parmenides (c. 425 B.C.E.) refuted the concept, asserting that the universe must have fixed boundaries. Others who supported Anaximander's ideas were Melissus (c. 450 B.C.E.), and Anaxagoras (c. 500–428 B.C.E.). ARISTOTLE (384–322 B.C.E.) equated the *aperion* with infinity. Because all matter could be divided infinitely, matter must be boundless.

Anaximander's theories are based on his "scientific" understanding of the world and do not derive from religious beliefs. Consequently, his work prefigured the modern scientific approach later developed by such notable cosmologists as Nicolaus Copernicus (1473–1543), Galileo Galilei (1564–1642), and the evolutionist Charles Darwin (1809–1882). All of these later scientists had to defend their theories against the pressure of religious traditions.

Clearly, Anaximander provides an early example of a philosopher–scientist who developed theories based on empirical evidence and provided theories that laid the foundation for much subsequent scientific analysis.

Renaud

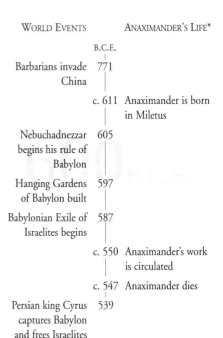

World Events	Anaximander's Life*
	B.C.E.
Barbarians invade China	771
	c. 611 Anaximander is born in Miletus
Nebuchadnezzar begins his rule of Babylon	605
Hanging Gardens of Babylon built	597
Babylonian Exile of Israelites begins	587
	c. 550 Anaximander's work is circulated
	c. 547 Anaximander dies
Persian king Cyrus captures Babylon and frees Israelites	539

For Further Reading:

Curd, Patricia, ed. *A Pre-Socrates Reader.* Indianapolis, Ind.: Hackett Publishing Co., 1996.

McKirahan, Richard D. *Philosophy Before Socrates.* Indianapolis, Ind.: Hackett Publishing Co., 1994.

* Scholars cannot date the specific events in Anaximander's life with accuracy.

Anselm of Canterbury, Saint

Archbishop of Canterbury;
Father of Scholasticism
c. 1033–1109

Life and Work

One of the most important theologians of the Middle Ages, Anselm of Canterbury is known for his use of reason to prove the importance of Christian beliefs.

Anselm was born of noble parentage in the Alpine village of Aosta, Italy. He wanted to become a monk as a young man but was refused admission to a monastery because of his father's objections. When he was 23 he left home to study and eventually became a pupil of the noted theologian, Lanfranc, then in the Abbey of Bec in Normandy. Anselm joined the Bec

WORLD EVENTS		ANSELM'S LIFE
Northern Sung Dynasty begins	960	
	c. 1033	Anselm of Canterbury is born
Schism between Roman Catholic and Orthodox Church	1054	
	c. 1059	Anselm arrives at Benedictine Abbey in Bec
	1059–63	Anselm studies with Lanfranc
	1078	Anselm becomes abbot of monastery at Bec; he develops ontological proof for God's existence
	1093	Anselm becomes archbishop of Canterbury
First Crusade	1095	
	1097– 1100	Anselm's first exile in Rome
Settling of Timbuktu, present-day Mali	c. 1100	
	1103–06	Anselm's second exile in Rome
	1109	Anselm dies in Canterbury
Islamic ruler of Egypt, Saladin, captures Jerusalem	1187	

community in 1060. Ten years later Anselm began writing at the request of the monks, who found his ideas useful in understanding and defending the faith. He became abbot in 1078.

In his writings, Anselm attempted to use reason to defend the Christian faith. In 1076, he completed the *Monologue on Rational Faith* in which he contends that God must exist because: 1) degrees of goodness require an absolute good, 2) everything that exists requires a cause and, ultimately, a superior cause, and 3) as there is not an infinite hierarchy of perfect beings, there must be one being superior to all others.

By 1078, Anselm had developed this proof further by proposing an ontological argument (one based on being itself) for the existence of God. He postulated that God is greater than that which can be thought. Such an entity must exist in reality as well as in understanding. If God existed in thought only, God could not be *greater* than that which can be thought.

Anselm's *Cur Deus Homo* (1097–1100) was one of the most significant works on the Atonement in medieval theology. In it Anselm attempts to explain why the all-powerful God, who could have saved humankind by any means he chose, became human and died for humanity's sins. Between 1080 and 1085, Anselm wrote *De grammatico (On Grammar)*, an introduction to logic, and *De veritate (On Truth)*, introduction to truth. In the latter, Anselm contends that there are three kinds of truth: truth in God, truth in things created by God, and the truth of the mind and the will. Toward the end of his life, Anselm focused on questions of freedom and God's grace.

In 1093 King William II of England appointed Anselm as archbishop of Canterbury, succeeding his mentor Lanfranc, who had died four years earlier. William had waited to fill the position in order to exploit its revenues. Anselm vigorously defended the freedom of the Church from political intrusion and, in 1097, went to Rome to ask for papal support. In his absence, William seized his church property and refused to allow him to return. When William died in 1100, Anselm returned to England only to be once more forced into exile in 1103 by Henry I, who challenged his authority. The king and the archbishop made peace in 1106. Anselm died in Canterbury on April 21, 1109.

Legacy

Anselm's insistence that Christian theology could be understood and defended solely by rational thought earned him the title the "Father of Scholasticism." Following the efforts of his teacher, Lanfranc, to provide a rational basis for describing the elements of the Lord's Supper (bread, wine), Anselm applied his pattern of logic to such Christian doctrines as the Trinity, the Incarnation, and redemption, showing that these doctrines are "necessary truths."

The idea that the Christian faith can seek defense in rational thought lies at the heart of Scholasticism. Anselm's mode of argument was adopted by such later theologians as William of Champeaux (c. 1070–1121), PETER ABELARD (1079–1142), and Hugh of St. Victor (c. 1096–1142). Scholasticism reached its height in the work of Peter Lombard (c. 1100–1160), whose *Sentences* became the standard theological textbook prior to the Protestant Reformation.

While Anselm's rational mode of argument found quick acceptance, he was not without critics. Shortly after his ontological proof appeared, Gaunilo, a monk from Marmourtier, challenged this proof with two objections. First, God's existence cannot be inferred from an unambiguous idea of the absolute good; second, existence in thought is no proof for existence outside of thought. Anselm replied to this challenge by insisting that he was focused on God as superior to the greatest being one can imagine. In later years, this challenge was continued by THOMAS AQUINAS, JOHN LOCKE, and IMMANUEL KANT. Nevertheless, Anselm found support from Bonaventure, Duns Scotus, RENÉ DESCARTES, Gottfried Leibniz, and GEORG WILHELM FRIEDRICH HEGEL.

von Dehsen

For Further Reading:
Evans, G. R. *Anselm and a New Generation.* New York: Oxford University Press, 1980.
Southern, R. W. *Saint Anselm: A Portrait in a Landscape.* New York: Cambridge University Press, 1990.

'Arabi, Ibn al-

Master of Islamic Sufi Mysticism
1165–1240

Life and Work

Ibn al-'Arabi was a philosopher of Islamic Sufi mysticism who insisted that the mystical union with the deity was not confined to a single moment but was a continuous, transformative process.

Ibn al-'Arabi was born on August 7, 1165, in Murcia, Spain. When he was eight years old, his parents moved to Seville, a center of Islamic learning. As a child, Ibn al-'Arabi was so extraordinarily bright that he impressed his father's friend, the noted philosopher AVERROËS (1126–1198).

In 1198, Ibn al-'Arabi had a vision in which he was instructed to leave Spain and to travel east. Over the next few years he wandered throughout North Africa and the Middle East. In 1202 he reached Mecca, Islam's holy shrine in present-day Saudi Arabia, to complete his *hajj*, the pilgrimage to Mecca obligatory for every Muslim once in a lifetime. After spending two years there, he continued traveling around the Mediterranean world.

During this period, Ibn al-'Arabi developed his religious thought, which transformed the Sufi static concept of mystical connection into a more dynamic one described by the phrase "perpetual transformation." According to Ibn al-'Arabi, one needs to distinguish the deity's perspective from eternity, in which all time is visible at once, from that of humanity's, which is trapped within the flow of time and which can see only that aspect of the divine revealed in the moment. True mystical connection consists in the "polishing of the mirror," the point where the mystic becomes so attuned to the deity that he or she completely reflects the multifaceted characteristics of the divine. The continual reimaging of the deity in the mystic suggests continual creation, as the deity, who wishes to interact with human beings, is realized in the mirror of human consciousness. Moreover, the unity of the deity and the mystic is so complete that there is no sense of "other," that is, of duality. Ibn al-'Arabi warns people against "binding" certain finite aspects

of the deity to their own static image of God. Such binding leads to idolatry, not to true mystical connection, which is always one of dynamic change.

Ibn al-'Arabi wrote over 200 books. Among his most important are *Interpreter of Desires* (completed 1215), *The Ringsettings of Wisdom* (begun in 1229), and *Meccan Openings* (completed 1238). In 1223 he settled in Damascus, where he spent the remainder of his life. He died there on November 16, 1240.

Legacy

Ibn al-'Arabi was an Islamic Sufi mystic who expanded the concept of mystical experience from one of static union, as was described by earlier mystics, to one of perpetual transformation. His ideas were the culmination of the third phase of Sufi mysticism, which had begun with thinkers such as RABI'AH AL'ADAWIYAH (c. 717–801) and continued in the works of AL-GHAZALI (1058–1111). He believed that the mystic, understood as a "polished mirror," continued to reflect the many aspects of the eternal deity. As a tribute to his great contributions, Ottoman Sultan Selim I reconstructed Ibn al-'Arabi's gravesite in 1518. His tomb has become an important pilgrimage site for Sufis.

Ibn al-'Arabi's thought first spread largely through the efforts of his students Sadr al-Din (1209–1274) and the poet 'Iraki (d. 1287). Sadr al-Din propagated his ideas throughout Anatolia (Turkey), where his works had their most profound influence. Over the centuries Ibn al-'Arabi's writings were used as texts and became the subject of commentaries. By the fourteenth century his concept of monism, that is, nondualism, had become central to Anatolian mystical philosophy. 'Iraki took Ibn al-'Arabi's thought as far as eastern Iran. Still others spread his teachings as far as Yemen and India.

Ibn al-'Arabi's ideas were not always well received. The great historian IBN KHALDUN (1332–1406) dismissed them as meaningless and heretical. In the last few centuries, his work has also been criticized by modernists who were influenced by Western thought as well as fundamentalists such as the Wahhabi sect dominant in Saudi Arabia. (Ibn al-'Arabi's books are banned in that country.)

Yet at the end of the twentieth century, many Islamic mystics are returning to his con-

cepts. Some even regard him as the "Grand Master" of Islamic mystical philosophy.

Ibn al-'Arabi's influence was not limited to the Islamic world. Many of his ideas were found in the writings of later European mystics, and he may have influenced thinkers such as Moses de Leon (d. 1305) and Meister Eckhardt (d.c. 1327).

von Dehsen

WORLD EVENTS		IBN AL-'ARABI'S LIFE
Settling of Timbuktu, c. 1100 present-day Mali		
	1165	Ibn al-'Arabi is born
Islamic ruler of Egypt, Saladin, captures Jerusalem	1187	
	1198	Ibn al-'Arabi leaves Spain and travels east
	1202	Ibn al-'Arabi reaches Mecca on pilgrimage
	1215	*Interpreter of Desires* is completed
	1223	Ibn al-'Arabi moves to Damascus
	1229	*The Ringsettings of Wisdom* is begun
	1238	*Meccan Openings* is completed
	1240	Ibn al-'Arabi dies
Hapsburg dynasty begins dominance in Holy Roman Empire	1273	

For Further Reading:

Chittick, William. *The Self-Disclosure of God: Principles of Ibn 'Arabi's Cosmology.* Albany: State University of New York Press, 1998.

Sells, Michael. *Mystical Languages of Unsaying.* Chicago: University of Chicago Press, 1994.

Arendt, Hannah

Philosopher of Totalitarianism
1906–1975

Life and Work

Hannah Arendt was a political philosopher who studied the nature of totalitarianism and the political role of citizens as members of a larger community.

Arendt was born in Hanover, Germany, on October 14, 1906, into a well-to-do family of nonreligious Jews. As a young student she studied with MARTIN HEIDEGGER and EDMUND HUSSERL at the University of Marburg, attended Frieburg University, and, in 1929, completed her doctoral degree at Heidelberg University. She completed her dissertation under Karl Jaspers on AUGUSTINE OF HIPPO'S view of love.

When Hitler came to power in Germany in 1933, Arendt moved to Paris, where she supported Jewish refugee organizations. As the Nazi troops approached Paris in 1940, she fled to the United States, where she continued to work for

WORLD EVENTS	ARENDT'S LIFE
	1906 Hannah Arendt is born
World War I 1914–18	
	1929 Arendt receives doctorate from Heidelberg University
	1933 Arendt moves to Paris
	1941 Arendt flees to United States to escape Nazis
World War II 1939–45	
Mao Tse-tung establishes Communist rule in China	1949
Korean War 1950–53	
	1951 *The Origins of Totalitarianism* is published
	1959 Arendt becomes first woman appointed full professor at Princeton University
	1963 *Eichmann in Jerusalem* is published
Six Day War between Israel and Arabs	1967
End of Vietnam War	1975 Arendt dies
Fall of Communism in eastern Europe	1989

several Jewish institutions. She became an American citizen in 1951.

The 1950s saw the publication of several books that brought Arendt widespread acclaim. In 1951, she produced her most important work, *The Origins of Totalitarianism*, in which she confronted the political abuses of Nazism and Stalinism. Such abuses, she theorized, stem from the dehumanization of people by considering them "interchangeable parts" in the context of the larger economy. Moreover, when people see themselves only as isolated individuals and not as citizens in a relationship of interconnectedness, they lose the collective power to resist totalitarian forces. Arendt developed these ideas further in *The Human Condition* (1958).

In 1962, Arendt traveled to Israel to witness the trial of the Nazi war criminal, Adolf Eichmann, for the *New Yorker*. She published her views of Eichmann, and by extension her view of evil, in *Eichmann in Jerusalem* (1963). For Arendt, Eichmann was an example of the "banality of evil." Eichmann blindly followed the orders of his superiors, without considering the consequences of his actions; his evil was generated by his indifference to the lives he took. That same year Arendt published *On Revolution*, in which she advocated human initiative as the proper impetus for revolution.

In 1959 Arendt became the first woman to be appointed a full professor at Princeton University. From 1963 to 1967 she taught at the University of Chicago. Arendt joined the faculty of the New School for Social Research in New York in 1967. She died in New York City on December 4, 1975.

Legacy

Arendt was a political theorist whose writings reexamined traditional views of the causes of totalitarianism and evil. Her analysis grew, in part, out of her personal experience of the Nazi terror in the 1930s and 1940s. On the basis of these events, she rethought the nature and responsibility of the citizen in society. Her concept of people as interrelated components of society challenged the notion of the person as autonomous individual prevalent in Western culture.

One of the strengths of Arendt's work was that it forced individuals to reevaluate their own roles in society without appeal to established tradition. (Such tradition could only stifle an open critique of established attitudes.) Thus, some

political philosophers believe that her ideas about the person as citizen and about the causes of revolution may have inspired those who effected the dismantling of communism in Eastern Europe in 1989.

Arendt's political philosophy has challenged scholars to revisit the question of how a new government arising out of revolution establishes its initial legitimacy (the consensus among citizens that its authority is to be obeyed). More broadly, scholars use Arendt's theories to explore the relationship between the individual, the "self," and the world. This question becomes extremely important when one considers her suggestion that passivity among the citizenry may breed the kinds of evil exemplified by the Nazis and, in particular, by Eichmann.

Despite her emphasis on human responsibility in the political realm, Arendt's theories have been hard to classify. Some scholars contend that Arendt tried to recast traditional ideas through the lens of her experiences as a women, thus providing a methodological model for feminist thought in the late 1970s and 1980s. Others counter that, as Arendt was not particularly focused on issues of gender identity, it would be hard to consider her work as a foundation for later feminism.

The original nature of Arendt's thought provided opportunities for more innovative uses of her work. For example, in 1984 Michael Sandel included portions from *On Revolution* in his anthology, *Liberalism and Its Critics*. The Yale Law School offered a course on Arendt's thought in its curriculum, even though Arendt herself never addressed legal philosophy.

von Dehsen

For Further Reading:

Hansen, Phillip Birger. *Hannah Arendt: Politics, History, and Citizenship*. Cambridge: Polity Press, 1993.

McGowan, John. *Hannah Arendt: An Introduction*. Minneapolis: University of Minnesota Press, 1998.

May, Larry, and Jerome Kohn, eds. *Hannah Arendt: Twenty Years Later*. Cambridge, Mass.: MIT Press, 1997.

Aristotle

Influential Greek Philosopher;
Opponent of Platonic Concept of
Forms

384–322 B.C.E.

Life and Work

Aristotle, a student of PLATO, developed ideas about logic and about the unity of matter and essence that challenged the Platonic concept of forms and opened alternate ways of viewing reality.

Born in Stageira, Macedonia, in 384 B.C.E., Aristotle was the son of the physician to King Philip of Macedon. From 367 to 347, he studied with Plato at the Academy in Athens. When Plato died in 347, Aristotle left Athens for Asia Minor, disappointed that he was not named the master's successor. Five years later, he returned to Macedonia as young Prince Alexander's tutor. When Philip was assassinated, Alexander ascended the throne and Aristotle returned to Athens in 336, founded his own school, the Lyceum, and remained there until Alexander's death in 323.

Like Plato, Aristotle spoke of forms. In contrast to Plato's idea that all forms are abstract and immaterial, Aristotle asserted that, with the exception of certain immaterial forms (e.g., God), all forms are composed of matter. Matter and form then become the tools for explaining the causes of change in the world, that is, how and why natural beings and artifacts come to be and pass away. Aristotle believed that the essence of a person or object cannot be separated from its material existence.

Human beings, according to Aristotle, can know the principles of the natural world, the general rules of human thought, conduct and society, and the nature of the "first cause" itself—Aristotle's nonreligious god described as the pure form of thinking that causes all universal motion. His many texts (collections of lecture notes, student notes, and other writings) contain his ideas about such various topics as logic, natural science, ethics, aesthetics, political science, and metaphysics; they include: *Physics, On The Soul, Nichomachean Ethics, Politics, Rhetoric,* and *Poetics.*

Aristotle was also the first philosopher to analyze the methods of argument and reasoning. He believed that all conclusions should be drawn from observed data. These basic ideas are preserved in a series of essays collected under the title *Organon.*

In 323, in the face of Athenian backlash against the rule of his patron, Alexander the Great, Aristotle, like SOCRATES before him, was charged with atheism. Aristotle fled the city, allegedly remarking, "I will not let Athens sin against philosophy twice." He died of natural causes in Chalkis in Euboea, Greece, the following year.

Legacy

The tension created by the dialogue between Aristotle and his mentor, Plato, over the nature of reality has shaped philosophical and theological discourse ever since. Aristotle's concept that the essence of a person or object cannot be separated from its material existence and that God is the "first cause" of all reality has provided a strong counterpoint to the Platonic concept of forms.

Aristotle's significance for Western thinking has not been uniform. Following Rome's decline, Western thinkers knew most of his writings primarily through surviving commentaries about them; only Arabic scholars in Moorish Spain and Constantinople had the texts. These scholars, such as AL-FARABI, AVICENNA, AL-GHAZALI, and AVERROËS, mirror the debate over the nature of existence and its origin from the perspective of Islamic theology. Thanks to the Crusades, Aristotle's writings were rediscovered in Europe, translated into Latin, and made the cornerstone of medieval learning.

THOMAS AQUINAS (1224–1274), influenced by his teacher, Albert the Great, drew heavily upon Aristotle, whom he considered *the* philosopher, for his great work, *Summa Theologica.* There Aquinas, following Aristotle's example, seeks to correlate faith and reason. He also asserts that one can discern the existence of God from the effects of God in the visible world—a variation of Aristotle's "first cause" argument. A younger contemporary of Aquinas, the poet Dante Alighieri (1265–1321) recognized in Aristotle's broad reach "the master of those who know."

By the fourteenth century, Aristotle's logic, his division of knowledge into theoretical, practical (moral), and productive (crafts), and his explanatory concepts of cause, matter, and form, became *the* investigative model for all advancement in learning. Even when science and philosophy became separate disciplines in the sixteenth century, the revolutionary theorists, such as Nicolaus Copernicus (1473–1543) and Galileo Galilei (1564–1642), acknowledged the power of this thinking in the force of their counterarguments.

In the late twentieth century, Aristotle's writings have not been ignored; ethicists, political scientists, and philosophers of logic around the world still mine their depths for new perspectives on age-old questions and fresh insights into contemporary challenges.

Magurshak

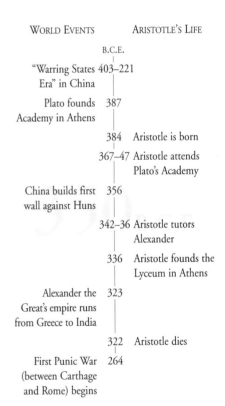

WORLD EVENTS		ARISTOTLE'S LIFE
	B.C.E.	
"Warring States Era" in China	403–221	
Plato founds Academy in Athens	387	
	384	Aristotle is born
	367–47	Aristotle attends Plato's Academy
China builds first wall against Huns	356	
	342–36	Aristotle tutors Alexander
	336	Aristotle founds the Lyceum in Athens
Alexander the Great's empire runs from Greece to India	323	
	322	Aristotle dies
First Punic War (between Carthage and Rome) begins	264	

For Further Reading:

Ackrill, J. L. *Aristotle the Philosopher.* New York: Oxford University Press, 1981.

Edel, Abraham. *Aristotle and His Philosophy.* Chapel Hill: University of North Carolina Press, 1982,

Rist, John M. *The Mind of Aristotle: A Study in Philosophical Growth.* Toronto: University of Toronto Press, 1989.

Arjun

Fifth Sikh *Guru*, Compiler of the *Adi Granth*
1563–1606

WORLD EVENTS		ARJUN'S LIFE
Reformation begins	1517	
	1563	Arjun is born
	1581	Arjun becomes Sikh *guru*
	1589	Arjun begins building Golden Temple at Amritsar
	1604	Arjun compiles *Adi Granth*
	1606	Arjun dies
Thirty Years' War in Europe	1618-48	

Life and Work

The fifth Sikh *guru* (teacher), Arjun compiled the Sikh sacred scripture, the *Adi Granth*, and established a center for Sikh worship at the Golden Temple in Amritsar, in present-day northwestern India.

Arjun was born on April 15, 1563, in Goindwal, India. Little is known of his early life. He inherited the position of Sikh *guru* upon the death of his father, *Guru* Ram Das in 1581. As youngest son of Ram Das, he ordinarily would not have succeeded his father, but his grandfather, *Guru* Amar Das, had predicted that Arjun would assume the office.

In 1589 Arjun began constructing the Golden Temple (the Hari Mandir) in the city of Amritsar. While Hindu and Muslim houses of worship were built on raised mounds, the Sikh temple was built on a low platform because he wanted to make the point that God was worshiped through bending low in submission. It had doors on all four sides, signifying that people of all castes, beliefs, and nationalities were welcome to worship there. Arjun made his permanent residence at Amritsar and was the first *guru* to become temporal as well as spiritual leader of the community.

Arjun also compiled the hymns and prayers of the previous *gurus*, together with some of his own, into the *Adi Granth (The First Book)*. The work, completed in 1604, became the earliest scripture of the Sikhs.

Toward the end of his life, Arjun unintentionally became involved in a power struggle between Emperor Jahangir and his son, Prince Khusrau. When the prince asked Arjun for help in ousting his father, the Sikh leader refused, saying a son should not rebel against his father. Jahangir did not believe that he had denied Khusrau aid and sentenced Arjun to death by torture. He died on May 30, 1606.

Legacy

Arjun helped Sikhism develop a distinct identity by compiling its important religious literature into the *Adi Granth,* its earliest scripture, and by establishing a geographic focus for believers, the Golden Temple at Amritsar.

By collecting the writings of the early *gurus*, Arjun brought together spiritual material from the Hindu and Islamic traditions out of which Sikhism had developed. The *Adi Granth* expanded from the base that Arjun 's compilation provided, and other literature was added, including the poetry of later *gurus* Tegh Bahadur (the ninth *guru*) and GOBIND SINGH (the tenth *guru*), who prepared the final version of the *Adi Granth* in 1704. Sikhs believe that the hereditary *gurus* were physical manifestations of the first *guru*, NANAK, as he repeated the cycle of death and rebirth. Before his death, Gobind Singh declared the line of *gurus* would end with him and that, henceforth, the *Adi Granth* would be the *guru.*

The *Adi Granth* promotes ethical uprightness as more important for spiritual growth than rituals and symbols. If one seeks God, who is Truth, then one has to conduct one's life ethically to attain union with God. It rejects all distinctions between people by caste or nationality and extols universal brotherhood. To achieve spiritual and ethical perfection, a Sikh needs to follow the guidance of the true *guru*. If successful, a Sikh can reach the state of *sahj* (balance), in which the mind becomes pure.

Over the years Arjun's Golden Temple became the principal shrine of Sikhism and Amritsar the center of a powerful Sikh state. In the mid-nineteenth century two wars resulted in British control of the region. Since Indian independence in 1947, Sikhs have attempted to restore their power base in Punjab. In 1984 Sikh separatists, demanding political autonomy, seized the Golden Temple. The Indian army ousted them only after slaughtering hundreds. In retaliation, Sikh fundamentalists assassinated India's Prime Minister Indira Gandhi later that year.

von Dehsen

For Further Reading:

Gangopadhyaya, Sunil. *Arjun.* New York: Viking Penguin, 1987.

Joshi, Mahindara Singha. *Guru Arjan Dev.* New Delhi: Sahitya Akademi, 1994.

Athanasius, Saint

Egyptian Bishop and Theologian; Developer of the New Testament Canon

c. 293–373

Life and Work

Athanasius the bishop of Alexandria, Egypt, championed traditional Christian teachings against the fourth century Arian heresy. He also helped determine the final canon (list of books) in the New Testament.

Athanasius was probably born to Christian parents in Alexandria. As a young man he was influenced by St. Anthony, a desert hermit who was a founder of Christian monasticism. He attended the celebrated catechetical school of his native city and was ordained a deacon. In 325, as secretary to Bishop Alexander of Alexandria, he attended the Council of Nicaea, which had been called to deal with the Arian heresy. (This heresy subordinated the Son to the Father in the Trinity.) There, he opposed Arius, the Alexandrian priest who taught that the Son was of a different substance from that of the Father and was merely more perfect than any other creature. Athanasius advocated the ultimately victorious doctrine expressed in the Nicene Creed (325), that Christ is *homoousios*, that is, of the same substance or essence as God the Father. Arius' teaching,

Athanasius maintained, denied the doctrine of the Trinity and led to polytheism—one god as creator and another created. Throughout his career he defended his position in his many books: *Against the Heathen* (c. 335), *On the Incarnation of the Word of God* (c. 335), *Apology Against the Arians* (c. 346), *Four Orations Against the Arians* (c. 356), *History of the Arians* (c. 360), and *On the Decrees of the Nicene Synod* (c. 350).

In 328 Athanasius was elected bishop of Alexandria, including all of Egypt and modern Libya. As a supporter of St. Anthony's ascetic ideas, he became spiritual head of the desert hermits as well. Athanasius immediately faced a revival of Arianism that occupied much of his life. The doctrinal controversy was entwined with imperial politics and, on five occasions, the Arian party convinced the emperor to exile Athanasius from Alexandria. During his third exile, 356–362, Athanasius lived with Egyptian hermits and wrote his greatest doctrinal work, *Discourses Against the Arians*. Through it all, he remained immovable in his adherence to the orthodox teaching of the Nicene Creed. In 366, Athanasius returned to Alexandria where he helped build a new Nicene faction to counter the Arians. To resolve a long-standing debate over the canon (list of books) of the New Testament, Athanasius provided what would become the definitive list of the 27 books of the New Testament in 367. He spent the remaining years of his life in Alexandria, working in peace until his death in 373.

Legacy

Called the "champion of orthodoxy," Athanasius fought against one of the greatest theological threats to the Christian church—Arianism. His firm defense of the nature and person of Christ became a permanent fixture in Christian teaching following the ultimate triumph over Arianism at the General Council of Constantinople in 381. Although he is not the author of the Athanasian Creed, which originated in the fifth or sixth centuries, its name pays tribute to his crucial defense of the doctrine of the Trinity.

Athanasius' support of St. Anthony and his ascetic life did much to spread the ascetic ideal in both East and West and contributed to the development of monasticism. In later years,

monasticism grew under the influence of such notables as AUGUSTINE OF HIPPO (354–430) and BENEDICT OF NURSIA (c. 480–547). Roman Catholic monasteries have also nurtured such people as MARTIN LUTHER (1483–1546) and MOTHER TERESA (1910–1997).

Athanasius' stand on the list of the canon of the New Testament set the stage for the authoritative list established by the North African Council at Carthage in 397. Martin Luther and Huldrych Zwingli raised the issue of the canon again during the Protestant Reformation of the sixteenth century when they questioned the inclusion of the books of James, Jude, Hebrews, and Revelations because they were not Christ centered. This renewed controversy compelled the Council of Trent in 1546 to reaffirm the list of books in Athanasius' canon, originally published in 367.

Olson

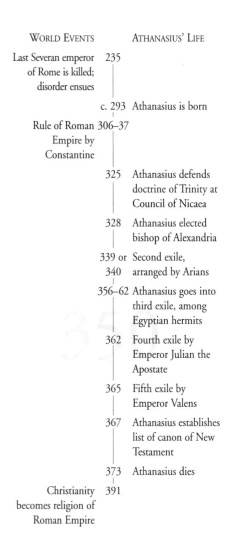

WORLD EVENTS		ATHANASIUS' LIFE
Last Severan emperor of Rome is killed; disorder ensues	235	
	c. 293	Athanasius is born
Rule of Roman Empire by Constantine	306–37	
	325	Athanasius defends doctrine of Trinity at Council of Nicaea
	328	Athanasius elected bishop of Alexandria
	339 or 340	Second exile, arranged by Arians
	356–62	Athanasius goes into third exile, among Egyptian hermits
	362	Fourth exile by Emperor Julian the Apostate
	365	Fifth exile by Emperor Valens
	367	Athanasius establishes list of canon of New Testament
	373	Athanasius dies
Christianity becomes religion of Roman Empire	391	

For Further Reading:

Barnes, Timothy David. *Athanasius and Constantius: Theology and Politics in the Constantinian Empire.* Cambridge, Mass.: Harvard University Press, 1993.

Kanneniesser, Charles. *Arius and Athanasius: Two Alexandrian Theologians.* Brookfield, Vt.: Grower Publishing Co., 1991.

Augustine of Hippo, Saint

Seminal Christian Theologian
354–430

Life and Work

Augustine of Hippo was a theologian whose work shaped Western Christianity.

Augustine was born in Tagaste (present-day Algeria) on November 13, 354. His father, Patricius, was a non-Christian; his mother, Monica, was a devout Christian. Augustine was not baptized as a child and until the age of 30 led a profligate life. He studied philosophy in Carthage (North Africa) and for nine years was a Manichaean, a member of a religious sect that believed there were two gods, one good and one evil. Eventually disillusioned by its principles, he became a skeptic. Around 383 he moved to Italy to teach rhetoric first in Rome and then in Milan. There he became interested in Neoplatonism, the belief that the whole world originates from as cosmic principle, and met Ambrose, whose sermons mixing Christian devotion with the Neoplatonic concepts drew Augustine to the Church; Ambrose baptized him in 387. The following year he returned to Tagaste, where he set up an ascetic community. He was ordained a priest in 391 and became bishop of Hippo (modern Annaba, Algeria) in 396.

As bishop, Augustine articulated his major theological themes in controversies involving three major heresies. Against the Manichaeans he asserted that there was only one, good God who, although creator of all, was not responsible for evil, which arose from Adam's willful disobedience. From 403 to 412 Augustine contended with the Donatists, who alleged that the moral character of the priest affected the validity of any sacrament he administered. The bishop countered that God's grace was not compromised by a priest's moral character. The Church would always be a "mixed" community, composed of the righteous and repentant sinners. It was holy because its purpose, not its people, was holy.

Augustine's most significant attack was leveled against the Pelagians who denied original sin and argued that human beings could contribute to their own salvation. Augustine rejected these teachings. He insisted that humanity inherited Adam's sin. Original sin was integral to human nature; even seemingly virtuous conduct was contaminated by it. Consequently, salvation can come only by God's grace. God in his mercy has predestined a minority of humanity for salvation. The empirical evidence of this salvation lies in goodness of character, which is also a gift from God.

Perhaps Augustine's two most famous writings are his *Confessions* (397) and *The City of God* (413–426). The former is an autobiography in which he candidly writes of his wanton youth and of his conversion to Christianity. In the latter he offers a theological philosophy of history: God works through events to achieve his ultimate purpose, redemption. Augustine illustrated his thesis using the metaphor of two cities: The City of God, a heavenly city, identified with the Church, which is governed by love, and the City of Earth, the pagan state, which is controlled by human selfishness. Ultimately the City of God will overcome the City of Earth. Augustine summarizes his views on how human beings know God.

Augustine died on August 28, 430, as Hippo was besieged by the Vandals from Northern Europe.

Legacy

Augustine's ideas had a seminal influence on Western Christian theology and shaped the course of European life for almost 1,000 years.

Augustine's thinking is central to both Roman Catholic and Protestant theology. Medieval thinkers appealed to him as authority, and his influence can be seen in the thought of ANSELM OF CANTERBURY, THOMAS AQUINAS and Peter Lombard, among others. The leaders of the Protestant Reformation relied heavily on his teachings. Augustine's teaching that individuals are saved by grace alone was central to MARTIN LUTHER's theology, while his theory of predestination strongly influenced JOHN CALVIN. The eighteenth-century reformer JOHN WESLEY also studied Augustine, although he ultimately rejected the African's focus on God's grace.

The influence of Augustine's work and thought extends beyond religious matters in a profound way. His understanding of PLATO dominated Europe until the discovery of ARISTOTLE in the thirteenth century. His theological interpretation of history provided the framework for historical writing until the Enlightenment. The ideas expressed in *The City of God* formed the basis for the medieval understanding of politics and the relationship between church and state. His view that heaven was the goal of life shaped social and economic attitudes. Even medieval attitudes toward sexuality were influenced by Augustine. His idea that original sin was bound in reproduction prompted society to look on marriage as a lesser state than the celibate religious life.

Augustine's teachings still dominate the Western Christian tradition. In recent years the commonality of these ideas has provided an important point of agreement in Christian ecumenical dialogues.

von Dehsen

World Events		Augustine's Life
Rule of Roman Empire by Constantine	306–37	
	354	Augustine of Hippo is born in Tagaste (Algeria)
	387	Augustine is baptized by Ambrose in Milan
Christianity becomes religion of Roman Empire	391	Augustine is ordained a priest
	396	Augustine becomes bishop of Hippo
	397	Augustine completes *Confessions*
	403–12	Augustine attacks Donatist heresy
	413–26	Augustine writes *The City of God*
	430	Augustine dies at Hippo
Fall of Roman Empire	476	

For Further Reading:

Chadwick, Henry. *Augustine.* New York: Oxford University Press, 1986.

Kirwan, Christopher. *Augustine.* New York: Routledge, 1989.

O'Donnell, James Joseph. *Augustine.* Boston: Twayne Publishers, 1985.

Aurobindo Ghose
(Sri Aurobindo)
Founder of Integral Yoga
1872–1950

Life and Work

Aurobindo Ghose, known to his followers as Sri Aurobindo, founded the spiritual discipline of Integral Yoga. This form of yoga grew out of his opposition to the British rule of India and a growing appreciation for India's Hindu traditions.

Aurobindo was born on August 15, 1872, in Calcutta. His father, eager for his son to absorb British culture, sent him to England for his education. He remained in England from the age of seven to 21, studying at St. Paul's School in London and King's College in Cambridge.

Aurobindo returned to India in 1893 thoroughly westernized and with little understanding of India's spiritual tradition but with a deep desire to end British rule. He worked as a teacher and educational administrator while immersing himself in Indian culture. Thrusting himself into Indian politics, he wrote articles criticizing colonialism and became a leader of the Extremists, a group that wanted the immediate end of British rule. From 1908 to 1909 he was jailed for sedition, during which time he began to practice yoga and experience anew some of the religious teachings of Hinduism. Aurobindo emerged convinced that India's spiritual tradition could serve the cause of independence. In 1910, fearing a second imprisonment, he fled to French Pondicherry in southern India. There he gave up his political struggles and dedicated his life to the spiritual transformation of India.

Over the next 40 years he formulated what became known as Integral Yoga. As a result of his resistance to the British, he recognized that India was a special spiritual place and that this spirituality could be nourished through the discipline of yoga. On August 15, 1914, Aurobindo founded the journal *Arya*, in which he began to formulate his concepts. These articles were the basis of his later writings, including *Essays on the Gita* (1928), *The Synthesis of Yoga* (1948), *The Life of the Divine* (1949), and *The Human Cycle* (1949).

Aurobindo believed that human beings could ascend to the *Brahman*, the Absolute Divine, through yoga. As humans progress toward the *Brahman*, they achieve higher and higher forms of consciousness. Once a person reaches the "Overmental Consciousness," then the *Brahman* descends to meet that consciousness to form an integration of the two. Moreover, this integration manifests itself in action. Therefore, Aurobindo saw his earlier political resistance as part of the way the *Brahman* acted in the world. Aurobindo claimed to have achieved this "integration" of consciousness himself on November 24, 1926.

Aurobindo taught these principles to his students at his ashram in Pondicherry, where he remained until his death on December 5, 1950. His last days were spent revising his epic poem on evolution, *Savitri*.

Legacy

Aurobindo's teachings about Integral Yoga became the founding principles of his ashram at Pondicherry, where his followers eventually honored him by founding Auroville, a city dedicated to the preservation of his teachings.

Perhaps Aurobindo's most important student was Mira Richard, who first visited the ashram in 1914 as a supporter of the journal, *Arya*. By 1920 she had devoted her life to Aurobindo and eventually became the manager of the community's day-to-day affairs. Aurobindo gradually came to view her as the earthly manifestation of the Divine Mother, and later referred to Mira as "Mother." Aurobindo asserted that "Mother's" consciousness so united with the consciousness of the Divine Mother that "Mother" was the deity's earthly manifestation. In effect, she had obtained the state of spiritual unity that was the essence of Integral Yoga.

To continue the work of Aurobindo, Mother established the Sri Aurobindo International Centre of Education at the ashram in Pondicherry. The school invites students to pursue means by which they might integrate all parts of their being—inner and outer—at their own pace.

Especially after the destruction of World War II, Mother worked with Aurobindo to usher the Overmind into the earthly realm to bring about the destruction of evil through social reform. (Aurobindo and Mother believed that their spiritual discipline during World War II had aided the Allies in their victory over the "Herren Volks," the German Nazis.)

When Aurobindo died in 1950, Mother continued her work to bring the Overmind to the earthly realm. On February 29, 1956, she experienced the "Supramental Manifestation," bringing the Supramental Light to Earth to effect social reform. Followers of the Mother credit this event as the cause of all subsequent social improvements. Mother also noted that the Supramental Light had affected her physically by requiring biological alterations to her body to retain her connection to the Divine Consciousness.

To bring Aurobindo's teachings to others throughout the world, Mother founded Auroville on February 28, 1968, near Pondicherry. The founding of this community was endorsed by both the Indian government and the United Nations.

The work of Aurobindo continued at Auroville after Mother's death in 1973. Its center is the ashram and it has spawned communities dedicated to Integral Yoga in India, Britain, and the United States.

von Dehsen

WORLD EVENTS	AUROBINDO'S LIFE
	1872 Aurobindo Ghose is born
	1893 Aurobindo begins work in Indian education
Spanish American War 1898	
	1914 Aurobindo founds journal, *Arya*
World War I 1914–18	
	1926 Aurobindo experiences integration of consciousness
World War II 1939–45	
Mao Tse-tung establishes Communist rule in China 1949	
	1950 Aurobindo dies
Korean War 1950–53	

For Further Reading:

Heehs, Peter. *Sri Aurobindo: A Brief Biography.* New York: Oxford University Press, 1989.

van Vrekhem, Georges. *Beyond Man: The Life and Work of Aurobindo and the Mother.* New Delhi: HarperCollins Publishers, 1997.

Averroës

(Ibn Rushd)

Islamic Theologian;
Interpreter of Aristotle and Plato
1126–1198

Life and Work

Ibn Rushd, more commonly known as Averroës, was an Islamic philosopher who both integrated ancient Greek concepts with Islamic theology and produced commentaries on the writings of ARISTOTLE and on PLATO's *Republic* that helped preserve their work.

Averroës was born in 1126 in Cordoba, Spain, to a respected family of legal scholars. Cordoba was the cultural center of western Islam, and he received an excellent education in law, medicine, religion, and Greek philoso-

WORLD EVENTS	AVERROËS'S LIFE
Settling of Timbuktu, c. 1100 present-day Mali	
	1126 Averroës is born
	1169 Averroës begins commentaries on Aristotle
	1182 Averroës becomes court physician to Abu Ya'qub Yusuf
	1184 *The Incoherence of "The Incoherence"* is published
Islamic ruler of Egypt, Saladin, captures Jerusalem	1187
	1198 Averroës dies
Hapsburg dynasty begins dominance in Holy Roman Empire	1273

phy. He became the *qadi* (judge) for Seville and Cordoba, a position previously held by his grandfather and, in 1182, was appointed court physician for Caliph Abu Ya'qub Yusuf.

At the caliph's request, between 1169 and 1195, Averroës completed commentaries on Aristotle's major works, including his *Organon, De Anima, Physica, Metaphysica,* and *Nichomachean Ethics* and on Plato's *Republic.* During this period he also developed his own philosophy, heavily influenced by Aristotle. In his works Averroës contends that there is only one truth, the law as understood by the philosopher, who can properly discern virtue, thus integrating Islamic theology with the Platonic concept of the philosopher-king, the ideal ruler. Averroës's primary focus was to show how the prophetically revealed truth of Islam, the *Shariah,* is best interpreted, not by Muslim theology, but by the principles of philosophy. He also agreed with Plato that women should share equal civil rights with men, even though this idea was directly contrary to traditional Islamic teaching. Like AL-FARABI (c. 878–950) and AVICENNA (980–1037) before him, Averroës presumed that gifted philosophers could discover and understand the inner meaning of the *Shariah.* Others less gifted could gain such understanding only through the enlightened stories and images provided by philosophers. Averroës's major work, *The Incoherence of "The Incoherence,"* (1184) was a rebuttal of the Islamic mystic AL-GHAZALI's attacks on Aristotelian philosophy and Neoplatonism made 90 years earlier.

Averroës's open teaching of Aristotelian philosophy eventually led his contemporaries in Cordoba to charge him with heresy in 1195. He was convicted and exiled to the North African city of Marrakech, where he died in 1198.

Legacy

Averroës's commentaries on Aristotle were central to the preservation and continued study of the Greek philosopher. In addition, Averroës's theories about the relationship of the material world to the Creator sparked a lively debate among scholars from various religious perspectives.

Averroës has had little impact on the Islamic world, where interest in philosophy declined

with the rise of mysticism. Nevertheless, he was honored as a scholar who tried to reconcile Islam and philosophy. His major influence was in the West, where his commentaries greatly influenced medieval Jewish and Scholastic philosophy.

One of the earliest critics of Averroës was MOSES BEN MAIMON (1135–1204), a Jewish philosopher. Moses ben Maimon rejected Averroës's rationalistic approach to the interpretation of Aristotle; instead, he favored the more theological approach of Avicenna, who emphasized the Aristotelian concept of God as the "First Cause." Another critic of Averroës was THOMAS AQUINAS (c. 1224–1274), who rejected Averroës's contention that all matter was eternal because this repudiated the belief that God created all things.

One of Averroës's first Christian followers was Siger of Brabant (1240–1284), a French philosopher and political activist among the faculty at the University of Paris. He developed what came to be known as "radical Aristotelianism" following the philosophical ideas of Avicenna and Averroës. Siger taught that the world and all of its living species are eternal, stemming from a single first cause. He also asserted that all human beings are components of a single active intelligence. Siger was thought to promote Averroës's ideas that there was a "double truth"—one from theology and the other from natural philosophy. For his ideas, Siger was accused of heresy in 1276; he was eventually acquitted of the charges.

Averroës's ideas also influenced those of Levi ben Gershom (1288–1344), a French philosopher known as Gersonides. His studies of Aristotle depended directly on the earlier ideas of Maimonides and Averroës. Gersonides disagreed with Averroës about the nature of truth; unlike the Spaniard, Gersonides contended that there was no difference between philosophical and revealed truth. He also challenged Averroës's theory that matter is eternal; Gersonides contended that the Creator shaped all matter from a primordial substance.

As a preserver and interpreter of the writings of Aristotle, and as a model for theologians and philosophers who seek to find points of contact between reason and religious teaching, Averroës's work has had great influence.

von Dehsen

For Further Reading:

Davidson, Herbert A. *Alfarabi, Avicenna, and Averroes: Their Cosmologies, Theories of the Active Intellect, and Theories of Human Intellect.* New York: Oxford University Press, 1992.

Leaman, Oliver. *Averroës and His Philosophy.* Richmond, United Kingdom: Curzon, 1998.

Wahba, Mourad, and Mona Abousenna, eds. *Averroës and the Enlightenment: The First Humanist-Muslim Dialogue.* Amherst, N.Y.: Prometheus Press, 1996

Avicenna

(Ibn Sina)

Islamic Philosopher;
Synthesizer of Greek Thought
980–1037

Life and Work

Ibn Sina, commonly known as Avicenna, was an Islamic philosopher and physician. Apart from his medical texts, he is best known for his attempts to synthesize Islamic theology and Greek philosophy. His work led not only to the preservation of the works of PLATO and ARISTOTLE, but his philosophical works also became a benchmark for others who struggled with the relationship between religious revelation and rational ideas.

Avicenna was born in 980 to a scholarly family in Bukhara in what is now modern Uzbekistan. His home was frequently the site of lively scholarly discussion sponsored by his father. By age 10, Avicenna had already memorized the Koran, the holy book of Islam. As a teenager, he studied logic and philosophy. By age 18, he was expert in Islamic law and in medicine. As a result of successfully treating Prince Nuh ibn Mansur, Avicenna was granted access to the royal library containing the writings of the ancient philosophers. At about this time, he also found a copy of *Metaphysics* by the Islamic philosopher, AL-FARABI, an interpreter of

Aristotle. By age 21, Avicenna was recognized as a philosopher, physician, and legal expert.

After the death of his father, Avicenna wandered throughout present day Iran. He held several important royal posts, including that of vizier (a representative of the court) and court physician in Hamadan, which allowed him both a comfortable existence and the freedom to pursue his philosophy with students. In 1022, the royal family was overthrown and Avicenna was banished for heretical thought. He fled to Esfahan, once again becoming a court official. During this time, he completed over 200 treatises, a medical work, *The Book of Healing,* and a collection of personal reflections, *Book of Devotions and Remarks.*

Avicenna's greatest theological contribution came in his synthesis of Islamic doctrine and Greek philosophy. Avicenna argued that the created world is not inherently necessary but is the result of the creative will of an absolute being and its spiritual emanations. This "indirect" manner of creation prevents the absolute from controlling creation and allows for the appearance of evil. He thereby correlated the Islamic concept of contingency (all that exists in the world depends on the intelligent will of a creator) with the Aristotelian idea of the first cause. For Avicenna, the first cause was Allah.

Avicenna died of colic in 1037. Ironically, his death was hastened by his aggressive treatment of his own illness.

Legacy

Avicenna's synthesis of Greek philosophy and Islamic thought proved to be a stimulus for later Islamic philosophers as well as for Christian theologians of the medieval period. His emphasis on the works of Plato and Aristotle also contributed significantly to their preservation for later generations.

Avicenna's thinking instigated an intense debate among later Islamic philosophers. The mystics Sana'i (d. 1150) and Jami (d. 1492) both vigorously opposed Avicenna as a corrupter of the faith. The religious philosopher AL-GHAZALI (1058–1111) challenged Avicenna from a more scholarly perspective. Specifically, he rejected the concept that Allah deals only indirectly with creation. For al-Ghazali, Allah dealt directly with creation and was involved in

particular aspects of life. In all cases, Avicenna seemed to have compromised the revelations of Allah by substituting for them human concepts.

Other Islamic thinkers, however, embraced and extended Avicenna's synthesis. Ibn al-'Arabi (d. 1240) seems to have been the first to integrate philosophy and theology with mysticism. The most important supporter of Avicenna was the Spaniard, AVERROËS (1126–1198), who became a staunch defender of Avicenna, even though he critiqued some of the former's interpretation of Aristotle.

In the West, Avicenna's integration of rational Greek philosophy and theology became a foundation for Scholasticism. Although AUGUSTINE OF HIPPO (354–430) had already suggested such a connection, the medieval theologians had access to the Greek philosophers thanks to the work of Islamic scholars. Moreover, many of Avicenna's basic ideas, such as the distinction between essence and existence and the identification of God as the first cause, inspired the work of Roscelin de Compiègne (c.1050–c.1125) and PETER ABELARD (1079–1142). Avicenna's writings directly influenced many medieval theologians. THOMAS AQUINAS (c. 1224–1274) embraced Avicenna's concept of God as the necessary being. For Duns Scotus (1266–1308), Avicenna become the theoretical point of departure for his own synthesis of faith and reason.

William of Ockham (c.1285–1347) built on Avicenna's thought to defend logic itself as an independent entity. Roger Bacon (c.1214–1293) thought Avicenna the greatest philosopher since Aristotle. In his *Inferno,* Dante Alighieri (1265–1321) even places Avicenna in Limbo along with other great non-Christian writers.

Finally, Avicenna is also valued as a scientist. His work is considered to be an important part of the foundation for the scientific revolution.

von Dehsen

WORLD EVENTS		AVICENNA'S LIFE
Northern Sung Dynasty begins	960	
	980	Avicenna is born
	c. 998	Avicenna already expert in Islamic law
	1022	Avicenna flees court of Hamadan; he becomes court official at Esfahan
	1037	Avicenna dies
Schism between Roman Catholic and Orthodox Church	1054	

For Further Reading:

Davidson, Herbert A. *Alfarabi, Avicenna, and Averroes: Their Cosmologies, Theories of the Active Intellect, and Theories of Human Intellect.* New York: Oxford University Press, 1992.

Fry, George. *Avicenna's Philosophy of Education: An Introduction.* Washington, D.C.: Three Continents Press, 1990.

Goodman, L. E. *Avicenna.* New York: Routledge, 1992.

Kemal, Salim. *The Poetics of Alfarabi and Avicenna.* Leiden, Netherlands: Brill, 1991.

Bacon, Francis

Philosopher of Science;
Originator of Inductive Method
of Scientific Inquiry
1561–1626

Life and Work

Francis Bacon was an English philosopher and scientist whose determination to expand and classify all human knowledge led him to develop the inductive method of scientific analysis.

The son of a close advisor to Queen Elizabeth I, Bacon was born on January 22, 1561, in London and educated at Cambridge University. In 1582 he turned to law, eventually becoming the legal advisor to the queen and then to her successor, King James I. James appointed him lord chancellor of England in 1618.

Although Bacon published several legal treatises, his most important works were in the field of the philosophy of science. He envisioned developing a complete system of all human knowledge that would include not only abstract disciplines such as mathematics, but also the skills associated with crafts and trades. His system was to be created through the collaborative effort of intellectuals who could then use it to solve human problems. Utilization of this system would lead to progress and the ultimate creation of a utopia he called New Atlantica.

Bacon proposed developing this system through inductive reasoning. Before drawing any conclusions, scientists must abandon any preconceived ideas, which he called idols, and must collect sufficient data through observation and experience to form tentative conclusions. As the amount of data increases and specific theories are confirmed, scientists can develop general theories that can be used to discern the basic principles of the universe. Bacon's method stood in sharp contrast to that used by medieval natural philosophers, who created systems based on logical deduction from a single philosophical principle.

Bacon first outlined his thoughts in *Advancement of Learning* (1605). In 1623 he revised and extended his arguments in a more scholarly version, *De Argumentis Scientiarum.* He published his most influential work on the subject, *Novum Organum,* in 1620.

Bacon applied his method to the study of history in 1622. His *Reign of Henry VII* examined the king's policies by tracing their causes back to the king's personality.

Convicted of accepting bribes in 1621, Bacon was briefly imprisoned and exiled from the royal court. He died near London on April 9, 1626, after contracting bronchitis.

Legacy

Bacon's use of induction as a method of collecting and organizing knowledge inspired the thinkers of the eighteenth-century Enlightenment and was a fundamental advance in science.

Bacon's idea that science was based on the collection and organization of evidence influenced the work of many seventeenth- and eighteenth-century scientists in Europe and the British North American colonies. Isaac Newton was one of the first scholars to acknowledge his indebtedness to Bacon's principles. He synthesized Bacon's approach with that of RENÉ DESCARTES, whose mechanical philosophy stressed deductive reasoning from a few basic axioms and, in so doing, developed the scientific or experimental method that underlies one of the most common approaches to modern scientific investigation.

Bacon's principles also had an influence on the development of philosophical empiricism, the theory that knowledge comes from experience rather than solely through the use of human ability to reason, as the opposing rationalist school contended. Empiricism was one of the foundations of the Enlightenment and was

articulated by philosophers such as JOHN LOCKE (1632–1704), whose theory of psychology centered all human knowledge around experience. Bacon's empiricism also influenced nineteenth-century philosophers such as JOHN STUART MILL (1806–1873).

Bacon's concept of collaborative scientific investigation was institutionalized with the founding of the Royal Society of London in 1660. This organization, which was dedicated to promoting Bacon's program, became one of the major scientific institutions of the Enlightenment, with members disseminating the latest scientific knowledge across Europe. The Society also opened some of its sessions to the public, promoting interest in and knowledge of science among the general population. Among its most prominent members were Newton, chemist Robert Boyle (1627–1691), and astronomer William Herschel (1738–1822).

Bacon's belief in progress and the perfectibility of humans as well as his scientific ideas became part of general Enlightenment thought through the work of the French author VOLTAIRE (1694–1778). The French political philosopher MONTESQUIEU (1687–1755) attempted to apply Bacon's ideas to the study of political society in *The Spirit of the Law,* which influenced the leaders of the American Revolution. DENIS DIDEROT (1713–1784) organized his *Encylcopédie,* intended to be a comprehensive presentation of all human knowledge, not only on Bacon's general principles but also on the specific classifications of knowledge that the English thinker had developed.

von Dehsen

WORLD EVENTS		BACON'S LIFE
Reformation begins	1517	
	1561	Francis Bacon is born
	1605	*Advances in Learning* is published
	1618	Bacon appointed lord chancellor of England
Thirty Years' War in Europe	1618-48	
	1620	*Novum Organum* is published
	1623	*De Argumentis Scientiarum* is published
	1626	Bacon dies
England's Glorious Revolution	1688	

For Further Reading:

Quinton, Anthony. *Francis Bacon.* New York: Hill and Wang, 1980.

Urbach, Peter. *Francis Bacon's Philosophy of Science: An Account and Reappraisal.* La Salle, Ill.: Open Court Press, 1987.

Zagorin, Perez. *Francis Bacon.* Princeton, N.J.: Princeton University Press, 1998.

Baha' Allah

(Mirza Hoseyn Ali Nuri)

Founder of Bahai Religion
1817–1892

Life and Work

Mirza Hoseyn Ali Nuri, commonly known as Baha' Allah ("glory of God"), was the founder of the Bahai religion.

The son of a noble family, Baha' Allah was born on November 17, 1817, in Tehran, Iran. He never received a formal education. A spiritual person, he was attracted to the teachings of the Bab (c. 1820–1850), who claimed to be the ultimate manifestation of the Islamic faith. His followers, known as Babi, formally broke with Islam in 1848. Following the Bab's execution for treason in 1850, Baha' Allah became one of the leaders of the movement.

In an attempt to eradicate the Babi, the Iranian government began a general persecution of the sect during which hundreds of thousands were slaughtered and Baha' Allah was imprisoned. While in jail he had a spiritual experience in which God chose him to be God's emissary. After his release in 1853, he spent the rest of his life as a political prisoner, exiled first to Baghdad, Iraq, then to Kurdistan, back to Baghdad, and eventually to Istanbul, Turkey. During his second visit to Baghdad in 1863, he declared himself as the one who fulfilled the Bab's promise as the one "whom God shall manifest."

The majority of Bab's followers, now known as "Bahais," accepted Baha' Allah as their inspired teacher. When a significant minority of the Bab's followers threatened discord because of Baha' Allah's claims, the Ottoman rulers banished him and his assemblage to Palestine. They arrived there in August, 1868, after which date they considered Palestine to be their Holy Land.

Although first imprisoned by the Ottoman rulers, he eventually settled in Haifa in 1880. From 1877 to 1884 he completed *The Most Holy Book,* a compilation of his teachings. Baha' Allah believed that religious truth was not absolute, but adaptable to the needs of the times. Therefore former religious figures—such as MOSES, JESUS, and MUHAMMAD—were links in a chain to spread God's message to a continually broader range of people. It was now the Baha' Allah's task to bring this message to the whole human race. He claimed that the soul was engaged in a continual process of unifying itself with God. Thus, there is no ultimate goal—heaven or hell—but an eternal seeking and movement toward God.

Because of his insistence on the unity of all people with God, Baha' Allah renounced all distinctions of race, gender, and social class. Moreover, he rejected the concept of sacraments and a hierarchy of priests. Instead, each member of the community of Bahais was encouraged to help others in their individual spiritual quests.

Baha' Allah died in Haifa, present-day Israel, on May 29, 1892.

Legacy

Baha' Allah founded the Bahai religion, which spread throughout the world in the twentieth century.

When Baha' Allah died, leadership of the group went to his son, 'Abbas Effendi (1844–1926). After a period of imprisonment, he traveled worldwide to establish Bahai communities in such places as Egypt (1910), Europe (1911), and North America (1912–1913).

The teachings of Baha' Allah became the core of the fundamental beliefs and practices of Bahai. This teaching has four basic components: 1) Bahais should come together every 19 days; 2) they should fast for 19 days during the Muslim month of 'Ala, which ends on March 21, the vernal equinox, which is their New Year's Day; 3) they must abstain from alcohol; and 4) they are to pray daily.

Baha' Allah's principles of equality lie at the heart of the democratic nature of Bahai communities. Built on the premise that the majority will expresses the will of God, community structure is pyramidal, growing upwards from the large base of the electorate to smaller, ruling councils. The electorate chooses a nine-member Local Spiritual Assembly each year. In turn, these local assemblies meet together to elect a nine-member National Assembly. Every five years, the national assemblies meet to elect the nine-member International House of Justice. This international body is the final arbiter of questions for all Bahais. It has the authority to revoke old, antiquated religious laws and to create new law as the circumstances warrant.

During the twentieth century, the number of followers of Bahai has increased dramatically. By 1985, there were 27,887 Local Assemblies and 143 National Councils overseeing a worldwide Bahai community of over 1.5 million. Although Bahai has no priesthood or public worship, followers are encouraged to build temples called *Mashriq al-Adhkar* ("a place where mention of the name of God arises at dawn"). These temples are nine-sided structures capped by a dome consisting of nine sections. The first of these temples, built in 1920, stands in 'Ishqabad, in present day Russia. Another, completed in 1953, is located just outside of Chicago in Wilmette, Illinois. In the last half of the twentieth century, other temples have arisen in Panama, Australia, Germany, Uganda, and Samoa. Still another is under construction in India.

von Dehsen

WORLD EVENTS	BAHA' ALLAH'S LIFE
Napoleonic Wars 1803–15 in Europe	
	1817 Baha' Allah is born
Greek War of 1821–29 Independence against Turkey	
Revolutions in 1848 Austria, France, Germany, and Italy	
United States 1861–65 Civil War	
	1863 Baha' Allah declares himself "he whom God shall manifest"
	1868 Baha' Allah arrives in Palestine
Germany is united 1871	
	1877–84 *The Most Holy Book* is written
	1892 Baha' Allah dies
Spanish American 1898 War	

For Further Reading:

Balyuzi, H. M. *Baha u'llah, the King of Glory.* Oxford: Ronald, 1980.

Hofman, David. *Bah'a 'ull'ah: Prince of Peace.* Oxford: Ronald, 1992.

Bakunin, Mikhail

Russian Revolutionary;
Founder of Modern Anarchy
1814–1876

World Events		Bakunin's Life
Napoleonic Wars 1803–15 in Europe		
	1814	Mikhail Bakunin is born in Tver, near Moscow
Greek War of 1821–29 Independence against Turkey		
	1840	Bakunin moves to Berlin and encounters "Young Hegelians"
Revolutions in Austria, France, Germany, and Italy	1848	Bakunin supports workers' revolts in France
	1849	Bakunin is extradited to Russia
	1861	Bakunin escapes from exile and flees to London
United States Civil War	1861–65	
	1863	*The Revolutionary Catechism* is published
	1867	*Federalism, Socialism, and Anti-Theologism* is published
Germany is united	1871	
	1876	Bakunin dies in Berne, Switzerland
Spanish American War	1898	

Life and Work

Mikhail Bakunin was a Russian revolutionary and founder of one of the major strains of nineteenth-century anarchism.

Bakunin was born on May 30, 1814, to an aristocratic family in Tver, northwest of Moscow. He studied philosophy in Moscow, where he began exploring radical political ideas, and in 1840 moved to Berlin to finish his education. There he encountered the "Young Hegelians," who advocated the necessity of putting political thought into action. Two years later, Bakunin published an article entitled, "The Reaction in Germany," in which he predicted the outbreak of revolutions in Russia. The Russian government tried and convicted him in absentia for this incendiary article.

Over the next few years, Bakunin traveled throughout Europe. He met KARL MARX but became a socialist only in 1848. He fought alongside Parisian workers during their uprising in February 1848 and that same year participated in the Slavic Congress, advocating the creation of Slavic republics after the overthrow of the Russian and German empires. Captured by authorities during a revolt in Dresden, Germany, in 1849, he was extradited to Russia, where he was imprisoned and then sent into exile in Siberia. He escaped in 1861 and spent the remainder of his life organizing revolutionary groups and insurrections in Europe. Eventually he promoted the idea of an international brotherhood of anarchists that would destroy all states and pave the way for world revolution.

Bakunin publicized his ideas through a series of articles and books including *The Revolutionary Catechism* (1863) and *Federalism, Socialism, and Anti-Theologism* (1867). Announcing that "the passion for destruction is also a creative passion," he called for the overthrow of all states because they were inherently unjust. Those who held positions in government formed a ruling class that would always pursue its own interests at the expense of the rest of society. And even if rulers were selfless, government could never pass laws for the common good because society was too complex for all to have the same needs and goals. He advocated constituting society from the bottom up through voluntary associations among workers. Bakunin saw the overthrow of the state as coming from a mass rebellion rather than through military action, which might lead to the establishment of an oligarchy. He sought to promote this rebellion through propaganda, strikes, and insurrection.

Bakunin's last few years were spent writing and supporting insurrections in Lyons (1870) and Italy (1874). He died in Berne, Switzerland, on June 1, 1876.

Legacy

Bakunin was one of the fathers of modern anarchism. He pushed anarchism in a collective direction, helping to radicalize worker movements in France, Spain, and Italy at the turn of the nineteenth century. By 1883 anarchists had organized their own International (a multinational organization) and they held their first convention in Amsterdam in 1907. Because of its philosophy, however, anarchism never was a highly organized movement.

In the first half of the twentieth century, anarchism found support among the oppressed labor unionists of the Industrial Workers of the World. This organization had chapters in France, Italy, and the United States. Anarchists had their greatest success in Spain, where they gained control of many areas during the opening years of the Spanish Civil War (1936–1939).

Bakunin never supported terrorism, yet his advocacy of violent revolution inspired the assassination of several prominent leaders by his more radical followers. In short succession assassins killed Czar Alexander II of Russia (1881), President F. M. Sadi Carnot of France (1894), Empress Elizabeth of Austria (1898), King Humbert of Italy (1900), and President McKinley of the United States (1901), as well as many lesser government leaders.

Bakunin's theories of anarchism continue to find some support among socialists and oppressed workers' groups that see the regime in power as the chief source of their oppression. The most effective anarchist movements of the last third of the twentieth century are principally focused on peace and justice issues and the ecological movement.

von Dehsen

For Further Reading:

Masters, Anthony. *Bakunin, The Father of Anarchism.* London: Sidgwick and Jackson, 1974.

Morland, David. *Demanding the Impossible?: Human Nature and Nineteenth Century Anarchism.* Washington, D.C.: Cassell, 1997.

Saltman, Richard B. *The Social and Political Thought of Mikhail Bakunin.* Westport, Conn.: Greenwood Press, 1983.

Barth, Karl

Christian Theologian and
Originator of Neo-Orthodoxy;
Active Opponent of Hitler
1886–1968

Life and Work

One of the most influential Christian theologians of the twentieth century, Karl Barth was the originator of neo-orthodoxy.

Born on May 10, 1886, in Basel, Switzerland, Barth was the son of Fritz Barth, a Reformed minister and scholar. He attended the universities of Bern, Berlin, Tübingen, and Marburg, where he studied with some of the leading liberal theologians of the day. From 1911 to 1921 he served as minister in the working-class parish of Safenwil, Switzerland.

Barth was deeply shocked by the horror of World War I and troubled by Christian churches' uncritical support of it. He questioned the easy optimism of liberal theology, which emphasized God's accessibility and equated humankind's work with God's activity. In 1919 Barth published *Commentary on the Epistle to the Romans,* which stressed God's sovereignty and glory. His work led to his appointment as professor first at the University of Gottingen (1921) and then at Munster (1925) and Bonn (1930).

Barth opposed Adolf Hitler and was one of the founders of the "Confessing Church," which fought the cooperation of the German Lutheran church with Nazi ideology. He wrote the draft of the 1934 Barmen Declaration, asserting the primacy of the traditional Gospel against the demands of the state and was expelled from Bonn that same year. His refusal to swear allegiance to Hitler cost him his chair in Bonn, and in 1935 he returned to Switzerland where he became professor of theology at the University of Basel.

Barth's objective was to lead the church away from what he saw as fundamentally erroneous liberal theology and back to the principles of the Reformation and the Bible. In his works, including his monumental *Church Dogmatics* (1932–62), he emphasized the great gulf between God and humanity and sinful man's inability to know God except through God's revelation. The Bible was not God's revelation, but the record of that revelation, which was JESUS CHRIST himself. It was only through the Word of God that God communicates with man. He rejected the liberals' belief that God could be understood through reason or human religious experience. "Religion," Barth insisted, "is the enemy of faith." By religion he meant man's attempt to enter into communion with God on his own terms.

Barth stressed the sinfulness of humanity. He dismissed the liberal thinking that sin was merely error or ignorance that could be overcome by education or human action. Instead, he asserted that sin was a basic condition of humankind that was overcome only by God's mercy and forgiveness. In his works Barth revived the doctrine of the Trinity and reasserted the Christology of the ancient church. He died in Basel on December 9, 1968.

Legacy

Barth was one of the most influential Christian theologians of the twentieth century, initiating a trend toward neo-orthodoxy (an attempt to restore traditional teachings in view of modern liberalism) in Protestantism that had a tremendous impact on later Christian thinkers.

Neo-orthodoxy emerged in the United States in mid-century in the writings of PAUL TILLICH and H. Richard and REINHOLD NIEBUHR. In H. Richard Niebuhr's *The Kingdom of God in America* (1937), he succinctly dismissed liberal theology, "A God without wrath brought men without sin into a kingdom without judgment through the ministrations of a Christ without a cross." These neo-orthodox theologians challenged the liberal tendency to associate the contemporary world with God's will and stressed that Christ is not a part of modern culture but challenges it. Tillich and Reinhold Niebuhr differed from Barth, however, in their understanding of revelation. While Barth insisted that revelation came only through God's revelatory event—the coming of Christ, the Americans asserted that human beings could have some understanding of God apart from Christ.

Ironically, radical theologians in the 1960s used Barth's work as a foundation upon which to build the so-called "Death of God" theology, a theology Barth would have disavowed. They accepted Barth's statement that Christianity was not a religion and questioned whether a society with no feeling for the transcendent could experience God.

Barth's work stimulated renewed interest in MARTIN LUTHER and SØREN AABYE KIERKEGAARD, and in JOHN CALVIN's reformed tradition. His writings have become a benchmark against which all subsequent Christian theology is measured. In developing new theological ideas, supporters and critics alike must engage his ideas.

Olson

WORLD EVENTS		BARTH'S LIFE
Germany is united	1871	
	1886	Karl Barth is born in Basel, Switzerland
Spanish American War	1898	
World War I	1914–18	
	1919	*Commentary on the Epistle to the Romans* is published
	1930	Barth is appointed professor at Bonn
	1932–62	Barth publishes *Church Dogmatics*
	1934	Barth writes draft of Barmen Declaration
		Barth is expelled from Bonn
World War II	1939–45	
Mao Tse-tung establishes Communist rule in China	1949	
Korean War	1950–53	
Six Day War between Israel and Arabs	1967	
	1968	Barth dies in Basel
End of Vietnam War	1975	

For Further Reading:

Anderson, William P. *Aspects of the Theology of Karl Barth.* Washington, D.C.: University Press of America, 1981.

Hunsinger, George, ed. *Karl Barth and Radical Politics.* Philadelphia: Westminster, 1976.

Jüngel, Eberhard. *Karl Barth, A Theological Legacy.* Translated by Garnett E. Paul. Philadelphia: Westminster, 1986.

Sykes, S. W. *Karl Barth.* Oxford: Oxford University Press, 1979.

Benedict of Nursia, Saint

Founder of Basic Structure of
Western Monasticism
c. 480–547

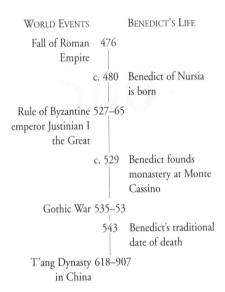

World Events		Benedict's Life
Fall of Roman Empire	476	
	c. 480	Benedict of Nursia is born
Rule of Byzantine emperor Justinian I the Great	527–65	
	c. 529	Benedict founds monastery at Monte Cassino
Gothic War	535–53	
	543	Benedict's traditional date of death
T'ang Dynasty in China	618–907	

Life and Work

Benedict established the rule that governed life in Western monasteries for over 1,500 years.

There is no contemporary account of Benedict's life. The sole source is the *Dialogues* of Pope GREGORY I, who obtained his information from several of Benedict's disciples. Benedict was born to a distinguished family in Nursia, in what is now central Italy, and spent his early years studying in Rome. Disillusioned by the moral laxity of the city, he decided to live the life of a religious hermit in a cave at Subiaco, east of Rome. Benedict soon developed a reputation for holiness and was asked to head a community of monks at nearby Vicovaro. When the monks objected to his strict rule and tried to kill him, he returned to Subiaco, where he was joined by numerous disciples. He organized them into 12 small communities over which he had general supervision.

Around 529 Benedict established a monastery at Monte Cassino, halfway between Rome and Naples. Church historians consider Monte Cassino the birthplace of Western monasticism. There Benedict developed his plans for reforming monasticism and wrote the rule by which his monks were governed.

Benedict's rule contains both the principles of monasticism and directives for the life of monks. It is practical rather than austere, stressing a balance between prayer, work, and study—with the Divine Office (the liturgy of the Mass) as the center of monastic life. The monks engage in physical labor, take their meals together, and avoid unnecessary conversation. The rule regulates sleep, meals, clothing, work, care of the sick and travelers, and the admission and training of members.

From his monastery Benedict counseled rulers and popes and looked after the local population during the chaotic period of the Gothic War (535–553). With his sister, Scholastica, he also founded a community for women. Benedict died at Monte Cassino in 543.

Legacy

Benedict developed the rule that served as the basic guide for all Western monasticism. In consequence, he had a profound influence on the development of Western European society during the Middle Ages, when many threatened aspects of civilization were preserved in monasteries.

Benedict's insistence that monks care for the sick and receive guests as Christ made monasteries centers of charity. The rule that all monks had to spend time in reading resulted in an emphasis on education and the growth of a literary culture that equipped the monasteries to become repositories of learning. His emphasis on the importance of the Divine Office led to the preservation and development of liturgical art and music.

The rule gradually spread throughout Europe. For two centuries after his death this rule was one of several from which abbots could choose when establishing a monastery. In the seventh century it was propagated in Gaul (France) by the Celtic monasteries, where it was combined with the Rule of Columban. In the eighth century, the Anglo-Saxon missionary monks, led by St. Boniface, carried the rule with them to Germany where they reestablished monasticism along Benedictine lines. The Synod of Aachen imposed the rule on all monasteries of the Holy Roman Empire in 817. Almost all the orders that sprung up in the Middle Ages were based on the rule, although several, such as the Cistercians, carried austerity further than the original rule permitted. By the twelfth century more than 3,000 communities were organized according to Benedict's rule.

Benedict's religious and cultural influences have been best expressed by historians who have called the period from 800 to 1200 the "Benedictine Centuries." In 1964 Pope Paul VI proclaimed, Benedict "father of Europe and patron of the Occident [West]" because of the impact monks under his rule had on European civilization.

The Reformation of the sixteenth century ended monasticism in northern Europe. In the late eighteenth century, government anticlericalism nearly destroyed all Benedictine foundations in the rest of Europe. Yet since 1830, the Benedictines have revived in Europe and America, and remain an important group within the Roman Catholic church.

Olson

For Further Reading:

Chapman, John. *St. Benedict and the Sixth Century, 1919.* Reprint. Westport, Conn: Greenwood Press, 1971.

Zimmermann, O. J., and B. R. Avery. *Life and Miracles of St. Benedict.* Westport, Conn.: Greenwood Press, 1980.

Hilpisch, Stephen. *Benedictinism Through Changing Centuries.* Collegeville, Minn.: St. John's Abbey Press, 1958.

Bentham, Jeremy

English Jurist and Philosopher;
Expounder of Utilitarianism
1748–1832

Life and Work

Jeremy Bentham was a British political reformer and philosopher who developed the idea of utilitarianism.

Bentham was born in London, February 15, 1748. A child prodigy, he entered Oxford University at 12, where he studied law and earned a master's degree in 1766. He became a lawyer in 1772 but quickly became disillusioned with the legal system, which he believed reflected broad social corruption. Independently wealthy, Bentham gave up the law and devoted his life to a broad range of social and political reforms. He campaigned for legal and penal reform and spoke of the paramount necessity of education. In 1817 he published *Catechism of Parliamentary Reform* in which he recommended extending the franchise and equalizing electoral districts. Bentham was an early champion of equal rights for women.

Bentham was convinced that the social corruption of his day was rooted in unsound Enlightenment theories of natural law, natural rights, and the social contract of government. These concepts had been based on the supposition that moral standards were self-evident and known by intuition. Bentham claimed that he could scientifically ascertain what was morally justifiable by applying the principle of "utility," which he defined as "that property in any object whereby it tends to produce benefit, advantage, pleasure, good, or happiness, or to prevent the happening of mischief, pain, evil, or unhappiness in the party whose interest is considered." He expounded this theory of utilitarianism in his greatest work, *Introduction to the Principles of Morals and Legislation,* published in 1789.

Humans, he argued, have two main motives, gain and pleasure, which ought to determine what we do. The legislator's chief concern is to decide what form of behavior would be most likely to bring the most happiness and what sanctions will be most likely to bring about such happiness. Right actions should not be determined by a continuation of past events but by a vision of the future state of affairs.

Actions were right if they tended to produce the greatest happiness for the greatest number of people. Bentham made happiness equivalent to pleasure. If values were based on pleasure and pain, then theories of natural rights and natural law were invalid. If all pleasures and pains were of the same order, a kind of moral–mathematical evaluation of moral, political, and legal activities (dubbed "hedonic calculus") is possible. He tried to apply these principles to prison reform. He proposed a plan for a modern prison, "the Panopticon," for the rehabilitation of prisoners. The plan was so complex, however, that it was abandoned by 1813.

He was the leader of the Philosophical Radicals, whose members included James Mill and his son, JOHN STUART MILL. In 1823, they founded the *Westminster Review,* dedicated to preaching philosophical radicalism.

Bentham died in London on June 6, 1832.

Legacy

Bentham wrote one of the eighteenth century's most influential works of moral philosophy, yet his legacy lives not only in his theories but also in the practical reforms that arose from them.

Through his attempts to place the development of law under scientific scrutiny, Bentham is remembered more as a critic of law and of judicial and political institutions than as a legal philosopher. His legacy remains in the tradition of political and legal reforms. The Reform Act of 1832, which took government out of the hands of the aristocracy by broadening the franchise, was the result of his influence. It was passed just two days after his death. Bentham was also responsible for the development of a civil service based on merit and the elimination of imprisonment for debt. His *Principles of Penal Law* contains the germs of most modern prison reforms, although his plan for a model prison, the "Panopticon," was not adopted. Bentham also popularized the idea that democracy was most likely to produce "the greatest happiness of the greatest number," a political concept which blossomed in the nineteenth and twentieth centuries. These concepts have also influenced cost-benefit analysis and policy development.

One of Bentham's lasting memorials is University College, London, which he helped found. To ensure that the institution adheres to his reformist principles, Bentham stipulated in his will that he be present at meetings of the college's governing board. His skeleton, fully clothed, provided with a wax head and seated in a glass case is present at all meetings.

Olson

WORLD EVENTS		BENTHAM'S LIFE
Peace of Utrecht 1713–15 settles War of Spanish Succession		
	1748	Jeremy Bentham is born
United States independence	1776	
French Revolution	1789	*Introduction to the Principles of Morals and Legislation* is published
Napoleonic Wars 1803–15 in Europe		
	1817	*Catechism of Parliamentary Reform* is published
Greek War of 1821–29 Independence against Turkey		
	1823	Bentham, James Mill, and John Stuart Mill establish the *Westminster Review*
	1832	Bentham dies in London
Revolutions in 1848 Austria, France, Germany, and Italy		

For Further Reading:

Dinwiddy, J. *Bentham.* Oxford: Oxford University Press, 1989.

Hart, H. L. A. *Essays on Bentham.* Oxford: Oxford University Press, 1982.

Berkeley, George

Founder of Idealism
1685–1753

World Events		Berkeley's Life
Thirty Years' War in Europe	1618–48	
	1685	George Berkeley is born
England's Glorious Revolution	1688	
English seize Calcutta, India	1690	
	1709	*An Essay Towards a New Theory of Vision* is published
	1710	Berkeley is ordained a priest in Church of England; *A Treatise Concerning the Principles of Human Knowledge* is published
Peace of Utrecht settles War of Spanish Succession	1713–15	
	1721	*De Motu* is published
	1728	Berkeley travels to North America
	1734	Berkeley becomes Bishop of Cloyne; *The Analyst* is published
	1753	Berkeley dies at Oxford
United States independence	1776	

Life and Work

George Berkeley was a major figure in the development of empiricism, the school of thought that dominated the psychological theories during the eighteenth century Enlightenment. He is considered to be the founder of the philosophical school of idealism.

The son of English parents, Berkeley was born in County Kilkenny, Ireland, on March 12, 1685. He studied philosophy at Trinity College, Dublin, where he was influenced by the ideas of English philosopher JOHN LOCKE, and became a fellow there in 1707. He was ordained a priest in the Church of England three years later. Berkeley quickly rose to prominence within the church and became closely associated with the cultural leaders of the day, including Jonathan Swift and Alexander Pope. He served as a lecturer in divinity at Trinity from 1721 to 1724, when he was appointed dean of Derry. In 1721 he also published *De Motu (On Motion),* a book challenging the theories of Isaac Newton. In 1728 Berkeley traveled to America in a vain attempt to found a missionary college for Native Americans. While in the colonies, he influenced the development of several universities, especially Yale and Columbia. He returned to Britain in 1732 and, in 1734, became bishop of Cloyne, County Cork, Ireland, where he founded the journal, *The Querist.*

Berkeley's philosophical interest centered on explaining the relationship between external reality and ideas. He accepted the basic idea of John Locke's theory of empirical psychology that experience, rather than innate reason, is the center of all human knowledge. Nevertheless, he rejected Locke's claim that sensory perception always leads to certain knowledge. Instead, Berkeley hypothesized that material objects exist only when they are perceived by the mind: *esse est percipi,* "to be is to be perceived." There is no reality outside the mind. Individuals cannot be certain that the ideas they develop from experience are always true. Only when the same experience yields the same perception can an individual guarantee the validity of an idea. This came to be known as the theory of immaterialism. Berkeley noted that people cannot always control their ideas and so claimed that there must be one mind that contains all ideas—the mind of God who perceives all things. Berkeley published his ideas in three important books: *An Essay Towards a New Theory of Vision* (1709), *A Treatise Concerning the Principles of Human Knowledge* (1710), and *The Analyst* (1734).

Berkeley retired to Oxford in 1752 and died there the following year.

Legacy

Berkeley is considered to be the founder of idealism. His contributions to empiricism greatly influenced the maturation of other psychological theories during the Enlightenment. Berkeley's philosophical system produced few followers, but his criticisms of arguments for a separate external world and of the concept of matter have influenced philosophers ever since.

Berkeley's theory of immateriality laid the groundwork for much of later existential philosophy. Once the premise is accepted that all reality is mental and that things only exist as perceived, it is a short step to assume that all reality exists only as the individual discerns it. This philosophy anticipates much of the thought of IMMANUEL KANT, FRIEDRICH WILHELM NIETZSCHE, and JEAN-PAUL SARTRE.

Berkeley's immaterialist argument against Newton in his *De Motu* of 1721 provided the theoretical framework for the scientific theories of Ernst Mach and the theory of relativity originated by Albert Einstein.

Berkeley's theory of idealism also had its detractors. For example, Kant argued that even the mind presumes itself to exist in an objective order containing external objects. Therefore, there must be a reality apart from the mind itself. Others argued that nature itself would not be affected if there were no one to perceive it. Samuel Johnson attempted to refute Berkeley by kicking a stone to demonstrate the stone's "objective" existence.

Nevertheless, Berkeley focused the question of knowing onto the knower and inspired Californians to name the city of Berkeley after him.

Olson

For Further Reading:

Dancy, Jonathan. *Berkeley: An Introduction.* New York: Blackwell, 1987.

Umson, J. G. *Berkeley.* Oxford: Oxford University Press, 1982.

Warnoc, G. J. *Berkeley.* Notre Dame, Ind.: University of Notre Dame Press, 1983.

Winkler, Kenneth P. *Berkeley: An Interpretation.* Oxford: Oxford University Press, 1989.

Bernadette of Lourdes, Saint

(Marie Bernarde Soubirous)

Roman Catholic Visionary
1844–1879

Life and Work

Marie Bernarde Soubirous, commonly known as Bernadette of Lourdes, professed to have seen a vision of MARY just outside the small town of Lourdes, in southwestern France. This vision led to the discovery of a mineral spring with healing powers. As a result, Lourdes has become one of the most prominent shrines to Mary in the Roman Catholic church.

Bernadette was born on January 7, 1844, in Lourdes. She was the oldest child of Louise and Francis Soubirous, a poor miller. As a young girl, Bernadette had no opportunity for formal education. She was also frequently in ill health, suffering from asthma and from cholera during the epidemic of 1854.

On February 11, 1858, Bernadette was collecting wood beside the Gave River, just outside of town, when she had a vision of the Virgin Mary standing above a cave. Her account of this vision brought the suspicion of her parents and of the local authorities. These visions continued daily from February 18 through March 4.

Despite constant resistance to her claims, Bernadette continued to obey the instructions of the Virgin Mary and discovered an underground spring where none had been before. Quickly, the spring became known for its healing powers.

On March 25, 1858, Bernadette experienced another vision, in which the Mary identified herself as the "Immaculate Conception." (This expression could refer either to the immaculate conception of JESUS or to the Roman Catholic teaching, issued by Pope Pius IX in 1854, that asserted that Mary herself was free from original sin.) Bernadette also stated that Mary instructed that a chapel be built on the site. The young girl continued to have visions until July 26 of that year.

These visions caused such controversy that Bernadette's parents and the local church authorities thought it best for her to leave Lourdes. She was placed in a boarding school run by the Sisters of Charity in the town of Nevers. In 1866 she became a sister of the order and remained at the convent in Nevers. Her health continued to be poor. She refused to avail herself of the healing waters of Lourdes, claiming that the "Lady" required penance from her. Bernadette died in Nevers on April 16, 1879; her body remains on view in the chapel there.

Legacy

Bernadette's vision transformed the town of Lourdes from an unknown village in the Pyrenees to one renowned for its shrine to the Virgin Mother and for its healing waters. Millions of people travel to this village annually to venerate Mary and sample the waters in search of healing. It quickly became one of the most visited pilgrimage sites of the Roman Catholic church.

Many of the people who visited the spring at Lourdes claimed to have experienced miraculous healing. Some of these healings have been investigated by Church and scientific authorities and have been verified as inexplicable, that is, as miraculous. In response to these healings, identified as miracles attributed to the intercession of Bernadette, she was canonized by Pope Pius XI on December 8, 1933. In the twentieth century, many Roman Catholic hospitals have been named after "Our Lady of Lourdes," that is, the Virgin Mary, to honor the healing nature of the spring.

The vision of Bernadette at Lourdes, and the identification of a shrine dedicated to Mary, is part of a larger pattern of Marian visions over the last several centuries. In 1531, Juan Diego, a recent convert to Roman Catholicism, received a vision of Mary in Guadalupe, Mexico. Catherine Laboure experienced a vision of Mary in Paris in 1830; Mary instructed her to have medals struck honoring the Immaculate Conception to inspire faithfulness.

In the twentieth century, several people have avowed to have had visions of Mary. On May 13, 1917, three young children, Lucian de Santos, and her two cousins, Francisco and Jacinta Marto, maintained that they saw "Our Lady of the Rosary." The Lady gave them several messages warning the world of the inevitable destruction it would face if people remained in sin. More recently, a group of young people in Medjugorje, in the former Yugoslavia, contend that they have received visions of Mary since June of 1981. In these visions, Mary issues messages focusing on peace, conversion, fasting, penance, and prayer.

The visions of Bernadette of the Virgin Mary have given hope and inspiration to many people. As a simple girl, her insistence that Mary spoke to her, identified herself as the "Immaculate Conception," and disclosed the healing waters have led countless Roman Catholic faithful to travel to Lourdes seeking both spiritual and physical well being.

von Dehsen

World Events	Bernadette's Life
Greek War of 1821–29 Independence against Turkey	
	1844 Marie Bernarde Soubirous is born
Revolutions in 1848 Austria, France, Germany, and Italy	
	1858 Bernadette receives visions of Mary and uncovers the spring
United States 1861–65 Civil War	
	1866 Bernadette becomes nun of Sisters of Charity
Germany is united 1871	
	1879 Bernadette dies
Spanish American 1898 War	

For Further Reading:
Laurentin, René. *Bernadette of Lourdes: A Life Based on Authenticated Documents*. Minneapolis, Minn.: Winston Press, 1979.
Ravier, André. *Bernadette*. Cleveland, Ohio: Collins, 1979.

Bernard of Clairvaux, Saint

Defender of Christianity
Against Rationalism
1090–1153

Life and Work

Bernard of Clairvaux, one of the most influential men of the twelfth century, had a significant impact on his age and on the thinking of the Christian church through the centuries.

Born to aristocratic parents near Dijon, France, Bernard took monastic vows in 1112 at the Cistercian monastery at Citeaux, a community founded to restore the strict observance of the Benedictine rule. Three years later, he established a new monastery at Clairvaux, which became one of the centers for the Cistercian order. Bernard was largely responsible for the rapid expansion of the Cistercians, not only founding monasteries but also shaping the spirituality of the order. A man with an electrifying personality who earned a reputation for scholarship and holiness, Bernard quickly became one of the major religious forces in Europe.

Eventually Bernard was involved in almost all the major religious and political events of his time. In 1128 he helped establish the Knights Templar as an arm of the Crusades. In 1130 he was instrumental in settling the disputed election between Pope Innocent II and the Antipope (a person who claimed to be the legitimate pope) Anacletus, thereby winning the acceptance of Innocent. His influence increased when Eugenius III, a former monk of Clairvaux, became Pope. At the Pope's request, Bernard roused all of Europe for a Second Crusade against the Turks in 1146. The crusade, however, ended in disaster, which Bernard attributed to the wickedness of the crusaders.

Severely orthodox in his theology, Bernard led campaigns against what he considered the major theological threats of the day. Believing that God should be approached through faith and prayer, not human reason, he opposed theologian PETER ABELARD's rationalist approach to Christianity and orchestrated Abelard's condemnation at the Council of Sens in 1140. At the request of Pope Eugenius, he preached against the Albigensians, who believed that Christ's redemptive work came from his teachings and not from his suffering. Toward the end of his life he denounced Gilbert de la Portee, who rejected the divinity of Christ.

A prolific writer, Bernard expounded his theology in more than 800 sermons, letters, and books. During his early days at Clairvaux he produced a small work on MARY entitled "Praises of the Virgin Mother." Among his most important books were *On the Love of God* (c. 1127) and *Sermons on the Song of Songs.* Bernard stressed the importance of freeing oneself from self-love, that is, attachment to one's own judgments and false ambitions, in order to achieve a closer relationship with God. Through a life of simplicity, seeking perfection through submission to God's will, one can achieve a mystical marriage with him.

Bernard died at Clairvaux in August 20, 1153. He was declared a saint of the Church in 1174 only 20 years after his death.

Legacy

Bernard's influence on the twelfth century was enormous, but his impact on the Christian church extended well beyond his own lifetime. Bernard's importance lies in the several seemingly divergent paths his life took.

First, was Bernard's influence in the spiritual realm. He was a champion of the contemplative, inner-directed life, providing models for those who wished to seek union with God and support the poor. His work helped shape the mystical thought of the Middle Ages. In addition, his sermons on biblical themes and his devotion to Mary exerted a strong influence on Christian spirituality.

Second, was Bernard's effect on the concrete world of both church and politics. His support of Popes Innocent II and Eugenius III shaped the future direction of the papacy. His support of the Second Crusade put Bernard at the center of a part of Christian history whose import is debated to this day, especially as it shaped the course of history of Turkey and the Middle East.

Finally, he remains significant in the history of biblical interpretation; his sermon series *On the Song of Songs* is a famous example of the allegorical method that became prominent among the Scholastics of the late medieval period. Bernard's emphasis on God's gracious justification by faith served as an early influence on the development of MARTIN LUTHER's theology. His opposition to Abelard's rationalism provided a basis for the Church's engagement with the Enlightenment in the eighteenth century.

The lasting importance of Bernard's teaching and personal example earned him the acknowledgment as the last of the Church Fathers—early theologians who shaped later doctrine. In 1830 he was more formally recognized as a Doctor (Teacher) of the Church.

Olson

WORLD EVENTS		BERNARD'S LIFE
Schism between Roman Catholic and Orthodox Church	1054	
	1090	Bernard is born
First Crusade	1095	
Crusaders capture Jerusalem during First Crusade	1099	
Settling of Timbuktu, present-day Mali	c. 1100	
	1112	Bernard enters monastery at Citeaux
	1115	Bernard establishes monastery at Clairvaux
	c. 1127	*On the Love of God* is published
	1128	Bernard helps organize Knights Templar
	1139	Bernard denounces Abelard
	1147–49	Bernard is instrumental in organizing Second Crusade
	1153	Dies at Clairvaux
	1174	Canonized
Islamic ruler of Egypt, Saladin, captures Jerusalem	1187	
	1830	Recognized as Doctor of the Church

For Further Reading:
Evans, Gillian R. *The Mind of St. Bernard of Clairvaux.* Oxford: Clarendon Press, 1983.
Leclercq, Jean. *Bernard of Clairvaux and the Cistercian Spirit.* Kalamazoo, Mich.: Cistercian Publishers, 1976.

Bihbihani, Aka Sayyid Muhammad Bakir

Influential Shiite Legal Scholar
c. 1705–c. 1792

Life and Work

Aka Sayyid Muhammad Bakir Bihbihani was a Shiite *mujaddid* (an inspired renewer of Islamic legal interpretation and practice). He established the role of the *mujtahid*, the authoritative practitioner of *ijtihad* (the rational interpretation of *Shariah*, Islamic law).

Bihbihani was born in about 1705 in Isfahan (in present-day Iran). When he was still a young boy, his father, Mulla Muhammad Akmal, took him to Karbala in Iraq, one of the *atabat*, or shrine cities, that contained the Shrine of Imam Husayn, the grandson of MUHAMMAD, who was murdered there in 640. (According to Shiite tradition, an imam is a leader in the succession of Muhammad.) Bihbihani had intended to return to Iran once his education was complete. However, before he could leave Karbala, he had a dream in which he was visited by the twelfth, and last, imam, Muhammad al-Mahdi (d. 941), who instructed him to settle there.

In Karbala Bihbihani led the Usuli school of legal interpretation against the then-dominant Akhbari school over the question of *fikh*, Islamic jurisprudence. The Akhbari school contended that no further interpretation of law was necessary apart from the traditions (*akhbar*) developed by the leaders from Muhammad through the twelfth imam. The Usuli, in contrast, asserted that the *mujtahid* could interpret the *Shariah* in light of new circumstances. Prior to Bihbihani's tenure as *mujtahid*, Shiites could not even walk in public with Usuli books visible.

Bihbihani broke Akhbari domination and established the supremacy of the Usuli *mujtahids*. His tactics ranged from scholarly writing and debate to blatant use of force. On the one hand, he produced many legal writings, including a strident refutation of the Akhbari theories in his most famous book, *al-Fawa'id*

al-Usuliyya. (English title for this volume is unavailable.) On the other hand, when he traveled he took along several *mirghadabs*, executors of punishment, to carry out the sentences he deemed appropriate for heretics. Bihbihani was also a fierce opponent of the Sufi mystics, who challenged the authority of the *mujtahid* by claiming direct divine revelation and rejecting the necessary direction of the *Shariah*. His attacks against them became so brutal that he earned the appellate, *sufikush*, Sufi-killer.

Bihbihani died in Karbala around 1792 and was buried near the tomb of Imam Husayn.

Legacy

Bihbihani's legacy is symbolized by his title *mujaddid*, renewer: his leadership secured the dominance of the Usuli school of Islamic jurisprudence over that of the Akhbari. He established a line of *mujtahid* jurists who were the religious rulers of the *atabat* until the last third of the twentieth century.

By establishing the Usuli *ijtihad* as the principal method of legal interpretation in the *atabat*, Bihbihani laid the foundation for the emergence of a dynamic and contextual approach to understanding the requirements of the *Shariah*. The insistence that a *mujtahid* did not need to rely on fixed interpretations but could apply his own reasoning and expertise to articulate the demands of the law allowed the *Shariah* to address concerns unforeseen in the ancient text. In the event that *mujtahids* from different communities developed different interpretations, they would acknowledge that their opinions were *zann*, debatable opinions. The community, in turn, was to practice *taqlid*, compliance with the rulings of the *mujtahid*. Thus, Bihbihani's model of jurisprudence constructed a community whose life was shaped by the *Shariah* but not stifled by it.

Bihbihani's suppression of the Akhbari school advanced Usuli theories in Iran. Many of the cities of the *atabat* provided places for Iranian *ulama* (religious scholars) to study. In Iraq, Bihbihani's ideas thrived among his students and the *mujtahids* who followed. Among these juridical leaders were his son, Mirza Muhammad 'Ali, and Shaikh Ja'far al-Najafi. In the middle of the nineteenth century, Shaikh Murtaza Ansari (d. 1865) consolidated religious authority by becoming the *marja'-i*

taqid, the sole legal authority for the entire Shiite community. The rule of the *mujtahids* continued until the death of Ayatollah Burujirdi, the last *marja'-i taqid*, in 1962.

von Dehsen

WORLD EVENTS		BIHBIHANI'S LIFE*
English seize Calcutta, India	1690	
		c. 1705 Aka Sayyid Muhammad Bakir Bihbihani is born
Peace of Utrecht settles War of Spanish Succession	1713–15	
United States independence	1776	
French Revolution	1789	
		c. 1792 Bihbihani dies
Napoleonic Wars in Europe	1803–15	

* Scholars cannot date the events of Bihbihani's life with accuracy.

For Further Reading:

Alger, Hamid. *Religion and State in Iran.* Berkeley: University of California Press, 1969.

Avery, Peter, and Stanley I. Grossman, eds. *The Cambridge History of Iran.* Vol. 7. Cambridge: Cambridge University Press, 1991.

Blavatsky, Helena Petrovna

Founder of the Theosophical
Movement
1831–1891

Life and Work

Helena Petrovna Blavatsky was the principal founder of the theosophical ("divine wisdom") movement, an attempt to bring together spiritual aspects of Eastern and Western religious beliefs. Through the use of spiritual practices, theosophy promotes the unity of all spirit and matter with the universal deity.

Blavatsky was born in 1831 in the Russian village of Ekaterinoslav. As a young girl she exhibited paranormal abilities and a charismatic personality. She received little formal education and, at 17, abandoned her husband and family to travel in Europe, America, India and Tibet. In Tibet she met the person she claimed was the "master," who taught her the secrets of Eastern spirituality. These ideas became the foundation of theosophy.

In 1873 Blavatsky moved to New York and became involved with the spiritualist movement, which attempted to overcome the limitations of earthly existence and to communicate with the spirits of the dead. Soon thereafter she began col-

laborating with Col. Henry S. Olcott, a lawyer and journalist, with whom she formed the Theosophical Society on November 17, 1875. Theosophy is a blend of Eastern and Western beliefs centered on three basic principles: 1) there is a universal Reality that embraces both matter and spirit; 2) there is a universal law of constant, cyclical evolution and change; and 3) all souls are intertwined with the universal Oversoul, a component of the Reality. Blavatsky developed her ideas in her book, *Isis Unveiled*, published in 1875.

In 1878, Blavatsky and Olcott left for India, where they founded *The Theosophist*, a journal devoted to merging Eastern spirituality with Western thought. As her ideas gained acceptance, Blavatsky became a controversial figure. Many denounced her claims to contact spirits as fraudulent, and, in 1885, the "Hodgson Report" from the London Society for Psychical Research accused her of having plagiarized a letter from the Tibetan master. That same year she returned to Europe.

During her remaining years, Blavatsky continued to develop and detail the precepts of theosophy, even though she suffered from poor health. In 1888, she completed her systematic presentation of theosophy, *The Secret Doctrine*. The following year she completed two more books, *The Voice of Silence* and *The Key to Theosophy* and started a new journal, *Lucifer*. She died on May 8, 1891, a date still honored by the Theosophical Society as White Lotus Day.

Legacy

As founder of the Theosophical Society, Blavatsky provided a foundation for the Theosophical movement's efforts to blend Eastern spirituality with Western religious traditions.

The Theosophical Society asserts the universality of humanity, the study of comparative religion, and the development of supernatural abilities in people. Clearly, these ideas stem from Blavatsky's own interest in establishing points of contact among all religions and her efforts at transcending the sphere of the natural world though spiritualism. Theosophy is also focused on exploring the interrelatedness of all beings. For example, theosophists carefully analyze religious symbols and narratives to broaden their understanding of internal spiritual knowledge and awareness. These spiritual exercises are designed to enlighten believers and to expand the believer's insight into the fundamental principles of the universe.

During her lifetime, Blavatsky never claimed to be the originator of any of her ideas. Rather, she maintained that her study of ancient religions and her own travels and experiences allowed her to find points of correspondence among seemingly unrelated religious concepts.

Blavatsky's insights have also been accepted by others not directly associated with theosophy. For example, the New Age movement of the last third of the twentieth century draws heavily on Blavatsky's spirituality and theosophical beliefs. Even though the New Age religions are more future-oriented than was theosophy, New Age thought looks to the development of inner spirituality. This spirituality promotes healing and a change in consciousness to overcome dualistic views of the cosmos, replacing them with a cosmic view that asserts the metaphysical interrelation of all aspects of the universe. By finding inner peace and wholeness, New Agers contend that they will also find universal peace through connectedness with the cosmos.

Finally, Blavatsky's attempts to find points of correspondence among divergent religious traditions paved the way to introduce those religions to Western culture. In 1907, Annie Wood Besant, a socialist who embraced theosophy, supported the development of Hinduism in her native Britain and other countries of the West. In 1917 the Indian National Congress honored her by electing her as their only non-Western president. In addition, Blavatsky's theories on the correspondence of religions anticipated scholarly interests in comparative religion during the twentieth century.

von Dehsen

WORLD EVENTS		BLAVATSKY'S LIFE
Greek War of Independence against Turkey	1821–29	
	1831	Helena Petrovna Blavatsky is born
Revolutions in Austria, France, Germany, and Italy	1848	
United States Civil War	1861–65	
Germany is united	1871	
	1875	Blavatsky and Henry S. Olcott form Theosophical Society
	1888	*The Secret Doctrine* is published
	1889	*The Voice of Silence* and *The Key to Theosophy* are published
	1891	Blavatsky dies
Spanish American War	1898	

For Further Reading:

Cranston, Sylvia. *HPB: The Extraordinary Life and Influence of Helena Blavatsky, Founder of the Modern Theosophical Movement*. New York: G. P. Putnam's Sons, 1993.

Marcos, Plino. *Madam Blavatsky*. Sao Paolo, Brazil: P. Marcos, 1988.

Meade, Marion. *Madam Blavatsky, The Woman Behind the Myth*. New York: Putnam, 1980.

Boethius, Anicius Manlius Severinus

Influential Medieval Philosopher; Architect of Scholasticism

c. 480–c. 524

Life and Work

Anicius Manlius Severinus Boethius was a Roman philosopher and Aristotelian translator whose work had a profound influence on the development of late classical and medieval philosophy.

Born into a noble Roman family about 480, Boethius was adopted by Symmachus, an extremely wealthy aristocrat, upon his father's death. He received an excellent education in Greek language and philosophy that shaped his future intellectual pursuits. Like many aristocrats, Boethius alternated between periods of private leisure and service to the state. His technical knowledge and skills led to a distinguished political career in the court of Theodoric, Gothic king of Italy, whom he served as consul (510) and as head of all government and court offices (520).

Wishing to reconcile the works of PLATO and ARISTOTLE, Boethius planned to translate and comment on all the philosophers' works, but the project was never completed. Instead, he translated only Aristotle's *Categories, Topics, Prior and Posterior Analytics, Sophistical Arguments,* and *On Interpretation.* He also translated Porphyry's *Isagoge,* a third century treatise on the logic of Aristotle. In his commentary on this work he tried to reconcile Aristotle's and Plato's theories of universals, that is, the reality of general concepts. While Plato pronounced universals real (realism) and Aristotle held them to be mental concepts (nominalism), Boethius suggested that the mind could recognize that immaterial universals manifest themselves in matter.

Boethius also wrote a number of original works on logic and mathematics as well as *De institutione musica.* In 520 he turned his attention to the question of the Trinity, using Aristotelian, rather than pure Christian, forms of reasoning to support the unity of the triune Christian deity. Using categories of relation-ships, he showed that God can exist in three relational forms, while remaining one unity.

Boethius wrote his greatest work, the five-volume *De Consolatione Philosophiae (Consolation of Philosophy),* while he was in prison on charges of treason for siding with the Eastern Roman emperor in a doctrinal dispute. In the work he wrestles with the problems of good and evil and divine foreknowledge and human freedom. While in prison, "Lady Philosophy" comes to console Boethius, telling him in Platonic fashion that true happiness comes not from possessions or power but from the pursuit of the highest good, which is God. If evil seems to triumph in life, order will be restored in the next. God's knowledge of our fate does not limit our free will.

Boethius was executed in Pavia c. 524.

Legacy

Boethius was one of the monumental figures in the history of medieval philosophy. His translations of Aristotle provided the medieval world with its knowledge of Greek philosophy and his original works set the course of medieval philosophical debate.

Scholars relied almost solely on Boethius's translations of Aristotle for their understanding of ancient Greek philosophy during the early Middle Ages. Although his translations were later found to be faulty, his works sustained the study of and interest in philosophy until the discovery of the whole Aristotelian corpus during the twelfth and thirteenth centuries.

Boethius's treatises on logic dominated medieval philosophy and provided the basic texts for medieval Scholasticism, a philosophy using reason to examine questions of the Christian faith. His discussion of universals, in particular, laid the foundation for the great philosophical debate between nominalism, supported by philosophers such as Jean Roscelin (1050–c.1125) and realism, advocated by thinkers such as ANSELM OF CANTERBURY (c.1033–1109). The structure of his academic thought provided the framework of later university curricula. He divided intellectual disciplines into two groups. The first, the *quadrivium,* consisted of arithmetic, music, geometry, and astronomy. The other, the *trivium,* contained grammar, rhetoric, and logic. *De institutione musica* became the predominant work on Greek music in the ninth century and was one of the first works on music to be published in Venice around 1491. While works on ecclesiastical music eventually replaced it, the book remains a significant source for information about the development of music theory.

The *Consolation of Philosophy* was the most widely read book in medieval Europe after the Bible, and it helped transmit Platonic ideas throughout the continent. King Alfred (849–899), king of Wessex, translated it into Anglo-Saxon. It also appeared in German in the eleventh century and in French in the thirteenth century. In the fourteenth century, Chaucer translated it into English.

Honigsberg

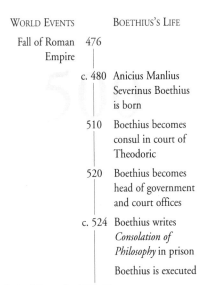

WORLD EVENTS		BOETHIUS'S LIFE
Fall of Roman Empire	476	
	c. 480	Anicius Manlius Severinus Boethius is born
	510	Boethius becomes consul in court of Theodoric
	520	Boethius becomes head of government and court offices
	c. 524	Boethius writes *Consolation of Philosophy* in prison
		Boethius is executed
Rule of Byzantine emperor Justinian I the Great	527–65	

For Further Reading:

McInery, Ralph M. *Boethius and Aquinas.* Washington, D.C.: Catholic University Press, 1990.

Reiss, Edmund. *Boethius.* Boston: Twayne Publishers, 1982.

Boff, Leonardo

Influential Liberation Theologian
1938–

Life and Work

Leonardo Boff was a Roman Catholic priest from Brazil who worked for the political and economic liberation of the poor and oppressed. His writings have become one of the major sources of Latin American liberation theology.

Boff was born in Concordia, Brazil, on December 14, 1938. His grandparents had immigrated to Brazil from Italy in the early 1900s. His father, an important early influence, held several jobs, including druggist, teacher, and accountant. He used these skills to help European immigrants acclimate themselves to Brazil, even establishing literacy programs to help newcomers learn Portuguese.

Boff was ordained a Roman Catholic priest in 1964. Later, he studied in Europe, receiving a doctorate in theology from the University of Munich in 1971. When he returned to Brazil, Boff began to serve parishes in poor communities. At that time he began to appreciate the

basic teachings of liberation theology, which emphasized the work, or praxis, of Christians on behalf of the oppressed in society; this work usually takes the form of political involvement. Liberation theology received official support at the Second Vatican Council (1964–1965) and at the conference of Latin American bishops at Medellín, Colombia in 1968.

Boff believed that theology should originate from "below," that is, it should be based on the experience of people suffering from the oppression of powerful, hierarchical, social, and political structures. He focused on the biblical images of JESUS' association with the poor, and Jesus' own suffering, to stress that all Christians should seek solidarity with the powerless. As a priest, Boff advocated social justice for marginalized people and the elimination of the structures that oppressed them.

Boff presented his liberation theology in many writings, notably in *Jesus Christ, Liberator* (1978), *Liberating Grace* (1979), and *Church: Charism and Power* (1981, [English translation, 1985]). As a result of this last book, which criticized the hierarchy of the Roman Catholic church, he was investigated by Cardinal Joseph Ratzinger, head of the Vatican's Sacred Congregation for the Doctrine of the Faith. On May 9, 1985, Ratzinger issued an order to ban Boff from teaching or writing his ideas. Although this ban lasted until March 29, 1986, less than a year, its impact was considerable. Boff's supporters rallied around him and thus brought more attention to their efforts on behalf of the poor.

On June 29, 1992, Boff resigned from the priesthood, although he continues to write, focusing especially on questions of environmental justice. In 1995 he co-authored *Ecology and Poverty: Cry of the Earth, Cry of the Poor.*

Legacy

Boff's emphasis on the special concern of Jesus for the poor and on the importance of "doing theology from below," has helped to inspire others to develop their own types of liberation theology, one of the major theological movements in the last third of the twentieth century.

Outside of Latin America, perhaps the most prominent advocate of liberation theology is DESMOND TUTU, the Anglican Bishop of

South Africa. Tutu focused on God's special bias for the poor in his opposition to South Africa's system of racial separation, commonly known as apartheid. Tutu's efforts contributed to the larger political movement to dismantle apartheid. These efforts culminated in the dismantling of apartheid and the election of Nelson Mandela as South Africa's president in 1994. For his work against apartheid, Tutu received the Nobel Peace Prize in 1984.

In North America, Boff's liberation theology helped inspire other forms of liberation theology: black theology among African Americans, feminist theology among women, Womanist theology among African-American women, and Mujerista theology among Hispanic women. Gays and lesbians have also appealed to the principles of liberation theology in their opposition to injustice. Liberation theology for each group flows from its own experience; some would maintain that it is best to speak of liberation theologies.

While liberation theology has grown among disenfranchised groups, it has been criticized as a religious brand of Marxism. Although its proponents vigorously deny this charge, such criticism tends to weaken its effectiveness, especially since the collapse of communism at the end of the twentieth century.

As an advocate of social justice and God's concern for the poor and the environment, Boff continues to press others to oppose the injustices of their social situation.

von Dehsen

WORLD EVENTS		BOFF'S LIFE
World War I	1914–18	
	1938	Leonardo Boff is born
World War II	1939–45	
Mao Tse-tung establishes Communist rule in China	1949	
	1964	Boff is ordained Roman Catholic priest
Six Day War between Israel and Arabs	1967	
	1971	Boff receives doctorate from University of Munich
End of Vietnam War	1975	
	1981	*Christ: Charism and Power* is published
	1985	Cardinal Ratzinger silences Boff
	1986	Boff's silencing is lifted
Fall of Communism in eastern Europe	1989	
Dissolution of Soviet Union	1991	
	1992	Boff leaves priesthood
Apartheid in South Africa is dismantled	1994	

For Further Reading:

Chopp, Rebecca. *The Praxis of Suffering: An Interpretation of Liberation and Political Theologies.* Maryknoll, N.Y.: Orbis Books, 1986.

Cox, Harvey. *The Silencing of Leonardo Boff: The Vatican and the Future of World Christianity.* Bloomington, Ind.: Meyer-Stone Books, 1988.

Ferm, Donald. *Third World Liberation Theologies: A Reader.* Maryknoll, N.Y.: Orbis Books, 1986.

Waltermire, Donald. *The Liberation Theologies of Leonardo Boff and Jon Sobrino.* Lanham, Md.: University of America Press, 1994

Bonhoeffer, Dietrich

German Theologian;
Influential Nazi Resister
1906–1945

Life and Work

Dietrich Bonhoeffer was a German theologian who lived out his own theology in resistance to Hitler and the Nazis.

The son of a prominent physician, Bonhoeffer was born on February 4, 1906, in Breslau, Prussia (present-day Wroclaw, Poland). He studied theology at the University of Tubingen and at the University of Berlin, where he received his doctorate. From 1930 to 1931 he did postgraduate work with REINHOLD NIEBUHR at Union Theological Seminary in New York. He then accepted a position as lecturer in theology at the University of Berlin.

For the rest of his life, Bonhoeffer struggled against Nazism, both in the German Lutheran church and in German society at large. By 1933 he had become disenchanted with the Church's unwillingness to speak out against Nazi abuses and accepted a position as pastor to a German congregation in London. He returned to Germany in 1935 to teach at a new seminary in Finkenwald, formed by the Confessing Church, which opposed Hitler's policies.

Bonhoeffer's writings theologically reflect what he was actually living. In his earliest book, *The Communion of Saints* (1930), he coordinated sociological reality with the basis of Christian teachings in revelation. Similarly, in *Act and Being* (1931), he contended that the church is the one community that is equipped to deal with the ever-changing circumstances of society. By 1937 his writing dealt more pointedly with the role of Christians facing the Nazi regime. That year he completed *The Cost of Discipleship*, in which he contrasts "cheap grace," the Christian belief that salvation concerns only the believer's personal relationship to God, with "costly grace," the grace that compels a Christian into the world's struggles without consideration of personal cost or risk. In 1939 he published *Life Together,* showing how some of the themes of his earlier works were lived out at the Finkenwald seminary.

The Gestapo closed the Finkenwald seminary in 1939, and Union Theological Seminary invited Bonhoeffer to return to New York. After only four weeks there, he felt compelled to return to Germany to become part of the resistance movement against the Nazis. On April 5, 1943, he was arrested on charges of suspicion to conspire against Hitler. Two years later, on April 9, 1945, he was hanged in Flossenberg prison.

Legacy

Bonhoeffer's life and work were intimately intertwined. His maturing theology led him to confront the passive Christian attitude of what he called "cheap grace," with the concept of "costly grace," the willingness to put all at risk to remain faithful in the face of demonic horror. Subsequent generations of Christians have considered him a model of faithfulness and have looked to his life and teachings as a source of inspiration and wisdom.

In the late twentieth century, Bonhoeffer's life and work became a standard by which Christian social responsibility was measured. Many pointed to his fateful decision to return to Germany in 1939 as a moment of courage and decision comparable to that of the early Christian martyrs who died for their faith. Surely Bonhoeffer must have anticipated his own imprisonment, if not death. Bonhoeffer's courage and commitment to the Christian faith became an inspiration to other Christians, including those living under the oppressive system of apartheid in South Africa, to continue their struggle for justice as an expression of "costly grace."

Many of Bonhoeffer's personal reflections on his situation as a Nazi prisoner became public only in 1951, six years after his death, with the publication of his *Letters and Papers From Prison.* This volume reveals his most private thoughts on the role of a Christian under persecution and shows how he came to accept the suffering required of a Christian as a disciple of Christ, who also suffered at the hands of an abusive power structure. The book contains some of his most pointed attacks on the Church's passivity in the face of the Nazis and the Holocaust. He argues that, in a "world come of age"—in a world mature enough to face reality without illusion—Christians ought to be mature enough not to hide from the evil before their eyes.

To keep his message alive, the International Bonhoeffer Society produces publications and sponsors lectures relating themes in Bonhoeffer's life and writings to the modern world. Union Theological Seminary remains devoted to his work; it has named an academic chair in his honor and frequently displays works related to his days of study there.

von Dehsen

WORLD EVENTS		BONHOEFFER'S LIFE
Spanish American War	1898	
	1906	Dietrich Bonhoeffer is born
World War I	1914–18	
	1930	*The Communion of Saints* is published
	1930–31	Bonhoeffer studies at Union Theological Seminary
	1935	Bonhoeffer teaches at Finkenwald seminary
	1937	*The Cost of Discipleship* is published
	1939	Bonhoeffer decides to return to Germany from New York
World War II	1939–45	
	1943	Bonhoeffer is arrested by Nazis
	1945	Bonhoeffer is hanged by Nazis
Mao Tse-tung establishes Communist rule in China	1949	
Korean War	1950–53	
	1951	*Letters and Papers From Prison* is published posthumously
Six Day War between Israel and Arabs	1967	

For Further Reading:

Bethge, Eberhard. *Dietrich Bonhoeffer: Man of Vision, Man of Courage.* New York: Harper & Row, 1977.

Feil, Ernst. *The Theology of Dietrich Bonhoeffer.* Philadelphia: Fortress, 1985.

Marsh, Charles. *Reclaiming Dietrich Bonhoeffer: The Promise of His Theology.* New York: Oxford University Press, 1994.

Buber, Martin

Religious Philosopher;
Developer of Jewish Existentialism
1878–1965

Life and Work

German–Jewish philosopher Martin Buber wrote on many subjects including Zionism, adult education, biblical commentary, and social reform. His most important idea—the one that informed all his other attitudes—centered on a person's relationship to God and to other people.

Martin Buber was born in Vienna, Austria, on February 8, 1878, into an assimilated Jewish family. He was educated at the universities of Leipzig, Zurich, and Berlin, receiving his doctorate in philosophy from the University of Vienna in 1904. Buber became active in the Zionist movement and in 1901

served as editor of the Zionist newspaper, *The World*. In 1916 he founded the journal *Der Jude (The Jew)*, which became the major forum for German–Jewish intellectual thought.

In 1901, Buber became interested in Hasidism, an eighteenth-century Russian–Jewish movement, which greatly influenced his conception of the relationship between humans and God. His important work *Ich und Du (I and Thou,* 1923) examines human relations in terms of I–It and I–Thou. In the I–It relationship, a person regards another from a distance, as a thing. In the I–Thou relationship, the person enters into a relationship with his whole being, having a genuine dialogue. For Buber, relationships between people reflected those between humans and God. Through the I–Thou relationship, a dialogue between humans and God is possible. But Buber remained skeptical of any religious dogma, organized church, or set rules of behavior and practiced a Judaism unique to himself.

In 1938 Buber left Germany after criticizing Hitler and settled in Palestine where he taught at Hebrew University until 1951. He reluctantly accepted the state of Israel and advocated a binational state in which Jews and Arabs lived culturally independent lives.

Among his many works is *Daniel* in 1913, in which Buber explores attitudes in relating to the world. In the 1923 *Talks On Judaism,* he explores the question, "Why do we call ourselves Jews?" With Franz Rosenzweig, another religious philosopher, he translated the Hebrew Bible into German between 1926 and 1937. His 1949 *Paths in Utopia* praised the Israeli kibbutz, or collective community, but criticized the largely secular inhabitants of the kibbutz as denying their relationship to God.

Buber died on June 13, 1965, in Jerusalem.

Legacy

Considered to be a member of the twentieth-century existential philosophical movement, Martin Buber combined the practical and the mystical in his philosophy, his teachings, and his thought. His emphasis on the authentic "I–Thou" relationship both between each person and the deity, and among human beings in relationships, echoed the existentialist focus on the individual and his or her responsibilities in the world.

Buber had a significant following among Jewish and Christian scholars in Europe and North America. Among Jewish theologians, Buber influenced Will Herberg, Arthur A. Cohen, and Eugene Borowitz. Buber also found support among such Christian theologians as PAUL TILLICH and H. Richard Niebuhr. Tillich focused on God as the believer's "Ultimate Concern," that is, the fundamental concern that is not dependent on any prior concern. Niebuhr's realistic approach to matters political certainly took seriously the matrix of interrelationships central to the political world and how these political concerns derive from the relationship with God. Buber's concepts of relationships also influenced the thought of psychiatrist Leslie Farber and philosopher Ernst Becker. Buber's influence even extended to the leaders of the United Nations. At the time of his death in 1961, Dag Hammarskjöld, the U.N. secretary general, was translating Buber's writings into Swedish.

Ironically, Buber had only limited impact in Israel. There his religious ideas as well as his stand on Arab–Jewish relations made him unacceptable to the majority. His influence was confined to kibbutzim (collective farms), whose movement he championed as the possible realization of a kind of utopian socialism. Many traditional rabbis rejected the noninstitutional orientation of his religious views.

Such was the esteem in which Buber was held that at his elaborate state funeral, a group of Arab students laid a wreath at his tomb, an unheard of sign of respect.

Saltz

WORLD EVENTS		BUBER'S LIFE
Germany is united	1871	
	1878	Martin Buber is born
Spanish American War	1898	
	1901	Buber edits Zionist newspaper; becomes interested in Hassidism
World War I	1914–18	
	1916	Buber founds periodical *Der Jude (The Jew)*
	1923	*I and Thou* is published
	1938	Buber immigrates to Palestine
	1938–51	Buber teaches at Hebrew University
World War II	1939–45	
Mao Tse-tung establishes Communist rule in China	1949	
Korean War	1950–53	
	1965	Buber dies
Six Day War between Israel and Arabs	1967	

For Further Reading:

Hodes, Aubrey. *Martin Buber: An Intimate Portrait.* New York: Viking Press, 1971.

Moore, Donald J. *Martin Buber: Prophet of Religious Secularism.* New York: Fordham University Press, 1996.

Buddha

(Siddhartha Gautama)

Founder of Buddhism

c. 600–c. 400 B.C.E.

Life and Work

Siddhartha Gautama, the "Buddha," was the founder of Buddhism. The word "buddha" is not a name but a title meaning "enlightened one."

According to ancient writings and legends, the Buddha Gautama was born Siddhartha Gautama in what is now Nepal in the fifth or sixth century B.C.E., a time of great social and religious change. The son of the king and queen of the Sakya kingdom, Prince Siddhartha was raised in a life of great luxury. At age 16 he married his cousin, Princess Yasodhara. When he was 29 he renounced his princely life and family and became a wandering ascetic in search of the way of truth. After learning all he could from several teachers, Gautama arrived at what is now Gaya, India. Legend has it that after almost six years of trying, and ultimately rejecting, a life of austerity and self-mortification, he achieved enlightenment and discovered the *dhamma* (truth, doctrine).

After meditating for several weeks on his discovery, he went to Isipatana, now called Sarnath, where he first preached the Four Noble Truths: first, that human existence is full of sorrow and suffering (*dukkha*); second, that the cause of this suffering is selfish desire or craving (*tanhu*); third, that there can be an end to this suffering (*nirvana*); and fourth, that the pathway to this liberation is the Noble Eightfold Path. This path is the middle, moderate path between self-indulgence and self-denial, and consists of right view, right intention, right speech, right conduct, right way of living, right endeavor, right mindfulness, and right concentration.

Gautama spent the rest of his life traveling the countryside, teaching disciples and creating a Buddhist community (the *sangha*). He died in his eightieth year at Kushinagara (now Kasia, India) among his disciples and followers.

Legacy

At his death, Gautama left the foundation for one of the world's great religions. After his death, according to legend, Gautama's followers collected his teachings (*dharma*), his sermons (*sutras*), and the codes of discipline (*vinaya*); relics were enshrined in buildings (*stupas*); and a cult of devotion (*bhakti*) developed around the *stupas* and other symbols and sites associated with the Buddha. Wandering monks formed monastic communities. Soon, however, doctrinal splits developed among followers and many different branches of Buddhism took root. Later thinkers such as Nagarjuna in the second century C.E. and the brothers Asanga and Vasubandhu in the fourth century C.E. both expanded and refined existing doctrine.

Within a few hundred years of Gautama's death, various forms of Buddhism began to spread throughout Asia. The Emperor Asoka (third century B.C.E.), a committed Buddhist, is said to have sent his son to Ceylon (now Sri Lanka) and missionaries to the East to spread the word. By the first century C.E. Buddhism had spread to China where it combined with Taoism to form a uniquely Chinese variation. In China, many new sects were formed and, by the thirteenth century, many of them—including Zen Buddhism—had been exported to Japan. In the seventh century, Tantric Buddhism, focusing on the interrelatedness of all things, was introduced into Tibet where it became the primary form of Buddhism practiced there. Ironically, because of its absorption by Hinduism and persecution by invading Muslims, by the thirteenth century Buddhism had disappeared from India, the land of its founding.

In the twentieth century, Buddhism in its traditional strongholds, i.e., China, Cambodia, Laos, Vietnam, Tibet, and North Korea, has been wiped out under communist regimes. In non-communist Asian countries, Westernization has also greatly diminished the influence of Buddhism. On the other hand, Buddhism has been growing in Western Europe and America, leading some to speculate that its future may actually lie in the West. It is estimated that there are some 300 million Buddhists worldwide today.

Saltz

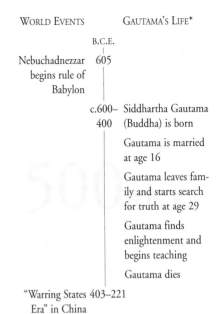

WORLD EVENTS	GAUTAMA'S LIFE*
B.C.E.	
Nebuchadnezzar begins rule of Babylon	605
	c.600–400 Siddhartha Gautama (Buddha) is born
	Gautama is married at age 16
	Gautama leaves family and starts search for truth at age 29
	Gautama finds enlightenment and begins teaching
	Gautama dies
"Warring States 403–221 Era" in China	

* *Scholars cannot date the specific events in the Buddha's life with accuracy. This chronology is based on Buddhist legends.*

For Further Reading:

Marshall, George N. *Buddha, the Quest for Serenity: A Biography.* Boston: Beacon Press, 1978.

Mitchell, Robert Allen. *The Buddha: His Life Retold.* New York: Paragon House, 1989.

Skilton, Andrew (Dharmacari Sthiramati). *A Concise History of Buddhism.* Birmingham: Windhorse, 1994.

Burke, Edmund

Influential Political Philosopher
1729–1797

Life and Work

E dmund Burke was a British statesman and political thinker who laid the foundation for conservative political thought.

Burke was born on January 12(?), 1729, in Dublin, Ireland, to a Catholic mother and a Protestant father. (Dates may be uncertain due to a calendar correction in the eighteenth century.) He was educated at Trinity College, Dublin, before briefly studying law in London. Following a short career as a literary journalist, he won a seat in Parliament in 1766. Over the course of three decades, he became one of its leading orators, skilled at putting the issues of the day in wider philosophical perspective.

Burke believed that politics should be based on the possible, not on abstract ideas. He criticized many of the political philosophers of the Enlightenment such as JEAN-JACQUES ROUSSEAU and JOHN LOCKE, denouncing their concept of natural rights as nonsensical and denying the assumption of ultimate human perfectibility that lay at the heart of their philosophy. For Burke rights came from laws based on custom and tradition, not theory.

Burke opposed radical political change and supported a political system based on a mature, evolving tradition. He viewed the unwritten English constitution, which granted Parliament ascendancy over the monarch, as the ideal system of government and the embodiment of the divine will. Burke thought social inequality unavoidable and maintained that rule by the aristocracy, whom he viewed as natural leaders, was the best means

for guaranteeing political liberty. He supported representative government but insisted that representatives be guided by their conscience and judgment rather than by the wishes of their constituents. Burke tempered his conservative views by advocating some of the basic principles of liberalism—religious tolerance, a belief in the possibility of upward mobility, and the importance of colonial powers respecting native traditions.

Burke defended the American colonies in their dispute with Great Britain because he believed that the colonists were trying to protect traditional rights and liberties. He denounced the oppressive penalties imposed on Catholics in Ireland and tirelessly criticized the despotic rule of the East India Company in Bengal.

Burke was particularly critical of the French Revolution, which he thought dangerous because it appealed to universal, abstract principles and sought to overthrow traditional authority. He set forth his criticisms in *Reflections on the Revolution in France* (1790) in which he also predicted that the republican experiment would lead to "democratic despotism."

Burke retired from Parliament in 1794 and died three years later, on July 9, 1797.

Legacy

B urke's ideas had a profound impact on both the practical politics and political theory of the late-eighteenth and early-nineteenth centuries, influencing British policy and establishing the basic concepts of conservative thought.

On a practical level, Burke's denunciation of the French Revolution stiffened the British government's anti-French policy, while his call for an international crusade against France provided justification for much of Europe going to war with the republic. Similarly, his backing of the American struggle led to the quick rapprochement between the two nations in the mid-nineteenth century, and his harsh criticism of the poor administration of Britain's East India Company prompted reform of colonial rule.

Ironically Burke was not a conservative, particularly in the modern sense of the word. His pamphlets and essays propounded reformist and liberal views. Yet his *Reflections on the Revolution in France,* with its opposition to revolutions based on abstract principles and its defense of established institutions, became the definitive statement of classical political conservatism.

Influenced by Burke, European statesmen such as Klemens von Metternich (1773–1859),

foreign minister of Austria, rejected the political principles of the Enlightenment, particularly the ideas of progress and equality. These men, who dominated the Congress of Vienna (1815), which remade Europe following the defeat of Napoleon, went beyond Burke: they were hostile to any political change, to republican government, and to the separation of church and state.

English conservatives, on the other hand, accepted change as inevitable and looked to conservative ideas to moderate radical demands. They supported the principle of parliamentary supremacy and, under the direction of leaders such as Prime Minister Benjamin Disraeli (1804–1881), established a tradition of conservative social reform. During the nineteenth century conservative ideas influenced such Americans as writers James Fenimore Cooper (1789–1851) and Henry Adams (1838–1915) as well as political theorist William Graham Sumner (1840–1910).

Over the course of two centuries conservatism changed. During the nineteenth century conservatives were preoccupied with the nature of change; for much of the twentieth century they focused on the struggle against socialism. By the end of World War II, conservatives had accepted secularism, equality, and representative government. Contemporary conservatives differ from liberals in the types of inequality they believe legitimate in democracies and in the role of government in remedying inequality. Conservative positions can be found in the Christian Democratic parties of Europe, the Republican Party in the United States, the Likud Party in Israel, and the Conservative Party in Great Britain.

von Dehsen

WORLD EVENTS	BURKE'S LIFE	
	1729	Edward Burke is born
	1766	Burke wins seat in House of Commons
United States independence	1776	
French Revolution	1789	
	1790	Burke publishes *Reflections on the Revolution in France*
	1794	Burke retires from Parliament
	1797	Burke dies
Napoleonic Wars in Europe	1803–15	

For Further Reading:

McCue, Jim. *Edmund Burke and Our Present Discontents.* London: Claridge Press, 1997.

Stanlis, Peter J. *Edmund Burke: The Enlightenment and Revolution.* New Brunswick, N.J.: Transaction Publishers, 1991.

Bushnell, Horace

Protestant Theologian; Father of American Religious Liberalism
1802–1876

Life and Work

Horace Bushnell was one of the most important and controversial thinkers in the history of American Protestantism. He provided the intellectual framework for theological modernism, which reshaped mainline Protestantism.

Bushnell was born in Bantam, Connecticut, on April 14, 1802. He joined the Congregational Church in 1821 and entered Yale College in 1823, graduating in 1827. He then studied law, becoming a member of the bar in 1831. However, after a religious conversion, he decided to enter the ministry and enrolled in Yale Divinity School. He graduated in 1833 and went to North Church in Hartford, Conn., where he was minister until he resigned in 1859 because of ill health.

Influenced by the liberal Calvinism of his teacher Nathaniel William Taylor, Bushnell was also drawn to the teachings of the liberal German theologian, Friedrich Schleiermacher and to the religious romanticism of RALPH WALDO EMERSON and Samuel Taylor Coleridge. He believed that God lived in every individual's soul and that people could recognize the existence of God on their own. In his first important writing, *Christian Nurture* (1847), he critiqued the central idea of Calvinism—that children were born lost sinners until they have a conversion experience. He believed that social context shapes character. Therefore, through Christian nurture the family and church could raise children who from their earliest days knew God. In *God in Christ* (1849) and *Christ in Theology* (1851) Bushnell argued that language was symbolic and, therefore, that the text of the Bible and of traditional Christian doctrine was not to be considered as literal, but as poetic, statements. Seven years later, in *Nature and the Supernatural* (1858) he presented what he called "Christocentric liberalism," Christ as the center of history, in response to new dis-

coveries in geology. These ideas caused an uproar among fundamentalists and religious conservatives. Bushnell was charged with heresy but the North Church withdrew from the larger church body, thus avoiding a heresy trial, and Bushnell remained its minister.

Bushnell resigned from North Church in 1859 because of ill health. He continued his writing and was active in theological activities until his death in Hartford on February 17, 1876.

Legacy

Often called the "father of American religious liberalism," Bushnell helped shape nineteenth-century American Protestantism. Although controversial and bitterly attacked during his life, Bushnell laid the foundation for what came to be known as "Progressive Orthodoxy" or the New Theology, which dominated American Protestantism after the Civil War.

Bushnell's ideas enabled religious thinkers to maintain a Christ-centered theology in the face of new challenges from science and biblical scholarship. Although he resisted Darwin's theory of evolution, his insistence that Christian progress came by growth, not conquest, enabled later theologians to accommodate new scientific discoveries. His view that language is symbolic and that doctrine should be based on experience rather than traditional dogma enabled believers to accept the results of evolving biblical criticism.

Bushnell's *Christian Nurture* was one of the most influential books ever published in America, shaping theories of Christian education throughout the century. His ideas on religious language as symbolic foreshadowed recent scholarship by such individuals as Joseph Campbell on the importance of myth and story in world religions.

Bushnell lived long enough to see his ideas influence the Social Gospel movement of the late nineteenth century—this movement sought to relate Christian principles to social reform and provided the ideological justification for programs of government-sponsored reform advocated by individuals such as Theodore Roosevelt and Woodrow Wilson.

Saltz

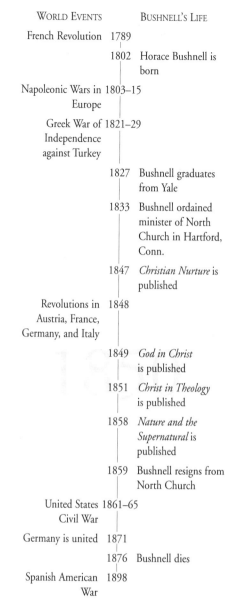

WORLD EVENTS		BUSHNELL'S LIFE
French Revolution	1789	
	1802	Horace Bushnell is born
Napoleonic Wars in Europe	1803–15	
Greek War of Independence against Turkey	1821–29	
	1827	Bushnell graduates from Yale
	1833	Bushnell ordained minister of North Church in Hartford, Conn.
	1847	*Christian Nurture* is published
Revolutions in Austria, France, Germany, and Italy	1848	
	1849	*God in Christ* is published
	1851	*Christ in Theology* is published
	1858	*Nature and the Supernatural* is published
	1859	Bushnell resigns from North Church
United States Civil War	1861–65	
Germany is united	1871	
	1876	Bushnell dies
Spanish American War	1898	

For Further Reading:

Edwards, Robert Lansing. *Of Singular Genius, of Singular Grace: A Biography of Horace Bushnell.* Cleveland, Ohio: Pilgrim Press, 1992.

Haddorff, David W. *Dependence and Freedom: The Moral Thought of Horace Bushnell.* Lanham, Md.: University Press of America, 1994.

Calvin, John

Theologian; Leading Protestant
Reformer
1509–1564

Life and Work

John Calvin was a preeminent reformer of the Christian church and a founder of the Reformed branch of Protestantism.

Born into a middle-class family in Noyon, France, on July 10, 1509, Calvin initially trained for the priesthood at the University of Paris, before studying law. He was gradually converted to the doctrines of the Reformation and in 1534 formally broke with the Roman Catholic church. His support of MARTIN LUTHER forced him to flee Paris in 1535.

While moving frequently to avoid Church authorities, Calvin wrote *Institutes of the Christian Religion* (1536), the first systematic statement of Protestant doctrine. Like other early Reformation leaders, Calvin stressed justification by faith and the authority of the Bible for religious teaching. Where he broke with reformers such as Luther was in his teaching of double predestination. Before God created the world, Calvin maintained, he preordained some for eternal life and others for condemnation. One could do nothing to change God's decree.

The *Institutes* gained Calvin immediate recognition. In 1536 he settled in Geneva to help organize the Reformation but was asked to leave the city two years later because of his strict doctrines. In 1541 he returned at the request of the citizens and proceeded to establish a theocratic regime organized along Old Testament lines. Government was in the hands of pastors, elders, and deacons, and the power of the state was used to compel religious conformity; opponents were expelled or burned at the stake.

Under Calvin's leadership Geneva served as the focal point for the defense of Protestantism throughout Europe and as a refuge for Protestant exiles from all of Europe. During the later years of his life, Calvin devoted himself to writing biblical commentaries. He died in Geneva on May 27, 1564, and was buried in an unmarked grave.

Legacy

Calvin's ideas have had such a wide impact on all areas of life that scholars consider him one of the makers of the modern mind.

Calvin's writings brought the scattered and unsystematic reformed opinions of the period into one body of doctrine, "Calvinism." During the sixteenth century Calvinism spread throughout Europe. It was particularly strong in Scotland and the Netherlands, where it became the established church. Calvin's doctrines are honored in the Presbyterian, Congregational, and Baptist churches as well as in segments of the Anglican communion. Seventeenth-century English Calvinists, known as Puritans, brought their beliefs to the "New World" where they became the dominant thread in American Protestantism. In the twentieth century, Calvin's theology shaped the social and political positions of such prominent theologians as KARL BARTH, Emil Brunner, and REINHOLD NIEBUHR.

Calvinism had a major role in Europe's transition from a medieval to a modern economy. The medieval church taught people not to labor for rewards in this life but to prepare the soul for heaven. Calvinism, on the other hand, looked to the present. No one knew who was

saved, but God would surely bless the elect in their worldly endeavors. Consequently, business and trade became acceptable professions and economic success was seen as a sign of God's favor.

Calvinism also contributed to the development of education by emphasizing the need for a scholarly clergy and an educated laity. The insistence that all read the Bible led to the development of public schools while a growing need for Calvinist-educated clergy resulted in the establishment of institutions of higher learning such as Harvard College.

Although Calvin believed that the church should dominate the state, his ideas on church structure helped prepare the way for representative democracy. Calvinist communions were organized in a pyramid with a hierarchy of elected representatives—both clergy and lay persons—all the way to the pinnacle of power. Thus authority moved up from local congregations, not down from a single figure as in the Roman Catholic church. This organization gave people practical experience in representative democracy.

Calvinism also played a major role in the formation of the American character. The Puritans established the Massachusetts Bay colony as an example to the rest of the world. Gradually the idea of Americans as the elect with a divine mission became part of the secular religion. By the time of the American Revolution, patriots justified independence in terms of the colonies' mandate to be an example of liberty to the world. That sense of special purpose continues in America today.

Olson

WORLD EVENTS		CALVIN'S LIFE
Columbus discovers Americas	1492	
Last Muslim state in Spain falls to Christians		
	1509	John Calvin is born in Noyon, France
Reformation begins	1517	
	1535	Calvin flees Paris
	1536	Calvin settles in Geneva; First edition of *Institutes of the Christian Religion* is published
	1538	Calvin is asked to leave Geneva
	1541	Calvin is recalled to Geneva
	1564	Calvin dies
Thirty Years' War in Europe	1618–48	

For Further Reading:

Bouwsma, William. *John Calvin, A Sixteenth Century Portrait.* New York: Oxford, 1988.
Parker, T. H. L. *Calvin: An Introduction to His Thought.* Louisville, Ky.: Westminster/John Knox Press, 1995.

Camus, Albert

Influential Existentialist Novelist
1913–1960

Life and Work

Although not an academic philosopher, Albert Camus promoted existential ideas of the absurdity of life through the characters of his fiction.

Camus was born in French Algeria on November 7, 1913, and raised by his widowed mother in extreme poverty. In 1930, he studied philosophy at the university in Algiers, although illness prevented him from completing his studies. In 1938 Camus became a journalist with *Alger-Republicain*.

During World War II he joined a resistance cell in France called "Combat" and for four years edited its clandestine newspaper, also called *Combat*. At that time he formulated his doctrine of the "absurd": the contrast between human need and the unreasonable silence of the world. Human life is rendered meaningless by the fact of death and the inability of the individual to make sense of his experience. The fundamental question becomes that of suicide. If life is absurd, why bother to live it further?

Camus expressed his beliefs in novels. In *The Stranger* (1942) the absurdist theme is illustrated by the atheist, Meursault, who is executed for accidentally killing an Arab, but whose existence is justified by not trying to be anything more than himself. The same theme is presented in *The Myth of Sisyphus* (1942): as there is no point to living, the individual can react with a "tenacious revolt." A person's dignity arises from a consciousness of death, an awareness that eternal values and ideas do not exist, and a refusal to give in to the notion of hope or to appeal to something supernatural. Sisyphus, an absurd hero, sentenced to rolling a rock to the top of a mountain ceaselessly and to watching its descent, is doomed to accomplishing nothing. Yet Sisyphus is victorious; his struggle itself justifies his existence.

In effect, Camus took a highly moral position: no matter how inexplicable human life might be, human life is sacred. In *The Plague* (1947), under the sentence of death, Dr. Rieux continues to perform his duty; his achievement is in the assertion of human dignity and endurance.

The Rebel (1951) is a collection of Camus's thoughts that criticize the eternal transcendence (otherworldliness) of Christianity and the historical transcendence of Marxism. It brought him into bitter controversy with the French existentialist philosopher, JEAN-PAUL SARTRE, a defender of Marxism.

For his body of work, Camus received the Nobel Prize for literature in 1957. Camus died in an automobile accident on January 4, 1960.

Legacy

Through his writing, in which his major characters embody individual existence, individual freedom, and choice, Camus expresses the insights of an "existential" philosopher. His untimely death in 1960 prevented him from developing his ideas more fully.

Camus was a central figure in the intellectual life of France after the war. He played a major role in the literature of the twentieth century. His characters not only presented the existential angst closely associated with the secularization of the last half of the twentieth century, they also offered hope for the struggle against despair. The consensus of the time was that Sartre's support of Marxism was the proper leftist attitude toward Stalinism in contrast to that of Camus. At the dawn of the twenty-first century, after the fall of communism, however, Camus is admired for having the vision to condemn Soviet absolutism.

Through his fiction, Camus became a popularizer of existentialist ideas; he continues to be a best-selling author. His passionate and lucid literary style have made him a successor to MICHEL EYQUEM DE MONTAIGNE (1533–1592), who said that all philosophical theories should be based on experience, and the classical moralists. Although he was also the author of plays, his main legacy is his brilliant body of short fiction in which he depicts the human condition against the background of his native Algeria. His themes can serve to illustrate the absurdity of human life even to those who do not share his pessimistic views.

Olson

World Events		Camus's Life
Spanish American War	1898	
	1913	Albert Camus is born
World War I	1914–18	
	1930	Camus studies philosophy at University of Algiers.
World War II	1939–45	
	1942	*The Stranger* is published
		The Myth of Sisyphus is published
	1947	*The Plague* is published
Mao Tse-tung establishes Communist rule in China	1949	
Korean War	1950–53	
	1951	*The Rebel* is published
		Camus engages in controversy with Jean-Paul Sartre over Marxism
	1957	Camus receives Nobel Prize for literature
	1960	Camus is killed in auto accident
Six Day War between Israel and Arabs	1967	

For Further Reading:

Rhein, Phillip. *Albert Camus*. Boston: Twayne Publishers, 1989.

Todd, Oliver. *Albert Camus: A Life*. New York: Alfred A. Knopf, 1997.

Channing, William Ellery

Early Unitarian Church Leader
1780–1842

Life and Work

William Ellery Channing was one of the principal figures in the establishment of the Unitarian Church in the United States.

Born in Newport, Rhode Island, on April 7, 1780, Channing graduated from Harvard College in 1798 and was ordained a Congregationalist minister in 1803. That year he became pastor of the Federal Street Congregational Church, Boston, where he served until his death in 1842.

Although he had been brought up as a strict Calvinist, Channing was unable to accept the Congregationalist doctrine, based on the teaching of JOHN CALVIN, that human beings are innately sinful. As a religious liberal, he insisted that all human beings had divinely given potential.

His sermon, "Unitarian Christianity," preached in Baltimore in 1819, articulated the liberal ideas that became the basis for early Unitarian theology. He considered the doctrine of the Trinity unbiblical and unacceptable; God was a "unity." In addition, he found no basis in scripture for a "jealous" God, original sin, or salvation by grace. Instead, he preached a "pure and reasonable Christianity": the goodness of God, the essential virtue and perfectibility of man, freedom of the will. Channing believed that God had inspired JESUS to lead people toward more moral lives and closer communion with him, but he rejected the orthodox Christian idea that Jesus' death atoned for humanity's sinfulness. In his crucial sermon, "The Moral Argument Against Calvinism," he argued against the doctrine of sin and in favor of the possibility that human beings were morally able to achieve their own salvation.

In 1820 Channing broke with the Congregationalists and organized the Berry Street Conference of liberal ministers. That group organized the American Unitarian Association in 1825, originally consisting of 125 congregations in Boston and environs.

Channing's belief in the perfectibility of humans led him to espouse many of the social reforms of the day—temperance, pacifism, and particularly abolition. In 1835 he wrote "Slavery," an influential indictment of the system of slavery, and just before he died in 1842 he published the "Address at Lenox," hoping to arouse anti-slavery sentiment in the North.

Channing died in Bennington, Vermont, on October 2, 1842.

Legacy

Channing's legacy lies in the development of the Unitarian Church, a distinct denomination, which emphasizes the oneness of God rather than the Trinity.

A faith that appeals to reason, it gained few converts and remained centered in New England. Nevertheless, its influence was well out of proportion to its numbers because its adherents were composed largely of the cultural, business, and civil elite of New England who had a dominant role in American life during the pre–Civil War period.

Although Channing was a critic of the New England Transcendentalists, whom he thought strayed too far from orthodox belief, his Unitarian ideas formed the basis from which the Unitarian movement would develop its ideas of direct communion with God apart from institutions and traditional belief systems. James Freeman Clarke (1810–1888), a nineteenth-century Unitarian leader, summarized the basic beliefs of this church as "The fatherhood of God, the brotherhood of man [sic], the leadership of Jesus, salvation by [individual] character, and the progress of mankind [sic] onward and upward forever." Among the writers associated with the "Channing Unitarians," were RALPH WALDO EMERSON, Henry Wadsworth Longfellow, James Russell Lowell, and Oliver Wendell Holmes.

Channing's liberal Unitarians found a companion in the Universalist movement, which had similar views but was concentrated in rural areas. Both movements arose out of a need to break free from the restraints of traditional doctrine and to emphasize the basic goodness of humanity. By the twentieth century, both of these movements were willing to accept people who had vastly divergent views of Christianity, bordering on agnosticism (doubt about the existence of God), and both were facing the financial difficulties of small membership. These two groups united in 1961 to form the Unitarian Universalist Association, a religious denomination committed to congregational autonomy, freedom of belief, and support of liberal political causes.

Olson

WORLD EVENTS		CHANNING'S LIFE
United States independence	1776	
	1780	William Ellery Channing is born
French Revolution	1789	
	1798	Channing graduates from Harvard College
Napoleonic Wars in Europe	1803–15	
	1803–42	Channing is minister of Federal Street Congregational Church, Boston
	1819	Channing delivers sermon on "Unitarian Christianity"
	1820	Channing breaks with Congregationalists
Greek War of Independence against Turkey	1821–29	
	1825	Channing helps to form American Unitarian Association
	1835	Channing writes "Slavery"
	1842	Channing dies in Bennington, Vt.
Revolutions in Austria, France, Germany, and Italy	1848	

For Further Reading:
Hudspeth, Robert N. *Ellery Channing*. New York: Twayne, 1973.
Wright, Conrad E. *American Unitarianism*, 1805–1865. Boston: Massachusetts Historical Society, 1989.

Columba, Saint

Founder of the Influential Christian Community at Iona
521–597

Life and Work

Columba established the great monastery at Iona off the coast of Scotland, from which missionaries spread Christianity and learning into areas of continental Europe.

Born on December 7, 521, to a family of royal descent in Gartan (Donegal), Ireland, Columba took an interest in the Church at a young age. He was ordained a deacon by Finnian of Clonard, studied with the bard Gemman, and was made a priest by Etchen, bishop of Clonfad, after entering the monastery of Mobhi Clarainech. When the plague forced the monastery to disband in 543, Columba spent the next decade founding monasteries throughout Ireland.

In 561 Columba started one of the bloodiest battles in Irish history. When the high king violated the law of monastic sanctuary to capture and execute a relative of Columba under his protection, he roused the Finnian clan to a battle in which 3,000 men were killed. He was excommunicated for a short period and in remorse promised to convert the same number of souls as those who had died in battle.

With 12 relatives, Columba sailed to Iona in 563, where he founded what would become one of the greatest monasteries in Christendom. Drawn by his reputation for holiness, followers came from all over Britain to join his community. From Iona he sent missionaries to spread the faith, and, by the time of his death, he had founded 60 monasteries in Scotland. Columba himself remained an active missionary, spending the rest of his life converting the Scots and Picts.

Columba would return to Ireland several times during his life. In 575 he attended the Synod of Drumceat in Meath to help secure an exemption for women from military service. He returned once more in 585, and in 587 he may have provoked the battle of Cuil Feda over the ownership of the church of Colethem.

Columba died in prayer on June 9, 597.

Legacy

Columba had an enormous influence on Western Christianity. He is chiefly remembered for the establishment of his monastery at Iona and for the missionary work that spread across Europe from there. Moreover, in the face of encroaching Roman traditions, Columba assisted in the preservation of Celtic culture.

Not quite 40 years after Columba's death, Aidan (d. 651), Columba's spiritual heir, brought Christianity to northern England. Other monks from Iona traveled to Greenland, Iceland, and many parts of Europe, converting the population to Christianity. Equally important for the intellectual development of the West, the Irish brought the ancient Greek and Roman learning they had preserved as the continent had fallen into the Dark Ages. They also brought with them Columba's rule of monastic life, which was widely practiced on the European mainland until it was eventually replaced by the rule of BENEDICT OF NURSIA.

Iona remained the religious center of northern and western Britain and a great center of learning for several hundred years after its founding. Viking attacks destroyed it in the ninth century and, although restored, it never regained its prominence.

Columba brought to Britain ecclesiastical customs at odds with those of Rome. Churches were led by presbyter-abbots instead of bishops, and Celtic and Roman calendars differed in the dating of Easter. In 597, the year of Columba's death, Augustine of Canterbury, with his ordered, continental style of Christianity, arrived in southern England. Within 100 years that tradition would sweep through the isles, culminating with the Council of Whitby (664) in which the Northumbrian king formally accepted Roman practices. But the seed of the Celtic church tradition that Columba had planted stayed alive, though as a tiny minority, in Ireland, in isolated places in England, and on the mainland of Europe.

In the twentieth century, a renewed fascination with Celtic culture has revived interest in Columba's life and work. Aidan's Northumbrian community has been restored and is revivifying Celtic traditions.

Honigsberg

WORLD EVENTS		COLUMBA'S LIFE
Fall of Roman Empire	476	
	521	Columba is born in Gartan (Donegal)
Rule of Byzantine emperor Justinian I the Great	527–65	
	561	Columba starts Finnian clan battle against high king
	563	Columba sails with 12 disciples to Iona
	575	Columba attends Synod of Drumceat in Meath, Ireland
	597	Columba dies
T'ang Dynasty in China	618–907	

For Further Reading:

Bourke, Cormak. *Studies in the Cult of St. Columba.* Dublin: Four Courts Press, 1997.

Cahill, Thomas. *How the Irish Saved Civilization: The Untold Story of Ireland's Heroic Role from the Fall of Rome to the Rise of Medieval Europe.* New York: Doubleday, 1995.

Jones, Norman L. *The Saint Columba Home Page.* January 4, 1998. http://www.usu.edu/~history/norm/columb-1.htm.

Van de Weyer, Robert. *Celtic Fire: The Passionate Religious Vision of Ancient Britain and Ireland.* New York: Doubleday, 1990.

Comte, Auguste

Founder of Sociology
1798–1857

Life and Work

Auguste Comte's theory of the law of three stages led to the development of philosophical positivism and the discipline of sociology.

Comte was born at Montpelier near Marseilles on January 19, 1798. At 14 he rejected the Roman Catholicism and royalism of his parents. Beginning in 1814, he was educated mainly at the Ecole Polytechnique in Paris, which he came to think of as a model for a future society directed by scientists and engineers. From 1817 to 1824 he served as secretary to the utopian Count Henri de Saint-Simon, director of the periodical, *Industrie*, from whom he learned the need for a unifying social science that would explain society and guide social planning.

From 1833 to 1842, while teaching at the Ecole, Comte addressed the need for a new social order in the *Course of Positive Philosophy*. Positivism concerns the method used in the theoretical and abstract sciences to deal with positive, observable facts. It concerns itself not with "why," but only with "how" of things. Comte assumed that human behavior obeyed strict laws and that social behavior can be directed toward specific desired ends. He resolved to analyze such behavior in the spirit of science, and thereby created a discipline he called "sociology." When "sociologists" know social laws, it is possible for them to act upon societies.

WORLD EVENTS	COMTE'S LIFE
French Revolution 1789	
	1798 Auguste Comte is born
Napoleonic Wars 1803–15 in Europe	
	1814 Comte enters Ecole Polytechnique
Greek War of 1821–29 Independence against Turkey	
	1830–42 *Course of Positive Philosophy* is published
Revolutions in 1848 Austria, France, Germany, and Italy	
	1851–54 *System of Positive Polity* is published
	1857 Comte dies
United States 1861–65 Civil War	

Comte's theory of human history and progress was based on the law of the three stages. First, every branch of human knowledge passes through the theological stage, in which supernatural agencies explain what cannot otherwise be explained. Next, the metaphysical stage, in which effects are attributed to abstract (albeit poorly understood) causes. The third stage is the "positive" stage in which the scientific laws that control the world are understood.

In 1845 he married Clothilde de Vaux. After her early death, he made himself the high priest of a secular positivist "Religion of Humanity," a scheme of salvation that emphasized reason and logic. The object of human worship, he believed, should be society as an organized whole.

In 1848 he founded a group called the Positive Society and expressed his views in free lectures, which were suppressed by the government in 1851. He determined arbitrarily that the ultimate foundation of positivism is love: the intellect must be governed by the heart. Ironically, his condemnation of metaphysics in the name of science culminated in the subordination of science to an irrational element. During this time he completed *The System of Positive Polity* (1851–1854).

Comte died insane on September 5, 1857.

Legacy

Comte's theories provided the foundation for philosophical positivism and for the principles of sociology.

Positivism is a philosophical movement characterized by an emphasis on science and scientific method as the only sources of knowledge, a sharp distinction between the realms of fact and value, and a strong hostility toward religion and traditional philosophy, especially metaphysics. His philosophical positivism was continued by Emile Littré in the journal, *The Positive Review*. He influenced thought, especially in the period of Louis Napoleon (1808–1873). His influence can be seen in the work of significant figures such as the novelist George Eliot, the philosopher JOHN STUART MILL, the psychologist Claude Bernard, and the historian Hippolyte Taine.

Comte's theories inspired the growth of logical positivism in the 1920s. This branch of philosophy accepted as true only that which can be verified by objective evidence. As such, it rejected the assertions of metaphysics, claiming that such assertions were beyond the control of empirical

data. His positivism underlies contemporary logical positivism, which seeks to find empirical data to verify its conclusions, and analytic and linguistic philosophy, which studies the structure of language to uncover the structure of the world.

Comte's views helped establish the discipline of sociology, which he thought should be governed by the methods of the natural sciences—observation, experimentation, and comparison. For him, the study of society preceded the study of the individual. The original units out of which societies grew were not individuals but families. Later social developments resulted from complex and interrelated institutional structures that came about when social functions were divided.

Shortly after Comte's death, others further developed his concepts of sociology. Herbert Spencer applied them to Darwinism in the *Principles of Sociology*. KARL MARX analyzed economic relationships from a political and sociological perspective. The modern study of sociology was founded by ÉMILE DURKHEIM, who studied society using empirical evidence, and by Max Weber, a theorist. In the United States, the discipline of sociology was advanced by Lester Frank Ward and William Graham Sumner.

More recently, scholars of the history of religions have relied on sociological methodology to investigate the growth and development of religious beliefs and practices. Such investigations presume that religions reflect human circumstances and address questions of human existence. In short, Comte's work has led such scholars to presuppose that all religions are "Religions of Humanity."

Olson

For Further Reading
Pickering, Mary. *Auguste Comte: An Intellectual Biography.* New York: Cambridge University Press, 1993.
Shariff, Robert C. *Comte After Positivism.* New York: Cambridge University Press, 1995.
Standly, Arlene Reilein. *Auguste Comte.* Boston: Twayne Press, 1981.

Cone, James Hal

Architect of Black Liberation
Theology
1938–

Life and Work

James Hal Cone, professor of systematic theology at Union Theological Seminary in New York City, is author of the first book in the field of black theology and one of the founders of the black liberation theology movement.

Cone was born on August 5, 1938, and raised by a staunchly independent family in Bearden, Arkansas, a small town about 50 miles from Little Rock. An excellent student throughout his schooling, Cone received his bachelor of divinity degree from Garrett Theological Seminary in 1961 and his Ph.D. from Northwestern University in 1965 in systematic theology. His dissertation was on KARL BARTH, one of the major figures in twentieth-century Protestant theology. Cone taught for a year at Philander Smith, a small black college in Little Rock, and then at Adrian College in Michigan. In 1969, he joined the faculty of Union Theological Seminary, where he became the Charles A. Briggs Distinguished Professor of Systematic Theology. Cone describes his teaching and research interests as "Christian theology, with special attention to black theology and the theologies of Africa, Asia, and Latin America, as well as twentieth-century European–American theologies."

Cone's early life focused on his family and the Macedonia African Methodist Episcopal church in "separate but equal" Bearden, where the white people held all the influential positions. After his years as a student during the civil rights era and social turmoil of the 1960s, Cone struggled to express the Christian gospel as experienced by the black church, to represent blacks without any "filtering" by whites. His manifesto, *Black Theology and Black Power* (1969), rocketed onto the scene as the first book on black liberation theology. In it Cone analyzed the meaning of black power, the church, the gospel, and concluded that black power was the central message of Christ to twentieth-century America. Writing the book in the summer of 1968 (the year MARTIN LUTHER KING, JR. was assassinated), he said, was a "conversion experience."

Cone's book *God of the Oppressed* (1975) advocated black power, retrieved historical texts of black liberation thought, and opened a dialogue with liberation traditions in a global context. It connected to the everyday struggles of people and worked to marry human dignity and social justice. Cone's other important work includes *Martin and Malcolm: A Dream or a Nightmare?* published in 1972.

Legacy

Cone's work is based on practice rooted in living traditions of faith and attentiveness to socio-political power structures that control access to significant resources. His contribution to black and American theology has been immense.

Calling into question elitism, racism, and socio-economic exploitation, black theology introduced new interpretations of biblical and traditional texts, always connecting abstract theological ideas to the concrete historical experience of black people and, to a large degree, rejecting the concept of "pure, timeless" theological ideas. Once Cone broke this new ground, much was written on the black church and its extraordinary religio-cultural accomplishments, including studies involving African traditions that the American black church managed to hold onto and "baptize" and the black church's clear grasp of the race-transcending universalism of the Christian gospel. A compendium of this scholarship and theology of the first generation of black theologians can be found in *Black Theology: A Documentary History* (1979), which Cone wrote with Gayraud S. Wilmore.

Several years after Cone's first work, prominent American church historian Sidney E. Ahlstrom wrote, "The basic paradigm for a renovation of American church history is the black religious experience, which has been virtually closed out of all synoptic histories written so far." Because of Cone's work and that of his peers and successors, however, this failure on the part of white theologians and church historians has become far more difficult to understand.

Many voices are now recording the contributions made to American Christianity by the power and originality of African-American Christian traditions. A second generation of scholars has been schooled on Cone's teachings

and that of his colleagues in the black theology movement. A prime example is Cornel West, currently professor of the philosophy of religion at Harvard Divinity School, who writes and teaches on black theology and related areas. One of his earliest books was *Prophesy Deliverance!* (1982); one of his most recent is *Restoring Hope: Conversations on the Future of Black America* (1999). West contributes essays to all areas of important scholarship on black culture, such as the recent and monumental *Norton Anthology of African-American Literature* (1996). West was a student and later a colleague of Cone at Union Theological Seminary.

K. T. Weidmann

WORLD EVENTS		CONE'S LIFE
Mao Tse-tung establishes Communist Party in China	1921	
	1938	James Hal Cone is born in Bearden, Arkansas
World War II	1939–45	
Mao Tse-tung establishes Communist rule in China	1949	
Korean War	1950–53	
	1965	Cone receives Ph.D. from Northwestern University
Six Day War between Israel and Arabs	1967	
	1969	*Black Theology and Black Power* is published; Cone joins faculty of Union Theological Seminary
	1972	*Martin and Malcolm: A Dream or a Nightmare?* is published
End of Vietnam War	1975	*God of the Oppressed* is published
Fall of Communism in eastern Europe	1989	
Dissolution of Soviet Union	1991	
Apartheid in South Africa is dismantled	1994	

For Further Reading:

Burrow, Rufus. *James H. Cone and Black Liberation Theology*. Jefferson, N.C.: McFarland & Co., 1994.

Cone, James H. *God of the Oppressed*. New York: Seabury Press, 1975.

Wilmore, Gayraud S., and James H. Cone. *Black Theology: A Documentary History*. New York: Orbis Books, 1979.

Confucius (K'ung Ch'iu)

Chinese Philosopher;
Founder of Confucianism
551–479 B.C.E.

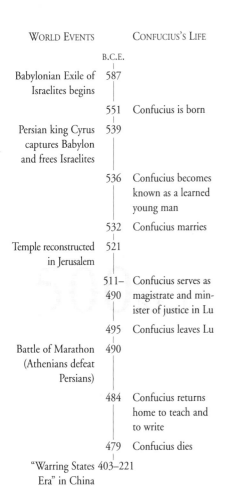

WORLD EVENTS	CONFUCIUS'S LIFE
	B.C.E.
Babylonian Exile of Israelites begins	587
	551 Confucius is born
Persian king Cyrus captures Babylon and frees Israelites	539
	536 Confucius becomes known as a learned young man
	532 Confucius marries
Temple reconstructed in Jerusalem	521
	511– Confucius serves as magistrate and minister of justice in Lu
	490
	495 Confucius leaves Lu
Battle of Marathon (Athenians defeat Persians)	490
	484 Confucius returns home to teach and to write
	479 Confucius dies
"Warring States Era" in China	403–221

Life and Work

Confucius was a Chinese philosopher and teacher whose vision of a well-ordered, harmonious society became the basis for East Asian culture.

K'ung Ch'iu, better known by his latinized name Confucius, was born to an aristocratic family in the Lu Province of China (now the Shantung Province) in 551 B.C.E. during the reign of Duke Hsiang. This period was marked by political agitation, with feudal lords challenging the ruling family of the Chou Dynasty (1059–249 B.C.E.) for control.

Confucius began to reflect on the problems of his time and tried to build upon ancient wisdom and values to find ways of restoring order and ensuring a harmonious society. Having a position in government service, he hoped to persuade the ruler that a good ruler, like a good father, guides his people by moral example.

He was also interested in developing other cultural aspects of society. Around the age of 35, he traveled to the nearby Chi Province, where he studied music and discussed his ideas about good government with the local ruler, Duke Ching. When he could not gain a government position in Chi, he returned to Lu and became a teacher, gathering disciples around him. Once again faced with political turmoil, he left Lu and journeyed to neighboring areas with his disciples. They traveled for 13 years, encountering communities in the area of present-day Shantung and Honan. In 484 B.C.E. he returned to Lu and, at age 65, was again appointed to a minor government post. During his remaining years, he devoted much time to discussion with his disciples about such matters as government, family, poetry, music, and ritual. He died in 479 B.C.E.

Confucius believed that a harmonious society was based on duty and virtue. All of human duty could be encompassed by five virtues: kindness, uprightness, decorum, wisdom, and faithfulness. These virtues formed the basis of the five fundamental relationships within society: father to son, elder brother to younger brother, husband to wife, elder to junior, and ruler to subject. To nurture these relationships and virtues, Confucius encouraged education for all members of society, not just for the ruling class, as had formerly been the custom.

Confucius's teachings are principally found in the *Analects*, a collection of conversations with his disciples compiled in the third century B.C.E. He is also credited with editing five classics: the *Shi ching* (*Book of Poetry*), the *I ching* (*Book of Changes*), the *Shu ching* (*Book of History*), *Li ching* (*Book of Rites*), and the *Ch'un-ch'ju* (*Spring and Autumn Annals*).

Legacy

Confucius is known as the first teacher in China who wanted to make education available to all men. He was instrumental in establishing the art of teaching as a vocation, indeed as a way of life. His birthday is an official holiday, "Teachers' Day," in Taiwan.

Confucius devoted his life to education in hopes of improving and even transforming society. He believed that all human beings could benefit from self-cultivation, but the primary focus of his teaching was the training of noblemen. Training programs for statesmen and studies in humanities for potential leaders were instituted at his urging. He believed education to be character building and a primary requirement for public service. These ideas about learning and its importance to public life became the basis for the educational system in China as well as in other East Asian countries.

Confucius consciously tried to reanimate the old order to attain the new. In fact, he helped preserve the continuity of the cultural values and the social norms that had worked so well for the civilization of the Chou dynasty in China. As the architect of Chinese and East Asian cultures and civilizations, his legacy was one of unity and continuity. This legacy can be observed to this day—in family structure, social hierarchy, and educational systems among many other areas.

Yang

For Further Reading:

Chan, Wing-tsit. *Neo-Confucian Terms Explained.* New York: Columbia University Press, 1986.
De Bary, William. *The Trouble with Confucianism.* Cambridge: Harvard University Press, 1991.

Cranmer, Thomas

Leader of the English Reformation
1489–1556

Life and Work

Thomas Cranmer was a leader of the English Reformation who helped establish the Church of England.

The son of a village squire, Cranmer was born on July 2, 1489. He attended Cambridge University, where he was influenced by the Renaissance humanists and continental reformers. In 1526, he received his doctorate, was ordained, and became a lecturer in divinity at Jesus College, Cambridge.

Cranmer rose quickly, primarily because he advised King Henry VIII that he need not wait for the Pope to grant an annulment of his marriage to Catherine of Aragon but could refer the question of its legality to scholars in England. Cranmer prepared Henry's argument before the universities of Oxford and Cambridge and, in 1530, went to Rome to explain Henry's position to the Pope.

Soon thereafter, Henry VIII recommended Cranmer to become the next Archbishop of Canterbury. Publicly renouncing any allegiance to the Pope, Cranmer was consecrated on March 30, 1533. Within two months, he nullified the marriage of Henry and Catherine and validated the marriage of Henry to Anne Boleyn (performed the previous January). In the next few years, Cranmer pronounced the

King of England head of the English church, consecrated bishops, and gradually assumed various duties previously reserved to the Pope.

During the last years of Henry's reign, Cranmer's increasingly reformist views clashed with those of the king and others who had no interest in changing the Church of England. Several times enemies attempted to have him convicted of heresy but were prevented by Henry's personal attachment to the archbishop.

When King Edward VI ascended the throne in 1547, Cranmer was able to implement reforms in teaching and practice that brought the Church of England closer to the Reformation churches on the European continent. One of his most significant acts was compiling the *Book of Common Prayer*, first issued in 1549. In 1552 he produced a second *Book of Common Prayer*. This book included a list of 42 articles of belief (later reduced to 39), which became the doctrinal statements of the early Church of England and echoed some of the theological principles of the European Reformation.

Following Mary Tudor's (Mary I) ascension to the throne in 1553, Cranmer was condemned to death for heresy and forced to disavow his Protestant teachings. At his execution, he rejected his own recantations. On March 21, 1556, as a sign of the wrongfulness of what his right hand had written in recanting his beliefs, he put it first into the fire that destroyed him.

Legacy

Cranmer was instrumental in establishing the Anglican church in England independent of the Roman Catholic church. Through his leadership, it retained continuity with Catholic tradition while affirming reformation.

Cranmer established some of the most significant elements of the Anglican church: its connection with the government and monarch; its accommodation of tradition and reform; and its stress on the importance of scripture and the witness of the early Church Fathers. Cranmer's ideas contributed to the Anglican church's emphasis on grace and on the importance of spirituality and ethics. In the 42 articles he outlined the Anglican church's position on some of the controversies of the Reformation. The language was carefully crafted to permit a wide variety of inter-

pretation. The articles' impact went far beyond the Church of England, forming the basis of the Methodist Twenty-Five Articles.

Cranmer's *Book of Common Prayer* presented a traditional liturgy but with a distinctly English emphasis. His liturgical forms became models, not only for Anglican churches throughout the world, but also for other English-speaking denominations. The prayer book, with its dignified, graceful language, had a lasting influence on the English language and literature. Although the language has since been modified, it remains central in Anglican life. After the Bible, it is the basic document of the Anglican church.

Osterfield

WORLD EVENTS		CRANMER'S LIFE
Ottoman Empire captures Byzantine capital, Constantinople	1453	
	1489	Thomas Cranmer is born in Nottinghamshire
Columbus discovers Americas	1492	
Last Muslim State in Spain falls to Christians		
Reformation begins	1517	
	1526	Cranmer is ordained
	1533	Cranmer is consecrated Archbishop of Canterbury; he declares Henry VIII's marriage to Catherine void, pronounces marriage to Anne Boleyn valid
Henry VIII dies; Edward VI is crowned	1547	
	1549	Cranmer compiles first *Book of Common Prayer*
	1552	Cranmer issues second *Book of Common Prayer* and 42 articles of belief
	1553	Cranmer recants reforms instituted earlier
	1556	Cranmer is executed by fire
Thirty Years' War in Europe	1618–48	

For Further Reading:

Brooks, Peter Newman. *Cranmer in Context*. Minneapolis, Minn., Fortress, 1989.
MacCulloch, Diarmaid. *Thomas Cranmer: A Life*. New Haven, Conn.: Yale University Press, 1996.

Cyril of Alexandria, Saint

Architect of Early Christian Christology
c. 375–444

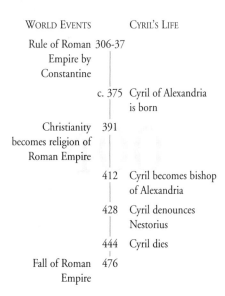

WORLD EVENTS		CYRIL'S LIFE
Rule of Roman Empire by Constantine	306-37	
	c. 375	Cyril of Alexandria is born
Christianity becomes religion of Roman Empire	391	
	412	Cyril becomes bishop of Alexandria
	428	Cyril denounces Nestorius
	444	Cyril dies
Fall of Roman Empire	476	

Life and Work

Cyril of Alexandria (Egypt) forged the early Christian Church's teaching on Christology, the doctrine describing the person and work of JESUS.

Cyril was born in Theodosiou, near Alexandria, around 375. His uncle, Theophilus, was the bishop of the city, and Cyril grew up during his uncle's campaign to root out heresy and paganism in Egypt. Cyril succeeded his uncle as bishop in 412, following a bloody, disputed election. A distinguished theologian but a deeply intolerant man, he continued his uncle's campaign against dissent and heresy. His actions ultimately led to riots among Christians, pagans, and Jews, culminating in the murder by a Christian mob of the distinguished philosopher, Hypatia.

Cyril achieved prominence as a theologian during his dispute with Nestorius, bishop of Constantinople, over the nature of Christ, about the way Jesus is both man and God. Nestorius strongly distinguished Christ's two natures and was particularly disturbed by groups calling MARY *Theotokos* (mother of God). To Nestorius she was the mother only of the human Jesus, not God the son. In 428, Cyril denounced Nestorius' views in a series of letters and 12 propositions in which he accused Nestorius of separating Christ into two beings—the human and the divine—and denying the singular human–divine nature of Christ. For Cyril, Christ was God and man at once; of one nature but "out of two natures."

The *Theotokos* dispute became entangled in Church politics when the emperor asked Nestorius to investigate a series of complaints against the Egyptian bishop. Angered that Nestorius would sit in judgment over him, Cyril began a campaign to discredit Nestorius and, by 431, had convinced Pope Celestine I (r. 422–432) to call a council at Ephesus in Asia Minor. Before all of the participants could arrive, Cyril forced the condemnation of Nestorius. Nestorius was removed from office and eventually exiled.

Cyril's literary work centered on Christological themes and biblical interpretation. He produced commentaries, known as *Glaphura*, focusing on Isaiah, the minor prophets, and interpretations of the Gospels of Matthew, Luke, and John. In these commentaries he promoted the allegorical and etymological interpretations prominent among Alexandrian scholars.

Cyril died in 444. On June 27, 1882, Pope Leo XIII pronounced Cyril a doctor of the Church.

Legacy

Cyril's work laid the foundation for the Church's development of Christological and Trinitarian teaching. His attacks on the Trinitarian concepts of Nestorius cemented the Church's teaching that Jesus was simultaneously divine and human.

The debate over the nature of Christ continued after Cyril's death. Nestorius' "two nature" formula was condemned by a second council at Ephesus in 449. Two years later the Council of Chalcedon adopted what became the traditional definition of Christ and understanding of the Trinity. It defined Christ as one person, perfect God and perfect man, known in two natures. The differences between Christ as God and Christ as man are preserved and both come together in the one fundamental unity of the person of Christ. The council developed this formula from several sources, among them two of Cyril's letters to Nestorius. Before concluding, it also condemned Nestorius and approved Cyril's writings. Later Church councils extended approval to all.

Not all churches accepted the decrees of Chalcedon. By the middle of the fifth century, the Monophysites, who believed that Christ had only one (*monos*) nature (*physis*), instead of two, appealed to the writings of Cyril to support their claims. The contemporary Coptic (Ethiopia), Jacobite (Syrian), and Armenian Orthodox churches subscribe to this doctrine.

von Dehsen

For Further Reading:

McGuckin, John Anthony. *St. Cyril of Alexandria: The Christological Controversy: Its History, Theology, and Texts.* Leiden, Netherlands, and New York: E. J. Brill, 1994.

Welch, Lawrence J. *Christology and Eucharist in the Early Thought of Cyril of Alexandria.* San Francisco: International Scholars Press, 1994.

Dalai Lama

(Tenzin Gyatso)

Spiritual Leader of Tibetan Buddhism
1935–

Life and Work

The spiritual and temporal leader of the Tibetan people, Tenzin Gyatso, the fourteenth Dalai Lama, is the late-twentieth-century personification of the nonviolent struggle for human rights.

Tenzin Gyatso was born July 6, 1935, in the small village of Takster in northeast Tibet (what is now Tsinghai province, China) to peasant farmers. At the age of two he was recognized as the reincarnation of the thirteenth Dalai Lama. Tibetans believe that the Dalai Lamas are manifestations of enlightened men who have been reincarnated to serve the Tibetan people. Traditionally they have been both the spiritual and temporal leaders (civil leaders) of Tibet. Tenzin Gyatso was enthroned in 1940 at the age of four and assumed political power in 1950, when he was only 16. Following the Chinese military occupation of Tibet in 1959, he fled into exile with 100,000 of his followers.

Granted political asylum in India, the Dalai Lama set up a government-in-exile in Dharamsala, in the Himalayan mountains. In 1963 he drafted a democratic constitution for Tibet. It permitted Tibetans throughout the world to elect representatives to the government in exile. Under the constitution the Dalai Lama was no longer absolute ruler and could be impeached.

While in exile the Dalai Lama has worked to free Tibet from Chinese domination through peaceful means. Throughout his campaign, he has emphasized the use of nonviolent action, asserting that he will win the battle through compassion. As a result of his appeals, the United Nations General Assembly adopted resolutions in 1959, 1961, and 1965 calling on China to respect Tibetan human rights and the people's desire for self-determination. In 1987 he proposed the creation of an autonomous Tibetan state in association with China. Although communist China has yet to relinquish Tibet, the Dalai Lama believes that, given the fall of communist governments in eastern Europe, Tibetan freedom is still possible.

While fighting to regain Tibetan independence, the Dalai Lama has led a campaign to preserve Tibetan identity, which the communist Chinese had attempted to destroy. He founded an educational system for refugee children and set up numerous monasteries and institutes to preserve the 2000-year-old Tibetan culture.

The Dalai Lama has played a major role in interfaith dialogues, meeting with other religious leaders to promote better understanding and respect among the world's faiths. His messages emphasize the common elements among faiths and the importance of love, kindness, compassion and the universal responsibility to respond to other people's suffering.

In 1989 he was awarded the Nobel Prize for Peace in recognition of his nonviolent campaign to end Chinese domination of Tibet.

Legacy

The Dalai Lama has been a significant political, religious and moral presence as he continues the struggle for Tibetan freedom through nonviolence.

As political leader of the Tibetans, the Dalai Lama has maintained the campaign for Tibetan independence for more than 35 years in the face of the indifference of many nations which were concerned about alienating China. When the Chinese invaded Tibet, they ruthlessly destroyed Tibetan culture in an effort to erase national identity. The Dalai Lama has led the fight to preserve that culture. In so doing he has introduced it to many throughout the world.

As the leader of Tibetan Buddhism he has brought that faith, once isolated in the Himalayas, to the world's attention. Since his exile, Tibetan Buddhism has spread to many nations. He has been a prominent figure in the promotion of religious tolerance. Preaching of triumph through compassion, the Dalai Lama is a successor of MOHANDAS KARAMCHAND GANDHI. He is a symbol of nonviolence and strength for all oppressed people in the world.

Yang

WORLD EVENTS		DALAI LAMA'S LIFE
Mao Tse-tung establishes Communist Party in China	1921	
	1935	Tenzin Gayatso is born
World War II	1939–45	
	1940	Tenzin Gayatso enthroned as the 14th Dalai Lama
Mao Tse-tung establishes Communist rule in China	1949	
Apartheid laws established in South Africa		
	1950	The Dalai Lama assumes political role as head of state and government
Korean War	1950–53	
	1959	Following Chinese invasion, the Dalai Lama flees to exile in India
Six Day War between Israel and Arabs	1967	
End of Vietnam War	1975	
	1987	The Dalai Lama proposes a creation of an autonomous Tibetan state
Fall of Communism in eastern Europe	1989	The Dalai Lama is awarded the Nobel Prize for Peace
Dissolution of Soviet Union	1991	

For Further Reading:

Pell, Claiborne, and Sidney Piburn. *The Dalai Lama, A Policy of Kindness.* Ithaca, N.Y.: Snow Lion Publication, 1990.

Tibetan Parliamentary and Policy Research Center. *The Spirit of Tibet, Vision for Human Liberation: Selected Speeches and Writings of HH the Dalai Lama.* Edited by A. A. Shiromany. New Delhi, India: Vikas Publishing House, 1996.

Warren, Bill, and Nanci Hoetzlein Rose. *Living Tibet: the Dalai Lama in Dharamsala.* Ithaca, N.Y.: Snow Lion Publications, 1995.

Daly, Mary

Influential Feminist Theologian
and Philosopher
1928–

Life and Work

Mary Daly is a radical feminist theologian and philosopher whose groundbreaking work in feminist thought was aimed at exposing the patriarchal (male-centered) biases in the Christian church and in Western society at large.

Daly was born in Schenectady, New York, in 1928. Her parents were Irish Catholics who sent her to parochial schools. Daly graduated from the College of St. Rose in Albany, New York, in 1950 and received a doctorate in religion from St. Mary's College, the women's college associated with Notre Dame University, in 1954. She wanted to study for an additional doctorate, this time in philosophy, at Notre Dame but was denied entrance because she was a woman. She received doctorates in both theology and philosophy in 1965 from the University of Fribourg in Switzerland. In 1966, Daly began her teaching career at Boston College, a Jesuit university. While there, she began to publish books articulating her feminist philosophy.

In her early works, *The Church and the Second Sex* (1968) and *Beyond God the Father: Toward a Philosophy of Women's Liberation* (1973), Daly critiqued the patriarchal structure

of Christianity, especially that of the Roman Catholic church, and the male-dominated imagery of God. Both of these books caused much controversy and brought Daly, and Boston College, unfavorable publicity. As a result of the publicity and the radical critique of the Church, in 1968, Boston College almost denied her academic tenure and in 1975 the college refused to promote her to full professor.

In her next two books, *Gyn/Ecology: The Metaethics of Radical Feminism* (1978) and *Pure Lust: Elemental Feminist Philosophy* (1984), Daly attacked patriarchy in the larger society. In *Gyn/Ecology* she asserted that women's liberation was an ontological movement, focusing on who women are in their patterns of thinking and acting and on breaking the patriarchal manipulation of those patterns. *Pure Lust* took this mode of thinking further, pointing to ways the ontological categories of *Gyn/Ecology* could be realized. Work on these books led to the creation of Daly's next book, *Webster's First New Intergalactic Wickedary of the English Language* (1987), a compendium of new vocabulary created to counter what she saw as the patriarchal English language.

In 1992, Daly published *Overcourse: A Be-Dazzling Voyage*, her philosophical autobiography. In 1998 she released *Quintessence—Realizing the Archaic Future: A Feminist Manifesto*. In the spring of 1999 she retired from Boston College after a battle over her long-standing practice of barring males from her classes.

Legacy

Daly's radical feminist philosophy challenged patriarchal assumptions dominant both in the Roman Catholic church and in Western society in general. Her work broke theological and philosophical ground, opening ways for other women to develop their own voices in addressing questions of patriarchal oppression.

Much feminist thought grows out of the personal experiences of the women who produced it and champions the premise that a woman's experience is an essential component of her feminist perspective. Daly's life and work certainly provide a striking example of this—her quest for a doctorate in philosophy and her rejection by male-dominated Roman Catholic institutions certainly were important factors in the drive to develop and articulate her radical feminist philosophy.

Daly's radical thought has inspired others to develop these ideas further. For example, her argu-

ment in *Pure Lust* that passion and reason must be renamed and, therefore, re-understood by women has helped other feminists to rediscover the role language plays in imposing patriarchal constraints upon women. By using language to objectify women's bodies and oppress them through brutality and pornography, language becomes a patriarchal weapon. This understanding of the use of language has influenced the work of such feminist scholars as Carol McMillan, Genevieve Lloyd, Marilyn Frye, and Luce Irigaray.

Daly's insistence that the lives of women are intimately connected with nature in the biosphere has contributed greatly to the movement known as "eco-feminism." Such scholars as Maria Mies, Irene Diamond, and Gloria Feman Orenstein have echoed Daly's themes in terms of protection for the environment and women's relationship to nature.

Other feminists have challenged the radical nature of Daly's thought. Hester Einstein, for example, believed that Daly so retreated into psychological individualism and so desired a feminist community separated from men that she ignored some of the political aspects of the feminist movement. Ruth Wallsgrove challenged Daly's concept that society is necrophiliac (death-loving) based on innate male characteristics. Wallsgrove argues that men, as well as women, develop a concept of life socially conditioned by the male's biological inability to bear children.

Whatever the response, Mary Daly's has become a significant voice in feminist thought. Her radical ideas continue to generate spirited responses among feminists and nonfeminists alike.

von Dehsen

World Events		Daly's Life
	1928	Mary Daly is born
World War II	1939–45	
Mao Tse-tung establishes Communist rule in China	1949	
Korean War	1950–53	
	1965	Daly receives doctorate from University of Fribourg
	1966	Daly begins teaching at Boston College
Six Day War between Israel and Arabs	1967	
	1968	*The Church and the Second Sex* is published
End of Vietnam War	1975	
	1978	*Gyn/Ecology* is published
Dissolution of Soviet Union	1991	
	1999	Daly retires from Boston College

For Further Reading:

Griffiths, Morwenna, and Margaret Whiteford, eds. *Feminist Perspectives in Philosophy.* Bloomington: Indiana University Press, 1988.
Ratcliffe, Krista. *Anglo-American Feminist Challenge to the Rhetorical Tradition: Virginia Woolf, Mary Daly, and Adrienne Rich.* Carbondale: Southern Illinois University Press, 1996.

David

Important Biblical Figure;
Founder of Jerusalem
Tenth Century B.C.E.

Life And Work

David was the second king of a unified Israel (Israel and Judah) and founder of a dynasty that ruled until the fall of Jerusalem to Babylon in 587 B.C.E.

Our only primary source for the life of David is the Hebrew Bible. He was the youngest son of Jesse and a resident of Bethlehem in Judah. The stories of his youth emphasize his shepherd life and musical talents, both foreshadowing themes of his reign. As a young man he was noted for his courage in battles against the Philistines as shown in his legendary encounter with Goliath. He served in the court of Israel's first king, Saul, but was forced into exile when Saul became jealous of his growing popularity. For several years David led a band of warriors serving various local rulers. Upon the death of Saul and his sons in battle in about 1,000 B.C.E., David became king of Judah and seven years later was anointed king of Israel, thus uniting the two kingdoms.

During his reign David engaged in a series of successful military campaigns against neighboring states that extended his kingdom and solidified it as an independent nation. One of his most significant conquests was the capture of the Jebusite (a local clan) town of Zion, which became the nucleus of his capital, Jerusalem. Under his direction the city became the political and cultural center of his kingdom.

The later years of David's reign were troubled by rebellions and confrontations with his children. David's eldest son, Absalom, led an unsuccessful rebellion against him. Later David became involved in a dispute with his surviving eldest son, Adonijah, who had himself proclaimed king after David had appointed his younger son, Solomon, as his successor. David was able to rally support in favor of his choice. David died shortly thereafter (c. 962 B.C.E.).

Legacy

David brought coherence to the twelve tribes of Israel. Later generations of Jews looked back upon his reign as the model for the people and God's promise for their future.

David brought the various "tribes" of Israel and Jerusalem together, thus encouraging the sharing of religious and political traditions. The concept of rule by kings was grafted onto the anti-monarchical political and religious beliefs of earlier Israelite and Judean clans. He expanded the territory of Israel and established a dynasty that ruled the united kingdom under his son Solomon and continued in Judah for some 400 years until 587 B.C.E. David is credited with organizing aspects of Israelite worship and writing many of the psalms.

After the fall of the Davidic kingdom and the exile to Babylon, hope for the future among some Jews was placed in the promise of an eternal reign for the line of David; thus began a long history of "recognition" of various figures as the promised successor of David. Zerubbabel, a political leader in the postexilic rebuilding of the Temple, was so identified. Over the next few centuries, the hope for a Messiah was mixed with other hopes for a renewed Israelite–Jewish people, as Judah suffered under various political overlords. The early Christian movement attached some of these hopes to JESUS (as is evidenced by the fact that "Christ" is a Greek translation of Messiah). With the separation of Christianity from Judaism (primarily after the fall of Jerusalem to the Romans in 70 C.E.), occasional outbreaks of messianic fervor swept portions of the Jewish people. Two famous examples of messianic pretenders are Bar Kokhba in 132 C.E. and Shabbetai Zevi in the seventeenth century C.E.

The place of Jerusalem in the lives and hopes of Jews through the ages is attributable primarily to David, who made the city central to the life of Judah and larger Israel. Jerusalem also became very important for the later Christian and Muslim communities, thus contributing to battles for Jerusalem over the millennia.

The tradition that David is the author of the biblical psalms encouraged their use in Jewish worship and devotion. This poetry, in the Hebrew and in various translations and paraphrases, has been formative in the worship of churches and synagogues.

Osterfield

WORLD EVENTS   DAVID'S LIFE *

B.C.E.

Fall of Troy c. 1150

c. 1000 David's rule begins
in Jerusalem

c. 962 David dies

Barbarians invade   771
China

* *Scholars cannot date the specific events in David's life with accuracy.*

For Further Reading:

Steussy, Marti J., *David: Biblical Portraits of Power*. Columbia: University of South Carolina Press, 1998.

Brueggemann, Walter. *David's Truth in Israel's Imagination and Memory*. Philadelphia: Fortress, 1985.

Carlson, R. A. *David, The Chosen King*. Uppsala, Sweden: Almquist and Wiksells, 1964.

Eisemann, Moshe. *A Pearl in the Sand: Reflections on Shavuos, Megilas Ruth and The Davidic Kingship*. Baltimore, Md.: M. M. Eisemann, 1997.

Derrida, Jacques

Postmodern French Philosopher;
Proponent of Deconstructionism
1930–

Life and Work

Jacques Derrida is a French philosopher whose work on the problems inherent in interpreting written texts contributed to the development of deconstructionism. This mode of interpretation insists that the meaning of a text derives solely from the interpreter.

WORLD EVENTS	DERRIDA'S LIFE
World War I 1914–18	
	1930 Jacques Derrida is born in French Algeria
World War II 1939–45	
Mao Tse-tung establishes Communist rule in China	1949
Apartheid laws established in South Africa	
Korean War 1950–53	
	1956 Derrida studies at Harvard
Six Day War between Israel and Arabs	1967 *Of Grammatology* and *Writing and Difference* are published
	mid-1970s Derrida helps establish International College of Philosophy
End of Vietnam War 1975	
	1976 *Of Grammatology* appears in English
Fall of Communism in eastern Europe	1989

Derrida was born on July 15, 1930, in French Algeria to a family of Sephardic Jews. He graduated from a Jewish lycee in 1948. Having first encountered philosophy through a French radio lecture, he began its formal study in 1950 and earned a master's degree in 1952 at the École Normale Supérieure in Paris. His thesis was written on EDMUND HUSSERL, a leading philosopher of phenomenology. He then studied the thought of MARTIN HEIDEGGER and GEORG WILHELM FRIEDRICH HEGEL and spent a year at Harvard in 1956. Returning to France, he taught at the Sorbonne and published a prize-winning translation of Husserl's *Origin of Geometry*. Husserl's work made him suspicious of the premise that universal truths could be discovered through philosophy.

In 1967 the publication *Of Grammatology and Writing and Difference* caught the French intellectual world's attention. At the same time, literary critics in North America began serious study of an academic paper Derrida presented a year earlier at a conference in Baltimore. By 1972, Derrida began teaching both in French and American universities. The next year his major works started appearing in English. *Of Grammatology* appeared in English in 1976, generating charges that his works are confusing and unphilosophical.

Derrida's association with deconstructionism has overshadowed his more serious critique of "mainstream" philosophical writings. In general, deconstructive reading maintains that any text, even philosophical ones, thoroughly embodies the social, historical, cultural, and linguistic assumptions of their times. Consequently, all texts are open to many, often conflicting, interpretations. Such largely unconscious assumptions predetermine what is discussed, what is considered reasonable, and what is "marginalized," or excluded, from social discourse. Deconstructive readings of any text, then, aim to explore the implicitly powerful constructions and presuppositions that operate in a text.

In the mid-1970s Derrida joined a group to reform the teaching of philosophy in France. He assisted in the establishment of the International College of Philosophy, a program open to a broader, interdisciplinary, approach to philosophical research. Major philosophical studies of Derrida's writings have

continued. His transatlantic teaching, writing, and fostering of lively philosophical debate continue to this day.

Legacy

Derrida posed questions about how texts are interpreted that opened ways for later scholars to explore the relationship between the text and the "contribution" of the reader to the meaning of the text. Under the broad category of deconstructionism, Derrida's thought has provided intellectual tools for others to examine how texts are used for political and social purposes.

Scholars identify Derrida's thinking as a fundamental component of a number of French intellectual perspectives loosely termed "Postmodern" or "deconstruction." Based on insights derived from FRIEDRICH WILHELM NIETZSCHE and Martin Heidegger, these various approaches call into question the ability of philosophy to stand apart from its cultural and historical context and to assert objective truths.

Over the last third of the twentieth century, feminist scholars have appropriated the techniques of Derrida to uncover the patriarchal bias within a text used to oppress women. This approach to a text is often called the "hermeneutics of suspicion," which is the uncovering of a male bias embedded in the text. Through the use of this hermeneutic, the bias within a text has been exposed and the authority of the text questioned. Such biblical scholars as Phyllis Trible have used "rhetorical criticism," a methodology derived from deconstructionism, to reclaim the text for women and men alike.

Passionate debates between Derrida, like-minded thinkers, and critics continue. Some extreme deconstructionists assert that no interpretation is better than any other in an endless, pointless play on words. Others contend that every truth is merely relative to the context. Derrida avoids such extremes by urging a careful reading of basic traditional works, suggesting that some interpretations are closer to the "interpreted facts" than are others. Philosophically, one may argue that while no truth presents its subject matter complete and pure, every well-founded truth provides a partial revelation of the world.

Magurshak

For Further Reading:

Caputo, John. *Deconstruction in a Nutshell: A Conversation with Jacques Derrida.* New York: Fordham University Press, 1997.

Norris, Christopher. *Derrida.* Cambridge, Mass.: Harvard University Press, 1987.

Solomon, Robert C., and Kathleen M. Higgins. *A Short History of Philosophy.* New York: Oxford University Press, 1996.

Descartes, René

Originator of the Framework of
Modern Philosophy
1596–1650

Life and Work

René Descartes was a French mathematician and philosopher who set the framework for philosophy in the modern period.

Descartes was born into an aristocratic family in La Haye (now Descartes), France, on
March 11, 1596. He was educated at the prestigious Jesuit College, La Fleche, and following
graduation in 1612, studied law at the
University of Poitiers. He then began a military career that took him across Europe. In
1628 he settled in Holland where he spent his
time exploring mathematical problems and
developing his systematic philosophy, which
made him renowned throughout Europe.

Dissatisfied with scholastic philosophy,
which emphasized the importance of authority
and reasoning, Descartes proposed a philosophical methodology derived from that used in science and particularly geometry. His basic rules
were: 1) accept only what is self-evident as true,
2) divide problems into their simplest parts, 3)
solve problems by proceeding from the simple
to the complex, and 4) recheck the reasoning.

Descartes's method is grounded in the idea
that knowledge based on senses or authority
must be doubted. The only thing that cannot
be doubted is one's own doubting. He
expressed this idea in his famous *cogito ergo
sum* ("I think, therefore I am").

From establishing the existence of a thinking
being, he offered proof of the existence of God.
He argued that the presence in his imperfect
mind of the idea of a supremely perfect being
could have been put there only by a being that
was supremely perfect, namely God. Through
God, who would not deceive beings by presenting illusions, Descartes establishes the reality of
the physical world. God created a reality composed of two types of substances: minds, or
thinking substances, and material bodies.
Descartes concluded that he was a mind in a
material body, and that the material world is
completely divorced from that of the mind (a
theory called Cartesian dualism). Descartes was
aware of the close connection between the mind
(ideas) and the brain (which was a material substance) and reasoned that the two interacted, but
he never explained how this interaction worked.

Descartes's philosophy was based on the
underlying assumption that reason is the
source of all knowledge, a theory called
rationalism. He applied his method to science
and, by the use of reason, created a system of
natural philosophy aimed at explaining the
operation of the physical world.

Descartes presented his ideas in a series of
works including *Discourse on Method* (1637),
Meditations on First Philosophy (1641), and
The Principles of Philosophy (1644).

In 1649, Descartes accepted an invitation
from Queen Christina of Sweden to be her
tutor in philosophy. He became ill in the harsh
climate and died in Stockholm on February
11, 1650.

Legacy

Descartes is often considered to be one of the
founders of the modern age. His ideas were
central to the intellectual revolution of the seventeenth century, which overthrew existing systems of thinking based on ancient Greek
philosophy. Descartes established the framework
for much of modern philosophical discourse and
gave it some of its most significant problems.

By focusing on the nature of the human mind
and the problem of true and certain knowledge,
Descartes made the relationship between the
mind and the world the starting point of philosophy. Although the philosophical distinction
between mind and body can be traced to the
Greek philosopher PLATO, Descartes is considered to be the father of what became known as
the mind–body problem. By contending that
the mind and body interacted even though they
existed in different realms, he posed one of the
major philosophical questions of the modern
age: What connects our minds to our brains?

Philosophers such as Nicholas Malebranche
(1638–1715), BENEDICT DE SPINOZA (1632–
1677) and Gottfried Leibnitz (1646–1716) all
formulated their theories about the relationship
of mind and body in response to Cartesian
dualism. Scientific discoveries made in the
nineteenth century fostered new interest in the
relationship between mind and brain for
philosophers such as WILLIAM JAMES (1842–
1910). All addressed the problems in terms of the
questions Descartes's ideas posed.

Descartes's rationalism, defined as the use of
reason as an intellectual tool, affected theory in
virtually all disciplines and was enthusiastically
received, particularly in Europe, during his lifetime. This rationalism was challenged by eighteenth-century Enlightenment philosophers
such as JOHN LOCKE (1632–1704) who
asserted that knowledge was based on experience and experimental observation. This theory
is called empiricism. Empiricism eventually
gained dominance, particularly in science.

Olson

For Further Reading:
Foster, John. *The Immaterial Self: A Defense of the Cartesian Dualist Conception of the Mind.* New York: Routledge, 1991.
Kearns, John T. *Reconceiving Experience: A Solution to a Problem Inherited from Descartes.* Albany: State University of New York Press, 1996.
Schouls, Peter. *Descartes and the Enlightenment.* Kingston, Ont.: McGill-Queens University Press, 1989.

WORLD EVENTS		DESCARTES'S LIFE
Reformation begins	1517	
	1596	René Descartes is born in La Haye, France
	1612	Descartes begins to study law at University of Poitiers
Thirty Years' War in Europe	1618–48	
	1637	*Discourse on Method* is published
	1638	Descartes settles in Holland and begins mathematical career
	1641	*Meditations on First Philosophy* is published
	1644	*Principles of Philosophy* is published
	1650	Descartes dies in Stockholm, Sweden
England's Glorious Revolution	1688	

Dewey, John

Father of Progressive Education
1859–1952

Life and Work

The father of progressive education, John Dewey revolutionized educational methods by connecting the teaching of abstract skills to solving problems of everyday life.

Dewey was born in Burlington, Vermont, on October 20, 1859. He received a B.A. from the University of Vermont in 1879 and a Ph.D. from Johns Hopkins University in 1884. For the next 10 years he taught at the University of Michigan, where he did research in the emerging science of child psychology.

From these studies Dewey developed a revolutionary theory of education. Children, he theorized, learned by absorbing the information they needed in their daily lives. Education, therefore, should center around problem solving rather than a rigidly structured curriculum. He also believed that education should prepare American children for life in a modern democratic society.

In 1894 he became the chair of the department of philosophy at the recently established University of Chicago, where he began putting his ideas into practice. He opened the Laboratory School, later called the Dewey School, in 1896 to test his theories. Each grade was assigned an age-appropriate activity, such as designing a farm or exploring prehistoric times, to teach such topics as mathematical and linguistic skills. This practical approach, sometimes called pragmatism, unites scientific knowledge and other ways of knowing. It also encourages such democratic values as cooperation among people from different classes and genders.

By 1904, the University of Chicago was no longer willing to underwrite Dewey's experiments and he moved on to Columbia University in New York, as professor of philosophy, where he taught until retirement. In 1919, he was instrumental in establishing the New School for Social Research in New York, and in 1933 he helped found the "University in Exile" for scholars displaced by the Nazis. Eventually, this institution became the New School Graduate Faculty of Political and Social Science.

Dewey announced his retirement from Columbia in 1927. To keep him active, Columbia appointed him its first professor emeritus. He spent his remaining years at Columbia writing and advising students.

Over his lifetime, Dewey produced a wealth of writing. Among the most important are: *Psychology* (1887), *The School and Society* (1899), *The Child and the Curriculum* (1901), and *Experience and Nature* (1925).

Dewey retired completely in 1951. He died of pneumonia in New York on June 1, 1952.

Legacy

Dewey revolutionized the methods of American education. He refocused educational goals from those of rote memorization of isolated facts and formulas in a context of fear to one in which students were encouraged to cooperate in practical activities linked to learning objectives.

This approach is not without its critics. Dewey's liberal education theories have been blamed for the malaise of American public education, its permissiveness, lack of discipline, and low academic standards. In a 1928 essay, "Experience and Education," Dewey himself criticized the misuse of his methods by teachers who attempted to entertain, rather than to

instruct, and fostered unfocused activity.

Nevertheless, Dewey has been called the father of American education and the originator of progressive education, a student-centered enterprise, emphasizing directed activity. The teacher functions as a guide and coworker, not as an authoritative dispenser of knowledge. The educational goal shifted away from the mere accumulation of information to the building of a positive self-image. Many of these concepts derived from his seminal work in psychology, emphasizing the whole person.

Dewey's collaboration in the founding of the New School for Social Research in New York carried his efforts at innovation to matters of postsecondary education. Founded in 1919, the New School departed from the political constraints on education imposed by World War I and provided a free and uninhibited atmosphere for the exploration of ideas. The emphasis was on open learning, not on the acquisition of grades and credits. Consequently, the New School has traditionally attracted adult learners; only a small portion of its student body matriculate to earn college credit. Over the years, it has branched out to embrace academic programs focused on such diverse areas as urban management and design. Thus, the school models Dewey's openness and provides a venue for experimental and nontraditional forms of education.

Dewey's efforts have touched all areas of American education. Not only have his theories charted new approaches to primary and secondary education, they have inspired "unconventional" methods for stimulating learning among adults as well.

Olson

WORLD EVENTS		DEWEY'S LIFE
	1859	John Dewey is born
United States Civil War	1861–65	
Germany is united	1871	
	1884	Dewey receives Ph.D. from Johns Hopkins University
	1896	Dewey establishes Laboratory Schools at University of Chicago
Spanish American War	1898	
	1904	Dewey becomes professor of philosophy, Columbia University
World War I	1914–18	
	1925	*Experience and Nature* is published
World War II	1939–45	
Mao Tse-tung establishes Communist rule in China	1949	
Korean War	1950–53	
	1952	Dewey dies
Six Day War between Israel and Arabs	1967	

For Further Reading:

Campbell, James. *Understanding John Dewey: Nature and Cooperative Intelligence*. Peru, Ill.: Open Count Publishing Co., 1995

Dykhuizen, George. *The Life and Mind of John Dewey*. Carbondale: Southern Illinois University Press, 1973.

Ryan, Alan. *John Dewey and the High Tide of American Liberalism*. New York: W. W. Norton and Co., 1997.

Diderot, Denis

Encyclopedist and Major Philosopher of the French Enlightenment
1713–1784

Life and Work

A prolific author and general editor of the *Encyclopédie*, Denis Diderot was one of the leaders of the French Enlightenment.

Diderot was born in Langres, France, on October 5, 1713. He was educated in Jesuit schools but gradually abandoned the Christian faith, ultimately becoming an atheist. After receiving a master of arts degree from the University of Paris in 1732, he eked out a living by writing and tutoring.

In 1747 Diderot became editor of the *Encyclopédie*, which was originally conceived as a translation of Ephraim Chamber's *Cyclopedia*. Diderot, however, vastly expanded the project in an attempt to cover all human knowledge. The work was grounded in his own philosophical belief that human reason, guided by the experience of the senses, could increase knowledge and thus the well-being of humanity. Its implicit criticism of the conservative political and religious establishment resulted in the official suppression of the first 10 volumes of the *Encyclopédie* in 1759. Undaunted by an injunction against further publication, Diderot worked with the major figures of the French Enlightenment to complete the project and had the remaining volumes printed secretly. The first volume was published in 1751 and the seventeenth and final volume of text was completed in 1765.

Although Diderot complained that the *Encyclopédie* took up most of his time, he was a prolific author, producing plays and novels as well as works on poetics, aesthetics, and science. His writings often reflected his materialist belief that life is nothing but matter acting according to scientific laws and consequently that there was no spiritual soul. The publication of *An Essay on Blindness* (1749), in which he questioned the existence of an intelligent God, led to a brief imprisonment for undermining established religious teachings.

Because he feared that many of his works would not pass the censors, Diderot did not attempt to publish many of them during his lifetime. Among those that appeared only posthumously was *d'Alembert's Dream* (1830), in which he discusses the origins of life without mentioning God and foreshadows Darwin's theory of evolution.

Toward the end of his life Diderot won the patronage of Empress Catherine the Great, the enlightened monarch of Russia. He died in Paris on July 31, 1784.

Legacy

Encyclopedist, philosopher, novelist, and art critic, Diderot contributed significantly to the spread of the ideas of the French Enlightenment.

Diderot's most influential work was the *Encyclopédie*, which reflected the Enlightenment belief in progress and the perfectibility of humankind through the acquisition of knowledge. He viewed it not only as a collection of knowledge but also as a means of bringing about a "revolution in Men's minds" by promoting a rational, materialistic view of the world. The *Encyclopédie* extended the ideas of the Enlightenment beyond the salons of Paris to the broader educated public. Although it was not the first encyclopedia published, it greatly modified the encyclopedic tradition in two ways. First, it relied on the collaboration of a wide group of experts to complete the project. Second, it was the first encyclopedia to include entries on such practical subjects as trade and crafts, a result of the Enlightenment emphasis on the utility of knowledge. This work, then, paved the way for future encyclopedias to address a wide range of topics based on rational analysis and scientific methodology.

As founder of the journal *Les Salons* (1759), which critiqued the biannual art shows at the Royal Academy of Art, Diderot is viewed as the pioneer of literary art criticism. In his novels he championed realism and expressed strong emotions, foreshadowing the romantic-realist revolt against classicism in the nineteenth century.

Because many of his most important works were not published until after his death, Diderot's significance was not generally recognized until the mid-nineteenth century. Among the first to acknowledge his work were Johann Wolfgang von Goethe, Honoré de Balzac, and Victor Hugo. Diderot's enormous curiosity and pursuit of knowledge led him to anticipate concepts that others later developed more fully. For example, the concept that the blind could read by touch, which he presented in his *An Essay on Blindness*, was actualized by the alphabet for the blind developed by Louis Braille. His ideas on heredity and genetics in *d'Alembert's Dream* foreshadowed twentieth-century science.

Diderot's thought also appealed to Marxists. For Friedrich Engels, Diderot's scientific approach coupled with his materialist emphasis could easily be applied to theories of economic determinism. Just as "biology is destiny," so too economic status became destiny.

von Dehsen

WORLD EVENTS		DIDEROT'S LIFE
English seize Calcutta, India	1690	
	1713	Denis Diderot is born
Peace of Utrecht settles War of Spanish Succession	1713–15	
	1747	Diderot becomes editor of *Encyclopédie*
	1749	Diderot completes *An Essay on Blindness*
	1751	First volume of the *Encyclopédie* is published
	1765	*Encyclopédie* is completed
United States independence	1776	
	1784	Diderot dies
French Revolution	1789	
Napoleonic Wars in Europe	1803–15	
Greek War of Independence against Turkey	1821–29	
	1830	*D'Alembert's Dream* is published posthumously
Revolutions in Austria, France, Germany, and Italy	1848	

For Further Reading:

France, Peter. *Diderot.* New York: Oxford University Press, 1983.

Mason, John Hope. *The Irresistible Diderot.* New York: Quartet Books, 1982.

Du Bois, W. E. B.

Black Nationalist Leader;
Founder of the NAACP
1868–1963

Life and Work

W. E. B. (William Edward Burghardt) Du Bois was one of the founders of the National Association for the Advancement of Colored People (NAACP) and one of most important African-American leaders of the twentieth century.

Du Bois was born on February 23, 1868, in Great Barrington, Massachusetts. He was educated at Fisk University, Harvard, and the University of Berlin in Germany, earning his doctorate from Harvard in 1895. A teaching appointment to the University of Pennsylvania led to a study of the local black community, *The Philadelphia Negro: A Social Study* (1899).

WORLD EVENTS		DU BOIS'S LIFE
United States Civil War	1861–65	
	1868	W. E. B. Du Bois is born
Germany is united	1871	
	1895	Du Bois receives Ph.D. from Harvard
	1897– 1910	Du Bois teaches at Atlanta University
Spanish American War	1898	
	1903	*The Souls of Black Folk* is published
	1909	Du Bois helps found the NAACP
	1910–34	Du Bois edits *The Crisis*
World War I	1914–18	
World War II	1939–45	
	1948	Du Bois breaks with NAACP
Mao Tse-tung established Communist rule in China	1949	
Apartheid laws established in South Africa		
Korean War	1950–53	
	1961	Du Bois moves to Ghana
	1963	Du Bois dies

In 1897 Du Bois was appointed professor at Atlanta University where he taught economics and history and published several books including *The Souls of Black Folk* (1903). In this influential work, Du Bois challenged BOOKER T. WASHINGTON's policy of accepting present discrimination while urging blacks to elevate themselves through education and economic development. Instead, Du Bois stressed the need for a more activist agenda to improve the lot of African Americans. In 1905 Du Bois founded the Niagara Movement to oppose Washington's program. Although short-lived, it led to the establishment of the National Association for the Advancement of Colored People (NAACP), which Du Bois helped found in 1909. In 1910 he left Atlanta to become the NAACP's publicity director and editor of its magazine, *The Crisis.*

By the time he was a member of the NAACP, Du Bois's philosophy included the more radical elements of black nationalism and separatism, even though he advocated racial integration. He was active in the Pan-African movement that advocated the end of colonialism in Africa and the unification of its people. He attended the first Pan-African Conference in London in 1900 and was a major figure at four other such international meetings between 1919 and 1927. Du Bois also advocated cultural nationalism, encouraging black literature and art, calling on African Americans to see "Beauty in Black."

In 1934 Du Bois resigned from the NAACP and returned to Atlanta University following a dispute over how to respond to the effects of the Depression on African Americans. The NAACP wanted to continue its legal struggle for integration; Du Bois wanted to temporarily abandon it in favor of an emphasis on economic advancement. Throughout his life, Du Bois was an advocate of socialist and Marxist ideas; following a 1926 visit to the Soviet Union, he became even more vigorous in his advocacy. In 1944 he returned to the NAACP as research director, but his radical ideas led to a final, bitter break in 1948. A victim of the communist witch-hunts of the late 1940s and 1950s, Du Bois was indicted for acting as an unregistered agent for a foreign power but was later exonerated. In 1961, vilified or ignored by his colleagues and harassed by the government for his views, an embittered Du Bois joined the American Communist Party and moved to Ghana. He became a citizen of Ghana where he died on August 27, 1963.

Legacy

Du Bois was the most important voice in black politics, philosophy, and literature during the first half of the twentieth century.

From his position in the NAACP he was able to exercise enormous influence on the African-American community and progressive whites. The NAACP became one of the leading champions for civil rights in the 1950s and 1960s. Its influence is still strong in the 1990s—it was one of the sponsors of the Million Man March in Washington, D.C., in 1995.

Du Bois's promotion of black artists and writers and his insistence that black writing reflect the unique African-American experience led to—the Harlem Renaissance—the flowering of black literature during the 1920s and early 1930s. Du Bois's own body of work, including many books, articles, speeches, and essays, and his support of other black writers and scholars laid the foundation for the traditions of twentieth-century black intellectualism. His writings include *Black Reconstruction* (1935) and *Dusk of Dawn: An Essay Toward an Autobiography of a Race Concept* (1940).

All twentieth-century black writers, intellectuals, and leaders owe something to Du Bois. Elements of Du Bois's thought—black nationalism and pride, his belief in black separateness along with efforts at integration—can be found in the policies and writings of every major twentieth-century African-American leader, from MARCUS GARVEY to MALCOLM X to MARTIN LUTHER KING, JR.

Saltz

For Further Reading:
Du Bois, W. E. B. (William Edward Burghardt). *The Souls of Black Folk.* New York: Modern Library, 1996.
Marable, Manning. *W. E. B. Du Bois: Black Radical Democrat.* Boston: Twayne Publishers, 1986.

Durkheim, Émile

Founder of Modern Methods
of Sociology
1858–1917

Life and Work

Émile Durkheim is considered to be the founder of the modern methods of sociology.

Durkheim was born on April 15, 1858, to the family of a rabbi in Epinal, France. As a child he was an outstanding student and graduated from the prestigious École Normale Supérieure in Paris in 1882. He worked as a teacher of philosophy in several smaller schools before joining the faculty of the University of Bordeaux in 1887. He taught social philosophy there until he joined the Sorbonne in 1902.

Much of Durkheim's work was deeply influenced by contemporary events. He saw France beset by a sense of rootlessness, which he called *anomie*, generated by the absence of social norms following a century of dramatic political, social, and technological change. In his doctoral dissertation, *The Division of Labour in Society* (1893), Durkheim showed how technology and industrialization were undermining ethical and societal structures. In *The Rules of Sociological Method* (1895), Durkheim established a scientifically rigorous methodology for sociological analysis. This work not only brought him scholarly acclaim, it also provoked the criticism of more conservative philosophers who were suspicious of this new methodology. Durkheim's *Suicide* (1897) is a groundbreaking work in which he first introduced the use of statistical analysis for the study of human groups.

By the turn of the century Durkheim had become more fully aware of growing anti-Semitism in France as a result of the Dreyfus Affair. (Alfred Dreyfus was a Jewish officer who was wrongly convicted of selling military secrets to the Germans.) Durkheim was active in the campaign to exonerate him and, in his later years, looked to religion and education to remedy the societal ills this event and his research had revealed.

In 1915 Durkheim completed his last important work, *The Elementary Forms of the Religious Life*, a study of native Australian religion. Durkheim's final years were marked by controversy—he was criticized for what some perceived as a German influence on his work and for making a religion of sociology. He died in Paris on November 15, 1917.

Legacy

Durkheim was the founder of the modern study of sociology. He was one of the first to recognize the social context for individual pathologies, and he warned of the perils of the lack of social connection.

It would be hard to overestimate Durkheim's contribution. He transformed the sociohistorical context of French liberalism into modes of action, mapped out how societies work, and showed the importance of society to the individual. Like KARL MARX (1818–1883), he focused not on the individual but on the social unit and how that social unit was affected by political, social, and educational policies of his time. He also went on to argue that technology and the Industrial Revolution endangered social structures. His work on suicide is considered to be a classic and still appears in sociology textbooks today.

What makes Durkheim's work all the more important was the intellectual rigor he brought to his analysis. He was the first to use statistical techniques in his research and established statistics as a necessary component of modern sociological study.

One of the earliest scholars to carry on Durkheim's work was Marcel Mauss (1872–1950). He employed Durkheim's methodology to produce a comparative study on forms of exchange and social structure. In 1925, Mauss founded the Ethnology Institute of the University of Paris. That same year he published *The Gift*, an analysis of the forms of exchange and contracts in Melanesia, Polynesia, and North America that focused on the legal and economic aspects of giving and receiving.

Another major scholar influenced by Durkheim's work was Claude Lévi-Strauss (1908–), who held the same academic chair as Durkheim at the Sorbonne. Lévi-Strauss conducted fieldwork among native groups in Brazil and published several major works, including *Structural Anthropology* (1961) and *The Elemental Structures of Kinship* (1967). Lévi-Strauss attempted to find essential structural elements of society in which to place individual pieces of information. For him, cultures were systems of communication; he used theories from structural linguistics and information to analyze them.

Renaud

WORLD EVENTS		DURKHEIM'S LIFE
Revolutions in Austria, France, Germany, and Italy	1848	
	1858	Émile Durkheim is born
United States Civil War	1861–65	
Germany is united	1871	
	1893	*The Division of Labour in Society* is published
	1895	*The Rules of Sociological Method* is published
	1897	*Suicide* is published
Spanish American War	1898	
	1902	Durkheim begins teaching at the Sorbonne
World War I	1914–18	
	1915	*The Elementary Forms of the Religious Life* is published
	1917	Durkheim dies
World War II	1939–45	

For Further Reading:

Fenton, Steve. *Durkheim and Modern Sociology.* Cambridge: Cambridge University Press, 1984.

Giddens, Anthony. *Durkheim.* London: Fontana, 1986.

Eddy, Mary Baker

Founder of Christian Science
1821–1910

Life and Work

Mary Baker Eddy was an American religious leader who, through her teachings, writings, and excellent organizational abilities, established Christian Science, its church, and its publications.

Eddy was born Mary Morse Baker in Bow, New Hampshire, on July 16, 1821. A sickly child, she nevertheless managed to educate herself. In 1843 she married George W. Glover, who died a year later. Eddy then married Daniel Patterson, a dentist, in 1853; the couple eventually divorced in 1873. Eddy suffered from continual spinal problems and, in 1862, she

consulted a healer named Phineas P. Quimby, a hypnotist who believed that sickness was mostly in the mind and could be cured without medication. Under Quimby's treatment, Eddy's health took a remarkable turn for the better and she moved near to Quimby to study his methods.

After Quimby's death in 1866, Eddy, now living in Linn, Massachusetts, was badly injured in a fall on the ice. Confined to her bed, she read the New Testament and shortly arose, miraculously cured, having experienced a revelation and discovering Christian Science. Eddy now worked as a traveling healer attracting followers and codifying her theology. In 1875 she published the result, the first version of *Science and Health*. While adopting some of Quimby's ideas, Eddy went much further in her belief that only God, not the human mind, possessed the power of healing based on her reinterpreting the Bible in light of Christian Science theology. Revised many times before her death, this book was eventually republished as *Science and Health with Key to the Scriptures*. This book, along with the Bible, is considered divine scripture by Christian Scientists.

During her lifetime, Eddy created a number of institutions and publications to teach about the new religion. In 1876 she founded the Christian Science Association and in 1881 the Massachusetts Metaphysical College, where she taught until it closed in 1889. She was, by all accounts, a brilliant teacher. Proving herself a master at public relations, Eddy founded the monthly *Christian Science Journal* in 1883; the *Christian Science Sentinel* in 1898, a weekly publication; and, in 1906, *The Christian Science Monitor*.

From 1875 onward she held meetings of her followers and, in 1877, married one of them, Asa G. Eddy. In 1879 Eddy took out a charter in Boston for the First Church of Christ, Scientist; this church was completed in 1895 and called the "Mother Church." In semi-retirement from 1887, Eddy turned the running of the church over to a board of directors who governed according to Eddy's *Church Manual*. Eddy remained active in church affairs until shortly before her death in Chestnut Hill, Massachusetts, on December 3, 1910.

Legacy

As the spiritual leader of Christian Science and through her indefatigable organiza-

tional efforts, at the time of her death Eddy left a newly created religion with about 100,000 adherents.

Eddy and Christian Science received much criticism during her lifetime, notably from Mark Twain. Twain wrote a book, *Christian Science* (1907), in which he pictured Eddy as a dictator who ruled over her subjects as a tyrant. Nevertheless, she managed to leave a healthy and growing church and a huge media organization to spread her teachings.

Controversial, even today, is the Christian Science practice of relying on the power of prayer instead of medical treatment to cure illness. Although the church claims not to condemn members who turn to medical science, it is clearly incompatible with members' religious beliefs. The right of parents to deny their children medical treatment has been challenged in the courts.

Throughout its history, women have played a prominent role in the movement. This prominence stands in contrast to that of many other religious organizations, which, until the last 20 years, restricted leadership opportunities for women.

Christian Science has some 2,200 branch churches in about 60 countries worldwide; numerous Christian Science reading rooms promote the group's literature. In addition, its newspaper, *Christian Science Monitor* is considered to be a very reliable source of information. Christian Science also spreads news and its message of spiritual healing worldwide through its broadcasts over shortwave radio.

Saltz

World Events	Baker's Life
Napoleonic Wars in 1803–15 Europe	
	1821 Mary Baker Eddy is born
Greek War of 1821–29 Independence against Turkey	
Revolutions in 1848 Austria, France, Germany, and Italy	
United States 1861–65 Civil War	
	1866 Eddy is injured in a fall
	Eddy conceives of Christian Science
Germany is united 1871	
	1875 First version of *Science and Health* is published
	1879 Eddy organizes Church of Christ, Scientist, in Boston
	1883 *Journal of Christian Science* begins publication
	1895 First Church of Christ, Scientist, in Boston is completed
Spanish American 1898 War	*Christian Science Sentinel* begins publication
	1906 *The Christian Science Monitor* is first published
	1910 Eddy dies

For Further Reading:
Cather, Willa, and Georgine Milmine. *The Life of Mary Baker G. Eddy: and the History of Christian Science*. Lincoln: University of Nebraska Press, 1993.
Powell, Lyman P. *Mary Baker Eddy: A Life Size Portrait*. New York: Powell, 1930.
Twain, Mark. *Christian Science*. Buffalo, N.Y.: Prometheus Books, 1986.

Einhorn, David

Theologian of Reform Judaism
1809–1879

Life and Work

David Einhorn provided the intellectual foundation for Reform Judaism in the United States in the late nineteenth and early twentieth century.

Einhorn was born in Dispek, Bavaria (present-day Germany), on November 10, 1809. He studied at an Orthodox yeshiva but, in a move highly unusual for his day, supplemented his religious education by attending secular universities. In 1826 he received his rabbinical certificate. Unable to find a position for almost a decade because of Orthodox opposition to his increasingly radical views, he finally found a post in Mecklenburg-Schwerin and in 1852 became rabbi of a congregation in Budapest. The Austro-Hungarian government closed the synagogue shortly after his arrival because of his support for the Hungarian Revolution.

Einhorn immigrated to the United States in 1855 and settled in Baltimore, Maryland, as rabbi of Temple Har Sinai, the first Reform congregation organized in the United States. He was forced to leave his post six years later after he was attacked for his opposition to slavery. He served as rabbi of Keneseth Israel in Philadelphia until 1866, when he became rabbi of Adath Jeshurun (later Temple Beth-El) in New York City.

As a rabbi Einhorn worked to provide a theological base for Reform Judaism. On the left of the Reform movement, he insisted that Judaism focus on its "imperishable spirit," its monotheistic God, and the moral law of the scriptures. He maintained that "all other divine ordinances are only signs of the Covenant [between God and the Jewish people]" that must change with the times. Consequently, he rejected ritual law, the belief in a coming Messiah, and the need for the establishment of a Jewish state in Israel.

Einhorn's views were reflected in *Olat Tamid,* a prayer book published in 1856. He remained rabbi of Adath Jeshurun until his death on November 2, 1879.

Legacy

Einhorn's ideas provided the intellectual foundation of American Reform Judaism and dominated the movement until the mid-twentieth century.

In the years following Einhorn's death, his ideas were championed by his son-in-law, Kaufmann Kohler (1843–1926), who eventually became chief spokesman for Reform Judaism. In 1885 Kohler called Reform rabbis to attend a conference designed to bolster the movement. Meeting in Pittsburgh, the rabbis produced a platform that determined the direction of Reform Judaism for almost 70 years. The Pittsburgh Platform declared Judaism a "progressive religion, ever striving to be in accord with the postulates of reason." It viewed the Bible as the source of religious and moral instruction but considered its statements on science and history to be the "primitive ideas of its own age." The platform rejected ancient laws regarding diet and purity as "not in keeping with the views and habits of modern civilization" and, while affirming the immortality of the soul, rejected bodily resurrection. One of the platform's most significant statements was that Jews were not a unique people but a "religious community" that did not need the reestablishment of a Jewish state in Palestine.

The Pittsburgh Platform resulted in a complete break between the American Reform movement and the more traditional elements of American Judaism. Its radical statements caused unease even among Reform adherents, most notably Isaac Mayer Wise (1819–1900), who had helped found the movement. As president of Hebrew Union College, he refused to have his institution endorse the platform. Nevertheless, Einhorn's ideas as reflected in the platform gradually became integrated into the Reform tradition. In 1892 the Central Conference of American Rabbis issued the *Union Prayer Book* based largely on Einhorn's *Olat Tamid.*

The influx of Orthodox Jews from Eastern Europe into the United States in the early twentieth century ultimately transformed Reform ideas. As the children of immigrants Americanized, some joined Reform congregations. Nevertheless, they were unwilling to give up many elements of Jewish culture and iden-

tity. In 1937 the movement adopted a new statement of principles. It abandoned its anti-Zionist stance and called for the creation of a Jewish homeland in Palestine. It also renounced Einhorn's idea that Jews were not a separate people, asserting that the Jewish people were held together by a common history and the heritage of faith. After World War II Reform synagogues became centers of both religious and cultural activities, with many of the symbols of traditional Judaism restored.

Einhorn's rationalism, taken to its logical conclusion, resulted in the development of the Ethical Culture Society. Guided by Felix Adler (1851–1933), the society eschewed specific religious confessions and focused on a shared ethical view reflected in political and social activities.

von Dehsen

WORLD EVENTS		EINHORN'S LIFE
Napoleonic Wars in Europe	1803–15	
	1809	David Einhorn is born in Dispek, Bavaria
Greek War of Independence against Turkey	1821–29	
	1826	Einhorn receives rabbinical certificate
Revolutions in Austria, France, Germany, and Italy	1848	
	1855	Einhorn immigrates to United States and becomes rabbi of Temple Har Sinai in Baltimore
	1856	Einhorn's *Olat Tamid* published
	1861	Einhorn forced to leave Baltimore
United States Civil War	1861–65	
	1866	Einhorn becomes rabbi of Adath Jeshurun in New York City
Germany is united	1871	
	1879	Einhorn dies
Spanish American War	1898	

For Further Reading:

Rutman, Herbert S. *Rabbi David Einhorn.* Baltimore: Jewish Historical Society of Maryland, 1979.
Sachar, Howard M. *A History of Jews in America.* New York: Knopf, 1992.

Elijah

Hebrew Prophet; Monotheist
c. 9th Century B.C.E.

* *Scholars cannot date the specific events in Elijah's life with accuracy. This chronology is based on the biblical account.*

Life and Work

The premier Hebrew prophet during the ninth century B.C.E., Elijah played a major role in the development of monotheism by insisting that the only true god was the God of Israel. In a period when most gods were associated with the forces of nature, he described a new spirituality that put the Hebrew god in a realm apart from nature.

Elijah lived during the reign of King Ahab and Queen Jezebel, a Phoenician princess who successfully promoted the worship of the Canaanite god Baal. At age 75 Elijah proclaimed that Yahweh had caused a drought and devastating famine as punishment for Israel's acceptance of the foreign god. He demanded that the people choose between Yahweh and Baal, and, in a contest with the prophets of Baal, he demonstrated that Yahweh is the only true god. The drought immediately ended, thus showing that only Yahweh is the god of creation.

Fearing the wrath of Jezebel, Elijah retreated to the Sinai where Yahweh further revealed himself. He showed Elijah that he is not contained by the forces of nature but stands apart from them.

In another narrative, Elijah is seen as the upholder of Israelite moral law. Jezebel had a man named Naboth unjustly executed so that Ahab could acquire his land. Elijah prophesied, correctly, that because of his part in the plot, the king would die a violent death. Later Elijah brought similar word of Yahweh's judgment to Ahab's son Ahaziah, who had abandoned Yahweh for the worship of foreign deities.

According to the biblical account, Elijah did not die but was carried to heaven in a chariot of fire, leaving behind his mantle for his successor Elisha.

Legacy

In an age marked by political, religious, and moral corruption, the prophet Elijah's radical monotheism and insistence that the people of Israel make up their minds to follow either Yahweh or the pagan god Baal demonstrated the uncompromising nature of Yahwistic faith. He had a central role in maintaining monotheism.

Elijah was not the only prophet vocal in Israel during his lifetime. Indeed, the prophet Obadiah is remembered in the Elijah account as a loyal prophet of the Lord. Obadiah risked his own life in hiding 100 followers of the Lord from Ahab and his men. Even though there were other prophets, Elijah stands out among them as the "man of God" with prophetic powers.

Elijah's involvement in criticizing the monarchies of Ahab and Ahaziah set the stage for other biblical prophets. The threats that Elijah was exposed to reflect the animosity between the prophets of Yahweh and the monarchy whenever the monarchy deviated from its allegiance to Yahweh. Prophets like Elijah helped ancient Israel maintain her theological identity and faithfulness to Yahweh, despite many years of political turbulence.

This devotion is also associated with Elijah as the forerunner of the Messiah. In Jewish tradition, the prophet is awaited at the seder (Passover) meal; a special place is reserved at the table for Elijah in anticipation of deliverance by the Messiah. In Christian tradition, John the Baptist is identified with the prophet; he is the one who prepares the way for JESUS the Messiah. Elijah is an important figure who is seen as a herald of the messianic age.

Harris

For Further Reading:
von Speyr, Adrienne. *Elijah.* Translated by Brian McNeil. San Francisco: Ignatius Press, 1990.
Wallace, Ronald S. *Elijah and Elisha: Expositions from the Book of Kings.* Edinburgh: Oliver and Boyd, 1952.

Emerson, Ralph Waldo

Pioneer of Transcendentalism
1803–1882

Life and Work

R alph Waldo Emerson was a religious philosopher who contributed to the development of "Transcendentalism," the attempt to find ultimate religious meaning by "transcending" the limitations of the physical world.

Emerson was born May 25, 1803, in Boston, Massachusetts. After graduating from Harvard in 1821, he attended Harvard Divinity School and was licensed to preach in the Unitarian community in 1826. Because of illness, he was not ordained a Unitarian clergyman until 1829. In a sermon in 1832, he rejected divine inspiration, thus rejecting traditional religious doctrine. Emerson resigned from the Unitarian ministry later in 1832. He then traveled to Europe, becoming acquainted with the various intellectual movements on the Continent.

After returning to the United States in 1834, Emerson settled in Concord, Massachusetts. Three of his works, *Nature* (1836), "The American Scholar," (1837) and his "Harvard Divinity School Address" (1838), led to the formation of a group of intellectuals called "Transcendentalists," a group that also included HENRY DAVID THOREAU (1817–1862). Emerson became the spokesman of the group.

The basic premise of these thinkers was that reality existed for the individual in his or her relation to nature. Therefore, they rejected all forms of established teachings, especially those promoted by established religion, as coercive and destructive of human freedom of thought. In 1840, Emerson helped begin *The Dial,* a magazine that presented the ideas of Transcendentalism to the nation. The magazine was short-lived.

In his early works he had attempted to integrate the philosophical implications of Isaac Newton's physics and JOHN LOCKE's psychology of sensation with an idealism that emphasized moral individualism and self-reliance. Emerson held that humans could transcend the material world and reach a consciousness of the spirit of the universe. This consciousness, which Emerson termed the "Oversoul," permeates the universe, nature, and all living things. Individuals find "enlightened self-awareness" by looking into their own souls and recognizing the ability to change their own world according to their ideals and conscience. Consequently, an individual can change society only through actions stemming from enlightened self-awareness and not through organized political action.

In the 1860s Emerson continued to give frequent lectures. In 1867 he also published a collection of poems, *May-Day*, that enhanced his reputation as a literary figure. By then a new generation had absorbed his teaching but did not recall the hostility that greeted his early rejection of most of traditional religion.

Emerson died on April 27, 1882, in Concord, Massachusetts. Upon his death, Emerson was transformed into the "Sage of Concord."

Legacy

E merson promoted two basic principles that influenced thinkers of later generations: 1) that the human spirit is related to that of nature, and 2) that external forces, such as religious tradition and social custom, are destructive to human freedom and individuality. Indeed, his emphasis on individualism and self-reliance became a call for human self-understanding in late twentieth-century Western cultures.

Much of contemporary environmental thought focuses on the building of a harmonious relationship between humans and nature. For example, in his 1973 article, "The Shallow and the Deep, Long-Range Ecology Movements," Norwegian philosopher Arne Naess inspired the

"Deep Ecology" movement, which expresses human relation to nature in terms of deeply felt religious experiences. This movement eventually generated an ecological system of thought similar to Emerson's, proposing that ecological renewal will be accomplished by spiritual transformation using poetry, ritual, and the arts to awaken greater sensitivity to the connection of humans to nature.

Similarly, many twentieth-century religious movements and philosophies, such as Christian Science, New Age Thought, and existentialist philosophy, find conceptual moorings in transcendental thought. The critique of traditional religious teaching coupled with the emphasis on self-reliance have anchored beliefs on spiritual healing and mental wholeness through individual spirituality. Existentialist philosophers draw upon transcendental concepts to develop their central focus on the importance of individual experience and responsibility.

Transcendental thought has influenced many later poets and thinkers. Such prominent figures as Robert Frost, Walt Whitman, Frank Lloyd Wright, FRIEDRICH WILHELM NIETZSCHE, and Gertrude Stein have built upon themes of Emerson and his colleagues.

Jurkovic

WORLD EVENTS		EMERSON'S LIFE
French Revolution	1789	
Napoleonic Wars in Europe	1803–15	
	1803	Ralph Waldo Emerson is born in Boston, Massachusetts
	1821	Emerson graduates from Harvard College
Greek War of Independence against Turkey	1821–29	
	1829	Emerson is ordained
	1836	*Nature* is published
	1838	Emerson gives Harvard address
	1840	Emerson helps establish *The Dial*
Revolutions in Austria, France, Germany, and Italy	1848	
United States Civil War	1861–65	
	1867	*May-Day* is published
Germany is united	1871	
	1882	Emerson dies
Spanish American War	1898	

For Further Reading:

McAleer, John J. *Ralph Waldo Emerson: Days of Encounter.* Boston: Little Brown, 1984.

New, Elisa. *The Regenerate Lyric: Theology and Innovation in American Poetry.* New York: Cambridge University Press, 1993.

Richardson, Robert D. *Emerson: The Mind on Fire: A Biography.* Berkeley: University of California Press, 1995.

Epictetus

Influential Stoic Philosopher
c. 50–c. 135

Life and Work

Epictetus was a Stoic philosopher who claimed that the universe was controlled by an overarching force called the Logos and that happiness and virtue derived from living in harmony with the Logos.

Epictetus was a slave born in Hierapolis in Phrygia (Asia Minor). Early in his life he was taken to Rome, where he became the slave of Epaphroditus, an administrative assistant to Emperor Nero. Epaphroditus recognized Epictetus' intellectual abilities and arranged for

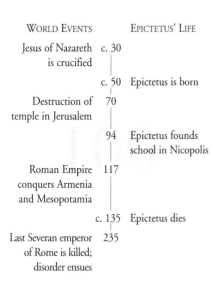

WORLD EVENTS		EPICTETUS' LIFE
Jesus of Nazareth is crucified	c. 30	
	c. 50	Epictetus is born
Destruction of temple in Jerusalem	70	
	94	Epictetus founds school in Nicopolis
Roman Empire conquers Armenia and Mesopotamia	117	
	c. 135	Epictetus dies
Last Severan emperor of Rome is killed; disorder ensues	235	

him to study with the renowned teacher, Musonius Rufus.

Epictetus eventually received his freedom, perhaps as a result of the death of Epaphroditus. When, in 94, the Emperor Domitian forced all philosophers to leave Rome, Epictetus fled to Nicopolis in northwestern Greece. There he lived in straitened conditions and founded a school for young men. Although he did not write any books, his words were preserved by Arrian, a student who recorded his master's teachings. Arrian left two books of Epictetus' philosophy: *Discourses* and *The Enchridion.*

For Epictetus, the goal of philosophy was to live a virtuous life. Such a life requires that a person distinguish between what a person can control and what a person cannot. Epictetus believed that the universe was controlled by an overarching force—the Logos. (In Greek logos means "reason" or "word.") In parallel fashion, each human being is governed by the individual's sense of reason.

For the wise person, individual reason functions in concert with the Logos. By acting according to the Logos, a person can achieve a harmonious and virtuous life. However, such union with the Logos requires that the person accept all the actions of the Logos, even when they are tragic (e.g., the death of a child). The Stoic's life must reflect the principle of *apatheia*, freedom from emotion. Only such *apatheia* can lead to true freedom in that the person is no longer controlled by individual desires and passions.

Epictetus considered the virtuous life to be that of a philosopher. As one who can discern the will of the Logos and not be distracted from union with the Logos by trivial wants and cravings, a philosopher can earn true freedom by living within the limits set by the Logos.

It is difficult to determine whether Epictetus equated the Logos with God. Like other Stoics, he identified God with nature, and, by extension, the Logos controlled nature. Nevertheless, there does not seem to be any direct link between the two.

Epictetus remained at his school in Nicopolis for the rest of his life. He died there around 135.

Legacy

Epictetus is one of the few Stoic philosophers whose work survived. He is often seen as the ideal model of a Stoic philosopher. His simple life, focused on discerning the will of the Logos, not on acquiring material comforts, proved an inspiration to others.

The next great Stoic philosopher was Emperor MARCUS AURELIUS (121–180). In his *Meditations*, Aurelius promotes *apatheia* by asserting that a person should not return evil for evil; evil can only harm a person who seeks revenge. One can only achieve freedom by accepting the will of Reason as part of the world order, which because it is rational by definition, must be good. As a philosopher, he would have much preferred a life unencumbered by external obligations and devoted to seeking truth. Yet, Aurelius, as a Stoic, accepted his own lot as emperor; the Logos must have placed him there for the good of the world.

Stoic thought may have also influenced Christian theology. In the opening verses of the Gospel of John, the author wrote: "In the beginning was the Logos." Here JESUS is identified as the one who existed at the beginning of the world and helped create it. This image clearly corresponds to that of the Stoic Logos, who controls the world by reason. (Although most translations open the Gospel of John with, "In the beginning was the Word," it would be just as accurate to translate this as, "In the beginning was Reason.") The Apostle PAUL may also have been drawing upon Stoic ideas when he encouraged the Corinthians to remain free from worldly concerns in awaiting the Second Coming of Christ (1 Corinthians 7:29–31).

Philosophers continue to ponder the ideas originally introduced by Epictetus and his fellow Stoics. For example, is there a governing principle of the universe, such as "laws of science" or "laws of history"? If so, how are human life and happiness related to such laws? If not, what does it mean to be human and what constitutes freedom? To some extent, the ideas of the Stoics have formed an essential component of much contemporary thought.

von Dehsen

For Further Reading:

Barnes, Jonathan. *Logic and the Imperial Stoa.* Leiden, Neth.: Brill, 1997.

Long, A. A. *Stoic Studies.* New York: Cambridge University Press, 1996.

Epicurus

Founder of Epicurean School of
Philosophy
341–270 B.C.E.

Life and Work

Epicurus was a Greek philosopher who promoted a pleasurable way of life unaffected by political events and devoted his efforts to the search for truth and the cultivation of friendship.

Epicurus was born on Samos in the Aegean in 341 B.C.E. He later moved to Colophon (west coast of present-day Turkey) where he studied the atomist philosophy of Democritus under Nausiphanes. At the age of 32 he went to Mytilene on the island of Lesbos and later to Lampsacus. In both places he established schools. In 307–306 B.C.E., he went to live in Athens where he bought a house with an attached garden. Since he did most of his teaching in the garden, his school became known as the Garden.

Epicurus lived with his followers, and their bonds of friendship became legendary. In the garden, Epicurus and his disciples (which included women and slaves) secluded themselves from the affairs of Athens and lived austerely.

So he could devote himself exclusively to the pursuit of philosophy, Epicurus never married and remained chaste. Pleasure was the ultimate goal of life, an idea that gave rise to the popular perception that Epicurus and his followers were hedonists given to excess. On the contrary,

Epicurus was more of an ascetic: too much pleasure would cause pain, and therefore would distract one from his or her contemplation of philosophy. Hence, the goal of life was *ataraxia*, freedom from disturbance and avoidance of pain.

According to Epicurus the purpose of philosophy was to secure a happy life. Pleasure, in fact, was the beginning and end of philosophy. Some pleasures, however, need to be distinguished from others, for they cause pain. Pleasure of the soul is more valuable. Fear was seen as an emotion that distracted people from their true purpose in life.

As a way to achieve the desired state of pleasure, Epicurus taught that death was not to be feared: all matter consists of atoms; once a living creature dies, that creature's atoms are dispersed into the universe again. While he admitted to the existence of gods, Epicurus claimed that his fellow Greeks need not fear them because the gods had little concern for people. Thus, humans beings are not subject to cosmic determinism but can exercise free will.

Little of his writing survives. We know about Epicurus through Diogenes Laertius, who devoted a whole book to him and to Lucretius who wrote the epic *De Rerum Natura (On the Nature of Things)*.

He died in Athens in 270 B.C.E., leaving disciples dedicated to his system of philosophy known as Epicureanism.

Legacy

Epicurus's system of philosophy, especially his ethical code, appealed to many. Diogenes Laertius (third century C.E.) claims that one could fill cities with the followers of Epicurus. In their number were Lucretius, Horace, and Julius Caesar. In fact, the word "epicure" has entered the English language to indicate a person who seeks pleasure.

Because little of his work has survived, it is not always easy to distinguish Epicurus's ideas from those articulated by his successors. It is clear, however, that he created a new and distinctive philosophical system. Further, he established the foundation and framework of Epicureanism. Those who followed him refined and furthered his basic ideas in three areas: ethics, knowledge, and physics.

Of the three parts of the Epicurean universe that Epicurus set forth, his ethical system has proved to be the most influential. People were to

engage in pleasure of the mind by avoiding the competitive life (politics, athletics, etc.). His ideas stressed the self-reliance of individuals: one was responsible for one's own happiness, not the outside world. The followers of Epicurus became the first proponents of free will. They also believed that social justice was based on an agreement between citizens for the common good. These ideas anticipated those later supported by such philosophers as JOHN LOCKE, THOMAS HOBBES, and JEAN-JACQUES ROUSSEAU. Other writers, such as the Roman writer and statesman Cicero, found much to praise, especially the friendship Epicurus and his followers shared.

Epicurus also addressed knowledge (logic). Perception was the way to knowledge. Because physical objects are made of indivisible atoms, the atoms of the object are transmitted to the atoms of the soul (mind). Therefore appearance is never false except when given in the form of opinions.

Physics was the third area he addressed. The world and beings came to be through collisions of suitable atoms and because they are composed of atoms, they will one day dissolve into atoms again. That is, what exists now will one day be destroyed in a great conflagration. (Many ancient philosophers believed that the basic element of the universe was fire. Ultimately, the universe would return to its original, fiery, state.) While scholars find fault with his materialistic conception of the world, they agree that his adaptation of Democritus's work was influential in how modern scientists view the world, in particular the work of Pierre Gassendi (1592–1655), a philosopher-scientist. Gassendi based his theories of the interaction of objects on Epicurean atomism.

Renaud

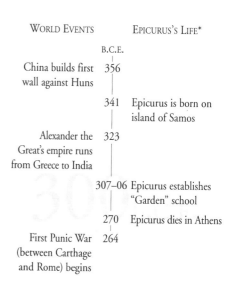

WORLD EVENTS		EPICURUS'S LIFE*
	B.C.E.	
China builds first wall against Huns	356	
	341	Epicurus is born on island of Samos
Alexander the Great's empire runs from Greece to India	323	
	307–06	Epicurus establishes "Garden" school
	270	Epicurus dies in Athens
First Punic War (between Carthage and Rome) begins	264	

* Scholars cannot date the specific events in Epicurus' life with accuracy.

For Further Reading:

Gordon, Pamela. *Epicurus in Lycia: The Second Century World of Diogenes Oenoanda.* Ann Arbor: University of Michigan Press, 1996.

Jones, Howard. *The Epicurean Tradition.* New York: Routledge, 1992.

Sharples, R. W. *Stoics, Epicureans, and Skeptics.* New York: Routledge, 1996.

Erasmus, Desiderius

Humanist Theologian and Scholar; Christian Proponent of Free Will
c. 1469–1536

Life and Work

Erasmus was the chief exponent of Christian humanism, the religious manifestation of the Renaissance that sought to unite Christian piety with classical learning in order to return to the sources of scripture and faith.

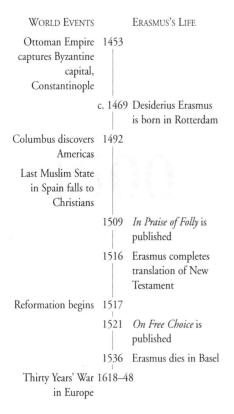

World Events		Erasmus's Life
Ottoman Empire captures Byzantine capital, Constantinople	1453	
	c. 1469	Desiderius Erasmus is born in Rotterdam
Columbus discovers Americas	1492	
Last Muslim State in Spain falls to Christians		
	1509	*In Praise of Folly* is published
	1516	Erasmus completes translation of New Testament
Reformation begins	1517	
	1521	*On Free Choice* is published
	1536	Erasmus dies in Basel
Thirty Years' War in Europe	1618–48	

Erasmus was born in Rotterdam, Netherlands, around 1469. He received his early education among the Brethren of the Common Life, a lay congregation that emphasized inner piety, and was ordained a priest in 1492. He later studied theology at the universities of Paris and Turin and was attracted to humanism, the Renaissance movement emphasizing the importance of human intellectual and cultural achievements. Uncomfortable with monastic life, he eventually lived as a secular scholar, making his living by tutoring and through the patronage of important individuals.

Erasmus was deeply disturbed by the contemporary Church, which he viewed as morally corrupt and theologically bankrupt. In serious and comic writings such as *In Praise of Folly* (1509), he attacked clerical ignorance and the Church's emphasis on meaningless ritual. He abhorred the constant bickering of theologians and was contemptuous of overly subtle systematic theology that he thought a poor substitute for true Christianity—a life lived in imitation of Christ.

Erasmus sought to reform Christian life through the "philosophy of Christ," combining internal piety with humanistic learning. He believed that the study of ancient secular texts was vital to the understanding of key Christian writings, many of which had been influenced by Greek philosophy. Much of his work involved producing new translations of the early church fathers such as JEROME and AUGUSTINE OF HIPPO. His masterwork was a translation of the New Testament (1516) that, because it significantly changed the meaning of some key biblical passages, provided a scholarly challenge to the practices and teachings of the medieval Church.

After 1517, Erasmus's career became enmeshed in the Reformation. Although he supported reform, he was deeply concerned that MARTIN LUTHER's efforts would divide the Church and sought to distance himself from the German theologian. Because of his contempt for theological bickering, he was reluctant to engage Luther directly. He eventually did so in 1521 with the publication of *On Free Choice,* a statement of his theological position in which he presented the humanistic idea that individuals have free will in all matters, including those of faith, a doctrine Luther opposed.

At the end of his life he was mistrusted by both the Roman Catholic church and the reformers. He died in Basel, Switzerland, on July 12, 1536.

Legacy

Erasmus's humanistic ideas not only formed the basis for European intellectual reform but also helped lay the foundation for the Protestant Reformation.

As the most respected scholar of his day, Erasmus spread the ideas of Christian humanism, showing contemporary Europe how Christian piety could be combined with the new learning of the Renaissance. Through his patrons and admirers, including SIR THOMAS MORE, King Henry VIII of England, and the Holy Roman Emperor Charles V, he had a profound effect on the thought of his day.

By discrediting conventional religious practices, Erasmus's critique of the contemporary Church made Europe receptive to the ideas of the Protestant Reformation. He failed in his goal of reforming the Roman Catholic church from within through gentle reason and tolerance. His "philosophy of Christ" lacked the popular appeal and theological vision of Luther's works, and he lived to see the Church torn by warfare, which he deplored. Yet he succeeded in establishing the critical foundations for a new understanding of scripture.

Erasmus's work marked an important step in the development of what came to be called textual criticism, the attempt to determine the original Greek text of the New Testament through the examination of various manuscripts, and provided the foundation for biblical scholarship into the nineteenth century. This Greek text served as the basis for Luther's German translation of the New Testament published in 1522 and also influenced the texts that were used to produce the English King James Bible in 1611.

Erasmus's disavowal of systematic theology has led some scholars to point to him as a source for modern non-dogmatic theology and for religious skepticism.

von Dehsen

For Further Reading:

Bainton, Roland H. *Erasmus of Christendom.* Tring, United Kingdom: Lion, 1988.

Bouyer, Louis. *Erasmus and the Humanist Experiment.* London: Chapman, 1959.

DeMolen, Richard L. *Essays on the Works of Erasmus.* New Haven, Conn.: Yale University Press, 1978.

McConica, James. *Erasmus.* New York: Oxford University Press, 1991.

Farabi, al-

First Theologian to Relate Islamic Theology to Greek Philosophy
c. 878–c. 950

Life and Work

Al-Farabi (also known as Abu Nasr al-Farabi) was the first Islamic theologian to develop concepts of the ideal Islamic state based on the Greek philosophy of PLATO and ARISTOTLE. His philosophical work promoted the correspondence between Greek rational ideals and Islamic theological principles.

Little is known of al-Farabi's life other than that he was born in Transoxiana (now Uzbekistan) of Turkish parents around 878. He studied first in Khorasan and then in Baghdad. It was in Baghdad that he encountered Syrian Christians who introduced him to Greek philosophy. Later he served at the court of Sagf ad-Dawiah in Syria.

Al-Farabi's views derive primarily from his study of Plato, Aristotle, and the Roman philosopher Plotinus. Building on the Platonic concept of the philosopher-king, al-Farabi believed that the ideal society was one governed by a wise philosopher. This person would use his intellect to develop insights based on his communication with the Active Intellect, the revelations of the first cause, who created the world on the basis of rational intellect. Others, not as intellectually able as the wise philoso-

pher, could serve as legislators. These legislators could enact, but not originate, the principles that ensure a virtuous and peaceful society. The majority of the people, however, would not be able to understand the basic principles directly. To such people the wise philosopher must speak in images or parables.

Without such a leader, societies risk becoming either ignorant—led by a ruler not wise enough to lead the people to true virtue—or wicked—led by a ruler who rejects the principles of virtue. In contrast to Greek philosophy, which rejects all except defensive war, al-Farabi's thought would allow for war to overthrow ignorant or wicked societies. His Islamic vision of a just society went beyond the Greek concept of the polis (the city-state); he envisioned a worldwide rule of peace and harmony.

Although many of al-Farabi's works have been lost, his writings *The Virtuous City* and *The Virtuous Religion* preserve many of his most important ideas. His interests also went beyond political theory. His *Catalog of Science* is the first Islamic attempt to systematize human knowledge.

Legacy

Al-Farabi was the first Islamic philosopher to ground Islamic political thought in Greek philosophical, rational concepts. In addition, his interest in Plato and Aristotle helped preserve their writings for future generations.

Writing from Cordova and Seville, Spain, Ibn Rushd, better known as AVERROËS (1126–1198), continued al-Farabi's work on Greek philosophers. Averroës wrote commentaries on both Aristotle and Plato. He alleged that the ideal ruler was a "physician-ruler," a person who best understands how to promote human happiness. In Averroës's commentary on Plato, he contends that the ruler should achieve a balance between virtues and the practical arts. The natural order achieved by this balance produces a regime that allows the best environment for the living of a good life. Averroës then correlates those theories with the principles found in the Koran, the holy scripture of Islam. As did al-Farabi, Averroës believes that the ruler is also responsible for presenting his theories in ways understandable to the majority of the populace.

After Averroës, the next Islamic scholar to consider the political theories of the ancient Greeks

was IBN KHALDUN (1332–1406). Thereafter, the Greek influence diminished until the nineteenth century, when these ideas were revived by JAMAL AD-DIN AL-AFGHANI (1838–1897), MUHAMMAD 'ABDUH (1849–1905), and Muhammad Igbal (1876–1938). Both al-Afghani and 'Abduh lived in Egypt. When al-Afghani was expelled for his political views, he traveled to London and Paris. He was joined in Europe by 'Abduh. In 1884 they returned to Egypt, where, in 1899, 'Abduh was appointed *mufti*, a Muslim political leader. Igbal, a poet, led the Pakistani movement for liberation from foreign domination. In both Egypt and Pakistan, the rulers rejected government by democratic rule for one led by an enlightened leader.

Al-Farabi's influence, therefore, extended into the twentieth century. His theories about an enlightened ruler form a bridge from the Greek concept of the philosopher-king of Plato to that of a ruler instructed by the teachings of the Koran who applies these insights to the actual situation of governing.

von Dehsen

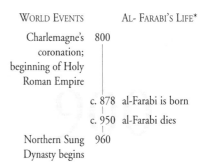

WORLD EVENTS		AL-FARABI'S LIFE*
Charlemagne's coronation; beginning of Holy Roman Empire	800	
	c. 878	al-Farabi is born
	c. 950	al-Farabi dies
Northern Sung Dynasty begins	960	

* *Scholars cannot date the specific events in al-Farabi's life with accuracy.*

For Further Reading:

Davidson, Herbert A. *Alfarabi, Avicenna, and Averroes: Their Cosmologies, Theories of the Active Intellect, and Theories of Human Intellect.* New York: Oxford University Press, 1992.

Kemal, Salim. *The Poetics of Alfarabi and Avicenna.* Leiden, Netherlands: Brill, 1991.

Fatimah Bint Muhammad

Daughter of Muhammad;
Matriarch of the Shiite Sect
c. 610–633

World Events		Fatimah's Life	
Rule of Byzantine emperor Justinian I the Great	527–65		
		c. 610	Fatimah Bint Muhammad is born
T'ang Dynasty in China	618–907		
Buddhism becomes official religion of China	624		
		c. 625	Fatimah marries 'Ali ibn Abi Talib
Muhammad conquers Mecca	630		
Islam established on Arabian Peninsula	c. 632		
		632–33	Fatimah resists Ibn al-'Arabi's attempt to control Islam after Muhammad's death
		633	Fatimah dies
Islamic expansion through North Africa and Spain	640–711		

Life and Work

Fatimah Bint Muhammad was the daughter of MUHAMMAD, the founder and chief prophet of Islam. Through her husband and children she continued the teachings of her father and helped establish the hereditary leadership of the Shiite sect of Islam.

Fatimah was born to Muhammad and his first wife, Khadijah, around 610. Little is known of Fatimah's early life prior to the *hegira* (migration) from Mecca to Medina in 622. All that is mentioned of her in this period comes from traditions that describe her intense sorrow at the death of her mother.

Fatimah married 'Ali ibn Abi Talib, the cousin of Muhammad and the son of one of his most loyal protectors, in around 625. The couple had two sons, Hasan and Husayn, who would become central figures in the Shiite movement after the death of their father. However, the marriage seems not to have been a happy one. During the harsh years of the early period in Medina, emotional and financial strains created tension. Hoping to restore the marriage bond of the couple, Muhammad intervened with emotional and material support. He even prevented 'Ali from taking another wife.

Fatimah's influence within the Muslim community increased after Muhammad's death in 632. She became embroiled in the dispute between Ibn al-'Arabi, the new caliph (religious and secular leader), who insisted that he was the rightful heir to the Prophet's mantle of authority. Fatimah resisted the attempt to usurp power from the bloodline of Muhammad and insisted that her husband, 'Ali, and her sons were the bona fide leaders of Islam.

Fatimah was not able to carry out this struggle for leadership long. She died in Medina in 633, less than one year after the passing of her father. (The exact date of her death is unknown. After she died, the family buried her in secret to prevent provoking undue tumult over her death.)

Legacy

Fatimah's battle with Ibn al-'Arabi for the control of Islam opened a rift in the Muslim world that continues to this day.

Because of her faith and loyalty to her father and family, she has become venerated by many devoted Shiites at shrines around the world.

The conflict over identifying the rightful religious heir of Muhammad eventually split Islam. Some agreed with Fatimah that her husband, 'Ali, was the legitimate *imam* (leader). Those who supported 'Ali became known as the *shi'at 'Ali* (party of 'Ali), which generated the name Shiite. They insisted that only he and Fatimah's descendants should rule the Muslim community. A larger group, the Sunnis, focused on the continuity of tradition (*sunnah*). The dispute began as a political split, but by the end of the eighth century the emphasis on rule by 'Ali and Fatimah's descendants became a cornerstone of Shiite belief.

In subsequent generations, as internal conflicts within Islam continued over questions of rightful succession, the role of the *imam* evolved from one of a simple descendant of the Prophet, to one of being the authoritative interpreter of the Koran. The first such *imam* was Muhammad al-Baqir (d. c. 735), the grandson of Hoseyn. The eleventh, Hasan al-'Askari, died in 874. Although he left no visible heirs, many Shiites believe that he had a son who, as an infant, was put into hiding. This son became the immortal twelfth *imam*, who appears from time to time in human form to guide the community. Because these people awaited the return of the twelfth *imam*, they became known as the "Twelver Shiites."

As the matriarch of the Shiites, Fatimah has herself become the object of veneration. She is considered sinless and is one of the 14 pure souls of Islam. Some of her titles may have arisen from a religious association between her and MARY. Some called her the "mother of the father"; this designation may be related to the Marian title, *Theotokos* (Mother of God). Although this expression seems to indicate that she is the mother of Muhammad, it is generally taken to mean that her last descendant will also have the name Muhammad. She also is known as, for example, *al-Zahra* (shining), "virgin," and "Mary the Greater."

In Shiite tradition, Fatimah is thought to take part in the final judgment. She is said to be the first person to enter Paradise and will stand beside Allah to judge the dead, consigning them to heaven or hell.

von Dehsen

For Further Reading:
Qazwini, Muhammad Kazm. *Fatima the Gracious.* Qum, Iran: Anssarian Publications, 1980.
Sayyid, Haadee Husayn. *Biography of Fatima Zahraa.* Karachi, Pakistan: Peermohomed Ebrahim Trust, 1981.

Fa-tsang

Systematizer of *Huayan* School of Chinese Buddhism
643–712

Life and Work

Fa-tsang was the third great master, or patriarch, of the *Huayan* (Flower Garland Scripture) tradition of Chinese Buddhism. His teachings emphasized the synthesis of ideas within the "omniverse," the range of interactions of all components of existence over time and space.

Fa-tsang was born in 643, perhaps in Samarkand in Central Asia. His father, Mi, was a high-ranking military officer in the Tang Dynasty. A devout young man, Fa-tsang burned off one of his fingers as an offering to the BUDDHA at age 16. He studied with Chih-yen (d. 668), later acknowledged as the second great *Huayan* master, and, at 28, took vows as a Buddhist monk.

Fa-tsang devoted his life to systematizing the basic teachings of the *Huayan* tradition into the fourfold *dharmadhatu*. All perceptions can be described according to this fourfold system. First, there are simple phenomena (events) taken by themselves. Next, there are the principles behind these phenomena, which disclose that each object by itself is empty and without inherent meaning. Third, the connection between the principle and phenomena reveals that the true nature of everything is its emptiness. Fourth, the consequence of the first three points is that all beings and objects interact with other beings and objects in causal relationships. Nothing has an essence of its own. That is, things have meaningful existence only in relationship with other objects. Fa-tsang explained these principles with illustrations called the "Ten Mysteries." The most notable of these is "Indra's Net." Imagine a net over the sky in which brilliant jewels are set at all intersections of the rope. Each jewel, then, would be reflected in the faces of many other jewels.

Finally, Fa-tsang systematized the *Huayan* tradition into five categories, which he called the *panjiao*. The five categories were: 1) *Hinayana* (early Buddhist tradition); 2) Initial Mahayana ("large vehicle"—that is, open to many people); 3) Final Mahayana; 4) Sudden Teaching of the One Vehicle (for the spiritually enlightened); and 5) Comprehensive Teaching of the One Vehicle (*Huayan* teachings).

A prolific writer, Fa-tsang expressed his ideas in several books, including *Essay on the Five Teachings of Huayan, The Hundred Gates to the Unfathomable Meaning of the Huayan,* and *Commentary on the Mahayana Awakening of Faith.*

Fa-tsang died in November 712.

Legacy

Fa-tsang is remembered as a synthesizer of the *Huayan* tradition of Chinese Buddhism whose thought helped articulate the *Huayan* concept of the "omniverse." His importance was noted immediately upon his death by the Emperor Hsün-tsung, who bestowed upon Fa-tsang the posthumous title of Hung-lu-ch'ing, director of palace ceremonies.

Fa-tsang's wealth of writings, clearly presented and persuasively argued, formed a body of work that became fundamental to the later development of *Huayan* Buddhism. His disciple Shimsang (d. 742) was one of the founders of *Huayan* Buddhism in Japan; his lectures motivated Emperor Shômu (r. 724–749) to build the Todai Temple in which the emperor placed the monumental statue of the Great Buddha. Fa-tsang's thought also influenced Li Tung-hsüan (c. 635–c. 730), whose work is characterized by original interpretations of *Huayan* themes.

The fourth great master of *Huayan* Buddhism, Ch'eng-kuan (738-c. 839), expanded Fa-tsang's thought to show how *Huayan* concepts could be compatible with other forms of Buddhism. The last *Huayan* patriarch, Tsung-mi (780–841), classified all Buddhist traditions in a hierarchical system and developed a comprehensive overview of doctrines and practices. He also advocated the unification of Ch'an (meditative) Buddhism with the more doctrinal *Huayan* tradition. By the ninth century, many of *Huayan's* concepts were incorporated into other Buddhist traditions, making it difficult to identify a distinctive tradition after this date. Nevertheless its impact can be found in a wide variety of East Asian traditions, including Ch'an, which came to dominate Chinese Buddhism, and Japanese Zen.

Fa-tsang's ideas were challenged by scholars who claimed that they violated the basic concept of Buddhism, that suffering could cease only if existence of any sort were dissolved into the emptiness of Nirvana. In the twentieth century a school calling itself "Critical Buddhism" emerged in Japan that did not consider any form of East Asian Buddhism to be Buddhism because of its reliance on Fa-tsang's ideas.

von Dehsen

WORLD EVENTS		FA-TSANG'S LIFE*
Islam established on Arabian Peninsula	c. 632	
Islamic expansion through North Africa and Spain	640–711	
	643	Fa-tsang is born
	c. 671	Fa-tsang takes vows as Buddhist monk
	712	Fa-tsang dies
Charlemagne's coronation; beginning of Holy Roman Empire	800	

* *Scholars cannot date the specific events in Fa-tsang's life with accuracy.*

For Further Reading:

Liu, Ming-wood. *The Teaching of Fa-Tsang: An Examination of Buddhist Metaphysics.* Ann Arbor, Mich.: University Microfilms International, 1979.

Fichte, Johann Gottlieb

Philosopher of Transcendental Idealism
1762–1814

Life and Work

Johann Gottlieb Fichte was a German philosopher who expanded the work of IMMANUEL KANT into what became identified as transcendental idealism.

Fichte was born on May 19, 1762, in Rammenau (now in Germany). He studied at the universities in Jena (1780) and Leipzig (1781–1784) and later in Zürich (1788) and Warsaw (1791).

Fichte was attracted to the idealism of Immanuel Kant (1724–1804), which contrasted objects in the material world, "things-in-themselves," with the world of perceptions found in the mind. Fichte sent a manuscript entitled *An Attempt at a Critique of All Revelation* to Kant. Kant was so impressed by Fichte's work that he

helped bring attention to the book, which was published in 1792.

In 1793, Fichte obtained a position at the University of Jena. Over the next few years, he produced several important philosophical works, including *On the Concept of the Theory of Science (Wissenschaftslehre)* in 1794, and *Wissenschaftslehre nova methodo* in the years 1796 to 1799.

In these books, Fichte tries to develop Kant's idealism by investigating ways that the mind interacts with the material world. Fichte argued that after recognizing itself as a "self," the "self" perceives its own limits imposed by existing in space and time. This observation led Fichte to address issues of political philosophy and ethics in two books: *Foundations of Natural Rights* (1796–1797) and *The System of Ethical Theory* (1798). For Fichte, natural rights are a condition of self-consciousness, whereas political order among people is governed by reason. Moreover, by seeing their limits, free individuals recognize that they must fulfill obligations to other free individuals. Consequently individuals in communities require ethical norms.

After a charge of atheism forced Fichte to leave Jena, he moved to Berlin in 1799. In Berlin, Fichte's writings focused on political topics (e.g., *Address to the German Nation*, 1808) and theological issues (e.g., *The Vocation of Man*, 1800, and *The Characteristics of the Present Age*, 1806). In the *Address* he calls for a national system of education and for German patriotism in light of Napoleon's aggression.

In his theological writings he not only saw God as the infinite moral will of the universe, he also saw the goal of the life of reason as the perception of the divine order of the universe. In *The Way Toward the Blessed Life* (1806), Fichte posits what seemed to be a mystical union between God and the human self.

Fichte spent his last years as the rector of the University of Berlin (1810–1812). He died on January 27, 1814, in Berlin.

Legacy

Fichte's contributions to the idealism of Kant provoked others to examine his own philosophy, which inspired some of the most important thinkers of the nineteenth century.

Friedrich Schelling (1775–1854) much admired the thought of Fichte and sent his first book, *On the Possibility and Form of Philosophy in General* (1795) to Fichte. Here Schelling equated God with the absolute ego of each person. After studying science in Leipzig, Schelling

became more critical of Fichte's view that nature was completely under human control. For Schelling, nature could direct itself toward the spirit. In 1800, he published the *System of Transcendental Idealism* in an attempt to coordinate Fichte's thought with his own. In this work Schelling focused on art as a means to connect the world of objects with the perceptions of the mind. Unfortunately, the book led to a rift between Fichte and his protégé.

GEORG WILHELM FRIEDRICH HEGEL (1770–1831) coedited *The Critical Journal of Philosophy* with Schelling when they both taught at Jena. In his articles for this journal, Hegel engaged the philosophies of Kant and Fichte. He hoped to systematize philosophical thought by addressing the role of reason in nature and in experience. However, instead of presupposing that reason begins in the mind and then relates to objective reality, Hegel posited that the mind first encounters reason only in its experience of the world. Moreover, Hegel modified Fichte's view of the Absolute; Hegel saw it not as a static reality but as a dynamic entity changing over time.

Fichte's concepts of transcendental idealism also affected the poetry of Friedrich von Hardenberg, commonly known as Novalis (1772–1801). Through his poetry, Novalis attempted to broaden Fichte's intellectual focus by applying his ideas to demonstrate that such concepts as faith, love, and imagination could be viewed as independent realms of the mind. Novalis claimed that poetic power was a sphere of awareness that complemented intellectual abilities, thereby uniting philosophy and poetry.

von Dehsen

WORLD EVENTS	FICHTE'S LIFE
Peace of Utrecht 1713–15 settles War of Spanish Succession	
1762	Johann Gottlieb Fichte is born
United States 1776 independence	
French Revolution 1789	
1792	*An Attempt at a Critique of All Revelation* is published
1793	Fichte begins teaching at Jena
1794	*On the Concept of the Theory of Science* is published
1796–99	*Wissenschaftslehre nova methodo* is published
1799	Fichte moves to Berlin
Napoleonic Wars 1803–15 in Europe	
1810	Fichte becomes rector of University of Berlin
1814	Fichte dies
Greek War of 1821–29 Independence against Turkey	

For Further Reading:
Rockmore, Tom, and Daniel Breazeale. *New Perspectives on Fichte.* Atlantic Highlands, N.J.: Humanities Press, 1996.
Zoller, Gunter. *Fichte's Transcendental Philosophy: The Original Duplicity of Intelligence and Will.* New York: Cambridge University Press, 1998.

Fortune, Dion

Founder of the Society of the
Inner Light
1890–1946

Life and Work

Dion Fortune was one of the leading occultists of the twentieth century and the first to try to understand the connection between occultism and psychology.

Fortune was born Violet May Firth on December 6, 1890, in Bryn y Bia Llandudno on the north coast of Wales. Her father, a lawyer, was a member of a family that had made its fortune manufacturing weapons for the British government. Firth later took the name she used in the occult community from the family motto, *deo non fortuna* (God, not luck).

Little is known of her childhood. She had dreams of what she thought were her previous lives as temple priestesses; she also showed some abilities as a medium (a person who is a channel of communication between the earthly world and that of the spirits). She briefly became involved in the Theosophical Movement of HELENA PETROVNA BLAVATSKY but left because she felt uncomfortable with its Eastern style of occultism. Following a nervous breakdown, she became a lay psychoanalyst, under the influence of Theodore Moriarty, who gave her basic training in the occult. In 1919 a dream prompted her to join the Stella Matutina, the outer order of the Hermetic Order of the Golden Dawn, an influential occult society whose members included poet William Butler Yeats. Three years later she founded the Fraternity of the Inner Light to recruit members for the Golden Dawn, but, following conflicts with the Order's leadership, she withdrew her group around 1926.

Fortune wrote a number of theoretical works and practical guides to the occult that were among the most important produced in the twentieth century. In 1935 she published *The Mystical Qabalah* in which she contends that the Kabbalah (the Jewish mystical system for interpreting scripture) can be a source of practical mysticism for Western audiences and suggests that the mind uses symbols to explore spiritual experience it cannot otherwise grasp. Five years later she wrote her autobiography, *Psychic Self-Defense*.

Fortune's most influential works have been her novels about magical practice. They assert the importance and power of women in the world of magic and use Freudian and Jungian psychology to explain the occult. Among her most notable works were *The Demon Lover* (1927) and *The Sea Priestess* (1938).

Fortune died of leukemia on January 8, 1946.

Legacy

Fortune took the romantic practices of Victorian spiritualism and elevated them to a form of religious and investigative science, making them accessible to a broader audience. She and the Fraternity of the Inner Light generated a movement to take seriously people's unexplainable supernatural experiences.

The Fraternity, later Society, of the Inner Light continued after Fortune's death. (In fact, her followers contend that she used mediums to guide it for a number of years from beyond the grave.) In the years immediately after her death it continued teaching Western occultism with a strong Christian focus. It also published a monthly journal, *The Inner Light Magazine*, that was devoted to what it termed "occult science" and the psychology of "superconsciousness." In more recent years it has become international and broadened its focus to include a wide variety of occult traditions.

Fortune trained a number of noted occultists, mystics, and psychics, including Gareth Knight and W. E. Butler, who established a school of occult science that, in 1972, became the School of the Inner Light. The group's goal is to teach what it calls the Western Mysteries, which it defines as "the true inner spiritual heritage of the West."

Fortune's life and work have influenced modern writers of occult fiction, including the best-selling fantasy works of Katherine Kurtz. Her work is popular among Neopagans, modern-day followers of ancient nature religions, although Fortune was not connected with that movement.

Honigsberg

WORLD EVENTS		FORTUNE'S LIFE
Germany is united	1871	
	1890	Violet Firth (later Dion Fortune) is born in Wales
Spanish American War	1898	
World War I	1914–18	
	1919	Fortune joins Stella Matutina
	1922	Fortune founds Fraternity of the Inner Light
	c. 1926	The Fraternity of Inner Light becomes independent
	1935	Fortune publishes *The Mystical Qabalah*
World War II	1939–45	
	1946	Fortune dies
Mao Tse-tung establishes Communist rule in China	1949	

For Further Reading:

Fielding, Charles, and Carr Collins. *The Story of Dion Fortune*. Dallas, Tex.: Star & Cross Publications/Samuel Weiser, Inc., 1985.

Richardson, Alan. *Priestess: The Life and Magic of Dion Fortune*. Wellingborough, England: Aquarian Press, 1987.

Foucault, Michel

Wide-ranging Twentieth-Century
Philosopher
1926–1984

World Events	Foucault's Life
World War I 1914–18	
	1926 Michel Foucault is born in Poitiers, France
World War II 1939–45	
Mao Tse-tung establishes Communist rule in China	1949
Apartheid laws established in South Africa	
Korean War 1950–53	
	1960 *Madness and Civilization* is published
	1966 *The Order of Things* is published
Six Day War between Israel and Arabs	1967
	1969 *The Archeology of Knowledge* is published
	1970 *Discipline and Punishment* is published
	Foucault is elected to the College de France
End of Vietnam War 1975	
	1976–84 *The History of Sexuality* is published
	1984 Foucault dies
Fall of Communism in eastern Europe	1989

Life and Work

Michel Foucault was a wide-ranging philosopher whose controversial writings have had a profound influence on a variety of twentieth-century thinkers.

Foucault was born on October 15, 1926, in the French city of Poitiers. He studied philosophy and psychology at the elite École Normale Supérieure in Paris, where he was a student of the Marxist philosopher Louis Althusser. During the 1960s Foucault taught at the University of Clermont-Ferrand and then at the the University of Paris-Vincennes. In 1970 he was elected to the College de France, where he took the title of Professor of the History of Systems of Thought. In the following years his international reputation grew as he lectured all over the world.

Foucault first rose to prominence with the 1960 publication of *Madness and Civilization*. In this book, Foucault traced the historical development of the concept of madness. His aim was to show that "madness" is not a fixed concept, but is, rather, an idea that has transformed radically over time. Our understanding of madness, he argued, is a historical construction, and one that is deeply interwoven with the systems of power that structure modern life.

Later important works include *The Order of Things* (1966), *The Archeology of Knowledge* (1969), and *Discipline and Punish* (1970). In these works, Foucault continued to trace the development of such concepts as "madness," "power," and "knowledge," and analyzed the ways in which such concepts function within a given social order.

Foucault's last years were marked chiefly by his voluminous and unfinished *History of Sexuality* (1976–84). As with his earlier works, Foucault examined the development of a concept over time (in this case the concept of "sexuality"), and the relationship of that concept to systems of power and social control. In 1984 Foucault died, at his home in France, of AIDS.

Legacy

Foucault was always a controversial thinker, and his legacy continues to incite debate among contemporary scholars. Foucault's impact upon academic thought has been substantial; the broad range of his work has influenced such diverse academic disciplines as philosophy, history, religious studies, and literature.

Among philosophers, the degree of Foucault's influence varies widely. His influence, as might be expected, has been strongest in France. Roland Barthes, Gilles Deleuze, and Felix Guattari are just a few French thinkers who have been deeply influenced by Foucault, though each has also taken issue with elements of Foucault's work.

Foucault's greatest impact in the Anglo-American world has been in the fields of literary and cultural studies. Critics influenced by Foucault tend to look at works of literature not as timeless classics but rather as products of specific historical moments. As a consequence, they are far less interested in celebrating the "eternal truths" of a literary work than in exposing the ways in which those supposed truths function within a given social order.

Smith

For Further Reading:
Dreyfus, Hubert L., and Paul Rabinow. *Michel Foucault: Beyond Structuralism and Hermeneutics.* Chicago: University of Chicago Press, 1982.
Sarup, Madan. *An Introductory Guide to Post-structuralism and Postmodernism.* Athens: The University of Georgia Press, 1993.

Fox, George

Founder of the Quakers
1624–1691

Life and Work

George Fox was the founder of the Religious Society of Friends, popularly known as the Quakers.

The son of a devout Puritan weaver, Fox was born in Leicester in July 1624, during a period of civil and religious unrest in England. He apprenticed to a cobbler but left his position in 1643, when he received a call from God telling him to search for spiritual enlightenment. His search led him to believe that there was an "Inner Light," the internal presence of God, in each individual. To find eternal truth people must rely not on the sacraments or the Bible but must look into their souls.

In 1647 Fox began preaching his message. A charismatic speaker and an excellent organizer, he attracted followers throughout England. He emphasized the Inner Light and true obedience to Christ. Because he believed that the spirit of God resided in all, he saw no need for a formal clergy. He developed no formal creed and his church services, called meetings, lacked a standard liturgy. Meetings were silent until God inspired someone to speak. Fox urged his followers to adopt simple dress, speech, and manner. They treated all equally and did not observe contemporary status distinctions, for example, refusing to take off their hats to their social "betters." Quakers refused to take oaths and would not pay taxes to support the established church. (The use of the term Quaker can be dated from 1650 when Fox urged one of his followers to quake at the Word of the Lord.) By 1660 they had become pacifists.

The Quakers' conduct led to their persecution. Fox was jailed eight times. Yet the movement prospered. Eventually Fox organized churches in Ireland, America, and the West Indies as well as England. By the time of his death in London on January 13, 1691, the Quakers had become an established religious movement.

Legacy

Fox developed the theology and laid the organizational foundation for the Religious Society of Friends. Although the church was never large, it has had an influence much beyond its numbers.

During the years of persecution, Fox gave his blessing for one of his followers, William Penn, to establish a colony in America as a refuge for believers and a "holy experiment," in living the Quaker ideals. Pennsylvania, founded in 1681, and its capital, Philadelphia, eventually became the center of the Quaker movement. Under Quaker leadership the colony flourished. The Quaker doctrine of religious tolerance attracted colonists from all over Europe, while the group's emphasis on thrift and strict honesty made the colony prosperous. Many Quakers became extremely wealthy. In the 1750s the Quakers removed themselves from the Pennsylvania government. The immediate reason was the desire of the legislature to wage a war against the Indians on the frontier, but the root cause was that the Quakers feared that their wealth and involvement in the world had eroded their spiritual values. In the years that followed, they withdrew from the world to cultivate what they called the "inner plantation" of the soul. Nevertheless, as a religious body they continued to have a significant impact on American society.

Quakers were early opponents of slavery. In the late seventeenth century Quaker meetings declared slavery a sin and during the eighteenth century Quakers would not permit slaveholders to join the denomination. Quakers were prominent in the abolitionist movement of the nineteenth century, both in the United States and England. In America they played an important role in the Underground Railroad, moving escaped slaves to safety in Canada.

Because Quakers believed that the divine spark could be found in anyone, women played an equal role in the denomination. The experience of equality led many Quaker women, including Susan B. Anthony and Lucretia Mott, to take leadership roles in the struggle for women's rights. Quakers were also involved in the temperance crusade, prison and education reform, and the movement for Indian rights.

Today the Religious Society of Friends, as it is known, is a thriving international religion with several hundred thousand members. The majority of its members are in the United States with sizable groups in England and East Africa.

Saltz

World Events		Fox's Life
Thirty Years' War in Europe	1618–48	
	1624	George Fox is born
	1643	Fox leaves home
	1647	Fox begins to preach
	1660	Fox announces Quakers' pacifism
England's Glorious Revolution	1688	
English seize Calcutta, India	1690	
	1691	Fox dies
Peace of Utrecht settles War of Spanish Succession	1713–15	

For Further Reading:

Fox, George. *The Journal of George Fox.* New York: Dutton, 1962.

Ingle, H. Larry. *First Among Friends: George Fox and Creation of Quakerism.* New York and Oxford: Oxford University Press, 1994.

Francis of Assisi, Saint

Founder of the Franciscan Order
of Friars
c. 1181–1226

Life and Work

Francis of Assisi was a self-appointed preacher who embraced a life of poverty and service to others in order to imitate the life of Christ. During his lifetime, he organized an order of friars that eventually became known as the Franciscans.

World Events	Francis's Life
Settling of Timbuktu, c. 1100 present-day Mali	
	c. 1181 Giovanni di Bernadone (later Francis of Assisi) is born
Islamic ruler of Egypt, Saladin, captures Jerusalem 1187	
	1202 Francis captured in war between Assisi and Perugia
	1208 Francis begins public preaching
	1209 Franciscan Order is established
	1212 Poor Clares is founded
	1224 Francis receives *stigmata*
	1226 Francis dies
	1228 Francis is canonized
Hapsburg dynasty begins dominance in Holy Roman Empire 1273	

The son of a wealthy cloth merchant, Francis was baptized Giovanni di Bernadone in Assisi, Italy. His father, who was absent at his son's baptism, changed the infant's name to Francis because of a fondness for France. As a youth, Francis was known for an exuberant love of good living. In 1202 he was captured in the war between Assisi and Perugia and held prisoner for over a year. Upon his return to Assisi, he began questioning his values and undertook a life of solitary prayer and almsgiving. His new life-style enraged his father, who brought him to court after Francis sold cloth he had taken from the store to raise funds to repair a chapel. At the trial Francis publicly renounced his patrimony. He divested himself of all his possessions and over the next two years lived the life of a hermit.

Responding to a call from God, Francis began publicly preaching in 1208. He soon attracted 11 followers who, in 1209, received permission from the Pope to establish a new monastic order known as the "Lesser Brothers." In 1212 Francis established an order for women, the Poor Clares, named after a noblewoman who had joined his movement.

Francis and his followers devoted themselves to lives of penitential preaching among the poor. Owning no property, they supported themselves by begging or practicing whatever trade they knew. His spirituality was characterized by compassion and a deep love for all of God's creation. It focused on the manifestation of God's goodness in sending Christ to redeem sinful humankind. Christ accepted the poverty of being human, becoming "poor for us in this world," and through his poverty and self-giving showed how people could experience God.

By 1223 Francis had resigned the administration of his order. In September 1224, while on a retreat, Francis beheld a vision of Christ after which he received the *stigmata* (wounds in his hands and feet and on his side corresponding to those Christ received on the cross). Francis died at Porziuncola, near Assisi, on October 3, 1226.

Legacy

Francis is remembered not only as the founder of the Franciscan Order, but also as a model of Christian piety and self-sacrifice in the service of others. These qualities inspired the Roman Catholic church to canonize him on July 15, 1228, only two years after his death.

The founding of the Franciscan Order was part of a general movement among the laity in the twelfth and thirteenth centuries to return to the simple life of the early Church and the example of Jesus. As the order grew, friars traveled throughout Europe carrying religious reform into areas beset by poverty and heresy. Growth, however, gradually changed the congregation and it increasingly began to resemble other religious orders. The Franciscans abandoned absolute poverty and settled in university towns where their training schools produced some of the great scholars of the Middle Ages, among them John Duns Scotus (d. 1308), William of Ockham (d. 1347), and Bonaventure (d. 1274), who reinvigorated the order during the thirteenth century.

A minority, known as the Spirituals, resisted these changes but were condemned by the pope in the early fourteenth century. Over the next several hundred years, the Franciscans' internal differences led to the creation of several subgroups. Toward the end of the fourteenth century, a reform movement, the Observants, reestablished the strict rule of poverty. They expanded throughout Europe under the direction of Bernadino of Siena (1380–1444) and John of Capistrano (1386–1456). By 1517 these groups formed the Friars Minor of the Observance. The Capuchins, a third absolutist group, formed in 1525. This congregation became successful preachers among the lower classes during the Counter–Reformation. After the sixteenth century the order lost the intellectual preeminence it had achieved during the Middle Ages, but remained in the vanguard of the Roman Catholic church's preaching and missionary activities. It was one of the orders that helped evangelize North and South America. At the end of the twentieth century the three congregations in the order contained about 35,000 members. The Order of Poor Clares numbered about 19,000.

The reverence for Francis continued into the twentieth century. In 1939, Francis became the patron saint of Italy. Pope John Paul II declared him the patron saint of ecology in 1979.

von Dehsen

For Further Reading:
Chesterton, G. K. *St. Francis of Assisi.* New York: Image Books, 1989.
Frugoni, Chiara. *Francis of Assisi: A Life.* London: SCM, 1998.

Gadamer, Hans-Georg

Philosopher of Hermeneutics
1900–

Life and Work

Hans-Georg Gadamer is a German philosopher whose views on such subjects as truth, beauty, and the nature of language have had a significant impact on philosophers and theologians.

Gadamer was born in Marburg, Germany, on February 11, 1900. He studied humanities at the universities of Breslau, Marburg, Freiburg, and Munich, and received his doctorate at Freiburg in 1922. His mentor at Freiburg was MARTIN HEIDEGGER, one of the most important philosophers of the twentieth century, whose thought had an enormous impact on Gadamer's own.

After graduating from Freiburg, Gadamer taught philosophy at the universities of Marburg (1933), Kiel (1934–35), and Marburg again (1936–38), where he was named extraordinary professor. In 1939 he moved to the University of Leipzig, where he was named full professor, and later taught at Frankfurt am Main (1947–49) and Heidelberg (1949). His emergence into international fame, however, came in 1960, with the publication of *Truth and Method*.

Truth and Method is a work of philosophical hermeneutics heavily influenced by the philosophies of Wilhelm Dilthey and Heideggar. "Hermeneutics" is, roughly, the science of interpretation; whereas the word was once used to apply only to biblical interpretation, Heideggar and others expanded the term to include the interpretation of texts generally and, indeed, the interpretation of all of human communication. In *Truth and Method*, Gadamer raised the question of how an individual interprets any communicative act. He argued that our understanding of reality is always framed by our "tradition"—that is, our history and our language—and that all interpretation takes place within this boundary. While the limitations of tradition are predetermined, they are also ever-changing, such that tradition may be viewed as constantly becoming other than it is.

In subsequent years, Gadamer continued to explore the ground he had laid in *Truth and Method* and expanded his range of inquiry to include aesthetics, ethics, and questions of religion. *Dialogue and Dialectic* (English translation, 1980) and *Reason in the Age of Science* (English translation, 1981) are two important collections of his later essays.

Legacy

Gadamer's impact on late twentieth-century philosophy and theology has been significant. He has led many thinkers to pay greater attention to the ways in which history and language frame even our most basic understandings of the world.

Gadamer is largely responsible for the revival of interest among many academics in the concept of tradition. Prior to *Truth and Method*, the debate over the value of tradition can be divided into two camps: a liberal, or Marxist, camp that saw tradition as inherently repressive and antirational, and a conservative camp that viewed tradition as socially beneficial, morally good, and the source of accumulated wisdom. Theologians in particular have been deeply divided along these lines, with liberals emphasizing the dangers of tradition while conservatives stress its value.

But Gadamer refocused the entire debate and has influenced many thinkers to do the same. The Catholic theologian and priest

David Tracy, for example, has followed Gadamer in affirming the central importance of tradition (indeed, arguing that human communication is impossible without it), while at the same time stressing that tradition, properly understood, is a fluid and a dynamic entity, constantly opening up new horizons for change and growth.

Smith

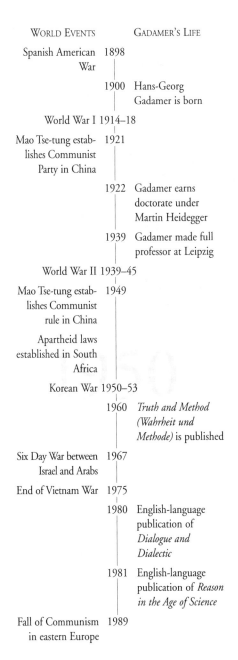

WORLD EVENTS		GADAMER'S LIFE
Spanish American War	1898	
	1900	Hans-Georg Gadamer is born
World War I	1914–18	
Mao Tse-tung establishes Communist Party in China	1921	
	1922	Gadamer earns doctorate under Martin Heidegger
	1939	Gadamer made full professor at Leipzig
World War II	1939–45	
Mao Tse-tung establishes Communist rule in China	1949	
Apartheid laws established in South Africa		
Korean War	1950–53	
	1960	*Truth and Method (Wahrheit und Methode)* is published
Six Day War between Israel and Arabs	1967	
End of Vietnam War	1975	
	1980	English-language publication of *Dialogue and Dialectic*
	1981	English-language publication of *Reason in the Age of Science*
Fall of Communism in eastern Europe	1989	

For Further Reading:

Roberts, David, ed. *Reconstructing Theory: Gadamer, Habermas, Luhmann.* Melbourne, Australia: Melbourne University Press, 1995.

Warnke, Georgia. *Gadamer: Hermeneutics, Tradition, and Reason.* Oxford: Polity Press, 1987.

Gandhi, Mohandas Karamchand (Mahatma)

Father of Indian Independence;
Leading Advocate of Nonviolent
Protest
1869–1948

Life and Work

One of the towering figures of the twentieth century, Mohandas Karamchand Gandhi won independence for India through a nonviolent revolution. He is one of the few individuals in history who used a philosophy of love and patience to change the world.

Born on October 2, 1869, in Porbander, India, Gandhi was the youngest son of the chief minister of the principality and an extremely religious mother. He grew up in a deeply religious Hindu home that emphasized pacifism and the sanctity of all living things. After studying law in England beginning in 1888, he returned briefly to India before moving to South Africa in 1893. There he found himself treated as a member of an inferior race. Over the next 20 years Gandhi threw himself into the struggle for civil liberties and political rights for Indians in South Africa. Eschewing violence, he launched a unique campaign, based on collective acts of civil disobedience and passive resistance, that forced the British to repeal several racial laws.

In 1914 Gandhi returned to India, where he became the preeminent figure in the struggle for independence. He became head of the Indian National Congress in 1921 and waged a successful campaign to include the masses in the independence movement, which had been dominated by the urban middle class. He also convinced the movement's leaders to use civil disobedience and passive resistance as their main tactics. In 1924, Gandhi withdrew from active politics, 23 years before India gained independence from Britain, but he remained India's most important political figure and a national symbol of a free India. The masses revered him for his ascetic lifestyle and his moral virtue. It was during this period that he became known as Mahatma, Sanskrit for "great-souled."

During the 1930s Gandhi waged a campaign against the Hindu caste system, a system of social hierarchy based on inherited membership in a social class. Although he was himself a member of the merchant caste, in 1932 he undertook a "fast unto death" to fight for the rights for Hindu "Untouchables," the lowest caste.

Gandhi was never able to convince India's Muslims that an independent India would respect their interests, and he reluctantly agreed to the partition of India. When the British granted independence in 1947, Pakistan broke away as a separate Muslim state. On January 30, 1948, Gandhi was assassinated by a Hindu fanatic who thought that

Gandhi's emphasis on nonviolence and compassion was weakening the Hindu nation.

Legacy

Gandhi was the father of Indian independence, but his legacy transcends politics. He was immensely revered as a towering figure of moral virtue. His teachings of nonviolence, civil disobedience, and passive resistance had a profound effect on freedom struggles around the world.

As the preeminent leader in India's struggle for freedom, Gandhi not only built an independent nation but also influenced India's democratic life for years following his death. His insistence that the masses be involved in the independence movement united India's various ethnic, political, and linguistic groups against a common adversary. By the time of independence, he had taught India to think as a nation rather than a group of principalities. Gandhi's philosophy also helped stabilize the fledgling democracy. His teachings inspired so many that for years opposition parties used nonviolent protests and mass mobilizations to influence government policy.

Gandhi's teachings inspired freedom movements around the world. MARTIN LUTHER KING, JR., employed his ideas of passive resistance and civil disobedience in the civil rights movement in the United States. The African National Congress used similar techniques during the early years of its struggle against apartheid in South Africa.

Yang

WORLD EVENTS		GANDHI'S LIFE
United States Civil War	1861–65	
	1869	Mohandas Gandhi is born
Germany is united	1871	
	1888	Gandhi begins law studies at University College, London
	1893	Gandhi settles in South Africa, begins campaign against discrimination
Spanish American War	1898	
	1914	Gandhi returns to India
World War I	1914–18	
	1921	Gandhi becomes head of the Indian National Congress
	1924	Gandhi retires from active politics
	1930s	Gandhi campaigns against caste system
World War II	1939–45	
	1947	British grant Indian independence
	1948	Gandhi is assassinated
Mao Tse-tung established Communist rule in China	1949	

For Further Reading:

Dalton, Dennis. *Mahatma Gandhi: Nonviolent Power in Action.* New York: Columbia University Press, 1993.

Fischer, Louis. *The Life of Mahatma Gandhi.* New York: Harper & Row, 1988.

Mehta, Ved. *Mahatma Gandhi and His Apostles.* New Haven, Conn.: Yale University Press, 1993.

Garrison, William Lloyd

Leader of Abolitionist Movement
1805–1879

Life and Work

William Lloyd Garrison was a crusading journalist who rose to prominence as the advocate for the immediate abolition of slavery; his stance grew out of his sense of Christian compassion.

The son of an itinerant seaman, Garrison was born on December 12, 1805, in Newburyport, Massachusetts. In 1828, he met the Quaker Benjamin Lundy, an early abolitionist who advocated the gradual emancipation of the slaves, and took up the anti-slavery cause. In 1829 Garrison became co-editor with Lundy of the *Genius of Universal Emancipation* in Baltimore, Maryland.

Garrison initially shared Lundy's views, but soon he adopted a much more radical stance toward abolition. In 1831 Garrison founded the journal *The Liberator*, which became one of the most influential papers of the pre–Civil War period. In his editorials, Garrison promoted his radical views; he labeled slavery a sin and un-American and demanded its immediate elimination.

Undaunted by the threats that his views generated, in 1833 Garrison helped found the American Anti-Slavery Society (AASS) to advocate the peaceful overthrow of slavery and racial equality. In 1837 Garrison embraced Christian

"perfectionism," a body of ideas that not only deplored slavery, but also advocated women's rights and pacifism. He denounced the established churches as siding with slave owners and refused to work within existing political institutions, which he thought "corrupted" by slavery. In 1840 the majority of the Society's more moderate members left to form two groups of their own, the American and Foreign Anti-Slavery Society and the Liberty Party, to push for political change.

After this split, Garrison's group of supporters grew fewer in number as his own ideas grew more radical. In 1844 he advocated that the North secede from the Union lest it be corrupted by the slave-owning South. He became increasingly hostile to the federal government, coming out against the Compromise of 1850 and the Dred Scott decision, in which the Supreme Court ruled that Congress had no authority to restrict slavery in the territories. He also displayed a more militant side, lauding radical abolitionist John Brown's raid as "God's . . . retribution upon the head of the tyrant." By 1850, he had also become an ardent advocate of women's rights, as evidenced by his attendance at the First National Women's Rights Convention in Worcester, Massachusetts. In 1854 he burned a copy of the U.S. Constitution in public.

At the outbreak of the Civil War, however, Garrison put aside his pacifism and supported the war. He enthusiastically supported Abraham Lincoln and pushed the president for immediate emancipation. With the passage of the 13th Amendment, which freed the slaves, in 1865, Garrison announced that his work was done and resigned from the Society. He spent the last years of his life in retirement and died in New York City on May 24, 1879.

Legacy

Garrison was for many the voice and personification of the American anti-slavery movement. His uncompromising morality and his relentless, fire-breathing denunciations earned him recognition both in the United States and in England, where his journal *The Liberator* was also circulated.

Garrison's radical stance had few followers, but his fiery editorials kept the issue of slavery before the nation. During the 1840s and 1850s his political influence declined, yet he continued to grow as a symbol of radical abolitionism. He was hailed as a prophet when civil war broke out. He and his fellow abolitionists were instrumen-

tal in making the war not only a struggle to preserve the union, as Lincoln perceived it, but also to abolish slavery. Although he did not take an active part in lobbying for the Civil Rights Acts that Congress passed in 1865 after the end of the Civil War, they and the 14th and 15th Amendments nevertheless have to be considered fruits of Garrison's years of effort. These acts gave freed slaves the right to own property, to become full citizens, to vote, and to equal protection under the law. Unfortunately, by the 1880s the climate in the United States had changed and further progress on civil rights was not to be made until well into the twentieth century.

Following emancipation has come more than a century of turbulence as former slaves, their descendants, and their allies have fought and continue to fight for complete equality and civil rights. A number of Garrison's beliefs were much ahead of their time. The cause of women's rights became a movement of its own later in the century and continues to this day. The principle of nonviolence was picked up in the twentieth century in other forms by leaders such as MOHANDAS GANDHI and MARTIN LUTHER KING, JR. Garrison's acts of defiance against the government were echoed in the 1960s as students burned flags to protest the Vietnam War.

Saltz

WORLD EVENTS	GARRISON'S LIFE
Napoleonic Wars 1803–15 in Europe	
	1805 William Lloyd Garrison is born
Greek War of 1821–29 Independence against Turkey	
	1828 Garrison becomes abolitionist
	1831 Garrison founds *The Liberator*
	1833 Garrison helps found American Anti-Slavery Society
Revolutions in 1848 Austria, France, Germany, and Italy	
United States 1861–65 Civil War	Garrison backs Lincoln during Civil War
	1865 Garrison resigns from Society after slaves are freed
Germany is united 1871	
	1879 Garrison dies
Spanish American 1898 War	

For Further Reading:
Dillon, Merton Lynn. *The Abolitionists: The Growth of a Dissenting Minority.* DeKalb: Northern Illinois University Press, 1974.
Grimke, Archibald Henry. *William Lloyd Garrison: The Abolitionist.* New York: Negro Universities Press, 1969.

Garvey, Marcus

Founder and Leader of the
Black Nationalist Movement
1887–1940

Life and Work

Marcus Garvey founded and led the first black nationalist mass movement in the United States, which, at its height, boasted nearly one million members.

Born on August 17, 1887, in St. Anne's Bay, Jamaica, Garvey was descended from escaped slaves. Living and working in the Caribbean and Central America, he came to believe that blacks could never expect fair treatment or

WORLD EVENTS		GARVEY'S LIFE
Germany is united	1871	
	1887	Marcus Garvey is born in Jamaica, West Indies
Spanish American War	1898	
	1914	Garvey organizes the Universal Negro Improvement Association (UNIA)
World War I 1914–18		
	1916	Garvey arrives in the United States
	1918	First issue of *Negro World* is published
	1919	Garvey forms the Black Star Line
	1920	First international meeting of UNIA
	1922	Black Star Line fails and Garvey is indicted for mail fraud
	1927	President Coolidge commutes Garvey's sentence and deports him to Jamaica
	1939–45	
World War II	1940	Garvey dies
	1949	
Mao Tse-tung establishes Communist rule in China		

help from whites. He believed they could achieve equality only through racial separation and the development of self-sufficiency through business enterprises combined with education and racial pride. Garvey also advocated the creation of an independent black state in Africa that would coordinate the development of a viable black economy worldwide.

In 1914, following two years in England, Garvey returned to Jamaica and organized the Universal Negro Improvement Association (UNIA), which was designed to unify and help the black community. In 1916 he went to the United States and organized a chapter of the UNIA in Harlem, New York City. Speaking engagements around the country gained him national support and led to the formation of more chapters of UNIA. In 1918 Garvey began publishing the newspaper *Negro World* in several languages so it could also be read in Africa, the Caribbean, and Latin America. In 1920 the first international meeting of UNIA in New York attracted thousands of followers from all over the United States and many foreign countries.

Garvey's ideas of racial pride extended to theology as well as politics and economics. He urged African Americans to think that God was black and with them in their struggle. He urged the formation of a separate black church with a religiosity free of white European domination.

In 1919 Garvey established the Black Star Line, a steamship company entirely owned and run by blacks. Its purpose was to provide transport to and from Africa and to trade black-manufactured goods with the rest of the world. He also formed the Negro Factories Corporation to promote African-American economic independence. In 1922 the Black Star Line failed and Garvey, who by this time had gained the unfavorable attention of the FBI, was indicted on what many felt were falsified mail fraud charges in connection with the company. He was eventually convicted and sentenced to five years in prison. In 1927 President Calvin Coolidge commuted Garvey's sentence and had him deported to Jamaica. There, in 1929, Garvey organized the last convention of UNIA. Greatly weakened by Garvey's absence while in prison and then exile, what was left of UNIA was ultimately

eliminated worldwide by the economic stress of the Depression.

Garvey's attempts to rekindle the UNIA were prevented by ill health and his death on June 10, 1940.

Legacy

Garvey was the first person to develop a mass movement among American blacks. His emphasis on racial roles and black nationalism had a profound influence on future militant black movements.

Garvey's ideas of black separatism and black nationalism later found roots in the Nation of Islam and MALCOLM X in the 1950s and early 1960s, the black power movement in the late '60s and in the racial pride and black consciousness movements of the 1970s. The black studies programs at many universities can look back to Garvey as one of their spiritual fathers. His separatist ideas are still preached by the controversial Louis Farrakhan, the leader of the Nation of Islam.

Garvey's support of black churches and his insistence that God is black and stands with African Americans in their struggle inspired such theologians as JAMES HAL CONE to develop what came to be known as "black [liberation] theology." For Cone, anyone who was oppressed or marginalized was "black"; such people attract the special concern of God for the alleviation of their social, political, and economic suffering.

Saltz

For Further Reading:

Cronon, Edmund David. *Black Moses: The Story of Marcus Garvey and the Universal Negro Improvement Association.* Madison: University of Wisconsin Press, 1981.

Sewell, Tony. *Garvey's Children: The Legacy of Marcus Garvey.* Trenton, N.J.: Africa World Press, 1990.

Ghazali, al-

Influential Islamic Theologian
and Mystic
1058–1111

Life and Work

One of the most influential Islamic theologians and mystics of the medieval period, al-Ghazali was able to combine Islamic scholastic and mystical idea systems to prevent an unbridgeable division within Islam.

Al-Ghazali was born in 1058 in Tus in present-day Iran. At the age of 19 he traveled to Nishapur to study at the Nizamiyah college under ʿAbd al-Malik al-Juwayni (d. 1085), one of the leading religious scholars of the period. While law was his primary focus, al-Ghazali also studied the philosophical writings of AL-FARABI (c. 873–950) and AVICENNA (980–1037). In 1091 al-Ghazali was named a professor at the university in Baghdad, a prominent Sunni Islamic institution, but left this post around 1095 and became a wandering mystic and ascetic. He returned to teaching about a decade later.

In his autobiography al-Ghazali describes his life as a search for truth from a succession of sources: Ashʿariyah scholars (rational theologians), Neoplatonic philosophers, and Sufi Islamic mystics. Dissatisfied with the rationalism of theologians, he ultimately turned to mysticism, with its emphasis on the development of the inner spirit, to satisfy the longing of his soul. This progression is visible in his works. He first embraced the philosophy of the Ashʿariyah. In his chief work, *The Golden Mean in Belief,* he offers his own philosophical concepts, including his proof for the existence of God. He then turned to the Neoplatonic writings of the earlier Islamic philosophers, al-Farabi and Avicenna. This study initially resulted in a synopsis of the thought of Avicenna: *The Views of the Philosophers.* Later, however, he produced a 17-point critique of Avicenna's religious views in *The Inconsistency of the Philosophers.* Specifically, he challenges three of Avicenna's central theories: 1) that there is no resurrection of bodies, only of spirits; 2) that God knows only universals, not particulars; and 3) that the world has existed forever (i.e., has not been created by God). Underlying his work is the conviction that the earlier philosophers had not proved their views by logic. Therefore he rejected their approach and ultimately turned to mysticism. Yet he never completely abandoned logic in defense of doctrine. His later work, the mystical *The Revival of Religious Sciences,* shows the continuing influence of Ashʿariyah philosophy.

In 1106, the Muslim year 500, friends convinced al-Ghazali that he was the "renewer" predicted by MUHAMMAD to manifest at the beginning of each century. Al-Ghazali accepted this role while also accepting a professorship at the university in Nishapur. In 1111, he returned to his hometown of Tus, perhaps because of ill health, where he died.

Legacy

Al-Ghazali was able to combine the scholastic and mystical schools of Islam to stop a growing division within the community and permit an emotional component in Islamic religious life.

He lived during a period when a gap was developing between *ulama* (learned men), who emphasized the law and believed that knowledge of God came from theological study, and the Sufi, mystics who stressed the inner attitude by which believers performed outward religious obligations. His efforts in mystical thought promoted the concept that strict observance of the *Shariah* enriches inner mystical experience. By linking mystical experience with ordinary activity, he made the mystical life more attractive to those who might have otherwise rejected ascetic discipline. Thus, he provided a model that one need not abandon the *Shariah* and sound teaching to pursue mystical enlightenment. In addition, al-Ghazali's insights made Sufi practice more acceptable to other Muslims and encouraged them to adopt moderate practices.

Al-Ghazali was not without his critics in the Arab world. In the West, Spanish-Arab philosopher AVERROËS (1126–1198) wrote his major work of systematic philosophy to refute al-Ghazali's *The Inconsistency of the Philosophers* and to defend pure Aristotelian thought.

Sufism grew rapidly after al-Ghazali's death. It won many converts in western Asia and North Africa, where Sufi missionaries carried the message of Islam, as well as among Shiite Muslims. In many areas Sufis became so dominant that the *ulama* were unable to limit their influence.

In 1842, *The Deliverer From Error* was translated into French, allowing many European scholars to examine al-Ghazali's ideas. His favorable reception among these scholars helped popularize his ideas and shape the Western view of Islam.

von Dehsen

WORLD EVENTS		AL-GHAZALI'S LIFE
Schism between Roman Catholic and Orthodox Church	1054	
	1058	Al-Ghazali is born
	1091	Al-Ghazali becomes professor at University in Baghdad
First Crusade	1095	
Crusaders capture Jerusalem during First Crusade	1099	
Settling of Timbuktu, present-day Mali	c. 1100	
	1106	Al-Ghazali recognized as "renewer"
	1111	Al-Ghazali dies
Islamic ruler of Egypt, Saladin, captures Jerusalem	1187	

For Further Reading:

Frank, Richard W. *Al-Ghazali and the Ash'arite School.* Durham, N.C.: Duke University Press, 1994.

Frank, Richard W. *Creation and the Cosmic System: Al-Ghazali and Avicenna.* Heidelberg, Germany: Carl Winter Universitatsverlag, 1992.

Smith, Margaret. *Al-Ghazali, The Mystic.* Lahore, Pakistan: Hijra International Publishers, 1983.

Gladden, Solomon Washington

Protestant Leader of Social
Gospel Movement
1836–1918

Life and Work

Solomon Washington Gladden was a liberal Protestant clergyman who was a leader of the Social Gospel movement, which began in the United States after the Civil War. The Social Gospel movement was an attempt to reform social institutions according to the Christian ethic.

World Events	Gladden's Life
Greek War of 1821–29 Independence against Turkey	
	1836 Solomon Washington Gladden is born
Revolutions in 1848 Austria, France, Germany, and Italy	
	1859 Gladden graduates from Williams College
United States 1861–65 Civil War	
Germany is united 1871	
	1875 Gladden begins pastoral work in Springfield, Massachusetts
	1877 Gladden helps during labor crisis
	1882 Gladden appointed pastor in Columbus, Ohio
	1886 *Applied Christianity* is published
Spanish American 1898 War	
	1902 *Social Salvation* is published
	1908 Federal Council of Churches is formed
	1914 Gladden retires
World War I 1914–18	
	1918 Gladden dies
World War II 1939–45	

Gladden was born on February 11, 1836, and brought up on a farm near Oswego, New York. He graduated from Williams College in 1859 and worked a short time for *The Independent,* an abolitionist newspaper that became the leading church newspaper after the Civil War. Although Gladden had no formal theological training, he spent the rest of his life in the Congregational ministry. From 1875 to 1882, he served as a pastor in Springfield, Massachusetts. There he became involved in the labor movement and, in 1877, during violent strikes resulting from an economic depression, Gladden acted as mediator between management and labor. In 1882, he was appointed pastor of the First Congregational Church of Columbus, Ohio, where he spent the rest of his career.

Influenced by liberal churchmen such as HORACE BUSHNELL, Gladden believed that for Christianity to continue developing in America, the ills of society would have to be cured through Christian principles. This emphasis became known as the Social Gospel. Some of the issues that Gladden addressed were higher wages for workers, poverty, the excesses of laissez-faire capitalism, the abolition of child labor, and race relations. Although he was not a socialist, he advocated public ownership of railroads and utilities and workers' ownership of corporations. First influenced by BOOKER T. WASHINGTON and then by W. E. B. DU BOIS, Gladden came to realize that economic well-being alone was not enough to achieve equality between the races—that political equality was also necessary. Gladden also advocated cooperation with not only other Protestant denominations but also with Jews and Roman Catholics, whom he saw as possible allies in his social activism. He was a leader of the Federal Council of Churches formed in 1908.

Among Gladden's many books are *Applied Christianity: Moral Aspects of Social Questions,* published in 1886, and *Social Salvation,* published in 1902.

Gladden retired in 1914 and died in Columbus on July 2, 1918.

Legacy

During his 50-year career, Gladden developed and spread the ideas of the Social Gospel, which had a significant influence on American religion and social reform in the twentieth century.

The Social Gospel helped develop the climate for progressive reform that dominated American society and politics during the first two decades of the twentieth century. Guided by its principles, reformers like Theodore Roosevelt, Woodrow Wilson, and Jane Addams viewed their crusades for social and political justice in moral terms.

The Social Gospel movement was always a minority movement within American Protestantism. Its most enthusiastic supporters were found within only four denominations—Congregationalists, Episcopalians, Methodists, and northern Baptists. It never won over the immigrant population it tried to serve, and it proposed few lasting solutions to the problems it sought to address. Nevertheless its commitment to social justice became an increasingly important thread in American Protestantism.

Gladden and the Social Gospel movement laid the foundation for ecumenical cooperation on social causes among churches that belonged to the Federal Council of Churches and its successor the National Council of Churches. Currently representing 32 Protestant and Orthodox churches with combined memberships of 42 million, the Council is involved in such issues as civil rights, world peace, racial strife, and famine and disaster relief.

Saltz

For Further Reading:

Curtis, Susan. *A Consuming Faith: The Social Gospel and Modern American Culture.* Baltimore, Md.: Johns Hopkins University Press, 1991.

Gorrell, Donald K. *The Age of Social Responsibility: The Social Gospel in the Progressive Era, 1900–1920.* Macon, Ga.: Mercer University Press, 1988.

Gobind Singh

Founder of Khalsa Sect of Sikhism
1666–1708

Life and Work

Gobind Singh (originally Gobind Rai) was the tenth, and last, *guru* of Sikhism and the founder of Khalsa, a militaristic Sikh faction.

Gobind Rai was born on December 26, 1666, in Patna, in the Bihar region of India. His father, Tegh Bahadur, was the ninth Sikh *guru*. When Gobind was nine, the Mughal emperor charged his father with extortion and sentenced him to death. Before the execution on November 11, 1675, Tegh appointed his son as the tenth *guru*.

Fearing the emperor, Gobind hid in the mountains at Paonta. There he received an education in Sanskrit, Persian, and in military techniques. Determined to root out evil and to exterminate tyrants so that the righteous might prosper, he organized his followers into a militia that waged war against the Mughals and the neighboring Hindu chieftains.

On April 13, 1699, while at prayer with his people, Gobind called for five men to offer themselves as sacrifices. He took the five out of the tent and soon returned with a bloodied sword, horrifying the worshipers. Shortly thereafter, the five entered the tent; Gobind had actually slaughtered five goats. These five men became the core of the Khalsa, a new, military community of "pure ones." As others joined, they shared in the "baptism" of drinking from a single bowl (symbolizing the breakdown of castes) liquid that had been stirred by a double-edged dagger. To solidify these "troops," he gave them aw new family name, Singh (lion), and created music, rituals, and discipline to forge them into an "army of saints."

After initial defeats, including the loss of all four of his sons, Gobind retreated to Mustar, where he attracted new recruits. There he prepared the definitive version of the *Adi Granth*, the scripture of the Sikhs. He also completed a book of his own writings, the *Dasam Granth*.

In late 1708, Gobind was mortally wounded. Before he died at Nander on October 7, he declared the line of *gurus* would end with him. Thereafter the Sikh *guru* would be the *Adi Granth*.

Legacy

Gobind, the last of the *gurus*, redirected the focus of the Sikh religion by replacing the veneration of the *gurus* with adoration of the *Adi Granth* and by founding the military sect known as Khalsa.

The Khalsa promoted purity, concentrating on the "five K's": *kesa* (uncut hair and beard), *kangha* (comb), *kacch* (short trousers), *kara* (steel bracelet), and *kirpan* (double-edged dagger). The members of Khalsa also pledged to abstain from alcohol, tobacco, adultery, and from meat not properly slaughtered.

The Sikhs continued their opposition to Mughal rule following Gobind's death. Under the leadership of the warrior Ranjit Singh, they established a powerful state in Punjab around 1800. The rule of the Khalsa was short-lived, however. In late 1845 and early 1846, they suffered defeat by the British in the First Sikh War. Another British victory in the Second Sikh War in 1849 solidified their control. The British dominated Punjab for the rest of the century.

Since Indian independence in 1947, Sikhs have attempted to restore their power base in Punjab, in the northwest of India. As their prosperity improved after the Indian–Pakistani War of 1965, religious tensions with the Hindus heightened. By 1980, the Shiromani Akali Dal, the political party of the Sikh fundamentalists, demanded political and economic improvements for their people. In 1984, Jarnail Singh Bhindranwale seized the Golden Temple, the most holy Sikh pilgrimage site, to publicize their concerns. The Indian army responded by assaulting the Temple and slaughtering hundreds of Sikhs. In retaliation, Sikh fundamentalists assassinated Prime Minister Indira Gandhi the following October. Since then, tensions between Sikhs and Hindus remain centered on the question of establishing a separate Sikh state.

Thus, the militaristic focus of Gobind continues to be a central force among the Sikhs.

von Dehsen

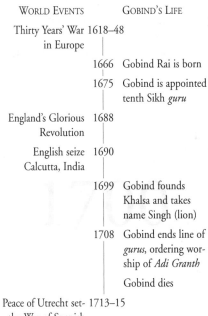

World Events	Gobind's Life
Thirty Years' War 1618–48 in Europe	
	1666 Gobind Rai is born
	1675 Gobind is appointed tenth Sikh *guru*
England's Glorious 1688 Revolution	
English seize 1690 Calcutta, India	
	1699 Gobind founds Khalsa and takes name Singh (lion)
	1708 Gobind ends line of *gurus*, ordering worship of *Adi Granth*
	Gobind dies
Peace of Utrecht set- 1713–15 tles War of Spanish Succession	

For Further Reading:

Joher, Surinder Singh. *Guru Gobind Singh*. New Delhi: Enkay Publishers, 1987.

Kohli, Surinder Singh. *The Life and Ideals of Gobind Singh: Based on Original Resources*. New Delhi: Munshiram Manoharal Publishers, 1986.

Singh, Dalip. *Guru Gobind Singh and Khalsa Discipline*. Amritsar, Punjab: Singh Bros., 1992.

Gregory I, Pope

Early Pope and Church Reformer
c. 540–604

Life and Work

Gregory I, later known as Gregory the Great, was a strong but compassionate Pope who, using his administrative skills, reformed the Catholic church administratively and liturgically. He was also a social and moral reformer.

Born about 540 in Rome into a wealthy, noble family, Gregory was a great-grandson of Pope Felix III. He spent two years as prefect of Rome from 573 to 575, and then founded a

WORLD EVENTS		GREGORY'S LIFE
Rule of Byzantine emperor Justinian I the Great	527–65	
	c. 540	Gregory is born
	c. 573	Gregory becomes prefect of Rome
	579	Gregory is appointed papal ambassador to Byzantine court
	590	Gregory is elected Pope
	596	Gregory sends mission led by Augustine to England
	604	Gregory dies and is declared saint
T'ang Dynasty in China	618–907	
Buddhism becomes official religion of China	624	
Muhammad conquers Mecca	630	

monastery, which he entered as a monk. He also built six other monasteries in Sicily. In 579 Pope Pelagius II chose him to be the papal nuncio (emissary) to Constantinople (now Istanbul), the capital of the Byzantine empire. He returned to Rome in 584 and became abbot of his monastery.

Desiring only to be a monk, Gregory reluctantly became Pope in 590. In a time of great turbulence in the Church and in Europe, Gregory immediately began to help refugees, the poor, and the starving with Church funds and grain. He reorganized and added to the Church's landholdings. An excellent administrator, Gregory set about reforming the Church administration by centralizing it and reforming monasteries, weeding out corruption. He also worked tirelessly to assert papal supremacy within the Church against challenges from the patriarch in Constantinople, the head of the Eastern Orthodox Church.

Gregory also asserted papal supremacy over secular matters. As the barbaric Lombards (Germanic occupiers of northern Italy) threatened Rome, he took the unprecedented step of bypassing secular authority and negotiating a peace treaty with their king. He began appointing governors of Italian cities and used Church funds to supply them with arms.

Gregory did much missionary work, trying to convert the Lombards and to strengthen and spread Catholicism to other lands. In 596 he sent approximately 40 missionaries to England with Augustine of Canterbury. In contrast to peaceful missionary work, Gregory also advocated conversion by war and coercion, laying the foundation for the Crusades of the Middle Ages.

Gregory reformed the Catholic liturgy as well, popularized miracles, and developed the concept of purgatory. His reform of the mass led to the adoption of plainchant, inaccurately called Gregorian chant.

Gregory died on March 12, 604, in Rome, and he is buried in St. Peter's Basilica.

Legacy

As Pope, Gregory laid the foundations for what would become the hallmarks of the medieval papacy, when the Pope assumed more and more secular power and when Gregory's liturgical and administrative reforms took root.

His assertions of papal primacy were taken up later by more authoritarian Popes, who used their power for imperialistic purposes.

Gregory's actions expressed a new vision of the world, not as individual kingdoms but as one churchly empire extending throughout a Europe ruled by the Pope. This vision played a central role in the politics of the Middle Ages as Popes asserted their power as arbiters in all lay affairs over the claims of emperors and kings. Gregory's assumption of secular power in Italy ultimately led to the establishment of the Papal States in 756 when the Pope became a temporal as well as a spiritual leader. These states remained significant in Italy until Italian unification in the nineteenth century.

Gregory's ecclesiastical reforms had a significant impact on the role of monks and nuns ("religious") and priests in the medieval Church. Gregory did away with the common practice of monks and nuns either living as hermits under rules they, themselves, devised or mixing freely with the community as they performed social services such as caring for the sick. He attempted to impose claustration (seclusion from the world) on religious communities and put secular officials in charge of their business affairs. He also ended the practice of dual monasteries, which were communities of both men and women. Spiritual care of the laity was left in the hands of priests. This enhanced the importance of the priesthood and was one factor in the increasing subordination of women in the Church.

By his advocacy of the use of plainchant during the mass to lend it dignity and gravity, Gregory played a part in the history of music; plainchant was the music from which evolved the future traditions of Western music. This form of liturgical music came to be known as "Gregorian Chant." The first to consider the social implications of the papacy, he believed that Church lands and money should be used to help the poor and needy.

His importance to the Church was recognized immediately upon his death. On September 3, 604, less than six months after his death, he was canonized, that is, declared a saint of the Roman Catholic church. A humble man, Gregory called himself *"servus servorum Dei"* (servant of the servants of God), a phrase that is still used to describe the papacy today.

Saltz

For Further Reading:

Richards, Jeffrey. *Consul of God: The Life and Times of Gregory the Great.* London and Boston: Routledge & Kegan Paul, 1980.

Straw, Carole Ellen. *Gregory the Great: Perfection in Imperfection.* Berkeley: University of California Press, 1988.

Gutiérrez, Gustavo

Originator of Latin American
Liberation Theology
1928–

Life and Work

Gustavo Gutiérrez, professor of theology and social sciences, is a Roman Catholic priest who coined the term "theology of liberation," and is a founder of the Liberation Theology movement.

Born on June 8, 1928, in Lima, Peru, Gutiérrez grew up poor and sick in a loving family. He trained for three years as a doctor, then, in 1951, he went to Europe to study for the priesthood. Gutiérrez returned as a priest to Lima in 1959, teaching theology (after earning his master's degree from University of Lyon in France that year) at the Pontifical Catholic University of Peru. After Vatican II, he formulated the thought on which liberation theology is based, using the term "theology of liberation" for the first time in a paper delivered in July 1968.

Gutiérrez's *A Theology of Liberation: History, Politics and Salvation,* the seminal book on liberation theology, was published in 1971. The book argued that theology should not be a systematic collection of static truths, but rather, it must be a dynamic and continuous struggle, involving the full human heart "weakened" and opened by the gospel, repelled by social injustice, and ready to act. Theology, it said, must be practiced, not sim-

ply thought—and must "at all times protest against injustice, challenge what is inhuman, and side with the poor and the oppressed."

Gutiérrez has continued to publish articles and books regularly. *The Power of the Poor in History* (1983) is an important collection of his essays that (among other things) pointed to DIETRICH BONHOEFFER, the German theologian martyred by the Nazis, as the twentieth-century visionary who cleared a theological path for liberation theology. Along with his direct involvement in the Liberation Theology movement, Gutiérrez continues to teach in Lima and around the world, preaches weekly, and lives in the slums rather than in comfort. In 1985, he received a doctorate in theology from Lyon, in recognition of the influence his work has had on twentieth-century Christian thought. He is regularly recognized through awards and honorary degrees for his work.

Legacy

Gutiérrez's "theology of liberation" shook the foundations of Christian theology in our time, becoming a rallying cry for the oppressed and Christians of the third world.

In the "first phase" of the movement, liberation theology was accepted worldwide, with some reservations concerning its relationship to Marxism. What may be the second most influential book on liberation theology published during this period was Clovodis and LEONARDO BOFF's *Introducing Liberation Theology* (1987). Short (100 pages) and still popular, this book was designed for the novice, outlining most facets of the sometimes complex world of liberation theology in a simple and direct manner. The popularity of and need for this book attests to the general prominence liberation theology gained within the first 15 years of its articulation.

The rise of liberation theology slightly precedes POPE JOHN PAUL II's work to establish a balanced policy on social injustice and political activism for Roman Catholic clergy. In the 1980s, Cardinal Ratzinger, head of the Vatican's Congregation for the Doctrine of the Faith, issued two major papers that explained, critiqued, and recommended certain aspects of the liberation theology agenda. The second paper went so far as to endorse armed struggle "as a last resort to put an end to an obvious and prolonged tyranny which is gravely damaging the common good."

Although they usually base their premises on biblical texts, liberation theologians are often accused of espousing Marxism; so they regularly argue that "Marxist analysis" is not the same as Marxism—an academically reasonable point of view. The fall of communism worldwide in the late 1980s has made discussions on both sides of this issue even more complicated. Another challenge to the movement is the recent large conversions of Latin American Catholics to Protestantism. This has raised questions such as, "Might liberation theology be too worldly and not spiritual enough?" As it enters this "second phase," the Liberation Theology movement is renewing itself on a number of fronts. How it will evolve in the next century remains a question for the future, but Gutiérrez's work will remain influential in shaping it.

K. T. Weidmann

World Events		Gutiérrez's Life
World War I	1914–18	
	1928	Gustavo Gutiérrez is born
World War II	1939–45	
Mao Tse-tung establishes Communist rule in China	1949	
Korean War	1950–53	
	1951	Gutiérrez leaves Peru to study in Europe
	1959	Gutiérrez begins teaching theology in Lima
Six Day War between Israel and Arabs	1967	
	1968	Gutiérrez coins phrase "theology of liberation"
	1971	*A Theology of Liberation: History, Politics and Salvation* is published
End of Vietnam War	1975	
	1985	Gutiérrez receives doctorate from Lyon
Fall of Communism in eastern Europe	1989	
Dissolution of Soviet Union	1991	
Apartheid in South Africa is dismantled	1994	

For Further Reading:

Boff, Leonardo and Clovodis. *Introducing Liberation Theology.* New York: Orbis Books, 1987.

Brown, Robert McAfee. *Gustavo Gutierrez: An Introduction to Liberation Theology.* New York: Orbis Books, 1990.

Gutiérrez, Gustavo. *A Theology of Liberation: History, Politics and Salvation.* New York: Orbis Books, 1971.

Hallaj, al-

Founder of the
Sufi Halladjiyya Sect
c. 858–922

Life and Work

Al-Hallaj was a Sufi mystic who preached a concept of *wahdat al-shuhud*, the "unity of being" in which the mystic experiences total unification with God.

Al-Hallaj was born in Tur in Fars (southwestern Iran) around 858. Tradition states that he was the grandson of Abu Ayyub, a companion of MUHAMMAD. His father, a wool carder,

WORLD EVENTS		AL-HALLAJ'S LIFE
Charlemagne's coronation; beginning of Holy Roman Empire	800	
	c. 858	Al-Hallaj is born
	c. 869	Al-Hallaj memorizes Koran
	c. 877	Al-Hallaj makes first pilgrimage to Mecca
	908	Al-Hallaj is tried in Baghdad
	913	Al-Hallaj is imprisoned
	922	Al-Hallaj is executed
Northern Sung Dynasty begins	960	

left Tur for Wasit, a town on the Tigris River in the midst of a textile region, where al-Hallaj met Sunni-Hanabali Muslims noted for their study of the Koran. By the time he was 12, he had memorized the Koran and begun his search for the inner meaning of its contents. At age 20, al-Hallaj left for Basra (present-day Iraq) where he became a Sufi, a member of a mystical Muslim sect that focused on the "inner way," the spiritual journey toward God. While on a pilgrimage to Mecca, al-Hallaj, acting counter to the Sufi tradition of secrecy, began publicly proclaiming the need for union with God. From Mecca he traveled throughout present-day Iran, India, and Turkistan, attracting hundreds of followers with his preaching that everyone should find God in their hearts.

Al-Hallaj eventually returned to Baghdad, where his preaching aroused popular emotions and engendered a movement for political and religious reform. He proclaimed not only his burning love of God, but also his desire to offer himself as a sacrifice, "accursed for his community." Ultimately he followed the Sufi path to its limit, announcing that he had found union with God, "I am [God] the Truth."

Sunni authorities rejected his assertion and attempted to try him for heresy, but initially the civil authorities refused to get involved in a religious trial. Al-Hallaj, himself, claimed that his mystical union placed him and his followers beyond the confines of both religious and secular law. Nevertheless, as concern over his influence grew, he was put on trial in 908 and imprisoned in 913. During that time he wrote several works suggesting that mystical union would bring a believer closer to God than even Muhammad had been able to achieve. His trial was reopened in 921, and he was sentenced to death by beheading. He was executed in Baghdad on March 27, 922.

Legacy

Al-Hallaj generated the branch of Sufi mysticism that broke ties with both Sufi traditions of secrecy and the accepted theology of the Sunni branch of Islam, the largest Muslim group.

Al-Hallaj became the *shaikh* (founding master) of the *tarikc* (religious community), known as the Halladjiyya, which continued his basic teachings. Central among these teachings was the commitment to preach publicly to attract new members. Their preaching focused on the concept of *wahdat al-shuhud*, the unity of being. The disciples of al-Hallaj believed that through their mystical practices they could unite their being directly with God, making them superior to others who were able to follow only the *Shariah*, the law of Islam.

Oddly, their "role models" were Iblis (the devil) and the Pharaoh who enslaved the Hebrew people. Both Iblis, who was a fallen angel, and Pharaoh suffered the wrath of God yet continued to pursue their goals. Iblis, especially, never rejected the majesty of God and refused to bow to Adam. Their transgressions of God's law led them to a relationship of love with God that became an archetype for the perfect Sufi based on a "higher law."

These teachings ran counter to the traditional religious norms both of the Sufis and the Sunnis. Since the time of the *shaikh* Nur, the Sufi, fearing persecution, observed a rule of silence. Thus, the open preaching of the disciples of al-Hallaj led to condemnation by their fellow mystics. Opposition from Sunni groups was directed at the teaching itself. Because the Sunnis believed that the teachings of Muhammad are the *direct teachings of Allah,* not only must the Prophet be revered, but the teachings themselves must also be obeyed. ("Islam" means "surrender," obviously, to the revealed will of Allah.) Thus, the contention that the mystic could become more perfect than the *Shariah* and Muhammad was tantamount to blasphemy.

The earliest followers of al-Hallaj suffered from the effects of these teachings. Immediately after the death of their master, his followers scattered. In 924 and 925, those who remained in Baghdad suffered the same fate as their *shaikh.*

Among those who fled, some traveled to Khurasan in eastern Iran, where they took part in the Hanafi-Maturidi reform movement. In most places where the Halladjiyya appeared, they were accused of holding extreme religious positions. In the twelfth century, the Halladjiyya attracted some philosophical adherents whose concept of reason corresponded to the mystical concept of the *Shariah*'s limits. By the twentieth century, there were no more formal followers of al-Hallaj, although some Sunnis have adopted portions of his thought.

von Dehsen

For Further Reading:

Mason, Herbert W. *Al-Hallaj*. London: Curzon Press, 1994.

Massignon, Louis. *The Passion of Hallaj: Mystic and Martyr of Islam*. Princeton, N.J.: Princeton University Press, 1982.

Mir Futurus, 'Ali. *Hallaj*. Encino, Calif.: Ketab Corp., 1987.

Han-fei-tzu

Major Scholar of Chinese
Legalist School
c. 280–c. 233 B.C.E.

Life and Work

Han-fei-tzu was a legal scholar who synthesized and articulated Chinese legal theory in what came to be called the Legalist School.

Han-fei-tzu was born to an influential family around 280 B.C.E. in the central Chinese state of Han. As a young man he studied with the Confucian scholar HSÜN-TZU (c. 298–238 B.C.E.). He had hoped to become a legal counselor to the king of Han, but met with no success. Frustrated, Han-fei-tzu defended his theories of government in at least 55 essays later collected under the title *Han fei Zi*. When the state of Qin was threatening war with the state of Han, the king of Han sent Han-fei-tzu to Qin to negotiate a peace. The king of Qin was so impressed with Han-fei-tzu's legal abilities that he thought of giving him a post in his own kingdom. Nevertheless, the ruler ultimately questioned his loyalty and, on the advice of Li Si, Han-fei-tzu's former schoolmate and the prime minister, ordered Han-fei-tzu's death.

Han-fei-tzu's legal theory is based on the premise that most human beings are motivated by self-interest. A ruler, thus, can construct a clear and distinct set of laws based on reward and punishment, the "two handles" of government, to preserve order and to repel chaos. Consequently, Han-fei-tzu became a critic of Confucianism, which builds on the assumed goodness of people and their ability to adhere voluntarily to beneficial and reciprocal social obligations.

Han-fei-tzu argued that there were three elements of good government: law, power, and statecraft. Law (*fa*) must provide clear and distinct rules for behavior in order to promote social stability. He likened the law to a chalk line drawn by a carpenter to cut a straight line. Just as a carpenter cannot tolerate a crooked cut, so also a society cannot tolerate deviant behavior. This concept leads to the second element: power (*shi*). A ruler must use swift and severe punishment to enforce the law. Such punishment ensures social conformity; lenient punishment only invites disrespect for the law. The final element is statesmanship (*shu*). Although the ruler should retain all power, he must learn to delegate it effectively without allowing the bureaucracy to amass power of its own.

Han-fei-tzu was forced to take poison around 233 B.C.E. in the state of Qin.

Legacy

Han-fei-tzu's theory of legalism had an immediate impact on the First Emperor, Qin Shi Huangdi (r. 221–210 B.C.E.), and became an important theoretical foundation for the Legalist School.

Ironically the First Emperor was guided by the counsel of Li Si, Han-fei-tzu's executioner and proponent of the very legalist principles Han-fei-tzu espoused. During his reign, the First Emperor became a ruthless autocrat who attempted to unify China under one ruler and one law. Following Han-fei-tzu's program for a strong government, he relocated citizens and troops throughout China to prevent rebellion against his harsh methods. He also issued an order to burn all books except those on such practical matters as agriculture and medicine. Those scholars who refused to comply with this order were buried alive.

After the demise of the First Emperor, the Legalist School fell out of favor. During the Han Dynasty (206 B.C.E.–220 C.E.), Confucian principles of social order through education, not coercion, became dominant. Only Han-fei-tzu's principles of statesmanship survived to help guide the organization of government and society.

Communist leader Mao Tse-tung revived the First Emperor's memory in 1958. Mao praised the First Emperor for exterminating his opponents, in essence using the emperor as a model of his own efforts to impose uniformity of law and culture upon China. After an attempt on his life in 1971 for being a modern-day First emperor, Mao inaugurated a program to rehabilitate the ruler's reputation. As part of this program, Mao ordered the emperor's tomb unearthed, disclosing the huge number of terra-cotta soldiers buried with the emperor to protect him.

von Dehsen

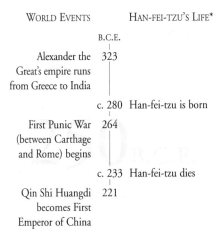

WORLD EVENTS		HAN-FEI-TZU'S LIFE*
	B.C.E.	
Alexander the Great's empire runs from Greece to India	323	
	c. 280	Han-fei-tzu is born
First Punic War (between Carthage and Rome) begins	264	
	c. 233	Han-fei-tzu dies
Qin Shi Huangdi becomes First Emperor of China	221	

* *Scholars cannot date the specific events in Han-fei-tzu's life with accuracy.*

For Further Reading:

Peerenboon, R. P. *Law and Morality in Ancient China*. Albany: State University of New York Press, 1993.

Wang, Hsia-po, and Leo Chang. *Philosophical Foundations of Han Fei's Political Theory*. Honolulu: University of Hawaii Press, 1986.

Hegel, Georg Wilhelm Friedrich

Pioneer of Dialectical Historical
Method
1770–1831

Life and Work

Georg Wilhelm Friedrich Hegel became the foremost Idealist philosopher and a major inspiration of modern historical studies.

The son of a revenue officer, Hegel was born on August 27, 1770, in Stuttgart, Germany. In 1788, he began theological studies at the University of Tübingen, joining the young poet J. C. F. Holderlin and his future philosophical rival Friedrich Schelling in celebrating Greek tragedy and the French Revolution. As a private tutor in Bern and Frankfurt, Hegel's passionate theological concerns fueled by IMMANUEL KANT's reflections on religion became more philosophical. Joining Schelling in Jena, Germany, in 1801, he gradually developed his comprehensive philosophical system through his lectures while writing *The Phenomenology of Spirit* (1807). He completed this seminal work as Napoleon's troops battled outside the city. While the principal of a Nuremberg gymnasium (college preparatory school in Germany) from 1808 to 1816, Hegel published his *Science of Logic* and, after a year as a professor at the University of Heidelberg,

accepted a prestigious professorship at the University of Berlin. Renowned throughout Europe and considered the "official" Prussian philosopher (Prussia was a German state in what is now eastern Germany), Hegel presented richly illustrated lectures on aesthetics, the philosophy of religion, and the philosophy of history. He eventually became the university rector in 1830.

In his philosophy Hegel interprets the Christian doctrine of the Trinity as the Father's eternal generation of the Son joined again in the Holy Spirit of love. He envisions every aspect of every kind of reality as a phase of a rationally unfolding absolute Spirit or Mind (*Geist*). This Spirit actualizes itself in the ever more complicated development of nature, consciousness, history, and philosophical thinking. Lacking existence apart from natural, human, and historical reality, the divine, infinite, rational Spirit constitutes the internal principle of dialectical development. Just as the inherent potential of a seed necessarily assures both its negation and preservation in the production of a blossom- and fruit-bearing tree, so too every finite, partial reality is negated, and yet preserved, as it advances toward a more complete, rational actualization. Inorganic reality produces life, life becomes conscious, and consciousness attains self-conscious expression in political organization, works of art, systematic religion, and ultimately in systematic philosophical knowledge of this entire process. When thinkers comprehend each historical phase of this dialectic as necessary to their own knowledge of it, they embody absolute Spirit's highest actualization—the freedom of knowing itself as manifested in every stage and aspect of the unfolding universe.

In the summer of 1831, Hegel and his family fled Berlin following an outbreak of cholera. He returned to Berlin only to die of the illness on November 14, 1831.

Legacy

Hegel stands both as the last great advocate of European rationalism and as the pioneer of a dialectical historical method that inserts humanity into all the tension-filled contradictions of complex concrete experience.

Seeking eternal rational principles in the churning flux of oppositions, Hegel spawns incredibly diverse and far-reaching intellectual and political offspring. In the 1840s, theologically conservative Hegelians defended the ideas of a separately existing God and of personal immortality against

Hegel's pantheism and his claim that mythic religious images such as God as father are more adequately expressed as Absolute Spirit. Others like David Strauss (1808–1874) argued that humanity itself, not JESUS alone, is God incarnate, or maintained with Ludwig Feuerbach (1804–1872) that humanity, alienated from its genuine potential, projects that potential in the idea of God only to reclaim it through the historical actualization of human potential. KARL MARX (1818–1883), however, contended that such dialectical development of religious ideas is the expression of the more basic unfolding of the historical–material conditions of humanity's production of life's necessities.

Marx, and many socialist and communist thinkers thereafter, argued that humanity's rational self-actualization will occur when people decide, historical circumstances permitting, to create by revolution an economic-political-social order that supports everyone's self-actualization.

Although such historical realization grows from the inner contradictions of historical economic conditions rather than from some metaphysical image called Spirit, Hegel's dialectical method is essential to such thinking because it recognizes that change necessarily flows out of present tension-filled circumstances. In Denmark, SØREN AABYE KIERKEGAARD (1813–1855) humorously opposed Hegelian-inspired Lutheran theology in the name of the concrete, existing believer alone before God while simultaneously offering dialectical reflections on the task of human realization.

Literate German immigrants fleeing the aftermath of the 1848 political turmoil (stemming from revolutions in France, Germany, and the Hapsburg Empire) transplanted Hegelian methods and ideas of history to American soil. Members of the St. Louis Philosophical Society interpreted American Western settlement as historically inevitable, and thinkers in Cincinnati such as August Willich and John Bernard Stallo later argued that labor unions and democracy manifested humanity's essential actualization.

The methodological and substantive influence of Hegel's thought waxed and waned in Europe, England, and America until 1945. Since then Marxists, existential thinkers, phenomenologists, and others reacting to the narrowly focused, abstract nature of much Anglo-American philosophy have returned to Hegel's provocative insights into logic, aesthetics, and political institutions, as well as his insights into the inescapably historical individual who, perhaps in spite of himself, still strives for complete and universal truth.

Magurshak

WORLD EVENTS		HEGEL'S LIFE
	1770	Georg Hegel is born
United States independence	1776	
	1788	Hegel studies at Tübingen
French Revolution	1789	
Napoleonic Wars in Europe	1803–15	
	1807	*The Phenomenology of Spirit* is published
	1818	Hegel becomes professor at University of Berlin
Greek War of Independence against Turkey	1821–29	
	1830	Hegel becomes rector at University of Berlin
	1831	Hegel dies
Revolutions in Austria, France, Germany, and Italy	1848	

For Further Reading:

Hodgson, Peter. *G. W. F. Hegel: Theologian of the Spirit.* Minneapolis, Minn.: Fortress, 1997.
Kainz, Howard. *G. W. F. Hegel.* New York: Twayne Publishers, 1996.

Heidegger, Martin

Influential Twentieth-Century
Existential Philosopher
1889–1976

Life and Work

Even in his lifetime, Martin Heidegger was one of the most famous and most controversial of twentieth-century philosophers. Dismissed by many Anglo-American philosophers as tortuously obscure and unphilosophical, his works have inspired significant trends in Western theology, interpretation theory, psychoanalysis, and philosophy as well as severe criticism for certain fascist undercurrents.

Born in Messkirch, Germany, in 1889, Heidegger grew up a Catholic and in 1909 entered the University in Freiburg-im-Breisgaw to prepare for the priesthood. Changing directions, Heidegger focused on Greek philosophy, its medieval development, and phenomenology. (While difficult to define, phenomenology is the attempt to analyze meaning from observations of the "phenomena" in the world.) From 1915 to 1923 he studied at Freiburg and taught there; he then taught at Marburg University from 1923 to 1928. There he completed his first major and most famous work, *Being and Time* (1927). The next year he returned to Freiburg to replace his doctoral advisor, EDMUND HUSSERL, a leading philosopher of phenomenology.

Heidegger continued to lecture in Freiburg until his retirement. His time there was interrupted twice. First, in 1933, the faculty elected him the university's rector, a post he resigned after 10 months but not before joining the Nazi party in 1934. The second break in his post at Freiburg came between 1945 and 1951 when the postwar government forbade him to teach because of his affiliation with the Nazis.

Heidegger's lectures and writings focused on the relationship between human existence and what he names Being (*das Sein*). Taking up ARISTOTLE's question, "What does the verb 'to be' mean in its various senses?," Heidegger explores the same question from several perspectives: through an analysis of classical philosophers, through a phenomenological, that is, descriptive analysis of human existence

as one self-consciously lives it, and through intense meditations on language, works of art, poetry, and culture (e.g., the effects of technology and scientific learning). In all of these open-ended efforts, Heidegger emphasizes that Being in its near incomprehensibility always discloses itself only partially to human beings and in various ways in different epochs. Being realizes itself in each moment, so that it is constantly "Becoming" as each moment passes into the next.

Toward the end of his life, Heidegger turned to questions of language and poetry and their ability to disclose Being. These ideas formed the basis of *Poetry, Language, Thought*, published in 1971. He died in Freiburg in 1976 while overseeing the publication of his collected works and in correspondence with scholars from Japan, India, and North America.

Legacy

Heidegger's impact on European and North American thought is yet to be fully appreciated; his work had a profound effect on existential thought and the philosophy of hermeneutics, the study of how people interpret texts and events.

Heidegger's writings, some yet to be published, continue to engage philosophers today. *Being and Time* redirected phenomenology, which was an abstract philosophical movement, toward a vivid, descriptive analysis of first-person experience even as it raised anew the question of Being.

In the 1930s and 1940s, European thinkers like Miguel de Unamuno (1864–1936), Gabriel Marcel (1889–1973), JEAN-PAUL SARTRE (1905–1980), and Maurice Merleau-Ponty (1908–1961) appropriated Heidegger's insights to construct their own insights into existential thought.

Heidegger's insights also became important for questions related to the interpretation of texts. In Germany, Heidegger's philosophy contributed to the demythologization of the Bible by Rudolf Bultmann (1884–1976), a biblical scholar, and the hermeneutical theories of HANS-GEORG GADAMER (b. 1900). In France, JACQUES DERRIDA (b. 1930) has made Heidegger's work a source for his version of deconstructive thinking—an attempt to analyze the question of meaning with respect both

to the text itself and the presuppositions of the reader. Ultimately, the question becomes whether or not a text can have an objective meaning at all.

By the 1960s, Heidegger's writings were receiving serious attention in North America and Japan, and this scholarship continues to grow. More recently, scholars everywhere have debated the link between Heidegger's brief involvement with the Nazis and his thought. Heidegger's support of the National Socialists has cast a shadow over the impact of his thought.

Magurshak

WORLD EVENTS		HEIDEGGER'S LIFE
Germany is united	1871	
	1889	Martin Heidegger is born in Messkirch
Spanish American War	1898	
World War I	1914–18	
	1927	*Being and Time* is published
	1933	Heidegger elected rector of University of Freiberg
	1934	Heidegger resigns from Freiburg
World War II	1939–45	
	1945–51	Heidegger prohibited from teaching
Mao Tse-tung establishes Communist rule in China	1949	
Korean War	1950–53	
Six Day War between Israel and Arabs	1967	
End of Vietnam War	1975	
	1976	Heidegger dies
Fall of Communism in eastern Europe	1989	

For Further Reading:

Caputo, John. *Demythologizing Heidegger*. Bloomington: Indiana University Press, 1993.

Krell, David. *Martin Heidegger: Basic Writings*. 2nd ed. New York: Harper and Row, 1997

Poggeler, Otto. *The Paths of Heidegger's Life and Thought*. Atlantic Highlands, N.J.: Humanities Press, 1997.

Herodotus

Father of European History
c. 484–c. 425 B.C.E.

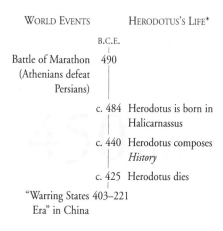

World Events	Herodotus's Life*
	B.C.E.
Battle of Marathon 490	
(Athenians defeat	
Persians)	
	c. 484 Herodotus is born in
	Halicarnassus
	c. 440 Herodotus composes
	History
	c. 425 Herodotus dies
"Warring States 403–221	
Era" in China	

* *Scholars cannot date the specific events in Herodotus's life with accuracy.*

Life and Work

Often called the father of history, Herodotus set the standards and focus of historical writing for centuries.

Herodotus was born in Halicarnassus, a Persian-controlled Greek city in what is now Turkey, around 484 B.C.E. Little is known of the specific events of his life, but it is believed that he was exiled in 457 because of his opposition to Persian rule. He then traveled widely in Asia Minor, Egypt, and the Middle East, gaining firsthand knowledge of the cultures of the Mediterranean world. Around 447 he settled in Athens, where he won the admiration of Athenian leaders, including the great statesman Pericles. In 443 he settled in Thuria, a Greek city in southern Italy, and devoted his life to writing his history of the Persian Wars.

Prior to Herodotus, writers such as Hecataeus (c. 500 B.C.E.) either wrote geographic treatises or presented the stories of the gods in mythical times. Herodotus abandoned these approaches and offered a largely secular, narrative history with a general theme. His *History* (Greek for "inquiry") was perhaps the first creative work written in prose. In a charming, anecdotal style, he traces the development of ancient civilizations to the inevitable clash between Greece, which he considers the center of Western culture, and Persia, the center of culture in the East. His account of the Persian Wars, which is the centerpiece of the work, is still used by modern historians to reconstruct the events of that conflict.

Herodotus's work draws heavily on the understanding of various civilizations he gained in his travels and on eyewitness accounts of recent events. He wrote history to show that the gods punish the evil and arrogant, but he assumed that fortune was so unstable that even the good might suffer. Herodotus emphasized the moral lessons to be learned from important events and viewed history as a means of political education.

Herodotus probably died in Thuria in c. 425 B.C.E.

Legacy

Herodotus produced the world's first comprehensive secular history and in so doing set the course of historical writing and study for centuries. His focus, methodology, and standards dominated historical study until the Middle Ages and were revived during the Renaissance.

Like Herodotus, ancient Greek historians such as the Thucydides (c. 460–400 B.C.E.) and Xenophon (c.430–355 B.C.E.) as well as Romans such as Cato the Elder (234–149 B.C.E.), focused on recent or near-recent political and military events; they left research into culture and society to philosophers. They stressed the importance of presenting history in elegant prose free from bias and had rigorous standards for truthfulness. All Greek and Roman historians attempted to draw moral lessons from important events.

Herodotus's focus on writing about secular events continued to dominate historical writing until the fourth century C.E., when Eusebius of Caesarea produced his *Ecclesiastical History* (c. 325) to present the history of the Christian church. In the following centuries most writers, including AUGUSTINE OF HIPPO (354–430) mixed religious and secular elements to present the relationship between God and humankind in history.

Herodotus's emphasis on secular history was revived in the late Middle Ages and Renaissance by men such as Jean de Joinville, Jean Froissart, and Leonardo Bruni. His stress on literary style became less important as Enlightenment historians in the seventeenth and eighteenth century focused on basic research, amassing collections of documents. Historical focus also broadened during this period as VOLTAIRE (1694–1778) included all aspects of civilization in his *Essay on Manners* (1756).

Contemporary historians have expanded the scope of their discipline beyond politics and have used other disciplines such as sociology, psychology, and anthropology to interpret history. They no longer try to draw moral lessons from past events. Nevertheless, they look to Herodotus as the founder of their discipline and continue to pursue his goal of bringing the past to life.

Renaud

For Further Reading:
Gould, John. *Herodotus*. London: Weidenfeld and Nicolson, 1989.
Hart, John. *Herodotus and Greek History*. New York: St. Martin's Press, 1982.

Heschel, Abraham Joshua

Influential Jewish Theologian and Social Activist

1907–1972

Life and Work

Abraham Joshua Heschel was a Jewish scholar whose work sought to find ways to relate traditional Jewish teachings to the modern world. He embodied his teachings through social activism, especially in the civil rights movement.

Heschel was born in Warsaw, Poland, in 1907 into a deeply religious family. His father was a direct descendant of Dov Ber, an important Hasidic leader. As a young man, he studied the Talmud (Jewish law) and rabbinic literature while developing an interest in Jewish mysticism.

Eager to acquire a secular, Western education, in 1925 Heschel entered the University of Berlin from which he received a doctorate in 1933. In 1938 the Nazis expelled all Polish Jews from Germany, forcing Heschel back to Poland. The following year, an invitation to teach at the Hebrew Union College in Cincinnati enabled him to leave Poland before the Nazi invasion. Heschel stayed in Cincinnati until 1945, when he was appointed a professor of ethics and mysticism at the Jewish Theological Seminary in New York.

Heschel's writings focus on the question of meaningfulness and the role of religion in the twentieth century. Faced with the dominance of reason and with such atrocities as the Holocaust, Heschel sought to develop an understanding of Judaism appropriate for the times. He rejected the proposition that Judaism should be based on reason alone; then it would be reduced to nothing more than a philosophy. He also rejected the proposition that Judaism should be focused on emotions; then it would be reduced to nothing more than psychology. Instead, he constructed a synthesis that built on both modes.

Heschel starts with the concept of "divine pathos." By this he means that God both suffers with and needs the world and its creatures. In turn, humans respond to this pathos by recognizing God's concern both as corresponding to their own and as a commission to carry out the divine commandments.

The way such commandments are manifest in the world is through ethics and, by extension, social action. Heschel himself manifested this teaching by becoming an ardent supporter of Soviet Jewry and a vigorous protester of the Vietnam War. He also worked closely with MARTIN LUTHER KING, JR. in the civil rights movement, standing near King during the March on Selma (Alabama) in 1965. In addition, Heschel helped foster Christian–Jewish relationships by working with Roman Catholic theologians to write "Declaration on the Relationship of the Church to Non-Christians," which emerged from Vatican Council II. This document absolved Jews for the death of Christ and denounced all forms of anti-Semitism.

Heschel wrote many books; the most important of which are *Man Is Not Alone: A Philosophy of Religion* (1951) and *God in Search of Man: A Philosophy of Judaism* (1956).

Heschel died in New York City on December 23, 1972.

Legacy

In the last quarter of the twentieth century, Heschel became the model of the Jewish thinker who wishes to represent both the deep spirituality of the mystical teachings and the rigorous scholarship of Jewish intellectual tradition.

Heschel's mystical background initially led some of his Jewish colleagues to conclude that he was out of step with the modern world. Yet, in post–World War II Judaism, Heschel's concept of divine pathos and his search for God and meaning apart from the limits of the modern world have moved some to go back to his writings as a source of guidance. That he exemplified the mystical strain both as a social activist in support of Soviet Jewry and as a protester against the Vietnam War allowed him to become a model for those who do not wish to compromise their social responsibilities in view of their spiritual feelings.

As a social activist Heschel is remembered as the one who marched with King in Selma. Yet his influence in the civil rights movement is not limited to political involvement. In many discussions with King, Heschel helped the civil rights leader recognize the importance of prophets such as Amos whose words, "But let justice roll down like waters, and righteousness like an everflowing stream," became the theme of the civil rights movement. He also influenced King's comparison of MOSES and the Israelites' escape from slavery in Exodus to the events of the civil rights struggle. Even after the death of both these men, such images remained central to the movement's theological focus. Moreover, Heschel's concept of divine pathos undergirded King's belief that God suffered with the oppressed.

Heschel's most enduring legacy is that his never-ending quest to synthesize the spiritual and intellectual aspects of Judaism in the context of the world's affairs helped others to understand those relationships as well.

von Dehsen

WORLD EVENTS		HESCHEL'S LIFE
Spanish American War	1898	
	1907	Abraham Joshua Heschel is born
World War I	1914–18	
	1933	Heschel receives doctorate from University of Berlin
World War II	1939–45	
	1945	Heschel joins Jewish Theological Seminary
Mao Tse-tung establishes Communist rule in China	1949	
Korean War	1950–53	
	1956	*God in Search of Man: A Philosophy of Judaism* is published
	1965	Heschel joins Martin Luther King in March on Selma
Six Day War between Israel and Arabs	1967	
	1972	Heschel dies
End of Vietnam War	1975	

For Further Reading:

Brown, Moshe. *The Life and Teaching of Rabbi Abraham Joshua Heschel.* Northvale, N.J.: Jason Aronson, 1997.

Kaplan, Edward K. *Abraham Joshua Heschel: Prophetic Witness.* New Haven, Conn.: Yale University Press, 1998.

Hildegard von Bingen, Saint

Major Figure in Medieval
Mystical Tradition
1098–1179

Life and Work

Called the "sibyl (ancient prophetess) of the Rhine," Hildegard von Bingen was one of the most influential religious women of the medieval period.

Born in 1098 in Böckelheim (in present-day Germany), Hildegard was the tenth child of a noble family who dedicated her to the Church at birth. At the age of eight she was placed in the care of Jutta von Spanheim, a religious recluse. Other girls gathered around Jutta and the group eventually formed a Benedictine community. Hildegard became prioress of the group following Jutta's death in 1136. About 11 years later she moved the convent to Rupertsberg, near Bingen, hence her surname.

In 1141 Hildegard had a vision in which God gave her the gift of instantaneous understanding of religious texts and directed her to record her mystical experiences. These visions became the basis for some of the most important mystical writings of the Middle Ages. Her most popular theological work, *Scivias (Know the Ways)*, writ-

ten in the 1140s, was a collection of her early visions designed to serve as a guide to Christians living in a fallen world. Its theology is generally conventional, but Hildegard stretched the bounds of accepted belief by suggesting that virgins dedicated to God as Brides of Christ are his spokespersons. At one point she even hinted that they are equal to the Church fathers. She wrote two other important books based on her visions: *Liber vitae meritorum (Book of Life of Merits)* and *Liber divinorum operum (Book of Divine Works)*, the latter a synthesis of her theological, philosophical, and scientific beliefs.

Not all Hildegard's works were mystical; she also wrote in fields as varied as medicine, physical science, and astrology. Many of these works also reflect her feminist thought. In an era when marriage was thought inferior to the celibate religious life, she extolled the institution and saw husbands and wives as loving, equal partners. Her medical work dealt frankly with female sexuality. She left behind some 300 letters, nearly 80 vocal compositions, and the *Ordo virtutum* (1152), a religious drama set to music that some historians suggest was the first morality play.

Hildegard died in Bingen in 1179.

Legacy

Hildegard was in the forefront of a mystical tradition in which women played a significant role during the Middle Ages and Renaissance. In the twentieth century many feminists extolled her forward-looking views and regarded her as a role model.

Hildegard transcended the role that the medieval Church had set for women. She carried on a voluminous correspondence with the political and religious leaders of the day, including Pope Eugenius (r. 1145–1153), leading theologian BERNARD OF CLAIRVAUX (1090–1153), and Emperor Frederick Barbarossa (r. 1155–1190). She also dared to enter the field of theology, traditionally reserved for men. In an era when nuns were cloistered and women were expressly forbidden to preach, she traveled to cathedrals and universities where her preaching, officially sanctioned by the Church, attracted thousands. Her works were circulated and read throughout Europe.

Hildegard was the first in a line of female mystics that began to blossom in the fourteenth century and culminated with TERESA OF ÁVILA in the sixteenth century. Elizabeth von Schonau

(Hildegard's intimate friend and frequent visitor), Hadewijch of Antwerp, Beatrice of Nazareth, and Mechthild of Magdeburg are to some degree indebted to her. They, in turn, foreshadowed Meister Eckhardt (1260–1328) and St. John of the Cross (1542–1591). Hildegard's works have been in print since the seventeenth century, and the German writer Johann Wolfgang von Goethe (1749–1832) mentions her.

The late twentieth century saw a renewed interest in Hildegard because of her forward-looking ideas, many of which resonated with the feminist movement. Historians studied her views on women's roles and were particularly interested in understanding how Hildegard, living in a period when women's lives were restricted, could have become a theologian, poet, scientist, musician, and healer. For many, the twelfth-century abbess was an inspiration in overcoming social, cultural, and gender barriers.

Hildegard's music also enjoyed a resurgence of popularity in the last decades of the twentieth century. It has found admirers not only among medievalists but also among composers of New Age music who responded to its ethereal qualities. To Hildegard, music represented the recaptured joy and beauty of Eden.

Hildegard was beatified after her death, but because those investigating miracles attributed to her intercession did not leave careful records, she was never canonized (made a saint). Nevertheless, her name is mentioned in Renaissance martyrologies (catalogues of saints) and she is frequently called St. Hildegard.

Renaud

WORLD EVENTS		HILDEGARD'S LIFE
First Crusade	1095	
	1098	Hildegard is born
Crusaders capture Jerusalem during First Crusade	1099	
Settling of Timbuktu, present-day Mali	c. 1100	
	1106	Hildegard is placed in care of Jutta von Spanheim
	1136	Hildegard becomes prioress of community
	1141	Hildegard has important vision
	1140s	Hildegard writes *Scivias*
	1179	Hildegard dies
Islamic ruler of Egypt, Saladin, captures Jerusalem	1187	

For Further Reading:

Flanagan, Sabina. *Hildegard of Bingen, a Visionary Life*. London: Routledge, 1989.

Newman, Barbara. *Sister of Wisdom: St. Hildegard's Theology of the Feminine*. Berkeley: University of California Press, 1987.

Weeks, Andrew. *German Mysticism from Hildegard of Bingen to Ludwig Wittgenstein: A Literary and Intellectual History*. Albany: State University of New York Press, 1993.

Hillel

Influential Rabbi; Interpreter of
Biblical Law

c. 60 B.C.E.–c. 20 C.E.

Life and Work

Hillel was a rabbi who provided the methods of interpretation that enabled Judaism to adapt its historical traditions and biblical teachings to a changing world.

Very little is known of Hillel's life. He was born and educated in Babylon in the first century B.C.E. He then went to Palestine to study with the leading scholars of his day while earning a meager living as a manual laborer. In time Hillel became a noted scholar and so impressed the Sanhedrin (the Jewish ruling court) with his interpretations of law and scripture that it chose him as leader. The second position in the court, traditionally held by the leader of a different interpretive school, eventually was given to the great scholar Shammai, his friend and ideological opponent.

Hillel generally took a more lenient point of view on moral and religious matters than did Shammai, who emphasized tradition. While Shammai stressed strict, literal obedience to the Torah (law), Hillel believed that biblical law could be interpreted to meet changing conditions. He is credited with applying seven basic rules of biblical interpretation, similar to those used by contemporary Hellenistic philosophers, that permitted the use of inference and analogy in understanding a text rather than following a literal interpretation. Later Jewish tradition would describe the differences between the two schools: the House of Shammai had its origin in might and the House of Hillel in mercy.

Hillel was noted for his humility, patience, and kindness as well as his wisdom. Legends grew up around him emphasizing his devotion to the Torah and his deep concern for the poor. One of Hillel's most important opinions illustrates his compassion for the underprivileged and his liberal interpretation of the Torah. The biblical regulation requiring the cancellation of all debts every seven years had the undesired result of making it impossible for the poor to secure a loan in the last years of each cycle.

Hillel established a legal concept, the *prosbul*, in which the loan was made eligible for collection at any time.

Traditionally Hillel has been credited with giving the "negative" Golden Rule. When a non-Jew challenged him to teach the whole of Judaism while standing on one foot, he replied "What is hateful to you do not do to your neighbor."

Legacy

Under the guidance of Hillel, the Jewish community experienced a revolution in its spiritual life that enabled it to deal successfully with the changing world. By teaching and example, he led Judaism to a flexible, but faithful, observance of tradition.

Although Hillel's views were accepted only gradually, their progressive approach, permitting the adaptation of inherited laws rather than literal application, came to dominate Judaism. This approach enabled Jews to maintain their traditions despite the different circumstances they encountered after their dispersal from Israel in the first century C.E. Hillel's approach permitted the further development of Jewish law and narrowed the differences between the dominant groups in the community. His rules for interpreting scripture were adapted and added to by later rabbis, who quoted him frequently in their works.

Hillel and Shammai became the last of the "pairs" (*zugot*) of teachers to lead Jewish life. For decades after their deaths, their influence was so great that the two primary parties of Jewish teaching were the "House of Hillel" and the "House of Shammai." Following Hillel's death, however, the Jewish community abandoned the *zugot* and in its place accepted a dynasty descended from Hillel that ruled the community for 400 years.

Hillel's personality, in which wisdom was combined with humility, patience, love of Torah, and social concern, became the model of conduct for future generations. He established the importance of intellect and interpretation along with tradition. In part because of Hillel, Judaism became a culture in which piety is connected with study. Scholarship and religion are not opposing forces, but go hand in hand.

Osterfield

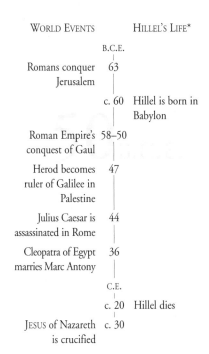

WORLD EVENTS		HILLEL'S LIFE*
	B.C.E.	
Romans conquer Jerusalem	63	
	c. 60	Hillel is born in Babylon
Roman Empire's conquest of Gaul	58–50	
Herod becomes ruler of Galilee in Palestine	47	
Julius Caesar is assassinated in Rome	44	
Cleopatra of Egypt marries Marc Antony	36	
	C.E.	
	c. 20	Hillel dies
JESUS of Nazareth is crucified	c. 30	

* *Scholars cannot date the specific events in Hillel's life with accuracy.*

For Further Reading:

Buxbaum, Yitzhak. *The Life and Teachings of Hillel.* Northvale, N.J.: Jason Aronson, 1994.

Charlesworth, James H. *Hillel and Jesus: Comparative Studies of Two Major Religious Leaders.* Minneapolis, Minn.: Fortress Press, 1997.

Hobbes, Thomas

Political Philosopher; Developer of the Social Contract Theory
1588–1679

Life and Work

Thomas Hobbes was a philosopher and political theorist who proposed a society based on a social contract and on scientific principles rather than on the religious principle of the divine right of kings.

The son of a clergyman, Hobbes was born on April 5, 1588, in Malmesbury, England. He was educated at Oxford, and, in 1608, became the tutor of the son of the Earl of Devonshire. He held this post, with one brief absence, until 1640. From 1634 to 1636 he took his student on an extended European tour, during which he met such notable scientific figures as RENÉ DESCARTES and Galileo Galilei. These encounters greatly influenced his future thought by

WORLD EVENTS		HOBBES'S LIFE
Reformation begins	1517	
	1588	Thomas Hobbes is born in Malmesbury, England
	1608–40	Hobbes becomes tutor to son of Earl of Devonshire
Thirty Years' War in Europe	1618–48	
	1634–36	Hobbes tours Europe and meets Descartes and Galileo
	1640	Hobbes flees to France and becomes tutor for future English king, Charles II
	1651	*Leviathan* is published in France
	1660	Hobbes returns to England
	1666	Parliament bans further publishing by Hobbes
	1679	Hobbes dies
England's Glorious Revolution	1688	

focusing his ideas on contemporary scientific methods and principles.

In 1640, Hobbes fled England, fearing for his safety because he had supported King Charles I in that monarch's unsuccessful conflict with Parliament. Hobbes spent the next 11 years in France as the tutor to the future King Charles II, son of King Charles I. By this time Hobbes had developed a scientific theory of the universe. He concluded that all matter, including the matter composing human beings, could be analyzed by the causes of its motion. For human beings, this causation was emotions. Hobbes especially considered the lust for power and the fear of death as the prime forces for understanding human life. He also abandoned any religious idea of the soul; for Hobbes human beings, like any other components of the universe, were soulless "machines" controlled by objective, scientific principles.

In *Leviathan*, published from France in 1651, Hobbes argues that the ideal form of government is created by people joining together under a social contract. People would agree to suppress their lust for power in exchange for the security and protection afforded by a strong society. To prevent internal dissension and to defend against external threats, Hobbes believed that society should be governed by an absolute sovereign who cannot be deposed. While it was first thought that *Leviathan* was written to defend the power of the king over Parliament, Hobbes never identified the sovereign with a monarch and rejected as unscientific any royal authority based on divine right.

Hobbes returned to England in 1660, when the throne was restored to Charles II. Although Hobbes enjoyed the king's favor, Charles could not protect him from the enemies his controversial theories had created. Parliament investigated *Leviathan* for atheistic tendencies and in 1666 prohibited Hobbes from further publishing. He died on December 4, 1679.

Legacy

One of the most important political philosophers of the modern age, Thomas Hobbes had a profound impact on subsequent political thinking through his ideas on the formation of political society.

Hobbes was one of the first Western political theorists to justify the state in secular rather than religious terms and to view it as arising from a voluntary association of the governed rather than from the divine right of kings. Ironically, this defender of absolutism laid the theoretical groundwork for such liberal political philosophers as JOHN LOCKE, MONTESQUIEU, and JEAN-JACQUES ROUSSEAU.

For all of these later philosophers, Hobbes's understanding of the social contract became the point of departure for their own theories. Rousseau refined Hobbes's theory by asserting that government is bound to follow the general will of the people and is legitimate only insofar as it does so. Locke went further, maintaining that people retain certain inalienable rights even after entering the contract and may revolt if government tramples these rights. Montesquieu put forth a theory of checks and balances limiting the power of the various branches of government to protect the citizenry from breach of the social contract. Through these later philosophers, Hobbes influenced such American political thinkers as THOMAS JEFFERSON and JAMES MADISON as well as leaders of the French Revolution.

Hobbes is also regarded as an important early contributor to psychology and sociology through his application of mechanical principles to human action. He was also an early influence on utilitarian philosophers (who believe that the value of an action is determined by its consequences) such as JEREMY BENTHAM and JOHN STUART MILL.

von Dehsen

For Further Reading:
Green, Arnold W. *The Cambridge Companion to Hobbes.* New Brunswick, N.J.: Transaction Publishers, 1993.
Sorell, Tom, ed. *Hobbes and Human Nature.* New York: Cambridge University Press, 1996.
Tuck, Richard. *Hobbes.* New York: Oxford University Press, 1989.

Hsün-tzu

Influential Confucian Moral
Philosopher
c. 300–c. 230 B.C.E.

Life and Work

Hsün-tzu was a Confucian moral philosopher who emphasized the importance of ritual and education to civilize inherently self-centered human beings.

Hsün-tzu ("Master Hsün") was born in about 300 B.C.E. in the Chinese state of Chao. Although little is known of his background, he probably studied at the respected Jixia Academy. Later he served in several important governmental positions, including advisor to the prime minister of the state of Ch'i, counselor to two kings in the state of Qin, and advisor to a senior minister in the state of Chao.

Hsün-tzu was a devoted follower of the teachings of CONFUCIUS, but he disagreed with some subsequent interpretations of the philosopher's writings. Specifically, he challenged the premise of MENCIUS (c. 371–c. 289 B.C.E.), a noted Confucian thinker, that human beings were basically good. The rituals and education at the heart of Confucianism principally served to nurture that innate goodness to form responsible and ethical citizens.

In contrast to Mencius, Hsün-tzu believed that human beings were essentially selfish and evil, seeking personal gain and pleasure even at the expense of others. Unlike animals, however, human beings also saw the need to construct civil societies and had the potential for rehabilitation through education and ritual. Such actions, however artificial, civilize people and instill in them the important Confucian concept of *li,* a sense of decorum and propriety. One of Hsün-tzu's chief maxims was, "The nature of man is evil; his goodness is acquired by training."

Hsün-tzu's model for such a process was that of the education of an artisan, who honed his craft through repetition of practice drills. Once skilled, such an artisan was able to impose harmony and order on unformed and chaotic raw material.

In good Confucian tradition, therefore, Hsün-tzu endorsed the creation of a harmonious society based on mutual respect and obligation within the context of a strict social order. Although he did not believe in supernatural beings, he taught that Heaven (*Ti'en*) was a moral force that guided the creation of such a society.

Much of Hsün-tzu's teachings were preserved in 32 essays, called chapters, in the volume entitled *Hsün Tzu.* He spent the final years of his life in the city of Lin-lang in Ch'u, where he died in about 230 B.C.E.

Legacy

Hsün-tzu was an influential Confucian moral philosopher whose premise that human beings were essentially evil provided an intellectual counterpoint to the traditional stance of Confucius and Mencius that human beings were inherently good.

The immediate impact of Hsün-tzu's teachings, however, was one he did not anticipate. Two of his most prominent students, HAN-FEI-TZU (c. 280–c. 233 B.C.E.) and Li Si (c. 280–208 B.C.E.), both of whom held prominent governmental positions during the "Warring States Period" (403–221 B.C.E.), took Hsün-tzu's teachings to an extreme in developing the principal ideas of the Legalist School of Thought. In contrast to their teacher, who saw education and ritual as a means for rehabilitating self-centered people, those of the Legalist School contended that the law must control all aspects of life to ensure a peaceful society. Law should impose clear consequences for action by establishing a strict system of rewards and punishments. These laws must be enforced by a strong central ruler, who has absolute control over his own administration and who is ruthless in extinguishing all opposition.

This theory was well carried out in practice. In c. 233 B.C.E. Li Si had Han-fei-tzu poisoned in prison, when Han-fei-tzu was on the verge of replacing him as the king's legal counselor. Later, Li Si became the chief advisor to the first emperor, Qin Shi Huangdi (r. 221–210 B.C.E.). Qin Shi Huangdi unified the six states that made up China and imposed strict imperial rule over the whole country, thus playing out on a large scale what the Legalist School prescribed for the strict rule of kingdoms.

Hsün-tzu's influence remained after the rule of the first emperor ended. His perspective on Confucianism was dominant during the Han Dynasty (206 B.C.E.–220 C.E.), and it was only in the T'ang Dynasty (618–907 C.E.) that the ideas of Mencius began once again to influence Confucian thought. By the time of the Neo-Confucian scholar Zhu Xi (1130–1200), the ideas of Mencius had completely overshadowed those of Hsün-tzu.

Hsün-tzu's most lasting influence may have been his practice of presenting his ideas in essay form. Previously, Confucian writing had consisted largely of collections of sayings from the masters derived from the notes of their students. Thus, Hsün-tzu's mode of writing transformed the basic style of Confucian scholarship.

von Dehsen

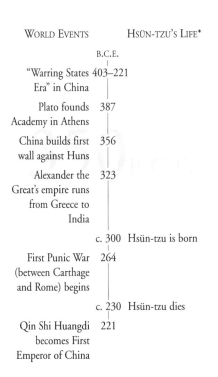

WORLD EVENTS		HSÜN-TZU'S LIFE*
	B.C.E.	
"Warring States Era" in China	403–221	
Plato founds Academy in Athens	387	
China builds first wall against Huns	356	
Alexander the Great's empire runs from Greece to India	323	
	c. 300	Hsün-tzu is born
First Punic War (between Carthage and Rome) begins	264	
	c. 230	Hsün-tzu dies
Qin Shi Huangdi becomes First Emperor of China	221	

* *Scholars cannot date the specific events in Hsün-tzu's life with accuracy.*

For Further Reading:
Berthrong, John H. *Transformations of the Confucian Way.* Boulder, Colo.: Westview Press, 1998.
Cua, A. S. *Ethical Argumentation: A Study in Hsün Tzu's Epistemology.* Honolulu: University of Hawaii Press, 1985.

Hubbard, L. Ron

Founder of the Church of
Scientology
1911–1986

Life and Work

L Ron Hubbard is the founder of the controversial Church of Scientology.

Born in March 1911 in Tilden, Nebraska, Hubbard came from a Navy family that moved often. In 1929 he enrolled at George Washington University, where he studied engineering and atomic physics while working as a photographer, singing on the radio, and writing dramas.

World Events		Hubbard's Life
Spanish American War	1898	
	1911	L. Ron Hubbard is born
World War I 1914–18		
	1929	Hubbard enrolls in George Washington University
World War II 1939–45		
	1941–45	Hubbard serves in U.S. Navy
Mao Tse-tung establishes Communist rule in China	1949	
	1950	First book on *Dianetics* is published
Korean War 1950–53		
	1954	Hubbard opens first Church of Scientology in Los Angeles
	1956	Hubbard begins opening branch churches in Europe
	1966	Hubbard resigns from his church
Six Day War between Israel and Arabs	1967	
End of Vietnam War	1975	
	1982	*Battlefield Earth* is published
	1986	Hubbard dies
Fall of Communism in eastern Europe	1989	

Hubbard wrote fiction from 1933 to 1938, turning out 138 adventure or science fiction novels. He served in the Navy during World War II.

While recuperating from war wounds, Hubbard helped to heal other patients, an experience that formed the basis for his system of psychotherapy called Dianetics. In 1950 he published his ideas in *Dianetics: The Modern Science of Mental Health,* which continued to be a bestseller through the end of the twentieth century. The goal of Dianetics is to erase the reactive mind, full of "engrams" (residual effects of past painful experiences) that prevent people from becoming more ethical, more aware, happier, and saner. This is accomplished by the use of "auditors" who use "E-meters" to monitor a person's recall of emotional experiences. Freed from engrams, an individual becomes a "Clear," or "an optimal individual."

In 1954 Hubbard established the first Church of Scientology in Los Angeles; its philosophy was based on Dianetics. Over the next several years Hubbard added a more spiritual element to his movement. He asserted the reincarnation of the "thetan," or spirit of a person, through eight "dynamics" and the ultimate release of the thetan from the enslavement of the body. His church later established programs to discourage the use of drugs for psychological therapy and to oppose certain traditional methods of psychotherapy.

During the next 12 years, Hubbard opened many branches of his church in the United States and Europe, but in 1966 he resigned from all Scientology organizations. Buying and living on ever larger yachts, Hubbard spent the next 10 years sailing, lecturing, and writing on many of his interests.

After moving to a California ranch in 1976, Hubbard returned to fiction, writing *Battlefield Earth,* a bestseller, in 1982. Hubbard died in California on January 24, 1986, leaving a $600 million estate.

Legacy

A t his death Hubbard left behind a religious movement surrounded by controversy.

Opponents have accused Scientologists of brainwashing their adherents and have pointed out that Hubbard's theories have never been proven scientifically. The church has been called a "cult of greed" for the high prices it charges adherents to its programs. Some have

alleged that Hubbard gave his movement a religious dimension in an effort to benefit from the tax-exempt status of churches. The church is so controversial that several countries, including Germany, limit its activities.

Hubbard, himself, remained controversial throughout his life. Critics accused him of everything from lying about his past accomplishments to wife beating, bigamy, drug addiction, forgery, and writing bad checks. Some charged him with harassing opponents and those who had left the movement. In the 1980s, Hubbard's wife and 10 leading Scientologists were imprisoned for interfering with a government investigation of the church.

In addition to his thriving church, Hubbard left a huge body of writing on many subjects, some of which were incorporated into Scientology. His system of organizational structure and management was used to run the church and was adopted by other companies and organizations around the world. His drug and criminal rehabilitation programs are now part of Scientology centers. He left books on educational methods and comprehension as well as music he had composed and writings on sound recording.

Since Hubbard's death the church has continued to grow, attracting celebrity members such as John Travolta and Tom Cruise. After 25 years the IRS finally granted the Church of Scientology tax-exempt status in 1993. The church now claims to have more than eight million members and 2,000 centers in more than 60 countries, though critics challenge the validity of those figures.

Saltz

For Further Reading:
Miller, Russell. *Bare-faced Messiah: The True Story of L. Ron Hubbard.* London: M. Joseph, 1987.
Corydon, Bent, and L. Ron Hubbard, Jr. *L. Ron Hubbard, Messiah or Madman?* Secaucus, N.J.: L. Stuart, 1987.

Hume, David

Major Enlightenment Philosopher;
Critic of Empiricism

1711–1776

Life and Work

One of the major figures of the Enlightenment, David Hume helped shape the philosophical and political thought of his era through his investigation into the nature of human knowledge.

Hume was born in Edinburgh, Scotland, on May 7, 1711. At the age of 12, he entered the University of Edinburgh, where he immersed himself in the classics. There his youthful doubts about the truth of Christianity were deepened by his philosophical studies, with the result that he became a thorough skeptic. Hume never graduated; instead he continued studying privately until he had a nervous breakdown at age 18. Following his recovery, he turned to business, but lost interest and began writing philosophy.

Hume's philosophical masterpiece was his three-volume *A Treatise of Human Nature* (1739–40) in which he attempted to use the scientific method of Isaac Newton and build on the ideas of philosopher JOHN LOCKE to explain how human beings acquire knowledge. His work was poorly received, in part because it was difficult to understand, and he later regarded it as immature.

Hume condensed and revised this work to clarify his ideas in *An Enquiry Concerning Human Understanding* (1748). In what became his most popular work, he argued that all knowledge can be reduced to impressions (sensations, passions, emotions) and ideas (faint images of the impressions). Ideas are either simple or complex and can be misleading; for example, a flying horse is a possible idea. Reason, he taught, can never demonstrate the connection of cause and effect, which is derived "from nothing but custom"—a combination of contiguity and succession in time. Like GEORGE BERKELEY, he distinguished reason from sensation, but, unlike Berkeley, he denied "spiritual substance." He even denied the existence of the individual self, which he dismissed as "a bundle of different perceptions."

Hume dismissed the argument for the existence of God by denying the plausibility of miracles. Here, he contradicted his own argument against causation (see above), because he presumed that reason can, in fact, uncover natural causes for what believers consider miracles.

In 1752 he published *Political Discourses* in which he developed economic theories on interest rates, money supply, and the free market. Between 1754 and 1762 he published his six-volume *History of England,* which broke with tradition in emphasizing the economic and social forces, rather than leaders, that shaped events.

Hume died in 1776 in Edinburgh. *Dialogues Concerning Natural Religion* was published three years after his death.

Legacy

Hume's interests in such disciplines as philosophy, history, and ethics helped shape the thought of the later Enlightenment, particularly in France and Germany.

Hume's influence in economics stems from his close friendship with his fellow Scot, ADAM SMITH. Having developed a monetary theory and ideas about international trade and population growth, Hume taught that wealth depends not on money but on commodities and called attention to the social conditions that influence economics. Smith's famous book, *Wealth of Nations,* published in 1776, the year of Hume's death, developed these ideas and may have been inspired by Hume's theories.

Hume's six-volume *History of England* was regarded as a classic. This work served as a model for later historical literature by documenting dispassionately the deeds of the most prominent people and the impact of the most significant events. Hume also set this historical data into the context of the intellectual life of the most notable citizens. His writing style was clear and intertwined lives and events smoothly. He, therefore, set the standard of excellence for the future writing of history for a general readership.

Although his thought was like that of the Deists, who denied that God interacted with the world, Hume can be better understood as an atheist; his works became a basis for opposition to religion. Belief, he taught, was a particular way of forming an idea. By carrying reason, as expressed in the empirical philosophy of John Locke and Berkeley (for whom all knowledge comes from experience) to its logical conclusion, Hume brought the philosophy of the Enlightenment to its dead end. Even the best thinking, even of science, was not capable of what the Enlightenment had expected. Reason had overstepped its reach and was bankrupt as an absolute judge of reality.

The logical consequence was that everything was uncertain. Hume thus blazed new philosophical directions and contributed to Utilitarian and Positivist philosophy. Both of these philosophies reject a focus on abstract principles in favor of the analysis of concrete data and observable results. He influenced the philosophers JEREMY BENTHAM, AUGUSTE COMTE, WILLIAM JAMES, George Santayana, BERTRAND RUSSELL, Johann Georg Hamann, and IMMANUEL KANT. Reading Hume, Kant testified, awakened him out of his "dogmatic slumber." Bertrand Russell believed that "[T]he growth of unreason in the nineteenth century was a natural sequence to Hume's destruction of empiricism."

Olson

WORLD EVENTS		HUME'S LIFE
English seize Calcutta, India	1690	
	1711	David Hume is born
Peace of Utrecht settles War of Spanish Succession	1713–15	
	1739–40	*A Treatise of Human Nature* is published
	1748	*An Enquiry Concerning Human Understanding* is published
	1752	*Political Discourses* is published
	1754–62	*History of England* is published
United States independence	1776	Hume dies
	1779	*Dialogues Concerning Natural Religion* is published posthumously
French Revolution	1789	

For Further Reading:

Fogelin, Robert. *Hume's Skepticism in the Treatise of Human Nature.* Boston: Routledge & Kegan Paul, 1985.

Norton, David Fate. *David Hume, Common-Sense Moralist, Sceptical Metaphysician.* Princeton, N.J.: Princeton University Press, 1982.

Passmore, John. *Hume's Intentions.* 3rd ed. London: Duckworth, 1980.

Hus, Jan

Czech Reformer of the Christian
Church
1372–1415

Life and Work

Jan Hus was a Bohemian church reformer who used scripture to challenge the authority of the Pope.

Of peasant origin, Hus was born in the small Bohemian town of Husinee and edu-

cated at the University of Prague, then a center of Czech nationalism and the movement for church reform. In 1398 he joined the faculty as a lecturer in theology. He was ordained a priest in 1400 and became dean of the philosophical faculty the following year. Influenced by the fourteenth-century Czech preacher Jan Milic as well as the English reformer JOHN WYCLIFFE, Hus became deeply involved in reform. In 1402, Hus became the preacher of the Bethlehem Chapel in Prague. He used this prominent pulpit to lead the Czech reform movement, denouncing moral corruption among the clergy and attempting to bring religion to the people by preaching in the vernacular (local language) instead of the traditional Latin. His sermons incorporated some of Wycliffe's teachings, including the assertion that Christ, not the Pope, was the true head of the Church and that the Bible rather than church leaders was the ultimate religious authority.

Initially Hus had the support of both the king and the archbishop of Prague, who, in 1406, selected him as the preacher to the Prague synod. However Hus's vigorous attacks on the moral laxity of priests soon provoked opposition among the clergy, who turned the archbishop against him. Under papal direction, the archbishop ordered Wycliffe's books burned and forbade preaching in private chapels, thus hoping to silence Hus. Hus continued to preach in defiance of the order. In 1410 Hus and his followers were excommunicated. He eventually lost the support of the king when he opposed the sale of indulgences in which the king had a financial stake.

By the time of his excommunication Hus had become a symbol of Czech nationalism as well as church reform. Thousands came to hear him preach and street demonstrators pledged him continuing support while denouncing his political and ecclesiastical detractors. Hus persisted in preaching until Prague was threatened with the papal interdict (withholding all sacraments and rites of the Church) in 1412, when he went into voluntary exile. During this time he wrote 15 books, including his most important *De ecclesia (Concerning the Church*, 1413).

In 1414 Hus accepted an invitation to attend the Council of Constance in Germany where he hoped to defend his teachings.

Although he was promised safe conduct, the Council imprisoned him and charged him with heresy. Found guilty, he was burned at the stake on July 6, 1415.

Legacy

Hus's attempt at reform, often called the First Reformation, served as a touchstone for the more successful attempts at reformation in the sixteenth century.

With his death, Hus became a martyr and a national hero. Noble supporters and Bohemian cities united to defend the reform movement. When the king tried to suppress them, a Hussite revolution broke out (1419) that eventually spread through all of Bohemia and parts of Moravia.

Sixteenth-century reformers from the conservative MARTIN LUTHER to the radical Thomas Müntzer embraced Hus as forerunner of their movement. In particular they pointed to his attacks on clerical abuses and immorality and to his principle that scripture is the ultimate authority of the Church. For these reformers Hus's contribution lay primarily in his call for moral reform. Hus had few doctrinal differences with the established Church. He supported the doctrine of transubstantiation, suggested that tradition and conscience had a role, albeit a subordinate one, in the development of doctrine, and believed that good works played a part in salvation—all stands challenged by the sixteenth-century reformers. Nevertheless, these men saw a clear connection to the earlier movement. In his last days Hus warned his captors that they may "roast this goose" (Hus means goose) but a swan will rise up. Luther adopted the swan as his symbol.

The Hussite movement splintered into several groups: The Utraquists (from the Latin for "each of two," referring to the bread and wine of the Lord's Supper), the Calixtine (meaning "goblet"), and the more radical Bohemian Brethren, who embraced more of Wycliffe's teachings. Czech Protestantism was suppressed after 1620, but supporters held fast to their beliefs until the Austrian emperor permitted open practice in 1781. In 1920 the Czechoslovak Hussite Church (or Czechoslovakian National Church) was established to continue the Hussite tradition.

von Dehsen

For Further Reading:
Bonnechose, Emile. *Reformers Before the Reformation.* New York: AMS Press, 1980.
Spinka, Matthew. John *Hus and the Czech Reform.* Hamden, Conn.: Archon Books, 1966.

Husserl, Edmund

Philosopher and Founder of
Phenomenology
1859–1938

Life and Work

Edmund Husserl was a mathematician and philosopher whose inquiries into the ways people comprehend the world resulted in the development of the philosophical theories of phenomenology.

Husserl was born in Prossnits in the present-day Czech Republic on April 8, 1859. He studied science and philosophy at the universities of Leipzig (in Germany), Berlin, and Vienna. After completing his doctorate in mathematics at Vienna, he taught at Halle, Germany, from 1887 to 1901. There he became interested in the psychology of mathematics and published his first book, *The Philosophy of Arithmetic,* in 1891. Later he taught at Göttingen (1901–1916) and Freiburg (1916–1928), both in Germany.

Husserl's curiosity about how the human mind thinks about mathematics led to the first investigations into phenomenology in his books *Logical Investigations* (1901) and *Ideas: General Introduction to Phenomenology* (1913). Husserl postulated that the human mind intends to know things (intentionality), whether or not those things exist in the external world. Things known by the mind are

"phenomena," hence the name "phenomenology." (For example, the words on this page are "objects in the world," but are only meaningful when a reader comprehends them. Further, the reader does not have to have the page available to comprehend the words; the reader can remember them as a phenomenon distinct from the ink on the page.) Husserl also maintained that encounters with any phenomenon, real or abstract, were the same. He further distinguished between ordinary encounters with the elements of the world and a person's reflection on those things.

Later in his life Husserl expanded his analysis to explore the questions of how people understand time, and how scientists deduce scientific and mathematical theories from the "life-world" in which they live.

Husserl developed these theories in two books written later in his career: *Formal and Transcendental Logic* (1929) and *Cartesian Meditations* (1931). Edith Stein and MARTIN HEIDEGGER collected and edited his papers and published them in *Lectures on the Phenomenology of Inner Time Consciousness* (1928).

Husserl died at Freiburg on April 26, 1938.

Legacy

Husserl's theories of phenomenology laid the groundwork for the thought of some of the most influential thinkers of the twentieth century.

Martin Heidegger (1889–1976) was perhaps Husserl's most prominent disciple. He actually replaced Husserl in his academic chair at Freiburg. Heidegger's classic work, *Being and Time* (1927), directly expands the thought of Husserl, while at the same time critiquing it. In answering the question of "being," Heidegger recast it to incorporate the question of meaning as well. His solution was to critique Husserl's premise that the mind could relate to real and abstract objects equally; he redirected phenomenology to focus on how one exists in the world. For Heidegger, "being-in-the-world" was a sufficient context for the mind to engage actual objects and to derive meaning from them. Similarly, the German theological ethicist Max Scheler used Husserl's phenomenological theories in analyzing how social emotions affect the ways people relate to each other.

The French existentialist JEAN-PAUL SARTRE (1905–1980) developed his philosophy of existential consciousness in response to the writings of Husserl. For Sartre, the conscious mind can be aware of itself only in relation to other objects. He returned to Husserl's thesis that the mind addressed real or abstract objects in the same manner. The French existentialist, Maurice Merleau-Ponty emphasized Husserl's theory of "life-world" to develop a theory of bodiliness in the world. As did Heidegger, he concentrated his studies on the way human beings inferred meaning from their relationships to the world.

Husserl's seminal ideas inspired divergent modes of interpretation and continue to find new applications. His theories are influential in the development of such various areas of scholarship as systems theory, literary theory, life-world sciences, concepts relating time and individual identity, and artificial intelligence.

von Dehsen

WORLD EVENTS		HUSSERL'S LIFE
Revolutions in Austria, France, Germany, and Italy	1848	
	1859	Edmund Husserl is born
United States Civil War	1861–65	
Germany is united	1871	
Spanish American War	1898	
	1901	*Logical Investigations* is published
	1913	*Ideas: General Introduction to Phenomenology* is published
World War I	1914–18	
	1928	*Lectures on the Phenomenology of Inner Time Consciousness* is published
	1938	Husserl dies
World War II	1939–45	

For Further Reading:

Bell, David Andrew. *Husserl.* New York: Routledge, 1989.

Hopkins, Burton C. *Husserl in Contemporary Context.* Boston: Kluwer Academic, 1997.

Kowlakowski, Lezlek. *Husserl and the Search for Certitude.* Chicago: University of Chicago Press, 1987.

Smith, Barry, and David W. Smith, eds. *The Cambridge Companion to Husserl.* New York: Cambridge University Press, 1995.

Ignatius of Loyola, Saint

Founder of the Society of Jesus
(Jesuits)
1491–1556

Life and Work

Ignatius of Loyola was the founder of the Roman Catholic Order of the Society of Jesus, commonly known as the Jesuits.

The youngest son of a wealthy noble family, Ignatius was born in the Loyola ancestral castle in the Basque area of Spain in 1491. In 1517 he became a knight in the service of the viceroy of Navarre, who used him in military and diplomatic positions. In 1521, during a battle at Pamplona, Ignatius was struck by a cannonball that badly injured his legs.

During a long convalescence at Loyola, he experienced conversion and decided to do penance for his sins. In early 1522 Ignatius went to Montserrat in Spain, made his confession, and abandoned his military garb. Dressed as a beggar he traveled to Manresa, where he spent the next year practicing austerity, deep meditation, and prayer. While at Manresa he began the first of his

important books, *The Spiritual Exercises,* outlining the essential components of his system of spirituality. The following year was spent on a journey to Jerusalem; he returned to Barcelona in March 1524, where he began his religious studies.

Ignatius spent the next 12 years studying in Spain, Paris, and, finally, in Italy, attracting a small group of followers. In 1534 he and six companions took vows of poverty, chastity, and obedience, and three years later Ignatius and his French companions were ordained in Italy. Ignatius said his first mass in Rome on Christmas Day 1538.

In 1540 Pope Paul III approved the formation of Ignatius's order, the Society of Jesus, which elected Ignatius as their general. Under Ignatius, the Society sent missionaries all over Europe as well as to India, Brazil, and Ethiopia. His interest in developing schools for religious and moral instruction led to the establishment of the Roman College, which later became the Gregorian University. He also founded a home for fallen women and another for converted Jews, both in Rome.

During his last years, Ignatius wrote the *Constitutions,* rules of the Society, in which he ordered members to abandon priestly clothes and many other traditions of religious life; he demanded lengthy training of his followers and forbade a female branch of the order. Jesuits take a special vow of obedience to the Pope.

After several years of illness, Ignatius died in Rome July 31, 1556. He was canonized by Pope Gregory XV in 1622.

Legacy

The Society of Jesus, founded by Ignatius, has become one of the most respected intellectual communities within the Roman Catholic Church. Its members have become leaders in education and chief advisors to church leaders.

Starting with seven members of the Society of Jesus, the Jesuits grew to more than 1,000 at the time of Ignatius's death. The order has flourished , acquiring much influence and remaining the subject of much controversy. The eminent role the Jesuits played as leaders of the Counter–Reformation, as defenders of the Pope, and as one of the most influential orders of the Church has made them a target.

During Ignatius's lifetime and after, the Jesuits took a large role in the Counter–Reformation, the response of the Catholic church to the Protestant Reformation. Known then and now

for their scholarship, they were instrumental in founding many schools. Today there are 90 Jesuit colleges in 27 countries and more than 430 high schools in 55 countries. The United States has 28 Jesuit colleges and universities. Among the Jesuit universities in the United States are Fordham University, Georgetown, and Loyola University of Chicago.

By 1750, the Jesuits were operating 30 astronomical observatories, had established the Gregorian calendar, and had charted five of the world's major rivers. They established important outposts in China, Russia, and South America, where they taught the natives agriculture, metallurgy, music, and printing. In China, the Jesuit Matteo Ricci helped established Christianity and began cultural and economic interchanges with Europe.

In 1773, Pope Clement XIV, under pressure form the Bourbon courts, suppressed and disbanded the order, closed its schools and destroyed its books. The Pope feared the loss of support and the possible loss of influence in other countries. Only in Russia, where Empress Catherine refused to obey the papal order, did the Jesuits remain intact. Restored 41 years later by Pope Pius VII, the Society quickly grew even larger than before.

Since then the Jesuits have provided many scholars, scientists, educators, writers, and explorers. Two of the most prominent of the Jesuits were Teilhard de Chardin (1881–1955), a paleontologist who tried to reconcile science and faith, and Gerard Manley Hopkins (1844–1889), a prominent English poet.

Saltz

World Events		Ignatius's Life
Ottoman Empire captures Byzantine capital, Constantinople	1453	
	1491	Ignatius is born
Columbus discovers Americas	1492	
Last Muslim State in Spain falls to Christians		
Reformation begins	1517	Ignatius becomes a knight
	1521	Ignatius undergoes conversion
	1523	Ignatius travels to Jerusalem
	1524	Ignatius begins religious training
	1537	Ignatius is ordained
	1540	Society of Jesus is formed
	1556	Ignatius dies
Thirty Years' War in Europe	1618–48	

For Further Reading:

Lacouture, Jean. *Jesuits: A Multibiography.* Translated by Jeremy Leggatt. Washington, D.C.: Counterpoint, 1995.

Tellechea Idigoras, Jose Ignacio. *Ignatius of Loyola: The Pilgrim Saint.* Translated, edited, and with a preface by Cornelius Michael Buckley. Chicago: Loyola University Press, 1994.

Israel ben Eliezer

(Baʻal Shem Tov)

Founder of the Jewish Hasidic
Movement

c. 1700–1760

Life and Work

Israel ben Eliezer, commonly known as Besht, an acronym for Baʻal Shem Tov, "Master of the Good Name," founded Hasidic Judaism. (Hasidism is a form of Jewish piety that focuses on the realization of the relationship with God in all aspects of life.)

Besht was born in the town of Okopy in the southern Ukraine in 1700. There are no historically verifiable sources that describe his life; what information is available about him comes largely from later legend.

Around 1738, Besht emerged from the Carpathian Mountains of Eastern Europe, preaching that God could be known through emotions as well as through the study of the Talmud. He was also a healer and exorcist. His powers as a preacher attracted many followers, including teachers of the Torah and Kabbalah (Jewish mysticism), among them Yaʻaqov Yosef of Polonnoye (d. 1782), whose works later became a source of Besht's teachings, and Dov Ber of Mezherich (d. 1772), a future leader of the movement.

Besht rejected the impersonal rabbinical tradition of Torah interpretation in favor of one advocating *devequt* (cleaving), spiritual union with God. Since for Besht there was no distinction between the holy and common, he asserted that *devequt* was possible not only through worship and prayer, but also through the ordinary activity of everyday life. Thus, *devequt* became for Besht the principal means for an individual attaining spiritual communion with the divine realm. He even believed that evil could be transformed into good by elevating it to the realm of God.

Besht was convinced that his own prayers had a special impact on God and could benefit others as well. He also believed that righteous ones would appear in each generation with similar mystical powers.

Some scholars contend that the Hasidic movement under Besht came as a response to the failed messianic claims of Shabbetai Tsvei (1626–1676), a messianic pretender who abandoned Judaism for Islam in 1666. Under Besht the Hasidic movement responded to the "Shabbetean crisis" by encouraging strenuous pietistic (Hasidic) obedience in all aspects of life to restore the religious confidence destroyed by Shabbetai. One legend has it that Besht tried to rescue Shabbetai from hell, but Besht only barely escaped Shabbetai's efforts to drag him down into hell.

Besht died in 1760, in Medzhibozh, in Podolia, Poland, where he lived for much of his later life.

Legacy

Through life and legend, Besht established a pattern of Jewish pietism that was to blossom into the Hasidic movement of the nineteenth and twentieth centuries. Hasidism has become a prominent component of twentieth-century Judaism.

Besht's idea of righteous ones in each generation formed the basis for the doctrine of the *tsaddiq* (righteous one) that later became central to Hasidic Judaism. Each Hasidic community is directed by such a holy person whose principal responsibility is to serve as an intermediary between the faithful and God. Free from sin, the *tsaddiq* works for the spiritual well-being of others. Moreover, like some forms of Jewish mysticism, Hasidic Judaism downplays the role of the Messiah, who would come from outside to liberate the community from its oppressors. Instead, the emphasis on spiritual well-being focused on the internal, individual process of developing a direct relationship with God.

In some respects, Hasidic communities have teachings no different from the official teachings of rabbinic Judaism. Nevertheless, the Hasidim emphasize that individual believers can achieve *devequt*, connection with God, not only through prayer and worship, but also through the ordinary acts of everyday life.

Immediately following the death of Besht in 1760, his disciples took up his mantle and continued the Hasidic movement in Mezhirich (present-day Poland). From 1760 to 1772, Dov Ber guided the community. After his death, several of Dov Ber's disciples established "courts," places for Hasidim to meet with the *tsaddiq* at the center of larger communities. From 1773 to 1812, the Hasidic movement spread dramatically, becoming a major force in Eastern European Judaism.

It was during this period that the Hasidim were persecuted by other Jewish groups, who feared the Hasidic emphasis on emotion would undermine the traditional social structure that valued scholars. While this persecution did not stunt its growth, it did precipitate the expansion of the Hasidic movement into the Ukraine. Over time, these Hasidic communities became the largest Jewish groups in Eastern Europe. This growth continued until the movement was almost destroyed by the Holocaust.

Several Hasidic groups migrated to the United States during and after World War II. The communities grew rapidly because of a high birth rate, but the American Hasidim number no more than 150,000. Nevertheless they have had an impact that far outweighs their number. They have reinvigorated American Orthodox Judaism, and their traditions and legends have become a part of the substance of American Judaism.

von Dehsen

WORLD EVENTS		BESHT'S LIFE*
English seize Calcutta, India	1690	
	1700	Israel ben Eliezer (Besht) is born
Peace of Utrecht settles War of Spanish Succession	1713–15	
	c. 1738	Besht begins preaching and healing
	1760	Besht dies
United States independence	1776	

* *Scholars cannot date the specific events in Besht's life with accuracy.*

For Further Reading:

Ben-Amos, Dan, and Jerome R. Mintz, eds. and trans. *In Praise of Baal-Shem Tov: The Earliest Legends About the Founder of Hasidism.* New York: Schocken Books, 1984.

Rosman, Murray Jay. *Founder of Hasidim: A Quest for the Historical Baʻal Shem Tov.* Berkeley: University of California Press, 1996.

James, William

Preeminent American Psychologist;
Philosophical Pragmatist
1842–1910

Life and Work

William James was a psychologist and philosopher whose work had a profound impact on both disciplines. His work in psychology opened doors for new methods of experimentation. As a pragmatist, James laid the groundwork for the study of the complex relationship between human beings and their interaction with the world around them.

Born in New York City on January 11, 1842, James was the son of theologian Henry James, Sr., and brother of future novelist Henry James. He earned a medical degree from Harvard in 1869; the following year, he joined the college's philosophy department. Ultimately James became interested in psychology. In 1880, he created the first experimental psychology laboratory in the United States and, in 1889, became professor of psychology at Harvard. Ten years later James published *The Principles of Psychology* (1890), a landmark in the transformation of that discipline from an abstract philosophy to an experimental science.

The study of psychology brought James, in turn, to questions of religion—the existence of God, the immortality of the soul, and free will versus determinism. James accepted the idea of free will. "My first act of free will," he wrote, "shall be to believe in free will." That decision was reflected in his discussions of psychology, philosophy, scientific method, human qualities, and the nature of reality. In *The Will to Believe* (1897), he argued that one can choose belief even beyond the reach of reason and evidence. The existence of divinity, he argued in *The Varieties of Religious Experience* (1902), was established by the record of human religious experience. "Like love, like wrath, like hope, ambition, jealousy, like every other instinctive eagerness and impulse it [religion] adds to life and enchantment, which is not rationally deducible from anything else."

Opposing all absolutes, James emphasized the importance of experience, calling his philosophical program "radical empiricism." A person does not experience events in isolation; rather, James argued, a person experiences the external world as a "stream of consciousness," linking experiences together. The meaning of an idea, he argued, can be found only in its experimental consequences. In *Pragmatism* (1907), he expanded on the ideas of Harvard philosopher CHARLES SANDERS PEIRCE, explaining pragmatic truth as whatever is "expedient in the way of our thinking." His *Essays in Radical Empiricism* (1912), published posthumously, advocated an integration of all experience as foundation for a phenomenalist analysis of human experience.

He died of heart failure in New Hampshire on August 26, 1910.

Legacy

James, who became the "guru" of philosophy in the English-speaking countries, bequeathed to his country a body of work of the first rank. From the perspective of Europe in the latter nineteenth century, the United States was a philosophical backwater. Nevertheless, his work gained the respect of many scholars on both sides of the Atlantic.

As popularizer of pragmatism, he influenced JOHN DEWEY (1859–1952) in the United States, BERTRAND RUSSELL (1872–1970) in England, and EDMUND HUSSERL (1859–1938) in Germany; each of these scholars continued the effort to connect the world of ideas with life, lived in the world of matter. Dewey built his theories on the premise that all education ought to be "pragmatic," that is, ought to link learning skills and abstract concepts with practical activities. Russell's theory of logic grew from the connection between knowledge and actual matter. Husserl founded the philosophical school of phenomenology, the attempt to analyze how external objects are perceived and how those perceptions influence the interpretation of those objects.

James also enjoyed wide influence on those outside philosophical circles—historians, literary critics, writers like Walt Whitman, and scientists such as Niels Bohr and Albert Einstein. These scientists strove to link the highly abstract theories of physics to the conclusions drawn from actual data collected by scientific observation. The "stream of consciousness" structure, characteristic of the works of James Joyce (1882–1941), Virginia Woolf (1882–1941), and William Faulkner (1897–1962), was probably inspired by James's use of the same expression. Together with the influence from the Moral Rearmament movement (Buchmanism, Oxford Movement), James is partly responsible for the "twelve step" program for curing alcoholism. This program grounds a practical method for overcoming addiction in a spiritual, or transcendent, set of beliefs.

James's ideas continue to be popular in America. His emphasis on religious experience rather than doctrine, for example, tends to legitimatize American religious pluralism. Therefore, people from different religious backgrounds could join together for a common religious experience.

James's hardheaded, practical, and optimistic philosophical pragmatism is particularly suited to the American psyche: ideas are true only when they are useful and have practical applications. After a century, James continues to be relevant in the discipline of psychology; his *Principles of Psychology* is still a best-seller.

Olson

WORLD EVENTS	JAMES'S LIFE
Greek War of 1821–29 Independence against Turkey	
	1842 William James is born
Revolutions in 1848 Austria, France, Germany, and Italy	
United States 1861–65 Civil War	
	1869 James earns M.D. from Harvard Medical School
Germany is united 1871	
	1889 James becomes professor of psychology at Harvard
	1890 *The Principles of Psychology* is published
	1897 James becomes professor of philosophy at Harvard
	The Will to Believe is published
Spanish American 1898 War	
	1902 *The Varieties of Religious Experience* is published
	1907 *Pragmatism* is published
	1910 James dies
	1912 *Essays in Radical Empiricism* is published posthumously
World War I 1914–18	

For Further Reading:

Barzun, Jacques. *A Stroll With William James.* New York: Harper & Row, 1983.

Levinson, Henry. *The Religious Investigations of William James.* Chapel Hill: University of North Carolina Press, 1981.

Simon, Linda. *Genuine Reality. A Life of William James.* New York: Harcourt Brace, 1998.

Jefferson, Thomas

Principal Author of the U.S.
Declaration of Independence
1743–1826

Life and Work

Thomas Jefferson was the principal author of the Declaration of Independence and a political thinker whose ideas influenced the course of United States history; he served as third president of the United States.

The son of a self-made planter, Jefferson was born in a log cabin on the western frontier of Virginia (now Albemarle County) on April 13, 1743. He attended the College of William and Mary but left before graduation to study law. He was admitted to the bar in 1767 and the following year won election to the House of Burgesses (the lower chamber of the Virginia legislature). There he became a member of the radical faction questioning British colonial policies.

Jefferson's forceful presentation of his views in *The Summary View of the Rights of British North America* (1774) resulted in his appointment to the Continental Congress, which asked him to draft the Declaration of Independence in 1776. Drawing on the intellectual tradition of the Enlightenment, he asserted that all "men" were created equal and born with certain natural rights, which governments were formed to protect. If governments failed to do so, the people had the right to overthrow them.

As governor of Virginia from 1779 to 1781,

Jefferson fought to disestablish the Anglican church in the state. (Established churches received public financial support.) A passionate proponent of the total separation of church and state, what he called "a wall of separation," he drafted the Virginia Statute for Religious Freedom. This measure, finally passed in 1786, guaranteed free expression of religion and prohibited the use of taxes to support religious institutions. It became the model for the First Amendment of the United States Constitution.

Expansion of personal liberty was the central theme of Jefferson's writing and career. He generally supported the Constitution of 1787 but called for carefully limiting federal powers to those expressly granted the national government by the Constitution. Most power, he maintained, should reside with the states, the segment of government closest to the people. Fearing that the strong national government created under the Constitution could lead to tyranny, he pushed for a bill of rights to protect individual liberty.

As secretary of state (1790–1793) and vice president (1797–1801), Jefferson led the opposition to attempts to expand federal power. Following passage of the repressive Alien and Sedition Acts in 1798, he drafted the Kentucky Resolutions suggesting that states had the right to nullify objectionable laws.

President from 1801 to 1809, Jefferson oversaw the vast expansion of the United States through the Louisiana Purchase (1803). He died on July 4, 1826—50 years after the signing of the Declaration of Independence.

Legacy

Jefferson's thought has had a profound impact on United States history. The ideas expressed in the Declaration of Independence are seminal to American political philosophy; his views on government shaped political debate in the United States; his belief in the importance of individual rights helped define the American concept of freedom; and his thoughts on religious liberty influenced American understanding of the relationship between church and state.

Historians have described the Declaration of Independence as "the American creed," the ideas that are the core of American civil values. Its prologue, "We hold these truths to be self-evident, that all men are created equal," has been the basis for America's great political struggles, including the women's suffrage and the civil rights movements.

Jefferson's narrow construction of the Constitution helped lay the foundation for the doctrine of states' rights. As this developed in the first half of the nineteenth century, men such as South Carolina's Senator John C. Calhoun argued that each state had the right to nullify any federal law it deemed unconstitutional. The Supreme Court used the states' rights position in *Dred Scot v. Sanford* (1857) when it supported the supremacy of state laws over federal statutes in governing slavery. Ultimately, the South employed the doctrine to justify secession in 1860.

An emphasis on individual freedom became a defining element of United States society. The Bill of Rights, which Jefferson advocated, played little role in citizens' lives during the nineteenth century, when Americans thought the right to property to be primary in preserving liberty. By the end of the twentieth century, however, personal rights became central in defining their concept of freedom. Beginning in the 1940s, the Supreme Court gave fundamental liberties such as freedom of speech and religion special protections, and in the 1960s it presided over a rights revolution that expanded individual freedoms beyond those specifically articulated in the Bill of Rights.

Jefferson used the phrase "wall of separation" to describe the relationship he envisioned between church and state. During the twentieth century most Americans accepted total separation, and the concept formed the foundation of Supreme Court decisions on religion and government, many of which included Jefferson's phrase.

von Dehsen

WORLD EVENTS		JEFFERSON'S LIFE
	1743	Thomas Jefferson is born
	1768	Jefferson wins election to Virginia's House of Burgesses
United States independence	1776	Jefferson writes Declaration of Independence
French Revolution	1789	
	1790–93	Jefferson serves as secretary of state
	1801–09	Jefferson serves as president of the United States
Napoleonic Wars in Europe	1803–15	
	1826	Jefferson dies
Revolutions in Austria, France, Germany, and Italy	1848	

For Further Reading:
Burstein, Andrew. *The Inner Jefferson: Portrait of a Grieving Optimist.* Charlottesville: University Press of Virginia, 1996.
Cunningham, Noble E., Jr. *In Pursuit of Reason: The Life of Thomas Jefferson.* Baton Rouge: Louisiana State University Press, 1987.
Malone, Dumas. *The Sage of Monticello.* Boston: Little, Brown, & Company, 1981.

Jeremiah

Biblical Prophet Influential in Diaspora Judaism
c. 645–c. 570 B.C.E.

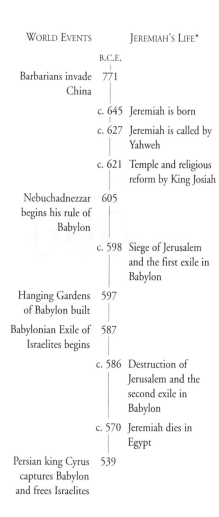

WORLD EVENTS		JEREMIAH'S LIFE*
	B.C.E.	
Barbarians invade China	771	
	c. 645	Jeremiah is born
	c. 627	Jeremiah is called by Yahweh
	c. 621	Temple and religious reform by King Josiah
Nebuchadnezzar begins his rule of Babylon	605	
	c. 598	Siege of Jerusalem and the first exile in Babylon
Hanging Gardens of Babylon built	597	
Babylonian Exile of Israelites begins	587	
	c. 586	Destruction of Jerusalem and the second exile in Babylon
	c. 570	Jeremiah dies in Egypt
Persian king Cyrus captures Babylon and frees Israelites	539	

* Scholars cannot date the specific events in Jeremiah's life with accuracy. This chronology is based on the biblical account.

Life and Work

Jeremiah was the biblical prophet who laid the theological foundations for the Judaism of the Diaspora (Jews living outside of Palestine).

Born into a priestly family in Anathoth, a town in the kingdom of Judah, Jeremiah began prophesying c. 627 B.C.E. His earliest datable prophecies condemned the believers in Yahweh for their lack of faith and social justice.

Jeremiah's thoughts matured during a period of social and religious reform led by King Josiah (ruled 639–609 B.C.E.), who sought to reestablish proper Temple ritual. Ultimately Jeremiah's own ideas went beyond mere ritual reform to anticipate a new covenant based on individual responsibility and not the Mosaic law. During the reign of Josiah's successor, Jehoiakim (609–598 B.C.E.), Jeremiah delivered his famous "Temple Sermon," in which he denounced the people's dependence on the Temple, arguing that Yahweh was not tied to a single place. This concept became central to the continuation of Judaism during the Diaspora.

Between the death of King Josiah in 609 B.C.E. and the sack of Jerusalem by the Babylonians in 586 B.C.E., Jeremiah's prophecies related largely to international politics. During this period, a series of Judean kings refused to pay tribute to their overlords in Babylon, eventually prompting an invasion. Jeremiah supported the unpopular idea of continued submission to Babylon in order to preserve peace. He predicted the conquest of Judah and subsequent removal of Jews to captivity in Babylon, interpreting these events as punishment from Yahweh for the people's unfaithfulness. For his views he was called a traitor and treated like a criminal, held captive first in an empty cistern and then under house arrest. Following the Babylon's capture of Jerusalem in 586 B.C.E., Jeremiah was forcibly taken to Egypt by a group of Judean rebels. He was probably murdered there in 570 B.C.E.

Legacy

Jeremiah had little impact on his contemporaries, who ignored his warnings. Nevertheless his influence on Judaism is significant. His Temple Sermon laid the theological foundation for Diaspora Judaism. Even though the temple in Jerusalem is destroyed, Yahweh, the God of Israel, still lives. This insight had direct bearing on the exiles in Babylon as well as on Jews all over in the world.

Moreover, the new covenant of individual responsibility championed by Jeremiah raises ethical responsibility to a new level and offers hope to God's people wherever they are. Jeremiah's exacting moral demands never compromised the radical demands of worshipping Yahweh as Lord and creator, thus providing later prophets and followers of Yahweh an insight into their religious responsibilities. He soundly condemned any outward show of piety that was not matched by a change of one's heart in the form of repentance. This concept of a new covenant (or "new testament") also profoundly influenced Jesus and early Christian writers as they looked for new ways to understand their relationship with God.

Although he is sometimes called the "prophet of wrath," Jeremiah continues to carry an overriding message of forgiveness for those who turn to Yahweh and trust in him. More than any other prophet, Jeremiah assures people that all is not lost—time yet remains for repentance. The importance of Jeremiah's legacy lies in his assertion that humanity's worst behavior toward the Lord and toward others is no match for the Lord's mercy or his desire for life and peace.

Harris

For Further Reading:

Bright, John. *Jeremiah: Introduction, Translation, and Notes.* New York: Doubleday and Company, 1965.

Carroll, Robert. *Jeremiah: A Commentary.* London: SCM Press, 1986.

Mays, James Luther, and Paul Achtemeier, eds. *Interpreting the Prophets.* Philadelphia: Fortress Press, 1987.

Jerome, Saint

Christian Theologian; Translator of the Bible into Latin

c. 347–419/20

Life and Work

One of the most significant and influential figures in the early Christian church, Jerome translated the Hebrew and Greek scriptures into Latin.

Jerome was born to a Christian family in what is now Slovenia. As a young man he studied the classics in Rome under pagan scholars and then traveled around the Mediterranean, sometimes as part of a group of ascetics—devout people who rejected earthly comforts and desires.

In 375, while very ill, he had a dream in which he heard himself accused of being a follower of the Roman philosopher Cicero rather than of Christ. He vowed to give up study of the ancient classics and went into the desert as a hermit. There he studied Greek and Hebrew so he could read the Bible and early Christian writings. He was ordained a priest in 378 and spent the next few years in extensive scriptural studies with the Eastern theologian Gregory Nazianzus. In 382, he returned to Rome, where he served as secretary to Pope Damasus. There he began revising the early Latin translation of the Gospels, Epistles, and Psalms on the basis of the best Greek manuscripts. He also wrote tracts interpreting biblical passages

and translated some of the works of ORIGEN (c. 184–c. 255), an African theologian and biblical scholar.

Jerome attracted many followers, including a noble Roman widow, Paula, who followed him to the Holy Land after the death of Pope Damasus in 385. By 389 Paula had built a monastery in Bethlehem headed by Jerome and three convents, which she headed. In Bethlehem Jerome continued his extensive study and writing, including the translation of the Old Testament into Latin. He also defended accepted belief from challenges by heretical groups. Among those who provoked his crushing polemics were the Pelagians (who emphasized good works as necessary to salvation) and the Arians (who denied the divinity of Christ). He also turned on Origenists (who emphasized spiritual knowledge mixed with mysticism and universalism) and tried to have Origen condemned.

Jerome died in about 419 and was buried in Bethlehem.

Legacy

Jerome's most lasting achievement was his translation of the Bible into Latin. Known as the Vulgate (*vulgata* means "common" in Latin), it was the standard text of the Roman Catholic church into the twentieth century. He was also important in the general development of the Western church.

Jerome's immediate influence resulted from his immense scholarship, which often contributed to the winning side in disputes over correct belief and practice. Through his translation of such Eastern Church Fathers as Origen, he contributed to the transmission of their ideas to European civilization. Yet Jerome, whose perspective was Western, was often critical of Eastern Christian traditions. His scholarship helped establish the Western, Latin church and gave it a confidence it had previously lacked as it faced the older churches of the East.

Jerome's translation of the Bible had a significant impact on the history of the Church. It provided some uniformity and continuity in the Western church's life that helped the Western church stay relatively united through several centuries. It also contributed to the differing theological emphases and ways of worship of the Eastern churches and the Western

church, and eventually to the split between them in the eleventh century.

During the Reformation, Christian churches split by language and nationality and reformers produced their own translations of the Bible. Although the early Protestant translations of the Bible were officially based on the original Hebrew and Greek texts, they reflect both Jerome's interpretations and the actual language of the Vulgate in many places. The Vulgate was modified over the centuries and today it has been supplanted by more accurate translations. Nevertheless, it is still viewed as a safe source of Roman Catholic teaching and beloved because of its long use in the Church.

Osterfield

WORLD EVENTS		JEROME'S LIFE
Rule of Roman Empire by Constantine	306–37	
	c. 347	Jerome is born in Slovenia
	375	Jerome has "Ciceronian" dream
	378	Jerome is ordained a priest
	382–85	Jerome serves as secretary to Pope Damasus
	389	Jerome completes translation of Old Testament into Latin
Christianity becomes the religion of Roman Empire	391	
	c. 419	Jerome dies
Fall of Roman Empire	476	

For Further Reading:

Kelly, J. N. D. *Jerome: His Life, Writings, and Controversies.* New York: Harper & Row, 1975.

Steinmann, Jean. *Saint Jerome and His Times.* Notre Dame, Ind.: Fides Publishers [1959?].

Jesus

Teacher, Healer, and Savior of the Christian Tradition

c. 4 B.C.E.–c. 30 C.E.

Life and Work

Jesus preached the "good news" about "the kingdom of God," taught an ethic of human relationships based on God as a caring parent, fostered a strong sense of kinship among his followers, and healed people. His teachings and actions led to the development of the Christian religion.

Jesus was born in the area of the Roman Empire that later became known as Palestine (present-day Israel and Jordan). The exact date of his birth and the events of his early life are unknown. He spent most of his life in Galilee, a farming region to the north of Jerusalem and Samaria.

Jesus had a deep and complex relationship to Judaism: he was born and raised a Jew and was immersed in its scriptures and traditions; at the same time, he felt distant, both literally and otherwise, from the center of religious power in Jerusalem. He also had a complex relationship with political and economic structures in Galilee: himself an artisan (*tekton*, perhaps best translated "builder"), he identified closely with the poor and marginalized, was critical of royal luxuriousness (see Luke 7:24–5), and during his ministry avoided cities—though he grew up only about three miles from a prominent city and may well have worked there.

Jesus' career as preacher, teacher, and healer lasted between one and three years. He was greatly influenced by a preacher named John, who baptized people as a way of symbolizing their once-and-for-all repentance and religious cleansing (other Jews periodically engaged in ritual bathing for cultic purposes). When he was baptized by John, Jesus experienced direct contact with God through the "holy spirit," which led him to begin a traveling ministry around Galilee. Meanwhile John was imprisoned and later executed by Herod Antipas.

Perhaps it was Jesus' use of "kingdom" language and his implicit questioning of governmental structures and of traditional ideas of family and cultic boundaries that got him into trouble. Or perhaps it was his insistence on engaging in some kind of public protest within the temple precincts in Jerusalem during a politically and religiously charged time of the year. Whatever the cause, Jesus was apparently seen as a threat both by the Jewish religious authorities and by the Roman governor. He was executed (c. 30) as an insurrectionist under the Roman governor, Pontius Pilate.

Legacy

Jesus' most obvious and enduring legacy is the Christian religion (within which he is considered "Christ," the Savior) and by extension various religious, political, and ethical movements growing out of Christianity. To what degree any of these is an expression of Jesus' intentions is a matter of debate.

Jesus left no writings. But he left behind people who remembered him and experienced his message and presence in different ways. Some began collecting and editing his sayings. Others had visions. Some of the sayings were remembered as having been self-referential: "This is my body. . . . This cup is the new covenant in my blood" (1 Cor. 11: 24–5). Soon these particular words were embedded in a ritual enacted "in remembrance of [Jesus]" (1 Cor. 11:25).

Over time these writings became authoritative and, by the second century, had been assembled into what became known as the New Testament. These writings collectively present various perspectives on the importance of Jesus and his ministry that form the basis of Christian theology. Each of the canonical Gospels is a kind of biography including many of Jesus' sayings, along with a report of his execution, resurrection, and postresurrection appearances (except Mark, in which the last are not reported). The Acts of the Apostles presents a kind of history of Jesus' followers from their fearful, early meetings in Jerusalem through the spread of their movement and its assuming of the name "Christian" (Acts 11:26). The letters bear the names of PAUL and some of Jesus' closest followers, including two of his brothers; they address Jesus' unique relationship to God and the moral and ethical implications of Jesus' actions. Finally, Revelation envisions a risen, heavenly Jesus (as a lamb still showing the marks of torture and execution) deposing all forces of evil and ruling over a new world. There are other records of Jesus and his sayings not found in the New Testament.

Perhaps Jesus' most enduring legacy is the positing of a "kingdom of God," which has been variously understood as a heavenly or earthly reality or potentiality. His best known sayings are the Lord's Prayer (Matthew 6:9–15 and Luke 11:2–4) and the Beatitudes (Matthew 5:3–12 and Luke 6:20–3).

As the message of the kingdom spread around the Mediterranean world, it generated groups of believers whose faith and teachings became the foundation for the worldwide growth of the Christian church. As the Church spread throughout Europe and Asia Minor, it became the dominant religious and political force until the Enlightenment. As such, its ideas and ethics became the foundation for Western civilization. While there are now numerous denominations of Christians, they all claim the life and teachings of Jesus as the foundation of their faith.

F. W. Weidmann

World Events	Jesus' Life*
	B.C.E.
Cleopatra of Egypt marries Marc Antony	36
	c. 4 Jesus is born
	C.E.
	c. 10–26 Jesus lives and works in Galilee
	27 Jesus is baptized by John; John is arrested
	27–30 Jesus conducts his ministry, primarily in Galilee
	30 Jesus teaches in temple precincts and is executed

* Scholars cannot date the specific events in Jesus' life with accuracy. The following chronology is based on the biblical account.

For Further Reading:

Meier, John P. *A Marginal Jew: Rethinking the Historical Jesus.* New York: Doubleday, 1991.

The New Testament

Sanders, E. P. *The Historical Figure of Jesus.* London: Penguin Press, 1993.

Joan of Arc, Saint

National Heroine and Patron Saint
of France

c. 1412–1431

Life and Work

Joan of Arc (Jeanne d'Arc in French) is revered as a model of Christian faith. Her religious conviction and courage in battle led to her eventual recognition as a national hero and as a saint of the Roman Catholic church.

Joan was born about 1412 in Domremy into a family of French peasants. The time was late in the Hundred Years' War, in which the English kings, allied with French dissidents, laid claim to the French throne. From the age of 13, Joan claimed to hear the voices of St. Michael, St. Catherine, and St. Margaret telling her to rid France of the English invaders. In 1429 she offered her services to the Dauphin (crown prince) Charles. To authenticate her claims, Charles had her examined for weeks by ecclesiastical authorities. Finally persuaded, he gave her troops to fight at Orleans, which had been besieged by the English for eight months. During eight days in May 1429, Joan, though wounded, led the French forces to victory at Orleans, lifting the siege and routing the English. Returning to the dauphin at Tours, Joan urged him to proceed to Reims to be crowned, but Charles vacillated. Meanwhile, Joan and the French

army cleared the English out of towns along the Loire and on the way to Reims. Finally, on July 17, 1429, the coronation of King Charles VII took place in Reims with Joan standing near the altar.

After an unsuccessful assault on Paris, Joan returned to the Loire. By this time, her exploits were well known throughout France and she was honored as the "Maid of Orleans." In May 1430, while trying to defend the town of Compiegne, Joan was captured and taken to the duke of Burgundy, an ally of the English. Held at various castles, and after several escape attempts, the British offered 10,000 francs to the duke to turn Joan over to Church authorities. By January 1431 she was in the hands of the bishop of Beauvais, charged with heresy, partly for her claims to have direct contact with God through visions, and with her trial set for Rouen.

At her trial beginning February 1431, she stubbornly refused to answer questions to the satisfaction of the Church. Finally, Joan signed a "confession," but a few days later, recanted. She was condemned once again as a heretic and turned over to the English and their French collaborators for execution. On May 30, 1431, Joan was burned at the stake in the market square of Rouen.

Legacy

It is probably as a symbol of great heroism and courage that is Joan's greatest legacy, particularly in France where she is a patron saint and national heroine.

Unfortunately, Joan was a victim of her own unsettled times and of the unfair nature of the proceeding against her—the Inquisition—which allowed her no counsel for her defense and whose decisions were often influenced by political considerations. Although Joan's victory at Orleans helped to bring more people to Charles's cause, the Hundred Years' War continued for another 20 years, ending only when the duke of Burgundy broke with the English. Twenty years after her death, King Charles VII, who had offered Joan no help after her capture, ordered an investigation into her trial. Ultimately, after a petition from her family, Pope Calixtus III began proceedings in 1455 that eventually revoked the sentence of the court.

Joan's brief but incredible story and her startling image in full armor, have been portrayed in many books, plays, films, operas, paintings, and sculpture in the centuries since her death, all of which have served to perpetuate the woman and her myth. There are monuments to her in many French cities including the Rouen square where she was burned. Her life was depicted on the stage in the play by George Bernard Shaw, *St. Joan*.

Joan was canonized by Pope Benedict XV on May 16, 1920. On June 24, 1920 the French parliament made the second Sunday in May a national festival in her honor.

Saltz

WORLD EVENTS		JOAN'S LIFE
Hong Wo establishes Ming Dynasty in China	1368	
	c. 1412	Joan of Arc is born
Beijing becomes capital of China	1421	
	c. 1425	Joan begins hearing voices
	1429	Joan routs English at Orleans
		Dauphin is crowned Charles VII
	1430	Joan is captured at Compiegne
	1431	Joan is condemned as heretic
		Joan is burned at stake
Ottoman Empire captures Byzantine capital, Constantinople	1453	
	1920	Joan is canonized

For Further Reading:

Gies, Frances. *Joan of Arc: The Legend and the Reality.* New York: Harper & Row: 1981.

Trask, Willard R, trans. and comp. *Joan of Arc: In Her Own Words.* New York: Turtle Point Press: 1996.

John XXIII, Pope

(Angelo Giuseppe Roncalli)

Pope and Modern Reformer of the Roman Catholic Church

1881–1963

World Events		John XXIII's Life
Germany is united	1871	
	1881	Angelo Giuseppe Roncalli is born in Sotto il Monte, Italy
Spanish American War	1898	
	1903	Roncalli is ordained to priesthood
	1905	Roncalli earns doctorate in theology
		Roncalli becomes secretary to Bishop Radini-Tedeschi of Bergamo
World War I	1914–18	
	1925 –44	Roncalli represents Vatican in Bulgaria and Turkey
World War II	1939–45	
Mao Tse-tung establishes Communist rule in China	1949	
Apartheid laws established in South Africa		
Korean War	1950–53	
	1953	Roncalli is named cardinal of Venice
	1958	Roncalli becomes Pope John XXIII
	1962	John XXIII calls first session of Vatican II
	1963	John XXIII dies in Rome
Six Day War between Israel and Arabs	1967	

Life and Work

John XXIII initiated the process of revitalizing the twentieth-century Roman Catholic church.

Angelo Giuseppe Roncalli was born to a family of farm workers on November 25, 1881, in Sotto il Monte, Italy. He was ordained a priest in 1904 and, after earning a doctorate in theology the following year, became secretary to the activist Bishop Radini-Tedeschi of Bergamo. Both he and the bishop were suspected of heresy during Pope Pius X's attack on modernism (abandoning traditional teachings and values in favor of more "modern" perspectives) in 1909. He served as a medical sergeant and chaplain in World War I.

Prior to the end of World War II Roncalli held administrative positions in Rome (1921–1925), Bulgaria (1925–1931), and Greece and Turkey (1934–1944). He gradually gained a reputation as a skilled diplomat with deep pastoral concern for his community and an interest in reform. During World War II Roncalli participated in the rescue of Jews from Nazi-controlled Hungary. At the end of the war he helped restore unity to the French Church divided by charges that its leaders had collaborated with the Nazis.

In 1953 Pope Pius XII named Roncalli a cardinal and head of the Church in Venice. When Pius XII died in October 1958, Roncalli was elected Pope. Seventy-seven at the time of his election, he was viewed as a caretaker who would maintain the Church until the next election when a dynamic younger man could be found.

John XXIII proved to be anything but an interim pontiff. He quickly put his life-long concerns into action. Within a month of his election he created 23 new cardinals, many from Africa and Asia, to open the Church to the rest of the world. Much to the dismay of the conservative Vatican Curia (Church leadership), he also laid plans for a great Church council.

The aim of this council, later called Vatican II, was to revitalize the Church's practices and to encourage Christian unity through broader ecumenical relationships. To secure widespread representation from the Catholic church, he gave the bishops the responsibility for organizing the conference. John XXIII also encouraged the Church's leadership to accept new methods of scholarship to interpret scripture and the

Church's teaching. Remembering his own brush with heresy charges, he granted theologians total freedom of expression at the council. He also invited Orthodox and Protestant leaders to act as official observers and to enter into dialogue with the participants. The first session of Vatican II occurred in October, 1962, and focused on Christian unity.

Unfortunately, John XXIII died June 3, 1963, three months before the second session of Vatican II was to begin.

Legacy

It may be impossible to underestimate the legacy John XXIII in transforming all aspects of the Roman Catholic church.

By the time of his death he had begun the process of what he called "opening the church's windows." His early decision to name many new cardinals had the immediate effect of formally recognizing the equality and importance of developing nations in the modern Church. In the long term it ensured that men with his vision would lead the Church in the next generation and choose a successor, Paul VI, who continued the process of reform.

John XXIII's most enduring legacy was the shifts in attitude reflected in the extensive reforms enacted in Vatican II. The council modernized the Church's religious orders, developed the concept of the universal responsibility of bishops for the whole Church, and reformed the Curia. It instituted extensive reforms in the liturgy, including removing the requirement for worship only in Latin and increased lay participation in worship. As a result of its work, the role of the laity increased in the Church.

John XXIII's support of consideration of new forms of biblical scholarship, much of which had been developed by European Protestants, allowed Catholic scholars more opportunities for research and debate to understand the scripture more fully.

John XXIII paved the way for rich engagement with other Christian communities. His efforts have blossomed in the series of dialogues between the Vatican and the Orthodox and such Protestant communities as the Anglicans, Lutherans, and Methodists. John XXIII transformed an attitude of fostering separation from other Christians into one of finding points of commonality.

von Dehsen

For Further Reading:

Hebblethwaite, Peter. *John XXIII, Pope of the Council.* London: G. Chapmen, 1984.

Zizola, Giancarlo. *The Utopia of Pope John XXIII.* Translated by Helen Barzolini. Maryknoll, N.Y.: Orbis Books, 1978.

John Paul II, Pope

(Karol Wojtyla)

Influential Roman Catholic Pope
1920–

Life and Work

The first non-Italian Pope in over 400 years, John Paul II increased the influence of the papacy in both religious and world affairs.

John Paul was born Karol Wojtyla in Wadowice, Poland, on May 18, 1920. He studied philosophy and literature at Jagiellonian University, where he developed an interest in acting. During World War II he worked in a quarry and then at a chemical plant while secretly studying for the priesthood. He was ordained in 1946. He earned doctoral degrees from Rome's Angelicum Institute and the Catholic University of Lublin; from 1953 to 1957, he taught ethics in Krakow and Lublin in Poland. He was appointed auxiliary bishop of Krakow in 1958, archbishop of Krakow in 1964, and in 1967 became a cardinal. He was elected Pope—the first Polish pope in the Church's history—in 1978 and took the name John Paul II.

John Paul's pontificate was shaped by his own experience in Poland under communism. There he saw the Church as a morally and politically unifying force countering the empty promises of modernism with its mixture of atheism and totalitarianism. He viewed his mission as restoring the moral authority of the Church in a divided, morally bankrupt world in order to establish the "Peace of God." Doctrinally he affirmed traditional teachings, condemning divorce, homosexuality, birth control, and abortion. He resisted the modernization of the Church, rejecting the ordination of women and dealing forcefully with doctrinal liberals.

In other aspects John Paul was progressive. He became an outspoken advocate for the poor and powerless and championed fundamental human rights and civil liberties. John Paul's mission led him to condemn repressive regimes of all types. In the late 1980s and early 1990s he played an important role in the fall of communism and the development of democracy in Eastern Europe.

A pontiff who emphasized the pastoral element of his office, John Paul traveled extensively in Africa, Asia, Europe, and the Americas. In ecumenical relations he continued dialogues with Anglican, Lutheran, and Orthodox churches and has attempted to heal the rift between Jews and the Vatican.

On May 13, 1981, he was gravely wounded but survived an assassination attempt by Mehmet Ali Agca, a Turk. After his recovery, he made many more pastoral visits to countries on every continent. In most cases, John Paul was the first Pope ever to visit those countries. In 1998, despite failing health, he made his eighty-first and eighty-second foreign visits to Cuba and Austria.

Legacy

John Paul II's legacy rests on his influence in the moral and doctrinal conservatism he espouses and in the international and political defense of traditional morality and human rights. He is an ardent anticommunist and is admired for his advocacy of democracy and justice, much to the discomfort of many authoritarian regimes.

John Paul's trips had the most success in third-world or developing countries where his speeches drew huge crowds and gave the people hope of a better life. For example, he made several visits to his native Poland in support of the workers' movement, Solidarity. At the end of 1998 he visited Cuba. As a result of that visit, Fidel Castro permitted the open celebration of Christmas in that officially atheist country. At the same time, he has been criticized for his conservatism in the liberal Western nations, where many Catholics ignore papal strictures against birth control and divorce.

John Paul's influence as a diplomat opened new avenues of discussion with religious and secular communities. His dialogues with Jews and Protestants have opened avenues of communication and led to better relationships between them and the Roman Catholic church. He also spoke out against many regional conflicts including those in Lebanon and the Persian Gulf. He opened diplomatic relations with Israel, Jordan, and South Africa. In 1994 John Paul's book, *Crossing the Threshold of Hope,* was published.

John Paul's devotion to MARY has awakened Marian devotion throughout the world. At present, there is in the Roman Catholic church a strong movement to have him issue an infallible teaching to declare Mary as co-redemptrix with Christ. (As the mother of Christ, Mary is believed to play an important role as an intercessory between believers and God. The supporters of this movement hope to have the Pope acknowledge this unique role through a special teaching.)

John Paul has also used his authority to elevate bishops from around the world to the status of cardinal. As cardinals serve for life, John Paul has not only made the college of cardinals more culturally diverse, especially by selecting cardinals from Africa and Asia, he has also ensured the continuation of his teachings long after his passing. He has tended to appoint men of the same ideological bent as himself—conservatives. John Paul will surely leave a legacy of a more activist Church, both in the political arena and in the conservative social and moral realm.

Saltz

For Further Reading:

Kung, Hans, and Leonard Swidler, eds. *The Church in Anguish: Has the Vatican Betrayed Vatican II?* San Francisco: Harper & Row, 1987.

Kwitny, Jonathan. *Man of the Century: The Life and Times of Pope John Paul II.* New York: Henry Holt and Co., 1997.

WORLD EVENTS		JOHN PAUL'S LIFE
World War I	1914–18	
	1920	Karol Wojtyla born
World War II	1939–45	
	1946	Wojtyla is ordained
Mao Tse-tung establishes Communist rule in China	1949	
Korean War	1950–53	
	1964	Wojtyla becomes archbishop of Krakow
Six Day War between Israel and Arabs	1967	Wojtyla becomes cardinal
End of Vietnam War	1975	
	1978	Wojtyla elected Pope and takes name John Paul II
	1981	John Paul wounded by assassin
Dissolution of Soviet Union	1991	

Junayd, Abu al-Qasim, al-

Architect of the First Theoretical
Foundations of Sufism
c. 825–c. 910

Life and Work

Abu al-Qasim al-Junayd was a master of
Sufism, a form of Islamic mysticism. He
was one of the first thinkers to try to relate
Sufism to traditional Islam.

WORLD EVENTS		AL-JUNAYD'S LIFE*
Charlemagne's coronation; beginning of Holy Roman Empire	800	
	c. 825	Abu al-Qasim al-Junayd is born
	c. 910	Al-Junayd dies
Northern Sung Dynasty begins	960	

* Scholars cannot date the specific events in
al-Junayd's life with accuracy.

Al-Junayd was born around 825 into a mercantile family in Baghdad. As a young man al-
Junayd came under the influence of his uncle,
Sari al-Saqati (d. c. 867), the acknowledged
founder of Sufism in the city. Al-Junayd became
interested in Sufism after exploring other forms
of Islamic thought, including *Shariah* (law),
hadith (tradition), and *kalam* (theology).

As a Sufi master, al-Junayd concentrated on
explaining the nature of the mystical union
with God. His teaching of *tawhid* (unification)
focused on distinguishing the eternal, timeless
nature of mystical union from the contingent,
everyday aspects of life. Once the soul becomes
detached from its earthly connections, it
returns to its original state, the one that existed
prior to its joining a physical body.

The nature of the soul in this pre-physical
state is central to al-Junayd's thought. Before it
entered the body the soul established a
covenant with God. When God asked, "Am I
your Lord?" the soul answered, "Yes." Thus the
mystical union of the soul with God reestab-
lishes the original relationship the soul had
with God before it joined its physical body.

Al-Junayd classified adherents of *tawhid* into
three categories, representing degrees of truth
and knowledge. First, there are ordinary
Muslims, who affirm God's oneness by reciting
the traditional confession, "There is no god, but
Allah." Next, there are theologians who apply
reason to faith. Finally, there are Sufis who not
only intellectually affirm God's oneness, but
also experience it through mystical union.

Al-Junayd sought to break down the barriers
that separated mainstream Muslims from the
Sufis, who often abandoned tradition and law
in favor of their private experiences. He contended that Sufis who had reached *tawhid*
must become involved in communal life under
the *Shariah*. Thus his form of Sufism became
known as "sober mind" because of his doctrine
of *sahw* (sobriety), which called for mystics to
guide others in establishing mystical union.

Al-Junayd wrote no books, but his ideas were
preserved in many letters and short treatises. He
died around 910, possibly in Baghdad.

Legacy

Al-Junayd was the first Sufi master to propose a theoretical understanding of
Sufism. His contention that the mystic must

be aware of *Shariah* and tradition, and that he
or she is obligated to serve the community and
to become a guide to others, helped bridge the
gap between Sufism and mainstream Islam.

Al-Junayd's efforts to discuss the mystical
union were continued by such later Sufi masters as AL-GHAZALI (1058–1111). Al-Ghazali
focused his work on trying to establish a relationship between reason and revelation. While
he favored revelation received through mystical experience over conclusions drawn by logic,
he nevertheless asserted that philosophy could
enhance a Muslim's understanding of the law
and theology. His efforts to combine Islamic
scholastic and mystical idea systems prevented
a division within the Islamic community and
permitted an emotional component in mainstream Islamic life.

Attempts to integrate Sufism into conventional Islam were continually met with opposition. Many "mainstream" Islamic thinkers
became suspicious of the intimate connection with God asserted by the mystic. Yet for
mystics, such identification is the goal of the
experience. For example, such Sufi mystics as
Abu Yaszid al-Bistami (d. 874) and AL-
HALLAJ (c. 858–922) openly declared their
union with God by announcing, "Glory be to
me!" Many Muslims viewed such declarations
as a violation of *shirk*, or the prohibition
against associationism (the "association," or
identification, of the human with the deity).
Moreover, the connection al-Junayd tried to
forge between mystical experience and traditional Islam often has been impeded by the
Sufis themselves because they see the union
as one of such intense identification with
God that that relationship supersedes any
limits set by the law. Naturally, other
Muslims view such an attitude as being contrary to the very essence of Islam, which is
based on the teachings of the Koran.

Even in the twentieth century, the tension
between Sufism and Islam remains. For example, the Wahhabi (the fundamentalist sect
dominant in Saudi Arabia) reject as un-Islamic
any practices not specifically authorized by the
Shariah. Contacts with the European secular-
ized world also have led many to become suspicious of mystical practices. Nevertheless, a
large number of Sufis continue to seek deeper
spiritual experiences.

von Dehsen

For Further Reading:
Burckhardt, Titus. *An Introduction to Sufism*. Wellingborough, England: Crucible, 1990.
Nicholson, Reynold Alleyene. *Studies in Islamic Mysticism*. New York: Kegan Paul International, 1998.

Kant, Immanuel

Leading Enlightenment Philosopher
1724–1804

Life and Work

Immanuel Kant was the foremost thinker of the Enlightenment and one of the most influential philosophers since 1600.

Kant was born into a pious Lutheran family on April 22, 1724, in Königsberg, Prussia. In 1740, he enrolled in the University of Königsberg, from which he received his doctorate in 1755. He spent most of his life at that university, where he was named a full professor in 1770.

Kant analyzed the powers and limits of reason while dismissing traditional claims to knowledge about God, immortality, or anything beyond sensory experience. Kant also argued that reason gives a basic moral law to each person. Moral law makes it reasonable to live as if God existed and as if one had an immortal soul that God would judge. Such faith is reasonable because these matters can be neither reasonably proved or refuted. Just as significant, Kant argues that one can have certain knowledge of basic scientific truths about the world—for example, every event has a cause.

Kant bases these claims on a revolution in philosophy so important that it can be compared to Copernicus's influence in astronomy. Copernicus solved certain astronomical problems by breaking with tradition: he asserted that the Earth is simply another planet that moves around the Sun. Similarly, Kant asserts, against philosophical tradition, that, instead of passively receiving its object of knowledge, the knower unconsciously but constructively organizes input from the senses spatially and temporally. That person then fits these perceptions into pre-given categories of the understanding following the mind's own rules. One thus knows a world of appearances constructed from received sensory data organized by the program of human sensibility, understanding, and reason. The world as it is apart from such construction is unknowable because knowledge arises only filtered through these constructs. Alleged realities such as God, the soul, or free will are also unknowable because they yield no sensory data. One may believe in them, however, based on considerations of morality and theoretical completeness.

Kant calls this philosophizing "critical" because it discloses the limits of knowing and "transcendental" because it involves structures of the mind that make experience and knowledge possible. Kant sets out these views in his three most significant but daunting works: *The Critique of Pure Reason* (1781), *The Critique of Practical Reason* (1788), and *The Critique of Judgment* (1790). These writings brought immediate renown and a flock of admiring students to the 60-year-old author and lecturer. However, the publication of his *Religion Within the Limits of Reason Alone* in 1793 led to controversies with the Prussian government. The government accused Kant of replacing traditional beliefs with rational argument and imposed teaching restrictions on the ailing professor.

Finally, after years of degenerative illness, Kant died on February 12, 1804, uttering the simple phrase, "It is good."

Legacy

Kant's philosophy was perhaps the most important of the Enlightenment and became the philosophical "point of departure" for the work of many others.

Ironically, Kant's efforts to defend the objectivity of scientific understanding while making room for objective moral principles, a reasonable faith in God, and immortality inspired two opposing non-Kantian philosophical directions emphasizing different aspects of his thought. Thinkers such as Hermann von Helmholtz (1831–1894) and Friedrich Albert Lange (1828–1875), who accepted the critical limiting of science to the world of rationally constructed appearances, pushed to deny even a reasonable faith. They argued that reality is ultimately a physical mechanism completely determined by independent causal relations. Others such as Heinrich Rickert (1863–1936), ever mindful of the limits of knowledge, wanted to reaffirm a knowledge of the world as it is and retain God, immortality, and free will as knowable based on the reality lying behind appearances.

Already in Kant's lifetime, metaphysical idealists like JOHANN GOTTLIEB FICHTE (1762–1814), Friedrich Wilhelm Schelling (1775–1854), ARTHUR SCHOPENHAUER (1788–1831), and above all GEORG WILHELM FRIEDRICH HEGEL (1770–1831) rejected Kant's limits on knowledge. Each in his own way argued that Kant's transcendental self, the unconsciously active spontaneous ego Kant assumed to lie behind the empirical self, is an aspect of an ultimate entity: a nonpersonal, non-corporeal unfolding Spirit, Mind, or Will. Every facet of reality—nature, human history and activity, and the divine—is irreducibly nonphysical, they argue, and a phase of a systematically knowable purposeful development. Because human knowledge, moral activity, and aesthetic appreciation are the most complete phases of this cosmic development, Kant's limits would disappear into an identity-in-difference (i.e., the recognition of one's own essential being in the other) of the knower and the known.

By the 1860s, such metaphysical pretensions to all-encompassing unity gave way to scientists who maintained that this kind of speculation could yield no knowledge. Helmholtz, Lange, and others down into the twentieth century endorsed knowledge only of a world of appearances, a fundamentally physical, deterministic, mechanized world that excluded empty ideas like God and free will. Later, a number of thinkers commonly called Neo-Kantians investigated the conditions for the possibility of cultural realities such as mythology and modified Kant's approach to encompass new psychological insights and post-Einsteinian science. In moral theory, Kant's idea of reason giving itself moral duties remains, with important modification, a viable account of moral obligation.

Kant's works prepared European thinking for such theories as KARL MARX's revolutionary economics, Albert Einstein's relativity, Sigmund Freud's analysis of the unconscious, and FRIEDRICH WILHELM NIETZSCHE's perspectivism. To paraphrase one thinker, one may philosophize for or against Kant but hardly without him.

Magurshak

For Further Reading:

Gulyga, Arsenii Vladimirovich. *Immanuel Kant: His Life and Thought.* Boston: Birkhauser, 1987.

Hoffe, Otfried. *Immanuel Kant.* Albany: State University of New York Press, 1994.

Kitcher, Patricia, ed. *Kant's Critique of Pure Reason.* Lanham, Md.: Rowman and Littlefield, 1998.

WORLD EVENTS		KANT'S LIFE
Peace of Utrecht settles War of Spanish Succession	1713–15	
	1724	Immanuel Kant is born
	1740	Kant enters University of Königsberg
	1770	Kant is named professor at University of Königsberg
United States independence	1776	
	1781	*The Critique of Pure Reason* is published
French Revolution	1789	
	1790	*The Critique of Judgment* is published
	1804	Kant dies
Greek War of Independence against Turkey	1821–29	

Kaplan, Mordecai Menahem

American–Jewish Theologian;
Founder of Reconstructionist
Judaism
1881–1983

World Events		Kaplan's Life
Germany is united	1871	
	1881	Mordecai Menahem Kaplan is born
Spanish American War	1898	
	1902	Kaplan graduates from Jewish Theological Seminary
		Kaplan ordained rabbi, serves Kehillat Yeshurun Synagogue
	1909	Kaplan joins staff of Jewish Theological Seminary
World War I	1914–18	
	1916	Kaplan organizes Jewish Center in New York City
	1922	Kaplan founds Society for the Advancement of Judaism
World War II	1939–45	
	1945	*Sabbath Prayer Book* is published
Mao Tse-tung establishes Communist rule in China	1949	
Korean War	1950–53	
	1963	Kaplan retires from Jewish Theological Seminary
Six Day War between Israel and Arabs	1967	
End of Vietnam War	1975	
	1983	Kaplan dies
Fall of Communism in eastern Europe	1989	

Life and Work

Mordecai Menahem Kaplan was a twentieth-century theologian who founded Reconstructionist Judaism.

Kaplan was born June 11, 1881, in Lithuania. His father was a scholar of the Jewish law who immigrated to the United States to become a member of the cabinet of the chief rabbi of New York. As a young man Kaplan began to have doubts about the reality of biblical miracles and MOSES' authorship of the Pentateuch but remained observant despite his doubts. In 1902 he graduated from the Jewish Theological Seminary (the academic arm of the Conservative Judaism) and received a Master's degree from Columbia University. He served briefly as an assistant rabbi in an Orthodox congregation and, in 1909, became dean of the Teachers Training Institute at the seminary. Shortly thereafter, he was appointed professor of homiletics (preaching).

Kaplan extended his influence beyond the seminary. He believed that a synagogue should be more than a religious institution and, in 1916, organized the Jewish Center in New York, the first synagogue to engage in social and cultural activities. His increasingly unorthodox views divided the congregation, and in 1922 he left to found the Society for the Advancement of Judaism, which became the nucleus of his evolving Reconstructionist view within Conservative Judaism.

Kaplan saw Judaism not merely as a religion but as "the evolving religious civilization of the Jewish people." His goal was to adapt it to modern life by removing supernatural elements. He understood God not in the traditional anthropomorphic sense but as the name for humankind's collective ethical idea. He rejected the idea of the Jews as a "chosen" people, which he thought implied superiority. Kaplan increased the participation of women in religious services and supported their ordination. He was also an ardent Zionist who saw the state of Israel as the spiritual center of Jewish life.

Kaplan presented his ideas in many books including *Judaism as a Civilization* (1934), which is considered to be one of the most influential books in American Judaism. In 1940 he published a new Passover service that discarded the traditional stress on miracles and emphasized the freedom embodied in the Exodus. His 1945 *Sabbath Prayer Book,* which changed prayers dealing with the supernatural, so infuriated the Orthodox rabbis that they excommunicated him.

After his retirement from the Jewish Theological Seminary in 1963, Kaplan split from the Conservatives and devoted his time to making Reconstructionism a strong and separate branch of Judaism. He died at the age of 102 in New York City on November 8, 1983.

Legacy

At his death Kaplan left a growing fourth branch of American Judaism (alongside the Orthodox, Conservative, and Reform) as well as a body of thought that has had a major impact on American Judaism.

Although initially considered radical, Kaplan's ideas have became widely accepted among American Jews. For example, both Conservative and Reform traditions now accept women's ordination. The fact that the ideas are so prevalent has weakened Reconstructionist Judaism as a denomination. One does not have to join a Reconstructionist congregation to find like-minded people. The more than 85 Reconstructionist congregations in 26 states as well as several in Canada sponsor an extensive cultural program featuring writers, artists, poets, and playwrights. Each congregation has a synagogue and a number of community programs, including Hebrew school and religious instruction, adult education courses, and family programming. The *Reconstructionist*, a periodical founded by Kaplan in 1935, is still published. Reconstructionists are inclusive and welcome people of all ages and family structures.

Reconstructionist Judaism has been so tied to Kaplan that his death has left its future uncertain. Yet Kaplan's legacy lives in his ideas that many have found religiously and intellectually satisfying.

Saltz

For Further Reading:

Goldsmith, Emanuel S., and Robert M. Seltzer, eds. *The American Judaism of Mordecai M. Kaplan.* New York: New York University Press, 1990.

Scult, Mel. *Judaism Faces The Twentieth Century: A Biography of Mordecai M. Kaplan.* Detroit, Mich.: Wayne State University Press, 1993.

Keynes, John Maynard

Influential Political Economist; Advocate of Government Intervention in Economic Affairs 1883–1946

Life and Work

John Maynard Keynes was a journalist, educator, and perhaps the most influential economist of the twentieth century. His economic theories based on government intervention and the effects of supply and demand overshadowed earlier theories based on the impact of economic cycles.

Keynes was born June 5, 1883, in Cambridge, England, to a Cambridge scholar and his highly educated wife. He attended Eton and Cambridge. While at Cambridge, he studied mathematics, politics, and economics, and became part of a circle of intellectuals that were later known as the Bloomsbury group, a culturally influential set of artists that included writers Virginia Woolf and Lytton Strachey, painter Duncan Grant, and art critic Clive Bell.

After leaving Cambridge he alternated teaching at Cambridge and working in government positions. During World War I he worked at the economic management of the war. After the war, he attended the Versailles Peace Conference as an economic advisor to British Prime Minister Lloyd George, but soon resigned, dismayed at the political maneuvering and the size of reparations being forced on a defeated Germany. In 1919 he published *The Economic Consequences of the Peace,* which had a scathing indictment of the Versailles agreement.

Keynes returned to Cambridge and in 1925 married the ballerina Lydia Lopokova. He became wealthy through wise stock investments and wrote articles for the *New Statesman, The London Times,* and the *Manchester Guardian.*

What ensured Keynes's fame was his response to the Great Depression of the 1930s. Most economists thought the Depression would be cured by the movement of the free market. Keynes, in *The General Theory of Employment, Interest and Money* (1936), argued that when demand was less than supply, suppliers would cut back on production, resulting in high unemployment and economic depression. The solution was government intervention designed to increase the money supply, which would result in lower interest rates and stimulation of business investment. Major depressions needed further government intervention to increase aggregate demand, which would in turn stimulate production and eventually employment. Such government action usually took the form of deficit spending—the creation of public works to provide employment to or outright welfare for the affected population.

In 1937 Keynes suffered a major heart attack. Weakened, he once more acted as advisor to the British treasury during World War II. In 1944 he attended the Bretton Woods Conference, which created the International Monetary Fund and the World Bank. At his death Keynes was a member of the Court of the Bank of England and a peer of the realm. He died on April 21, 1946, in Firle, Sussex, England.

Legacy

Keynes's economic insights established the theoretical foundation for much of the economic analysis and governmental policy in the Western nations for the rest of the twentieth century.

Keynes had an enormous influence on economic policy after World War II. His revolutionary approach to depression economics and business cycles was adopted almost immediately by many economists, especially in the United States and England. One result in the United States was the Employment Act of 1946 that established the Council of Economic Advisors and exhorted President Truman to promote policies of "maximum employment, production, and purchasing power." The Keynesian economic approach could be seen in the 1960s as the Kennedy and Johnson administrations increased government spending, for traditional Keynesian reasons of stimulating overall demand, but for military reasons as well.

But some disagreed with Keynes's policies. Influential, conservative economists such as Milton Friedman argued for traditional laissez-faire, free market policies to maintain a strong economy. The 1970s brought a period of high unemployment coupled with high inflation and periods of recession. It was a situation not anticipated by Keynes. During the 1980s, increased aggregate demand (more on military spending than social programs) continued to take the form of deficit spending and indeed stimulated the economy again. By the 1990s the national debt was so high that the only economic goal was to balance the budget, excluding any possibility of deficit spending.

However, a number of economists today hold Keynes's theories in high regard and point to Japan and Asia as examples of economies that could benefit from Keynes's approach.

The complete works of Keynes have been published in 29 volumes by the Royal Economic Society.

Saltz

WORLD EVENTS		KEYNES'S LIFE
Germany is united	1871	
	1883	John Maynard Keynes is born
Spanish American War	1898	
World War I	1914–18	
	1919	*The Economic Consequences of the Peace* is published
	1925	Keynes marries Lydia Lopokova
	1936	*The General Theory of Employment, Interest and Money* is published
	1937	Keynes suffers heart attack
World War II	1939–45	
	1944	Keynes attends Bretton Woods Conference
	1946	Keynes dies
Mao Tse-tung establishes Communist rule in China	1949	

For Further Reading:

Felix, David. *Biography of an Idea: John Maynard Keynes and the General Theory of Employment, Interest and Money.* New Brunswick, N.J.: Transaction Publishers, 1995.

Skidelsky, Robert Jacob Alexander. *Keynes.* Oxford and New York: Oxford University Press, 1996.

Khaldun, Ibn

Originator of the Sociological
Approach to History
1332–1406

Life and Work

Ibn Khaldun revolutionized the study of history by analyzing events from the perspective of economic, sociological, and cultural factors. He is considered to be the first historian to promote a scientific approach to historiography (the theory of historical writing).

Ibn Khaldun was born on May 27, 1332, in Tunis in North Africa. His family's roots were in Spain, where his ancestors held important

WORLD EVENTS		IBN KHALDUN'S LIFE
Muscovite state, present-day Russia, established by Ivan I	1325	
	1332	Ibn Khaldun is born
The Plague (Black Death) in Europe	1347–53	
Hong Wo establishes Ming Dynasty in China	1368	
	1375–79	Ibn Khaldun completes first draft of *An Introduction to History*
	1382	Ibn Khaldun settles in Egypt
	1406	Ibn Khaldun dies
Beijing becomes capital of China	1421	

political and military positions. His grandfather settled in Africa in 1248 following the Christian reconquest of Seville, Spain. His father was an administrator and soldier, but later devoted his life to the study of theology and law. In 1349, the Black Plague hit Tunis, claiming both his parents. By age 20, Ibn Khaldun found a position at the Tunis royal court; three years later he became a secretary for the sultan of Morocco. Over the course of his career he served in various diplomatic and administrative posts throughout North Africa, frequently switching allegiances as his political fortunes changed.

In 1375 Ibn Khaldun abandoned his political life and sought refuge among the tribe of Awlad 'Arif in what is present-day Frenda, Algeria. There he found the peace to write his most important work, the *Muqaddimah (An Introduction to History)*, a theoretical preparation for the writing of a universal history. In the work Ibn Khaldun strove to establish a philosophical basis for the scientific investigation of history. He was the first to contend that a historian must examine the "science of culture," that is, the cultural and social forces that generate historical change. He argued that social cohesion, enhanced by religious ideology, provided the impetus for a particular group to achieve power. Over time this power was weakened by economic, social, and cultural forces and an empire accordingly declined. He concluded that historical change ultimately could be envisioned as an endless cycle of social growth and decline. By 1379 he had not only completed the first draft of the *Introduction*, but he had also begun work on the *Kitabal-'ibar*, his comprehensive history of the Muslims of North Africa.

In 1379 he returned to Tunis, where he finished the *Kitabal-'ibar*. By 1382 he had moved to Cairo where, with several interruptions, he held professorships for the rest of his life. He died in Cairo on March 17, 1406.

Legacy

Ibn Khaldun's use of cultural and sociological evidence to construct a scientific historiography marks him as one of the most important and original historians of all time. As historian Yves Lacoste wrote, "If Thucydides is the inventor of history, Ibn Khaldun introduces history as a science."

Ibn Khaldun's major works, *An Introduction to History* and *Kitabal-'ibar*, have proved to be important both for the writing of history and for the history of Muslims in North Africa. In *An Introduction to History*, Ibn Khaldun was the first to promote a scientific methodology for analyzing historical events by investigating the complex social and economic factors that make up a society. From these factors he hoped to provide a rationale for historical change. Noted twentieth-century historian Arnold Toynbee acclaimed Ibn Khaldun's philosophy of history as "the greatest work of its kind."

Ibn Khaldun was such an original thinker that it took several centuries for scholars to recognize the importance of his theories. While his students in Egypt, such as al-Maqrizi, applied some of Ibn Khaldun's theories to their own scholarship, the full impact of his ideas was not appreciated until much later. (Al-Maqrizi analyzed the impact of rampant inflation and the social conditions of his time.) Ibn Khaldun's work became a focus of interest among the historians of the Ottoman Empire of the sixteenth and seventeenth centuries. However, his theories of history first attracted widespread interest only after the 1860s, when they were translated into French.

In the twentieth century the principles of economic and social analysis have become the methodological staple of many popular as well as scholarly historians. Writers as diverse as David M. Kennedy in his popular history of the Great Depression, *Freedom From Fear* (1999), and Gerd Theissen in his scholarly examination of New Testament communities, look to sociology to understand historical events. The approach is so widely accepted that the curriculums in U.S. schools mandate that history be viewed in terms of broad social, economic, and religious developments, not just political events shaped by an elite.

Ibn Khaldun's *Kitabal-'ibar* remains the best single work on the history of Muslims in North Africa. Although some have criticized this work for not having met the rigorous methodological demands for historiography promoted in the *Introduction* and it has been shown to have some factual inaccuracies, it still serves well as a source of historical data for its period.

von Dehsen

For Further Reading:
'Azmah, 'Aziz. *Ibn Khaldun in Modern Scholarship*. London: Third World Centre for Research and Publishing, 1981.
Brett, Michael. *Ibn Khaldun and the Medieval Maghrib*. Aldershot, England: Ashgate Variorum, 1999.
Lacoste, Yves. *Ibn Khaldun: The Birth of History and the Past of the Third World*. London: Verso, 1984.

Khomeini, Ruhollah

Influential Twentieth-Century
Islamic Leader
c. 1900–1989

Life and Work

Ruhollah Khomeini was the Iranian religious and political leader who made Islam a major force in the politics of the Middle East during the last decades of the twentieth century.

Khomeini was born around May 17, 1900, to a Shiite cleric who was murdered while his son was still an infant. A deeply religious and precocious child, he could recite passages from the Koran by heart when only six. In 1918 he began studying theology and by the 1930s he had gained a reputation as a brilliant scholar and teacher. In the 1950s Khomeini was acclaimed an ayatollah (great religious leader) and became grand ayatollah in 1961.

Khomeini first came to national prominence with the publication in 1944 of *The Key to Secrets,* in which he attacked the shah of Iran's secular reforms, denounced Western influence, and called for a return to Islamic purity. During the early 1960s he began publicly criticizing government policy, including the emancipation of women and land reform that reduced religious estates. His views led to his imprisonment in 1963 and forced exile the following year. Eventually he settled in Iraq. There he developed his theory of Islamic government in which he advocated the founding of a republic under the "Guardianship of the Jurist," that is, rule by the clergy. He asserted that

the infallible *imams* (highest leaders in Shiite Islam), who were descended from the Prophet MUHAMMAD, had transferred their political authority to the Shiite clergy, particularly the masters of Islamic religious law. These men were to be the supreme authority in the state; any government that refused to defer to religious authority was illegitimate and must be overthrown.

Iraq deemed Khomeini's ideas dangerous and expelled him in 1978. He found refuge in France, from where he escalated his calls for the overthrow of the shah. The Iranian monarchy collapsed in January 1979, and Khomeini triumphantly returned to Iran the following month. In December 1979, when Iran became an Islamic republic, Khomeini was named the supreme religious and political leader who was above the formal institutions of the state. Believing that "there is not a single topic in human life for which Islam has not provided instruction and established norms," he remained the ultimate arbiter of all political and religious issues in Iran until his death on June 3, 1989.

Legacy

Khomeini played a dominant role in the 1978–79 Iranian Revolution and in making Islamic fundamentalism a major force in Middle East politics

Khomeini's beliefs resonated with many of the people in the region who had fought Western political and cultural domination throughout the twentieth century. Nations achieved political freedom following World War II, but these new states discovered that they were still closely linked to the West by economic and military concerns. Just as significant, the conservative populations of these nations found themselves ruled by Western-educated elites who cared little for Islam and who were determined to reduce the role of Islam in society. In response, Muslims began reasserting Islamic values and developing an Islamic vision of the state. They insisted that independence was only the first step in obliterating all aspects of Western culture—Western law, secular learning, and decadent practices.

The Iranian Revolution was the most dramatic and successful attempt to break with the Western mold. Khomeini oversaw a cultural revolution that eventually transformed Iran into a fundamentalist Islamic society. Women were required to wear the veil, Western music was banned, *Shariah* (Islamic law) became the law of the state, and study of the Koran became the basis of education. Khomeini

dismissed Western representative government as invalid, insisting that sovereignty belonged to God rather than to the people. He tried to develop a "theodemocracy" of "limited popular sovereignty under a paramount God." He was never able to implement his desire for popular rule—if he ever intended to do so. Instead, Iran became an authoritarian state with terror an acceptable tool of government to ensure Islamic unanimity.

The success of Khomeini's Islamic revolution inspired Islamic-based opposition movements in other Middle Eastern countries. Many received aid from Iran in response to the ayatollah's belief that his Islamic revolution had to be exported in order to lay the foundation for a world Islamic state. Khomeini's drive helped destabilize the Persian Gulf and contributed to antigovernment activities in Saudi Arabia and Lebanon as well as Iraq and the Philippines. Following the Persian Gulf War of 1991, a wave of Islamic fundamentalism swept over North Africa. Fundamentalists became a strong force in Morocco and Tunisia and also became increasingly important in Turkey and Egypt. In the mid-1990s Muslim fundamentalists took control of Afghanistan and imposed a strict Islamic regime that severely curtailed civil rights and personal liberties.

von Dehsen

WORLD EVENTS		KHOMEINI'S LIFE
Spanish American War	1898	
	c. 1900	Ruhollah Khomeini is born
World War I	1914–18	
	1918	Khomeini begins theological study
World War II	1939–45	
	1944	Khomeini publishes *The Key to Secrets*
Mao Tse-tung establishes Communist rule in China	1949	
Korean War	1950–53	
	1963	Khomeini is imprisoned
	1964	Khomeini is exiled
Six Day War between Israel and Arabs	1967	
End of Vietnam War	1975	
	1979	Khomeini is named Iran's supreme religious and political leader
Fall of Communism in eastern Europe	1989	Khomeini dies
Dissolution of Soviet Union	1991	

For Further Reading:

Bakhash, Shaul. *The Reign of the Ayatollahs: Iran and the Islamic Revolution.* New York: Basic Books, 1984.

Montazam, Mir Ali Asghar. *The Life and Times of Ayatollah Khomeini.* London: Anglo–European Publishers, 1994.

Kierkegaard, Søren Aabye

Influential Existentialist
Philosopher
1813–1855

Life and Work

Søren Aabye Kierkegaard's writings are a major source of philosophical and Christian existential thought, a form of philosophy emphasizing individual existence, freedom, and choice.

World Events	Kierkegaard's Life
Napoleonic Wars 1803–15 in Europe	
	1813 Søren Aabye Kierkegaard is born
Greek War of 1821–29 Independence against Turkey	
	1830 Kierkegaard enters university
	1840 Kierkegaard awarded theology degree
	1841 Kierkegaard studies in Berlin
	1843 *Either/Or* and *Fear and Trembling* are published
	1844 *The Concept of Dread* is published
	1846 *Concluding Unscientific Postscript* is published
Revolutions in 1848 Austria, France, Germany, and Italy	
	1849 *The Sickness unto Death* is published
	1855 Kierkegaard dies
United States 1861–65 Civil War	

Born in Denmark on May 5, 1813, the youngest child of a retired businessman, Kierkegaard received from his father a challenging education and an anxiety-ridden Lutheran piety; in addition his fertile imagination was fired by his father's dramatic storytelling. He began university studies in 1830; in 1840 he received his theology degree, resolved to become a minister, and became engaged. A year later he decided against both marriage and the ministry, studied philosophy in Berlin, and began to write critical philosophical and religious works in Copenhagen, where he would remain until his death on November 11, 1855. In that time, he wrote Christian discourses under his own name; under several pseudonyms, he wrote significant philosophical works such as *Either/Or* and *Fear and Trembling* (1843), *The Concept of Dread* (1844), *Concluding Unscientific Postscript* (1846), and *The Sickness unto Death* (1849), each of which represented distinct spheres of existence: the aesthetic, the ethical, and the religious.

Kierkegaard's main concern was "how to become a Christian in Christendom." He contrasted the automatic, thoughtless acceptance of Denmark's established religion with the need for individuals alone before God to commit themselves to living each day with the unprovable belief of Christ as God-made-man. He also opposed Danish theologians' tendency to follow the German philosopher GEORG WILHELM FRIEDRICH HEGEL, who claimed to have developed a systematic, rational understanding of life and history. Kierkegaard believed philosophy was the result of intense self-examination and that existence could not be systematized. Kierkegaard, devout Christian and admirer of SOCRATES OF ATHENS, argues that the "truth for which I can live and die"—not systematic, merely intellectual truth—is most significant for an individual's life.

Kierkegaard recognizes three basic possible styles of living: aesthetic, ethical, and religious. He develops different characters, his pseudonyms, who write about these styles as their living representatives. His aesthetic individuals are concerned only with personal satisfaction, the ethical with moral obligation and commitment to others, and the religious with their living, daily relationship with God. His books present these ways of life as possibilities from which the reader must choose and live daily life accord-

ingly. By such choices, a person creates his or her own life, and for the Christian Kierkegaard, complete self-actualization is possible only when an individual is committed to a daily life shaped by faith in Christ the God-man.

Legacy

Kierkegaard is often viewed as the first existentialist, even though the term did not become prominent until after World War II.

Kierkegaard's influence was initially confined to Scandinavia, but as existentialism developed widely, his impact spread. His existential ideas also influenced a wide variety of work including the plays of August Strindberg, the novels of Walker Percy, the philosophies of MARTIN HEIDEGGER and JEAN-PAUL SARTRE, and the theology of KARL BARTH.

Along with FRIEDRICH WILHELM NIETZSCHE, Kierkegaard helped shape and define existential philosophy by emphasizing the concerns of the individual as he or she struggled with the anxiety and uncertainty of day-to-day existence. De-emphasizing abstract theory and impersonal truths, Kierkegaard inspired subsequent generations to think about life as a task based on the free, responsible choices of individuals who must detach themselves from commonly held worldviews to discover life's meaning for themselves. This approach to concrete human issues has borne fruit among religious and nonreligious thinkers alike as new studies and translations of Kierkegaard's work continue to appear today.

Magurshak

For Further Reading:

Bretall, Robert. ed. *A Kierkegaard Anthology.* Princeton, N.J.: Princeton University Press, 1946.

Gouwens, David Jay. *Kierkegaard as Religious Thinker.* New York: Cambridge University Press, 1996.

Kierkegaard, Søren. *The Point of View for My Work As an Author.* Translated by Walter Lowrie. New York: Harper Torchbooks, 1962.

Kindi, Yaqub ibn Ishaq as-Sabah, al-

Islamic Philosopher and
Synthesizer of Greek Thought
c. 800–c. 873

Life and Work

Yaqub ibn Ishaq as-Sabah al-Kindi was one of the first Islamic scholars to preserve the ancient wisdom of the Greeks and to relate the teachings of Islam to questions of reason and science.

Al-Kindi, as he is commonly known, was born of a noble family in Basra in present-day Iraq in about 800. Educated in Baghdad, he held the influential positions of tutor and astrologer in the caliphates of al-Mamun (r. 813–833) and Mu'tasim (r. 833–842). Al-Kindi's prominent positions gave him the opportunity to preserve and translate valuable philosophical texts, especially those of PLATO and ARISTOTLE.

Al-Kindi sought to synthesize Islamic teachings and Greek rational thought. In *On First Philosophy*, he asserts that philosophy can lead to the knowledge of the First Truth and the First Cause. Using astronomical arguments, he contends that the universe is composed of finite matter in finite time. Such a circumstance could come to be only from a First Cause—an infinite creator.

In *On the Number of Aristotle's Books*, al-Kindi addresses the relationship of philosophy to prophecy. In contrast to philosophers, who analyze issues according to the precepts of reason and logic, prophets receive knowledge intuitively. While al-Kindi develops these differences, he does not fully investigate points of convergence.

Despite this Aristotelian bent, al-Kindi focused intensely on the life and teachings of SOCRATES OF ATHENS. In his book, *Treatise on the Witness of Socrates*, al-Kindi revered Socrates for having led an ideal life, forgoing material comforts in the search for truth in the daily lives of his fellow citizens.

Al-Kindi illustrates the ideal life free from the burden of material possessions in *Treatise on the Device for Driving Away Sorrows*. Life is analogous to a trip on a ship. When the captain docks at a port, people quickly depart. When the captain calls them back, those who have nothing come back quickly and find the best accommodations. Next, those with few goods also return promptly and also find comfortable seats. However, those with many goods return late and are crowded in by their acquisitions. Finally, there are those who are so absorbed in their purchases that they do not hear the captain's call and miss the ship altogether.

Although it is claimed that al-Kindi wrote over 250 works, only about 40 survive, many of which are in poor condition.

Al-Kindi died in Baghdad in about 873.

Legacy

Although his thought was surpassed by that of later Islamic scholars, al-Kindi is remembered as the first scholar who advocated the acceptance of the rational principles of the Greek philosophers among Islamic thinkers.

Al-Kindi's disciples formed an important link in the larger attempt to synthesize Islamic teaching and Greek philosophy. Among his early disciples were as-Sarakhsi (d. 899) and al-Âmiri (d. 992). Following al-Kindi's lead, these later philosophers introduced Greek philosophers to an Islamic audience and developed points of synthesis between their philosophy and Islamic doctrine. Al-Kindi's work on Socrates may have also influenced the thought of al-Razi (865–925) in his book, *On the Philosophic Life*. Further, al-Razi's book may have been the spark that eventually led to the thought of AL-FARABI (870–950) and the development of Islamic political philosophy.

Al-Kindi's philosophical study proved important to the future course of Western philosophy and both Islamic and Christian theology. Over the next few centuries, Arab philosophers continued to try to find a synthesis between Islamic teaching and rational philosophy. AVICENNA (Ibn Sina, 980–1037) built on al-Farabi's thought and suggested ways in which a coherent system could be fashioned out of Islamic doctrine and Aristotelian principles. Avicenna's work was roundly challenged by AL-GHAZALI (1058–1111), who rejected Avicenna's principle of coherence. In turn, a later Islamic thinker from Spain, AVERROËS (Ibn Rushd 1126–1198), picked up Avicenna's mantle and defended him against the critique of al-Ghazali. It was through the work of these Islamic philosophers that the Greek writings entered the Christian world and contributed to the Scholastic movement of the medieval period, which saw similar attempts to synthesize faith and reason among Christians. Most notably, the work of these Islamic scholars inspired much of the thinking of THOMAS AQUINAS (1225–1274).

Al-Kindi's work, therefore, inaugurated a line of scholarship that engaged the difficult question of the relationship of reason and faith, a question that still occupies philosophers, theologians, and scientists at the dawn of the twenty-first century.

WORLD EVENTS	AL-KINDI'S LIFE*
Islamic expansion 640–711 through North Africa and Spain	
Charlemagne's coronation; beginning of Holy Roman Empire c. 800	Yaqub ibn Ishaq as-Sabah al-Kindi is born
c. 873	Al-Kindi dies
Northern Sung Dynasty begins 960	

* Scholars cannot date the specific events in al-Kindi's life with accuracy.

For Further Reading:

Atiyeh, George. *al-Kindi : The Philosopher of the Arabs*. Rawalpindi, Pakistan: Islamic Research Institute, 1966.

Butterworth, Charles E. *The Political Aspects of Islamic Philosophy: Essays in Honor of Mushin S. Mahadi*. Cambridge, Mass.: Harvard University Press, 1992.

King, Martin Luther, Jr.

Preeminent Civil Rights Leader
1929–1968

Life and Work

Martin Luther King, Jr., was the preeminent black civil rights leader of the 1950s and 1960s. His leadership of the civil rights movement led not only to the enactment of legislation but also to a fundamental shift in perspectives on race relations.

King was born on January 15, 1929, in Atlanta, Georgia, and grew up in the tradition of the Southern black ministry—both his father and maternal grandfather were Baptist preachers. After graduating from Morehouse College in Atlanta in 1948, he studied at Crozer Theological Seminary in Chester, Pennsylvania, and received a doctorate in theology from Boston University's School of Theology in 1955. While a student, he married Coretta Scott in 1953.

As a Baptist, King believed in individual conversion, but he insisted also on economic and political change for the disenfranchised, the poor, and the racially persecuted. For him, Christian faith necessitated an active struggle against injustice and suppression, to establish "the Beloved Community."

King advocated "nonviolent resistance." His methods were an original mixture of the theol-

ogy of WALTER RAUSCHENBUSCH, who taught a Social Gospel, and of the insights of HENRY DAVID THOREAU, which had convinced him of the possibility of eliminating social evil. From REINHOLD NIEBUHR he learned political realism concerning social conditions and power structures. To his Christian motivation he applied the Hindu doctrine of *satyagraha* (devotion to truth), the theoretical basis of the success of MOHANDAS GANDHI, who led Indians in their efforts to drive the British out of India. "Christ showed us the way," King said, "and Mahatma Gandhi shows us its practical realization." His aim was to wear down political and economic oppressors by the capacity of blacks to suffer under discriminatory treatment. Applying moral pressure to the consciences of white Americans, he was able at the same time to win them over.

His leadership of a bus boycott in Montgomery, Alabama, in 1955 led to a Supreme Court decision that declared laws requiring segregated seating on buses unconstitutional and brought him national fame. To coordinate civil rights activities, he founded the Southern Christian Leadership Conference (SCLC) in 1957. In the 1960s the SCLC, the national political branch of the black church, was able to effect great changes in the relationship of the races. King became even more prominent after the March on Washington in 1963. In 1964, King received the Nobel Peace Prize for his nonviolent leadership of the civil rights movement. Over the next few years his labors resulted in the passage of the Civil Rights Act of 1964 and the Voting Rights Act of 1965.

In his last years, King agitated against America's war in Vietnam, emphasizing the anomaly of young black men fighting for freedom abroad that they had never experienced at home. Spearheading a "poor people's campaign," he joined a protest of sanitation workers in Memphis, Tennessee, where he was assassinated on April 4, 1968.

Legacy

More than any other black leader of his day, King personified the African-American struggle for civil rights. His assassination in 1968 simultaneously highlighted the significance of his life and symbolized his own willingness to suffer for the sake of human rights.

Able to translate local conflicts into moral issues of nationwide concern, King became the conscience of a nation. His strategy of nonviolent

resistance awakened moral concern and the allegiance of blacks and whites in all parts of the country and effectively ended legal racial segregation in the United States; it has persisted against the rival "Black Power" movement, which advocated the use of force. King's speech, "I Have a Dream," at the Lincoln Memorial during the 1963 March on Washington is remembered as an American classic. His most tangible achievement was the U.S. Voting Rights Act of 1965.

After King's death, many of his close associates continued the struggle for civil rights and became prominent public leaders in their own right. Andrew Young was elected mayor of Atlanta; John Lewis was elected to Congress from King's home state of Georgia. The Rev. Jesse Jackson helped to galvanize African-American political action in recent years through inspirational speeches and his own campaigns for national office.

King's life also inspired others to try to articulate his ideals of freedom in other contexts. In the early 1970s, JAMES CONE developed "black theology" to articulate the demands for justice of the oppressed. Later these themes were expanded to address the needs of African-American women through the "womanist" theology of such scholars as Jaclyn Grant and Delores Williams. In the 1980s, King's life and message became a foundation of the struggle against apartheid in South Africa led by Bishop DESMOND TUTU. Wherever the oppressed seek freedom and justice, people recall the life and words of King as an inspiration for their struggle.

His birthday was made a federal holiday in 1986.

Olson

WORLD EVENTS		KING'S LIFE
	1929	Martin Luther King, Jr., is born in Atlanta
World War II	1939–45	
Mao Tse-tung establishes Communist rule in China	1949	
Korean War	1950–53	
	1955	King organizes bus boycott in Montgomery, Alabama
	1957	King organizes Southern Christian Leadership Conference
	1963	King leads March on Washington
Six Day War between Israel and Arabs	1967	
	1968	King is assassinated in Memphis, Tennessee
End of Vietnam War	1975	

For Further Reading:

Ansbro, John. *Martin Luther King, Jr.: The Making of a Mind*. Maryknoll, N.Y.: Orbis Books, 1982.

King, Martin Luther, Jr. *A Testament of Hope: The Essential Writings and Speeches of Martin Luther King, Jr.* Edited by James M. Washington. San Francisco: Harper, 1991.

Lewis, David L. *King: A Biography*. 2nd ed. Urbana: University of Illinois Press, 1978.

Lao-tzu

Founder of Taoism
c. 570–490 B.C.E.

Life and Work

Lao-tzu is the reputed founder of Taoism, a Chinese religious and philosophical system aimed at assisting its followers to achieve harmony within themselves and with the energy of the universe.

Little is known about the life of Lao-tzu (possible meaning: "The Grand Old Master") other than what is preserved in legend. The Chinese historian, Ssmu-Ch'ien (c. 145–86 B.C.E.), noted that Lao-tzu was a man deep in wisdom and understanding. He may even have been a teacher of CONFUCIUS.

Lao-tzu was born in the Chinese province of Henan. As a young man, he may have been a minor governmental official and a teacher of how to live the good life, stressing the need to live in tranquillity with nature. When he was older, he mounted a water buffalo and headed toward Tibet. Legend has it that when he approached the gate at the Hankao Pass, the gatekeeper, Yin Hsi, persuaded him to write all of his teachings in a book. The result was the *Tao Te Ching (The Way and Its Power)*, a short book of about 5,000 Chinese written characters containing the essence of Lao-tzu's teaching. (Many scholars believe that the *Tao Te Ching* is actually a compilation of teachings from several authors.)

The basic theme of the *Tao Te Ching* is to aid people seeking the "Way," the *Tao*, hence the name "Taoism." The *Tao* can be understood as the ultimate reality, so beyond ordinary experience that it cannot be captured in words. The first line of the *Tao Te Ching* is: "The *Tao* that can be spoken is not the true *Tao*." The *Tao* is the way of the universe, the rhythm and balance of nature. In some sense, the *Tao* is the way of human life.

Within the body are three forces to assist the achievement of harmony: the generative force (the *ching*), vitality (the *ch'i*), and the spirit (the *shen*). To bring these forces into balance, the Taoist must master *wu-wei*, a concept of inactivity or of taking no action contrary to nature. The image of flowing water is frequently used to picture this concept. As water flows it does not expend needless energy to move obstacles; it simply flows around them. The traditional symbol for the goal of Taoism to bring competing forces into balance is the *yin–yang* (symbol ☯).

There is no certain information about the death of Lao-tzu, although some sources indicate that he may have died around 490 B.C.E.

Legacy

It is often said that a Chinese person is a Confucian in his or her public affairs and a Taoist in private life. Only Confucianism, as a religious or philosophical system, has had a stronger impact on Chinese society. Indeed, only the Bible has been translated into more languages than the *Tao Te Ching*.

After Lao-tzu's death, many began to think of him as a deity. At Lu-i, traditionally considered his birthplace, Emperor Huan (r. 147–167 C.E.) authorized sacrifices to Lao-tzu. An advisor to the emperor, Hsiang K'ai, declared that Lao-tzu had been reincarnated as the BUDDHA. In the fourth century, Po Yüan, a Buddhist monk, and Wang Fou published a treatise identifying Lao-tzu with the Buddha.

In 1907, Sir Aurel Stein uncovered an ancient document, *Scriptures on the Transformations of Lao-Tzu*, in the Kansu province of China. This document depicts Lao-tzu as the governing ruler of the spiritual realm who has had many transformations in human form. In contrast, Chang Tao-ling (c. 142 C.E.) considered Lao-tzu a spiritual figure who revealed truths to his earthly followers, the Celestial Masters.

Over time, the impact of the *Tao Te Ching* grew, inspiring many commentaries. Three basic systems of Taoist thought emerged: philosophical, religious, and "practical." Philosophical Taoism sought to uncover and impart the wisdom that promotes harmony and balance in life. It aims at the avoidance of conflict and tension and at the conservation of energy. Religious Taoism, influenced by Buddhism and Chinese folk religion, incorporated some of those practices into Taoism and institutionalized the religion during the second century B.C.E. Religious Taoists consider Lao-tzu a deity. "Practical" Taoism seeks to find ways to increase the power of the Tao in a person. Sometimes such Taoists experiment with different foods to enhance the body's ability to receive and apply the cosmic force of the Tao. Other times, they use meditative practices, such as the movements incorporated in the *tai chi chuan*, designed to draw *ch'i* (vitality) from the cosmos. At times, some Taoists practice forms of yoga to align their bodies with cosmic forces.

Whether or not the teachings of Lao-tzu were embellished by legend, the teachings preserved in his name have become an essential component of Chinese life and culture.

von Dehsen

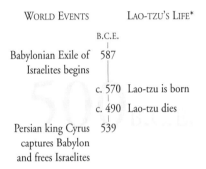

WORLD EVENTS	LAO-TZU'S LIFE*
	B.C.E.
Babylonian Exile of Israelites begins	587
	c. 570 Lao-tzu is born
	c. 490 Lao-tzu dies
Persian king Cyrus captures Babylon and frees Israelites	539

* Scholars cannot date the specific events in Lao-tzu's life with accuracy.

For Further Reading:

Blofeld, John. *Taoism: The Road to Immortality.* Boston: Shambhala, 1985.

Kohn, Livia, ed. *Lao-tzu and the Tao-te-ching.* Albany: State University of New York Press, 1998.

Maspero, Henri. *Taoism and Chinese Religion.* Amherst: University of Massachusetts Press, 1981.

Lee, Ann (Mother Ann)

Founder and Spiritual Leader of
the Shakers
1736–1784

Life and Work

Ann Lee and a small group of seven followers fled religious persecution in England and immigrated to America where she founded the United Society of Believers in Christ's Second Appearing, commonly known as the Shakers, one of the few indigenous American religions.

Lee was born on February 29, 1736, in Manchester, England, the daughter of a blacksmith. There she worked in a factory and as a cook. In 1758 she joined a religious sect, an off-shoot of the Quakers, known as the "Shaking Quakers" because of their trembling and shaking during worship. Lee married in 1762 and had four children, none of whom lived past infancy.

In 1770 she was imprisoned for her unorthodox views and her strange dancing and speaking in tongues. About that time, Lee had a vision that sexuality was the root of all sin and that only through celibacy could men and women reach perfection on Earth. Obeying another vision, Lee, her husband, and six other followers immigrated to the American colonies in 1774. In 1776 they settled in Watervliet, New York, where they lived a life of seclusion, attracting a few followers from the surrounding area. Her followers considered Lee to be the female Messiah, the second coming of Christ in female form. The Shakers believed that "Mother Ann," as Lee came to be called, represented the female side of God's dual nature.

The Shakers welcomed those who wished to join. They lived apart from society, practiced celibacy, separation but equality of the sexes, common ownership of property, and devotion to God. Children were raised communally. Their worship included trances, trembling, dancing, and shouting. Persecuted for her pacifism during the Revolutionary War, Lee was briefly imprisoned in 1780. In 1781 Lee began traveling around the country making converts but also inspiring fear and hatred and further persecution from some quarters. She died on September 8, 1784, in Watervliet, from beatings she received while trying to spread her faith.

Legacy

Founders of religions do not appear very often, and a woman in such a role is an extreme rarity. Although Lee did not live to see the growth of Shakerism, her vision and spirituality have provided the inspiration and guidance for 200 years of Shaker communities.

Following Lee's death, the Shaker movement, led by James Whittaker and Joseph Meacham, grew rapidly. Meacham went on to establish approximately 50 Shaker communities and to codify Shaker law. By the mid-nineteenth century, at its height, there were about 5,000 members in a number of Shaker communities as far west as Kentucky and Ohio, doubling the number of members at Lee's death.

The Shaker communities were highly organized and industrious, with codes for dress and behavior, a belief in simplicity, and with all their work consecrated to God. The Shakers approved of technology and laid great emphasis on the practical. The Shakers' inventions were many, including the clothespin, the flat broom, the circular saw, and the washing machine. They had an international garden seed business, dealt in herbal medicines, and were known for their farming methods. Shaker architecture is distinctive, their belief in the equality of the sexes shown in the symmetry of some of their buildings. Their craftsmanship is evident in their famous furniture, still valued and collected today for its simplicity of design. The Shakers also left a large body of their hymns and songs.

After the Civil War the number of Shakers declined. By 1908 Shaker membership had dwindled to about 1,000. Today there is only one Shaker community left, in Sabbathday Lake, Maine, where a few aged members live. However there are a number of preserved Shaker villages and museums that may be visited in New England and as far west as Kentucky.

Saltz

For Further Reading:

Andrews, Edward D. *The People Called Shakers*. New York: Oxford, 1953.

Campion, Nardi R. *Ann the Word: The Life of Mother Ann Lee, Founder of the Shakers*. Boston: Little, Brown, 1976.

Campion, Nardi R. *Mother Ann Lee: Morning Star of the Shakers*. Hanover, N.H.: University Press of New England, 1990.

Kirk, John T. *The Shaker World: Art, Life, Beliefs*. New York: Harry N. Abrams, 1997.

Locke, John

Architect of Classical Political
Liberalism
1632–1704

Life and Work

John Locke was a political philosopher whose concept that a government derives its authority from the governed had a profound effect upon liberal political thought.

Locke was born in Somerset, England, in 1632. His family was Anglican with Puritan leanings. He attended Westminster School in London and studied medicine and philosophy at Christ Church, Oxford. In 1667 he became physician to Lord Shaftesbury. That same year his *Essay Concerning Toleration* was published. Suspected of complicity in Shaftesbury's attempt to exclude Charles II's Roman Catholic brother, James (later James II), from ascending to the throne, Locke fled to Holland in 1683. After the "Glorious Revolution" of 1688–1689, in which Parliament replaced James with William and Mary, Locke returned to England.

Locke was best known as the first systematic theorist of classical political liberalism. In his most important political work, *Two Treatises of Government* (1690), he attacked "the divine right of kings," arguing that government was based on natural rights of individuals, not divine decree. Locke argued that people in nature were happy and free and had certain fundamental rights to

life, liberty, and property that could not be taken from them. Locke further maintained that people joined together in a social contract to protect those rights. In forming governments they voluntarily gave up some of those rights to preserve their society. Yet absolute sovereignty continued to reside with the people who had the right—and sometimes the duty—to overthrow governments that threatened or failed to protect liberty. Locke's ideas contrasted with those of THOMAS HOBBES, who thought that people were brutish in nature and, to secure self-preservation, that they surrender all of their rights to an absolute ruler.

In his *An Essay Concerning Human Understanding* (1690), Locke criticized the Platonic notion of "innate principles," as a means by which Hobbesians, Enthusiasts, and Roman Catholics imposed their opinions on others. All knowledge (except, perhaps, logic and mathematics) is empirical: it comes through experience, by sensation and reflection.

In 1691 he retired to Essex. In the last years of his life, he was the intellectual leader of the Whigs and wrote extensively on biblical themes. His *The Reasonableness of Christianity* (1695) was a plea for a liberal, nondogmatic Christianity; he has been called Socinian (denying the divinity of Christ and the Trinity) or Unitarian and deistic. "Revelation," he argued, "must be judged by reason." He died at Oates in Essex in 1704.

Legacy

Locke's ideas were central to the Enlightenment and became the fundamental principles behind the two great revolutions of the eighteenth century: the American Revolution and the French Revolution.

Locke's natural rights philosophy influenced THOMAS JEFFERSON, who used his arguments to justify revolution in the Declaration of Independence. Through the Declaration, Locke's concepts became central to what has become known as America's "civil religion," the ideas that unite to define Americans. Locke also influenced the more moderate wing of the French Revolution and his impact can be seen in the French Declaration of the Rights of Man (1791).

Locke's argument that the individual was the basic unit of society was the foundation of the classical political liberalism of the eighteenth and nineteenth centuries. For liberals, government was a necessary evil and it had to be limited through

institutional restraints. This thinking took its most concrete form in the U.S. Constitution, which established a federal government characterized by a system of checks and balances.

In his *An Essay Concerning Human Understanding*, Locke originated eighteenth-century empirical philosophy, which spread over England, France, and Germany. Called "the founder of the analytic philosophy of mind," he was the dominant philosophical influence until IMMANUEL KANT. He is sometimes also called the father of English skepticism. His epistemology (theory of knowledge) also became a standard for eighteenth-century Deism, the concept that God created the universe, set it in motion, and has not intervened since.

A major influence on modern philosophical and political thought, Locke epitomized the faith of the Enlightenment in the middle class, the new science, and in human goodness. For a century, the English Whig party was dominated by his ideas, and much of the liberal social, economic, and ethical theory of the eighteenth century was rooted in his theories of social contract. He influenced such later philosophers as DAVID HUME and GEORGE BERKELEY.

Because of their importance to the eighteenth-century liberal revolutions and to later political thought, Locke's ideas became central to Western democratic principles in the nineteenth and twentieth centuries.

Olson

WORLD EVENTS		LOCKE'S LIFE
Thirty Years' War in Europe	1618–48	
	1632	John Locke is born
	1667	Locke is named physician to Lord Schaftesbury
		Essay Concerning Toleration is published
	1683	Locke flees to Holland
England's Glorious Revolution	1688	
English seize Calcutta, India	1690	*Two Treatises of Government* is published
		An Essay Concerning Human Understanding is published
	1704	Locke dies
Peace of Utrecht settles War of Spanish Succession	1713–15	

For Further Reading:

Lloyd Thomas, David. *Locke on Government.* New York: Routledge, 1995.

Rogers, G. A. J. *Locke's Enlightenment: Aspects of the Origin, Nature, and Impact of his Philosophy.* New York: G. Olms, 1998.

Spellman, W. M. *John Locke.* New York: St. Martin's Press, 1997.

Luther, Martin

Principal Figure in the Protestant
Reformation
1483–1546

Life and Work

Martin Luther was a sixteenth-century German theologian whose call for the reform of the Roman Catholic church helped precipitate and shape the Protestant Reformation. Ultimately, his efforts led to establishment of the Lutheran church.

Luther was born in Eisleben, Germany, on November 10, 1483. He studied law at the University of Erfurt but, following a religious crisis in 1505, entered an Augustinian monastery. In 1512, he earned his doctorate in theology and was appointed to the chair of biblical theology at Wittenberg University. He became the focus of controversy, when, on October 31, 1517—the traditional beginning date for the Reformation—he issued 95 theses opposing the sale of indulgences and disputing the theology that supported them. (Indulgences offered release from temporal punishments for sins.)

Luther set forth his evolving theology in a series of pamphlets published in 1520. Widely disseminated through the newly invented printing press, they quickly spread his ideas throughout Europe. The most important of these pamphlets were *Address to the Christian Nobility of the German Nation, The Babylonian Captivity of the Church,* and *On the Freedom of a Christian Man.*

Luther's primary theme was justification by faith in contrast to "works righteousness," which taught that people could earn salvation through good works. Concerned about how weak humankind can be saved in face of the demands of God's law, Luther found an answer in the Epistle to the Romans. According to PAUL, the "righteousness of God" (Romans 1:17) is right-

eousness by grace alone (*sola gratia*). What was required for salvation, then, was not strict obedience to divine law, but a response of faith that accepted God's gift. Luther also rejected the established view of the Lord's Supper. In contrast to the traditional teaching that the bread and wine of the sacrament were transformed into Christ's body and blood (transubstantiation), he contended that the elements simultaneously remained bread and wine and became Christ's body and blood (consubstantiation).

Luther's defense and refusal to recant ultimately led to his excommunication in January 1521. Condemned following the Diet of Worms that April, he was secretly conveyed to Wartburg Castle where he was protected by Frederick of Saxony. There he began his translation of the New Testament into German. He returned to Wittenberg the following year, where he continued writing and overseeing ecclesiastical and liturgical reform. In 1524 he became embroiled in the violent Peasant's Revolt, which he condemned as a distortion of his teachings. In 1525 he broke the regulation for clerical celibacy by marrying Katharina von Bora, a former nun. He died in Eisleben on February 18, 1546.

Legacy

Luther's cause, the reformation of the Church, helped to launch the modern era. In varying measures, all modern "Protestants" rely on Luther's teaching. Almost 60 million of them throughout the world belong to churches that identify themselves as "Evangelical-Lutheran." Luther's legacy is traceable in many areas—political, economic, literary—but his central concerns were religious.

Immediately after Luther's death, PHILIPP MELANCHTHON continued Luther's work. Considered a compromiser, Melanchthon was able to chart a course among various radical factions to codify the basic theological teachings of what eventually became known as Lutheranism. By 1580, these teachings were collected in the *Book of Concord,* which became the standard for Lutheran theology.

Luther's association with the Germanic princes also led to a drastic political and religious realignment of Europe. The conflict over religious and political reform resulted in the Peace of Augsburg (1555), in which each prince was enabled to declare the religion of his province.

Thus, by the end of the sixteenth century, the countries of Scandinavia and the northern provinces of Germany were largely Lutheran, while areas closer to Italy remained Catholic.

Luther also left a strong legacy in biblical interpretation. He encouraged Bible reading among the laity. His German translation, commonly called the Luther Bible, made scripture available to ordinary believers. In preparing this translation, Luther drew upon forms of German from throughout all of the Germanic kingdoms. Thus, this translation had the added effect of providing the foundation for a common German language.

Luther's focus on Bible study and theological clarity began a distinguished line of theological inquiry. Among theologians who focused on scripture were such scholarly notables as F. C. Baur (1792–1860), Rudolf Bultmann (1884–1976), and Ernst Käsemann (twentieth century). Because biblical interpretation became the basis for church teaching, Luther's legacy also includes many important Protestant theologians, among them Albrecht Ritschl (1822–1855) and PAUL TILLICH (1886–1965). DIETRICH BONHOEFFER (1906–1945), a Lutheran pastor and theologian, continued Luther's emphasis on God's engagement with the world. Bonhoeffer was imprisoned, and eventually hanged, for his opposition to Hitler and the Third Reich during World War II.

Finally, Luther's emphasis on worship left an enduring liturgical legacy. Perhaps the most significant Lutheran composer was J. S. Bach (1685–1750) who composed music for the Thomas Kirche (the Thomas Church) in Leipzig.

Olson

WORLD EVENTS		LUTHER'S LIFE
	1483	Martin Luther is born in Eisleben
Columbus discovers Americas	1492	
Reformation begins	1517	Luther posts "95 theses" on indulgences
	1521	Luther refuses to recant at Diet of Worms; he begins translation of New Testament into German
	1546	Luther dies at Eisleben

For Further Reading:

Baton, Roland. *Here I Stand: A Life of Martin Luther.* New York: Abingdon-Cokesbury, 1950.

Boehmer, Heinrich. *Martin Luther: Road to Reformation.* New York: Meridian Books, 1967.

Kitteson, James M. *Luther the Reformer: The Story of the Man and His Career.* Minneapolis, Minn.: Augsburg, 1996.

Oberman, Heiko. *Luther: Man between God and the Devil.* New Haven, Conn.: Yale University Press, 1989.

Machiavelli, Niccolò

Founder of Modern Political
Science
1469–1527

Life and Work

Niccolò Machiavelli was a political theorist whose primary work, *The Prince*, presents a theory of governmental control that advocates that a ruler retain power by any means necessary.

Machiavelli was born in Florence, Italy, on May 3, 1469. Because he came from a poor family unable to send him to the university, Machiavelli was largely self-taught. At the time of his birth, Italy was not a unified nation, but a collection of city-states, each of which was controlled by a separate ruler. The small size of these city-states left them vulnerable to attack from the larger northern European kingdoms. To protect themselves from attack, the Italian states often sought support from foreign rulers.

In 1469, Florence was ruled by the Medici family. In 1494, Florence was invaded by Charles VIII of France and, by 1498, it was governed by the Soderini family, who established a republic. During this time, Machiavelli held several important offices, including minister of defense and diplomatic emissary. In 1512, the Spanish invaded Florence and restored the Medicis to power. Machiavelli was imprisoned.

The Medici held power until 1526. It was during this period, 1512–1526, that Machiavelli wrote his two most important works: *The Discourses* (1513–1517) and *The Prince* (1514).

The Discourses, a commentary on Livy's *History of Rome* was written between 1513 and 1517; it contains Machiavelli's arguments in favor of a republic. This form of government, states Machiavelli, promotes a commitment to the general well-being and to public participation in state affairs. The ruler pursues his own interests only insofar as such interests bolster republican values.

By the end of 1513, Machiavelli decided to ingratiate himself to the new Florentine regime by modifying his theory in *The Discourses* in hopes of obtaining a political post. The result was

the completion of *The Prince,* in which Machiavelli contends that an intelligent ruler knows that his self-interest requires that he provide his subjects with tangible results to ensure the survival of his regime. Such a ruler consolidates his power as he executes the ordinary duties of his office and is not bound by traditional values. In fact, the sole objective of the ruler is to retain power at all costs. Machiavelli dedicated *The Prince* to Lorenzo the Magnificent of the Medici family and sent it to him as a gift in 1514.

Machiavelli's tactic was successful and, in 1520, he was named historiographer of Florence by Lorenzo's successor, Cardinal Giulio de Medici. In 1523, Cardinal de Medici became Pope Clement VII and appointed Machiavelli to several Vatican offices. By the time that Charles V, the Holy Roman Emperor, conquered Rome in 1527, Machiavelli had lost all political support. He died in Florence on June 21, 1527.

Legacy

Machiavelli is most frequently identified as advocating a political theory that holds that success justifies whatever means is used to achieve it. Yet his legacy was far broader than a single political theory. Machiavelli is often called the father of modern political science.

Prior to Machiavelli, history and political science were viewed as branches of theology. Their major goal was to interpret events in terms of God's great plan for humanity's salvation. Medieval historians and political scientists treated people and events as unique and did not try to theorize from them. Their craft was based on faith and reason rather than empirical evidence. Machiavelli, on the other hand, developed general theories about political behavior that were not connected to specific times and cultures. He encouraged a secular and realistic approach to history and political science in order to understand, through empirical evidence, the functioning of a successful state.

Machiavelli's commitment to republicanism is found in *The Discourses*. He contributed at least two original thoughts to the Renaissance: 1) sovereignty should reside with the people, and 2) governmental actions are not necessarily bound by the same values as those of individuals. The sixteenth century viewed his ideas as radical and his name became a synonym for

atheism and cynical brutality. The description, "Machiavellian," entered European discourse as a slanderous term shortly after he died. The character of Barnabas, in Christopher Marlowe's *The Jew of Malta* (c. 1592), is a broad caricature of Machiavelli, who was viewed as the essence of evil.

Machiavelli's works had a profound impact on political thought and influenced individuals as varied as the sixteenth-century French queen Catherine d'Medici, the seventeenth-century English philosopher THOMAS HOBBES, and the twentieth-century Soviet dictator, Joseph Stalin, who reportedly kept a copy of *The Prince* by his bedside. "Machiavellian" has now come to be applied broadly to all persons engaging in unprincipled practices in private, as well as public, life.

Jurkovic

WORLD EVENTS		MACHIAVELLI'S LIFE
Ottoman Empire captures Byzantine capital, Constantinople	1453	
	1469	Niccolò Machiavelli is born in Florence, Italy
Columbus discovers Americas	1492	
Last Muslim State in Spain falls to Christians		
	1498– 1512	Machiavelli serves in government posts under Soderini family
	1512	Machiavelli is imprisoned
	1513	Machiavelli begins *The Discourses*
	1514	Machiavelli completes *The Prince* and dedicates it to Lorenzo de Medici
Reformation begins	1517	
	1520	Machiavelli becomes historiographer of Florence
	1523	Machiavelli becomes Vatican official
	1527	Machiavelli dies in Florence
Thirty Years' War in Europe	1618–48	

For Further Reading:

Donaldson, Peter S. *Machiavelli and Mystery of State.* New York: Cambridge University Press, 1988.

Masters, Roger D. *Fortune Is a River: Leonardo da Vinci and Niccolo Machiavelli's Magnificent Dream to Change the Course of Florentine History.* New York: Free Press, 1998.

Skinner, Quentin. *Machiavelli.* New York: Oxford University Press, 1981.

Madhva

Founder of Hindu School of
Dvaita Vedanta
c. 1199–c. 1278

Life and Work

Madhva was a thirteenth-century Hindu teacher who founded the Dvaita (dualistic) school of Vedanta, the study of the Vedas (early Hindu scriptures).

The basic traditions about Madhva state that he was born around 1199 to a Brahmin (upper caste) family in Rajatpitha, a town in South India. He was educated by Achyutrapeksha, a follower of SHANKARA, a ninth-century proponent of *advaita* (nondualism). Achyutrapeksha believed that the world of material objects was *maya* (illusion); reality is uncovered when the *maya* is unmasked; when this occurs total unification

WORLD EVENTS		MADHVA'S LIFE*
Islamic ruler of	1187	
Egypt, Saladin,		
captures Jerusalem		
	c. 1199	Madhva is born
Hapsburg dynasty	1273	
begins dominance		
in Holy Roman		
Empire		
	c. 1278	Madhva dies
Muscovite state,	1325	
present-day Russia,		
established by Ivan I		

* *Scholars cannot date the specific events in Madhva's life with accuracy.*

with the deity is possible. Not convinced by this non-dualistic approach, Madhva left Achyutrapeksha to study the Vedas.

Based on this study, Madhva rejected Shankara's *advaita* in favor of *dvaita* (dualism). (The word *dvaita* stems from the Sanskrit word *dvi*, meaning "two.") Madhva started from a commonsense observation. Everyday experience demonstrates that there is a distinction between the person who sees an object and the object itself, hence a dualism. Moreover, he contended that this *dvaita* reveals both a difference among the entities in the world and a mutual dependence among them. These characteristics of difference and dependence can be illustrated by thinking about a human being, composed of soul and body. While both of these attributes are different from each other, they are dependent on each other for life in the world. Only God, whom Madhva worshiped in the form of Vishnu, is totally independent.

Madhva's concepts of *dvaita* and the independence of God shaped his theories about the relationship between human beings and God. God created all human beings and all things, thus they are dependent on God and different from one another. Souls, then, seek *moksha* (release from the cycle of reincarnation) by exercising their free will to seek detachment from the world and knowledge of God. To attain such knowledge a person must engage both in serious study and disciplined meditation. Nevertheless, only by the grace of God is such knowledge granted to the seeker. Therefore Madhva supported a principle of predestination in which God preordains some for heaven and some for eternal damnation.

Madhva developed these ideas in 37 books, including *Commentary on the Brahma-sutra* and *Commentary on the Gita*. To spread his ideas and to practice devotion to Vishnu, he established a monastery at Udipi in South India. He died there around 1278.

Legacy

Madhva's concept of *dvaita* marked a radical change in the way the Vedas were interpreted and formed the basis of Dvaita Vedanta.

Prior to Madhva, the dominant forms of Vedanta were those of Shankara (700?–750?)

and RAMANUJA (c. 1017–1137). Both asserted *advaita* in that *moksha* involved total immersion into the deity so that there was no longer a distinction between the person and God.

Madhva's teaching was in stark contrast to that of these earlier Vedanta teachers and provided the foundation for a significant new school of thought among the modes of interpreting the Vedas. The monastery he established in Udipi has become the center of the continuing development of Dvaita Vedanta. His followers there even took the name Madhvas and deified him as an *avataara* (incarnation) of Makhya Praana, the god of life.

Perhaps his most important early follower was Sri Ananda Tiirtha (1239–1319), who at times claimed to be Madhva reincarnated. Sri Ananda Tiirtha is credited with developing Madhva's concept of differences and dependency into a fivefold doctrine known as Tattvavaada (the doctrine of real entities). Sri Ananda Tiirtha believed that three different kinds of entities inhabited the universe: insentient (unconscious matter and animals), sentient (conscious beings), and Vishnu (God). These three entities produced five dualistic relationships: 1) sentients and Vishnu, 2) insentients and Vishnu, 3) two separate and distinct sentients, 4) two separate and distinct insentients, and 5) sentients and insentients. Sri Ananda Tiirtha taught that once a person understands these five sets of relationships, a person can understand the whole universe. Further, the better one understands the universe, the better one understands God and moves closer to *moksha*.

Following Sri Ananda Tiirtha, there have been other important leaders of Dvaita Vedanta, including Sri Jayatiirtha, Sri Vaadiiraaja Tiirtha, and Sri Raghavendra Tiirtha. Both Sri Jayatiirtha and Sri Vaadiraaja Tiirtha were great scholars who wrote commentaries on the works of Sri Ananda Tiirtha. Sri Raghavendra Tiirtha is venerated as one who brought comfort to those who suffer.

The followers of Dvaita Vedanta have maintained their sanctuary at Udipi into the twentieth century through an unbroken succession of abbots, a testament to Madhva's influence and importance in contemporary Hindu thought and practice.

von Dehsen

For Further Reading:
Sharma, B. N. Krishnamurti. *The History of the Dvaita School of Vedanta and Its Literature: From the Earliest Beginnings to Our Own Time.* Delhi: Motilal Banarsidass, 1981.
von Galsenapp, Helmuth. *Madhva's Philosophy of the Vishnu Faith.* Bangalore, India: Dvaita Vedanta Studies and Research Foundation, 1992.

Madison, James

Principal Architect of the United
States Constitution
1751–1836

Life and Work

James Madison was the principal architect of the United States Constitution; he served as fourth president of the United States.

Born on March 16, 1751, on a plantation near what is now Port Conway, Virginia, Madison studied history, government, and law at the College of New Jersey (now Princeton University). Following graduation in 1771, he became committed to the establishment of an independent American republic. In 1776 he helped draft Virginia's state constitution and prepared its declaration of rights. His experiences while serving in the Continental Congress and Virginia Assembly in the late 1770s and early 1780s convinced him that the national government as defined under the Articles of Confederation was incapable of meeting the challenges to the new republic.

As delegate to the Constitutional Convention of 1787, the 36-year-old Madison played the major role in convincing the other delegates to create a new government in which sovereignty rested with the people rather than with the states, as it did under the existing system. He put forward a plan that outlined three branches of government joined in a shared-power system to prevent tyranny. His proposed system called for a strong chief executive and a bicameral national legislature elected by proportional representation (the size of each state del-

egation determined by population). The Virginia Plan, as it was called, served as the outline for the convention's debates and formed the basis of the document ultimately adopted after compromises to accommodate the small states. (The most notable compromise was the provision for state legislatures to elect senators.)

Although Madison was disappointed with some elements of the Constitution, he worked tirelessly for its passage. He coauthored *The Federalist Papers*, a collection of essays explaining the political theory behind the new system, and led the bitter struggle for ratification in Virginia. Madison had thought that the Constitution contained sufficient protection to ensure individual liberty but eventually became convinced of the need for a bill of rights, which he drafted in 1789.

From 1789 to 1797 Madison served in the House of Representatives, where he helped give life to the new system and led the fight for the adoption of the Bill of Rights. He was secretary of state from 1801 to 1808 and served as president from 1809 to 1817. At his death on June 28, 1836, he was the last survivor of those who had attended the Constitutional Convention.

Legacy

As the "Father of the Constitution," Madison played a major role in shaping the American system of government.

Madison devised a governmental system that provided the new republic with a central government powerful enough to address the problems facing the young nation, yet one in which individual liberty was protected by a unique system of shared powers and checks and balances. Over the years the system proved remarkably adaptable as the United States evolved from a small agricultural nation into an industrial power and as citizens changed their perceptions of and demands on government. The Constitution serves not only as an outline of government but also as a binding code of supreme law. As the core element in America's civil religion, it has become the symbol of national unity and continuity of the nation's basic ideals amid change. In place for over 200 years the United States Constitution is the world's longest-lived constitution and has been imitated by many nations across the world who have newly established democratic systems of government.

Historians believe that *The Federalist Papers*, which Madison wrote with Alexander Hamilton and John Jay in defense of the Constitution, had little influence on the public opinion of the day.

Yet the 85 articles of the *Papers* are now considered to be the most important work of political thought ever produced in the United States. Along with the voluminous notes Madison kept during the Constitutional Convention, the *Papers* continue to serve as the primary resource for understanding the intentions of the Constitution's framers. The Supreme Court frequently refers to them in developing opinions, and thus they have had a profound influence on modern constitutional interpretation.

The Bill of Rights that Madison created had little bearing on the lives of most Americans during the first 100 years of the republic. In the late eighteenth and early nineteenth centuries, Americans viewed the right to property as their most important civil liberty because they believed it vital for maintaining individual independence and preventing government tyranny. Over the course of the twentieth century, however, personal rights became central to the American concept of freedom and the Bill of Rights became the primary safeguard of liberty. In mid-century the Supreme Court began applying the protections of the Bill of Rights to the states and gave fundamental liberties such as freedom of speech and religion special protections. During the 1960s it presided over a rights revolution that expanded individual freedoms beyond even those specifically articulated in the Bill of Rights.

von Dehsen

For further reading:
McCoy, Drew R. *The Last of the Fathers: James Madison and the Republican Legacy*. New York: Cambridge University Press, 1989.
Rutland, Robert A. *James Madison: The Founding Father*. New York: Macmillan, 1987.

WORLD EVENTS		MADISON'S LIFE
Peace of Utrecht settles War of Spanish Succession	1713–15	
	1751	James Madison is born
United States independence	1776	Madison helps draft Virginia's constitution
	1787	Madison leads Constitutional Convention
French Revolution	1789	
	1789–97	Madison serves in U.S. House of Representatives
Napoleonic Wars in Europe	1803–15	
	1809–17	Madison is president of United States
Greek War of Independence against Turkey	1821–29	
	1836	Madison dies
Revolutions in Austria, France, Germany, and Italy	1848	

Maharishi Mahesh Yogi

Founder of Transcendental
Meditation
1911(?)–

Life and Work

The Maharishi Mahesh Yogi has devoted his life to spreading the benefits of transcendental meditation to the modern world.

Little is known of the Maharishi's early life, because he believes that it his teachings that are important, not the facts of his personal life. According to most accounts, he is a Hindu monk, who may have been born in 1911 and whose career began in relative seclusion studying with a Hindu religious leader (*guru*) of northern India. Before that, the Maharishi apparently studied physics at the University of Allahabad around 1932 and was for a time a factory worker, presumably under his own name, since "maharishi" means "enlightened spiritual one." From about 1940 to 1952, the Maharishi worked with his *guru* (Guru Dev) whose teachings are said to constitute the foundation of transcendental meditation (TM). After Guru Dev died in 1952, the Maharishi may have gone into nearly complete seclusion for two years, after which he began to organize a movement to spread TM throughout the world. The first world tour took place in 1959 and the movement grew slowly until the late 1960s when the Beatles and other celebrities began to join. At about that time, the Maharishi began to create TM educational centers in Europe, as well as in India.

In *The Science of Being and Art of Living* (1963), which may be considered his fundamental "philosophical" treatise, the Maharishi provides a "summation . . . of the Vedic (traditions) of ancient India and the growth of scientific thinking in the present-day Western world." In that and other books and lectures, he teaches that the nervous systems of individuals and the entire human race can evolve rapidly toward a state where "life is lived at full potential and in accord with the highest human aspirations."

How pervasive the Maharishi's teachings and the techniques of TM became in a short period can be shown by the invitation extended to him from the American Association of Higher Education (AAHE) to give the keynote address at its annual convention. Amidst the activities of his "Dawn of the Age of Enlightenment" world tour in 1973, the Maharishi addressed 3,000 prominent educators at the AAHE convention who met to explore the relationship of the quality of life to higher education.

The Maharishi is still active.

Legacy

Through the work of the Maharishi and his organization, the techniques of transcendental meditation and other applied "Vedic technologies" have been handed along to many around the globe.

TM remains a popular form of relaxation, especially in the United States. TM, originally taught only by the Maharishi today has thousands of teachers worldwide. TM is not a set of religious beliefs but a specific technique of meditation. Learning the technique involves a number of sessions of formal instruction, followed by a ceremony in which the applicant makes monetary and other offerings to the teacher and receives a mantra. TM practitioners, then, sit for 20 minutes twice a day completely focusing on the mantra. Only a formally initiated teacher can give a mantra to the student. Practitioners say (and many scientific studies seem to confirm) that TM brings deep relaxation, vitality, and creativity.

The Marharishi's influence has spread beyond TM since 1980, as its techniques have been applied beyond personal relaxation to regimens of holistic medicine, management of global corporations, and systems of academic instruction. Faculty at schools and centers in a number of countries teach this applied knowledge. In addition, scientific research has shown positive results from the new systems of applied transcendental meditation. This research has tested a variety of formalized theories, such as "consciousness-based learning" and "science of creative intelligence." Many of the experiments were done by the various Maharishi educational and medical institutions, but many were also conducted independently, substantiating, perhaps, the Maharishi's belief that ancient Indian wisdom can be productively joined to modern technology and expertise.

Founded in 1973 by the organization known today as the "Maharishi Vedic Education Development Corporation," the Maharishi International University was the first of the organization's schools to attract significant public notice in the United States when it was established on the site of the former Parsons College in Fairfield, Connecticut. In the years since then, the Maharishi Vedic Education Development Corporation has created manifold educational enterprises, working with trademarks (such as "Transcendental Meditation" and "Science of Creative Intelligence") and through privately owned schools and teaching centers. Some of the schools currently owned by the corporation are Maharishi International University, Maharishi School of the Age of Enlightenment, Maharishi Vedic University, Maharishi Medical Center, and Maharishi University of Management.

K. T. Weidmann

WORLD EVENTS	MAHARISHI'S LIFE*
	1911 (?) Maharishi is born
World War I 1914–18	
	c. 1932 Maharishi enters University of Alahabad to study physics
World War II 1939–45	
Mao Tse-tung establishes Communist rule in China 1949	
Korean War 1950–53	
	c. 1954 Maharishi founds TM movement
	1959 Maharishi's first world tour
	1963 Maharishi publishes *The Science of Being and Art of Living*
Six Day War between Israel and Arabs 1967	
	1973 Maharishi International University is founded in Fairfield, Connecticut
End of Vietnam War 1975	
Dissolution of Soviet Union 1991	

* Scholars cannot date the specific events in Maharishi's early life with accuracy.

For Further Reading:

Fagan, John. *Genetic Engineering: The Hazards. Vedic Engineering: The Solutions.* Fairfield, Conn.: Maharishi International University of Management Press, 1995.

Mahesh Yogi, Maharishi. *The Science of Being and Art of Living.* New York: New American Library, 1963.

Mason, Paul. *The Maharishi: The Biography of the Man Who Gave Transcendental Mediation to the World.* Rockport, Mass.: Element, 1994

Mahavira (Vardhamana)

Founder of Jainism
c. 599–c. 527 B.C.E.

Life and Work

Mahavira, also known as Vardhamana, was the founder of Jainism, a religion devoted to ascetic practices as a means of respecting all life forms. The goal of Jainism is for individuals to achieve *kevala*, a state of perfection free of all harmful *karma*.

Mahavira, Sanskrit for "The Great Hero," was born in northeast India to a family of the Kshatriya, or warrior, caste of Hinduism. His father, Siddhartha, was probably a prince; his mother, Devananda, may have been a member of the Brahman priestly caste, the highest of all the castes. Both were thought to have followed the teachings of Parshva, an ascetic who had lived 200 years earlier. During Mahavira's youth, opposition grew to Brahman cultural domination. In an era when the doctrines of nonviolence and reincarnation (linking animals and humans in a cycle of birth and rebirth) were spreading, many also objected to large-scale animal sacrifice.

In response, both Mahavira and his contemporary, BUDDHA (Siddhartha Gautama), sought release from Brahman control by redirecting religious activity inward and placing it in control of the individual through meditative and spiritual disciplines. At age 30, Mahavira renounced family and friends and took the life of a wandering ascetic.

After 12 years of living as an ascetic, Mahavira is said to have achieved the state of *kevala*, or purification from all evil *karma*. *Kevala* is the release from evil *karma* and is the ultimate focus of Jainism. Jains believe that *karma* is a sticky substance that clings to life. To achieve *kevala*, souls must pass through 14 stages until all evil *karma* is repelled. This spiritual achievement earned him the title *Jina*, or "Victor," which inspired the name of the religion that grew out of his teachings: Jainism.

Mahavira initially drew upon Hindu and Parshva teachings as the foundation for his teaching. From Hinduism, Mahavira built on the doctrine of reincarnation. If all souls traverse the path to Nirvana through various life-forms, then it holds that all life-forms are of equal value. From Parshva, Mahavira adopted the four ascetic disciplines—nonviolence, truthfulness, repudiation of greed, and denial of earthly attachments. He may have added sexual abstinence to the list. Tradition claims that 11 Brahman priests joined Mahavira and became his *ganadharas*, or disciples. Each of these *ganadharas* also attained *kevala*. During his lifetime. Mahavira is credited with attracting over 500,000 disciples.

Mahavira died around 527 B.C.E. in Pava, in the Bihar province of India.

Legacy

Western scholars view Mahavira as the founder of historical Jainism. (Jains consider him the latest of the prophets.) Mahavira, the *Jina*, became the model of the perfect life. Before he died, Mahavira entrusted his teaching to his *gadanharas*, the most prominent of whom were Gautama Indrabhuti and Sudharman. The latter taught his own disciple, Jambu, the sayings of Mahavira, thus securing the line of oral tradition.

Later Jains further refined Mahavira's teachings by separating the universe into two distinct realms: the nonliving (*ajiva*) and the living (*jiva*). Life-forms pervade all matter, plants, and animals; each higher form is progressively more complex than the form below it. Only the higher life forms are able to attain *kevala*. This teaching also leads to absolute respect for all life. As a result, most Jains are vegetarians. One can even see Jain monks and nuns walking carefully and wearing masks to avoid inadvertently injuring insects on their path.

Over the next few centuries, Jain teachings and traditions became relatively stable. In 79 C.E.,

Jainism split into two groups: Digambara and Svetambara. The Digambara (literally, "sky-clad") rejected all possessions, even clothing. Over time, the Digambara became allies of the ruling families in Karnataka and the Deccan, allowing Jainism to thrive. This royal support gave the Digambara the freedom to produce much poetry and philosophical writing from the sixth to twelfth centuries C.E. During this same period, the Svetabara (literally, "white clad"), who allowed minimal possessions, lived in relative peace in the north. They also had a significant literary yield.

By the twelfth century, the Digambara monks had begun to construct temples and monasteries. They became somewhat attracted to material comforts, giving rise to a reform movement and to the eventual loss of influence. During this time the Svetambara monks fell victim to the Muslim invasions. Although the influence of these groups waned over the next centuries, they did generate important internal reform movements, such as the one led by Sthanakavasi in the eighteenth century.

In the twentieth century Jainism has become influential in such political movements as nuclear disarmament and the objection to the use of animals for scientific research. MOHANDAS KARAMCHAND GANDHI noted that Jainism influenced his own nonviolent form of political protest.

von Dehsen

WORLD EVENTS		MAHAVIRA'S LIFE*
	B.C.E.	
Nebuchadnezzar begins rule of Babylon	605	
	c. 599	Mahavira is born
Hanging Gardens of Babylon built	597	
Babylonian Exile of Israelites begins	587	
	c. 569	Mahavira becomes wandering ascetic
	c. 557	Mahavira attains *kevala*
Persian king Cyrus captures Babylon and frees Israelites	539	
	c. 527	Mahavira dies
Temple reconstructed in Jerusalem	521	

For Further Reading:
Dundas, Paul. *The Jains*. London: Routledge, 1992.
Tobias, Michael. *The Life Force: The World of Jainism*. Berkeley, Calif.: Asian Humanities Press, 1992.

* *Scholars cannot date the specific events in Mahavira's life with accuracy.*

Malcolm X

(Malcolm Little)

Militant Black Activist; Minister of
the Nation of Islam
1925–1965

Life and Work

Malcolm X was a minister of the Nation of Islam who fought for the civil rights of African Americans.

Malcolm X was born Malcolm Little in Omaha, Nebraska, on May 19, 1925. In 1931 Malcolm's father, Earl Little, a follower of black

World Events	Malcolm's Life
World War I 1914–18	
1925	Malcolm X is born Malcolm Little
1931	Malcolm's father is murdered
World War II 1939–45	
1946	Malcolm sentenced to 10 years in prison
Mao Tse-tung establishes Communist rule in China 1949	
Korean War 1950–53	
1952	Malcolm is paroled and joins Nation of Islam
1954	Malcolm appointed minister of Temple Number 7 in Harlem
1954–64	Malcolm is national spokesman for the Nation of Islam
1964	Malcolm breaks with Nation of Islam and travels to Mecca
1965	Malcolm moderates his views on black separatism
	Malcolm is assassinated in New York City
	The Autobiography of Malcolm X is published
Six Day War between Israel and Arabs 1967	

nationalist MARCUS GARVEY, was brutally murdered by members of a racist group. His mother was unable to cope alone with her large family, and Malcolm was placed in foster care. Although he was a good and popular student, he dropped out of school after the eighth grade, moved to Boston, and turned to such crimes as selling drugs and illegal gambling. In 1946 he was sentenced to prison for 10 years for burglary.

In prison, he began a process of self-education and came under the influence of the teachings of ELIJAH MUHAMMAD, leader of the Nation of Islam, known widely as the Black Muslims. Malcolm was impressed with Muhammad's message that whites were the devil and that blacks could only better their lives by living separately from whites.

Paroled in 1952, Malcolm went to Detroit where he became a disciple of Elijah Muhammad. Playing an increasingly active role in the Nation of Islam, he adopted the strict moral code and ascetic lifestyle of its members and received the surname "X" to replace the name forced on his slave ancestors. In 1954 he was appointed minister of Temple Number 7 in New York City's Harlem and, until 1964, was the Nation of Islam's controversial national spokesman. He was given to inflammatory speechmaking that struck fear in the white population and offended the majority of blacks who, along with MARTIN LUTHER KING, JR., favored integration by peaceful means.

Malcolm's description of President John F. Kennedy's assassination as a "case of chickens coming home to roost" led to his suspension from the Black Muslims, and he broke with the group in 1964. He made a pilgrimage to Mecca and traveled throughout the Middle East and Africa, where he learned that classical Islam advocated racial equality and included among its adherents people of all races. Influenced by Islamic thinking, Malcolm abandoned his call for racial separation and began to promote more cooperation between the races. This transformation was cut short in New York City on February 21, 1965, when he was shot to death while addressing a rally of his newly formed Organization for Afro-American Unity.

Legacy

In the more than 30 years since his death, as the progress of civil rights and equality for

blacks has seemed to falter and, for some, even taken a backward step, the symbol of Malcolm has become, if anything, increasingly potent as a rallying cry among the disaffected black community.

While idolized by his followers, after his death Malcolm was remembered in both the white and black press as a militant revolutionary, an incendiary racist, harmful to the cause of integration and accommodation favored by most of the leaders of the civil rights movement. His death, however, preceded by one year the rise of the black power movement of the late 1960s which looked to Malcolm as one of its inspirations. During the race riots of 1965–68, the name of Malcolm X was often invoked while American cities burned. The black consciousness and black pride movements of the 1970s also had their roots partly in the black nationalism preached by Malcolm.

His fascinating, brief life has become the subject of books, plays, opera, and film. *The Autobiography of Malcolm X* and books of his speeches have been in print continuously since his death.

Today it seems that Malcolm's complexities of thinking and his turn toward moderation near the end of his life are largely overlooked or ignored. He is remembered and admired for his fiery style and as a black man who stood up for his people. When his name is invoked today, it is usually as a symbol of militancy and defiance against a hostile and unfair white world.

Saltz

For Further Reading:

X, Malcolm. *The Autobiography of Malcolm X.* With the assistance of Alex Haley. New York: Grove Press, 1965.

X, Malcolm. *Malcolm X Speaks: Selected Speeches and Statements.* Edited with prefatory notes by George Breitman. New York: Grove Weidenfeld, 1990.

Cone, James H. *Martin & Malcolm & America: A Dream or a Nightmare?* Maryknoll, N.Y.: Orbis Books, 1991.

Mani (Manes; Manichaeus)

Founder of Manichaeism
216–c. 274

Life and Work

Mani, also known as Manes and Manichaeus, was the founder of Manichaeism, a dualistic religious belief system that asserts that there are two realms of existence, one good and one evil. Although ultimately rejected by Christian theologians as a heresy, Manichaeism spread throughout the Mediterranean and to the east as far as China.

Mani was born on April 14, 216, in southern Babylonia, part of modern–day Iraq. Patek, his father, was from Hamadan, and believed in the practices of baptism and of extreme self-discipline. His mother, also named Mani, was a distant relative of the Parthian royal family. He had his first spiritual vision at the age of twelve (c. 228); later he claimed to have had visions of the Holy Spirit, who revealed divine mysteries to him.

On April 19, 240, at age 24, Mani received a divine commission to preach his beliefs publicly. He considered himself the "final prophet" in the line of prophets such as Adam, BUDDHA, ZOROASTER, and JESUS. The Persian king, Shapur I (242–273), became a convert to Mani's teachings and permitted him to preach throughout the Persian Empire.

Mani hoped to develop a religion based on universal truths expressed in the teachings of the earlier prophets. Each of these earlier prophets had access only to partial truths; Mani, for the first time, was able to integrate these teachings into a complete religious system. His teaching was also related to that of earlier Gnostics, such as Basilides and Valentinus, who taught that the material world was inherently evil. Only by receiving the proper spiritual knowledge, or *gnosis*, could a believer escape this evil realm and reunite with the Divine Spirit. For Mani this gnostic framework implied that souls originated in the realm of the God of light. Once trapped by the evil, material world, they required special knowledge to free themselves and reunite with God. Mani is also thought to have rejected the Christian

sacraments, since the use of "earthly elements" (water, bread, wine) tied these rituals to the material world. As not all believers have the same spiritual abilities, the people in Mani's churches were designated either as the "elect" or as the "hearers" (disciples) still learning the spiritual abilities.

Although Mani received support from King Shapur I, when the king died he was succeeded by Bahram I (274–277). Soon thereafter, the Zoroastrian priests denounced Mani's teaching. Around 274, the king imprisoned him at Gundeshapur (Belapet), where Mani died.

Legacy

Mani's teaching, commonly known as Manichaeism, quickly spread to Europe and east Asia. Wherever it took hold, it generated religious movements that promoted both Mani's dualistic teachings and his emphasis on breaking down barriers between religious communities.

Merchants carried Mani's teachings throughout the Roman Empire, and, by the fourth century, his ideas had reached Rome itself. Manichaean communities formed in Spain and Gaul (France) and especially along the Mediterranean coast of North Africa. During this period, the young Augustine of Carthage, destined to become a prominent Christian theologian, came under the influence of Manichaeism through his mother, Monica. Manichaeism soon came under attack from Christian theologians because it denied both that the world was created by God and that Jesus was human. By the end of the sixth century it had disappeared almost entirely from the Roman Empire.

In the East, Persian traders carried Manichaeism along the caravan routes. It first prospered in East Turkistan, and, in 762, it became the state religion of the Uigur kingdom on the northern border of China. Manichaeism also reached China where missionaries introduced it to the royal court in 694; a 732 edict granting freedom of religion allowed it to grow. Although the Emperor Wuzong persecuted adherents in 845, Manichaean communities existed, particularly in the southeast, until the fourteenth century. Manichaean beliefs may

have influenced the White Lotus Secret Society, a Buddhist sect that led rebellions against the Ming (1368–1644) and Qing (1644–1911) dynasties.

During the Middle Ages, so-called neo-Manichaean sects appeared in such places as Armenia (seventh century), Bulgaria (tenth century), and southern France (twelfth century).

The appeal of Manichaeism in these various locales stems in part from its commitment to ecumenical and universal religious principles. Based on the spiritual teachings of such important religious personages as Zoroaster, Buddha, and Jesus, this religion could adapt itself well to cultures dominated by Christianity, Buddhism, and Taoism.

von Dehsen

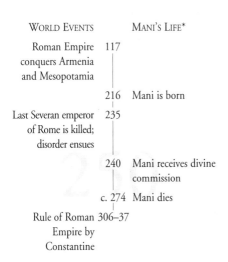

WORLD EVENTS		MANI'S LIFE*
Roman Empire conquers Armenia and Mesopotamia	117	
	216	Mani is born
Last Severan emperor of Rome is killed; disorder ensues	235	
	240	Mani receives divine commission
	c. 274	Mani dies
Rule of Roman Empire by Constantine	306–37	

* Scholars cannot date the specific events in Mani's life with accuracy.

For Further Reading:

Reeves, John C. *Heralds of That Good Realm: Syro-Mesopotamian Gnosis and Jewish Traditions.* New York: E. J. Brill, 1996.

Widengren, George. *Mani and Manichaeism.* London: Weidenfeld and Nicholson, 1965.

Mann, Horace

Educational Philosopher
and Reformer; Advocate of
Free Public Schools
1796–1859

Life and Work

Horace Mann was the first strong advocate in the United States for public schools that would be free, open to everyone of all classes, religions, and races, organized along democratic lines, and staffed by trained professionals.

Mann was born on May 4, 1796, in Franklin, Massachusetts. He had little formal schooling but managed to educate himself enough at the local library to gain admittance to Brown University, from which he graduated with honors in 1819. He went on to study law at Litchfield, Connecticut, and was admitted to the bar in 1823.

Mann had a quick legal mind, was an excellent speaker, and had an interest in many humanitarian and social causes. In 1827 he was elected to the Massachusetts House of Representatives, where he served until 1833. While there, he helped established the nation's

first state hospital for the insane. Serving in the state Senate from 1835 to 1837, he helped enact legislation establishing the first state board of education in the country and, in 1837, accepted an appointment to that board as secretary. In 1843 he traveled to Europe to study its educational institutions and methods. From his observations in France and Prussia he returned to the United States enthusiastic about supporting teacher education and eliminating the authoritarian, often cruel, methods of teaching.

As secretary of the board, Mann published the *Common School Journal* for educators, spoke convincingly about education to the public, and issued influential yearly reports that were widely read in the United States as well as in South America and Europe. Mann's critics were the clergy who advocated religious schooling and those who thought that education was the province of the church, the home, or private institutions. In 1848 Mann left the board to fill the seat of former President John Quincy Adams in the U.S. House of Representatives, where he served from 1848 to 1852. There he took up the anti-slavery cause and achieved a national reputation as an outspoken abolitionist.

In 1853 Mann accepted the post of president of the newly formed Antioch College in Yellow Springs, Ohio. Antioch was a liberal school that was nonsectarian, coeducational, and racially integrated. There Mann spent the remainder of his life and died on August 2, 1859.

Legacy

Mann promoted programs of educational reform that have become the foundation for contemporary educational practice. He was one of the first in North America to call for teacher education and to insist that all children, regardless of economic status, receive a decent education in publicly run schools.

Mann's campaign for schools run by the state, and not by private, usually religious, institutions was foundational for the development of American public school systems. After he returned from Europe in 1843, Mann began to push for special institutions to train teachers. Although roundly criticized, his actions ultimately led to the founding of hundreds of teachers colleges and the establishment of professional standards for educators.

The principle that all children have an equal

opportunity for an education was expanded after his death to include education at all levels. In 1879, James B. Angell, the president of the University of Michigan, appealed to Mann's ideals to endorse the concept that all are entitled to the opportunity for a university education.

Mann emphasized the practical in education and in so doing developed some of what has become standard educational practice today. For example, he founded school libraries containing books of practical interest. He also encouraged instruction in music and drawing and established programs in primary reading. He had less of an impact on the curriculum, where his desire to educate students for jobs led him to recommend abandoning abstract subjects such as history and geometry in favor of courses like surveying.

Massachusetts, thanks to Mann's educational leadership, was at the forefront of public education in the United States. By 1861 most of the northern states had state education offices; by 1900 about half of all states had established such offices. While Mann's emphasis was on the primary school, free public secondary schooling began to take hold in the 1870s. Compulsory schooling was in place countrywide by the 1920s. Today the United States has more than 89,000 public elementary and secondary schools and over 16,000 school districts. About 46,300,000 students are enrolled in the public schools.

Mann had little lasting impact on the development of the curriculum, but his legacy extends into all aspects of modern practice related to the institution, organization, administration, and public attitudes about education.

Saltz

World Events	Mann's Life
French Revolution 1789	
	1796 Horace Mann is born
Napoleonic Wars 1803–15 in Europe	
	1819 Mann graduates from Brown University
Greek War of 1821–29 Independence against Turkey	
	1827–37 Mann serves in Massachusetts legislature
	1837–48 Mann serves as secretary of Massachusetts Board of Education
Revolutions in 1848 Austria, France, Germany, and Italy	
	1848–52 Mann serves in U.S. House of Representatives
	1853–59 Mann is president of Antioch College
	1859 Mann dies in Ohio

For Further Reading:

Mann, Mary Tyler Peabody. "Mrs. Horace Mann." *Life of Horace Mann*. Centennial edition in facsimile. Washington, D.C.: National Education Association of the United States, 1937.

Tharp, Louise Hall. *Until Victory: Horace Mann and Mary Peabody*. Boston: Little, Brown, 1953.

Marcion

Influential Early Christian Heretic
1st–2nd Century C.E.

Life and Work

Marcion was a Christian heretic whose challenge to traditional theology motivated the Church to define orthodox doctrine and produce the biblical canon (list of books).

Marcion is known almost totally from the writings of his opponents. He was born in the late first century C.E., at Sinope in the Black Sea area of what is today Turkey. He was a member of the Christian community there; indeed, his father is reputed to have been bishop of Sinope. Marcion became a prosperous shipowner who seems to have traveled extensively. He left home after being excommunicated from the Church and settled in Rome, where he joined the Christian community in that city.

Marcion presented his theology in the Antithesis of his *Instrumentum*, which listed the contradictions in the Old and New Testament to prove that there were two Gods: the God of the Jews (the Demiurge) and the God of JESUS. The God of the Hebrew scriptures was angry, often vacillating. This God brought evil into what he viewed as a miserable world. The God of Jesus was kind and loving. The world knew nothing about this God until Jesus began his ministry. Marcion rejected the traditional stories of Jesus's birth, believing that anything associated with human reproduction was disgusting; he found it inconceivable that Jesus was born. Instead, he asserted that Jesus first appeared as an adult.

Because there was no connection between the Demiurge and the God of Jesus, Marcion rejected Hebrew scriptures and edited the Christian documents to remove the work of what he called "Judiasers," who saw continuity between the two.

Church authorities in Rome rejected his views and formally excommunicated him in 144. He then began to organize communities of followers throughout the Roman Empire, establishing Marcionite churches with their own clergy, sacraments, and rules. Because

Marcion believed that the world of the flesh was evil, his followers practiced asceticism and remained celibate. Unlike the traditional Church of the time, the Marcionite community opened its services to unbelievers and permitted women to serve as priests and bishops. Marcion's churches had numerous members for several centuries.

Nothing is known of the circumstances of Marcion's death.

Legacy

Marcion was a serious threat to the early Church. Much of what is now viewed as orthodox beliefs developed in response to his teachings.

Marcion was the first to establish a scriptural canon. He accepted as authoritative the Gospel of Luke and 10 Pauline letters, all edited to reflect his opposition to the creator God. In response, the Church was forced to develop a list of approved texts from diverse, unorganized material. The Church affirmed the authority of both a larger collection of Christian writings, the New Testament, and a collection of Jewish scriptures, the Old Testament.

A large portion of early Christian writing responds to Marcion. Polycarp (c. 160) called him the "firstborn of Satan," and Tertullian (c. 190) wrote *Against Marcion* in five volumes. Marcion's teachings even influenced the prologues written for the books of the Bible through the Middle Ages. Some of the Church's strong early affirmations explicitly deny Marcion's views. The emphasis on the Trinity and the continuity between the Old and New Testaments rejects Marcion's view of two Gods and the inferiority of the Old Testament deity. The affirmation of Jesus' humanity and birth from the Virgin MARY rejects the Marcionite view that Jesus was not born but appeared as an adult in Capernaum.

Marcionite church practices also influenced the traditional Church. The Church refused to demand celibacy but did follow in prizing celibacy above marriage. In so doing, the Church recognized that Marcion continued to maintain standards of holiness that other "heretical" groups denied. The Church also eventually allowed those not yet baptized to attend all services.

In the twentieth century, Marcion provides an example of someone who understands the Old Testament literally and who denies it any authority. Others have appealed to Marcionite openness to marginalized groups in the ordained ministry as an example for our time. Moreover, Marcion is often appealed to by the supporters of women's ordination; similarly, some opponents of women's ordination cite Marcion's excommunication as a reason for rejecting leadership roles for women.

Osterfield

WORLD EVENTS		MARCION'S LIFE*
Destruction of temple in Jerusalem	70	
	c. 85	Marcion is born
Roman Empire conquers Armenia and Mesopotamia	117	
	c. 140	Marcion arrives in Rome
	c. 144	Marcion repudiates Christian community in Rome and is expelled from Church as heretic
	c. 160	Marcion dies
Last Severan emperor of Rome is killed; disorder ensues	235	

* Scholars cannot date the specific events in Marcion's life with accuracy.

For Further Reading:

Harnack, Adolf von. *Marcion: The Gospel of the Alien God.* Translated by John E. Steely and Lyle D. Bierma. Durham, N.C. : Labyrinth Press, 1990.

Hoffmann, R. Joseph. *Marcion, on the Restitution of Christianity: An Essay on the Development of Radical Paulinist Theology in the Second Century.* Chico, Calif.: Scholar's Press, 1984.

Wilson, Robert Smith. *Marcion.* New York : AMS Press, 1980.

Marcus Aurelius

Roman Emperor; Stoic
"Philosopher–King"
121–180

Life and Work

Marcus Aurelius was a Roman emperor and Stoic philosopher who became the living example of the "philosopher–king" for Western political theorists and philosophers.

WORLD EVENTS		AURELIUS' LIFE
Roman Empire conquers Armenia and Mesopotamia	117	
	121	Marcus Aurelius is born in Baetica (now Spain)
	145	Aurelius marries emperor's daughter Annia Galeria Faustina
	161	Aurelius becomes emperor of Rome
	180	Aurelius dies in Vindobona (Vienna)
Last Severan emperor of Rome is killed; disorder ensues	235	

Aurelius was born on April 20, 121, into a wealthy, patrician family from Baetica (now Spain). He was the nephew of Emperor Antoninus, who, recognizing Aurelius' unusual abilities, adopted him and groomed him to succeed. During this apprenticeship, in 145, Aurelius married his cousin, the emperor's daughter Annia Galeria Faustina.

Aurelius became emperor in 161 and spent virtually half his reign waging war against barbarian tribes. A humanitarian, he instituted many reforms to improve social welfare and make the legal system more humane. When plague and famine hit the empire, he sold his personal possessions to help the victims. Yet he vigorously persecuted Christians, whom he believed were the empire's chief enemies.

In his *Meditations*, Aurelius expresses his Stoic philosophy. All of existence is governed by reason, considered as god, and life is well-lived if one lives in harmony with reason. This acceptance of the will of reason leads first to the willingness to accept the events, good or ill, of everyday life. It is the inner response of the individual—to accept or to contend with the unfortunate events of life, not the events themselves—that results in happiness or pain.

On a public level, Aurelius considered it his destiny to be emperor and saw himself obligated by reason (or god) to carry out his duties according to the dictates of universal law, not the law of Rome. He may have been emperor of Rome, but he viewed himself as a citizen of the world. As the "philosopher–king," it was his duty to govern according to his philosophical insights. To do less would be to ignore his own purpose and to contradict the requirements of universal reason.

On March 17, 180, Aurelius died of the plague in Vindobona, present day Vienna.

Legacy

Aurelius' legacy lies primarily in his philosophy and example, which has influenced Western theorists into the twentieth century.

As emperor, Aurelius had no lasting impact. Despite his efforts to defend Rome's frontiers, the barbaric tribes made increasing inroads into the empire, which fell to them in 476. The eighteenth century English historian Edward Gibbon, in *The Decline and Fall of the Roman Empire,* considered the death of Aurelius to be the beginning of Rome's decline.

Aurelius highly influenced early Christian thought through his idea of scrutinizing one's inner self and his belief that people have the divine spark within them. Although Aurelius' writings were little noted during the Middle Ages, William Xylander revived interest in them in 1559 when he translated the *Meditations* from Greek into Latin, the language of scholarship. For NICCOLÒ MACHIAVELLI (1469–1527), Aurelius served as the classic philosopher–king and the model of an ideal ruler for an already existing state. In contrast, the Emperor Severus (193–211) became the model of a ruler who employs cruelty to establish a kingdom. In fact, Machiavelli considered the period of the Roman Empire from Nerva to Aurelius (96–181) to be an exceptional era in which personal thought was not limited by authoritarian restrictions.

Aurelius also served as the embodiment of the philosopher–king, the ideal vision of kingship, for many Enlightenment philosophers of the eighteenth century. This king would be wise and gentle, yet powerful. He would pursue philosophical understanding as well as political power and as such would bring peace and prosperity to his subjects.

In more recent times, Aurelius influenced the transcendental ideas of HENRY DAVID THOREAU and RALPH WALDO EMERSON. Both of these later philosophers emphasized trusting one's own sense of morality instead of relying on external authority. Aurelius has also become an important resource for people engaged in recent discussions on diversity and multiculturalism.

Renaud

For Further Reading:

Birley, Anthony. *Marcus Aurelius, a Biography,* rev. ed. New Haven, Conn.: Yale University Press, 1987

Hadot, Pierre. *The Inner Citadel: The Meditations of Marcus Aurelius.* Cambridge: Harvard University Press, 1998.

Marx, Karl

Originator of Marxism
1818–1883

Life and Work

The ideas of Karl Marx and Friedrich Engels (1820–1895) established Marxism, which provided the political and economic principles for the development of socialism and communism in the twentieth century.

Marx was born on May 5, 1818, in Trier, Prussia (Germany), into a liberal Jewish family. He attended the universities of Bonn and Berlin and received a doctorate in philosophy from the University of Jena in 1841. In 1842 he was forced to leave the *Rheinische Zeitung* when his radical articles on social and economic issues led Prussian authorities to suspend publication of the newspaper. In 1844 Marx immigrated to Paris, where he met Friedrich Engels and began a collaboration that lasted his lifetime.

Both Marx and Engels were influenced by the analytical method of GEORG HEGEL (1770–1831). Hegel contended that every idea (thesis) had an opposite idea (antithesis). The clash of these ideas produced a new result (synthesis), which itself became a new thesis. Marx and Engels applied this method to the history of class struggle. The clash of social and economic classes produced social reform. They called this social and political analysis "dialectical materialism"; this method became the basis of their work.

Marx and Engels published their principles in the *Communist Manifesto* in 1848. The first systematic statement of socialist thought, it described history as a class struggle and predicted that the conflict between workers and capitalists would end with the workers creating a classless, utopian society. Exiled from Europe in the wake of the liberal revolutions that spread across the continent in 1848, Marx settled in England, where he spent the rest of his life. While in London he produced his most important work *Das Kapital* (1867–94). (The third volume was published in 1894, 11 years after Marx's death.)

Marx believed that economics was the primary force in history, and he saw human history as a continuing struggle between classes. Throughout history a ruling class, which owned the means of production (land or capital or people) and controlled the state, had been challenged and replaced by another class that had a more effective means of production. Thus, the capitalist middle class (bourgeoisie) had replaced the feudal nobility. The bourgeoisie, in turn, would be replaced by the oppressed working class (proletariat) who would revolt and claim their rightful share of the fruits of their labor.

Marx proposed the ultimate establishment of a democratic, classless society in which the coercive powers of the state would wither. The means of production would be owned in common and goods and services distributed justly. Because the transition to communism was radical, Marx foresaw an interim political stage in which the state would be under the control of a revolutionary dictatorship of the proletariat.

Marx died in London on March 14, 1883.

Legacy

Marx's influence on economics and politics has been profound. Initially, a number of communist parties were formed, each with a different interpretation of Marx's theories. In this century, Marxism became, with variations, the basis of a number of communist governments and one of the world's leading political forces.

Although Marx predicted that the workers' revolution would come in advanced, industrialized countries, this proved not to be the case. When the Bolshevik revolution finally happened in 1917, it was in Russia, a country with a small industrial working class but a large rural peasant class. The leader of the revolution, Vladimir Lenin, did not trust Marx's workers and peasants to reform the economic system and government, and led the revolution with professional revolutionaries. Communism's rise led to the abolition of private property, the collectivization of farms, and the government takeover of industry. For the next 74 years, especially during Joseph Stalin's regime (1924–1953), the U.S.S.R. suffered under the yoke of repression and totalitarianism. After World War II, Stalin imposed communism on the countries of Eastern Europe.

The Chinese Revolution of 1949 was another attempt at communism that has proven to be dictatorial. Mao Tse-tung, presiding over a largely agricultural society, took Marx's ideas of class struggle a step further in trying to stamp out any cultural influences from the past. A number of other countries in Asia, Africa, and Latin America have flirted with or actually imposed communist political and economic systems.

With the collapse of the U.S.S.R. in 1991, communism has been largely discredited. Although it still exists in places like Cuba and North Korea, its future, if any, is unclear.

Marx's ideas also had a profound effect on politics in many industrial nations. They shaped the criticism of the prevailing system, encouraged the development of potent labor reform efforts worldwide, influenced the development of important socialist parties, and forced governments to improve the working of liberal capitalism.

On the abstract level, Marxism has had a tremendous impact on all the social sciences. Schools of thought based on Marxist ideas became prominent in disciplines such as history, economics, and sociology during the early and mid-twentieth century.

Marxism may be dying as a political ideology, but the issues Marx raised and the approach he took are likely to remain important in a wide variety of academic studies.

Saltz

For Further Reading:
McLellan, David. *Karl Marx: A Biography.* London: Papermac, 1995.
Reiss, Edward. *Marx: A Clear Guide.* London and Chicago: Pluto Press, 1997.

WORLD EVENTS		MARX'S LIFE
	1818	Karl Marx is born
Greek War of	1821–29	
Independence		
against Turkey		
	1841	Marx receives doctorate in philosophy
	1844	Marx travels to Paris, meets Friedrich Engels
Revolutions in	1848	*Communist Manifesto* is published
Austria, France,		
Germany, and Italy		
	1867	First volume of *Das Kapital* is published
Germany is united	1871	
	1883	Marx dies
Spanish American	1898	
War		

Mary

Mother of Jesus;
Object of Catholic Veneration
1st Century B.C.E.–1st Century C.E.

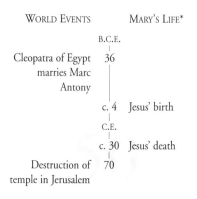

WORLD EVENTS	MARY'S LIFE*
	B.C.E.
Cleopatra of Egypt marries Marc Antony	36
	c. 4 — Jesus' birth
	C.E.
	c. 30 — Jesus' death
Destruction of temple in Jerusalem	70

* *Scholars cannot date the specific events in Mary's life with accuracy. This chronology is based on the biblical account.*

Life and Work

Mary was the mother of JESUS. Although not always a supporter of her son, she was at Jesus' crucifixion and was among the leaders of the early Church after his resurrection.

Mary is known only from biblical passages that speak of events in her life only in connection with her son, Jesus. According to Gospels of Matthew and Luke, Mary was in Bethlehem with Joseph to whom she was betrothed (a status closer to marriage than to our "engagement") when she gave birth to Jesus. Luke prefaces his tale with stories of the announcement by an angel to Mary of this birth (the Annunciation) and Mary's visit to her cousin Elizabeth, during which she praises God in what became known as the Magnificat. Luke also tells of Mary's trips to the Temple soon after the birth (for Jesus to be recognized by faithful Jews) and later when Jesus was 12 (for him to affirm his divine sonship). Matthew emphasizes the role of Joseph. He indicates that Joseph took Jesus and Mary with him to Egypt to avoid Herod's attempt to kill Jesus; later he took them to Nazareth, where they might live more safely than in Bethlehem.

The Gospel of John does not name the mother of Jesus, but she appears in very significant passages: the wedding at Cana, when she prompts Jesus to turn water into wine; and, the crucifixion, when Jesus gives her into the care of "the beloved disciple," traditionally understood to be John.

The last clear biblical reference to Mary is Acts 1:14, where Mary joins the apostles in the upper room after the Ascension, waiting for the coming of the Holy Spirit to empower the missionary activity of the new Church. There is no biblical information about her death.

Legacy

Little is known of Mary; she left no body of work and developed no new ideas. Yet she has had a profound impact on Western civilization in the various ways Christians have perceived her through the ages. All Christians honor Mary as the ultimate example of God's humble, trusting servant. She has also been a source of comfort to countless numbers of people who have prayed to her.

The Christian understanding of Mary changed through the centuries and reflected important themes of the times. Second-century Church Fathers perceived of sexuality as a grave danger and fatal flaw. Consequently, they emphasized Mary's virginity and her sinless nature. During the fourth century Mary was proclaimed *Theotokos* (God-bearer or Mother of God), in response to the controversy over the identity of Christ.

In the twelfth century, the age of chivalry, Mary became the ideal Lady, pure and faithful. The Church in the later middle ages (thirteenth to fifteenth centuries) so emphasized the divinity of Jesus that people saw a need to declare Mary their intercessor who brought the prayers of sinners to her son. The leaders of the Protestant Reformation of the sixteenth century saw her as a sterling example of faith in God's word. Many modern Christians, drawing on the words of the Magnificat, view her as an example of the liberation for the poor and downtrodden.

The Roman Catholic church has defined four articles of faith concerning Mary. Her divine motherhood and her virginity were accepted in the early years of the Church. In 1854 the doctrine of the Immaculate Conception—that Mary was conceived without sin—became binding on believers. In 1950, the Church declared the idea that Mary's body was assumed immediately into heaven (the Assumption) to be doctrine.

Although only officially defined for Roman Catholics, most of these teachings about Mary are also commonly held in the Eastern Orthodox churches. Some Protestant groups deny all of these later teachings, claiming either that they are contrary to scripture or unreasonable superstitions. Other Protestant churches, following the lead of early reformers such as MARTIN LUTHER, allow some (or all) of these teachings as acceptable personal beliefs.

Mary's inference far transcends theology. She had a profound impact on Western culture, inspiring men to raise great cathedrals and create sublime liturgies in her honor. Medieval cathedrals (*Notre Dame* means Our Lady) were named after her, and she became the subject of some of the world's greatest art.

Osterfield

For Further Reading:

Brown, Raymond E. et al., eds. *Mary in the New Testament.* Philadelphia: Fortress and New York: Paulist, 1978.

Cunneen, Sally. *In Search of Mary: The Woman and the Symbol.* New York: Random House, 1996.

Pelikan, Jaroslav. *Mary Through the Centuries: Her Place in the History of Culture.* New Haven, Conn.: Yale University Press, 1996.

Matta ibn Yunus

Early Arabic Commentator
on Aristotle
d. 940

Life and Work

Matta ibn Yunus was one of the earliest scholars to translate the works of ARISTOTLE into Arabic and provided some of the earliest commentaries on the Greek philosopher available to Islamic theologians.

Little is known of his life. He was a Nestorian Christian (one who believed that the two natures of Christ—the human and divine—were distinct and separate), who both studied and taught at Dayr Kunna (in present-day Syria) at the school in the convent of Mar Mari. His early teachers were Syrian Christians and Muslims from whom he learned logic and natural philosophy and who introduced him to the basic writings of Aristotle.

Aristotle's works so intrigued Matta ibn Yunus that he undertook both to translate them from Syriac, which he had used in school, into Arabic and to prepare commentaries on the texts. Among the works he translated were the *Analytics, Poetics,* the *Organon*, and portions of the *Metaphysics*. His commentaries took the form largely of marginal notes or appendixes to the translated text. His translations became the most complete and authoritative available to the Arab world of his time. As a result, he sparked among Arabic scholars a reawakening of philosophical interest in Aristotle.

Matta ibn Yunus was respected as a thinker as well as a translator and was viewed as the foremost scholar of logic of his day. Nevertheless, his emphasis on logic and reason as the means for discovering universal truths was attacked by the religious establishment, which questioned the validity of logic as a tool. Matta ibn Yunus defended himself by asserting that logic was a "universal grammar" that enables one to distinguish truth from falsehood.

Matta ibn Yunus moved to Baghdad around 934 and died there on June 20, 940.

Legacy

Matta ibn Yunus made many of Aristotle's writings available to later Islamic schol-ars. His work provided the scholarly material that generated both an interest in the relationship of reason and the Islamic faith and a debate over the proper use of reason to gain truth and knowledge about God.

One of the first scholars to develop a theoretical system to apply the rational principles of the Greek philosopher to the Islamic understanding of a just society was Matta ibn Yunus's student, AL-FARABI (c. 878–c. 950). Al-Farabi used the Greek concept of the philosopher-king to assert that the ruler must be a "wise philosopher" who would govern based on rational precepts revealed by the Absolute Intellect, the first cause, who created the world on the basis of those precepts. Only such a wise ruler could establish a just and peaceful society and prevent it from falling victim to the ignorant or wicked. Al-Farabi's theories went beyond those of the Greek philosophers, who were only interested in constructing a polis (city-state), by envisioning a worldwide rule of peace.

Al-Farabi's writings became an important source of inspiration for AVICENNA (Ibn Sina 980–1037), whose introduction to Aristotelian thought came from al-Farabi's work on Aristotle's *Metaphysics*. Avicenna attempted to synthesize Islamic doctrine and Greek philosophy by correlating the Islamic concept of contingency (all that exists in the world depends on the intelligent will of a Creator) with the Aristotelian idea of the first cause. For Avicenna, the first cause is Allah.

Avicenna's work generated its own set of responses. The Islamic mystic AL-GHAZALI (1058–1111) contested Avicenna's thesis that the world was created indirectly from God through spiritual emanations. He defended the traditional Islamic view that the world was created directly by God. The Spanish Islamic philosopher, AVERROËS (Ibn Rushd, 1126–1198) and the Arabic Sufi philosopher IBN AL-'ARABI (1165–1240) both relied heavily on Avicenna's thought in developing their philosophical theories. Averroës attempted to show how the prophetically revealed truth of Islam, the *Shariah*, is best interpreted, not by Muslim theology, but by the principles of philosophy. Ibn al-'Arabi transformed the Sufi static concept of mystical connection into a more dynamic one described by the phrase "perpetual transformation."

It was through the translations and commentaries of some of these Islamic philosophers that later Christian theologians, such as PETER ABELARD (1079–1142) and THOMAS AQUINAS (c. 1224–1274) first had access to Greek philosophy. These men helped shape the course of medieval thought by exploring ways to use philosophical insights in aid of theology.

von Dehsen

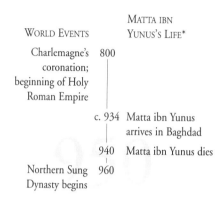

WORLD EVENTS		MATTA IBN YUNUS'S LIFE*
Charlemagne's coronation; beginning of Holy Roman Empire	800	
	c. 934	Matta ibn Yunus arrives in Baghdad
	940	Matta ibn Yunus dies
Northern Sung Dynasty begins	960	

* *Scholars cannot date the specific events in Matta ibn Yunus's life with accuracy.*

For Further Reading:

Fakhry, Majid. *A History of Islamic Philosophy.* New York: Columbia University Press, 1983.

Nasr, Sayyid Hossein, and Oliver Leaman, eds. *History of Islamic Philosophy.* New York: Routledge, 1996.

Melanchthon, Philipp

Humanist and Reformation Theologian; Author of Influential Lutheran Documents
1497–1560

Life and Work

Reformer and educator Philipp Melanchthon was the author of several of the foundational documents of the Lutheran church and led the church following MARTIN LUTHER's death.

Born Philipp Schwarzerd on February 16, 1497, in Bretten, Germany, Melanchthon (the Greek translation of his surname, which means black earth) entered the University of Heidelberg at the age of 12. When he was 21 he was appointed to teach Greek at the University of Wittenberg. His inaugural address called for a program of Christian humanism, combining classical and Christian learning to return to the sources of faith and reform society.

At Wittenberg, Melanchthon became a close friend and associate of Martin Luther, with whom he set forth the basic doctrines of the Reformation—salvation through faith alone and scripture as the sole source of theological authority. In 1521 he published *Loci communes theologici (Commonplaces of Theology),* the first

systematic presentation of Lutheran theology. Melanchthon differed from Luther in several key areas. He believed that Christ was spiritually, not physically, present in the bread and wine of the sacrament of the Lord's Supper and concluded that individuals could play a small part in salvation by accepting God's grace, while Luther maintained that even acceptance of grace was a gift of God. (Luther held that Christ was both spiritually and physically present in the bread and wine.) When Luther was placed under the papal ban in 1521, Melanchthon became the spokesman for the Reformation at Wittenberg.

Melanchthon was the principal author of the *Augsburg Confession* (1530), a summary of Reformation theology on such central concepts as justification by faith, the church and the sacraments, which was presented to Emperor Charles V in an attempt to reconcile differences with the Roman Catholic church. He defended the Confession against criticism that it went too far toward compromise in his *Apology of the Augsburg Confession* (1531), one of the finest theological writings of the Reformation.

As a humanist scholar, Melanchthon was interested in reforming education. In 1528 he developed a widely used plan for Protestant schools that emphasized a rounded education, using classical learning to enhance the understanding of religion. He also helped establish the universities of Marburg and Jena and made fundamental reforms at a number of universities, including Heidelberg and Tubingen.

After Luther's death in 1546, Melanchthon led the "Lutheran" churches in Germany, finding theological compromises to keep the church together in the face of political attack. Because of his differences with Luther and his willingness to compromise, he was bitterly attacked as a corrupter of Lutheranism. He died in Wittenberg on April 19, 1560, and was buried beside Luther.

Legacy

Melanchthon's life and work had a profound effect on the subsequent development of the Lutheran church and on the educational system of Germany.

Perhaps no other document shaped the teaching of the Lutheran church more than the *Augsburg Confession.* It became the normative statement of Lutheran theology and subse-

quently defined Lutheranism. Melanchthon's *Loci communes theologici,* the first attempt to present Christian teachings in a systematic manner based on scripture, became the model for much later theological writing. Prior to this time, the basic theological text had been the *Sentences* of Peter Lombard, a compilation of disconnected theological assertions that also relied on the authority of Church teaching. Melanchthon demonstrated how scripture alone could be the foundation for doctrine.

Melanchthon's humanistic perspectives also had a profound effect on the course of education in Europe. By affirming that human reason has its proper place in the realm of human affairs, he promoted the release of the curriculum from its control by the church. Melanchthon's emphasis on the importance of studying such topics as languages, philosophy, and rhetoric enabled students to analyze texts, including scripture, on their own. His education program eventually was enacted into law and became the basis for the Protestant public school system in Germany.

Melanchthon's attempt at compromise continued to generate controversy after his death. In 1577 those who considered themselves "true" Lutherans completed the "Formula of Concord," an elaborate restatement of Lutheran teachings. In 1580 all of the basic Lutheran documents, from the ancient creeds to *The Augsburg Confession* and the Formula, were collected in the *Book of Concord.* Since then, the writings in this book have served as the foundation for subsequent Lutheran theology.

von Dehsen

WORLD EVENTS		MELANCHTHON'S LIFE
Columbus discovers Americas	1492	
Last Muslim State in Spain falls to Christians		
	1497	Philipp Melanchthon is born in Bretten, Germany
Reformation begins	1517	
	1518	Melanchthon joins University of Wittenberg
	1521	*Loci communes theologici* is published
	1530	*The Augsburg Confession* is presented to Emperor Charles V
	1531	Melanchthon writes *Apology of the Augsburg Confession*
	1560	Melanchthon dies in Wittenberg

For Further Reading:

Kolb, Robert. *Confessing the Faith: Reformers Define the Church, 1530–1580.* St. Louis, Mo.: Concordia, 1991.

Kusukawa, Sachiko. *The Transformation of Natural Philosophy: The Case of Philipp Melanchthon.* New York: Cambridge University Press, 1995.

Wengert, Timothy. *Human Freedom, Christian Righteousness: Philipp Melanchthon's Exegetical Dispute with Erasmus of Rotterdam.* New York: Oxford University Press, 1998.

Mencius (Meng K'o)

Confucian Moral Philosopher and
Interpreter
c. 371–c. 289 B.C.E.

Life and Work

Meng K'o, commonly known as Mencius (from the title of his major work, *Meng-Tzu*), was a Confucian moral philosopher whose emphases on the innate goodness of people and on the role of government and education to foster that goodness, made him one of the earliest important interpreters of CONFUCIUS.

All that is known of Mencius' life comes from his major work, the *Meng-Tzu*. He was born around 371 B.C.E. in the Chinese province of Tsou and probably studied with a follower of K'ung Chi, the grandson of Confucius. From 320 B.C.E. on, he traveled extensively, lecturing on Confucianism and unsuccessfully urging rulers to exercise power for the good of the common people.

Mencius' major contribution to Confucian thought is found in the *Meng-Tzu*. The work is an unconnected collection of short sayings and lengthy conversations that his followers compiled, perhaps with his help. Mencius' central principle was that human beings are inherently good. They do not need to be taught goodness from without, but they need external structure and encouragement to develop their inherent goodness. Ancient rituals, therefore, should be retained as a long-standing reflection of that goodness. Government should provide for the welfare of ordinary citizens and promote peace. A ruler must rule by *jen*, benevolence; a corrupt ruler loses the right to govern and may be deposed. Education is also important in guiding young people to develop their own innate righteousness, divided into four components: kindness (*jen*), dutifulness (*i*), propriety (*li*), and knowledge of right and wrong (*chih*).

Mencius emphasized the development of the *hsin*, the heart-mind, which distinguishes right from wrong. The *hsin* is an inner attribute, not one learned from the outside. By emphasizing the *hsin*, Mencius attempted to refute the ideas of the Taoists Yang Chu and Mo-tzu, who asserted that moral enlightenment was acquired from others.

Little is known of the end of Mencius' life, although it is thought that he died around 289 B.C.E.

Legacy

As one of the earliest interpreters of Confucius, Mencius served as a strong advocate for the Confucian ideal of inner goodness and of the responsibility of family and society to encourage the growth of that goodness. His thought also provided a defense for Confucian teachings in the face of the growing influence of Taoism and Buddhism.

Toward the end of Mencius' life, another interpreter of Confucius, HSÜN-TZU, contended that humans are inherently evil and that heaven did not assist the continuation of good government. Humans can overcome this natural evil only when the government enforces the rules of *li* (decency) and *yi* (moral guidelines). Initially, Hsün-tzu's approach became dominant, overshadowing the teachings of Mencius. Only later did the Chinese government revive the teachings of Mencius to thwart the teachings of Buddhism and Taoism.

Mencius' writings greatly influenced Han Yü, an eighth-century government official and Confucian scholar who laid the foundation for a revival of Confucianism known as Neo-Confucianism during the Sung dynasty (960–1279 C.E.). The Neo-Confucian scholar Chu Hsi (1130–1200) wrote a major commentary on the *Meng-Tzu* and added it to three other works to form the canonical Four Books of Confucianism. These became the fundamental texts studied by scholars and were the basis for the examinations for the imperial civil service.

The moral philosophy of Mencius also provided a response to the teachings of Taoism and Buddhism. Both of these religions emphasize the isolation of the individual through meditation and discipline to overcome the distractions of the present world and achieve inner harmony and balance. While Mencius did not deny the individualistic emphasis, his Confucian emphasis on the role of family and society in the development of innate goodness was able to moderate the strict individualism of the other two and to provide a means for the preservation of the communal ideals of Confucianism.

von Dehsen

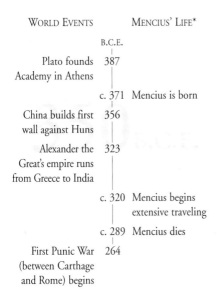

WORLD EVENTS		MENCIUS' LIFE*
	B.C.E.	
Plato founds Academy in Athens	387	
	c. 371	Mencius is born
China builds first wall against Huns	356	
Alexander the Great's empire runs from Greece to India	323	
	c. 320	Mencius begins extensive traveling
	c. 289	Mencius dies
First Punic War (between Carthage and Rome) begins	264	

* Scholars cannot date the specific events in Mencius' life with accuracy.

For Further Reading:
Ivanhoe, P. J. *Ethics in the Confucian Tradition: The Thought of Mencius and Wang Yang-ming.* Atlanta, Ga.: Scholar's Press, 1990.
Shun, Kwong-lui. *Mencius and Early Chinese Thought.* Stanford, Calif.: Stanford University Press, 1997.

Mill, John Stuart

Pioneer of Utilitarianism
1806–1873

Life and Work

British philosopher and social reformer John Stuart Mill was a leading theorist of utilitarianism and liberal political thought.

Born on May 20, 1806, in London, Mill was the son of utilitarian philosopher James Mill, a disciple of JEREMY BENTHAM (1748-1832), the English utilitarian philosopher. The elder Mill carefully supervised his son's home-based education in Greek, Latin, mathematics, philosophy, and economics. From exposure to his father's philosopher companions, Mill early resolved to be a "reformer of the world" and embraced the utilitarian belief that society should be based on the principle of the greatest happiness for the greatest number. Mill wrote for the Benthamist journal, *Westminster Review*, from 1824 to 1828, but, following a nervous breakdown in 1826–27, he modified his utilitarian views, emphasizing the importance of the *quality* as well as the quantity of happiness.

In 1843 Mill published *A System of Logic*, an exposition of the epistemology (ways of knowing the world) of empiricism, which holds that knowledge is derived from experience, and injected new life into that movement. As ARISTOTLE did for formal logic, Mill's work systematized the inductive method of experimental science. He identified four methods of inductive reasoning: agreement, difference, residue, and concomitant variations.

He denied that truths external to the mind can be known by means of intuition. All knowledge, he argued, comes from experience, even mathematical knowledge. Rather than relying on syllogisms (logical sequences of thought), he stressed inference from the known to the unknown.

Some of Mill's most influential works dealt with political theory. Initially he championed universal suffrage and frequent elections but gradually he began to doubt that democratic elections produced assemblies with the intellectual ability to govern effectively. In *Considerations on Representative Government* (1861), Mill proposed setting up a commission, drawn from the intellectual elite, to frame legislation that would then be voted on by democratically elected assemblies, thus ensuring popular control of government.

Mill was deeply concerned with the preservation of personal liberty and in his 1859 essay "On Liberty" warned against the tyranny of the majority, which he characterized as a collective mediocrity slavishly following convention. An egalitarian, Mill was an early supporter of women's rights and, in *On the Subjection of Women* (1869), argued against claims of innate male superiority.

Mill put many of his ideas into action as a member of Parliament from 1865 to 1868, championing the extension of voting rights, land reform in Ireland, and women's suffrage.

Mill died in Avignon, France, on May 8, 1873.

Legacy

Mill left a body of work that influenced a wide variety of disciplines from philosophy and scientific methodology to political science. For his contributions to political theory, scholars have called him a founding father of liberal thought and he is considered a prime architect of utilitarianism.

Mill's work had a significant impact on both the practical politics and political theory of the nineteenth century. His work for the expansion of the franchise (voting rights) resulted in a series of Reform Acts, passed during the course of the century, that gave Britain universal male suffrage. He also pushed for women's suffrage, but he did not see universal suffrage for women during his lifetime; however, his writings helped to lay the foundation for the women's movement of the late nineteenth and twentieth century. His thought influenced British political theorists such as Walter Bagehot (1826–1877), who also was concerned about expanding the franchise to the uneducated masses and urged educational reform to prepare new voters for their responsibilities. In the twentieth cen-

tury Libertarians, who espouse restricting government powers, owe much to Mill's thought.

Utilitarianism had a profound effect on the British socialist movement of the 1880s and 1890s. The movement was especially influential in the United States and France. German philosopher FRIEDRICH WILHELM NIETZSCHE (1844–1900), however, scoffed at it saying, "Man does not live for pleasure. Only the Englishman does." Utilitarian ideas influenced U.S. philosopher WILLIAM JAMES (1842–1910) and U.S. educator JOHN DEWEY (1859–1952), who substituted intelligence for happiness as the supreme value. Mill's ideas are evident in the work of BERTRAND RUSSELL (1872–1970) and the logical positivists, a prominent movement of the 1930s and 1940s.

Mill's four methods of inductive reasoning (agreement, difference, residue, and concomitant variations) have molded later scientific methodology. These methods provided the researcher with a dispassionate way for organizing and analyzing a vast amount of data. In some respects, Mill's methodology becomes a preemptive strike on the kind of methodological problem exemplified by what later became known as the "Heisenberg uncertainty principle." Werner Heisenberg articulated this principle after his investigations into particle physics. Others have used this principle to discuss uncertainty factors in other kinds of experiments. In its most general form, the uncertainty principle asserts that a researcher may unknowingly affect the outcome of an experiment. Thus a debate continues about the possibility of conducting objective experiments. Moreover, Mill's methodology also serves other fields of study, by cautioning against drawing overly biased conclusions.

Olson

WORLD EVENTS	MILL'S LIFE
	1806 John Stuart Mill is born in London
Greek War of 1821–29 Independence against Turkey	
	1824–28 Mill writes for *Westminster Review*
	1843 *System of Logic* is published
Revolutions in 1848 Austria, France, Germany, and Italy	
United States 1861–65 Civil War	
	1865–68 Mill is elected member of Parliament
Germany is united 1871	
	1873 Mill dies
Spanish American War 1898	

For Further Reading:
Ryan, Alan. *John Stuart Mill*. New York: Norton, 1997.
Stafford, William. *John Stuart Mill*. Basingstoke, England: Macmillan, 1998.

Montaigne, Michel Eyquem de

Influential French Philosopher
and Essayist
1533–1592

Life and Work

Michel Eyquem de Montaigne was a French philosopher and essayist who focused on the limits of human knowledge.

Montaigne was born on February 28, 1533, to a wealthy family in the Bordeaux region of France. As a young boy, he was educated at home, learning to speak Latin before he could speak French. He later attended the University of Toulouse, where he studied law. Following his family's tradition, Montaigne entered public service. In 1557, he became a member of the Parliament of Bordeaux, but in 1571, after the death of a very close friend, he sold his seat in Parliament and retired to his estate the following year.

Once retired, Montaigne began the composition of his major work, the *Essays* (1580; 1588). The *Essays* were written during a period of intense turmoil in Europe when religious persecution and wars shattered the optimism engendered by the Renaissance. In part, Montaigne was responding to this chaotic time and to his own physical ailments (kidney stones) by reflecting on the frailty of humanity through the lens of his own experience. He summed up his focus by saying, "I am myself the matter of the book." The essays are not organized according to any pattern, but rather express his thoughts as he explored them. Perhaps the most notable of them is entitled "Apology for Raymond Sebond." (Sebond was a Spanish monk and scientist.) Here Montaigne offers his famous question, *"Que sais-je?"*—"What do I know?" He asserts that people are unable to ascertain what they know or to know what they do not know. Ultimately, all that people can know is themselves. In other essays he concludes that as a duality—for example, body/soul, happiness/torment—a human being must accept his or her limitations and suffering. This concept of duality leads an individual to explore the relationship between the interior (private) and exterior (public) aspects of life. Both must be nour-ished, for example, through introspection and public service, respectively. In still another essay he comments that children are best taught through concrete activities.

Some scholars argue that in the essays Montaigne is preparing himself for his own death. That inevitable event occurred on September 13, 1592, in Bordeaux.

Legacy

Montaigne's varied personal thoughts, collected in his *Essays*, articulated the philosophical skepticism that became prominent in Europe during the late sixteenth and seventeenth centuries. This philosophy asserted that because certainty was beyond the dream of human knowledge, individuals should avoid judgment on all matters of knowledge.

Despite his later association with skepticism, the earliest scholars considered Montaigne's thought a form of Stoicism. Such a label is easy to understand—the ancient Greek Stoics believed that a harmonious life was one lived passively in accordance with the divine Logos (Reason). Similarly, Montaigne's concept of acceptance of human limitations has Stoic overtones, but his concept of active engagement with the world through public service would counterbalance the Stoic aspects.

By the seventeenth century, Montaigne had inspired a variety of responses. Some acknowledged Montaigne as a *honnete hommes,* a gentleman of wisdom and elegance. Others, such as Francis de Sales (1567–1622) and BLAISE PASCAL (1623–1662), labeled Montaigne a skeptic for his uncertainty about the ability of humans to know anything. In his *Pensées* (1670) Pascal attacks Montaigne's absolute skepticism by contending that it is not impossible to attain knowledge. Pascal defended the paradox that humans can know things even though they are not able to establish all forms of knowledge by rational means. Some knowledge comes through intuition and divine revelation.

By the eighteenth century, Montaigne had become a model of free thought for such scholars as VOLTAIRE (1694–1778) and DENIS DIDEROT (1713–1784). Moreover, Voltaire built on Montaigne's skepticism by suggesting that people should be content with the limited knowledge derived from everyday experience and from science. Montaigne's self-analysis appealed to JEAN-JACQUES ROUSSEAU (1712–1778), who saw Montaigne as the master of the self-portrait. Montaigne's style of self-reflection also found followers in the twentieth century, including the authors André Gide and Roland Barthes.

Perhaps Montaigne's most enduring contribution comes not from the content, but from the style of the *Essays*. From the French word *essais,* or "attempts," Montaigne named the genre of writing that is now known as "essays"—short, informal *attempts* in prose to explore a subject—a style most common by the end of the twentieth century.

von Dehsen

World Events		Montaigne's Life
Reformation begins	1517	
	1533	Michel Eyquem de Montaigne is born
	1557	Montaigne becomes a member of the Parliament of Bordeaux
	1571	Montaigne retires to write *Essays*
	1580	First edition of *Essays* is published
	1588	Revised edition of *Essays* is published
	1592	Montaigne dies
Thirty Years' War in Europe	1618–48	

For Further Reading:
Hoffmann, George. *Montaigne's Career.* New York: Clarendon Press, 1998.
Tetel, Marcel. *Montaigne.* Boston: Twayne Publishers, 1990.

Montesquieu, Baron de la Brède et de

(Charles Louis de Secondat)

Originator of the Theory of the Separation of Powers

1689–1755

Life and Work

Charles Louis de Secondat, Baron de la Brède et de Montesquieu, was a political philosopher whose theory of the separation of powers had a profound influence on modern political theory.

Montesquieu was born on January 18, 1689, in Bordeaux, France. He received his legal education at the universities of Bordeaux and Paris and in 1716 inherited a judgeship. (In France at that time, judgeships were purchased by families and passed from one generation to the next.) As a noble and a magistrate, Montesquieu held a privileged position in French society. Nevertheless, he questioned the established institutions of his day, reflecting some of the larger concerns of the Enlightenment. He viewed the despotic rule of the French kings as a plague on the nation. Married to a Calvinist who faced persecution for practicing her religion, he opposed the role of the established Roman Catholic church and championed religious tolerance.

Montesquieu gained immediate acclaim with his first literary work, *Persian Letters* (1721), a satire of French society and politics. Shortly after its publication, he moved to Paris where he became active in the intellectual salons of his day. After a tour of Europe in 1728, he spent two years in England where he became impressed with the British system of constitutional monarchy. While on his travels he began gathering the material and exploring the themes that he presented in *Considerations on the Causes of the Greatness of the Romans and Their Decline* (1734) and his greatest work, *The Spirit of Laws* (1748).

Montesquieu's primary concern was with preventing abuse of power while preserving the rule of law. In presenting his arguments he combined evidence drawn from his analysis of various modern and ancient societies with theory based on vitalism, a contemporary scientific idea that the body was a complex union of parts. Montesquieu envisioned the ideal society based on analogy to the human body. As a healthy body maintains a balance and harmony among its various parts, so also must a society maintain a structural balance to prevent one component of it from gaining absolute control. For Montesquieu the best example of this balance was the English political system, where the monarchy and Parliament divided governmental power. This separation of powers achieved both balance and limits on absolute power through a series of checks and balances—each branch of government could block the improper acts of the others. Montesquieu contended that for laws to be effective, they must be rooted in the spirit of the people and thus social reforms were only possible by changing the character of the people.

Montesquieu's ideas were denounced by the Roman Catholic Inquisition and his *The Spirit of Laws* was banned by Roman Catholic authorities. Yet it was widely read and enthusiastically received throughout Europe and in the American colonies. He died on February 10, 1755.

Legacy

Montesquieu's legacy lies primarily in his articulation of the theory of separation of powers and the need for checks and balances in government, but he was also influential in the development of sociology and history.

Montesquieu's political thought was central to the development of the U.S. Constitution and the French Constitution of 1791, both of which established systems based on separation of powers. His theories were used by JAMES MADISON, John Jay, and Alexander Hamilton in *The Federalist Papers,* written to promote the ratification of the Constitution. In the United States, Montesquieu's ideas were implemented within a republican system. In France his ideas were more strictly followed with the establishment of a constitutional monarchy. The French constitution was abandoned as the French Revolution became more radical. The U.S. Constitution, with its system of checks and balances, is one of the oldest constitutions in the world and has served as an example for many other nations.

Montesquieu's history of the fall of Rome began a new era in historical scholarship. Traditionally historians had explained events in theological terms. Montesquieu substituted a secular understanding, presenting history as the interaction of humans with the world rather than as God's will manifest on Earth. His work directly inspired Edward Gibbon's interpretation of Roman history in *The Decline and Fall of the Roman Empire* (1776–1788), which became the standard analysis of the last years of the Roman Empire. Because he emphasized the importance of social and environmental factors in shaping political culture, some scholars call Montesquieu the father of modern sociology.

von Dehsen

For Further Reading:

Conroy, Peter V. *Montesquieu Revisited.* New York: Twayne Publishers, 1992.

Shklar, Judith. *Montesquieu.* New York: Oxford University Press, 1987.

Starobinski, Jean. *Montesquieu.* Paris: Seuil, 1989.

Montessori, Maria

Educational Philosopher; Originator
of the Montessori Method
1870–1952

Life and Work

Maria Montessori was an Italian educational philosopher who developed the controversial theory of education, centered on self-direction, that bears her name.

Montessori was born on August 31, 1870, near Ancona, Italy. The first woman to receive a medical degree in Italy, she graduated from the University of Rome in 1894 and then worked at the university's psychiatric institute, where she became interested in the education of mentally retarded children. From 1896 to 1908 she taught pedagogy and anthropology at the University of Rome while continuing her studies in education.

In 1907 Montessori founded a school for children age three to six from the slums of Rome. There she developed the educational theories that bear her name. During the next two years she founded another four schools and published her most famous work *The Montessori Method* (1909).

Montessori's research led her to conclude that children learn primarily by working by themselves and, consequently, she based her educational philosophy on individual initiative. She scorned the traditional classroom with a teacher lecturing to rows of students. Instead she advocated creating an environment in which the student would be able to learn informally by using what she called the "didactic apparatus"—tools

such as cylinders, blocks, and beads, which she discovered taught children basic pre-mathematical and reading skills while holding their interest. A specially trained teacher was to demonstrate the materials but remain in the background, intervening only when absolutely necessary to help the self-learning process.

Montessori believed that children pass through certain "periods of sensitivity," corresponding to age, in which they are most ready and interested in acquiring certain types of knowledge. The task of the educator, and parent, was to provide an environment that the child could exploit for independent learning of the appropriate skills.

Montessori spent most of her life traveling in Europe, Asia, and the United States, lecturing on her educational methods, founding schools and establishing teacher-training programs. She expanded her basic theories in a series of works including *The Advanced Montessori Method* (1917–18), *The Secret of Childhood* (1936), and *The Absorbent Mind* (1949). She was appointed inspector of Italian schools in 1922 but left the country 12 years later to escape the Fascist regime.

Montessori eventually settled in the Netherlands, where she died in Noordwijk aan Zee on May 6, 1952.

Legacy

Montessori developed a successful educational method that significantly influenced early childhood education in the twentieth century.

Montessori's theories emerged in the wake of the kindergarten and child study movements, which advocated informal learning and adjusting the classroom setting to the child's natural interests. Her ideas became very popular throughout Europe and the United States, where Anne George, one of her pupils, opened the first Montessori school in Tarrytown, New York, in 1912. *The Montessori Method* appeared in English that year and became a best-seller in the United States, bought by parents who had been warned by some prominent educators that a constrained environment would hinder their children's development.

By 1914 opposition to Montessori's program arose from the advocates of JOHN DEWEY's school of progressive education. William Heard Kilpatrick, in particular, denounced what he considered to be the permissiveness of her methods that often left children unattended to learn or not as they chose. Instead, he urged close

teacher supervision of children in an atmosphere of experience-based learning. His opposition, presented in *The Montessori Method Examined* (1914), precipitated the rapid decline of her movement, which effectively disappeared in the United States by the end of World War I.

During the 1950s Montessori's method experienced a resurgence in the United States, where pediatrician Benjamin Spock was urging parents to use kindness rather than discipline in nurturing children. The American Montessori Society was established in 1960, and 15 years later the first public school utilizing Montessori's methods opened in Cincinnati, Ohio. By the mid-1990s approximately 100 public school districts had some sort of Montessori program. At the end of the twentieth century the American Montessori Society had certified 800 U.S. schools, with thousands utilizing Montessori's name without authorization.

von Dehsen

WORLD EVENTS		MONTESSORI'S LIFE
United States Civil War	1861–65	
	1870	Maria Montessori is born
Germany is united	1871	
	1894	Montessori receives a medical degree from the University of Rome
Spanish American War	1898	
	1907	Montessori founds her first school
	1909	*The Montessori Method* is published
World War I	1914–18	
	1917–18	*The Advanced Montessori Method* is published
	1922	Montessori is appointed government inspector of schools
	1934	Montessori leaves Italy
World War II	1939–45	
Mao Tse-tung establishes communist rule in China	1949	
Korean War	1950–53	
	1952	Montessori dies
Six Day War between Israel and Arabs	1967	

For Further Reading:
Chattin-McNichols, John. *The Montessori Controversy.* Albany, N.Y.: Delmar Publishers, 1992.
Standing, E. M. *Maria Montessori: Her Life and Work.* New York: Penguin USA, 1998.

Moon, Sun Myung

Evangelist and Founder of the
Unification Church
1920–

Life and Work

Sun Myung Moon is the founder of the Holy Spirit for the Unification of World Christianity, more popularly known as the Unification Church.

Moon was born January 6, 1920, in Kwangju Sangsa Ri, in what is now North Korea. In 1936, when he was 16, Christ appeared to him in a vision and told him to finish JESUS' work and usher in the Kingdom of God on Earth. Moon interpreted this command as saving the world from Satan and began a complete study of the Bible. Moon began preaching in North Korea in 1945 and in 1947 was excommunicated from the Presbyterian Church. He was imprisoned several times by the North Korean communists but in 1950 he escaped to South Korea.

In 1952 Moon published *The Divine Principle,* a book of his beliefs that has since become the scripture of his church. Moon teaches that humans are born with a fallen nature that resulted from Eve having spiritual sexual relations with Lucifer and then having physical sexual relations with Adam. Jesus had come to redeem humankind but was murdered before he could marry. According to Moon, marriage would have allowed Christ to go beyond spiritual salvation to the physical salvation of the world. Moon sees himself as the Messiah who has laid the foundation for the restoration of God's kingdom through his marriage. Through ritual purification, his followers can ensure that their children will not be born with a fallen nature.

In 1954 Moon founded what was to become the Unification Church in South Korea, building congregations in South Korea and Japan. In addition to his religious activities, he built an international financial empire that produces and sells such items as machinery, tea, paint, and arms.

In the early 1970s Moon came to the United States. Moon's church was criticized by the media and came under increased governmental scrutiny. In 1981 the church's application for tax-exempt status as a religious organization was rejected by the appellate court, which decided that the church was a political rather than a religious entity. In 1982 Moon was convicted of tax evasion.

The Unification Church claims some three million members worldwide, about 45,000 of them in the United States.

Legacy

Sun Myung Moon is one of the most controversial leaders of new religious groups in the contemporary world. Moon himself has been accused of brainwashing his disciples and of sexual and financial misconduct. He has been criticized for his control over church events like the mass weddings of couples matched by him from photographs and applications. In 1992 in Seoul, for example, he married 30,000 couples simultaneously. In addition, charges (including one by one of his children) have been made that his public image is a far cry from his personal behavior.

Many Americans view Moon's church suspiciously as a cult with its members pejoratively referred to as "Moonies." Parents of young members have accused the organization of brainwashing their children.

A 1978 Congressional subcommittee report accused Moon of wanting to establish a world theocracy with himself as leader, thereby doing away with separation of church and state. It accused him of violations of foreign exchange laws when moving cash and other assets in and out of the United States, and of flouting immigration laws by illegally importing foreign nationals to help with the running of his church. In spite of these controversies, Moon's prison sentence was protested as harassment by a large number of religious groups including the National Council of Churches. The Unification Church has survived and Moon remains revered by his followers as the Messiah. He and his wife are viewed as Father and Mother of the divine family with God as the "True Parent."

Moon's long-term legacy has yet to be written. Whether his Unification Church will survive him remains to be seen.

Saltz

World Events	Moon's Life
World War I 1914–18	
	1920 Sun Myung Moon born
	1936 Moon has vision of Christ
World War II 1939–45	
	1945 Moon begins preaching
	1947 Moon excommunicated from Presbyterian Church
Mao Tse-tung establishes Communist rule in China 1949	
Korean War 1950–53	
	1952 Moon publishes *The Divine Principle*
	1954 Moon establishes Unification Church
Six Day War between Israel and Arabs 1967	
End of Vietnam War 1975	
	1981 Unification Church's application for tax-exempt status is denied
	1984 Moon serves 11-month prison term for tax evasion
Fall of Communism in eastern Europe 1989	
Dissolution of Soviet Union 1991	
	1992 Moon marries 30,000 couples simultaneously in Seoul
Apartheid in South Africa is dismantled 1994	

For Further Reading:

Bromley, David G., and Anson D. Shupe, Jr. *Moonies in America: On the Road to the Millennium.* Beverly Hills, Calif.: Sage Publications, 1979.

Chryssides, George D. *The Advent of Sun Myung Moon: The Origins, Beliefs, and Practices of the Unification Church.* New York: St. Martin's Press, 1991.

More, Sir Thomas, Saint

Author of Utopia; Defender of the
Roman Catholic Faith
1477–1535

Life and Work

Humanist writer, statesman, and chancellor of England, Thomas More was a product of the English Renaissance and is considered to be one of the most intelligent men of his time. His book, *Utopia*, served as a blueprint for those hoping to create an ideal community.

Born in London on February 7, 1477, the son of a lawyer, More was educated at Oxford. In 1494 he returned to London, where he studied law, becoming a full barrister in 1501. Attracted to the religious life, More lived in a monastery for four years. Ultimately deciding to remain a lay Christian, he always retained his monastic habits of early rising, fasting, and prayer. He became a successful lawyer and international negotiator and, from 1510 to 1518, he served as undersheriff of London.

From 1513 to 1518 More wrote *History of King Richard III,* left unfinished, and in 1515–1516 wrote his masterpiece, *Utopia.* Translated into many languages, *Utopia* established More as one of the foremost proponents of humanism, which is the emphasis on the worth and dignity of human beings. In the book he imagines an ideal community whose

citizens live peacefully through the rule of reason. This community implicitly posed a critique of the social, political, and economic inequities of the European class structure.

In 1518 he became a member of the king's council and a confidant of Henry VIII. Five years later he became speaker of the House of Commons, where he championed free speech. That same year he criticized MARTIN LUTHER's view of the sacraments in *Responsio ad Lutherum* by defending the traditional teaching and authority of the Roman Catholic church. After years of distinguished political service, More was made lord chancellor in 1529. During his tenure in this office he completed several other books defending the Roman Catholic faith: *The Confutation of Tyndale's Answer* (1532), *Apology* (1533), and *Debellacyon* (1533).

More vigorously opposed King Henry VIII's attempts to justify divorcing Catherine of Aragon. In 1533 he further incurred the king's wrath by not attending the coronation of Anne Boleyn, Henry's second wife. Several attempts to take revenge on More with false charges backfired until 1534, when he refused to take an oath that repudiated the supremacy of the Pope. For that he was imprisoned on April 17, 1534. While in prison he completed *A Dialogue of Comfort against Tribulation.* He was tried on July 1, 1535, and convicted of treason on perjured evidence. He was beheaded on July 6, 1535.

Legacy

More is largely remembered as the creator of *Utopia* and as the author of several books defending the Roman Catholic church. Because of his execution, he has also became a model for those willing to make the ultimate sacrifice in defense of their faith while facing overwhelming hostility. The English writer and theologian, G. K. Chesterton, considered him to be one of the great historical personages in British history.

The death of More, whose writings and reputation were widely known, shocked and dismayed the rest of Europe. Even the Protestant world did not believe in his guilt. His friend, the Dutch philosopher DESIDERIUS ERASMUS, eulogized him as a man with a pure soul and great genius. Erasmus called More, "a man for all seasons." This phrase became the title of the play about More's struggle with Henry VIII written by Robert Bolt in 1960.

Unfortunately, the rise of the Anglican Church in England obscured the stature and works of More for many years. However, the eventual publication of More's state papers provided a clearer picture of this man who had been described as a model of an intellectually rounded individual, who lived simply, enjoyed life's pleasures, was an excellent speaker, a good and generous friend, and who, despite his full professional schedule, still found time for prayer.

Perhaps the most influential of More's writings was *Utopia*. Its major themes—the abolition of class struggle and the development of social reform and governmental programs such as public education and penal reform—anticipated social reform movements of later centuries. In fact, the title of the book, *Utopia*, has entered the English language as a word that means an ideal, trouble-free, and just place to live.

More's martyrdom for Catholicism did not go unnoticed by Rome. He was beatified in 1886 and canonized by Pius XI in 1935. His memory is preserved in London through monuments to him at Westminster Hall, the Tower of London, and the Chelsea Embankment.

Saltz

World Events		More's Life
Ottoman Empire captures Byzantine capital, Constantinople	1453	
	1477	Thomas More is born
Columbus discovers Americas	1492	
Last Muslim State in Spain falls to Christians		
	1501	More becomes barrister
	1516	*Utopia* is published
Reformation begins	1517	
	1518	More becomes member of king's council
	1523	More becomes speaker of House of Commons
	1529	More becomes lord chancellor
	1534	More refuses to repudiate supremacy of Pope
	1535	More convicted of treason and executed
Thirty Years' War in Europe	1618–48	

For Further Reading:
Ackroyd, Peter. *The Life of Thomas More.* London: Chatto & Windus, 1998.
Marius, Richard. *Thomas More: A Biography.* New York: Knopf, 1985.

Moses

First Leader and Lawgiver of the
Ancient Israelites
c. 13th century B.C.E.

WORLD EVENTS	MOSES' LIFE*
B.C.E.	
Pyramids at Giza c. 2500 are built	
	c. 1200 Moses is born
	Moses is called by God
	The Ten Plagues
	The Crossing of the Red Sea
	The Covenant at Mt. Sinai and the 10 Commandments
	Moses dies
Fall of Troy c. 1150	

Scholars cannot date the specific events in Moses' life with accuracy. This chronology is based on the biblical account.

Life and Work

The towering figure of the Old Testament, Moses is known as the leader and lawgiver of the Exodus, the fleeing of the Jews from slavery in Egypt. He stands as the premier individual associated with the founding of the Israelite people, ancient and modern.

Moses was probably born in Egypt to an Israelite couple in the thirteenth century B.C.E. Because of a decree by an unidentified Pharaoh (probably Ramses II) that all male Hebrews were to be put to death at birth, Moses' mother hid him in a makeshift boat among the reeds along the Nile. The Pharaoh's daughter discovered the child and raised him as her own. Despite his association with the royal court, Moses never lost his own sense of being a Hebrew. As an adult he killed an Egyptian who was beating two Hebrews and was forced to flee Egypt. He settled in the land of Midian (in northwestern Arabia), where he became a shepherd.

When he was 80 Moses received a call from God at a burning bush, commanding him to lead the Hebrews from slavery. As God's representative, Moses directed a series of plagues against Egypt to force Pharaoh to release the Israelites. The plagues culminated in the First Passover, in which God caused the death of the Egyptians' first-born sons while "passing over" Hebrew children. In what is remembered as the Exodus, Moses led the Israelites from Egypt and through the Red Sea, which parted at his command.

Over the next 40 years Moses guided the contentious Hebrews through the wilderness to the promised land of Canaan (in modern day Israel). During this period he received the law (the Torah), including the 10 Commandments, on Mt. Sinai. Moses never entered the promised land but only saw it from afar. As biblical tradition has it, the place and time of Moses' death remain unknown. According to Deuteronomy, God buried him somewhere in a valley in the land of Moab.

Legacy

No other Old Testament figure matches the influence that Moses had on the formation of ancient Israelite society and modern Western law and morality. Through Moses and the special role he played in receiving the Torah (Jewish law) on Mt. Sinai, the ancient Israelites, as well as Western society, received the traditions that form the core of Jewish and Christian religious ethics and Western legal traditions. As for the biblical generation that entered the Land of Canaan, Moses' leadership and role as intercessor between God and the people made it possible for the former slaves to experience a form of national identity and purpose.

Moses never entered the Promised Land, suffering the same punishment from God as did his rebellious Israelite contemporaries, who rebelled in the desert. His abiding hope that God would fulfill his promises has made Moses a symbol of the modern-day attempts by Jews and Palestinians to lay claim to the land of Canaan, the Promised Land. Moses guiding the Israelites from the oppressive slavery in Egypt provided vivid images for American folklore and African slaves. For the early settlers of North America, the figure of Moses and the covenant God made with Israel were read as foreshadowing the same quest for freedom from the oppressors in Europe. Similarly, in the music and belief of African slaves are found vivid images of the same desire to flee from oppressive slavery and to obtain freedom. More recently, the same Mosaic traditions played a large part in the formation of modern day Israel and the return of Jews from the "exodus" of living in foreign lands.

According to tradition, Moses recorded the Torah in the first five books of the Old Testament, referred to by many as the Pentateuch. Under the leadership of Joshua, who was Moses' successor, the Israelites carried with them not just the remembrance of Moses as their leader but the Torah itself, which is called in Joshua 1:7 "the law which Moses my servant commanded you." The Torah, along with its development in the Mishnah and the Talmud, lies at the heart of Jewish religious thought, both past and present. As the law of God, the Torah has also profoundly influenced the moral and religious ideas of Christianity and Islam.

Harris

For Further Reading:

Boice, James Montgomery. *Ordinary Men Called by God.* Grand Rapids, Mich.: Kregel, 1998.

Buber, Martin. *Moses.* Oxford: East and West Library, 1946.

Childs, Brevard. *The Book of Exodus: A Critical, Theological Commentary.* Philadelphia: Westminster Press, 1974.

Moses ben Maimon

(Maimonides)

Medieval Jewish Philosopher;
Codifier of Jewish Law
1135–1204

Life and Work

The foremost intellectual figure of medieval Judaism and an important influence on the Western philosophical tradition, Moses ben Maimon, more commonly known as Maimonides, codified Jewish law and attempted to harmonize philosophy and religion.

Maimonides was born Moses ben Maimon on March 30, 1135, in Cordova, Spain, a cultural center for Arabs, Christians, and Jews. His family contained eight generations of rabbis and Jewish scholars. In 1148 the fanatic Almohads invaded Cordova and forbade any non-Muslim public worship. Maimonides's family eventually fled and lived in Fez in North Africa, where Maimonides continued his studies in Greek philosophy, rabbinics, and medicine. Following a brief stay in Palestine, the family finally settled in Old Cairo, Egypt. There Maimonides became physician to the court of Sultan Saladin and a leader of the Jewish community.

A prolific writer, Maimonides is noted for three major works: *Commentary on the Mishnah, Mishnah Torah,* and *Guide to the Perplexed.* All reveal his preoccupation with approaching Judaism rationally, using philosophical method-

ology to confirm its basic beliefs and understand traditional law. Maimonides completed his *Commentary on the Mishnah* (oral Torah or rabbinic law) in 1168. This work includes the "Thirteen Articles of Faith," in which he discusses the existence and essence of God, Jewish law, prophecy, his belief in the divine revelation of the Torah (the first five books of the Old Testament), and his thoughts about divine providence and the coming of the Messiah. Ten years later he completed *Mishnah Torah* (1178) a 10-volume codification of all Jewish law, including those laws no longer relevant since the exile from Israel. The code gives a clear explanation of each law and the legal decisions proceeding from it.

Maimonides's greatest and most controversial work was *Guide to the Perplexed* (1190), an exposition of Jewish faith for the educated. In it he tries to reconcile Aristotelian philosophical thought (using reason and logic to analyze data) with a religion based on law and tradition. Maimonides views reason as preeminent; the intellect is the highest aspect of the soul. The highest form of religion is the intellectual contemplation of the divine, which he equates with the "love of God." The proper understanding of Judaism, he asserts, comes only through Aristotelian thought, other approaches are a form of idolatry.

Maimonides was also a highly respected medical writer who frequently interjected his medical opinions into his religious and philosophical writings. He wrote treatises on subjects as varied as poisons and asthma and was interested in preventive medicine and the connection between body and mind.

Maimonides died on December 13, 1204, in Egypt and was buried in Tiberias in Palestine.

Legacy

Maimonides had a profound influence not only on Jewish thought but also on the Western philosophical tradition through his attempts to reconcile philosophy and religion.

Maimonides's "Thirteen Articles of Faith" was the first formulation of Jewish dogma, which had been scattered throughout various Jewish teachings. It eventually became part of the liturgies of both Ashkenasic (Eastern and Northern European) and Sephardic (Southern European and Middle Eastern) Judaism. A poetic version became a well-known hymn. Maimonides's *Mishnah Torah* became a standard work of Jewish law.

Maimonides's attempts to harmonize religion and philosophy generated controversy even during his life. Jews living in Christian countries were alienated by his rejection of the traditional, irrational faith. The orthodox denounced him as a heretical egotist and forbade their followers to read any of his philosophical works. For centuries Judaism was divided between the Maimonists and the anti-Maimonists but the controversy died over time and today his writings have won universal acceptance.

Within the larger philosophical tradition, Maimonides influenced THOMAS AQUINAS, who attempted to reconcile Christian revelation with philosophic thought. Through Aquinas he influenced the Scholastics of the Middle Ages, including Duns Scotus and Meister Eckhardt, both of whom quoted him. The seventeenth-century Jewish philosopher BENEDICT DE SPINOZA reacted to Maimonides, pointing to the weaknesses in trying to join philosophy and religion. Maimonides also influenced the great seventeenth-century rationalist thinker Gottfried Wilhelm Leibniz.

Maimonides's medical writings emphasizing preventative medicine are considered advanced for their time. His works, written in Arabic, were translated into Hebrew and Latin. They were highly regarded by Muslims and were studied in European universities into the seventeenth century.

Saltz

WORLD EVENTS		MAIMONIDES'S LIFE
Settling of Timbuktu, present-day Mali	c. 1100	
	1135	Maimonides is born
	1148	Almohads conquer Cordova
	c. 1159	Maimonides's family leaves Cordova, settles in Fez, North Africa
	c. 1165	Maimonides begins to practice medicine
	1168	*Commentary on the Mishnah* is completed
	1178	*Mishnah Torah* is completed
Islamic ruler of Egypt, Saladin, captures Jerusalem	1187	
	1190	*Guide to the Perplexed* is completed
	1204	Maimonides dies
Hapsburg dynasty begins dominance in Holy Roman Empire	1273	

For Further Reading:
Heschel, Abraham Joshua. *Maimonides: A Biography.* Translated by Joachim Neugroschel. New York: Farrar, Straus, Giroux, 1982.
Rambam. *Readings in the Philosophy of Moses Maimonides.* Translated with Introduction and commentary by Lenn Evan Goodman. New York: Viking Press, 1976.

Muhammad

Prophet and Founder of Islam
c. 570–632

Life and Work

Muhammad founded one of the great religions of the world, Islam, whose central writing, the Koran, is believed by Muslims to be the word of God (Allah) as revealed to Muhammad.

Muhammad was born about 570 in Mecca in what is now Saudi Arabia. His father had died before his birth and, at age six, he lost his mother. He lived in poverty until he was about 25, when he married a wealthy older woman, Khadijah, and became a successful merchant.

About 610, while on a religious retreat on Mount Hira near Mecca, Muhammad had a vision calling upon him to preach the word of God. Further visions throughout his life make up the text of the Koran. Drawing freely on Jewish and Christian beliefs as well as Arabic and Gnostic traditions about the separation of spirit and flesh, Muhammad preached that there was one almighty, just, and merciful God, Allah, in whom alone is hope. Believers should submit and pray to Allah alone. On judgment day Allah will reward the faithful in heaven and condemn the infidels, the nonbelievers, to hell. Muhammad taught that Allah had sent prophets, including MOSES and JESUS, to nations throughout history but that he was the final prophet, superseding the earlier ones.

The pagan Meccans greeted Muhammad's message with ridicule; ultimately Muhammad found it impossible to preach there. In 622, fearing a murder plot, he and about 70 disciples left Mecca for Yathrib (later named Medina), a migration known as the *hegira* ("flight" in Arabic), from which date the Muslims begin their calendar.

In Medina, Muhammad emerged as a powerful religious and political leader, organized a Muslim community, and sent raiding parties to cripple Meccan commerce. Mecca peacefully surrendered to Muhammad and his army in 630.

Muhammad continued to consolidate his religious and political authority until he died on June 8, 632.

Legacy

By the time of his death, Muhammad had established one of the world's great religions and laid the foundations for a mighty Islamic empire.

Muhammad was succeeded by his brother-in-law, Abu Bakr, who became the first Caliph (successor to Muhammad and head of Islam), and began the spread of Islam. By 656 Islam could claim the entire Arabian peninsula and much of the Middle East. Under the fourth Caliph, Ali, the husband of Muhammad's daughter, FATIMAH, the Muslim community split into the Shiites and the Sunnis, a rift that remains today.

One hundred years after Muhammad's death, Islam had conquered North Africa and Spain and was established in the borders of China and India. By the sixteenth century, Islam, under the Turks, was at the gates of Vienna, challenging the heart of Christian Europe. Since the sixteenth century, Islam has spread to more of Africa, much of southeast Asia, and the Indian subcontinent and made major inroads in Western Europe and North America thanks to immigration and conversions.

In recent years, fundamentalist groups have arisen in some Muslim countries, trying to depose their secular governments and impose Islamic law (Sharia). This has led to many terrorist acts against, for example, the governments of Egypt and Algeria and a general hatred among fundamentalists for the West, particularly the United States, whose spreading culture they see as encroaching on Muslim values and whose support of Israel has helped displace their Palestinian brethren.

Muhammad's life has had profound significance for Muslims throughout history. In the centuries following his death, theologians developed the doctrine that Muhammad had lived a life of sinlessness, and his actions were considered the perfect embodiment of the God's will. He provides the *sunna*, or example, of the perfect life each Muslim tries to emulate.

Saltz

For Further Reading:
Hitti, Philip Khuri. *The Arabs: A Short History.* Washington, D.C.: Regnery Publishing, 1996.
Malik, Ghulam. *Muhammad: An Islamic Perspective.* Lanham, Md.: University Press of America, 1996.

Muhammad, Elijah
(Elijah Poole)

Leader of the Nation of Islam
1897–1975

Life and Work

Elijah Muhammad was the leader of the Nation of Islam (the Black Muslims) who preached racial separation and black self-reliance.

The son of a poor Baptist preacher, Elijah Poole was born on October 7, 1897, in Sandersville, Georgia. To help support his family, Poole dropped out of school in the fourth grade to work as a sharecropper. He married and eventually moved to Detroit, where he worked in various factories until he lost his job at the onset of the Depression. From 1929 to 1931 his family lived on welfare. Poole never forgot this period, which motivated him to later insist on self-reliance for his followers.

Around 1931 Elijah Poole became a follower of Wallace D. Fard, the founder of the First Temple of Islam, a forerunner of the Nation of Islam. Fard preached that Islam was the true religion of African Americans and that blacks owed no allegiance to a nation that had enslaved them. He appointed Poole his chief lieutenant and instructed him to abandon his "slave name"—Poole—and to accept his true Islamic name, Muhammad.

Fard disappeared mysteriously in 1934 and, shortly thereafter, tensions between his assistants forced Muhammad, who feared for his life, to move to Chicago. There he established a temple that became the headquarters of the Nation of Islam. He declared that Fard was the earthly manifestation of Allah come to bring the truth to black people, and that he, Elijah Muhammad, was the principal Messenger of Allah. From his base in Chicago, Elijah Muhammad rebuilt Fard's organization and gained control of the movement. During World War II his opposition to the draft—he urged blacks not to fight other people of color (the Japanese)—earned him four years in jail.

After the war, Elijah Muhammad promoted a program of racial separatism and self-reliance. He believed that African Americans must never depend on the oppressive white power structure but, instead, develop and support their own economic and political power bases. Under his leadership, the Nation of Islam founded stores, restaurants, and other businesses to encourage economic self-reliance. He also advocated the establishment of a separate state for Black Muslims.

In the mid-1960s scandals erupted over Muhammad's sexual relationships with his secretaries. At the same time a schism developed between him and Malcolm X, who questioned the focus on racial separatism and challenged Muhammad's teachings and practices. After Malcolm X was assassinated in 1965, Muhammad selected Louis Farrakhan to be his chief spokesman. The movement weakened and membership declined.

Elijah Muhammad died in Chicago on February 25, 1975. He was succeeded as the head of the Nation of Islam by his son, Wallace Deen Muhammad.

Legacy

Elijah Muhammad's legacy is varied and complex. His emphasis on racial separation ultimately divided his movement, but his encouragement of economic development improved the situation of many of his followers.

The Nation of Islam grew rapidly after the war, reaching its peak around 1963, when it had approximately 500,000 members and millions of sympathizers. The growth was largely attributable to the work of MALCOLM X, whom Elijah Muhammad had recruited in 1947 and made national spokesperson of the Nation of Islam.

When Wallace Deen Muhammad, Elijah Muhammad's son, took the helm of this group in 1975, he tried to soften its radical nature by tempering its insistence on racial separation and by admitting non-black members. (Islam itself believes that Allah is the God of all people and does not make racial distinctions.) He also dedicated the group to strict Islamic religious practices. Wallace Deen Muhammad eventually renamed the group the American Muslim Mission.

Louis Farrakhan remained loyal to the teachings of Elijah Muhammad and broke with the American Muslim Mission, forming a splinter group that he renamed the Nation of Islam. This restored group has continued Elijah Muhammad's emphasis on racial separation and self-reliance for African Americans, both as individuals and as families.

The Nation of Islam has attracted many prominent African Americans, such as Muhammed Ali, Kareem Abdul-Jabbar, and Mike Tyson, to its fold. It has also sponsored events to restore the African-American family and community, most notably the Million Man March in Washington, D.C., in 1995.

von Dehsen

WORLD EVENTS		MUHAMMAD'S LIFE
Germany is united	1871	
	1897	Elijah Poole is born in Sandersville, Georgia
Spanish American War	1898	
World War I	1914–18	
	1931	Poole meets Wallace Fard, founder of First Temple of Islam; he takes name Elijah Muhammad
	1934	Elijah Muhammad establishes temple in Chicago
World War II	1939–45	
	1947	Elijah Muhammad recruits Malcolm X
Mao Tse-tung establishes Communist rule in China	1949	
Korean War	1950–53	
	1965	Elijah Muhammad selects Louis Farrakhan as chief spokesman
Six Day War between Israel and Arabs	1967	
End of Vietnam War	1975	Elijah Muhammad dies in Chicago
Fall of Communism in eastern Europe	1989	

For Further Reading:

Clegg, Claude A. *An Original Man: The Life and Times of Elijah Muhammad*. New York: St. Martin's Press, 1997.

Kepel, Gilles. *Allah in the West: Islamic Movements in America and Europe*. Stanford, Calif.: Stanford University Press, 1997.

Nanak

Founder of Sikhism
1469–1539

Life and Work

The founder of Sikhism, Nanak was a follower of the Hindu *bhakti* (devotional) tradition; he developed Sikhism based on his personal religious insights combining Hinduism and the teachings of Islam.

Nanak was born on April 15, 1469, in the Punjab region of present-day northwestern India. His father was a government official and a member of the Hindu warrior caste. As a young man, Nanak worked as an accountant for the local sultan. During this time, he came to know Mardana, a Muslim minstrel. Together they conducted religious meetings featuring hymns with Nanak's lyrics set to Mardana's melodies.

At age 29, Nanak disappeared while bathing in a local stream. When Nanak returned after three days, he claimed that he had had a vision in which God commissioned him to preach

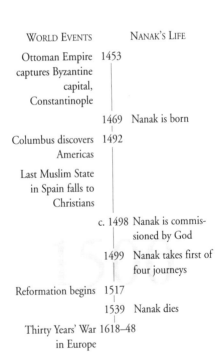

WORLD EVENTS		NANAK'S LIFE
Ottoman Empire captures Byzantine capital, Constantinople	1453	
	1469	Nanak is born
Columbus discovers Americas	1492	
Last Muslim State in Spain falls to Christians		
	c. 1498	Nanak is commissioned by God
	1499	Nanak takes first of four journeys
Reformation begins	1517	
	1539	Nanak dies
Thirty Years' War in Europe	1618–48	

the holy word (*nam*) and to teach others how to pray. As a result of this mystical experience, Nanak proclaimed, "There is no Hindu; there is no Muslim."

To fulfill this commission, Nanak took four journeys. The first was in 1499 to the east, where he visited many pilgrimage sites of the Hindus. On the second journey, he went southward as far as Sri Lanka. Upon his return to Punjab, he founded the city, Kartarpur, which became the first center of Sikhism. On the third journey, he traveled north. On the final journey, he returned to the west of India, traveling to the prominent Muslim holy cities of Mecca, Medina, and Baghdad.

Nanak's teachings borrowed from both Islamic and Hindu traditions. A monotheist, Nanak believed that there was one God who created the world. At creation, God also fabricated good and evil, so that people would have to choose good and reject evil in order to achieve salvation. Nanak also believed in *samara*, the Hindu teaching about reincarnation. He contended that it took a soul many lifetimes before it attained the spiritual perfection needed for *moksa*, the release from the eternal cycle of birth and death and the complete unity with God.

To achieve *moksa*, each *sisyas* (disciple, hence the name Sikhism) needed a *guru* (teacher) as a spiritual guide. The *guru* helped disciples attain righteousness and *moksa* through learning the teachings and practicing the devotions on *nam*, the divine word or name, by saying prayers and singing hymns. Moreover, the true *guru*, the *satguru*, was just slightly below God.

Nanak died in Kartarpur, on September 22, 1539.

Legacy

Nanak's death led to the recognition of nine subsequent *gurus*, whose teachings and religious and secular expansion of Nanak's initial teachings led to the development of Sikhism as an independent religion.

Angad (1504–1552), the second *guru*, formalized Kartarpur as the seat of Sikhism and compiled a hymnal based on the music of Nanak. Using the available legends, Angad also tried to assemble a biography of the founder. The next *guru*, Amar Das (1479–1574), split the Sikh community into two groups for the

purpose of collecting the 10% religious tax more efficiently. The fourth *guru*, Ram Das (1534–1581), established a new town that contained a large tank of water known as Amritsar, the tank of immortality. This new town soon became a center of commerce in Punjab. He also made the office of *guru* hereditary so that it remained in the Sodhis family.

The fifth *guru*, ARJUN (1563–1606), produced the *Adi Granth*, a collection of writings taken from those of the first four *gurus*, the Hindu and Muslim saints, coupled with his own writings. The *Adi Granth* became the Sikh sacred scripture and helped establish an independent Sikh identity. Arjun also built a new temple at Amritsar, the "Golden Temple," which became the most holy Sikh shrine. He also increased his revenue through trade and taxation, making him the *sacha padshah*, the ruler of the Sikh community.

Before his death, Arjun named his son, Hargobind (1594-1644), to be the sixth *guru*. Hargobind increased his temporal power and was criticized by his disciples for being too militant. The next two *gurus*, Har Rai (1630–1661) and his son Hari Kishan (1656–1664), tried to maintain peace, but came into conflict with Emperor Aurangzeb. When these *gurus* died of smallpox, the emperor captured and beheaded the ninth *guru*, Tegh Bahadur (1621–1675). His son, GOBIND SINGH (1666–1708) became the tenth and last *guru*. He is principally remembered for the creation of the military brotherhood known as the *Khalsa* and the establishment of the *Adi Granth* to replace the *guru* in Sikh devotion.

By 1800, the Sikhs had established a powerful kingdom in Punjab that threatened British domination. Nevertheless, the British were able to control internal dissension and annex Punjab in 1849. In 1947, Indian independence split Punjab between India and Pakistan. After migration to India, the Sikhs were allowed to form their own state in Punjab. Nevertheless, tension remained between the Sikhs and Hindus, resulting in hostilities leading to the seizure of the Golden Temple in 1984 and the assassination of Indira Gandhi in retaliation. They remain a militant religious group within the larger matrix of Indian society.

von Dehsen

For Further Reading:
Singh, Inderpal, and Madujit Kadur. *Guru Nanak: A Global Vision*. Amritsar: Guru Nanak Dev University, 1997.
Singh, Taran. *Guru Nanak: His Mind and Art*. New Delhi: Bahri Publications, 1992.

Niebuhr, Reinhold

Political Theologian; Advocate of
Christian Political Activism
1892–1971

Life and Work

Reinhold Niebuhr was a Christian theologian who profoundly influenced mid-twentieth-century theology and politics through his attempt to relate Christian values to political involvement and social justice.

Niebuhr was born to a German-American family in Wright City, Missouri, on June 21, 1892. The son of a pastor, Niebuhr knew by the time he was 10 that he wanted to enter the ministry. He received a B.A. in 1914 and a nM.A. in 1915 from Yale Divinity School and was ordained in the Evangelical and Reformed Church. He soon became pastor of Bethel Church in Detroit, which grew rapidly under his direction. Niebuhr quickly earned a reputation as a social activist, opposing racism, backing labor causes, and embracing pacifism. In 1928, Niebuhr's activist efforts won him a position on the faculty of Union Theological Seminary in New York City.

At Union, Niebuhr emerged as a nationally renowned Christian thinker and social critic. A man of constant action, he was involved in countless liberal organizations. In 1930 he founded the Fellowship of Social Christians; five

years later he established its journal *Radical Religion*, later renamed *Christianity and Society*. In 1940 he launched *Christianity and Crisis* to present his liberal, anti-Nazi views. In 1944 he became a founder of the Liberal Party in New York state. After World War II Niebuhr was an advisor to the State Department, helping shape America's response to the emerging Cold War. He delivered a major address at the first meeting of the World Council of Churches in 1948. In 1949 he contributed to the establishment of the liberal group, Americans for Democratic Action. Through his writings and friendships with political leaders such as Eleanor Roosevelt and Hubert Humphrey, he influenced public policy into the 1960s.

Never a systematic theologian, Niebuhr's primary concern was how to apply Christianity to the issues of the moment. For Niebuhr, Christ's message was realized in human institutions by the quest for justice tempered by love. Although influenced by liberal theology and the political emphasis of the Social Gospel in his early ministry, Niebuhr ultimately rejected the optimism and utopianism of these schools in favor of what he termed Christian Realism. He thought individuals and nations inherently sinful, a condition manifest in the belief that one has all knowledge and the right to impose it on others. He called this belief utopianism and urged people to reject it through activism. He saw true faith as inevitably leading to involvement in political affairs. He presented his thoughts in countless sermons and speeches as well as many books, the most important of which were *Moral Man and Immoral Society* (1932) and *Nature and Destiny of Man* (1941).

Niebuhr retired from Union in 1960. In 1964 President Lyndon Johnson awarded him the Medal of Freedom for his life's work. Niebuhr died in New York City on June 1, 1971.

Legacy

Niebuhr's life was dedicated to relating Christian faith to issues of social, political, and economic justice. Although his numerous writings do not disclose a consistent pattern of thought, they do reveal the work of a man who sought to apply the Christian principles of love and justice to the concerns of the day.

Niebuhr's ideas never became the foundation for a unique "Niebuhrian" school of thought. Nevertheless they became an integral part of late twentieth-century Christianity. Niebuhr's legacy rests on those who promote liberal causes as an expression of Christian faith. His insistence that society support the powerless and marginalized applies as well today as it did in his time. His periodical, *Christianity and Crisis,* continues to be published to promote such liberal views.

At Union, Niebuhr inspired countless students and scholars to make their faith real through action. He did not foster utopian ideals, but real engagement in a tarnished world where imperfect action led to continual struggle for justice. This mode of engagement not only lives on through those whom he inspired personally, but also in those more secular institutions such as Americans for Democratic Action and the Liberal Party. Niebuhr casts a long shadow over those who grapple with the issues of the day and attempt to relate faith to justice.

von Dehsen

WORLD EVENTS		NIEBUHR'S LIFE
	1892	Reinhold Niebuhr is born
Spanish American War	1898	
World War I	1914–18	
	1928	Niebuhr joins Union Theological Seminary
	1932	*Moral Man and Immoral Society* is published
World War II	1939–45	
	1941	*Nature and Destiny of Man* is published
	1948	Niebuhr addresses first assembly of the World Council of Churches
Mao Tse-tung establishes Communist rule in China	1949	Niebuhr helps establish Americans for Democratic Action
Korean War	1950–53	
	1964	Niebuhr receives Medal of Freedom from President Lyndon Johnson
Six Day War between Israel and Arabs	1967	
	1971	Niebuhr dies in New York City
End of Vietnam War	1975	

For Further Reading:

Beckley, Harlan. *Passion for Justice: Retrieving the Legacies of Walter Rauschenbusch, John A. Ryan, and Reinhold Niebuhr.* Louisville, Ky.: Westminster/John Knox Press, 1992.

Brown, Charles C. *Niebuhr and His Age: Reinhold Niebuhr's Prophetic Role in the Twentieth Century.* Philadelphia: Trinity Press International, 1992.

Stone, Ronald H. *Professor Reinhold Niebuhr: A Mentor for the Twentieth Century* Louisville, Ky.: John Knox Press, 1992.

Nietzsche, Friedrich Wilhelm

Influential Philosopher and Critic
of Judeo–Christian Tradition
1844–1900

Life and Work

No philosopher has influenced twentieth-century philosophy, theology, and literary criticism more significantly than Friedrich Wilhelm Nietzsche.

Nietzsche was born in Rocken, Germany, on October 15, 1844, to a cultured, middle-class family. His father, a Lutheran minister,

died before Nietzsche turned five. In 1864 he took up theology and classics in Bonn. The next year he renounced his Christian faith and followed his teacher Friedrich Wilhelm Ritschl to Leipzig to continue studying classical languages. Because of his brilliant work, in 1869 the Swiss University of Basel called him to teach—before he finished his doctorate. He taught there until 1879 when health problems forced him to retire. From then until his complete mental and physical breakdown in 1889, he lived a mostly solitary, nomadic existence and wrote his most influential works. After his collapse, he lived quietly with family members who managed the publication of his work without understanding most of it.

Nietzsche's first book, *The Birth of Tragedy*, appeared in 1872 and, like most of his work, was either ignored or much misunderstood. Such misunderstanding eventually led to uninformed interpretation of his work and the later Nazi misrepresentation of certain passages taken out of context.

As the greatest poetic philosopher since PLATO, Nietzsche, in aphoristic, image-filled works like *Dawn* (1881) and *The Gay Science* (1882), announced that "God is dead." Western culture must face the consequences of its general lack of faith in a supernatural world of absolute being, truth, and value, and it must become strong enough to create its own values and meaning. In his key work, *Thus Spoke Zarathustra* (1883–85), Nietzsche portrays a wise teacher, ZOROASTER (Zarathustra), who learns how to live life joyfully in spite of all its suffering through a self-disciplined, creative acceptance of his own unique existence. Lacking guidance from absolute truth, such an "overman" shows power not by political domination but through a self-mastery so affirming of life that he wants to live this exact same life forever. Ultimately, Nietzsche's insightful reflections on such self-actualization outweigh his negative attitudes about women and democracy, and his complete dismissal of Christianity.

He died in Weimar, Germany, on August 25, 1900, oblivious to the impact of his thinking in European universities.

Legacy

During his days of active scholarship (1872–1889), Nietzsche's influence upon his contemporaries was limited; few people actually read his works and fewer still understood them. Yet right before his breakdown, his work was well received in a series of lectures in Copenhagen, and by 1914 his work was so well known in Germany that a copy of *Thus Spoke Zarathustra* became standard issue for every German soldier in World War I.

Nietzsche's critique of Judeo-Christian culture influenced poets like Rainer Maria Rilke and William Butler Yeats, novelists such as Thomas Mann and Herman Hesse and important twentieth-century philosophers like MARTIN HEIDEGGER and ALBERT CAMUS. Furthermore, Sigmund Freud and other noted psychoanalysts admired Nietzsche's depth of self-knowledge, while important religious thinkers like PAUL TILLICH and MARTIN BUBER acknowledged his influence.

Nietzsche's writings have become even more significant since the 1960s. In the United States his work has inspired the "God-is-dead" theology of Thomas Altizer and many serious philosophical interpretations of his major works and ideas. Meanwhile major French Postmodern philosophers and literary critics, among them JACQUES DERRIDA and MICHEL FOUCAULT, have created a new wave of Nietzschean dialogue and interpretation critical of modern culture. In his intellectual autobiography *Ecce Homo*, published in 1908 after his death, Nietzsche observed that "some are born posthumously"; this, perhaps, cannot be said more truly of any other thinker.

Magurshak

WORLD EVENTS	NIETZSCHE'S LIFE
Greek War of 1821–29 Independence against Turkey	
	1844 Friedrich Wilhelm Nietzsche is born
Revolutions in 1848 Austria, France, Germany, and Italy	
	1849 Nietzsche's father dies
United States 1861–65 Civil War	
	1864 Nietzsche's university education begins
Germany is united 1871	
	1872 *The Birth of Tragedy* is published
	1879 Nietzsche retires from teaching
	1881 *Dawn* is published
	1882 *The Gay Science* is published
	1883–85 *Thus Spoke Zarathustra* is published
	1889 Nietzsche suffers a complete mental and physical breakdown
Spanish American 1898 War	
	1900 Nietzsche dies
World War I 1914–18	

For Further Reading:

Alderman, Harold. *Nietzsche's Gift.* Athens: Ohio University Press, 1977.

Hollingdale. *Nietzsche: The Man and His Philosophy.* London: Ark Paperbacks, 1985.

Kaufmann, Walter. *Nietzsche: Philosopher, Psychologist, Antichrist.* 4th edition. Princeton, N.J.: Princeton University Press, 1974.

Origen

(Oregenes Adamantius)

Synthesizer of Early Christian Theology

c. 185–c. 255

Life and Work

Origen was one of the most important thinkers of the early Christian church. He developed the first systematic and speculative theology of Christianity and introduced patterns of thinking that have become fundamental to subsequent Christian thought.

Born in Alexandria, Egypt, to Christian parents, Origen was educated primarily by his father Leonides, who was beheaded in 202, during Roman Emperor Septimius Severus' persecutions of the Alexandrian Christians. Origen was left with a deep opposition to pagan, i.e., Greek and Roman, philosophy and culture. Nevertheless, he studied "pagan" philosophy, and the influence of PLATO and the Stoic school (see ZENO OF CITIUM) is evident in his most important works. During the persecution of the Alexandrian Christians in 215, he made his way to Caesarea in Palestine, where he was ordained and where he remained for most of his life. Tortured in the empire-wide persecutions in 251, Origen eventually died as a result at age 69 in Tyre, in northern Palestine.

Origen's works can be divided into four major areas: critical (*Hexapla*), exegetical (commentaries of Old and New Testaments), doctrinal (Christian theology), and apologetic (works in defense of Christianity against attacks by pagan philosophers). One of the most accomplished biblical scholars of the early Christian church, Origen developed the *Hexapla*, a synopsis of six versions of the Old Testament. Origen attacked scholars who believed that the Bible must be interpreted literally. For him the prime mission of scripture was not to convey historical facts but spiritual truths. He thought that each scriptural passage could have many layers of meaning that could be understood through *logos*, divine reason.

In his doctrinal works, Origen sought to make the Christian view of the universe compatible with Greek thought. He developed a systematic theology in the Greek philosophical tradition, but it was distinctively Christian in other ways. Origen acknowledged that Plato said many wise things but did not see him as inspired to discover divine truth. For Origen, revelation came only from the Bible.

His indebtedness to the ideas of Plato and other Greek philosophers is evident especially in *On First Principles,* a treatise on the Christian concept of the universe. In it Origen maintained that the soul consisted of both material and spiritual forms, with the former being transitory and subject to death—an approach in keeping with Platonic teachings. His dualistic approach to theology (there is a spiritual world that is superior to the material world) is also evident in his belief that there were two churches: the real, physical one on Earth and the spiritual one, the Church of Christ. Origin also believed that, within the Trinity, the Son and the Spirit were subordinate to the Father. He wrote of universal salvation in which hell was a temporary place where unpure souls were cleansed for heaven and where the Devil would repent of his sins. Many of the ideas in *On First Principles* were later declared heretical.

Legacy

One of the most original thinkers of the early Christian church, Origen offered the first theory of knowledge and the universe from a Christian perspective. His works influenced all later Christian theologians and writers.

The Church debated the validity of Origen's ideas for centuries. Shortly after his death, he was attacked as a heretic. Controversy continued for the next three centuries, during which his ideas were widely misinterpreted and misunderstood. In the sixth century, the Emperor Justinian declared Origen a pernicious heretic, and in 543 a council at Constantinople (present-day Istanbul) issued an edict listing theological errors attributed to him. Ten years later The Second Council of Constantinople condemned Origen's teachings. By that point, the doctrines condemned had little relation to Origen's original thought.

His exegetical (interpretive) works on the Bible were one of the standards for the early Christian period. In fact, his influence on biblical criticism and systematic theology persisted into the Middle Ages. Origin's insistence that God's word comes through scripture influenced theologians through the Middle Ages, including JEROME, AUGUSTINE OF HIPPO, and MARTIN LUTHER.

Renaud

WORLD EVENTS		ORIGEN'S LIFE
Roman Empire conquers Armenia and Mesopotamia	117	
	c. 185	Origen is born
	202	Origen's father is martyred
	c. 212	Origen begins compiling his *Hexapla*
	230	Origen is ordained in Caesarea
Last Severan emperor of Rome is killed; disorder ensues	235	
	251	Origen is tortured by Romans during empire-wide persecution of Christians
	c. 255	Origen dies
Rule of Roman Empire by Constantine	306–307	

For Further Reading:

Chadwick, Henry, *The Early Church.* New York: Penguin Books, 1967.

Johnson, Paul. *A History of Christianity.* London: Weidenfeld and Nicolson, 1976.

Kannengiesser, Charles, ed. *Origen of Alexandira: His World and His Legacy.* Notre Dame, Ind.: University of Notre Dame Press, 1988.

Palmer, Phoebe Worrall

Founder of the Holiness Movement
1807–1874

Life and Work

Phoebe Worrall Palmer was a lay evangelist of the Methodist church and one of the early founders of the Holiness movement. The members of this movement believed that the faithful could achieve complete freedom from sins in this life.

Phoebe Worrall was born on December 18, 1807, in New York City. At 19, she married Walter C. Palmer, a physician. In 1835, her sister, Sarah Worrall Lanford, began a series of prayer meetings in the Palmer home. These meetings, originally intended for Methodist women and later open to men as well, became known as the "Tuesday Meeting for the Promotion of Holiness." These meetings emphasized Bible study, personal testimony, and prayer. They soon became the focal point for the growing "Holiness movement."

The pivotal moment for Palmer came on July 26, 1837, the event she later called "the day of days." On that day, she experienced complete sanctification, the total forgiveness of all her sins. This moment of holiness redirected Palmer's life to one of writing and preaching about holiness.

Palmer wrote 10 books, the most important of which was *The Way to Holiness,* published in 1843. From 1862 to 1874, she edited the magazine *Guide to Holiness* to spread her beliefs. The magazine eventually attracted about 30,000 subscribers. Palmer's message was simple and direct. Holiness was available to everyone who accepted Christ as a personal savior. Following conversion to Christ, a believer experienced consecration, by placing his or her whole life on the altar of Christ. This simple and straightforward message found many welcoming ears.

Coupled with Palmer's evangelical efforts were programs in social reform, bringing her message of complete sanctification to the poor and down-trodden. Among her most significant projects was her work in the poor and notorious neighborhood of "Five Points" in New York City. She also established a mission house in 1850 as a member of the Ladies' Home Missionary Society of the Methodist Episcopal church.

In 1857 and 1858 Palmer and her husband became active participants of the Prayer Meeting Revival in many northern states. These revivals were part of the larger spiritual revival that swept urban America at this time. After the Civil War, the "Tuesday Meetings" continued in her home.

Never fully in good health, Palmer believed that God spared her an early death to be of divine service. She died in New York City on November 2, 1874.

Legacy

Palmer's spiritual experience on her "day of days" sparked the Holiness movement, a revivalist movement emphasizing personal conversion and social reform.

Although founded from within the Methodist church, the Holiness movement soon developed organizations of its own. By the 1870s the National Holiness Association, founded in 1867, began to emerge as an independent group. This association grew out of Methodist revival meetings in Vineland, New Jersey, led by John Inskip and William B. Osborn. In addition, John P. Brooks, editor of the *Banner of Holiness,* broke with the national Methodist church and denounced any Christian denomination that would suppress holiness. (Most Protestant denominations would not agree that complete sanctification was possible in this life. Even though they are forgiven, believers are still tempted to continue in sin and needed continual forgiveness.)

The Holiness movement produced several new denominations. In 1881, wishing to free himself from the constraints and regulations of the national church organization, Daniel Sidney Warner established the Church of God in Christ in Anderson, Indiana. This congregation eventually developed into a larger body; by the end of the twentieth century, the national Church of God had over 200,000 members.

Founded as a local congregation in Los Angeles by Phineas Bresee in 1895, the Church of the Nazarene quickly gained a reputation as one that welcomed the poor. Once again, this local group blossomed into a national organization, claiming over 550,000 members by 1991. Also in Los Angeles, the Holiness movement inspired the Azusa Street revival in 1906 under the direction of William J. Seymour. While Seymour's Holiness roots led him to promote personal commitment to Christ, he broadened his teaching by requiring that believers verify their faith by demonstrating a gift of the Holy Spirit, such as speaking in tongues or healing.

The holiness movement also influenced the Salvation Army, founded in Britain and transported to the United States in 1880. The "battlegrounds" for this army were those areas inhabited by the poor. By providing food and necessities, the soldiers hoped to gain their trust and lead them to Christ.

From Palmer's home in New York, to the streets of Los Angeles, the Holiness movement brought Phoebe Palmer's gospel of personal salvation to hundreds of thousands of people.

von Dehsen

World Events		Palmer's Life
	1807	Phoebe Worrall is born
Greek War of	1821–29	
Independence against Turkey		
	1835	"Tuesday Meetings" begin in Palmer home
	1843	*The Way to Holiness* is published
Revolutions in	1848	
Austria, France, Germany, and Italy		
	1857–58	Palmers participate in the Prayer Meeting Revival
United States	1861–65	
Civil War		
Germany is united	1871	
	1874	Palmer dies
Spanish American War	1898	

For Further Reading:

Dieter, Melvin E. *The Holiness Revival of the Nineteenth Century.* Metuchen, N.J.: Scarecrow Press, 1980.

White, Charles Edward. *The Beauty of Holiness: Phoebe Palmer as Theologian, Revivalist, Feminist, and Humanitarian.* Grand Rapids, Mich.: F. Asbury Press, 1986.

Parham, Charles Fox

Founder of American Pentecostalism
1873–1929

Life and Work

Charles Fox Parham founded American Pentecostalism.

Parham was born in the farming community of Muscatine, Iowa, on June 4, 1873. At the age of 13, having undergone a religious conversion, he became active in the Methodist church. In 1890, he began studying for the ministry at Southwest Kansas College. Even though poor health forced him to leave college before completing his studies, he was ordained into the Methodist ministry in 1893. By 1895, he left the Methodist church and joined the Holiness movement, a revival movement that linked personal salvation (justification) with holiness of life (sanctification). It was during this time that Parham's health improved, a circumstance that moved him to emphasize healing.

By 1900, Parham established the Bethel Bible School in Topeka, Kansas. From his study of the account of Pentecost in the second chapter of the Acts of the Apostles (New Testament), he concluded that baptism in the Holy Spirit is followed by glossolalia, speaking in tongues (recognizable foreign languages). These gifts of the Spirit could be used to spread the gospel to other regions of the world.

On January 1, 1901, Parham claimed that a miracle occurred. Not only did he see fire fall from heaven, but his student, Agnes N. Ozman, began to speak in tongues. In the following months, Parham and other students received the gift of glossolalia, calling attention to the school. He soon organized the Apostolic Faith Missions, attracting over 25,000 people to "Pentecostalism."

In 1905, Parham opened a Bible institute in Houston, Texas, which William J. Seymour briefly attended in 1905. Seymour was to foster the growth of Pentecostalism in 1906 through the establishment of the Azusa Street Revival in Los Angeles.

Parham's hold over the Pentecostal movement soon faded. By 1907 his reputation was tarnished over charges of sexual immorality.

He spent his remaining years serving a small parish in Baxter Springs, Kansas. He died there on January 29, 1929.

Legacy

Although Parham's leadership of the Pentecostal movement lasted only a few years, the movement itself grew into one of the major components of Christianity in the United States.

The traditional starting point for the growth of Pentecostalism was the Azusa Street Revival in Los Angeles, an African-American Holiness church. A student of Parham, William J. Seymour, established the church in 1906 and preached the Pentecostal beliefs that he had learned from Parham in Houston. Pentecostalism quickly appealed to many because of its dramatic demonstrations of the power of the Holy Spirit through speaking in tongues and healing.

Although the impact of the Azusa Street Revival had diminished by 1909, it had generated interest in the Pentecostal movement, an interest that spread across the country. For example, a newly energized C. H. Mason returned from Azusa to his congregation in Memphis, Tennessee. He began to hold meetings emphasizing speaking in tongues and healing. Mason's evangelistic fervor eventually led to the founding of the Churches of God in Christ, an African-American Pentecostal communion. Mason remained at the head of this church until 1961.

In 1908, A. J. Thomlison established the Church of God, another Pentecostal community centered in Cleveland, Tennessee. By 1911, a third Pentecostal church, the Pentecostal Church International, was launched by merger of two Holiness churches in South Carolina. Once again the Azusa Street Revival had inspired a leader, Gaston B. Cashwell. Other Pentecostal groups followed. In 1914, William Durham organized the Assemblies of God from churches in the Midwest and South. In 1923, Aimee Semple McPherson established the International Church of the Foursquare Gospel in Los Angeles.

After World War II, Oral Roberts moved Pentecostalism into mainstream America through efforts to attract people from the mid-dle class. In 1953, he began the Full Gospel Business Men's Fellowship International. He also took his message to the airwaves, becoming one of the earliest "televangelists."

In the last half of the twentieth century the various Pentecostal churches have made many efforts to promote racial integration. These efforts resulted in the decision in 1994 to create an interracial alliance among the major Pentecostal groups (e.g., Assemblies of God; the Church of God in Christ). At the end of the twentieth century, the spiritual movement begun by Parham in Kansas has grown to a Christian denomination containing several million adherents.

von Dehsen

WORLD EVENTS		PARHAM'S LIFE
Germany is united	1871	
	1873	Charles Fox Parham is born in Muscatine, Iowa
	1886	Parham experiences religious conversion
	1893	Parham is ordained Methodist minister
Spanish American War	1898	
	1901	Parham experiences miracles of falling fire and glossolalia
	1905	Parham founds Bible institute in Houston, Texas
World War I 1914–18		
	1929	Parham dies in Baxter Springs, Kansas
World War II 1939–45		

For Further Reading:

Anderson, Robert Mapes. *Vision of the Disinherited: The Making of American Pentecostalism.* New York: Oxford University Press, 1989.

Goff, James R. *Fields White Unto Harvest: Charles F. Parham and the Missionary Origins of Pentecostalism.* Fayetteville: University of Arkansas Press, 1988.

Parham, Sarah E. *The Life of Charles F. Parham: Founder of the Apostolic Faith Movement.* New York: Garland Press, 1985.

Pascal, Blaise

Influential Mathematician,
Theologian, and Philosopher of
Science
1623–1662

Life and Work

A major figure in the history of mathematics and science, Blaise Pascal is also known for his religious and philosophical thought, particularly as an exponent of the Augustinian theology of the Jansenists.

Pascal was born on June 19, 1623, at Clermont-Ferrand, France. As a young man, his initial intellectual accomplishments were in the areas of mathematics and physics. In order to help his father compute tax revenues, in 1639 he built the first digital calculator. In 1640 he completed an important study on geometric conic sections, leading to Pascal's Theorem; between 1647 and 1648 his work on vacuums and atmospheric pressure led to Pascal's Law.

Pascal's scientific outlook changed dramatically after November 23, 1654. On that night he was crossing the Seine during a storm and had an intense religious experience. From that day on he dedicated his life to religious and philosophical concerns. In January 1655 he entered the religious community at Port-Royal de Paris. This community was devoted to Jansenism, a form of Catholicism based on AUGUSTINE OF HIPPO's (354–430) teachings

on predestination and God's grace. Although Pascal never took religious vows, he directed his energies to clarifying the community's theology.

Pascal's work at Port-Royal resulted in two major books. During 1656 and 1657, he wrote 18 letters defending Jansenist ideas from Jesuit criticism. These letters, later collected under the title, *The Provincial Letters,* provide a pointed and caustic attack on the perceived hypocrisy and moral corruption of the Jesuits. During 1657 and 1658, Pascal began writing preliminary notes and short essays to be included in a larger work on the Christian religion. Although the work was never completed, the notes were published posthumously in 1662 under the title, *Pensees (Thoughts).* Here Pascal takes on the skepticism of MICHEL EYQUEM DE MONTAIGNE (1533–1592), who claimed that people were unable to know anything for certain. Pascal, in response, argues that reason alone is insufficient to acquire complete knowledge. In addition, he maintained that knowledge can come through intuition and divine revelation.

From these last ideas Pascal proffered his famous "wager." Given the possibilities that God does or does not exist, it is better to bet that God does exist. For, if one bets that God does exist and lives a morally upright life, there is nothing really to lose if God does not exist. But, if one loses the bet that God does not exist, there is Hell to pay!

During the last years of his life, Pascal was in ill health. He died at Port-Royal on August 19, 1662.

Legacy

Pascal's abilities were so broad that he influenced almost all the intellectual disciplines he entered. For example, Pascal's Theorem contributed to the study of conic geometry, and Pascal's Law illuminated the science of atmospheric pressure and of vacuums. However, his influence stretches beyond science, into the fields of literature, theology, and philosophy.

Many acknowledge the influence of *Les Provincials* on subsequent French literature. The 18 letters were written in a precise style characterized by variety and economy of language. This style stood in stark contrast to the then typical French style marked by pompous and labored phraseology. Nicolas Boileau

(1636–1711), an early French literary critic, considered *Les Provincials* the starting point of French literary prose.

Les Provincials became immensely popular among those who joined the criticism of the Jesuits in defense of Jansenism. After Pascal's death, the convent at Port-Royal continued its promotion of this Augustinian theology. This defense raised the ire of the French Catholic hierarchy and, in 1705, Pope Clement XI forced the closure of Port-Royal. Eight years later Clement XI formally condemned Jansenism

Pascal's philosophical influence arises principally from his *Pensees,* in which he attacks the absolute skepticism of Montaigne and asserts the value of intuitive and religious knowledge. His synthesis of rational and nonrational forms of knowledge helps to temper the trend toward total reliance on scientific learning by creating an openness to other forms of knowledge. Moreover, this appeal to personal forms of knowing anticipates some of the forms of existential theory that were developed in the twentieth century.

Finally, many people have responded to the challenge of Pascal's wager. While it is clear that Pascal's point was to promote the perfected moral life of Christians as he saw it, his wager has faced criticism on at least two fronts. First, it could apply to any religious tradition that sees itself as the exclusive way to God's favor. Second, it posits a God who legalistically applies a moral system of rewards and punishments, a position that, if taken to its logical conclusion, actually contradicts the concept of grace that underlies Pascal's basic theological premise.

von Dehsen

WORLD EVENTS	PASCAL'S LIFE
Thirty Years' War 1618–48 in Europe	
	1623 Blaise Pascal is born
	1654 Pascal has intense religious experience
	1655 Pascal enters religious community at Port-Royal de Paris
	1656–57 Pascal composes 18 letters published as *The Provincial Letters*
	1657–58 Pascal writes notes later published as *Pensees*
	1662 Pascal dies
	Pensees is published posthumously
England's Glorious 1688 Revolution	

For Further Reading:

Davidson, Hugh M. *Blaise Pascal.* Boston: Twayne Publishers, 1983.

Krailsheimer, A. *Pascal.* New York: Oxford University Press, 1980.

Patañjali

Traditional Author of the *Yoga-Sutras*
c. 220 B.C.E. to c. 400 C.E.

Life and Work

Patañjali is the original codifier of early yogic meditation techniques and is considered to be the traditional author of the *Yoga-Sutras*. This work has made possible the philosophy and practice of yoga as we know it today.

Little is known of Patañjali's background. Scholars think that he was a grammarian, but they have not been able to conclusively determine when he lived; he may have lived as early as the third century B.C.E., or even as late as the fifth century C.E. Further, scholars suspect that many individuals may have written under the name Patañjali, thereby resulting in a composite authorship for the *Yoga-Sutras*. Scholars now generally agree that the author of the *Yoga-Sutras* is not exclusively Patañjali; he simply may have been the original codifier of them. (It seems likely, also, that the *Yoga-Sutras* was written or compiled in the third century C.E. This date has been established by looking closely at certain terms used in the text and comparing those with Buddhist and Jain texts whose dates are known.)

The *Yoga-Sutras* compiled the wisdom and meditative experience of centuries and the ancient esoteric practices of Indian ascetics and mystics. In Sanskrit, "yoga" (formally considered one of the six orthodox fields of Indian thought) means "bind together." "*Sutra*" (originally "thread") means a memorizable aphorism written to encapsulate a philosophical doctrine. The *Yoga-Sutras* is made up of 195 aphorisms, an example of which is #2: "Yoga is the cessation of the turnings of thought." The *sutras* in the book "probe" timeless problems of cognition with the purpose of clearing a practitioner's mind of memories and other "attachments" that bind humankind to this world of pain. The book is divided into four sections; the first section contains 51 aphorisms (*sutras*) that deal with "disengaging the trap of thought" and cultivating pure contemplation. The second section contains 55 aphorisms, explaining the eight aspects of the practice of yoga and ways to practice successfully. The third section, with 55 aphorisms, gives greater detail on the final three of the eight aspects, describing the extraordinary knowledge and powers involved in them. The 34 aphorisms of the fourth section discuss the nature of absolute spiritual freedom, the goal of yoga.

Legacy

Through the work of Patañjali, who originally collected and encapsulated an enormous set of ancient yogic teachings, yoga became a living and organized "system of philosophy" used to teach and encourage spiritual discipline.

Patañjali's text provided the basis for the further refinement of yogic traditions and doctrines. Many instrumental commentaries have been added to the literature, helping to elucidate Patañjali's original meaning and adding new doctrine of their own. Because of the pithiness of *sutras*, commentaries were indispensable for understanding them. In fact, commentaries constitute the major form of philosophical writings in many traditions of orthodox Indian thought. Vyasa wrote the earliest and most famous commentary on Patañjali's *Yoga-Sutras*, probably in the sixth century C.E. It contains the key to many of the more enigmatic aphorisms and has served as the foundation for all subsequent efforts to explain Patañjali's text. The important SHANKARA commentary, an annotation of the Vyasa commentary that preserved several variant readings of Vyasa's earlier work, was written c. 800 C.E. In the early eleventh century, King Bhoja wrote an important commentary that gives insights into certain yoga practices.

Certain aspects of Patañjali's yoga, which is referred to as Raja Yoga, have "spun-off" into other yogas over the centuries. The prime example is Hatha Yoga, devoted to the practice of physical positions. From the middle of the nineteenth century, yoga has become increasingly popular in the West; RALPH WALDO EMERSON (1803–1882) and HENRY DAVID THOREAU (1817–1862), for instance, were intrigued with it. The first organization formed for the study and practice of yoga in the United States was the New York Vedanta Society, founded by an Indian swami, VIVEKANANDA, in 1899. By the end of the twentieth century, instruction in both the physical and spiritual aspects of yoga could be found in manifold organizations, both "religious" and non-sectarian, and on television throughout the United States and Europe. The living tradition of Patañjali continues to flourish, as witnessed by the recent English translations of two important sources, Vyasa's commentary published in 1983 and Shankara's commentary published in 1990.

K. T. Weidmann

WORLD EVENTS	PATAÑJALI'S LIFE*
	B.C.E.
Great Wall of China constructed	215
	200 (?) Patañjali begins to codify Yoga practices
Maccabean Revolt begins in Palestine	167

* Scholars cannot date the specific events in Patañjali's life with accuracy.

For Further Reading:

Eliade, Mircea. *Patanjali and Yoga*. New York: Schocken Books, 1969.

Feuerstein, Georg. *The Philosophy of Classical Yoga*. Manchester, England: Manchester University Press, 1980.

Patañjali. *Yoga: Discipline of Freedom (The Yoga Sutra Attributed to Patanjali)*. Translated by Barbara Stoler Miller. New York: Bantam Doubleday Dell, 1998.

Patrick, Saint

Patron Saint and National Apostle
of Ireland

c. 390–c. 461

Life and Work

Patrick is credited with bringing Christianity to Ireland.

Details of his life are known only from his own works; he is thought to have been born in 390 in Britain—which was then under Roman rule—to a Romanized family. His father was a minor local official. At the age of 16 he was kidnapped by Irish raiders and sold into slavery in Ireland. Working as a shepherd, he turned for inner strength to his faith. Patrick escaped after six years in cap-

tivity and fled back to Britain, where his sufferings continued before finally being reunited with his family. He then traveled to Gaul (modern-day France) to study for the priesthood. He was ordained and served 15 years in a church at Auxerre.

Patrick's life as a slave instilled in him a strong Christian faith and the motivation to spread that faith among the Irish. He was made bishop in 432 and sent to evangelize. Although Patrick had many doubts about his ability to carry out his task because of his lack of education, once there, he thrived.

Never an intellectual, he was known as a hard working pastor with excellent organizational and diplomatic skill. He wandered around the countryside preaching, gaining acceptance of Christianity, and converting both peasants and nobility. Patrick also set up the basic church structure in Ireland by training local clergy, convening church councils, creating dioceses, and introducing monasticism. His cathedral church at Armagh became the center of the Irish Church. Despite his diplomatic skills in dealing with the non-Christians, Patrick was jailed several times and lived in constant fear of his life.

When British King Coroticus attempted to haul away spoils and slaves from the shores of north Ireland, Patrick appealed to British Christians to pressure the king to stop. In response, he was accused by some in England of going to Ireland for self-serving ends. To defend himself against these charges, he wrote his *Confessions*, which shows a man of great simplicity, humility, and spirituality. It is thought that Patrick died around 461.

Legacy

Patrick is the patron saint of Ireland and its national apostle, who, more so than any individual, shaped the course of Irish history.

As the missionary to the first land outside of the Roman Empire, Patrick found a country peopled by warring lords, accustomed to lax morality, and embedded in the practices of slavery and human sacrifice. By the end of his life, Patrick had brought relative peace to his adopted island, and inspired people to study Latin literature; he also convinced them to adopt more rigorous moral standards and to abolish slavery and human sacrifice.

Although probably from a later date, the "Prayer of St. Patrick," also known as "St. Patrick's Breastplate," captures the central idea of his teaching. Specifically, it expresses the belief that all of nature reveals God's grace and love. This idea transformed the ancient Druid premise that the world was filled with spirits into one in which the world becomes the area of life and peace. In so doing, Patrick's form of Christianity embraced the non-Roman traditions of the Celts and paved the way for Christianity and culture to flourish on the Emerald Isle.

Within 200 years of his death, Patrick's deeds became legendary to the Irish. For example, he is credited with removing all the snakes from Ireland. He is also said to have used the three-leafed shamrock to help explain the Holy Trinity. Today the shamrock is the national flower of Ireland and one of its national symbols.

His ministrations in Ireland took strong root. At present, except in the north, Ireland is still overwhelmingly Roman Catholic. The Catholic church in Ireland is still very traditional and comparatively strict. For years, its power prevented the passage of such secular-minded legislation on matters like abortion and divorce.

With the exception of Saint Nicholas, better known as Santa Claus, Saint Patrick is perhaps the most popularly remembered saint of the Catholic church, whose feast day, March 17, is celebrated with large parades in Ireland and all over the United States. The cathedral in New York City is named in his honor.

Saltz

WORLD EVENTS		PATRICK'S LIFE
Rule of Roman Empire by Constantine	306–37	
	c. 390	Patrick is born
Christianity becomes religion of Roman Empire	391	
	c. 406	Patrick is captured and sold into slavery
	c. 412	Patrick escapes and returns to Britain
	432	Patrick is appointed bishop of Ireland
	c. 461	Patrick dies
Fall of Roman Empire	476	

For Further Reading:
Hanson, Richard Patrick Crosland. *The Life and Writings of the Historical Saint Patrick.* New York: Seabury Press, 1983.
Proudfoot, Alice-Boyd, ed. *Patrick: Sixteen Centuries With Ireland's Patron Saint.* New York: Macmillan, 1983.

Paul (Saul of Tarsus)

Influential Early Christian Thinker and Missionary

c. 5 B.C.E.–c. 64 C.E.

Life and Work

Paul was a convert to Christianity whose writings, incorporated into the New Testament, form the basis for much of Christian theology.

Around 5 B.C.E., Saul of Tarsus was born a Jew in the capital city of the region of Cilicia (southeast Turkey). The Roman name "Paul" (which means "small") may be a nickname given because of Saul's physical stature or because of its closeness to his Hebrew name; it may also be a proper name and bespeak Roman citizenship (Acts 16:37). If the latter, then Paul's family, like other Jewish families, had benefited from a liberalizing of the ranks of citizenship and from Caesar's exemption of Jews from obligations conflicting with their religion.

Little is known of his early life. He was a Pharisee, meaning he was one of that group known for its broad application of Jewish law for reasons of religious devotion. He claims to have "advanced in Judaism beyond many among [his] people of the same age, for [he] was far more zealous for the traditions . . . " (Galatians 1:14). In his particular case, such "zeal" seems to have led him "to persecute" and "to try to destroy" the relatively new Christian movement (Gal. 1:13; Philippians 3:6) in c. 30–34.

Then, around 34, Paul had a vision in which, he remembers, God "revealed" JESUS, "so that I might proclaim him among the nations" (Gal. 1:15–16). And so, intermittently conferring with Christian authority figures in Jerusalem and in Syria (particularly Damascus and Antioch), Paul began a series of missionary enterprises to Christian communities west of the Jordan River, in Syria and Cilicia, and then farther west through Asia Minor (Turkey), Macedonia, and Greece (50–62). When he was absent from these churches he wrote them letters to address problems and give encouragement. Hardship of various kinds, including imprisonment, hounded Paul over the years. Around 61, he returned a final time to Jerusalem only to be arrested and then deported to Rome. Paul was probably executed in Rome around 64.

Legacy

Paul is arguably the most influential theologian in and for the Christian religion. The early strain of Christianity that came to predominate was heavily characterized by Pauline thought. His letters are preserved within the New Testament, a collection of writings that is authoritative for the Christian religion.

To a large degree, Paul's writings shape Christian scripture. Of the 27 documents in the New Testament, 13 are letters bearing Paul's name, and a fourteenth (Hebrews) was—and still is—considered by many to have been written by Paul. About half of the Acts of the Apostles treats Paul and his ministry. Other documents may have been influenced by Pauline thought, including the Gospels. Further, there are other ancient, nonbiblical Christian documents about, and purportedly by, Paul (e.g., *The Acts of Paul and Thecla*).

The New Testament letters are written to Christian communities experiencing particular problems and/or successes; they provide a fascinating window both on an early, fledgling movement and on the ruminations of an active leader trying to codify a faith system and apply ethical principles. As such, they have provided an authoritative model for subsequent Christian communities, especially in theology and ethics.

Throughout the ages those seeking change within Christianity have tapped Paul's writings for inspiration and support, from MARCION (second century) to MARTIN LUTHER (sixteenth century) to MARY DALY (twentieth century), to name only a few. Paul's writings may be used to argue for a more traditional (1 Corinthians 14:34: "Let it be that women are silent in the churches . . . they should be subordinate") or less traditional (Galatians 3:28: "There is no longer Jew or Greek, no longer slave or free, no longer male and female, for all of you are one in Christ Jesus") expression of religiosity and ethics. Paul's understanding of the human condition is that "there is no distinction" among people in terms of God's love: the death and resurrection of Jesus Christ is an expression of "[God's] grace as a gift" (Romans 3:22, 24). On the human side the hallmark of the God–human relationship is "faith in Jesus" (Romans 3:26); Paul casts heroes of Jewish scripture such as ABRAHAM as models of faith (Romans 4:1–12).

Paul's writings are full of debate and argumentation. That characteristic may account for some of the confusion about what it is that Paul really means to say, since he often quotes or summarizes other people's arguments.

F. W. Weidmann

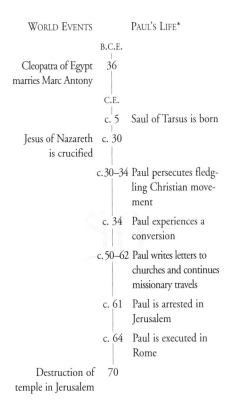

WORLD EVENTS		PAUL'S LIFE*
	B.C.E.	
Cleopatra of Egypt marries Marc Antony	36	
	C.E.	
	c. 5	Saul of Tarsus is born
Jesus of Nazareth is crucified	c. 30	
	c.30–34	Paul persecutes fledgling Christian movement
	c. 34	Paul experiences a conversion
	c.50–62	Paul writes letters to churches and continues missionary travels
	c. 61	Paul is arrested in Jerusalem
	c. 64	Paul is executed in Rome
Destruction of temple in Jerusalem	70	

* *Scholars cannot date the specific events in Paul's life with accuracy. This chronology is based on the biblical account.*

For Further Reading:

Furnish, Victor Paul. *Theology and Ethics in Paul.* Nashville, Tenn.: Abingdon Press, 1982.

Murphy-O'Connor, Jerome. *Paul: A Critical Life.* Oxford: Clarendon Press, 1996.

The New Testament.

Peirce, Charles Sanders

Founder of Pragmatism
1839–1914

Life and Work

Charles Sanders Peirce, a man of many interests, including philosophy, logic, science, and mathematics, is perhaps best known as the founder of the philosophical movement known as pragmatism.

The son of Benjamin Peirce, a professor of mathematics and astronomy at Harvard University, Peirce was born on September 10, 1839, in Cambridge, Massachusetts. He studied at Harvard, graduating summa cum laude in 1863 with a graduate degree in chemistry. Beginning in 1861 Peirce worked with the U.S. Coast and Geodetic Survey for 30 years while simultaneously pursuing his many other interests. During his years with the Survey, he worked on determining the shape of the Milky Way and headed a project to precisely measure the Earth's elliptical shape. His work on gravity measurement won him international fame among scientists.

WORLD EVENTS	PEIRCE'S LIFE
Greek War of 1821–29 Independence against Turkey	
	1839 Charles Peirce is born
Revolutions in 1848 Austria, France, Germany, and Italy	
	1861 Peirce begins working for Geodetic Survey
United States 1861–65 Civil War	
	1863 Peirce graduates from Harvard
	1867 Peirce is elected to Academy of Arts and Sciences
Germany is united 1871	
	1877–78 Peirce introduces pragmatism
	1891 Peirce resigns from Geodetic Survey
Spanish American 1898 War	
	1914 Peirce dies
World War I 1914–18	

But Peirce's main interest was in logic. He lectured at Harvard and Johns Hopkins University in Baltimore on logic but was never appointed to a permanent teaching position as the field was not yet recognized as a distinct discipline. Peirce developed a connection between logic and semiotics, the science of signs, and his major work, left unfinished, was on that subject.

In a series of articles in 1877–78 entitled "Illustrations of the Logic of Science," Peirce first introduced pragmatism. Peirce's belief was that the meaning of an idea could be found by observing the "practical consequences," that is, observable consequences, resulting from that idea. He extended his theories to analyze language, distinguishing between propositions and assertions and analyzing the logical aspects of acts of assertive speech.

In 1867 Peirce was elected to the American Academy of Arts and Sciences; in 1877 to the National Academy of Sciences. Between 1878 to 1911 he presented 34 papers to the National Academy, mostly on logic, but also on psychology, geodesy, physics, and mathematics. In 1880 he was elected to the London Mathematical Society.

In 1887 he moved to Milford, Pennsylvania, and continued to write articles and give occasional lectures. Peirce resigned from the Geodetic Survey in 1891 because of policy differences and never again held a regular position. He died on April 19, 1914, in Milford after years of poverty and illness.

Legacy

A man of many intellectual achievements, Charles Peirce laid the foundation for the branch of philosophy called pragmatism.

While the world has been slow in appreciating the work of Peirce, he is now recognized as having one of the most original minds in America. Peirce never wrote a book, but many volumes of his collected papers have been published. His writing was mostly on abstruse and technical subjects and understandable only to experts, another reason he was unknown by the general public. Peirce wrote in so many fields, and his knowledge and interests were so wide, that specialists in any one field are usually familiar with only a small part of his work. He produced papers that contain insights into psychology, computer science, history, aesthetics, language, metaphysics, religion, phenome-

nology, as well as cosmology, mathematics, chemistry, physics, and scientific method.

His pragmatist philosophy became influential in the twentieth century, made popular by WILLIAM JAMES. James was a lifelong friend of Peirce's, but Peirce was never happy with James's and others' definitions of pragmatism. James seemed to temper Peirce's radical empiricism with a sense of abstract idealism.

Students of Peirce's carried his pragmatism into other intellectual areas. In the areas of ethics, logic, and education, JOHN DEWEY advocated the use of practical projects to teach skills and ideas. George Herbert Mead, a social theorist, focused on stimulus and response as described by actual conduct to explain human behavior. Clarence Irving Lewis's theory of knowledge contends that the certainty of a judgment about reality depends on the congruence of justified judgments.

In the area of science, Peirce can be seen as the developer of what is now called the hypothetico-deductive method of scientific inquiry. He can be credited with cofounding the science of semiotics; he was also an important contributor to the philosophy of language. As a logician, he did much work on relations, created "existential graphs," and was a founder of quantification theory, which attempts to translate sentences into quantifiable formulas.

Peirce has become known by many as a thinker of enormous breadth and depth, one with a profound influence in the areas of his many interests.

Saltz

For Further Reading:
Brent, Joseph. *Charles Sanders Peirce: A Life.* Bloomington: Indiana University Press, 1993.
Brunning, Jacqueline, and Paul Forster, eds. *The Rule of Reason: The Philosophy of Charles Sanders Peirce.* Toronto: University of Toronto Press, 1997.

Pestalozzi, Johann Heinrich

Influential Educational
Philosopher and Reformer
1746–1827

Life and Work

Johann Heinrich Pestalozzi was a Swiss educational reformer whose ideas about teaching young children revolutionized educational methods.

Pestalozzi was born on January 12, 1746, in Zürich, Switzerland. He received his education at the University of Zürich, where he first encountered the thought of JEAN-JACQUES ROUSSEAU. Rousseau's novel, *Émile* (or *On Education*), depicted the education of the young man based on his experiences. The insights Pestalozzi found in this novel charted the course for his own work in educational theory.

Pestalozzi formulated an educational method that focused on the distinctive characteristics of each child. The educational goal was to guide each child's development individually to help that student become an independent thinker. He advocated participatory activities such as writing, drawing, and mapmaking, which allowed each student to learn at his or her pace, working from concrete experience and observation to abstract concepts. He grouped students by ability rather than by age and opposed the traditional use of punishment as a motivator. Pestalozzi also endorsed the formal training of teachers as part of a scientific approach to education.

In 1774, Pestalozzi first tried to put these concepts into practice in a school for orphans he opened in Neuhof. He focused on teaching the children practical skills such as weaving to help them become self-sufficient. Although the school failed financially, it provided Pestalozzi with enough information and experience to formulate his ideas in three books over the next two decades: *The Evening Hours of a Hermit* (1780), *Leonard and Gertrude* (4 vols., 1781–1787), and *My Inquiries Into the Course of Nature in the Development of Mankind* (1797).

In 1798 Pestalozzi opened another school for orphans in Stans. Although it, too, failed financially, his third school, which opened in 1799 and admitted the wealthy as well as the poor, was a success. The school at Yverdon was the first in Europe to teach children from different social and economic classes together and became a model for public education. Yverdon became a laboratory for Pestalozzi's ideas and a magnet for educators from around the Western world. In 1801, Pestalozzi published much of what he learned from this experience in *How Gertrude Teaches Her Children*.

Pestalozzi died in Brugg, Switzerland, on February 17, 1827.

Legacy

The educational theories of Pestalozzi sparked much of the development of educational theory in the nineteenth century. His school at Yverdon provided a model for state-managed public education. Once Pestalozzi's reputation became widespread, many significant educational theorists visited him at Yverdon and built on his insights.

Both Friedrich Froebel (1782–1852) and J. F. Herbart (1776–1841) traveled to the school to learn Pestalozzi's methods. Froebel, a German educator, opened the first kindergarten in 1816 in Grieshaeim, Germany. By 1837, he had established several others in Germany. In 1873, Susan E. Blow, a student of Froebel's, took her teacher's ideas to the United States. Following Pestalozzi, Froebel's kindergartens encouraged children to engage in such activities as reading, singing, and playing with geometric objects to promote intuitive learning. Herbart used Pestalozzi's insights to develop his "five formal steps" of learning. These steps provide ways of preparing students, based on their learning levels, for the introduction of new material.

Pestalozzi's advocacy of education across social and economic classes had a significant impact on American educators HORACE MANN (1796–1859) and Catharine Beecher (1800–1878). Mann is considered to be the "father of public education," especially in the northeastern United States. As a lawyer, he became involved with programs of social reform and, in 1837, helped to establish the first public school system in Massachusetts. In 1839, Mann was also involved in establishing the first teacher's college in the United States in Lexington, Massachusetts. From the Bay State, he promoted the development of public schools in much of the Northeast. In 1852, he moved to Ohio to become the first president of Antioch College, the first college in the United States to admit all qualified students without discrimination, putting Pestalozzi's theories into practice in the realm of higher education.

Beecher was influential in promoting education for women. In 1823 she opened the Hartford Female Seminary, where courses in such traditionally male-dominated fields as science and languages were made available to women. By 1831, her institution in Hartford had become her base of operations for establishing other such institutions for women around the United States. In 1833, she inaugurated the Western Female Institute in Cincinnati. Her work also contributed greatly to the prominence of women in the teaching profession.

Through such educational reformers as these, Pestalozzi's educational concepts gained wide acceptance and, eventually, formed the theoretical basis for much contemporary education methodology.

von Dehsen

WORLD EVENTS	PESTALOZZI'S LIFE
Peace of Utrecht 1713–15 settles War of Spanish Succession	
	1746 Johann Heinrich Pestalozzi is born
	1774 Pestalozzi opens school for orphans in Neuhof
United States independence 1776	
	1780 *The Evening Hours of a Hermit* is published
French Revolution 1789	
	1797 *My Inquiries Into the Course of Nature in the Development of Mankind* is published
	1799 Pestalozzi opens school in Yverdon
	1801 *How Gertrude Teaches Her Children* is published
Napoleonic Wars 1803–15 in Europe	
Greek War of 1821–29 Independence against Turkey	
	1827 Pestalozzi dies
Revolutions in 1848 Austria, France, Germany, and Italy	

For Further Reading:

Gutek, Gerald Lee. *Joseph Neef: The Americanization of Pestalozzianism.* Tuscaloosa: University of Alabama Press, 1978.

Jedun, Dieter. *Johann Heinrich Pestalozzi and the Pestalozzian Method of Language Teaching.* Las Vegas, Nev.: P. Lang, 1981.

Philo Judaeus

(Philo of Alexandria)

Hellenistic Interpreter of
Jewish Law

c. 20 B.C.E.–c. 50 C.E.

WORLD EVENTS	PHILO'S LIFE*
B.C.E.	
	c. 20 Philo is born
C.E.	
Jesus of Nazareth is crucified	c. 30
	39 Philo Judaeus leads delegation to Rome
	c. 50 Philo dies
Destruction of temple in Jerusalem	70

* Scholars cannot date the specific events in Philo's life with accuracy. This chronology is based on the biblical account.

Life and Work

The greatest Jewish philosopher of his era, Philo was the first religious thinker to explain and defend the Hebrew religion using the techniques of Hellenistic philosophy.

Little is known of Philo's life. A native of Alexandria in northern Egypt, he was born around 20 B.C.E. into a wealthy Hebrew family strongly influenced by its Hellenistic surroundings. Both of his brothers, Alexander and Tiberius, held prominent government positions that brought them into contact with the people of Palestine and Rome. The only known incident in his life occurred in 39 C.E., when he led a delegation to Rome to implore the emperor to end the religious persecutions of Jews in Alexandria. From his philosophical sophistication and his use of literary imagery, it seems clear that he had a solid grounding in Hellenistic literature.

Philo hoped to defend the Hebrew religion to a Hellenistic–Gentile audience by using allegorical interpretive techniques. In his works *On Creation* and *The Allegorical Interpretation of the Laws,* he argued that central figures, such as ABRAHAM, Isaac, Jacob, and MOSES, actually embodied universal ideas and virtues. This technique allowed Philo to link the concrete elements of Jewish tradition with the Hellenistic premise that reality existed chiefly in abstract, spiritual ideas imperfectly reflected in the objects of the material world.

Philo further cemented this link by asserting that true knowledge of God comes through the spiritual nature of the mind; those who experience God through the material world have an imperfect knowledge of God. For Philo, God was a being that exists beyond human earthly reality whose highest earthly manifestation was in the human rational intellect, making humans closer to God than are other living creatures and making the mind the true point of contact between God and humans. The human soul is itself a fragment of divine reason (the Logos) encased in a fleshly tomb. The truly wise person was "citizen of the world," one who has overcome the confining distinctions of earthly existence (e.g., ethnic distinctions).

Although there is no reliable date for his death, Philo probably died around 50 C.E.

Legacy

Philo was perhaps the first person to recognize that Jewish thought must engage the ideas of the larger world. His work provided the link between Hellenism and Hebrew thought that both rabbinic Judaism and Christianity would need after the destruction of the Temple in Jerusalem in 70.

Hellenistic thought depends on a dualistic mode of thinking that insists that the real world is the abstract world of ideas, sometimes thought of as the spiritual world. The material world is, at best, an imperfect reflection of that other world. In contrast, Judaism promotes no such dualism; the world perceived by the bodily senses is God's only creation and, hence, the only real world. Philo's use of symbolism and allegory attempts to harmonize these contrasting views of reality to build a bridge between them. Such a bridge ultimately allowed Judaism and Christianity to branch out into the Hellenized world of the Mediterranean basin.

Although it is hard to show that Philo's writing directly influenced the work of later theologians, his efforts at making Jewish ideas intelligible to a Hellenistic world was continued by the writings of such early Christians as PAUL, Clement of Alexandria, Ambrose, and the allegorical interpretations of Justin Martyr. Moreover, Philo's allegorical mode of interpretation became the prevailing method of biblical interpretation found in such later writers as ORIGEN, JEROME, and AUGUSTINE OF HIPPO. His concept that the connection that humans have to God is chiefly spiritual, not material, later became the dominant manner for viewing the relationship between God and human beings.

Philo was an intellectual pioneer, facing the challenge of synthesizing the Jewish religion with the philosophical patterns of Hellenistic thought.

von Dehsen

For Further Reading:

Borgen, Peder. *Philo of Alexandria: An Exegete for His Time.* Leiden, Netherlands: Brill, 1997.
Runia, David. *Exegesis and Philosophy: Philo of Alexandria.* Brookfield, Vt.: Gower, 1990.
Williamson, Ronald. *Jews in the Hellenistic World: Philo.* New York: Cambridge University Press, 1989.

Piaget, Jean

Pioneer of Developmental
Child Psychology
1896–1980

Life and Work

Jean Piaget is considered by many to be the foremost leader in the field of developmental child psychology in the twentieth century.

Piaget was born on August 9, 1896, in Neuchatel, Switzerland, and developed an early interest in zoology. Piaget studied zoology and philosophy at the Neuchatel University, receiving a doctorate in philosophy in 1918. His interest turned to epistemology (the study of the nature and theory of knowledge), which he studied in Zürich with Carl Gustav Jung and Eugen Bleuler. In 1919 he entered the Sorbonne in Paris for two years of study. In 1921 he was appointed director of the Institut J. Rousseau in Geneva. After three years of teaching philosophy at the University of Neuchatel (1926–29), he became professor of child psychology at the University of Geneva, where he remained until 1955. In that year he founded and became director of the International Center of Genetic Epistemology in Geneva.

While in Paris, Piaget began his life-long study of how children learn that ultimately led to his theory of cognitive development. According to Piaget, a child goes through four different developmental stages: the sensorimotor stage (from birth to two years), when the child learns to use physical objects and becomes aware of him- or herself as a separate physical being; the preoperational stage (from two to six years), in which the child learns to associate objects with words and to speak, but cannot yet conceptualize abstractly; the concrete operational state (from seven to 12 years), in which the child starts to think logically, to understand numbers and time, and begins to conceptualize; and the stage of formal operations (age 12 and up), when the child begins thinking as an adult—logically and abstractly—and learns to hypothesize. Each of these stages should be nurtured by an appropriate social and emotional environment.

The pace of cognitive development, said Piaget, is a genetically predetermined progression from the baby's state of dependency and total egotism to the ability to formulate abstract concepts.

Piaget wrote over 60 books and hundreds of articles on many subjects including philosophy, biology, logic, sociology, and epistemology. Among them are *The Language and Thought of the Child* in 1923, *Judgment and Reasoning in the Child* in 1924, *The Formation of Symbols in the Child* in 1946, and *The Origins of Intelligence in Children* in 1948, and the three-volume *Introduction to Genetic Epistemology* in 1950. He left a vast body of work on the various ways children see, relate to, and comprehend the world.

Piaget died on September 17, 1980.

Legacy

Piaget's theories, that a child's performance is based on past experiences and develops according to a predictable series of genetic stages, resulted in a rethinking of how children learn and had a profound impact on educational methods and also on linguistics and physics.

If Piaget's theories are true and the development of a child's comprehension follows a genetically determined pattern, there would be no point in trying to teach a child something before the child reached the stage to be able to understand it. However, Piaget believed that intellectual development was the major force in social and emotional development. The role of teachers, therefore, is not just to transmit information, as they have for hundreds of years, but also to guide the child toward both self-discovery and the outside world according to the child's ability to learn. His theories have encouraged educators to develop new curricula appropriate to the child's age and stage of development. Educators have also become more aware of the impact of a child's environment on cognitive development.

In the last half of the twentieth century these theories have generated a lively response. Jerome Bruner (1915–), a psychologist and founder of the Harvard Center for Cognitive Studies, disagreed with Piaget's basic premise that children travel through stages of intellectual development. He asserted instead that a child and adult scholar have the same ability to think abstractly. Bruner argued that children and adults differ only in experience and amount of knowledge.

Others embraced Piaget's theories enthusiastically. Morris Janowitz, a sociologist, promoted the aggregatational model of education. This model is considered "holistic," in that it proposes that classroom teachers are supported by curricular specialists to provide age-appropriate programs for children. John Goodlad (1921–), director of the Center for Educational Renewal at the University of Washington in Seattle, also endorsed holistic education. Goodlad advocated a curriculum based on a broad array of educational goals in which the ecology of the school is multiple, not linear (e.g., based on the awarding of grades), to create positive interaction between educators and students. More recently, Piaget's theories have served as the basis for the Head Start programs in the United States. This program intends to prepare prekindergarten children for formal education and has benefited over 13 million children since its introduction in 1964.

Piaget's theories have revolutionized the principles upon which teaching curricula are designed. His theories, once considered radical, now provide the basic structures for contemporary curricula development.

Saltz

For Further Reading:
Evans, Richard I. *Jean Piaget, the Man and His Ideas.* Translated by Eleanor Duckworth. New York: E. P. Dutton, 1973.
Sutherland, Peter. *Cognitive Development Today: Piaget and His Critics.* London: Paul Chapman Publishing, 1992.

WORLD EVENTS	PIAGET'S LIFE
1896	Jean Piaget is born
Spanish American 1898 War	
World War I 1914–18	
1918	Piaget receives doctorate in philosophy
1924	*Judgment and Reasoning in the Child* is published
World War II 1939–45	
1948	*The Origins of Intelligence in Children* is published
Korean War 1950–53	
Six Day War between 1967 Israel and Arabs	
1980	Piaget dies
Dissolution of 1991 Soviet Union	

Plato

Influential Greek Philosopher
c. 428–c. 347 B.C.E.

Life and Work

Plato's philosophy had a seminal impact on Western philosophy and the Western intellectual tradition.

Born to an aristocratic Athenian family, Plato may have had political ambitions, but he became disillusioned when the Athenian democracy executed his friend SOCRATES OF ATHENS in 399 B.C.E. Plato left Athens, only to return in 387 to found the Academy, which some consider the first European university. From then until his death Plato wrote philosophical dialogues and perhaps taught philosophy to a small student body whose most famous member was ARISTOTLE. He died around 347 B.C.E.

With a few exceptions, Plato wrote dialogues—artistically staged imaginary conversations between Socrates and his acquaintants covering a broad range of philosophical issues.

WORLD EVENTS	PLATO'S LIFE
	B.C.E.
Battle of Marathon (Athenians defeat Persians)	490
	c. 428 Plato is born
	407 Plato becomes pupil of Socrates
"Warring States Era" in China	403–221
	387 Plato founds the Academy
	367 Plato journeys to Sicily to tutor its ruler Dionysius the Younger
China builds first wall against Huns	356
	c. 347 Plato dies
Alexander the Great's empire runs from Greece to India	323

Scholars divide these writings into early, middle, and later dialogues. The early dialogues portray a historically accurate Socrates engaged in open-ended questioning. The middle dialogues use Socrates merely as a mouthpiece for Plato's own theories. The later ones often cast a self-critical eye on these very ideas.

Throughout much of his writing, Plato asserts a dualistic reality. Inspired by mathematical knowledge and moral concerns, Plato argues that there exists an ever-changing, temporal world of physical objects accessible to the senses as well as a timeless world of ideal Forms graspable by the mind only through abstract thinking. These Forms have three functions: 1) as models or patterns for physical objects, e.g., a chair imitates or somehow participates in the form "chairness;" 2) as standards of conduct, e.g., if one understands the definition of justice itself, one knows how to be just; and 3) as the objects of genuine knowledge, e.g., knowledge of beauty is not gained by recognizing beautiful people or art, but by intellectually grasping the permanent, eternal form of beauty itself.

Human beings, to be sure, inhabit the transient world of becoming because they are flesh and blood. However, Plato argues that they also possess, akin to the Forms, an eternal soul that exists both before birth and after death. Accepting the idea of reincarnation, he suggests that one fulfills the purpose of life by pursuing knowledge of eternal reality, giving up inessential physical satisfaction, and finally earning release from the cycle of birth and death into the eternal realm of Good itself. He articulates this vision of reality in perhaps his most famous dialogue, *Republic*, in which he develops his political ideas about the nature of justice and sketches a blueprint for an ideal city and for a just citizen of that city.

Legacy

It is nearly impossible to exaggerate the significance that Plato's writings have for Western philosophy and the Western intellectual tradition. His works are the West's first disciplined, sustained effort to understand the nature of the universe and human beings' role in it. Plato's discussions of reality, knowledge, and the purpose of existence—in rational, political, and mythical contexts—began a philosophical and theological conversation that stretches unbroken to the present day. To paraphrase one twentieth-century philosopher, all phi-

losophizing since Plato is in one way or another merely a series of footnotes to his work.

Plato's influence on Western thinking began immediately through Aristotle, his best student, whose major philosophical work is often a modification or a well-organized rejection of Plato's positions. By the first century, Plato's ideas of nonphysical reality and personal immortality influenced PHILO JUDAEUS'S Jewish theology and later early Christian theologians like ORIGEN and Clement of Alexandria; the ideal realm of Forms becomes the standard of creation in the mind of God. With Plotinus in the third century, a school of thought called neo-Platonism emerged to revive Plato's thought. It influenced the writings of AUGUSTINE OF HIPPO and later medieval thinkers like Bonaventure. In the fifteenth-century Florentine Academy, a Renaissance interest in Plato's political ideas inspired the works of Marcilia Ficino and SIR THOMAS MORE; among the Cambridge Platonists of seventeenth-century England, Platonic idealism influenced theories of poetry.

During the 1800s Plato's works were translated into German and English, and since that time Western philosophers and theologians have kept up a disciplined scholarly conversation about Platonic views on nearly every subject but particularly about the nature of "universal" concepts and the serious issues raised by Plato's political ideas. After nearly 24 centuries, Plato's writings still challenge and inspire any serious thinker to put forth his or her best effort. If one thinks seriously, then one has to contend with Plato.

Magurshak

For Further Reading:

Crombie, I. M. *Plato, The Midwife's Apprentice.* New York: Barnes and Noble, 1965.

Rutherford, R. B. *The Art of Plato: Ten Essays in Platonic Interpretation.* Cambridge, Mass.: Harvard University Press, 1995.

Taylor, A. E. *Plato: The Man and His Work.* New York: Routledge, 1960.

Trundle, Robert. *Ancient Greek Philosophy: Its Development and Relevance to Our Time.* Brookfield, Vt.: Avebury, 1994.

Pythagoras

Pre-Socratic Philosopher of
Mathematical Realism
c. 580–c. 500 B.C.E.

Life and Work

Greek philosopher and mathematician, Pythagoras founded a religious brotherhood and scientific school that tried to integrate all aspects of his knowledge into a system that reduced all reality to mathematics.

Pythagoras was born in Samos, Ionia (Greece), about 580 B.C.E. Little is known of the events of his life. As a young boy he traveled widely with his father, Mnesarchus, a merchant. He may have studied under the noted philosopher–scientists THALES OF MILETUS and ANAXIMANDER.

In about 532 Pythagoras went to southern Italy where he founded his religious/scientific society in Croton (present-day Crotona in southern Italy). The members of the the Semicircle, as it was known, kept to a strict code of secrecy and silence, in the Egyptian mystery school tradition, attributing all their work to the master. The fundamental concept of Pythagoreanism was that all reality is mathematical in nature. For example, the relationship of the sides of a right-angle triangle can be expressed by the formula $(a^2 + b^2 = c^2)$. This is known as the Pythagorean Theorem, which states that the square of the hypotenuse equals the sum of the squares of the other two sides. Similarly, Pythagoras noticed that the notes played by the strings of a lyre vibrate in relationships that can be expressed in mathematical terms. From these mathematical concepts, Pythagoreanism postulates that the cosmos is governed by sets of opposites that act upon each other. Even human souls can be reduced to mathematical concepts. As such, the soul "transmigrates" from one form of life to another, until it achieves perfection. All of these theories can, in turn, be applied to astronomy. The distance of planets from the Earth corresponds to a set of musical intervals, producing the "harmony of the spheres." Moreover, he believed that this set of intervals can directly influence human life.

Around 500, a conspiracy caused Pythagoras to flee to Metapontum, where he died in about 500.

Legacy

The ideas attributed to Pythagoras by his students have become the point of departure for many philosophical and scientific theories.

Shortly after his death, schools devoted to Pythagoras' teachings surfaced in southern Italy and Greece. By the fourth century B.C.E., PLATO and his students at the Academy in Athens saw themselves as the heirs to Pythagoras' thought. Philosophically, it is not a great leap from saying that all reality can be reduced to a mathematical concept to the fundamental Platonic concept that the basic element of reality is the abstract form reflected in material objects. By the Hellenistic Age, Pythagoreanism had become widespread and much apocryphal literature (writings attributed to the name of an ancient, usually dead, worthy to lend authority to that literature) was produced in his name.

By the first century C.E., a revival of Pythagorean thought, known as Neo-Pythagoreanism, developed. Chief among these Neo-Pythagoreanists was Apollonius of Tyana, who attempted to promote the concept of the ideal life and who claimed to be the reincarnation of Pythagoras himself.

Because of its affinity to Platonic thought, Neo-Pythagoreanism soon merged with Neo-Platonism, and lost its distinctive identity. Nevertheless, Pythagorean ideas may have influenced those of early Christianity. The so-called "household codes" found in Colossians 3:18–4:1 and Ephesians 5:21–6:9 may reflect the Pythagorean ideal of harmonious relationships. Pythagoras' ascetic ideals may have provided grist for the theological mills of such early theologians as Clement of Alexandria (c. 150–215) and ORIGEN (185–254).

Many of his concepts inspired similar concepts elsewhere. Pythagoras' concepts of opposing pairs are shared by many Eastern traditions such as Indian Ayurveda, Muslim Inani, and Buddhist medicines. His mathematical concepts of the cosmos continued into the Syrian and Egyptian monastic/mystical traditions in the works of Syrian-born and Egyptian-trained Evagrius Pontus (346–399). His musical theories were the basis of a book on the subject by ANICIUS MANLIUS SEVERINUS BOETHIUS (c. 480–c. 525) that was used into modern times.

In the sixteenth century, Pythagorean thought reemerged in the form of the scientific principles of Nicolas Copernicus (1473–1543). By asserting that the Earth revolved around the Sun, Copernicus saw himself as a Pythagorean, substantiating Pythagoras' notion of the "harmony of the spheres" through discovering ordered mathematical relationships between and among those cosmic bodies.

The last philosopher to consider himself a Pythagorean was Gottfried Leibniz (1646–1716), one of the founders of modern-day calculus. Leibniz avowed that all reality could be reduced to components consisting of colors, numbers, words, etc.

Honigsberg

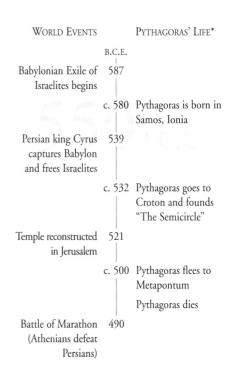

WORLD EVENTS		PYTHAGORAS' LIFE*
	B.C.E.	
Babylonian Exile of Israelites begins	587	
	c. 580	Pythagoras is born in Samos, Ionia
Persian king Cyrus captures Babylon and frees Israelites	539	
	c. 532	Pythagoras goes to Croton and founds "The Semicircle"
Temple reconstructed in Jerusalem	521	
	c. 500	Pythagoras flees to Metapontum
		Pythagoras dies
Battle of Marathon (Athenians defeat Persians)	490	

* Scholars cannot date the specific events in Pythagoras' life with accuracy.

For Further Reading:

Bamford, Christopher, ed. *Homage to Pythagoras: Rediscovering Sacred Science.* Hudson, N.Y.: Lindisfarne Press, 1994.

Gorman, Peter. *Pythagoras, A Life.* Boston: Routledge and K. Paul, 1979.

O'Meara, Dominic, J. *Pythagoras Revived: Mathematics and Philosophy in Late Antiquity.* New York: Oxford University Press, 1989.

Pythagoras of Samos. 1999. http://www-groups.dcs.st-and.ac.uk/~history/Mathematicians/Pythagoras.html.

Rabi'ah al'Adawiyah

Architect of Sufi Asceticism
c. 717–801

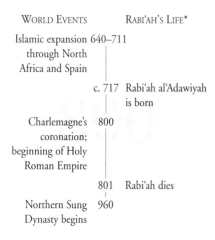

WORLD EVENTS	RABI'AH'S LIFE*
Islamic expansion 640–711 through North Africa and Spain	
	c. 717 Rabi'ah al'Adawiyah is born
Charlemagne's 800 coronation; beginning of Holy Roman Empire	
	801 Rabi'ah dies
Northern Sung 960 Dynasty begins	

* Scholars cannot date the specific events in Rabi'ah's life with accuracy.

Life and Work

Rabi'ah al'Adawiyah inspired a form of Islamic mysticism that synthesized ascetic practices with theological concerns.

While little is known of her early life, Rabi'ah was probably born in Basra (Iraq) around 717. Her name implies that she was the fourth (*rabi'ah*) daughter of her father. Although she had become a slave to a family in Basra, her intense devotion to Allah moved her master to grant her release. For the rest of her life she lived as a strict ascetic and became noted for her undivided love for Allah. (An ascetic is a person who renounces all worldly pleasure and comfort to seek a spiritual connection to the deity.)

Many of the legends that arose about Rabi'ah pitted her in debate against the much older Muslim scholar, Hasan of Basra. These stories are historically questionable because Hasan died in 728, when Rabi'ah was still a young girl. Nevertheless, they show the profound nature of her mystic insights. The conversations illustrate both her total devotion to Allah and the ways in which her life embodied the ascetic practices she espoused.

Rabi'ah's central concept was that nothing at all should distract a person from devotion to Allah. She emphasized sincere love (*sidq*), trust in Allah (*tawakkul*), and absolute acceptance (*rida*) as the pillars of her teaching. Sincere love involved committing one's entire being to Allah. Trust in Allah required turning one's life over to him, so much so that a person would not even think of making plans for the future. Absolute acceptance of Allah's will means that one asks nothing of either Allah (for Allah already knows what people need) or of other people (for that belies a trust in Allah). Her ultimate goal was the extinction (*fana*) of the ego-self in the Divine Being.

Rabi'ah is thought to have written many prayers and poems. She spent the majority of her life in Basra, where she died in 801.

Legacy

Through the legends about her, Rabi'ah became the model of one who manifested her mystical devotion to Allah through an ascetic life. Her ability to couple ascetic practice with the tenets of Islamic theology encouraged some to consider her teachings to be the foundation of Sufism, the mystical branch of Islam.

Rabi'ah 's life and teachings influenced the practices of Dhu al-Nun al-Misri (d. 859), who continued her style of mystical poetry. He also built on her idea of seeking divine unity by emphasizing the idea of the "conjunction of opposites." According to this theory, the same Allah who shows love and compassion is also the Allah of wrath and punishment.

In the ninth and tenth centuries, Sufi mystics drew on Rabi'ah's ideas to elucidate their analysis of what actually happens during the mystical experience. Their point of departure was Rabi'ah's assertion that divine love was the essence of the mystical experience. The driving questions of this quest for clarity were: "Does mystical union completely absorb the individual into the Divine Being?" or "Does the individual still preserve his or her own identity while within the sphere of mystical union?" This debate culminated with the claims of Abu Yazid (d. c. 874). He contended that the mystical union resulted in total absorption of the lover (individual) with the Beloved (Allah). In fact, such a mystical union so identified the mystic with the Divine Being that the mystic could shout, "Glory be to me!" or "How great is my majesty!" To those outside of the mystical circles, these cries seemed heretical because they equated the believer with Allah.

AL-HALLAJ (c. 858–922) also built on Rabi'ah's concept of mystical unity. He was a Sufi mystic who preached a concept of *wahdat al-shuhud*, the "unity of being" in which the mystic experiences total unification with Allah. Ultimately he followed the Sufi path to its limit, announcing that he had found union with Allah, "I am [Allah] the Truth." He wrote several works suggesting that mystical union would bring a believer closer to Allah than even MUHAMMAD had been able to achieve.

Rabi'ah's focus on the state of complete mystical union with the divine sparked a line of mystical reflection that eventually became the heart of Sufism.

von Dehsen

For Further Reading:
El Sakkakini, Widad. *First Among the Sufis: The Life and Thought of Rabia al-Adawiyya, The Woman Saint of Basra.* London: Octagon Press, 1982.
Smith, Margaret. *The Life and Work of Rabi'a and the Women Mystics of Islam.* Oxford: Oneworld, 1994.

Ramakrishna

(Gadadhar Chatterji)

Hindu Mystic Reformer
c. 1835–1886

Life and Work

Ramakrishna was a mystic who fostered the resurgence of Hinduism in India during the nineteenth century. The name Ramakrishna is a combination of the divine names, Rama and Krishna. These gods are manifestations of the god, Vishnu. The combined name suggests that Ramakrishna was an *avatar*, a human manifestation of the god.

Born Gadadhar Chatterji around 1835 in Bengal, India, Ramakrishna grew up in a poor brahman (upper caste) family whose tradition nurtured ecstatic devotion to the deities. As a young man, Ramakrishna already showed extreme emotional sensitivity, occasionally falling into a trance when overwhelmed by beauty or emotion. In 1852 he moved to Calcutta where his brother was the high priest at a temple dedicated to the Divine Mother, Kali. The temple also contained shrines to other major Hindu deities, thus combining the major devotional traditions of Hinduism. When his brother's health failed in 1855, Ramakrishna became a priest to Kali.

The death of his brother pushed Ramakrishna into a devotion to the Divine Mother so intense

that he lost consciousness at times. He later revealed that his frenzied longing for Kali drove him to the brink of suicide. Around 1860 Ramakrishna forsook the world and for 12 years lived the life of an ascetic in a forest. While there he learned the Tantric rituals designed to enable one to experience the divine directly. By so doing, he realized that all aspects of existence are manifestations of the divine productive power. Totapuri, a master of non-dualism (the concept that no distinction exists between the individuals and the universe), taught Ramakrishna that the sole reality of the impersonal Absolute could only be realized in a state of consciousness devoid of all conceptual forms. Thus Ramakrishna had to separate himself from devotion to his beloved Divine Mother in order to encounter the Absolute in a transcendental state. Eventually Ramakrishna devoted himself to the worship of Allah and Christ, during which he had visions that led him to view Christianity and Islam as alternate paths to the Absolute.

Ramakrishna's experiences enabled him to integrate the often conflicting ideas of world religions as well as the various branches of Hinduism. He stressed that there is only one reality and that everything that exists is a manifestation of that reality. He urged his followers not to negate the differences in religions but to embrace them. The good news of all religions lay not in the fact that they all lead to the realization of the Absolute but that all were manifestations of one truth and reality.

By the mid-1870s Ramakrishna had become the focal point of a resurgence of Hinduism, particularly among Westernized intellectuals. He eventually gathered an organized group of followers, led by his pupil VIVEKANANDA, who continued his work following his death on August 16, 1886.

Legacy

Ramakrishna was one of the leaders of the Hindu Renaissance of the late nineteenth century.

Ramakrishna lived during a period when many Indian intellectuals were confronting the challenges of Western culture and religion. Deeply nationalistic, they saw their religion as central to Indian identity but were uncomfortable with contemporary Hinduism, which focused on external rituals. Ramakrishna

returned them to the essential spirit of Hinduism and enabled them to understand how Western culture and traditional beliefs could exist side by side. In the long run it also opened ways for more harmonious relationships between Hinduism and other religious traditions.

Ramakrishna's ideas were extended to the West by his student, Vivekananda. In 1893, Vivekananda was the spokesman for Hinduism at the World Parliament of Religions. There Vivekananda's message of universalism was so well received that he attracted widespread support. He eventually established the Vedanta Society to spread the universal truths of Hindu philosophy and formed the Ramakrishna Order, a monastic society that not only promoted Ramakrishna's ideas of religious pluralism but also emphasized social service to the poor, who, as manifestations of the Divine Mother, were deserving of living devotion and service.

Ramakrishna's openness to the universal nature of the divine provided a conceptual foundation for such Indian leaders as MOHANDAS GANDHI to unify a multifaceted society. His ideas encouraged many scholars, such as John Cobb and John Hicks, to explore other ways of breaking down religious barriers erected by various religious traditions.

von Dehsen

For Further Reading:

Isherwood, Christopher. *Ramakrishna and His Disciples*. London: Shepheard-Walwyn, 1986.

Jackson, Carl T. *Vedanta for the West: The Ramakrishna Movement in the United States*. Bloomington and Indianapolis: The Indiana University Press, 1994

WORLD EVENTS		RAMAKRISHNA'S LIFE
Greek War of Independence against Turkey	1821–29	
	c.1835	Ramakrishna (Gadadhar Chatterji) is born in Bengal, India
Revolutions in Austria, France, Germany, and Italy	1848	
	1852	Ramakrishna moves to Calcutta to be with his brother, a high priest
	1855	Ramakrishna becomes high priest to Divine Mother, Kali
United States Civil War	1861–65	
	mid-1870s	Ramakrishna leads reform of Hinduism in Calcutta
Germany is united	1871	
	1886	Ramakrishna dies
Spanish American War	1898	

Ramanuja

Founder of Vishishtadvaita
Vedanta

c. 1017–1137 (traditionally)

World Events	Ramanuja's Life*
Northern Sung Dynasty begins	960
	c. 1017 Ramanuja is born
Schism between Roman Catholic and Orthodox churches	1054
First Crusade	1095
Settling of Timbuktu, present-day Mali	c. 1100
	1137 Ramanuja dies
Islamic ruler of Egypt, Saladin, captures Jerusalem	1187

* Ramanuja's birth and death dates are based on tradition. Scholars cannot date the specific events in Ramanuja's life with accuracy.

Life and Work

Ramanuja interpreted the Hindu scriptures, the *Upanishads*, to allow for a distinction between the *Brahman* (God) and human beings. In so doing, he established one of the principal schools of Hindu philosophy, which emphasizes the importance of *bhakti*, devotion to God.

According to tradition, Ramanuja was born around 1017 in Shriperumbudur in southern India to a family of the *brahman* (priestly) caste. As a young man he went to Kanci to study with Yadvaprakasha, a teacher who promoted absolute monism (complete unity with God), but Ramanuja ultimately rejected this philosophy and fell under the influence of several *alvars* (mystical poet-saints) of southern India. As a temple priest, he began preaching the importance of the worship of a personal god, the god Vishnu, rather than an impersonal Absolute Deity.

Ramanuja eventually developed a form of *Vedanta* (interpretation of the Upanishads) known as Vishishtadvaita (qualified non-dualism) Vedanta. His basic premise was that individuals ought to attain a relationship with God that intimately unites humans and God (non-dualism) and, simultaneously, retains the distinctions between the two (the qualification).

For Ramanuja, the relationship between God and humans in creation is comparable to that between the body and the soul of a person. Just as body and soul—distinct entities—act on one another and cannot exist without one another, so too God, souls, and matter are all one in creation, and no one component can exist without the other. Yet each of the components—God, soul, matter—is distinct from the others. Ramanuja summed up this complex relationship with the expression "identity-in-difference."

Ramanuja further believed that a person attains freedom only through work, knowledge, and *bhakti*. By work, he means the rituals prescribed by the ancient texts, the *Vedas*. Knowledge is the *Vedanta*, the correct interpretation of the *Upanishads*. *Bhakti* includes meditation and prayer. Still, the devotee is totally dependent on the grace of God for acceptance of the acts of devotion. Ramanuja's beliefs are preserved in three writings: *Commentary on the Brahma Sutra, Commentary on the Gita,* and *Compendium of Vedic Topics.*

According to tradition, Ramanuja died around 1137.

Legacy

Ramanuja founded a branch of Hinduism known as Vishishtadvaita Vedanta, which not only charted a new course between extreme monism and dualism, but also emphasized devotion (*bhakti*) as an important component of Hindu philosophy and piety. This emphasis on *bhakti* as a means of salvation helped break down barriers among castes, and, consequently, helped Vishishtadvaita Vedanta attract a large following.

The initial followers of Ramanuja eventually formed the Shrivaisnava sect, named after Shri, the consort of Vishnu. Tradition has it that Shri was Vishnu's first student. Similarly, the founders of Shrivaisnava were Ramanuja's initial students. The sect reached its peak round the turn of the eleventh century, when its influence spread from its base in southern India to the north.

In the late fourteenth century a controversy about the role of God's grace split the sect. One group followed Vedantadeshika (1268–1370), who interpreted *prapatti* (surrender to the grace of God) as requiring some effort on the part of the believer. His teaching became the basis for the Vadakalai emphasis on human cooperation in the attainment of unity with God. This group illustrated its teaching with the "analogy of the monkey." Just as a baby monkey must exert effort to cling to its mother while feeding, so too must a person exert effort to "cling" to God. The Vadakalai believers are often referred to as the northern sect of Shrivaisnava.

The second group, known as Tenkalai, followed Ramanuja's interest in the *alvars*, the mystic poets of southern India. The Tenkalai accentuated the complete grace of Vishnu; the person practicing *bhakti* does not need to make any effort to submit to the will of Vishnu. For them, the best analogy was that of the cat. Helpless and totally dependent on its mother, a kitten is carried about and wholly cared for by its mother.

Both of these sects continue to thrive in India. The most important locale for the Vadakalai sect is Mysore; the Tenkalai sect is centered in Nanganur, in the Tamil Nadu state.

von Dehsen

For Further Reading:

Lata, Prem. *Ramanuja*. Delhi: Summit Publications, 1980.

Veliath, Cyril. *The Mysticism of Ramanuja*. New Delhi: Munshiram Manoharlal Publishers, 1993.

Rauschenbusch, Walter

Leader of the Social Gospel
Movement
1861–1918

Life and Work

Walter Rauschenbusch was a Christian minister and theologian who developed the Social Gospel to focus on Christian responsibility for the poor and oppressed.

Rauschenbusch was born on October 4, 1861, in Rochester, New York. His father, August, a Baptist minister, was descended from a long line of Lutheran ministers. While a teenager, Rauschenbusch had a deep religious experience that convinced him to enter the ministry. He graduated from Rochester Theological Seminary in 1886 and became the pastor of Second German Baptist Church in New York City. The church was located in "Hell's Kitchen," a deeply impoverished immigrant neighborhood where Rauschenbusch first encountered the hardship of the turn-of-the-century urban poor. In response, he studied and wrote on economic and social problems and began to develop the theological concepts that eventually came to be known as the Social Gospel. He drew inspiration from a number of sources including British and European Christian socialists, eventually becoming a committed socialist.

In 1897 Rauschenbusch returned to Rochester Theological Seminary first as a professor of New Testament (1897–1902) and then as professor of church history (1902–1918). At Rochester he began to systematize his earlier thinking and publish his ideas. In 1907 he produced his most influential work, *Christianity and the Social Crisis,* often called the "bible" of the Social Gospel movement. He published his most systematic expression of the movement in *A Theology for the Social Gospel* (1917).

Rauschenbusch was disturbed that many Christians were silent in the face of the social injustices and economic disparity that accompanied the rise of industrial capitalism in the late nineteenth century. He believed that institutions, like individuals, were afflicted with sin and in need of salvation, what he termed social redemption. In its prophetic role, the church was witness to this need. For Rauschenbusch, the central idea of JESUS' teaching was the establishment of the Kingdom of God. He argued that Jesus' promise of the Kingdom ought not be related solely to the spiritual realm. God desired that the Kingdom be realized on Earth as well. This could be achieved by the church united with modern democracy to promote social and economic justice for the poor. These ideas became the basic principles of his theology of the Social Gospel.

Rauschenbusch died of cancer on July 25, 1918.

Legacy

Rauschenbusch's insistence that the gospel of Jesus emphasize the development of the Kingdom of God through human efforts at social reform had a profound effect on the political theology of the twentieth century.

The Social Gospel provided the theological underpinnings of the progressive reform movement that dominated American politics at the turn of the century. Its ideas enabled reformers such as Theodore Roosevelt to present their crusade for social, economic, and political change in moral terms. The movement took institutional form with the founding of the Federal Council of Churches in 1908. It and its successor institution, the National Council of Churches, have worked to promote the social justice Rauschenbusch envisioned.

Although the Social Gospel faded after 1920, its commitment to social justice became an increasingly important theme in American religion. REINHOLD NIEBUHR, perhaps the preeminent political theologian of the mid-twentieth century, was inspired by Rauschenbusch's Social Gospel. He dismissed Rauschenbusch's optimistic idea that humans could help bring about the Kingdom of God but emphasized Christian social and political responsibility. In the latter four decades of the twentieth century, the endeavors of Christians to carry out Jesus' instructions on justice and to care for the marginalized in society (the poor, minorities, women) have become the cornerstone of the civil rights movement, liberation theology (both in Latin America and in the United States), and the anti-apartheid movement in South Africa.

von Dehsen

WORLD EVENTS		RAUSCHENBUSCH'S LIFE
Revolutions in Austria, France, Germany, and Italy	1848	
United States Civil War	1861–65	
	1861	Walter Rauschenbusch is born in Rochester, New York
Germany is united	1871	
	1886	Rauschenbusch becomes pastor of Second German Baptist Church
	1897	Rauschenbusch joins faculty of Rochester Theological Seminary
Spanish American War	1898	
	1907	*Christianity and the Social Crisis* is published
World War I	1914–18	
	1917	*A Theology for the Social Gospel* is published
	1918	Rauschenbusch dies
World War II	1939–45	

For Further Reading:

Beckley, Harlan. P*assion for Justice: Retrieving the Legacies of Walter Rauschenbusch, John A. Ryan, and Reinhold Niebuhr.* Louisville, Ky.: Westminster/John Knox Press, 1992.

Handy, Robert. *The Social Gospel in America, 1870–1920.* New York: Oxford University Press, 1966.

Minus, Paul. *Walter Rauschenbusch, American Reformer.* New York: Macmillan, 1988.

Smucker, Donovan E. *The Origins of Walter Rauschenbusch's Social Ethics.* Montreal: McGill-Queen's University Press, 1994.

Reid, Thomas

Founder of the Philosophical
School of Common Sense
1710–1796

Life and Work

Thomas Reid was a Scots philosopher who developed the philosophical school of common sense.

WORLD EVENTS		REID'S LIFE
English seize Calcutta, India	1690	
	1710	Thomas Reid is born
Peace of Utrecht settles War of Spanish Succession	1713–15	
	1751	Reid becomes lecturer at King's College
	1764	*Inquiry into the Human Mind on the Principles of Common Sense* is published
United States independence	1776	
	1785	*Essays on the Intellectual Powers* is published
	1788	*Essays on the Active Powers* is published
French Revolution	1789	
	1796	Reid dies
Napoleonic Wars in Europe	1803–15	

Reid was born in Strachan, Scotland, on April 26, 1710. He was educated at Marischal College in Aberdeen, Scotland, and, like his father, became a Presbyterian minister. He worked as a librarian in Aberdeen for 10 years and then served a parish in New Machar until 1751, when he became a lecturer at King's College in Aberdeen. In 1764 he succeeded ADAM SMITH as professor of moral philosophy at the University of Glasgow.

Reid developed his philosophy in response to DAVID HUME's skepticism. In answering the question of how human beings gain knowledge of the external world, Hume had posited that knowledge was derived from human sensory experience (impressions) that reason abstracted into ideas. Pointing to the fact that children had ideas before they developed reason, Reid dismissed Hume's theory. He argued that the mind intuitively knows certain principles, including moral principles, without the need for external stimuli. Sense perceptions are interpreted on the basis of these principles and yield knowledge of the external world. Responding to his critics, Reid later attempted to base his theories in science by describing how common sense produces perception. He identified 30 powers that he asserted exist in all minds and provide common knowledge to all human beings.

Reid's common sense also moved him to endorse individual liberties. He argued that the mind had the capacity to originate ideas, to recognize freedom, and the will to act upon them. Therefore, no external authority had the right to prevent that action.

Reid presented his philosophy in three books: *Inquiry into the Human Mind on the Principles of Common Sense* (1764); *Essays on the Intellectual Powers* (1785); and *Essays on the Active Powers* (1788). In 1780 he stopped lecturing and devoted himself to writing. Reid died on October 7, 1796, in Glasgow.

Legacy

Reid founded the school of philosophy known as common sense, which came to define orthodox British philosophical thought during the early nineteenth century.

Initially, Reid's philosophy was coolly received by his contemporaries. It was popularized in England by the Scots poet and philosopher James Beattie (1733–1803) but attacked in Scotland by men such as English scientist and philosopher James Priestley (1733–1804). Nevertheless, by 1785 it had begun to dominate British philosophy. Reid's philosophy was disseminated by a number of Scotsmen, the most successful of whom was Dugald Stewart (1753–1828). Through Stewart, Reid's thoughts influenced Franz Joseph Gall (1758–1828), who used them in developing his own theory of phrenology (the belief that the formation of the skull is indicative of character and mental faculties). Reid's ideas spread to the United States, where his vision of human nature influenced the leaders of the American Revolution. They also were widely taught in early-nineteenth-century France and were read in Germany by IMMANUEL KANT (1724–1804).

William Whewell (1794–1866) built on Reid's theories by acknowledging that the mind can associate preconceived ideas with a set of data. However, this association is subject to three tests of verification: 1) the ideas must fit all the data; 2) the ideas must be able to predict correctly the application of this idea to data not yet available; and 3) the idea must exhibit *consilience*, that is, it must be able to "jump together" with other ideas originally thought to be unrelated. More recently, Edward O. Wilson (1929–) has used Whewell's concept of *consilience* to try to establish connections between separate areas of knowledge (e.g., environmental policy, ethics, social science, and biology).

Reid's common sensism also influenced the thinking of the moral philosopher, Henry Sidgwick (1838–1900). Sidgwick developed his theories about morality on the premise that moral principles were self-evident, immediately available to the mind. He notes that human beings usually can determine intuitively what is morally right and what ought to be right in general. This principle encourages people to strive for what is good in general, thus linking common sense to utilitarianism, where a good outcome signifies a good principle.

Reid was not without his critics. One of the most important was JOHN STUART MILL (1806–1873). Mill contended that any appeal to intuition or self-evidence was a covert way of promoting self-interest.

von Dehsen

For Further Reading:

Dalgarno, Melvin, and Eric Matthews, eds. *The Philosophy of Thomas Reid.* Boston: Kluwer Academic Publishers, 1989.

Lehrer, Keith. *Thomas Reid.* New York: Routledge, 1989.

Rowe, William. *Thomas Reid on Freedom and Morality.* Ithaca, N.Y.: Cornell University Press, 1991.

Rousseau, Jean-Jacques

Political Philosopher; Developer
of the Social Contract Theory
1712–1778

Life and Work

One of the most original thinkers of the Enlightenment, Jean-Jacques Rousseau made significant contributions to political theory, education, and the arts.

Rousseau was born in Geneva, Switzerland, on June 28, 1712, and raised by his widowed father, a watchmaker and rebel who was once exiled for clashing with Genevan authorities. At 16 he ran away from Geneva and was taken in by the wealthy Barone Louise de Warrens, who became his mentor, benefactress, and lover. In 1742 he settled in Paris, where he entered the social world of Enlightenment intellectuals and became a close friend of encyclopedist DENIS DIDEROT.

In 1750 Rousseau published *A Discourse on Sciences and the Arts* in which he presented a theme that would recur throughout his work: people were inherently good but had been corrupted by civilization. His theory, which went counter to the prevailing Enlightenment view that humanity had progressed in civilization, won him instant fame. He developed these ideas further in *The Discourse on the Origins of Inequality*, published in 1755, in which he charged that inequality arose when humans

founded societies and was furthered by institutions such as private property.

Rousseau left Paris in 1756 and eventually settled in the small French town of Montmorency. There he produced his most significant works, *Emile* (1762) and *The Social Contract* (1762), both of which offer solutions to what he considered the pernicious effects of civilization. *Emile* deals with the issue from the perspective of the individual while *The Social Contract* focuses on society. In *Emile* Rousseau presented a revolutionary theory of education, insisting that the molding of a child's feelings and sentiment should precede intellectual training, a sequence that he asserted mirrored the development of humankind in nature.

In *The Social Contract* Rousseau offered a model for a virtuous society to replace the corrupt contemporary order. Like English philosopher JOHN LOCKE, he believed that political society was formed when humans joined together in a social contract, agreeing to give up some of their natural rights in return for certain benefits. But while Locke equated liberty with the preservation of individual rights, Rousseau saw freedom and equality coming from people giving up those rights and living under self-imposed laws. These laws emerged from what he termed the General Will, the collective desires of society upon which the legitimacy of the political order was based.

While at Montmorency Rousseau also produced an immensely popular novel, *The New Eloise* (1761), written in a free style without the artificial constraints of contemporary literature. In it he explores the tensions between reason and feeling.

Rousseau's attack on divine revelation in *Emile* led to his expulsion from France. He spent the years 1762 to 1770 avoiding arrest by moving to Switzerland and then to Great Britain. Permitted to resettle in France in 1770, he died on July 2, 1778, in Ermenonville.

Legacy

A towering figure in European thought, Rousseau was a bridge between eighteenth-century Enlightenment, with its emphasis on reason, and nineteenth century Romanticism, with its stress on emotion and subjective experience.

His opinion that art should be free in expression influenced first the opera reformer Christoph Gluck and later the composers and writers of the

Romantic period. Rousseau's stress on the benevolence of nature and humankind's goodness in the natural state found expression in Romantic literature, including the works of American Transcendentalists HENRY DAVID THOREAU and RALPH WALDO EMERSON. His call for more emotional and less restrained relationships anticipated not only Romantic art and literature but also the change in attitudes toward public decorum.

Rousseau's political ideas had a significant impact on nineteenth- and twentieth-century political theory. His assertion that the state was based on a General Will rather than the divine right of kings was taken up by French revolutionaries to justify democracy. Conversely, his insistence that people subordinate themselves to the General Will was used to justify twentieth-century totalitarian regimes such as Nazi Germany.

Rousseau's theories on education had great influence on the way nineteenth-century parents both raised and educated their children. They were cited by nineteenth-century reformers, such as Friedrich Froebel and JOHANN PESTALOZZI, when advocating a child-centered education.

Saltz

WORLD EVENTS		ROUSSEAU'S LIFE
English seize Calcutta, India	1690	
	1712	Jean-Jacques Rousseau is born
Peace of Utrecht settles War of Spanish Succession	1713–15	
	1742	Rousseau arrives in Paris
	1750	*A Discourse on the Sciences and the Arts* is published
	1755	*Discourse on the Origin of Inequality* is published
	1762	*Emile* and *The Social Contract* are published
		Rousseau is expelled from France
	1770	Rousseau resettles in France
United States independence	1776	
	1778	Rousseau dies
French Revolution	1789	

For Further Reading:
Cranston, Maurice William. *The Noble Savage: Jean-Jacques Rousseau, 1754–1762*. Chicago: University of Chicago Press, 1991.
Havens, George Remington. *Jean-Jacques Rousseau*. Boston: Twayne, 1978.

Roy, Ram Mohun

Reformer of Hinduism;
Founder of Brahmo Samaj
1772–1833

Life and Work

Ram Mohun Roy was a reformer of Hinduism who promoted belief in one deity (monotheism) and the abolition of idol worship. He is best remembered as the founder of the Brahmo Samaj (Congregation of *brahman*), the first modern Hindu reform movement.

Roy was born on May 22, 1772, in Radhanager, West Bengal, India, to a family of devout Hindus sympathetic to Western religious and social ideas. He was educated in Patna, a center of Islamic learning. There he encountered the Islamic emphasis on monotheism and the critique of Hindu image worship.

Eventually, he went to Banaras to study Sanskrit and Hindu sacred literature. In 1803, he procured a position with the British East India Company and rose to the height of the Bengal civil service. He was so successful as a businessman that he was able to retire in Calcutta at the age of 42 and pursue his interests in religious reform.

As early as 1804 Roy advocated monotheism in his first book, *A Gift for the Monotheist.* He claimed that all people, by natural reason, believe in one creative divine being. However, religious leaders deceive people into abandoning this belief in favor of idol worship. In 1815 Roy published *Vedantagrantha*, a study of the Hindu Vedanta, (Hindu philosophy) and, from 1816 to 1819, he translated several major Upanishads (ancient Hindu writings emphasizing the oneness of the deity) to defend his belief in one *brahman* (divine being). In 1820 he completed *The Precepts of Jesus* in which he endorsed JESUS' ethical teachings but opposed the Christian doctrine of the Trinity.

From 1824 to 1828, Roy's belief in monotheism attracted him to Unitarian Christian services in Calcutta. Dissatisfied with Unitarianism, in 1828 he established the Brahmo Samaj to worship the *brahman* and to renounce Hindu idol worship. His exposure to Christian ethical teachings led him to promote social reform, especially education and women's rights. He was particularly critical of the Hindu custom of *sati*, the expectation that a widow will cremate herself on her husband's funeral pyre.

In 1830 he traveled to England to pursue his interests in European rational thought. On September 22, 1833, the victim of a sudden illness, he died in Bristol, England.

Legacy

Roy had such a profound influence on Indian social and political reform that he is often called the "father of modern India."

Roy's emphasis on religious monotheism and on religious and social reform were continued by the Brahmo Samaj and those it ultimately inspired. The Brahmo Samaj was a major force in shaping the Indian response to Western secular and religious influence and laid the foundation for the Hindu Renaissance of the late nineteenth century. The movement showed Indians how Western culture could exist side by side with Hinduism and even strengthen it. It also developed a new leadership class eager for political, social, and religious reform. By the end of the nineteenth century, the Brahmo Samaj had become one of the most important catalysts in the Indian movement for independence from the British. Roy's social reform program became a foundation of the thought of MOHANDAS GANDHI, underlying his campaign against social inequities in South Africa and India.

Under Roy, the Brahmo Samaj was a force for monotheism and Hindu religious reform. Roy's opposition to priestly authority opened the way for other members of influential castes to become religious leaders, such as Roy's successors in Brahmo Samaj: Debendranath Tagore (1817–1905) and Keshab Chandra Sen (1838–1884).

From 1843 to 1858 Tagore greatly increased the organization's membership, campaigned against Christian missionary work, and systematized the group's teachings. Sen, originally a banker, stressed the efforts of Brahmo Samaj at social reform and intensified the group's opposition to priestly authority.

Although the influence of the Brahmo Samaj diminished after Sen's death in 1884, its efforts continued through people inspired by the organization's reform platform. Roy's commitment to monotheism and his opposition to the priesthood motivated, for example, VIVEKANANDA at the end of the nineteenth century to promote meditation as a means to embrace the divine reality without the aid of ritual. Vivekananda ultimately became recognized as the person who introduced Hinduism to the West.

Roy's teaching, as promulgated by those aligned with the Brahmo Samaj, became the foundation for both religious and social reform movements that helped shape modern Indian culture.

von Dehsen

WORLD EVENTS	ROY'S LIFE
Peace of Utrecht 1713–15 settles War of Spanish Succession	
	1772 Ram Mohun Roy is born in Radhanagar, West Bengal
United States 1776 independence	
French Revolution 1789	
	1803 Roy is employed by British East India Company
Napoleonic Wars 1803–15 in Europe	
	1804 *A Gift for the Monotheist* is published
	1815 *Vedantagrantha* is published
	1816–19 Roy translates Upanishads
	1820 Roy completes *The Precepts of Jesus*
Greek War of 1821–29 Independence against Turkey	
	1828 Roy establishes the Brahmo Samaj
	1830 Roy travels to Europe
	1833 Roy dies in England
Revolutions in 1848 Austria, France, Germany, and Italy	

For Further Reading:

Dasa, Harihara. *The Indian Renaissance and Raja Rammohan Roy.* Jaipur, India: Pointer Publishers, 1996.

Dasgupa, B. N. *The Life and Times of Rammohun Roy.* New Delhi: Abika, 1980.

Robertson, Bruce Carlisle. *Raja Rammohan Roy: The Father of Modern India.* Delhi: Oxford University Press, 1995.

Russell, Bertrand

Influential Twentieth-Century
Philosopher; Founder of Logicism
1872–1970

Life and Work

Bertrand Russell was one of the most influential British philosophers of the twentieth century. Through writings intended both for academics and the general public, he promoted theories of empiricism based on models of mathematical reasoning.

A grandson of Lord John Russell, a former prime minister of England, Russell was born on May 18, 1872. He was orphaned by age three and was raised by his paternal grandparents, a rigidly puritanical couple with politically liberal views. Russell rejected his family's moral and religious views but held to their progressive politics. In 1890 he entered Cambridge University, where he won honors in mathematics and philosophy. After graduation he taught there.

By 1900 Russell had embraced empiricism, the philosophy that all knowledge should be based on practical experience, not theory. In collaboration with Alfred North Whitehead, he published the three-volume *Principia Mathematica* in 1910, 1912, and 1913, which argued that mathematics could be derived from principles of logic. In 1914, he completed *Our Knowledge of the External World,* in which he attempted to break all logical statements down into their independent,

component parts. For his pacifism during World War I, Russell was fired from his Cambridge teaching post and jailed for six months in 1918.

In the 1920s Russell wrote many books for both academics and professionals on ethics and political and social issues, including *Analysis of the Mind* (1921) and *Analysis of Matter* (1926). In 1927 he and his wife started a permissive experimental school that lasted until 1939. In 1931, on the death of his older brother, he became the third Earl Russell. During World War II Russell modified his pacifism, acknowledging that Hitler had to be defeated. He also continued his academic work by examining the basis of human knowledge in *Human Knowledge: Its Scope and Meaning* (1948). Here he retreated from his earlier conclusions that all knowledge is verifiable and adopted a more compromising position that some conclusions must be based on unverifiable presuppositions.

After the war, Russell became even more well known through television appearances and by his high visibility in political causes, usually left-leaning. In 1950 he won the Nobel Prize for Literature. His citation praised him as a philosopher who attacked weighty problems with wit and style. He was militantly opposed to nuclear proliferation and headed the Pugwash Conference of international scientists encouraging disarmament. He also opposed the war in Vietnam.

While living with his fourth wife, Russell completed his *Autobiography* in 1969. He died at age 98 on February 2, 1970, in Wales.

Legacy

Russell had one of most far-reaching minds of the twentieth century. His ideas became part of the foundation of analytic philosophy and sparked vigorous debate in areas ranging from logic to politics. After World War II, Russell's theory of knowledge went out of fashion as other movements in linguistics and philosophy took its place.

Although concerned with many subjects, Russell's primary influence lay in philosophy, especially logic. His *Principia Mathematica* has been acclaimed by logicians and mathematical philosophers as the most important work on logic in the twentieth century—even by those who do not agree with Russell's theories. This book is viewed as a foundational work in logic, although it has been criticized for not having

fully proven that mathematics can be derived from self-evident principles.

Russell became a standard-bearer for the political left. His high visibility in England and the United States, combined with his attachment to controversial left-wing causes, alienated him from the establishment while making him more attractive to the young. The publication of his religious views in the 1927 *Why I Am Not a Christian* alienated many. His opposition to the Vietnam war led directly to the convening of the International War Crimes Tribunal to protest alleged atrocities.

It is too early to predict what Russell's long-term influence will be, but during a career spanning three generations, his impact was enormous. His healthy skepticism, his willingness to question and modify his own ideas, his openness of mind, his need to investigate any unproved supposition, and the stringency of his analysis more than warrant his designation as one of this century's finest philosophical minds. In addition, Russell's willingness to write for the average citizen and the amazing variety of his interests extended his renown far beyond the academic world and made him one of the most famous, widely read, and influential minds of the last century.

Saltz

WORLD EVENTS		RUSSELL'S LIFE
Germany is united	1871	
	1872	Bertrand Russell is born
	1890	Russell enters Cambridge
Spanish American War	1898	
	1910–13	*Principia Mathematica* is published
World War I	1914–18	
	1927	Russell and his wife open experimental school
World War II	1939–45	
Mao Tse-tung establishes Communist rule in China	1949	
	1950	Russell wins Nobel Prize for Literature
Korean War	1950–53	
Six Day War between Israel and Arabs	1967	
	1969	*Autobiography* is completed
	1970	Russell dies
End of Vietnam War	1975	

For Further Reading:

Moorehead, Caroline. *Bertrand Russell: A Life.* New York: Viking, 1993.

Wood, Alan. *Bertrand Russell the Passionate Skeptic: A Biography.* New York: Simon & Schuster, 1958.

Russell, Charles Taze

Founder of the Jehovah's Witnesses
1852–1916

Life and Work

Charles Taze Russell was a lay evangelist and religious leader who founded the Zion Watch Tower Bible and Tract Society, a movement that later took the name Jehovah's Witnesses.

WORLD EVENTS		RUSSELL'S LIFE
Revolutions in Austria, France, Germany, and Italy	1848	
	1852	Charles Taze Russell is born
United States Civil War	1861–65	
Germany is united	1871	
	1872	Russell forms Bible study class
	1879	*Watchtower* begins publication
	1884	Zion's Watch Tower Bible and Tract Society is founded
Spanish American War	1898	
	1908	Russell separates from his wife
World War I	1914–18	
	1916	Russell dies
	1931	Jehovah's Witnesses becomes name of movement
World War II	1939–45	

Russell was born on February 16, 1852, in Allegheny, Pennsylvania, near Pittsburgh. He was raised as a Presbyterian but suffered a religious crisis while a teenager because he was unable to reconcile the Calvinist notion of eternal damnation with a just and merciful God. He came under the influence of the Adventists who encouraged him to study the Bible to understand God's plan for salvation and particularly to determine the date of the second coming of Christ, which would end the world. Russell formed a Bible study class in 1872 and began to distribute literature containing his own unique interpretations of the Bible.

Russell's beliefs differed from those of most Protestant denominations in that he rejected the concept of the Trinity, maintaining that JESUS was not God incarnate. He preached that Jesus had already returned invisible to Earth in 1874 and predicted that the world would end in 1914 with an apocalyptic battle that, when finished, would usher in the thousand years of God's kingdom on Earth. In 1879, Russell started publishing *Zion's Watchtower and Herald of Christ's Presence,* a magazine now published as the *Watchtower.*

In 1884 Russell founded the Zion's Watch Tower Bible and Tract Society to spread his message. Through his prolific writings and wide travels, he was successful in forming many groups of "Russellites."

In spite of the lack of an apocalypse in 1914 (World War I notwithstanding) and a number of scandals and lawsuits including separation from his wife in 1908, Russell managed to keep his flock together. He died suddenly while on an evangelizing trip in Pampa, Texas, on October 31, 1916.

Legacy

Russell laid the foundation for the Jehovah's Witnesses, a movement that now includes millions of adherents around the world.

During his lifetime, more than 1,200 Russellite communities were formed and millions of his books and pamphlets were printed. Some 2,000 newspapers published his weekly sermons.

After his death, Russell was succeeded by Joseph Franklin Rutherford, who led the organization from the Watch Tower Society in Brooklyn, New York. He revised some of

Russell's most important ideas, asserting that Christ had returned in spirit in 1914 and that the end of the world was in the distant future. The organization changed its name to Jehovah's Witnesses in 1931.

The religion as practiced today is still a millennialist group, although they adhere to no specific date for the Second Coming. Witnesses try to avoid any resemblance to traditional churches. They have no formal organization; the Watch Tower Society is their publishing organ. Regarding each member as God's messenger, the group has no clergy.

Witnesses believe that both the civil and ecclesiastical governments of the world are ruled by Satan and consequently it is their duty to remain aloof from them. This belief has made them controversial and led to clashes between civil authorities and believers. During the Nazi era, for example, thousands were sent to concentration camps. Witnesses have had a great impact on American society because their legal challenges to existing laws have won significant victories for the freedoms of religion and speech.

Today there are some six million members worldwide (according to 1997 statistics), with about a million in the United States. There are more than 85,000 congregations around the world of which some 11,000 are in the United States. The Witnesses have branches in more than 200 countries and have distributed billions of copies of the *Watchtower* in over 200 languages. They have also distributed some 50 million copies of the English Bible.

Saltz

For Further Reading:

Horowitz, David. *Pastor Charles Taze Russell: An Early American Christian Zionist.* New York: Philosophical Library, 1986.
Penton, M. James. *Apocalypse Delayed: The Story of Jehovah's Witnesses.* Toronto and Buffalo: University of Toronto Press, 1985.

Sa'adia ben Joseph

Jewish Talmudic Scholar and
Synthesizer of Faith and Reason
882–942

Life and Work

An outstanding scholar and leader of Babylon's Jewish community, Sa'adia ben Joseph was one of the first Jewish thinkers to propose ways of synthesizing faith and reason.

Sa'adia was born in 882, in Upper Egypt. At age 23 he left Egypt for Palestine, but not finding a congenial intellectual climate there, he settled in Babylon. By the time he left Egypt, he had already finished a Hebrew–Arab dictionary that later became known as the *Sefer ha-argon*.

Welcomed by Babylon's Jewish community as a noted scholar, Sa'adia defended traditional Judaism against Gnostic challenges, which rejected strict monotheism in favor of a dualism that pitted a good God against an evil God. He also championed the primacy of Babylonian over Palestinian rabbinical authorities in the ongoing struggle for control of Jewish teaching. A prolific author, he wrote numerous works on law and theology and translated the Pentateuch into Arabic.

Sa'adia was named *gaon*, leader, of the Academy at Sura in 928. One of his first tasks in that post was to sort the numerous topics of the Talmud (the rabbinical commentary on the Torah and Mishnah) by subject. In 932 his refusal to support David ben Zakkai, the exilarch (head) of the Babylonian Jewish community, led to a bitter conflict in which each excommunicated the other. Ben Zakkai convinced the Muslim ruler of Babylon to remove Sa'adia from office three years later.

Sa'adia retreated from public view and produced what is probably his most important work, *The Book on Beliefs and Opinions*, which he completed around 936. In this book he proposed three sources of truth: 1) sense perception, 2) rational intuition, and 3) valid conclusions drawn from this data. He suggested that revelation could serve as a source for those not sufficiently intellectually equipped to master logical argumentation. Sa'adia argued that a finite world could have only one finite creator (God) who administers justice by establishing both rational and traditional laws. Humans are judged on the basis of those laws. While some judgment occurs in the present as immediate punishment, and while some suffer in the present to test their faithfulness, the end time will bring the final judgment, separating the righteous from the wicked.

By 937, the exilarch and Sa'adia had reconciled, and Sa'adia returned to his post as *gaon*. He died in Sura in 942.

Legacy

Sa'adia had a major impact on later Jewish philosophy by demonstrating how reason and revelation could work in concert to explain and defend Jewish teachings. Moreover, his enthusiastic use of reason to undergird all aspects of Jewish thought—from organizing the Talmud, to settling legal disputes, to defending the oneness of God—gave a lasting legitimacy to his theories about the correspondence of reason and faith.

Sa'adia's Hebrew–Arab dictionary, translations, and commentaries have been a lasting influence on biblical studies. To the present day Yemenite Jews couple his Arabic translation of the Hebrew scriptures with the *Targum Onkelos* (an Aramaic paraphrase of the Hebrew biblical text) in a book called the *Taj (Crown of the Torah)*.

As a rational philosopher, Sa'adia won the praise of the later Jewish rationalist, MOSES BEN MAIMON (Maimonides, 1135–1204), who wrote, "If it were not for Sa'adiah, the Torah could well have disappeared from among the Jewish people." Moses ben Maimon, himself, provided the most widely recognized appeal to reason among Jewish scholars. In his *Guide to the Perplexed* (1190), he expanded the themes about the nature of God and God's relation to creation that Sa'adia inaugurated in *The Book on Beliefs and Opinions*. Moses ben Maimon contended that: 1) God has an external will and is not subject to natural laws; 2) God created the world and established its order; 3) humans can know only what they are not; and 4) God is an intellect.

Sa'adia's contribution to Talmudic study helped establish the primacy of the Babylonian Talmud over the Jerusalem Talmud as the principal source of rabbinical Torah interpretation. In both cases, the Talmud is a commentary on the "oral Torah," the Mishnah, which is a collection of rabbinical interpretations on various aspects of Jewish law. (A Talmudic page has the Mishnah text connected to the Gemara, further rabbinical commentary on the Torah. This further discussion became important as the Torah must be reinterpreted to address questions arising from new times and circumstances.) As it gained prominence, the Babylonian Talmud became an authoritative guide that helped shape Judaism.

von Dehsen

World Events		Sa'adia's Life
Charlemagne's coronation; beginning of Holy Roman Empire	800	
	882	Sa'adia ben Joseph is born
	928	Sa'adia named *gaon* of Academy at Sura
	935	Sa'adia is removed from office after dispute with Exilarch David ben Zakkai
	c. 936	Sa'adia completes *The Book on Beliefs and Opinions*
	942	Sa'adia dies
Northern Sung Dynasty begins	960	

For Further Reading:

Cohn-Sherbok, Dan. *Fifty Key Jewish Thinkers*. New York: Routledge, 1997.
Jospe, Raphael. *Paradigms in Jewish Philosophy*. Madison, N.J.: Fairleigh Dickinson University Press, 1997.

Sartre, Jean-Paul

Preeminent Twentieth-Century
Existentialist
1905–1980

Life and Work

Jean-Paul Sartre, one of twentieth-century Europe's foremost thinkers, introduced phenomenology, the attempt to extract meaning from the phenomena of the world, and coined the term "existentialism." As a political activist, he wrote phenomenological studies, novels, plays, and Marxist political essays.

Born in Paris on June 21, 1905, Sartre spent his childhood in a world of books. Intellectually brilliant, he graduated from the École Normale Supérieure in Paris at 22. He then spent a year in Berlin studying the philosophy of MARTIN HEIDEGGER and EDMUND HUSSERL. Returning to France in 1934, he taught at various institutions until 1939, when he was drafted. In 1938, his novel, *Nausea*, was published. From 1940 to 1941 he was a prisoner of war under the Germans. During the rest of the war he served the

French Resistance while a professor in Neuilly and Paris. In 1943 his play, *The Files*, was published, followed the next year by his play, *No Exit*.

In 1943 he published his most significant philosophical work, *Being and Nothingness*, a work heavily influenced by his life companion, Simone de Beauvoir (1908–1986). Later works included an existential biography of the French writer Jean Genet, entitled *Saint Genet* (1952), *Critique of Dialectical Reason* (1960), and a four-volume philosophical-social biography of Gustave Flaubert (1960-1971), a French novelist who lived from 1821 to 1880.

Throughout his work Sartre emphasized the radical freedom of every human individual. Using phenomenological analyses and descriptions of lived human experiences, Sartre argues that no God exists, no purpose for one's life precedes one's own choices made in everyday situations. Each person is "condemned" to take responsibility for all aspects of life, including the free choices a person makes in response to the given circumstances of human existence. For Sartre, all values proceed from those choices; only at death can others evaluate the overall meaning of another's life.

Suffering from lung cancer and progressive blindness, Sartre remained politically aware until his death in 1980. Twenty-five thousand people followed his body through Paris to his grave site.

Legacy

Sartre expanded and systematized existential ideas for a wider audience.

Sartre's ideas were embraced by others during his lifetime. In 1948, Simone de Beauvoir published *The Ethics of Ambiguity*, an existentialist work heavily influenced by Sartre. There she argued that human ethics are based on freedom projected into the future. In *The Second Sex* (1949), de Beauvoir built a philosophical case for the equality of women with men derived from the proposition that women ought not passively to accept their societal roles (immanence), but actively to take the responsibility for their lives in superseding those roles (transcendence).

Sartre's view of freedom leads to a bleak view of human relationships: in every interaction, one person becomes dominant as the other lets himself be dominated, because one's choice always objectifies what it engages. Furthermore, people can cooperate in mutual respect only if they focus on a third party as the "enemy."

Such views have sparked serious philosophical and psychological discussions, both in Europe and North America. These discussions have focused on the nature of human freedom, human relationships, and political engagement. Sartre's writings have also inspired the practice of an existential form of psychotherapy as well as fresh perspectives in literary and biographical analyses. While many scholars rightly criticize Sartre's existentialist tendency and eccentric points of view, many of his critics fall to extreme positions. Ironically, they also build upon insights and descriptions of the complexity of everyday thinking, choosing, and acting.

Sartre's concepts continue to draw attention. *Nausea* has become a twentieth-century classic; *No Exit* is still performed. Serious discussions of human freedom spring from, and contemporary Marxism contends with, Sartre's contributions. Sartre distrusted Marxism as a philosophy that forced contemporary life to fit a predetermined universal model of collective life. Existentialism, in contrast, asserts that current existence must determine how people live their lives individually.

Sartre's essay, "Existentialism And Humanism" (1946), stirred the criticism of Martin Heidegger (1889–1976). In his *Letter on Humanism* (1947), Heidegger challenges Sartre's focus on human reality as opposed to a central focus on absolute Being.

To some degree, Sartre's kind of existentialism has become the dominant mode of thought in Western culture. More so than ever, ordinary people view themselves not as under the influence of some transcendent power, but as independent agents, free to make their own choices to live a responsible life.

Magurshak

WORLD EVENTS | SARTRE'S LIFE

1905   Jean-Paul Sartre is born in Paris

World War I 1914–18

1938   Sartre's first novel, *Nausea*, is published

World War II 1939–45

1940–41 Sartre is held prisoner of war by the Germans

1943   *The Flies* is published

Being and Nothingness is published

1944   *No Exit* is published

Mao Tse-tung establishes Communist rule in China   1949

Korean War 1950–53

1960   *Critique of Dialectical Reason* is published

Six Day War between Israel and Arabs   1967

End of Vietnam War   1975

1980   Sartre dies

Fall of Communism in eastern Europe   1989

For Further Reading:

Raymond, Diane. *Existentialism and the Philosophical Traditions.* Englewood Cliffs, N.J.: Prentice Hall, 1991.

Solomon, Robert C., and Kathleen M. Higgins. *A Short History of Philosophy.* New York: Oxford University Press, 1996.

Savonarola, Girolamo

Italian Church Reformer;
Millenarian Prophet
1452–1498

Life and Work

Girolamo Savonarola was a flamboyant preacher whose apocalyptic fervor moved him to reform the Roman Catholic church of Florence and to establish, if only temporarily, a rule for that city by religious authority.

Savonarola was born in Ferrara, Italy, in 1452. In 1475, after a brief effort to study medicine, he entered the Dominican Order of Preachers in Bologna. Once he completed his novitiate (trial period), he attended the Dominicum Studium Generale. In 1482, he left for Florence, where he became a reader at the Observant Dominican convent of San Marco.

Two years later, Savonarola came to the realization, based on his study of scripture, that the Church had to be cleansed and reformed to avoid the imminent wrath of God. During his Lenten sermons in the spring of 1485, and again the following year, he made public his apocalyptic insights.

After a brief return to Bologna, Savonarola came back to San Marco in 1490 at the request of Lorenzo de Medici, the most powerful citizen of Florence. Elected prior of the convent, Savonarola focused his energies on reforming both the Church and secular authorities, emphasizing the judgment of God. Although Savonarola most likely irritated the ruling powers, his success at strengthening the convent persuaded the Medicis to allow him to continue his radical preaching.

In 1494, France's King Charles VIII (r. 1483–1498) invaded Italy and conquered Florence. When the ruler, Piero de Medici, fled the city, Savonarola took charge. His preaching, now grounded in spiritual visions, guided his decisions in governing. Savonarola emphasized moral reform and urged ascetic practices upon the populace. He envisioned Florence as the New Jerusalem and as the center of widespread religious and social reform.

Savonarola's teachings ultimately incurred the displeasure of the Pope, who ordered him to Rome. When he refused, the Pope excommunicated him and threatened anyone who might give him aid and comfort. In 1498 he was declared guilty of heresy and political conspiracy. Along with two other members of his order, Savonarola was executed in a public square in Florence on May 23, 1498.

Legacy

Savonarola's apocalyptic visions of secular and ecclesiastical reform not only continued to be influential in Florence, but emboldened other reformers as well.

Even though he died in 1498, Savonarola's reform government remained in power in Florence until 1512, when the Medicis, supported by Spanish forces, restored their rule. In 1527, a revolt, generated by reform principles originated by Savonarola, called *piagnone*, began at San Marco. Once again the Medicis were expelled and social and moral reforms imposed upon the city.

Although the Medicis again assumed power in 1530, Savonarola's ideas spread to other parts of Italy and into France and Germany. Savonarola's banner of religious and social reform was raised by Giovanfrancesco Pico and Gasparo Contarini, of Venice, who incorporated his ideas for fundamental Church reform in their own programs. In the mid-sixteenth century, Savonarola's teachings helped shape the religious renewal of individuals and the bridges to emerging Protestantism promoted by Italian evangelism. Marguerite d'Angoulème, sister of King Francis I, disseminated Savonarola's insights into the courts of France. MARTIN LUTHER, the German reformer, may have been influenced by Savonarola's teachings on the doctrine of justification, his emphasis on individual faith, and compassion for the poor. A statue of the Italian was erected in Luther's hometown of Wittenberg.

Finally, Savonarola may have had further influence through his students at San Marco. These students translated the original Greek and Hebrew of the Bible into Italian, thereby making those texts available to a wider audience. Moreover, contact between the "Savonarolans" and the French, especially at Lyons, helped to establish a system of relief for the poor in France.

von Dehsen

WORLD EVENTS		SAVONAROLA'S LIFE
Beijing becomes capital of China	1421	
	1452	Girolamo Savonarola is born
Ottoman Empire captures Byzantine capital, Constantinople	1453	
	1484	Savonarola decides to reform Roman Catholic Church
	1485–86	Savonarola delivers Lenten sermons on reform
Columbus discovers Americas	1492	
Last Muslim State in Spain falls to Christians		
	1494	Savonarola rules Florence
	1498	Savonarola is executed
Reformation begins	1517	

For Further Reading:

Ridolfi, Roberto. *The Life of Savonarola.* New York: Knopf, 1959.

Roeder, Ralph. *The Man of the Renaissance: Four Lawgivers, Savonarola, Machiavelli, Castilione, Aretino.* Cleveland, Ohio: Word Publishing Co., 1958.

Schneerson, Menachem Mendel

Head of the Habad–Lubavitch Sect
of Hasidic Judaism
1902–1994

Life and Work

The rabbinical leader of the influential Orthodox Habad–Lubavitch sect, Menachem Mendel Schneerson had a tremendous influence on contemporary American Judaism.

Schneerson was born on April 18, 1902, in Nikolayev, Russia, in what is now the Ukraine. He was a descendant of the founder of the Habad sect and, by the time of his bar mitzvah,

WORLD EVENTS		SCHNEERSON'S LIFE
Spanish American War	1898	
	1902	Menachem Mendel Schneerson is born
World War I	1914–18	
	1929	Schneerson marries in Poland
World War II	1939–45	
	1941	Schneerson immigrates to United States
Mao Tse-tung establishes Communist rule in China	1949	
	1950	Schneerson becomes head of Lubavitchers
Korean War	1950–53	
	1950–92	Schneerson widens influence and size of Lubavitchers
Six Day War between Israel and Arabs	1967	
End of Vietnam War	1975	
Dissolution of Soviet Union	1991	
Apartheid in South Africa is dismantled	1994	Schneerson dies

was considered a Torah scholar. Russian persecution drove the family to Poland where, in 1929, Schneerson married the daughter of the reigning Habad rabbi. In an action that was highly unusual for an Orthodox religious scholar, he received his higher education at secular universities, studying at the University of Berlin and the Sorbonne, from which he graduated with an engineering degree. Following the outbreak of World War II, Schneerson immigrated to the United States in 1941, where he joined his father-in-law and settled in Brooklyn, New York. Upon his father-in-law's death in 1950, Schneerson became the seventh Lubavitch rabbi.

While other Hasidic groups practiced their religion quietly in separate communities divorced from contemporary society, the Lubavitch under Schneerson was an active, proselytizing sect, always seeking to make converts and bring non-observant Jews back into the fold. Converted campers known as "Mitzvah Mobiles" traveled around New York City, their occupants trying to entice surprised pedestrians into them for a prayer. Schneerson himself, an intense, patriarchal figure, granted audiences several times a week and gave advice through the mail in any of the 10 languages in which he was fluent. The rebbe, as he was known, extended his outreach to practicing and nonpracticing Jews around the world, sending his followers to spread his philosophy not only in countries such as Israel, with large Jewish populations, but also to areas such as the Caribbean, with tiny Jewish communities. His openness toward nonobservant Jews distinguished him from the rest of the Orthodox community.

Schneerson's activism was grounded in Habad messianic desire and belief that there was a divine spark in everyone. Religious actions would bring Jews closer to God and make the world more hospitable for the promised Messiah.

In 1992 Schneerson suffered a stroke and spent the last two years of his life in frail health. He died on June 12, 1994.

Legacy

Schneerson had an influence on contemporary Judaism far greater than pure numbers would suggest.

Starting with a congregation that was decimated in the Holocaust, the Lubavitcher claimed more than 200,000 members world-

wide by the 1990s. This was done through the vast outreach program begun under Schneerson's direction. While sect members looked old-fashioned in their frock coats, they were not averse to using the latest in technology to promote their cause. To this end, they used every modern means at their disposal, including satellite and cable TV, radio, toll-free phone numbers, magazines, the Internet, bumper stickers, and full-page newspaper ads.

Schneerson's influence was felt far beyond the United States. He believed that Israel was a land for the Jews. Although he never visited the country, he had many followers there and through them was able to influence Israeli politics. The Lubavitchers have a small political party there that helps support hard-line governments through coalitions with other parties. In the United States, he was able to inspire support and funding not only from believers, but also from secular, nonobservant Jews who nevertheless saw Schneerson and the Lubavitchers as ensuring the continued existence of Jewish culture in the United States.

The Lubavitch is a messianic sect and many in the group thought that Schneerson himself was the Messiah. This claim (not made by Schneerson) reached its height during the late 1980s and early '90s after a number of Schneerson's predictions came true. At his death he left a grieving congregation without a successor and divided among themselves. There were those who still believed that Scheerson would be revealed as the Messiah, even after his death. So far, he has not.

Saltz

For Further Reading:
Dalfin, Chaim. *Conversations with the Rebbe, Menachem Mendel Schneerson: Interviews with 14 Leading Figures About the Rebbe.* Los Angeles: JEC Publishing Company, 1996.
Hoffman, Edward. *Despite All Odds: The Story of Lubavitch.* New York: Simon & Schuster, 1991.

Schopenhauer, Arthur

Exponent of the Metaphysical
Doctrine of the Will
1788–1860

Life and Work

Arthur Schopenhauer, a German philosopher whose theories focused on the nature of the will as it relates to the external world, was known for his philosophy of pessimism.

Schopenhauer was born on February 22, 1788, in Danzig, Prussia (present-day Gdansk, Poland), to a prosperous merchant family. In 1793, the family moved to Hamburg, where Schopenhauer was privately educated. After Schopenhauer's father died suddenly in 1805, his mother and sister moved to Weimar, where they became part of the city's famous literary circle that included writers such as Johann von Goethe. Schopenhauer remained in Hamburg to prepare for university. He attended the universities of Gottingen and Berlin and, in 1813, earned a doctorate in philosophy from the University of Jena. He then spent the next few years in Weimar, where he not only discussed philosophy with Goethe, but also became acquainted with the religious and philosophical thought of India through Friedrich Majer.

In 1819, Schopenhauer completed his major work, *The World as Will and Idea* (revised 1844 and 1859). Based upon concepts drawn largely from PLATO and IMMANUEL KANT, he attempts to distinguish between the external world and human perceptions of it. In the first two sections, which focus on philosophy and nature, Schopenhauer argues that the external world exists only as a representation; it is not, as Kant alleged, a "thing in itself." For Schopenhauer, the only "thing in itself" is the will, a person's inner desire. Because the will engages the external world, an inherently evil place, the individual encounters suffering and, ultimately, death. Thus, the only true freedom arises from the denial of the will. In the last two sections, aesthetics and ethics, Schopenhauer asserts that the arts, especially music, enable the will to transcend this existence and become "will-less." Similarly, ethics, conceived as selfless compassion, extricates the will by subduing it for the sake of the other. Thus, the saint becomes the model of an ideal will-less person.

For the rest of his life Schopenhauer developed and clarified these themes. Following a brief stint as a professor at the University of Berlin (1819–1825), he settled in Frankfurt-am-Main to write and study. There he produced several other books, including *On the Will in Nature* (1836) and *Parerga and Paralipomena* (1851). He died there on September 21, 1860.

Legacy

Although little known in his own lifetime, Schopenhauer's philosophy of aesthetics and the will influenced the work of such notable artists and philosophers as Richard Wagner (1813–1883), FRIEDRICH WILHELM NIETZSCHE (1844–1900), and LUDWIG WITTGENSTEIN (1889–1951).

Wagner first came across Schopenhauer's *The World as Will and Idea* in 1854, after he had already completed six operas and was in the middle of composing his famous *Ring des Nibelungen*. To some degree Schopenhauer's concepts helped Wagner sharpen his own, already formulated, ideas. He confirmed Wagner's insights on such themes as the suffering of this life and the denial of the will as the ultimate goal of the individual. Nevertheless, Wagner had previously seen art as that which expressed reality for the masses. Schopenhauer's ideas moved him to assert the transcendent nature of art, especially music, and to trust his aesthetic instincts as the assertion of his unconscious will. In fact, in his later years, Wagner became much more aware of the importance of music as an independent component of his work, not just as a support for the libretto.

In similar fashion, Nietzsche considered Schopenhauer his chief educator. In 1865, as a 22-year-old student in Leipzig, Nietzsche came across a copy of *The World as Will and Idea* in a secondhand book shop. He was drawn to Schopenhauer's thought from the opening pages. For Nietzsche, the will stood at the center of human existence. As Nietzsche's thought matured, however, he began to dispute Schopenhauer's contention that the will ultimately must be suppressed. In direct contrast to the selfless saint, Nietzsche's model is the "Superman," whose will is so strong that it is no longer bound by custom or mores. Instead, it is totally free to assert itself without limit. Nietzsche's final work, which he never completed, was titled *The Will to Power*.

Wittgenstein's encounter with Schopenhauer came very early in his development as a philosopher. He read Schopenhauer as a young man and that influence stayed with him throughout his career. While Wittgenstein never directly engages Schopenhauer's ideas, they are prevalent in such works as *Notebooks 1914–1916* and *Tractatus* (1921), where they form part of Wittgenstein's theory of language.

These examples actually reflect a larger group, including Sigmund Freud and Thomas Mann, who are indebted to Schopenhauer. The Schopenhauer Society, founded in Frankfurt in 1911, has continued to spread his ideas.

von Dehsen

WORLD EVENTS		SCHOPENHAUER'S LIFE
United States independence	1776	
	1788	Arthur Schopenhauer is born
French Revolution	1789	
Napoleonic Wars in Europe	1803–15	
	1805	Schopenhauer's father dies
	1819–25	Schopenhauer lectures at University of Berlin
Greek War of Independence against Turkey	1821–29	
	1836	*On the Will in Nature* is published
Revolutions in Austria, France, Germany, and Italy	1848	
	1851	*Parerga and Paralipomena* is published
	1860	Schopenhauer dies
United States Civil War	1861–65	

For Further Reading:
Hamlyn, D. W. *Schopenhauer, The Arguments From the Philosophers*. Boston: Routledge and Kegan Paul, 1980.
Janaway, Christopher. *Schopenhauer*. New York: Oxford University Press, 1983.
Magee, Bryan. *The Philosophy of Schopenhauer*. New York: Oxford University Press, 1997.

Seton, Elizabeth Ann, Saint

First American-Born Saint;
Founder of the Sisters of Charity
1774–1821

Life and Work

Elizabeth Ann Seton was the first native-born American to be canonized by the Catholic church. Also known as the mother of the American parochial school system, she was the founder of the first American religious society.

Elizabeth Seton was born Elizabeth Bayley in New York City on August 28, 1774. Her family were well-to-do Episcopalians, her father a doctor. Her mother died when she was three and she had a lonely, introspective childhood. In 1794 she married William Magee Seton, a businessman, with whom she had five children. In 1800 her husband's business went bankrupt, and by 1803 he had contracted tuberculosis. Elizabeth, William, and their eldest daughter traveled to Europe in the hope that the climate would help William, but he died while in Italy. Italian business friends of William Seton sheltered the grieving Elizabeth at their home in Leghorn. His family was Catholic and Seton was enthused by her first encounter with Roman Catholicism.

In 1804 Seton returned to New York, and in March 1805, in the face of much family opposition, converted to Catholicism. She moved to Baltimore in June 1808. The following September she opened the Paca Street School, a Catholic girls school, with other women who had been put in her charge and with whom she formed a religious congregation. Seton took first vows and received the name "Mother" during the spring of 1809. In June 1809 the group moved to Emmitsburg, Maryland, where, in February 1810, she opened an elementary school. Tragedy struck soon after when two of Seton's daughters died of tuberculosis—one in 1812 and another in 1816.

In 1812 the community's rules were formally adopted, the other women took vows, and the order, called the Sisters of Charity of St. Joseph, was officially founded on July 19, 1813. It was the first American religious society. The rules of the order, modeled on those of the Daughters of Charity in France, were adapted by Seton and Archbishop John Carroll to allow her to retain guardianship of her children and to conform to American customs. Seton continued as head of her order until she died, also of tuberculosis, in Emmitsburg on January 4, 1821.

Legacy

Although Seton's Emmitsburg school was not the first religiously based school in the United States, she is generally credited as the founder of the American Catholic parochial school system. The Sisters of Charity was the first Catholic religious community in the United States.

At the time of Seton's death, the Sisters of Charity had grown from 17 to 50 members with branches in many communities. There are now 13 congregations of the Sisters of Charity Federation, with 7,000 members and branches in 45 states, 10 Canadian provinces, and 12 countries in Asia, the Caribbean, and Central and South America.

Following Seton's original mission, the Sisters of Charity take vows of poverty, chastity, and obedience and provide many services to their communities. Their traditional activities are in education, health care, and social services with an emphasis on serving the poor. Over the years, their ministries have come to include orphanages and child welfare, AIDS care and counseling, alcoholism treatment, teaching from kindergarten to university, providing low-income apartments for the elderly and disabled, and nursing homes. Today her work is continued by her spiritual descendants in religious communities such as The New York Sisters of Charity of Mount Saint Vincent on the Hudson, the New Jersey Sisters of Charity of Convent Station, and the Cincinnati Sisters of Charity of Mount Saint Joseph.

In 1968, in advance of Seton's canonization, her relics were moved into a newly built shrine in Emmitsburg, the site of her "Mother House" and her first school. The shrine may be visited by the public. On September 14, 1975, Pope JOHN PAUL II canonized Elizabeth Seton, the first native-born American to be named a saint.

Saltz

WORLD EVENTS	SETON'S LIFE
Peace of Utrecht 1713–15 settles War of Spanish Succession	
	1774 Elizabeth Bayley is born
United States 1776 independence	
French Revolution 1789	
	1794 Bayley marries William Seton
	1803 William Seton dies
Napoleonic Wars 1803–15 in Europe	
	1805 Seton converts to Catholicism
	1809 Seton becomes a nun
	1810 Seton opens a school in Emmitsburg, Maryland
	1813 Sisters of Charity of St. Joseph is founded
	1821 Seton dies
Greek War of 1821–29 Independence against Turkey	

For Further Reading:

Dirvin, Joseph I. *Mrs. Seton, Foundress of the American Sisters of Charity.* New York: Farrar, Straus, & Giroux, 1962.
Melville, Annabelle M. *Elizabeth Bayley Seton.* New York: Scribner, 1951.

Shafi'i, Abu 'Abd Allah, ash-

Preeminent Islamic Legal Scholar
767–820

Life and Work

Abu 'Abd Allah ash-Shafi'i, more commonly known ash-Shafi'i, was an Islamic legal scholar who wrote the first treatise of jurisprudence in Islam. His theories led to the development of the Shafi'iyah school of interpretation of Islamic law.

Little is known of ash-Shafi'i's early life. He was probably born in 767 in Gaza or Ashkelon on the coast of Palestine and was 10 when his father died. Shortly thereafter his mother took him to Mecca, the central city of Islam, where he began his formal study of the *Shariah* (Islamic law).

At age 20, ash-Shafi'i traveled to Medina to continue his studies with Malik ibn Anas (d. 796), the leading Islamic legal scholar of the day. Ten years later, he so impressed the governor of Yemen that the governor offered him a post. When it was alleged that ash-Shafi'i had supported an opponent of the ruling Abbasid dynasty, he was sent to Baghdad for trial. There he was successfully defended by al-Shaybani, a leading jurist of the Hanafi school, who instructed him in its teachings.

From 804 to 810, ash-Shafi'i traveled to Syria and Hejaz in modern-day Saudi Arabia. He ultimately developed his own legal theories and settled in Egypt, where he would spend the rest of his life, teaching and dictating his legal works to his students.

Ash-Shafi'i's legal theories focused on determining what constituted the authoritative principles of Islamic law and how those principles could be applied in new circumstances. Ash-Shafi'i believed that the only true sources of the law were the Koran and the hadith, the bona fide non-Koranic sayings and traditions attributed to the Prophet MUHAMMAD. New laws could be derived from the basic tenets of these sources through the application of legal reasoning (*ijtihad*) and consensus (*ijma*). In his major writing, *Treatise on the Source of the Law*, completed in Egypt, ash-Shafi'i describes how

authentic hadith can be distinguished from the inauthentic. (In contrast, his teacher, Malik, argued that all hadith traditions from Medina were authentic.) When pressed about the difficulty of using consensus as a legal source, ash-Shafi'i contended that he meant the consensus of the community. While in Egypt, he completed his other major work, *Treatise on the Legal Precepts of the Koran*.

Ash-Shafi'i died in Cairo on January 20, 820, from injuries received from a follower of Malik who had just lost a legal dispute.

Legacy

Ash-Shafi'i's legal theories attracted many disciples in Egypt. After his death, many of these students preserved his writings and spread his ideas to other lands, forming the basis of what would become known as the Shafi'iyah school of Islamic legal interpretation.

Until ash-Shafi'i became prominent, the dominant modes of legal interpretation were those of Malik and the Hanafi. All three agreed on the authority of the Koran and hadith. The earlier schools had added to these the authority of local customs and practices. Because his legal theory focused directly on common sources, and because it did not allow for other traditions to supplement the authentic ones, ash-Shafi'i's methodology was seen as limiting those established methods. Moreover, Malik claimed that where consensus was needed, that consensus ought to be that of the legal scholars in Medina. The Hanafi school insisted that consensus should be subordinated to the use of analogy (*qiyas*) to connect Islamic law to the present situation. In contrast to both, ash-Shafi'i held that the consensus of the community could express the will of Allah, and, therefore, provide a normative filter for applying older teachings. This mode of legal interpretation was clearly "transportable" and was eventually widely accepted among the diverse communities within the Islamic world.

Within 100 years of his death, ash-Shafi'i's legal theories found acceptance in Syria and central Asia. Under Sultan Saladin (d. 1169), ash-Shafi'i's thought became the controlling legal theory in Egypt. By the sixteenth century, ash-Shafi'i's teachings had spread throughout much of the Ottoman Empire. At present, his theory anchors the legal thought of Islamic

communities in Egypt, Syria, the countries of the Persian Gulf, western and southern Asia, and east Africa.

One controversy, however, continued into the twentieth century. Given that ash-Shafi'i pointed to the consensus of the community as a basis for interpretation, how might that consensus be determined? In 1924, Shaykh Rashid Rida in his book, *The Caliphate and the High Imamate*, proposed a solution that gained wide acceptance: the consensus would be discovered through the deliberations of an elected body of men conversant with the *Shariah*. By itself, this decision witnesses to the spirit of ash-Shafi'i's pursuit of clarity in legal philosophy.

von Dehsen

WORLD EVENTS	ASH-SHAFI'I'S LIFE
Islamic expansion 640–711 through North Africa and Spain	
	767 Ash-Shafi'i is born
	777 Ash-Shafi'i travels to Mecca
	787 Ash-Shafi'i studies law with Malik in Medina
Charlemagne's 800 coronation; beginning of Holy Roman Empire	
	814 Ash-Shafi'i establishes legal school in Egypt
	820 Ash-Shafi'i dies
Northern Sung 960 Dynasty begins	

For Further Reading
Gleave, R., and E. Kermelli. *Islamic Law: Theory and Practice*. New York: I. B. Tauris Publishers, 1997.
Stewart, Devin J. *Law and Society in Islam*. Princeton, N.J.: Markus Wiener Publishers, 1996.

Shang Yang

(Kung-sun Yang)

Chinese Philosopher of
Legalist School
c. 390–338 B.C.E.

* Scholars cannot date the specific events in Shang Yang's life with accuracy.

Life and Work

Shang Yang was one of the earliest philosophers of the Chinese Legalist school of thought, which devised concepts to solve the problems of society and government. As the prime minister of Qin, he built the state into a military power that unified China during the third century B.C.E.

Originally named Kung-sun Yang, Shang Yang was born around 390 B.C.E. in the Chinese province of Wei. A descendant of a royal concubine, he became an assistant to the prime minister of Wei, who endorsed Shang Yang as his successor. However, the king denied the appointment and in 356 B.C.E. Shang Yang became prime minister to King Xiao of Qin. (Qin was an independent state that amassed significant power during the "Warring States Period"—403–221 B.C.E.)

As prime minister, Shang Yang followed Legalist political theory in administering the state. He consolidated power by centralizing administration and developing a powerful military machine. He created a new military aristocracy to replace the hereditary nobility and organized families into groups, each of which had to provide an assigned number of young men to the military. He also implemented policies permitting peasants to buy land, thereby attracting settlers and more young men for the military. He asserted that military service led to *zhong* (loyalty of the subjects to the ruler) and *xiao* (filial piety).

Shang Yang contended that rulers should have absolute power and should rule their subjects by harsh means. In his view, a peaceful and moral society could be created only by well-defined laws (*fa*) that were clearly written and that mandated a strict system of rewards and punishments. These laws were necessary because human beings were essentially selfish, vicious, and fearful of death.

Shang Yang's followers summarized his ideas in the *Book of Lord Shang*. Following King Xiao's death in 338, Shang Yang's numerous enemies had him arrested. He was captured while attempting to flee and executed. His body was then dismembered.

Legacy

Shang Yang provided theories about law and government that served as the foundation for the Chinese Legalist school. His ideas also became the basis for policy formation during the Qin Dynasty.

Despite the harsh reaction to Shang Yang's policies and the brutality of his death, his ideas were adopted by subsequent Qin rulers who continued consolidating power through military might and strategic alliances. Legalist thinkers such as HAN-FEI-TZU (c. 280–c. 233 B.C.E.) and Li Si (280–208 B.C.E.) provided the theoretical justification for their actions. Han-fei-tzu built on earlier Legalist thought by proposing that good government contains three elements: law (*fa*), power (*shi*), and statecraft (*shu*). The government preserves order by wielding its "two handles," reward and punishment. He criticized Confucianism, one of China's dominant thought systems, because it presupposed that people are inherently good and would construct a peaceful society by voluntarily adhering to a code of mutual obligations and duties.

Li Si provided the rationale for the brutal regime of Emperor Qin Shi Huangdi (259–210 B.C.E.), who proclaimed the unification of China during his reign. Using Legalist techniques, the First Emperor, as he came to be known, centralized power, standardized weights and measures, unified the tax system, and developed a single currency for China. To forestall rebellion against his authoritarian practices, he relocated many people and executed scholars who criticized him.

Subsequent rulers eventually repudiated such totalitarian practices and replaced them with the more compassionate principles of Confucianism. However, communist leader Mao Tse-tung revived the First Emperor's memory in 1958. Mao praised him for exterminating his opponents, in essence using the emperor as a model for his own attempts at imposing uniformity of law and culture upon China. After an attempt on his life in 1971 for being a modern-day First Emperor, Mao inaugurated a program to rehabilitate the ruler's reputation. Ironically, the chairman of the "People's Republic" revived the autocratic practices of Legalist scholars such as Shang Yang.

von Dehsen

For Further Reading:

Fu, Zhengyuan. *China's Legalists: The Earliest Totalitarians and Their Art of Ruling.* Armonk, N.Y.: M. E. Sharpe, 1996.
Peerenboon, R. P. *Law and Morality in Ancient China.* Albany: State University of New York Press, 1993.

Shankara

Founder of Advaita Vedanta
Hinduism
c. 700–c. 750

Life and Work

Shankara was a Hindu teacher who articulated the theory of Advaita Vedanta, the non-dualistic interpretation of the Vedas, the Hindu scriptures.

While little is known of Shankara's life, he is thought to have been born in about 700 in Kaladi, India. His family came from the highest Indian social caste, the Brahmans. At a young age he studied with Govinda, who was a pupil of the noted scriptural interpreter Gaudapada, and then traveled around India, debating with other teachers and attempting to reform errant teachings and practices.

Through this training and encounters with others, Shankara developed a system that came to be known as Advaita (non-dualistic) Vedanta. The goal of these teachings was to lead people to *moksa*, release from the eternal cycle of birth and death known as reincarnation, and complete union with the Absolute God, the Brahman, a non-dualistic reality. All essence comes from the Brahman and is with the Brahman, even the souls of people, the *atman*. Moreover, once the *atman* is united with the Brahman, it becomes indistinguishable from it. In other words, the realm of the Brahman is that

of non-duality. (It is as if one places a drop of water in the ocean. That drop becomes so united with the water of the ocean that they are indistinguishable. Apart from the ocean, the drop does not have a separate existence.)

Shankara starts with the concept of *badha*, sublation. Once a person perceives an error, then that person can replace the error with a correct teaching. The Brahman, however, is the truth that cannot be replaced by any other (or it would not be absolute!). Nevertheless, the world of experience and material is dualistic. This world can only be sublated to the absolute reality of the Brahman. Finally, there is the world of illusion, perceiving something to be what it is not.

Using these concepts, Shankara then describes the movement from dualism to non-dualism. Whenever human beings perceive that the world of matter and experience is the real world, they are in error. The world is an ever-changing stream of appearances created by the Brahman. Once a person perceives the error of perception about the world, that person can replace that error with union with the Brahman. His teachings were preserved in several writings, including his *Commentary on the Bhagavad Gita* and his *Commentary on the Brahma Sutra*.

Shankara died around 750 in Kedarnatha in the Himalayas.

Legacy

Shankara's philosophy of non-dualism became known as Advaita Vedanta. This belief system became one of the six major Vedantas of modern Hinduism.

Shankara's teachings found a wide following among Hindus. Among his direct pupils in the ninth century were Sureshvara, who wrote the *Varttika*, or "Gloss," as commentaries on Shankara's teaching, and Padmapada, the author of *Pañcapadika*, another set of commentaries. The debates that these students had over issues not settled by Shankara himself laid the groundwork for later debates that divided the Avaita Vedanta.

By the twelfth century a serious split had erupted among Shankara's followers. Some backed the *Vivarana*, a commentary on Padmapada's writings; others supported the teachings of Vacaspati, the ninth-century philosopher who wrote the commentary on

Shankara's writing known as *Bhamati*. The dispute arose over the question of where the focus of ignorance could be found. The adherents of the *Bhamati* considered the individual as the focus of ignorance. They believed that human beings stem from a beginningless sequence of reincarnations burdened by ignorance. This avoided concluding that the individual is the cause of ignorance and that the Brahman was the source of ignorance. This latter concept was held by the subscribers of the *Vivarana*. Although they did not acknowledge that the Brahman would itself create ignorance, they did argue that when people were confronted with the pure Brahman consciousness, they became aware of their own ignorance.

These schools of thought also disagreed over the descriptions of the individual. The Bhamati school concluded that a person is a limitation of the Brahman. They used the analogy of a room. Just as the floor, ceiling, and walls of a room enclose and limit a big space, so too do humans provide limits to the manifestation of the Brahman. The *Vivarana* followers saw human beings as many reflections of the unified Brahman.

Despite these internal differences, the non-dualistic teachings of Shankara continue to be an essential component of their religion for many contemporary Hindus.

von Dehsen

WORLD EVENTS	SHANKARA'S LIFE*
Islamic expansion 640–711 through North Africa and Spain	
	c. 700 Shankara is born
	c. 750 Shankara dies
Charlemagne's 800 coronation; beginning of Holy Roman Empire	

* According to Hindu tradition, Shankara was born c. 788 and died c. 820. However, most recent scholarship suggest that he was born c. 700 and died c. 750.

For Further Reading:
Isaeva, N. V. *Shankara and Indian Philosophy.* Albany: State University of New York Press, 1993.
Shastri, Udayavira. *The Age of Shankara.* Gaziabad, India: Virjanand Vedic Research Institute, 1981.

Smith, Adam

Philosopher and Political
Economist; Originator of Modern
Liberal Economic Theory
1723–1790

Life and Work

A dam Smith was the Scots philosopher and
political economist who first developed the
concept of a laissez-faire, free market economy.

Smith was born in Kirkcaldy, Scotland, on
June 5, 1723, and raised by his widowed mother.
Educated at the University of Glasgow and
Oxford University, he became professor of logic
at the University of Glasgow in 1751 and
assumed the chair of moral philosophy in 1752.
Following the publication of his acclaimed
Theory of Moral Sentiment (1759), Smith
resigned from the university to become tutor to
the young duke of Buccleuch. With the noble-
man, he toured Europe, meeting many of the

World Events	Smith's Life	
Peace of Utrecht 1713–15 settles War of Spanish Succession		
	1723	Adam Smith is born
	1751	Smith becomes professor of logic at University of Glasgow
	1752	Smith becomes professor of moral philosophy at University of Glasgow
	1759	Smith publishes *Theory of Moral Sentiment*
United States independence	1776	Smith publishes *Wealth of Nations*
	1778	Smith is named commissioner of customs in Edinburgh
	1787	Smith becomes lord rector of University of Glasgow
French Revolution	1789	
	1790	Smith dies
Napoleonic Wars 1803–15 in Europe		

important figures of the French Enlightenment
including the Physiocrats, who had developed
the first system of economic analysis. Smith
retired after his return to Scotland in 1766 to
concentrate on writing what became his most
important work, *Wealth of Nations* (1776).

In *Wealth of Nations* Smith presented a unified theory to explain and justify the operation
of commercial societies, particularly that of
Great Britain. Smith argued that social harmony
and economic progress could best be preserved
in a society in which people were free to pursue
their own economic interests. He reasoned that
self-interest would lead individuals to produce
goods and perform services that would be most
beneficial to themselves and to the general welfare. In pursuing their goals, they would be
guided by the "Hidden Hand," the natural laws
and forces that preserved economic equilibrium.
Natural human benevolence would provide a
check on the potential harm that might arise
from the pursuit of unrestrained self-interest.

Smith opposed government regulation,
arguing that the free exercise of economic self-
interest would ultimately guarantee the greatest prosperity. He criticized the contemporary
British mercantile system, which encouraged
state regulation and monopolies, and, instead,
advocated a laissez-faire system under which
competition would have free rein without government restrictions and tariffs. Smith saw
government's role as confined to three areas:
providing defense; ensuring justice; and developing vital public works and institutions that
could not be provided by market forces.

Smith was named commissioner of customs
in Edinburgh in 1778 and was appointed lord
rector of the University of Glasgow in 1787. He
died in 1790.

Legacy

O ne of the world's most influential thinkers,
Smith provided the foundation for the
subsequent development of modern liberal economic theory and practice and helped shape
classical liberal political thought.

Smith's economic thought became influential only in the early nineteenth century,
when it provided the intellectual justification
for the Industrial Revolution. During that
period the British government gradually
lifted economic regulation and established
the first capitalist economy. From England

capitalism spread to many Western nations,
including the United States.

The adoption of unrestricted capitalism ushered in economic cycles of expansion followed
by depression and resulted in the emergence of
the modern working class, individuals with little
property or skills who traded labor for low
wages. KARL MARX developed his theory of communism in response. Despite the serious problems that emerged from capitalism, it became
the dominant economic system in the nineteenth century because it generated enormous
wealth that raised general living standards.

Smith's economic ideas were closely entwined
with liberal political philosophy. Classical liberal
thought, accepted by such men as JAMES
MADISON, the primary architect of the United
States Constitution, was grounded in the belief
that government could not know what was best
for individuals. Consequently, people should be
free to pursue their own goals. Liberals accepted
Smith's idea that ownership of property was vital
for maintaining liberty. It encouraged responsible participation in government and gave individuals economic freedom that would ensure
independent political thought. Over the course
of the nineteenth century, however, liberals
began to view unrestrained industrial capitalism
as an obstacle to freedom, and leaders such as
U.S. president Theodore Roosevelt advocated
limited government action to ensure equality of
economic opportunity.

Smith's laissez-faire system was generally abandoned in the face of the Great Depression of the
1930s. In response to worldwide economic collapse, thinkers such as British economist JOHN
MAYNARD KEYNES urged aggressive government
activity to mitigate economic cycles. Keynes's
theories ushered in the era of "Big Government,"
with its tremendous growth of bureaucracy and
regulation. In the United States, for example,
President Franklin D. Roosevelt's New Deal
restructured the financial system, imposed government regulation on industry, and laid the
foundation for the modern welfare state.

"Big government" lasted until the 1980s,
when political leaders such as Margaret Thatcher
in the United Kingdom and President Ronald
Reagan in the United States called for a return to
a freer economy. With the fall of communism in
the 1990s, the newly formed governments of
Eastern Europe embraced capitalism, extending
the influence of Smith's ideas.

von Dehsen

For Further Reading:
Campbell, Roy H., and A. S. Skinner. *Adam Smith*. New York: St. Martin's Press, 1982.
Griswold, Charles L., Jr. *Adam Smith and the Virtues of Enlightenment*. Cambridge, Mass.: Cambridge University Press, 1998.
Muller, Jerry Z. *Adam Smith in His Time and Ours: Designing the Decent Society*. Princeton, N.J.: Princeton University Press,

Smith, Joseph

Founder of the Mormon Church
1805–1844

Life and Work

Joseph Smith was a religious visionary who founded the Church of Jesus Christ of Latter-day Saints (also known as the Mormon Church).

Smith was born on December 23, 1805, in Sharon, Vermont. When he was 10 years old, his family settled in Palmyra, New York. At the age of 14, Smith experienced the first of a number of visions of God and of figures from the Old and New Testaments. In an 1823 vision, he claimed that an angel named Moroni told him of golden plates containing hieroglyphics buried in Manchester, New York. In 1827 Smith dug up and translated the plates. The result he called the *Book of Mormon*, which was published in 1830. Smith claimed that the plates contained the writings of ancient Israelites who had migrated to North America.

On April 6, 1830, Smith founded the Church of Jesus Christ, later called the Church of Jesus Christ of Latter-day Saints, in Fayette, New York. The church was supposedly a restoration of the ancient Christian church. Among Smith's first converts was his own family. His charismatic personality attracted many other converts, but his claims of divine communion and his *Book of Mormon* also inspired

much antagonism and outright attacks on Smith and his followers. His writings, including *The Book of Commandments* (1833), an expanded version entitled *Doctrine and Covenants* (1835), and *The Pearl of Great Price*, published in 1851, are, along with the Old and New Testaments and the *Book of Mormon*, considered divine scripture by Mormons.

To escape persecution, the Mormons traveled westward until they reached Commerce, Illinois, in 1839, which they renamed Nauvoo. There the Mormons were finally accepted and issued a city charter by the state of Illinois. However, rumors that Smith and some of the elite church members were practicing polygamy created dissension both within and outside the Mormon community. Smith himself was rumored to have up to 50 wives, although he admitted to only one.

In 1844 Smith announced his campaign for the presidency. A dissenting group of Mormons published an anti-polygamy, anti-Smith article. Smith ordered their press destroyed and for this was arrested and jailed in Carthage, Illinois. On June 27, 1844, Smith and his brother Hyrum were both murdered by a lynch mob in the Carthage jail.

Legacy

Smith's legacy is the Mormon church, which, in 1997, only 167 years after its creation, claimed almost 10 million members worldwide, about half in the United States.

Smith considered Mormonism not just a religion but an entire way of life that, if followed, would lead to a utopian existence. Smith emphasized family life and education, and advocated physical health and a communal economy. His followers gathered in communities built by themselves, operated cooperative farms and industries, erected churches they called "temples," and built universities.

After Smith's death, the dissent within the Mormon community led to a split within the church. Another Mormon offshoot was called the Reorganized Church of Jesus Christ of the Latter-day Saints, which eventually moved to Independence, Missouri, and is still headquartered there. In 1998 it claimed approximately 250,000 members. Unlike the larger church, this branch has been led continuously by descendants of Joseph Smith. The main body of

Mormons followed BRIGHAM YOUNG, its new leader, to the Great Salt Basin in Utah, where they founded Salt Lake City and set up their temple and headquarters. The main church headquarters remain there to this day.

During his life and after, Smith has been either hailed as a true prophet or vilified as a charlatan. Whatever the truth, he remains one of America's most interesting and influential religious leaders.

Saltz

WORLD EVENTS	SMITH'S LIFE
Napoleonic Wars in 1803–15 Europe	
	1805 Joseph Smith is born
	1819 Smith receives first revelation
Greek War of 1821–29 Independence against Turkey	
	1823 Existence of gold plates is revealed to Smith
	1827 Smith unearths and translates gold plates
	1830 *Book of Mormon* is published
	Smith founds Church of Jesus Christ
	1839 Smith and followers settle in Nauvoo, Illinois
	1844 Smith announces his candidacy for president
	Smith is killed by lynch mob
Revolutions in 1848 Austria, France, Germany, and Italy	

For Further Reading:

Bushman, Richard L. *Joseph Smith and the Beginnings of Mormonism.* Urbana: University of Illinois Press, 1984.

Smith, Joseph. *An American Prophet's Record: The Diaries and Journals of Joseph Smith,* 2d ed. Edited by Scott H. Faulring. Salt Lake City, Utah: Signature Books, 1989.

Socrates of Athens

First Greek Philosopher of the Western Tradition; Developer of Socratic Method

c. 469–399 B.C.E.

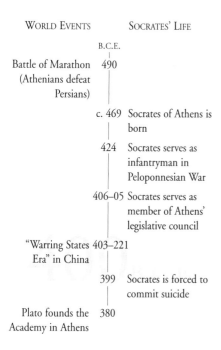

World Events	Socrates' Life
	B.C.E.
Battle of Marathon (Athenians defeat Persians)	490
	c. 469 Socrates of Athens is born
	424 Socrates serves as infantryman in Peloponnesian War
	406–05 Socrates serves as member of Athens' legislative council
"Warring States Era" in China	403–221
	399 Socrates is forced to commit suicide
Plato founds the Academy in Athens	380

Life and Work

Socrates of Athens was the first philosopher in the Western tradition to logically examine questions about moral conduct and the meaning of life.

Socrates was born around 469 B.C.E. in the Greek city-state of Athens and matured during "the Age of Pericles," the period of greatest Athenian political power and cultural development. His family was friends with the leaders of Athens, and he served with distinction in the Peloponnesian War between Sparta and Athens. No system of formal higher educational existed, thus Socrates, like other privileged young men of Athens, learned from noted teachers who traveled among the city-states. For a fee, these teachers instructed young men in everything from successful debating techniques to the nature of the universe. Socrates himself became such a teacher but with two important differences: he claimed never to have taught any specific doctrine and never to have charged anyone a fee.

As a teacher, Socrates significantly redirected the content and method of Greek philosophical questioning. Philosophers prior to Socrates discussed the basic elements of reality and the causes of natural occurrences; Socrates focused upon pressing human concerns such as the nature of wisdom, human excellence, and a morally good life. Furthermore, he claimed that genuine wisdom was knowing that one knew nothing for certain. In pointed dialogues, he raised moral questions with anyone interested and embarrassed prominent people by pointing out that they really didn't know what they claimed to know. Such tactics made some powerful enemies. In 406–405 B.C.E., Socrates served as a member of Athens' legislative council; but, after 70 years of living as a loyal Athenian, a courageous soldier, and a well-known figure in his city, Socrates was indicted for impiety. Convicted, he was sentenced to death, forced to drink poisonous hemlock, and died in 399 B.C.E.

Legacy

Socrates was one of the three renowned ancient Greek philosophers (along with Plato and Aristotle) who laid the foundation for Western thought. Although Socrates wrote nothing himself, his personality and teachings, vividly depicted in the writings of others, especially in Plato's *Dialogues*, have remained a significant model of Western philosophical inquiry.

In his own day, Socrates inspired men like Plato and Aeschines to establish schools and to write philosophy in dialogue form. He gave Western education the Socratic method—the process whereby instructor and student pose a question, proffer an answer, and then test the acceptability of the answer through further questioning. However, because our knowledge of Socrates comes only from writers who often use him as a mouthpiece for their own ideas, it is difficult—but not impossible—to describe his actual long-term legacy.

Scholars generally agree that Socrates exemplifies, even today, the attitude that humbly acknowledges how little one really knows about important moral questions. Convinced that an unexamined life was not worth living, he showed Western philosophers from Plato and Aristotle to the present how to seek general definitions of concepts such as moral excellence and justice that might guide them in living well. His example suggests that concern for moral character is more important than material success. In both its dialogical form and moral content, Socratic discussion remains a mainstay of much contemporary education.

Finally, Socrates inspires others as one who lived what he taught, who prized justice more than prosperity and survival, who sought good reasons before accepting opinions, and who nonetheless enjoyed life as a moderate, good-humored seeker of truth.

Magurshak

For Further Reading:

Luce, John Victor. *An Introduction to Greek Philosophy*. London: Thames and Hudson, 1992.

Plato. *The Trial and Death of Socrates*. Translated by G. M. A. Grube. Indianapolis, Ind.: Hackett Publishing Co., 1975.

Vlastos, Gregory. *Socrates, Ironist and Moral Philosopher*. New York: Cornell University Press, 1991.

Spinoza, Benedict de

First Philosophical Defender
of Democracy
1632–1677

Life and Work

Benedict de Spinoza (also known as Baruch Spinoza) was one of the major rationalist philosophers of the seventeenth century, a modern exponent of pantheism (equating God with the forces of nature), and the first political philosopher to construct a comprehensive defense of democracy.

Spinoza was born on November 24, 1632, in Amsterdam, Holland. His parents were prosperous Jewish merchants who had recently fled Portugal, fearing religious persecution. He attended traditional Jewish schools while receiving private tutoring in secular subjects. He later learned the craft of lens grinding, which he used to support himself while writing philosophy.

Spinoza challenged many established religious ideas, especially the authority of scripture. In consequence Jewish leaders expelled Spinoza from the synagogue in July 1656. Shortly thereafter, the rabbis convinced the civil authorities to banish him briefly from Amsterdam.

Spinoza's first published work was *Principles of the Philosophy of René Descartes* (1663). Disagreeing with DESCARTES' dualism of mind/spirit and body, Spinoza identified God with nature. He believed that there were universal mathematical and rational principles that governed all aspects of the universe, which itself was composed of divine material. Once these principles were discovered, they could become the basis for constructing a society most conducive to human well-being.

Much of Spinoza's theories appear in *Theologico-Political Treatise*, published anonymously in 1670. Like THOMAS HOBBES, Spinoza believed that humans, in the "state of nature," could not provide individually for all of their needs for survival and defense against external threats. Therefore, people banded together to form societies. Unlike Hobbes, who thought that such societies should be ruled by a strong central force, Spinoza argued that reason required that such societies be democratic. As all people needed reason to curb their passions and as differences among people gave rise to various ideas, the only way to allow reason to rule and to prevent the tyranny of any single idea was to promote democracy and freedom of speech. Religion, while somewhat opposed to reason, can promote the well-being of society through the advocacy of virtue as the foundation of civic society.

Several of his works were published posthumously, including *Short Treatise on God, Man, and His Well Being* (written in 1662), *Treatise on the Correction of the Understanding* (written in 1662), and *Ethics* (written from 1663 through 1677).

Spinoza died in The Hague on February 21, 1677, after a long battle with tuberculosis.

Legacy

Spinoza created no philosophical school, but he has had a pervasive influence on modern philosophy. He was the first philosopher to defend principles of democracy and free speech on the basis of scientific reasoning. His work forms a bridge between the Enlightenment's critique of monarchical rule by divine right and the foundation of democratic societies in the United States and France.

Philosophers were largely hostile to Spinoza's philosophy until the second half of the eighteenth century. His early critics argued that Spinoza supported a form of cosmic determinism in which people's ideas and lives were controlled by some cosmic force, as implied by the universal mathematical rational principles. Some of his early critics, such as the French skeptic Pierre Bayle (1647–1706), employed the term Spinozist to denote an atheist and materialist. (A materialist is one who asserts that matter is the only basic reality.) Gottfried Leibniz (1646–1716) also rejected Spinoza's determinism, but embraced other aspects of his thought.

In 1780, a debate, known as the *Pantheismusstreit* (Pantheism Quarrel), arose between the novelist Friedrich Jacobi (1743–1819) and the Jewish philosopher Moses Mendelssohn (1729–1786) over Spinoza's work. Jacobi accused the German dramatist and theologian Gottfried Lessing (1729–1781) of "Spinozism"; Mendelssohn came to Lessing's defense. This debate brought to light some of the less prominent aspects of Spinoza's thought. As a result, Johann von Goethe (1749–1832) and Johann Herder (1744–1803) became enamored with Spinoza's concepts and used them as a foundation for *Naturphilosophie* (nature philosophy), as a component of Romanticism. Ironically, Romanticism opposed the rational concepts of the Enlightenment. For example, instead of viewing the universe as being governed by cosmic principles, the Romantics view all humans as unique and independent individuals.

Spinoza's political thought, with its emphasis on a contractual democracy grounded in free debate, had a profound influence on French political theorist JEAN-JACQUES ROUSSEAU (1712–1778). His synthesis of the classical idea of virtue as the supreme good and the Enlightenment concept of the natural rights of the individual influenced German idealists such as IMMANUEL KANT (1724–1804), GEORG HEGEL (1770–1831), and KARL MARX (1818–1883).

Spinoza's influence continued through the writing of such diverse thinkers as Heinrich Heine, George Eliot, Sigmund Freud, and Albert Einstein. His work on the unity of matter influenced metaphysics and psychological concepts of mind-body identity.

von Dehsen

For Further Reading:
Balibar, Etienne. *Spinoza and Politics.* New York: Verso, 1998.
Garrett, Don, ed. *The Cambridge Companion to Spinoza.* New York: Cambridge University Press, 1996.
Harris, Errol E. *The Substance of Spinoza.* Atlantic Highlands, N.J.: Humanities Press International, 1994.

WORLD EVENTS	SPINOZA'S LIFE
Thirty Years' War 1618–48 in Europe	
	1632 Benedict de Spinoza is born
	1656 Spinoza is expelled from synagogue
	1663 *Principles of the Philosophy of René Descartes* is published
	1670 *Theologico-Political Treatise* is published
	1677 Spinoza dies
England's Glorious 1688 Revolution	

Stowe, Harriet Beecher

Prominent Abolitionist; Author of
Uncle Tom's Cabin
1811–1896

Life and Work

Harriet Beecher Stowe was a fervent opponent of slavery whose novel, *Uncle Tom's Cabin,* helped mobilize anti-slavery forces in the antebellum North.

Harriet Beecher was born in Litchfield, Connecticut, on June 14, 1811. Her father, Lyman Beecher, was a nationally known Congregationalist minister. In 1832, Rev. Beecher moved his family to Cincinnati, Ohio, to become president of Lane Theological

Seminary. In 1836, Harriet Beecher married Calvin E. Stowe, a professor of biblical studies at the seminary. Stowe encouraged his wife to pursue her writing. Over the next few years, she contributed to many local literary publications. In 1843, she published *The Mayflower,* a book about the descendants of the Pilgrims.

Outraged at the passage of the Fugitive Slave Act of 1850, designating slaves as property belonging to their masters even in states where slavery was forbidden, she wrote her most famous novel, *Uncle Tom's Cabin,* in 1851. This book first appeared in serialized form in the *National Era,* a Washington, D.C., newspaper. By 1852, the entire work was published in book form. In 1853, 1.2 million copies of the book were in print and the story reached the stage as a play.

The novel depicts a slave, Tom, who endures passively the punishment inflicted by his master. While some criticized Stowe for the passivity of Tom, she hoped that he would be recognized as a Christ-like figure, whose suffering ultimately leads to salvation. To substantiate some of her presentation of slavery, in 1853 she published the *Key to Uncle Tom's Cabin,* documenting the factual basis of the story. When she met President Lincoln during the Civil War, he reportedly said, "So you're the little woman who wrote the book that made this great war."

Stowe never stopped writing. In 1857 she helped found the literary journal, *The Atlantic Monthly,* to which she contributed several articles. In 1859, she wrote the book, *The Minister's Wooing,* to criticize the Calvinists because they condemned her unchurched son, Henry, to eternal damnation following his untimely death.

Stowe spent many of her last years in Florida. Toward the end of her life she moved to Hartford, Connecticut, where she died on July 1, 1896.

Legacy

Stowe's novel, *Uncle Tom's Cabin,* brought home the evils of slavery to a large number of Americans and increased the sectional tensions that ultimately led to the Civil War.

While it overstates the case to follow the wit of President Lincoln and credit *Uncle Tom's Cabin* with starting the Civil War, the

book helped to galvanize a country deeply split over the question of slavery. Both North and South viewed the book as containing accurate depictions of slavery. In the North it became a focal point for the abolitionist struggle against slavery. In the South it became a rallying point for resistance to the attempts to abolish their "peculiar institution." Long after the Civil War, *Uncle Tom's Cabin* provides insight into the horror of slavery and into the impassioned, and ultimately violent, efforts to remove it and to restore human dignity to African Americans.

Unfortunately, however, Stowe's portrait of Tom as a passive slave who quietly endures the hardships imposed by his master did not immediately bring to mind the Christ-like suffering she had hoped it would. Instead, the epithet "Uncle Tom" has come to mean a shiftless, passive person who never asserts his own value or rights. In essence, Stowe's concept of Tom has been turned on its head and transformed from one who endures with dignity to one who lacks the capacity to stand up for his or her own rights.

Finally, Stowe's contribution in helping to establish *The Atlantic Monthly* ought not to be overlooked. Since its inception in 1857, this periodical has offered the insights of some of the most prominent thinkers of the day on topics ranging from art to politics. Among those who have contributed to the journal are Frederick Douglass, Nathaniel Hawthorne, Mark Twain, Theodore Roosevelt, Woodrow Wilson, and Emily Dickinson.

von Dehsen

WORLD EVENTS	STOWE'S LIFE
Napoleonic Wars 1803–15 in Europe	
	1811 Harriet Beecher is born
Greek War of 1821–29 Independence against Turkey	
	1836 Beecher marries Calvin E. Stowe
Revolutions in 1848 Austria, France, Germany, and Italy	
	1851 *Uncle Tom's Cabin* is serialized
	1852 *Uncle Tom's Cabin* is published as in book form
	1857 Stowe helps to found *The Atlantic Monthly*
United States 1861–65 Civil War	
Germany is united 1871	
	1896 Stowe dies
Spanish American 1898 War	

For Further Reading:

Hendrick, Joan. *Harriet Beecher Stowe: A Life.* New York: Oxford University Press, 1994.

Holmes, Edward. *Harriet Beecher Stowe: Woman and Artist.* Orono, Me.: Northern Lights, 1991.

Strong, Josiah

Promoter of the Social Gospel;
Leader of the Ecumenical
Movement
1847–1916

Life and Work

Josiah Strong was at the forefront of the ecumenical movement in the United States and a proponent of the Social Gospel. He was one of the first religious leaders to encourage cooperation among Protestant Christians to work for the betterment of urban communities.

Strong was born on January 19, 1847, in Naperville, Illinois, just outside of Chicago. He graduated from Western Reserve College in 1869 and then studied at Lane Seminary from 1869 to 1871, both in Ohio. In 1871 he was ordained a Congregationalist minister. Over the next 15 years he served parishes in Wyoming and Ohio; from 1881 to 1884 he was also a regional secretary for the Congregational Home Missionary Society.

In 1885, while a pastor at a church in Cincinnati, Strong published his most important book, *Our Country: Its Possible Future and Its Present Crisis*. Here Strong analyzed urban social problems and proposed solutions. The book won Strong national recognition. That same year, Strong's congregation sponsored an interdenominational Christian conference to examine ways in which churches could combat social ills. The conference attracted many prominent leaders and led to similar conferences in 1887, 1889, and 1893.

In 1886, Strong became the general secretary of the Evangelical Alliance, an ecumenical organization for social reform. Hoping to expand the role of the church in social action, Strong founded the American League for Social Service in 1898.

In all his capacities, Strong believed that coordinated efforts of the churches within a community could best identify and address the social problems of their people. As his interests in this area expanded, he served on the Commission on the Church and Social Service of the Federal Council of Churches.

Strong devoted his life to bringing Christians together to marshal their resources in the service of compassion and social justice. He died in New York City on April 28, 1916.

Legacy

Strong's vision of a united Christianity directed at overcoming social ills provided a theological foundation and inspirational model for much ecumenical work in the twentieth century.

Strong was one of the first Christian ministers to seek cooperation among Protestant churches to work for social action. His own efforts not only inspired others to continue his emphasis, they also charted a course of action that led to the establishment of such Christian ecumenical groups as the National Council of Churches of Christ and the World Council of Churches.

Strong's book, *Our Country*, provided some of the basic principles for what became known as the Social Gospel movement. The advocates of the Social Gospel were Christian activists who applied Christian principles of compassion and justice in attempts to accomplish social reform and to help the poor. In the early decades of the twentieth century, this movement attracted such preeminent church leaders as WALTER RAUSCHENBUSCH, whose own book, *Christianity and the Social Crisis* (1907) grew out of his work in New York's Hell's Kitchen. By the 1920s this movement had representatives in Washington attempting to influence legislation and social policy. By the end of the twentieth century aspects of the Social Gospel emphasizing social reform for the oppressed could be found in such movements as black theology, feminist theology, and liberation theology.

Strong's vision of a united Christianity fighting social ills was realized in the Federal Council of Churches of Christ. After Strong's death in 1916, this organization continued Strong's work of cooperative Christian efforts. In 1951, the federation expanded by including additional church communions, for example Lutherans, and other agencies, such as Church World Service and the Protestant Radio Commission, and reorganized itself as the National Council of Churches of Christ. The member churches of the National Council set aside their doctrinal differences to combine resources in various social programs, such as those opposing poverty and advocating human rights. The World Council of Churches, founded in 1948, pursues the same agenda on a worldwide scale.

von Dehsen

WORLD EVENTS		STRONG'S LIFE
Greek War of Independence against Turkey	1821–29	
	1847	Josiah Strong is born
Revolutions in Austria, France, Germany, and Italy	1848	
United States Civil War	1861–65	
Germany is united	1871	Strong is ordained as Congregationalist minister
	1885	*Our Country: Its Possible Future and Its Present Crisis* is published
Spanish American War	1898	Strong founds American League for Social Service
World War I	1914–18	
	1916	Strong dies
World War II	1939–45	

For Further Reading:

Gorrell, Donald K. *The Age of Social Responsibility: The Social Gospel in the Progressive Era, 1900–1920*. Macon, Ga.: Mercer University Press, 1988.

Handy, Robert T. *The Social Gospel in America, 1870–1920*. New York: Oxford University Press, 1966.

Teresa, Mother

(Agnes Gonxha Bojaxhiu)

Founder of the Order of the
Missionary Sisters of Charity
1910–1997

WORLD EVENTS		TERESA'S LIFE
Spanish American War	1898	
	1910	Agnes Bojaxhiu (Mother Teresa) is born
World War I	1914–18	
	1928	Teresa joins Sisters of Loreto
	1937	Teresa takes final vows
World War II	1939–45	
	1946	Teresa decides to leave convent to live with poor
	1948	Teresa gets Vatican permission to leave convent
Mao Tse-tung establishes Communist rule in China	1949	
	1950	Teresa establishes Missionary Sisters of Charity
Korean War	1950–53	
	1952	Teresa opens home for the dying destitute
Six Day War between Israel and Arabs	1967	
End of Vietnam War	1975	
	1979	Teresa wins Nobel Prize for Peace
Dissolution of Soviet Union	1991	
Apartheid in South Africa is dismantled	1994	
	1997	Teresa dies

Life and Work

Mother Teresa was a Roman Catholic nun who devoted herself to the care of the poor, the ill, the destitute and the dying, first in India, and then worldwide.

Teresa was born Agnes Gonxha Bojaxhiu in August 1910, in what is now Skopje, Macedonia, but was then part of Albania. At a young age, Teresa decided she wanted to help the poor, particularly in India. In 1928 she joined the Sisters of Loreto, an Irish Catholic order that was active in India. After studying English for a few weeks, she went to India to begin her religious training in Darjeeling. She later trained and worked as a teacher, learned to speak Bengali and Hindi, and, after taking her final vows in 1937, was appointed principal of a school in Calcutta.

In 1946 she received a second calling to leave the convent to live and work among the poor. In 1948 she received permission from Rome to do so, took further training as a nurse, and opened her first school in the Calcutta slums. In 1950 Teresa received the Church's permission to establish a new order, the Missionary Sisters of Charity. In addition to the usual vows of chastity, obedience, and poverty, members of this order take a fourth vow of service to the poor. In 1952 Teresa opened the Pure of Heart Home for Dying Destitutes where the terminally ill destitute could die in dignity. A year later she opened her first orphanage. Since 1957 the order has been working with lepers and in the 1960s built a leper colony near Asansol, India. As her order grew, many more facilities were opened in India and other countries to serve many causes. Teresa used her increasing fame around the world to gain support and funding for her many projects. She was awarded many high honors in her life, including the Nobel Prize for Peace in 1979.

Following a number of years of declining health, Teresa died on September 5, 1997, in Calcutta, where she received a state funeral.

Legacy

At the time of her death, Teresa's order had grown to over 4,500 nuns, more than 400 priests and brothers, and hundreds of

thousands of lay workers worldwide. Her order, the Missionary Sisters of Charity, serves the poor at over 550 sites in 126 countries.

The interests of Teresa and her order are manifold. The order helps abandoned children, the aged, and the homeless. It provides soup kitchens, mobile health clinics, homeless shelters, drug and alcoholism treatment centers, hospices for AIDS victims, and centers for victims of spousal abuse. Teresa helped orphans in war-torn Beirut in 1982, fed the hungry in Ethiopia, treated radiation victims of Chernobyl, and helped people following earthquakes and floods.

Teresa did have her critics—who complained that ministering to the poor without ever trying to better their lot was really putting a kind face on their exploitation. She herself refused to criticize anyone who supported her cause and accepted help from individuals such as Haitian dictator Claude (Baby Doc) Duvalier. Although she lived and worked in one of the world's most populous countries, Teresa was unwavering in her condemnation of birth control and abortion.

Teresa's short-term legacy is a vast one. She left an enormous network of facilities throughout the world to help the sick and needy. Only the future will tell whether her order will continue to grow without her charismatic leadership. Already called "Saint Teresa" during her lifetime, she is believed to be an excellent candidate for Catholic sainthood.

Saltz

For Further Reading:

Sebba, Anne. *Mother Teresa: Beyond the Image.* New York: Doubleday, 1997.

Spink, Kathryn. *Mother Teresa: A Complete Authorized Biography.* San Francisco: Harper, 1997.

Teresa of Ávila, Saint

Christian Mystic; Founder of the Order of Barefoot Carmelites
1515–1582

Life and Work

Teresa of Ávila was one of the Christian church's great mystics, author of several important spiritual works and founder of the religious order of the Discalced (Barefoot) Carmelites.

Teresa was born on March 28, 1515, to a wealthy, noble family in Ávila, Spain. She was a sickly child and would remain plagued by poor health throughout her life. In 1535 she entered the local Carmelite convent and, over the next 20 years, became increasingly drawn to mysticism. Mystics believe that they can come into direct contact with God through spiritual and physical techniques. In 1555–56 she began to have visions of Christ and to experience pain that she said came from an angel's lance piercing her heart.

Long troubled by the slack discipline into which the Carmelites had lapsed, she determined to devote herself to reforming the order. In 1562 she overcame the bitter opposition of her immediate ecclesiastical superiors and founded, at Ávila, the first community of Barefoot Carmelite nuns. Her reform required complete withdrawal from the world so that the nuns could exercise what she termed "our vocation of reparation" for the sins of mankind. In 1567 she was authorized to establish similar religious houses for men. Five years later Pope Gregory XIII recognized the Barefoot Carmelites as an independent monastic body. A gifted organizer despite her frail health, Teresa founded 30 Discalced houses in her lifetime. Teresa died in Alba de Tormes on October 4, 1582.

Teresa wrote several works that have become classics of spiritual literature. Her *Autobiography* (1565) recorded the evolution of her spiritual life and delineated her plans for reform of the Carmelite Order. In *The Interior Castle* (1577), her mystical masterpiece, she analyzed the stages in the process of reaching God. She portrayed the human soul as a castle containing seven "abodes." In the innermost abode dwells God, the Lord of the castle. Through seven degrees of prayer an individual can reach this abode and be absorbed into the divine essence. *The Way of Perfection* (1573) offered advice to her nuns on how to achieve perfection in their religious life.

Teresa was made a saint in 1622 and was proclaimed a Doctor of the Church in 1970, the first woman to be so named.

Legacy

Teresa was a major figure in the history of spirituality and played an important role in the renewal of the Roman Catholic church following the Reformation.

Teresa profoundly influenced the development of Spanish mysticism, including such mystics as St. John of the Cross, who wrote major mystical works and worked with her to reform the Carmelite order. Teresa was the first person to discuss the existence of various states of prayer in the inner journey of souls toward God. She also methodically described the life of prayer as it progressed from meditation to what she termed "spiritual marriage."

Teresa's works concentrated on spiritual development within the contemplative life of a cloistered religious. In the seventeenth century St. Francis de Sales, the bishop of Geneva, modified her ideas to show how one could lead a saintly life in the world.

Teresa also gave spiritual direction to the Counter–Reformation (1534–1685), that period in which the Roman Catholic church was trying to face the challenges posed by the Protestant Reformation. She made the spiritual life a high priority in an age given to the idea of religious triumph through conquest and the Inquisition.

Teresa's legacy lives not only in her religious thought but also in her life. An intelligent, hard-headed yet charming woman, deeply spiritual but still active in the world, she became a model for religious women through the centuries.

Yang

WORLD EVENTS		TERESA'S LIFE
Last Muslim State in Spain falls to Christians	1492	
	1515	Teresa of Ávila is born
Reformation begins	1517	
	1535	Teresa enters local Carmelite Convent of the Incarnation
	1555–56	Teresa has visions of Christ and undergoes a spiritual awakening
	1562	Teresa founds Community of Barefoot Carmelites
	1567	Teresa is authorized to establish Barefoot Carmelite communities for men
	1582	Teresa dies
Thirty Years' War in Europe	1618–48	
	1622	Teresa is canonized
England's Glorious Revolution	1688	

For Further Reading:
Lincoln, Victoria. *Teresa: A Woman: A Biography of Teresa de Avila.* Albany: State University of New York Press. 1984.
Weber, Alison. *Teresa of Avila and the Rhetoric of Femininity.* Princeton, N.J.: Princeton University Press. 1990.

Thales of Miletus

Originator of the Foundations of
Greek Philosophy and Science
c. 624–c. 546 B.C.E.

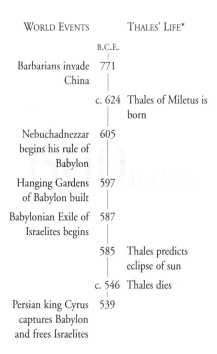

WORLD EVENTS		THALES' LIFE*
	B.C.E.	
Barbarians invade China	771	
	c. 624	Thales of Miletus is born
Nebuchadnezzar begins his rule of Babylon	605	
Hanging Gardens of Babylon built	597	
Babylonian Exile of Israelites begins	587	
	585	Thales predicts eclipse of sun
	c. 546	Thales dies
Persian king Cyrus captures Babylon and frees Israelites	539	

* *Scholars cannot date the specific events in Thales' life with accuracy.*

Life and Work

Thales of Miletus was the first person in Western history to explain the universe in rational rather than mythical terms. His work established the foundations of Greek science and philosophy.

Thales was born in Miletus, the premier city of Archaic Greece (modern Turkey), but little else is known about him. HERODOTUS, a Greek historian from the fifth century B.C.E., and ARISTOTLE are the main sources for his life and work. Even though little is known about his life, Thales came to be known as the first of the "Seven Sages" (wise men) of the ancient world.

While details of his education and early years remain unknown, it is clear that Thales learned astronomy from the Chaldaeans at Babylon. The Milesian philosopher is noted for his contributions in this field as well as those of geometry and cosmology (study of the origins of the universe). According to Herodotus, Thales predicted a full eclipse of the sun. Nineteenth-century astronomers have dated the eclipse to 585 B.C.E., the only relatively secure dating of Thales' life. Thales is said to have introduced geometry to Greece and to have developed the abstract geometry of lines.

Aristotle claimed Thales as the first person to propose natural, rather than mythical, causes for the creation of the *kosmos* (world). In developing a rational theory of the kosmos, Thales asserted that water was the first princi-ple (*arkhe*); that is, water is the material cause of all things. Further, he said that the Earth was a mass that floated on water and that, when earthquakes occurred, they were caused by disturbances in the water. Until Thales, most Greeks supposed that the god Poseidon was responsible for earthquakes; Poseidon, the god of the sea, would strike the Earth with his trident, causing the Earth to shake. Thales based his assertions on observation and specu-lation; he did not test his theories. He is also considered to be the founder of the Milesian school of science. All future natural philoso-phers were indebted to him.

Legacy

Thales was the first known individual to question commonly held assumptions about the physical world. He was also the first person in Western history to propose natural, rather than mythological, causes for the cre-ation and workings of the world. His work led the way for later Greeks to explain the universe and nature in rational terms rather than as caprices of the gods.

Thales introduced a way of thinking based on rational thought and inquiry that domi-nated Greek philosophy and sciences for cen-turies. His approach to philosophy was continued by such members of the Milesian school as Anaximenes and ANAXIMANDER and influenced PLATO and Aristotle. He initiated the process of intellectual inquiry that has fos-tered Western thought through the ages.

Renaud

For Further Reading:
Anglin, W. S. *The Heritage of Thales*. New York: Springer, 1995.
Barnes, Jonathan. *The Presocratic Philosophers*. Boston: Routledge and Paul, 1979.
McKirahan, Richard D. *Philosophy Before Socrates: An Introduction with Texts*. Indianapolis, Ind.: Haskett Publishing Co., 1994.

Thomas Aquinas, Saint

Christian Theologian;
Synthesizer of Faith and Reason
c. 1224–1274

Life and Work

One of the most important theologians of the Roman Catholic church, Thomas Aquinas is most noted for his attempts to synthesize faith and reason.

Aquinas, born of nobility in Aquino, Italy, around 1224, first studied at the Benedictine abbey of Monte Cassino. He later attended the university at Naples and, at 20, joined the Dominicans.

As a monk, he studied in Paris and Cologne from 1246 to 1252 with Albert the Great, a leading scholar who used Aristotelian philosophy in support of Christian teaching. He returned to Paris in 1252 as a student and lecturer. Between 1255 and 1259, Aquinas made early attempts at synthesizing Aristotelian logic with Christian teachings in *On Being and Essence* and *On Truth*. From 1258 to 1268 he taught near Rome in a school sponsored by the papal court. Before his death in 1274, Aquinas once again returned to Paris, engaged in contemporary religious controversies, and continued to write many philosophical and theological trea-

tises. He wrote his greatest work, the three-part *Summa Theologica*, between 1265 and 1272.

Aquinas followed the philosophical tradition of his day and pursued philosophy as the "handmaiden of theology." He studied ARISTOTLE and synthesized Aristotelian commentaries with theological writings, showing that rational arguments complemented and supported basic theological truths. God revealed what natural reason could not know experientially, and these revelations, believable with God's grace, would not contradict reason.

Aquinas argued that particular individuals, not Platonic universals, really exist, that each individual consists both of essence and existence, and that non-corporeal individuals such as immortal souls, angels, and God exist as well. The intellect recognizes and abstracts universal ideas from particular individuals but such ideas exist only in the mind. Furthermore, the fact of one's existence for Aquinas differs from what one is. A definition, for example, denotes the essence of a dragon, what it is, even when no such thing exists.

Aquinas argues that beings such as angels and souls exist, but he is most renowned for the much-debated five ways in which he claims to show the plausibility of God's existence as the non-corporeal, eternal first cause and continuing sustainer of everything that exists. However, questions like whether the universe is eternal or how God relates to creation are unanswerable without revelation. Similarly, while Aquinas maintains that any human being can by reason and conscience discover a natural moral law, other ethical matters such as duties to God require revelation.

In 1274, Pope Gregory X summoned Aquinas to the council at Lyons, France. While en route, Aquinas died on March 7 at the monastery in Fossanuova.

Legacy

The impact of Aquinas extends until the present. Both his efforts to synthesize faith and reason and his insight into Aristotelian philosophy continue to engage the interest of contemporary theologians and philosophers.

In 1277, only three years after his death, Aquinas's assertion that human beings are essentially a unity, not a duality of soul and body, was condemned as heresy by Archbishop Robert Kilwarby of Oxford, England. Only after 1323,

when Aquinas was canonized, were these condemnations withdrawn.

In his own age, Aquinas's synthesizing of faith and reason was but one controversial, creative interpretation of Aristotle among others; John Duns Scotus and William of Ockham (1285–1347) would follow their own paths. Blessed by the Church, though, his assertion that one could know reality exactly as it is through sense perception and intellectual abstraction, that is, that one could understand an individual's essence apart from its existence, remained intellectually dominant until the sixteenth century. Aquinas's thought was superseded by that of such philosophers as RENÉ DESCARTES (1596–1650) and GEORG HEGEL (1770–1831), who argued that the human knower, rather than passively receiving information, actually creatively organized and shaped reality in knowing it. Thomistic thought remained significant only in Spain (until 1700) and in Roman Catholic circles.

In 1850, the Roman Catholic church, in affirming the right and capacity of human reason to attain knowledge, endorsed and encouraged a revival of Aquinas's worldview as an approach more satisfying than current philosophies. In this century, thinkers such as Jacques Maritain, Etienne Gibson, and Bernard Lonergan, sympathetic both to contemporary philosophy and to Aquinas's nontheological insights, have sparked renewed interest beyond Catholic circles in Aquinas's "this-worldly" relevance and the questions of faith and reason. Indeed, preeminent philosophers of religion like Alvin Plantinga maintain that the works of Aquinas still merit and reward careful philosophical scrutiny.

Magurshak

For Further Reading:
Bradley, Denis J. *Aquinas on the Twofold Human Good: Reason and Human Happiness in Aquinas's Moral Science.* Washington, D.C.: Catholic University of America Press, 1997.
O'Meara, Thomas F. *Thomas Aquinas: Theologian.* Notre Dame, Ind.: University of Notre Dame Press, 1997.
Selman, Francis John. *Saint Thomas Aquinas: Teacher of Truth.* Edinburgh: T & T Clark, 1994.

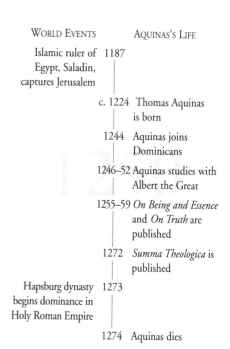

WORLD EVENTS		AQUINAS'S LIFE
Islamic ruler of Egypt, Saladin, captures Jerusalem	1187	
	c. 1224	Thomas Aquinas is born
	1244	Aquinas joins Dominicans
	1246–52	Aquinas studies with Albert the Great
	1255–59	*On Being and Essence* and *On Truth* are published
	1272	*Summa Theologica* is published
Hapsburg dynasty begins dominance in Holy Roman Empire	1273	
	1274	Aquinas dies

Thoreau, Henry David

Leading Transcendentalist
Philosopher
1817–1862

WORLD EVENTS	THOREAU'S LIFE
Napoleonic Wars 1803–15 in Europe	
	1817 Henry David Thoreau is born
Greek War of 1803–15 Independence against Turkey	
	1837 Thoreau graduates from Harvard
	1845–47 Thoreau lives in cabin by Walden Pond
	1846 Thoreau is jailed for not paying poll tax in protest against slavery and Mexican War
Revolutions in 1848 Austria, France, Germany, and Italy	
	1849 *A Week on the Concord and Merrimack Rivers* is published
	1854 *Walden, or Life in the Woods* is published
United States Civil War 1861–65	
Germany is united	1862 Thoreau dies
	1871

Life and Work

Henry David Thoreau was a writer, naturalist, and practical philosopher, a champion of individual liberties, and one of America's foremost Transcendentalists.

Thoreau was born in Concord, Massachusetts, on July 12, 1817. After graduating from Harvard in 1837, he was encouraged by his friend and mentor RALPH WALDO EMERSON to become a writer. In 1845 he built a small cabin near Walden Pond in Concord, where he lived for two years, writing, observing nature, and attempting to live "the simple life." During this time he composed two books, *A Week on the Concord and Merrimack Rivers* (1849) and *Walden, or Life in the Woods* (1854). The latter consisted of a series of 18 essays chronicling his life at Walden Pond and has proven to be his most enduring work.

In July 1846, while still at Walden, Thoreau refused to pay his poll tax as a protest against slavery and the Mexican War, and was sent to jail. Out of this experience emerged an essay, "Resistance to Civil Government," better known as "Civil Disobedience." In this essay Thoreau argued that an individual should obey the dictates of conscience over and above the dictates of civil law, and further advocated "passive resistance" against unjust authorities.

Thoreau's years at Walden constituted the height of his career, but Thoreau continued to write throughout the rest of his life. Always a committed abolitionist, Thoreau's activism intensified late in life and he helped escaped slaves on their way to Canada, lectured against slavery, and publicly defended the radical abolitionist John Brown.

Thoreau died on May 6, 1862, as a result of a long bout with tuberculosis.

Legacy

Thoreau's vision of "the simple life" and, more important, his willingness to not simply preach it but live it have inspired many people—writers, activists, philosophers, and countless others—to take up the challenge of *Walden*, experimenting with new ways of acting and thinking in the world.

During his own lifetime, Thoreau was often dismissed as a mere imitator of Emerson, and even Walden, his most popular book, was a commercial failure. Thoreau was little known in his own lifetime, and virtually forgotten after his death.

By the twentieth century, however, Thoreau's fame had grown. A new interest in the importance of nature led many to Thoreau's writings. Nature writer and conservationist John Muir (1838–1914), for example, was deeply indebted to Thoreau, as were other early conservationists Brenton MacKaye and Lewis Mumford. Today, countless conservationists and environmentalists are deeply influenced by Thoreau's life and thought.

Thoreau has also spoken to the utopian impulse among twentieth-century Americans. During the 1960s and 1970s, in particular, many were drawn by the spirituality of *Walden* and sought to create similar experiments in individual or group living.

Finally, Thoreau's essay "Civil Disobedience" has profoundly influenced the shape of social activism in the twentieth century. MOHANDAS GANDHI was deeply impressed by this essay, and particularly by Thoreau's idea of "passive resistance" to unjust laws. Gandhi used the principle of passive, or nonviolent, resistance in the struggle for the liberation of India from English rule. Similarly, MARTIN LUTHER KING, JR., utilized Thoreau's idea in the civil rights movement of the 1960s.

Smith

For Further Reading:
Bloom, Harold, ed. *Henry David Thoreau: Modern Critical Views.* New York: Chelsea House Publishing, 1988.
Harding, Walter. *The Days of Henry Thoreau.* Princeton, N.J.: Princeton University Press, 1993.

Tillich, Paul

Theologian and Philosopher;
Reconciler of Christian Thought
with Modern Culture
1886–1965

Life and Work

Through his many books, articles, and sermons, Paul Tillich sought to reconcile Christian faith with modern culture. He is generally considered to be one of the twentieth century's most influential theologians.

Tillich was born on August 20, 1886, in the town of Starzeddel, in the German province of Brandenburg. His father was a theologically conservative Lutheran pastor. Tillich himself studied theology at the universities of Berlin, Tübingen, and Halle, and in 1912 was ordained a minister in the Evangelical Lutheran Church. During World War I, Tillich served as an army chaplain, an experience that opened his eyes to the profound problems of modern society and increased his despair over conventional secular and religious solutions. Society, he said, was experiencing a collapse of cultural values that might lead to profound spiritual transformation. During this period he wrote many essays on politics, religion, and history, and published his influential work *The Socialist Decision* (1932), a critique of Hitler's Nazism.

Tillich was always a fervent opponent of the Nazis, and when they came to power in 1933 his opposition to their policies led to his dismissal from the professorship at the University of Frankfurt. He was the first non-Jewish professor "to be so honored," as he put it. Following his dismissal, Tillich immigrated to the United States, teaching first at Union Theological Seminary in New York City (1933–55), then at Harvard University (1955–62), and finally at the University of Chicago (1962–65). His international reputation grew with the publication of several important works, including *The Courage to Be* (1952), *Dynamics of Faith* (1957), and *The Eternal Now* (1963). Probably his greatest achievement, however, was a work entitled *Systematic Theology,* published in three volumes between 1951 and 1963. As the title suggests, this work was the most complete expression of Tillich's thought on religious faith and its ultimate realization in Christian doctrine.

Tillich's last years were spent teaching and writing; he died in Chicago on October 22, 1965.

Legacy

Tillich saw himself as occupying the border between the modern world and conventional religious belief, and his understanding of this border-territory has helped to shape theology, particularly in the United States, since the mid-1950s. His works have encouraged many religious believers to reexamine their faith and inspired some to take committed action for social and spiritual change in their communities.

Tillich's work has been especially influential among Christians who have felt conventional religious explanations to be inadequate to the experience of modern life. Tillich himself rejected the traditional concept of a personal, anthropomorphic God, and he often used terms such as "Ground of Being" or "the Ultimate" rather than "God" to describe the divine. Tillich's radical departure from traditional theology on this point has led some theologians to accuse him of agnosticism or atheism. But others have argued that Tillich simply provides a fuller vision of the divine than that offered by traditional religious understandings.

Tillich also helped shift much of theological debate away from issues of scriptural authority or metaphysical speculation (questions about the nature of reality) and toward a greater emphasis on human experience. This form of "existential theology" has been championed by many theologians in the latter half of the twentieth century, liberation theologian GUSTAVO GUTIÈRREZ and feminist theologian Beverly Wildung Harrison among them. But it has also come under attack from theologians who stress the centrality of Scripture (such as KARL BARTH) as well as those who stress the importance of metaphysical proof (such as Charles Hartshorne).

Smith

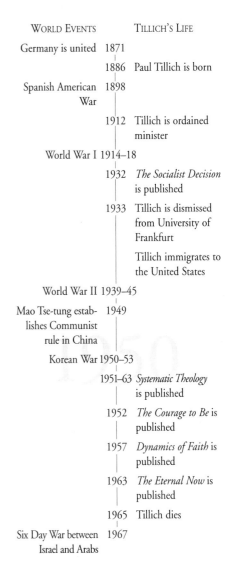

WORLD EVENTS		TILLICH'S LIFE
Germany is united	1871	
	1886	Paul Tillich is born
Spanish American War	1898	
	1912	Tillich is ordained minister
World War I	1914–18	
	1932	*The Socialist Decision* is published
	1933	Tillich is dismissed from University of Frankfurt
		Tillich immigrates to the United States
World War II	1939–45	
Mao Tse-tung establishes Communist rule in China	1949	
Korean War	1950–53	
	1951–63	*Systematic Theology* is published
	1952	*The Courage to Be* is published
	1957	*Dynamics of Faith* is published
	1963	*The Eternal Now* is published
	1965	Tillich dies
Six Day War between Israel and Arabs	1967	

For Further Reading:

Gilkey, Langdon. *Gilkey on Tillich*. New York: Crossroad Publishing Company, 1989.

Kelsey, David H. *The Fabric of Paul Tillich's Theology*. New Haven, Conn.: Yale University Press, 1967.

Newport, John P. *Paul Tillich*. Edited by Bob E. Patterson. Waco, Tex.: Word Books, 1984.

Pauck, Wilhelm. *Paul Tillich: His Life and Thought*. New York: Harper & Row, 1976.

Torquemada, Tomás de

First Grand Inquisitor of Spanish Inquisition
1420–1498

Life and Work

Tomás de Torquemada was the first grand inquisitor of Spain. His name has become synonymous with the horror and bigotry of the Inquisition, the council established by the Roman Catholic church to deal with heresy.

Torquemada was born in Valladolid, Spain, in 1420, most likely to a family of *conversos* (Jewish converts). He entered the Dominican order at a young age, later serving as the prior of the monastery of Santa Cruz in Segovia for 22 years. He was the Infanta (princess) Isabella's confessor and remained so after her marriage to Ferdinand of Aragon in 1469. When Isabella ascended the throne of Castile in 1474, Torquemada became one of her counselors.

In 1478, Pope Sixtus IV empowered Spain independently to convene the Inquisition to deal with the problem of Marranos and Moriscos (Jewish and Muslim converts, respectively) whom the Church believed insincere in their conversion to Christianity. In 1482 Torquemada became an assistant inquisitor and the following year he became grand inquisitor of Castile and Aragon.

As the head of the Inquisition, Torquemada drew up the 28 articles used to question suspects under torture so severe that death was offered as a reward for confession. These articles sought out not only "infidels," but also those who committed such offenses as sorcery, sexual immorality, blasphemy, and usury. In 1484 and 1488 Torquemada added further charges to his list. Once convicted, the prisoners received their sentences at the autos-da-fé, sumptuous public ceremonies in which heretics were condemned and executed. The regular form of punishment was to be burned at the stake. Some estimate that during Torquemada's lifetime over 2,000 such burnings occurred.

Although himself from a *conversos* family, Torquemada was viciously hostile to Jews and began a propaganda campaign that in 1492 persuaded Ferdinand and Isabella to expel all Jews who refused baptism. Those expelled sought refuge largely in Rome and Turkey.

In 1494 Pope Alexander VI (Rodrigo Borgia) tried to restrain Torquemada's juggernaut, but the Inquisition and the Spanish monarchs resisted over issues of sovereignty and money (goods plundered from their victims filled their coffers). As the Pope had the French and the Germans at his doorstep, he had few troops available to send to Spain to enforce his wishes.

Torquemada died in Avila on September 16, 1498.

Legacy

The Spanish Inquisition greatly affected the religious and cultural map of Spain and of much of Europe.

Although Ferdinand and particularly Isabella viewed the Inquisition as a weapon to maintain religious orthodoxy, it was also a major political weapon in the development of royal absolutism, inspiring conformity through terror. The Inquisition waned after Isabella's death in 1504, but was revived in 1520, broadening its focus to include suspected Protestants and unorthodox Catholics. In the sixteenth century it turned its attention to censoring books and enforcing religious and moral standards. Together with the state's prohibition against study abroad, the Inquisition contributed to Spain's intellectual isolation from the rest of Europe. Joseph Bonaparte suppressed the Inquisition in 1808, but it reemerged in 1814 and was finally extinguished by 1834.

Not all Jews were expelled from Spain in 1492. Many *conversos* who were orthodox Roman Catholics remained and contributed significantly to the Spanish renaissance of the sixteenth century. Nevertheless, their position remained precarious. Many suspected that these *conversos* harbored hidden Jewish loyalties and over the course of the sixteenth century statutes regarding *limpieza*, the purity of blood, were issued prohibiting any with the "taint" of *conversos* blood or with ancestors convicted of heresy from ecclesiastical appointments. While these laws helped prevent heresy, their emphasis on ancestry was ultimately a blight on Spanish society.

As a result of the Jews' expulsion from Spain, Jewish culture returned with new life to areas where it had been long absent—especially Turkey and the Holy Land, where they founded the city of Safed as a renowned center of mystical Judaism. This city was also the home of the famous rabbis Moses Cordovero (1522–1570), Joseph Karo (1488–1575), and Isaac Luria (1534–1572), three pillars of Kabbalah. The treasures of those communities remain to instruct and serve as reminders on both sides of this tragic chapter in the histories of Spain, the Roman Catholic church, and Judaism.

Torquemada's fanaticism left a legacy of fear, hatred, and mistrust that persisted throughout Spain for a long time. Unfortunately, much of the great literature and rich culture (music, paintings, dances) of Spain's multicultural heritage was lost and the damage has not yet been fully repaired. Beautiful old synagogues and mosques, whole towns, still lie abandoned throughout the Spanish countryside. Some of this cultural heritage is finally being recovered and revived by tenacious artists in Europe, the United States, and South America.

Honigsberg

WORLD EVENTS		TORQUEMADA'S LIFE
Hong Wo establishes Ming Dynasty in China	1368	
	1420	Tomás de Torquemada is born
Beijing becomes capital of China	1421	
Ottoman Empire captures Byzantine capital, Constantinople	1453	
	1474	Torquemada becomes Queen Isabella's counselor
	1482	Torquemada is appointed assistant inquisitor
	1483	Torquemada becomes Grand Inquisitor of Castile and all of Spain
	1484	Torquemada sets down "28 articles"
Columbus discovers Americas	1492	Torquemada compels expulsion of Jews from Spain
Last Muslim State in Spain falls to Christians		
	1498	Torquemada dies
Reformation begins	1517	

For Further Reading:
Paris, Erna. *The End of Days: A Story of Tolerance, Tyranny, and the Expulsion of the Jews from Spain.* Amherst, N.Y.: Prometheus Books, 1995.
Perez Galdos, Benito. *Torquemada.* New York: Columbia University Press, 1986.

Tutu, Desmond

Anglican Archbishop of South
Africa; Fighter Against Apartheid
1931–

Life and Work

Desmond Tutu was the first black archbishop of Cape Town, South Africa, and
a Nobel Peace Prize winner who was victorious
in his fight against the South African policies
of apartheid, or racial separation.

Tutu was born on October 7, 1931, in
Klerksdorp, Transvaal, South Africa. His father
was a teacher in mission schools, where Tutu
began his education. Tutu wanted to become a
physician but could not afford the training. In
1953 he received a teacher's degree and from
1954 to 1958 taught in various high schools.
From 1958 to 1960 he trained for the
Anglican priesthood; he was ordained a deacon
in 1960 and as a parish priest in 1961. From
1965 to 1967 he lived and worked in England,
where he received a master's degree in theology
from Kings College in London. After his
return to South Africa, he became lecturer at a
Johannesburg theological seminary.

After another stay in England from 1972 to
1975 as associate director of the World
Council of Churches, Tutu was made the dean
of Johannesburg cathedral in 1975. In 1976 he
was appointed bishop of Lesotho, South
Africa, and in 1978 he became the first black

general secretary of the South African Council
of Churches. Under his direction, the Council
played a leading role in the fight against
apartheid, and Tutu became an internationally
recognized spokesman for black African rights
by advocating nonviolent opposition to
apartheid. In 1984, he won the Nobel Peace
Prize for his anti-apartheid struggle.

In 1985 he became the first black bishop of
Johannesburg. For his installation, he needed
special permission to enter the white neighborhood where the ceremony was held.

In 1986 Tutu was elected the first black archbishop of Cape Town, becoming the head of the
Anglican church in South Africa. After the
repeal of the apartheid laws in 1991 and the
release from prison of Nelson Mandela, he
remained a spokesman for black causes and tried
to end black township violence. Tutu retired as
archbishop in 1996 and that same year became
chairman of the controversial Truth and
Reconciliation Commission that heard confessions of crimes committed under apartheid.

Legacy

Tutu's contributions to the history of South
Africa have been enormous. Using his
prestigious positions and international
celebrity, he became the foremost and most
credible critic of the apartheid system, ultimately helping to bring about its downfall.

Tutu was instrumental in bringing international condemnation on apartheid, gaining economic sanctions against, and foreign companies'
disinvestment from, South Africa. Sanctions
contributed to a larger policy that resulted in the
eventual dismantling of apartheid. He also
inspired expressions of black activism like work
stoppages and economic boycotts.

The Truth and Reconciliation Commission
under Tutu was an attempt to heal the many rifts
in South Africa caused by years of apartheid.
People confessed to crimes they had committed
under apartheid and sought amnesty for their
admissions. The Commission's report, issued in
October 1998, did grant amnesty to some but
recommended prosecution for others. It was
criticized both by the black government for calling attention to its excessive violence in trying to
overthrow the apartheid regime, and by the former white government, which thought it would
stir up resentment by blacks against whites.

In addition to the Nobel Prize, Tutu has
received many honorary degrees from universities in a number of countries. Several books of
his speeches and sermons, including *The
African Prayer Book* of 1976, *Crying in the
Wilderness* of 1982, and *Hope and Suffering* of
1983, have been published.

Saltz

WORLD EVENTS	TUTU'S LIFE
World War I 1914–18	
	1931 Desmond Tutu is born in Klerksdorp, Transvaal
World War II 1939–45	
Mao Tse-tung estab-lishes Communist rule in China 1949	
Korean War 1950-53	
	1954 Tutu begins teaching
	1961 Tutu is ordained an Anglican priest
Six Day War between Israel and Arabs 1967	
	1972 Tutu becomes associ-ate director of World Council of Churches
End of Vietnam War 1975	Tutu is made dean of Johannesburg cathedral
	1976 Tutu becomes bishop of Lesotho
	1984 Tutu receives the Nobel Peace Prize
	1985 Tutu is appointed bishop of Johannesburg
	1986 Tutu is elected archbishop, heading South African Anglican church
Dissolution of Soviet Union 1991	
Apartheid in South Africa is dismantled 1994	
	1996 Tutu becomes chairman of Truth and Reconciliation Commission

For Further Reading:
Tlhagale, B., and I. Mosala, eds., *Hammering Swords into Ploughshares: Essays in Honour of Archbishop Mpilo Desmond
Tutu*. Johannesburg: Skotaville Publishers, 1986.
Tutu, Desmond. *The Essential Desmond Tutu*. Compiled by John Allen. Johannesburg: Thorold's Africana Books, 1997.

Urban II, Pope
(Odo of Lagery)
Initiator of the Crusades
c. 1035–1099

Life and Work

Urban II was the Pope who inaugurated the Crusades. He also continued Pope Gregory VII's opposition to the lay investiture of Church officials (the practice of princes conferring spiritual offices) and to the practice of simony, the purchase or sale of religious offices.

World Events		Urban II's Life
Northern Sung Dynasty begins	960	
	c. 1035	Odo of Lagery is born in France
Schism between Roman Catholic and Orthodox Church	1054	
	1073	Odo becomes prior of monastery at Cluny
	1079	Odo named cardinal archbishop of Ostia
	1088	Odo becomes Pope Urban II
	1089	Urban II denounces lay investiture and simony
First Crusade	1095	Urban II launches First Crusade
Crusaders capture Jerusalem during First Crusade	1099	Urban II dies in Rome
Settling of Timbuktu, present-day Mali	c. 1100	

Odo of Lagery was born around 1035 in Chatillon-sur-Marne, France. As a young man, Odo studied with Bruno, founder of the Carthusian religious order. Around 1070 he became a Benedictine monk at Cluny, France. He was named prior of the monastery in 1073.

In about 1079, Pope Gregory VII named Odo cardinal archbishop of Ostia, Rome's port town. From 1084 to 1085 he served as the Pope's legate (official representative) in Germany. In 1088 he ascended to the papacy upon the death of Gregory VII.

Taking the name Urban II, the new Pope faced opposition from the "antipope," Clement III, who occupied the papal throne with the support of Henry IV, the Holy Roman Emperor. Urban II remained in Melfi in southern Italy until 1094, when Henry's power diminished and Urban was able to oust Clement III and move to the papal throne in Rome.

As pontiff, Urban continued and extended the reforms of Gregory VII. He opposed lay investiture and simony. In 1095, he issued a law requiring clerical celibacy.

Urban II's most notable contribution, however, was the initiation of the Crusades. Hoping to unite Western and Eastern Christianity and to defend Byzantine (Eastern Roman) Emperor Alexis I against encroachment from the Seljuk Turks, on November 27, 1095, Urban II preached a passionate sermon to a large crowd at the Council of Clermont, France, to mobilize Christian troops to reclaim the Holy Land of Palestine from the Muslims. The soldiers became known as Crusaders from the large red cross that adorned the front of their uniforms. On July 15, 1099, Crusaders from across Europe claimed Jerusalem.

Urban II never received the news of this victory. He died in Rome just two weeks later on July 29, 1099.

Legacy

Urban II's marshaling of forces for the First Crusade and his ecclesiastic reforms vaulted the power of the papacy to the forefront of Western Christendom.

Through his efforts, Urban II consolidated political power in the papacy. His victory in the investiture controversy and his ousting of Clement III strengthened the role of the papacy in Europe. No longer could temporal authorities entice the loyalty of subjects with the promise of ecclesiastical offices. The right to name bishops was now placed primarily within the Roman Catholic church. The conflict over investiture, however, continued long after Urban II's pontificate, surfacing in France in the seventeenth century and in Spain into the twentieth century

Urban II's most notable legacy, however, remains the initiation of the Crusades. While no Crusade was as successful as the First (1096–1099), they still aroused enthusiasm over the next few centuries. The Second Crusade (1147–1149) was inspired by the preaching of BERNARD OF CLAIRVAUX. As a result, King Louis VII of France and Conrad III of Germany led troops into Palestine, where they suffered defeat. Later Crusades (1189–1192, 1202–1204, 1217–1221, 1248–1254) resulted in similar losses. These Crusades provided a world stage for such European luminaries as King Richard the Lionhearted of England and King Louis IX, St. Louis, of France. They also occasioned the origin of such military orders as the Templars, Hospitalers, and Teutonic Knights. Nevertheless, they produced little permanent change in the political geography of Asia Minor and Palestine. Moreover, whatever benefit the Crusades had in encouraging religious fervor in Europe seems to have been matched by a similar fervor among Muslims to defend their territory.

Despite their apparent failure, the Crusades had more subtle influences. With increased contact with the Muslim world came an increased respect and knowledge of Islam. To encourage missions among these people, the Council of Vienna in 1311 promoted the study of Eastern languages. Further, this contact also allowed European Christians to become acquainted with Islamic advances in the fields of science, medicine, and philosophy. Europeans also encountered the preserved works of such ancient Greek philosophers as PLATO and ARISTOTLE. Thus, the intellectual advantages gained by the Crusades may have ultimately overshadowed the military and political disappointments.

For his contributions to the Church, Urban II was beatified in 1881.

von Dehsen

For Further Reading:
Foss, Michael. *People of the First Crusade.* New York: Arcade Publishing, 1997.
Riley-Smith, Jonathan. *The Crusades: A Short History.* New Haven, Conn.: Yale University Press, 1987.

Vivekananda

(Narendranath Datta or Dutt)

Promoter of Hinduism in
Western Society
1863–1902

Life and Work

Often called the first Hindu missionary to the West, Vivekananda nurtured the development of Hinduism in the West and was a major force in the revival of Hinduism in India.

Born Narendranath Datta in Calcutta, India, on January 12, 1863, Vivekananda was the son of a prosperous lawyer. In 1884 he graduated from Calcutta College and began to prepare to study law. However, his father's death soon thereafter created a spiritual crisis that impelled him on a religious quest.

During his college years, Narendranath belonged to the Brahmo Samaj (Congregation of *brahman*), a movement of Westernized Indians that rejected traditional Hindu polytheism in favor of the monotheism of early Vedanta (religious) texts and that sought to purify Hinduism by removing such elements as temple rituals and image worship. In 1881, he met RAMAKRISHNA, a Bengali mystic who taught him the principles of Advaita Vedanta Hinduism, chief among them the belief in the formlessness of god, that all manifestations of gods were actually a form of the Ultimate Reality. By 1885, Narendranath

accepted Ramakrishna as his guru, or teacher. Ramakrishna appointed him his successor and when the guru died the next year, Narendranath became the guide to the other disciples.

To strengthen his own weakening convictions, in 1890 Narendranath began a pilgrimage throughout India. This pilgrimage led him to develop a way to bring together his own non-dualistic philosophy (a belief that all living beings ultimately merge with the Ultimate Reality), his deep commitment to social concerns, and Ramakrishna's devotional insights.

In 1893, after taking the Sanskrit name Vivekananda ("bliss of discerning knowledge"), he traveled to the United States to address the World Parliament of Religions in Chicago about the universal truth of Hinduism. He insisted that all religions were the manifestation of one Ultimate Reality and that the Brahman (deity) had been incarnated in many forms—Christ, Buddha, as well as Krishna. His speeches attracted widespread support, and he began to develop a worldwide Hindu religious movement. In 1895, he established the Vedanta Society in New York City. It was the first Hindu missionary organization in America. Soon he had chapters of this society in London and Boston, each under the direction of swamis (teachers) from India.

By 1896, Vivekananda had returned to India, where he established the Ramakrishna Mission in Calcutta in 1897, a monastic order focused on education and social service. Its goal was to spread the truths of Hindu philosophy and reform society through love. By the time of his death, the order was organized worldwide. Vivekananda died in India on July 4, 1902.

Legacy

Vivekananda helped shape the Western understanding of Hinduism and reform Hinduism in India.

Vivekananda presented Hinduism as a religion with a place in the modern world and was particularly successful in explaining traditional Hindu ideas in terms accessible to Westerners. He coupled the mystical principles developed by Ramakrishna with the stimulus for social action and promoted a form of Hinduism that appealed both to those who focused on meditation and those who preferred practical involvement in their religion. He transplanted these

reform Hindu concepts to the West in the form of the Vedanta societies that are still active today. His form of "practical Vedanta" became the foundation for the acceptance of Hinduism in Western society. Among his adherents was the writer Christopher Isherwood whose work did much to popularize Hinduism.

Vivekananda also influenced the development of Hinduism in India, where his ideas challenged traditional doctrines and helped shape the Hindu response to secularization and European domination. His impact was felt not only through the Ramakrishna missions but also through his influence on following generations of Hindu thinkers including AUROBINDO GHOSE, who developed a new system of Vedanta—Integral Non-dualism—during the first half of the century, and Sarvepalli Radhakrishnan, the Indian philosopher who served as president of India in the 1960s.

Undergirding all of his efforts was the insight, first learned from Ramakrishna, that all religions were alternate paths to the same god. This theme has become the theoretical foundation for the work of such present-day theologians as Houston Smith, John Cobb, and John Hicks.

von Dehsen

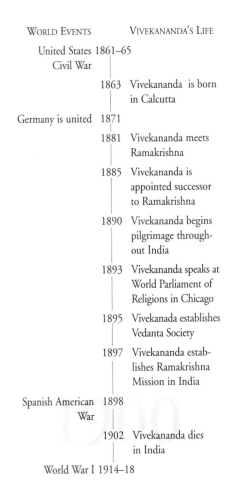

WORLD EVENTS	VIVEKANANDA'S LIFE
United States 1861–65 Civil War	
	1863 Vivekananda is born in Calcutta
Germany is united 1871	
	1881 Vivekananda meets Ramakrishna
	1885 Vivekananda is appointed successor to Ramakrishna
	1890 Vivekananda begins pilgrimage throughout India
	1893 Vivekananda speaks at World Parliament of Religions in Chicago
	1895 Vivekanada establishes Vedanta Society
	1897 Vivekananda establishes Ramakrishna Mission in India
Spanish American 1898 War	
	1902 Vivekananda dies in India
World War I 1914–18	

For Further Reading:

Isherwood, Christopher. *Ramakrishna and His Disciples.* London: Shepheard-Walwyn, 1986.

Jackson, Carl T. *Vedanta for the West: The Ramakrishna Movement in the United States.* Bloomington and Indianapolis: The Indiana University Press, 1994.

Voltaire

(François-Marie Arouet)

Leading Philosopher of the French
Enlightenment
1694–1778

Life and Work

Author and philosopher, Voltaire was one of the dominant figures of the French Enlightenment. Through his writings, he popularized the movement's ideas and promoted the use of reason to overcome what he thought to be the ignorance and superstition of religious teaching.

Born François-Marie Arouet in Paris on November 21, 1694, Voltaire came from a prosperous family. He was educated at Louis le

WORLD EVENTS		VOLTAIRE'S LIFE
English seize Calcutta, India	1690	
	1694	François Marie Arouet (Voltaire) is born
Peace of Utrecht settles War of Spanish Succession	1713–15	
	1726	Voltaire travels to England
	1733	*Letters Concerning the English Nation* is published
	1734–37	*Treatise on Metaphysics* is completed
	1738	*Elements of Newton's Philosophy* is published
	1750–55	Voltaire is court philosopher to Prussia's King Frederick the Great
	1759	*Candide* is published
United States independence	1776	
	1778	Voltaire dies
French Revolution	1789	

Grand, a Jesuit college, an experience that left him deeply hostile to established religion. While in prison for mocking the Duc de Rohan, the regent for King Louis XV, he completed his first play, *Oedipe* (1718), which won him immediate acclaim. It was at this time that he adopted the pen name Voltaire.

After another imprisonment in 1726, Voltaire traveled to England, where he experienced the country's political freedom and religious diversity and was introduced to the works of JOHN LOCKE, Isaac Newton, and GEORGE BERKELEY. He returned to France in 1729 determined to introduce English ideas into his own country. In 1733, he published *Letters Concerning the English Nation,* advocating liberal democratic principles as the basis for human development. A satiric and ironic criticism of royal and religious French authorities, this book won Voltaire the designation *philosophe,* denoting a critic of accepted ideas and customs. The angered response to this work forced Voltaire to flee to eastern France, where he remained for the next 15 years. During this time he completed *Treatise on Metaphysics* (1734–37), *Elements of Newton's Philosophy* (1738), and the novel *Zadig* (1748). Still in exile, he was named a member of the prestigious French Academy.

In 1750, Voltaire became the court philosopher to the Prussian king, Frederick the Great. Voltaire's satire of the Prussian court brought another exile in 1755, this time to Geneva. There, he began writing his most famous novel, *Candide.*

Candide (1759) encapsulates Voltaire's philosophical ideas. Here Voltaire contends that God, if God exists at all, is either unwilling or unable to intervene in human affairs. In fact, Voltaire further believed that the Jewish–Christian religious traditions, which had penetrated all of European culture and education, were the cause of human evil. He maintained that European society should shed its religious shackles and, in their place, embrace the rational principles of the Greek and Roman philosophers. Through these principles, humans can take control of their society by shedding rules based on religious, social, and class distinctions.

Voltaire returned to France in 1758, where he became a leading champion of humanistic causes. He died in Paris on May 30, 1778.

Legacy

Voltaire was one of the "fathers" of the French Enlightenment and a dominant figure of the Age of Reason. His defense of rational humanism, his advocacy of new scientific ideas, and his rejection of royal and religious authority placed him at the forefront of the Enlightenment, which changed the Western world's perception of nature and society.

Voltaire turned a critical eye on many of the major received traditions of France—political theory, science, and, above all, established religion. All were subject to his penetrating analysis and scathing wit. Although he was not a unique thinker, he had an immense impact as a popularizer, disseminating ideas beyond the boundaries of highly educated society and thus contributing to the general transformation of European thinking.

Voltaire's introduction of the ideas of the English Enlightenment into France helped shape the French experience. In his *Letters Concerning the English Nation,* he popularized English institutions and political thought, particularly that of John Locke. Together with BARON DE LA BRÈDE ET DE MONTESQUIEU, he prepared the ground for the political debates about the nature of government that would swirl around the French Revolution of 1789. Voltaire also played a major role in spreading the new philosophy and ideas of science to the general public of continental Europe. He helped move these ideas out of the realm of scientific specialists and into the popular consciousness, where they provided the basis for a new, secular view of the natural world. His historical works pioneered a new approach to historical writing. Rather than present the lives of great men, his writings emphasized broad cultural, political, and social trends and stressed culture and economics as much as politics and war.

Above all, Voltaire provided the model for the enlightened intellectual, a social and political critic of the existing order whose wide-ranging intelligence could solve the basic problems of existence through the use of reason. Voltaire and others who followed him generated an optimism in European society that no problem is too difficult, no ill too severe that it cannot be mastered by human ingenuity guided by rational thought.

von Dehsen

For Further Reading:

Andrews, Wayne. *Voltaire.* New York: New Directions, 1981.

Ayer, A. J. *Voltaire.* London: Weidenfeld and Nicolson, 1986.

Richter, Peyton E. *Voltaire.* Boston: Twayne Publishers, 1980.

Washington, Booker Taliaferro

Influential Educator and Spokesperson for African Americans

1856–1915

Life and Work

Booker T. Washington was the most important African-American leader of his time and the first president and principal developer of the Tuskegee Institute.

Washington was born into slavery and extreme poverty on April 5, 1856, in Franklin County, Virginia. Following the Civil War, his family moved to Malden, West Virginia, where, starting at age nine, Washington went to work in the coal mines, receiving virtually no education. In 1872 he enrolled at the Hampton Normal and Agricultural Institute, working as a janitor to support himself. (A "normal" school is one that trains teachers.) After further studies at the Wayland Seminary in 1878 and 1879, he began teaching at Hampton.

In 1881, Washington was asked to teach at Tuskegee Normal, a newly established school for blacks in Alabama. Washington became president of the school and devoted the rest of his life to its expansion.

This post-Reconstruction period (c. 1877) was one of intense racial bias and increasing segregation, especially in the South. Washington felt that the best way for blacks to better themselves in those times was by learning a craft or trade to gain economic security. Only through the acquisition of money and education, he contended, could blacks hope to win equality with whites. He urged that blacks temporarily put aside their efforts to win political and civil rights; it would be their education and wealth that would gain the respect of the white community and eventual acceptance as equals.

A noted speech at the Atlanta Exposition in 1895, where he advocated social separateness, but cooperation for "mutual progress," gained Washington the attention of the white community. Most blacks at that time were illiterate farm workers; they accepted his ideas, and his nonthreatening stance gained him great acceptance among whites. He became an important fund-raiser for black causes and an advisor to Presidents Theodore Roosevelt and William Howard Taft. He received honorary degrees from Harvard in 1896 and Dartmouth in 1901. Washington died on November 14, 1915, in Tuskegee, Alabama.

Legacy

Although Washington has a mixed legacy as a spokesman for racial equality, he was an ardent believer in the power of education and devoted his working life to expanding the Tuskegee Institute, which now stands as his greatest legacy.

When Washington arrived at Tuskegee, he was the only teacher for 30 students, and the institute's budget was $2,000 per year. When he died, the institute had 100 buildings, a faculty of almost 200 instructing in 38 professions and trades, a student body of about 1,500, and a $2 million endowment. Today Tuskegee University (as it is now called) has a student body of more than 3,000 and contains colleges of arts and sciences, agriculture, home economics, business, education, engineering and architecture, nursing and allied health, and veterinary medicine. Its large campus is a historic landmark.

During his lifetime, Washington's moderate views made him the most influential black spokesman to both the black and white com-

munities. He was strongly opposed by more militant spokesmen such as W. E. B. Du Bois, who demanded immediate political equality, but most people—black and white—then seemed more at ease with Washington's views.

In addition to Tuskegee University, Washington's legacy comprises several books including an autobiography, *Up from Slavery*, published in 1901 and printed in many languages.

Washington's ideas about compromises among racial groups can be viewed historically as a forerunner of the more vigorous efforts to obtain civil rights undertaken during the latter half of the twentieth century. In essence, Washington blazed a path toward racial harmony later followed by others and has remained high in the pantheon of African-American leaders.

Saltz

WORLD EVENTS		WASHINGTON'S LIFE
Revolutions in Austria, France, Germany, and Italy	1848	
	1856	Booker T. Washington is born
United States Civil War	1861–65	
Germany is united	1871	
	1872	Washington enrolls at Hampton Institute
	1878–79	Washington attends Wayland Seminary
	1879	Washington begins teaching at Hampton
	1881	Washington begins teaching at Tuskegee Normal School
	1895	Washington gives noted speech at Atlanta Exposition
	1896	Washington receives honorary degree from Harvard
Spanish American War	1898	
	1901	*Up from Slavery* is published
World War I	1914–18	
	1915	Washington dies

For Further Reading:

Harlan, Louis R. *Booker T. Washington: The Making of a Black Leader, 1856–1901.* New York: Oxford University Press, 1972.

Harlan, Louis R. *Booker T. Washington: The Wizard of Tuskegee, 1901–1915.* New York: Oxford University Press, 1983.

Washington, Booker T. *Up from Slavery: An Autobiography.* New Brunswick, N.J.: Transaction Publishers, 1997.

Wesley, John

Anglican Clergyman;
Founder of Methodism
1703–1791

Life and Work

Having a deep desire to realize his faith in acts of compassion, John Wesley initiated a renewal movement within the Church of England (Anglican church) that eventually led to the formation of the Methodist church.

The son of an Anglican clergyman, Wesley was born on June 17, 1703, in Epworth, England. He was educated at Christ Church College, Oxford, and in 1728 was ordained a priest. He served as his father's curate for two years before returning to Oxford as a fellow at Lincoln College. There he joined a student "Holy Club," dedicated to earnest study, support of the poor, and instruction for poor children. This group was also known derisively as "methodist" for its methodical adherence to its religious principles.

In 1735 Wesley became a missionary to the new American colony of Georgia. During his trip he met Moravians, German pietists whose emphasis on good works as visible expressions of their faith greatly impressed him. The main themes of their pietism—rebirth, atonement, and sanctification—had a significant impact on the development of his theology.

Wesley's mission to Georgia proved a failure, and he returned to England in 1738 to continue his missionary work. Preaching the doctrine of personal salvation through Christ, he attracted huge crowds, particularly from the working class, who were disturbed by the established church's formalism and rationalism. Wesley emphasized sanctification, the process by which one becomes holy, and the belief that the sanctified could lead lives free from conscious sin. He also stressed the importance of manifesting divine love through service to others. He set forth his teachings in four volumes of *Sermons* (1744–1760) and *Explanatory Notes upon the New Testament* (1755), works that form the basis of Methodist theology

Wesley's activities alienated the established church and made separation inevitable. In 1739, he began to organize a Methodist society in London. Although he never formally renounced his ties to the Church of England, he continued to organize Methodist societies during the 1740s and in 1784 provided for the legal incorporation of the movement.

Wesley died on March 2, 1791.

Legacy

Wesley's missionary activity led to the foundation of the Methodist church, one of the major branches of Western Christianity.

The Methodist church did not officially separate from the Anglican church until after Wesley's death in 1791. Schisms arose within the denomination in the early nineteenth century, with each group maintaining its own version of the Wesleyan tradition. These divisions, however, were restored over time, culminating in the formation of the Methodist church in 1932.

In Britain, Methodism initially attracted people of humble origin, although their Puritan virtues frequently brought them prosperity. The church was a stabilizing force for the working class, and some historians have argued that it helped Britain escape the social conflict that erupted in continental Europe during the first half of the nineteenth century. Methodism was centered in the industrial regions of the nation and, as a result, it established strong historical ties with the British labor movement. The church's emphasis on lay leadership provided trade union leaders with experience in administration and organization.

Methodism was transported to the American colonies in the 1760s and soon became an important part of American religious life. Methodists played a prominent role in the Second Great Awakening, the religious revival that swept the United States from 1790 to 1830, and their circuit riders were missionaries during the country's westward expansion. Methodist camp meetings and revivals became a part of the national tradition. The Methodist Episcopal church, formally organized in 1784, did not remain united for long. During the early nineteenth century African Americans formed the African Methodist Episcopal church in response to the denomination's insistence on segregation. The largest schism occurred in 1844 over the issue of slavery, when the church split along North–South lines. The twentieth century saw reunification with the ultimate formation of the United Methodist church in 1968.

Wesley's emphasis on sanctification and his teaching that Christians may achieve moral perfection and lead lives free from conscious sin gave impulse to the theological holiness movement of the mid-nineteenth century. Revivalists such as Charles G. Finney, preaching that Christians could overcome sin, attracted Quakers, Congregationalists, and Baptists, as well as Methodists to the movement. Ultimately the movement led to the formation of the Church of the Nazarene and the Wesleyan church.

A testament to Wesley's influence, Methodist churches existed in such diverse countries as Canada, India, Australia, Japan, and Zambia by the end of the twentieth century. There are approximately 50 million Methodists worldwide.

Olson

World Events		Wesley's Life
English seize Calcutta, India	1690	
	1703	John Wesley is born in Lincolnshire
Peace of Utrecht settles War of Spanish Succession	1713–15	
	1726	Wesley becomes Fellow at Lincoln College, Oxford
	1728	Wesley is ordained priest of Church of England
	1735–38	Wesley becomes missionary in colony of Georgia
	1739	Wesley establishes first Methodist society in London
	1744	Wesley calls first Methodist Annual Conference
United States independence	1776	
	1784	Wesley provides for legal incorporation of Methodism
French Revolution	1789	
	1791	Wesley dies
Napoleonic Wars in Europe	1803–15	

For Further Reading:

Baker, Frank. *John Wesley and the Church of England*. Nashville, Tenn.: Pantheon, 1966.

Heitzenrater, Richard P. *Wesley and the People Called Methodists*. Nashville, Tenn.: Abingdon Press, 1995.

Wana, W. Reginald. *The Protestant Evangelical Awakening*. Cambridge: Cambridge University Press, 1992.

White, Ellen Gould

Founder and Spiritual Leader of
the Seventh-Day Adventists
1827–1915

Life and Work

Ellen Gould White was the principal founder of the Seventh-Day Adventist Church. Through her writings, administrative gifts, and teaching, White formulated the doctrinal foundations of the church and fostered the growth of the denomination.

White was born Ellen Gould Harmon on November 26, 1827, in Gorham, Maine. In 1840 she, along with thousands of others, was converted to the Adventism of William Miller. Miller, a Baptist preacher, predicted that the second coming of Christ would occur on October 22, 1844. When that day passed uneventfully, most of Miller's disappointed followers drifted away but Harmon was not discouraged.

After a bout of serious illness, Harmon had the first of some 2,000 religious visions and began to write and teach among the remnants of Miller's followers in New England. In 1846 she married an Adventist preacher, James White. He began publication of the first church paper, *The Advent Review and Sabbath Herald*, in 1850.

In 1855 the Whites moved to Battle Creek, Michigan, and established the Adventist headquarters there. Five years later the loosely associated Adventist churches adopted the name Seventh-Day Adventists, and in 1863 the congregations were formally organized with a membership of about 3,500.

Over the years White wrote and preached what became the tenets of the denomination. Central to Adventist faith is the belief that the Sabbath should be observed on Saturday instead of Sunday; that the Bible is the word of God; that Christ's return to Earth is imminent; and that White's writings "are a continuing and authoritative source of truth. . . ." Because of White's experience with serious illness, health concerns play a prominent role in the denomination's thinking. Adventists practice vegetarianism and do not use tobacco, coffee, tea, alcohol, or drugs.

Under White's direction the Adventists expanded their program to build health and educational institutions. In 1866 she oversaw the establishment of a sanitarium, the Western Health Reform Institute. She founded Battle Creek College in 1875 and the College of Medical Evangelists in 1906.

White wrote about many subjects including religion, health, social concerns, education, evangelism, publishing, nutrition, and management. Her two most important books are a five-volume study of the conflict between good and evil, *Conflict of the Ages,* published in 1888, and *Steps to Christ* (1892), a step-by-step course on how to become and remain a Christian.

Beginning in 1874, White sent Adventist missionaries to other countries. Following her husband's death in 1881, she began traveling around the United States, Europe, Australia, and New Zealand. White moved to California in 1900 and died there on July 16, 1915.

Legacy

At her death, White left an expanding church, a body of writing including some 5,000 articles and 49 books, and a number of institutions serving the community and reflecting her interests in health reform and education.

Many of the institutions founded by White and her husband in the nineteenth century are still in existence and have served as the basis of many more. The Western Health Reform Institute was the first of a number of sanitariums built by the church and is a model of its kind. Battle Creek College is now Andrews University and the College of Medical Evangelists became the Loma Linda University and Medical Center in southern California. White's emphasis on health and nutrition had an indirect impact on contemporary American society. One of her followers, James Kellogg, created a breakfast cereal empire in Battle Creek.

White's writing, probably because of the church's extensive publishing program, has been translated more than any other author in literary history. James White's paper is still published today as the *Adventist Review* along with many other church periodicals in many languages.

As of June 1997, church statistics listed more than 42,000 churches worldwide, including some 4,700 in North America. In addition, the Adventists can boast over 5,400 schools and universities, more than 600 hospitals, sanitariums, and other medical facilities, and some 55 publishing houses and branches throughout the world. The church claims about 10 million members in more than 200 countries.

Saltz

World Events	White's Life
Greek War of 1821–29 Independence against Turkey	
	1827 Ellen Gould Harmon is born
	1846 Harmon marries James White
Revolutions in 1848 Austria, France, Germany, and Italy	
	1850 *The Advent Review and Sabbath Herald* is first published
	1860 Adventist churches adopt name Seventh-Day Adventists
United States 1861–65 Civil War	
	1863 Adventist church is formally organized
Germany is united 1871	
	1888 *Conflict of the Ages* is published
Spanish American 1898 War	
World War I 1914–18	
	1915 White dies in California

For Further Reading:
Damsteegt, P. Gerard. *Foundations of the Seventh-Day Adventist Message and Mission.* Grand Rapids, Mich.: Eerdmans, 1977.
Numbers, Ronald L. *Prophetess of Health: Ellen G. White and the Origins of Seventh-Day Adventist Health Reform.*
Knoxville: University of Tennessee Press, 1992.

Wise, Isaac Mayer

Founder of American
Reform Judaism
1819–1900

Life and Work

One of the most important figures in American Jewish life, Isaac Mayer Wise was the founder and early leader of American Reform Judaism.

Born on March 29, 1819, in Steingrub, Bohemia (now the Czech Republic), Wise had an unconventional education for a Central European Jew, studying German philosophy along with traditional religious texts. He became a rabbi in 1843 and served a congregation in Radnice, Bohemia, for two years. Unhappy with traditional Judaism and with European prejudice, he immigrated to the United States in 1846. He became rabbi of Congregation Beth El, in Albany, New York, where he cautiously began to introduce his reforms, among them eliminating the traditional separation of the sexes during worship services. His ideas were so controversial that they divided the congregation and he resigned in 1850. In 1854, Wise accepted a rabbinical position in Cincinnati, Ohio. The congregation was receptive to his ideas, and in time Cincinnati became the center of American Reform Judaism.

Over the years Wise oversaw a dramatic revision in Jewish practice. He ignored traditional dietary laws, saying Judaism did not reside in "the victuals." Wise conducted services in English rather than Hebrew, eliminated traditional symbols, did away with two-day Jewish holidays and introduced the use of choirs and organs. In 1857 he published the *Minhag America (American Usage)*, a prayer book in which he tried to bring the service in line with the times. He publicized his reforms through an English-language periodical, the *American Israelite*, and the German-language *Die Deborah*.

Although progressive in practice, Wise remained theologically conservative. He accepted the Torah (the first five books of the Old Testament) as the revealed word of God and authoritative law, but he believed that only the 10 Commandments were binding on individuals. The remainder of the Torah and the writings of the rabbis he thought open to interpretation.

In 1873 Wise helped form the Union of American Hebrew Congregations (UAHC), an association of synagogues in the South and Midwest. Two years later he became president of the newly created Hebrew Union College, a rabbinical school associated with the UAHC. He remained its president until his death. In 1889 he became president of the Central Conference of American Rabbis, the governing body of Reform Judaism, another post he kept until his death.

Wise died in Cincinnati on March 26, 1900.

Legacy

Wise's organizational skills and his drive to create a modern American Judaism gave institutional form to Reform Judaism. Primarily a man of action rather than a theologian, Wise developed the practices and created the organizations that form the core of contemporary Reform Judaism. Hebrew Union College, now known as the Hebrew Union College–Jewish Institute of Religion, still trains Reform clergy. The Union of American Hebrew Congregations eventually outgrew its Southern–Midwestern roots and became a confederation of American and Canadian Reform temples.

In 1894 *The Union Prayer Book* was published superseding Wise's *Minhag America*. Although Wise did not have an active part in compiling it, it came about largely because of Wise's outspoken, life-long call for it. The book is still used today in Reform services.

At the time of Wise's death, the Reform movement dominated American Judaism. The movement lost that position with the influx of Orthodox Eastern European Jews around the turn of the century. The Orthodox viewed Reform Jews as pagans, while Reform Jews looked upon the newcomers as superstitious rabble. As the Eastern Europeans assimilated into United States society, the tensions between the communities died and many of the immigrants' children joined Reform congregations, pushing the movement in a more conservative direction. For example, symbols of traditional Judaism were reintroduced. In contrast to the early Reform leaders who emphasized that Judaism was a religious community not a nation, the contemporary Reform movement increased emphasis on Jewish culture. In fact, the Conservative branch of Judaism began under the leadership of Solomon Schechter to find a middle way between Reform and Orthodox Judaism.

Today Reform Judaism is a large and vibrant part of Jewish life in the United States with two million members in over 850 congregations.

Saltz

For Further Reading:

Silverstein, Alan. *Alternatives to Assimilation: The Response of Reform Judaism to American Culture, 1840–1930.*
Hanover, N.H.: Published for Brandeis University Press by University Press of New England, 1994.
Temkin, Sefton D. *Isaac Mayer Wise, Shaping American Judaism.* Oxford and New York: Published for the Littman
Library by Oxford University Press, 1992.

Wittgenstein, Ludwig

Major Philosopher of the Twentieth Century
1889–1951

Life and Work

Ludwig Wittgenstein was a philosopher at Cambridge University in England; his work concentrated on "reality" and language, postulating different relationships between these terms as he continued to think about them over the course of his career.

Wittgenstein was born on April 26, 1889, in Vienna. Schooled in Austria until age 17, he studied in Berlin to be an engineer and, in 1908, went to England to experiment with the manufacture of airplane engines. Becoming fascinated by mathematics, Wittgenstein enrolled at Cambridge in 1911 to study mathematics and logic with BERTRAND RUSSELL, author of *The Principles of Mathematics*. While in the Austrian army during World War I, Wittgenstein kept a notebook, which was published in 1921 as his first great work, *Tractatus Logico-philosophicus*. His most acclaimed work, *Tractatus* considers a vast range of topics in a scant 75 pages. It posits a strict relationship between language and the physical world, saying: a sentence that says something (a proposition) is a "picture of reality"; so by arranging simple signs (words, letters, and punctuation), language can be said to "touch reality."

Wittgenstein did not return to Cambridge for 10 years after writing *Tractatus*. During this time, he gave away a large fortune inherited from his father, worked as a teacher, battled depression, and spent two years building a mansion in Vienna for his sister. In 1929, he became a fellow at Cambridge University's Trinity College, where he developed a philosophy contradictory to his earlier thinking. Wittgenstein was appointed to the chair in philosophy at Cambridge in 1939. During World War II, he worked at an English hospital. Shortly after the war, he left his university chair to concentrate on writing.

His second major work, *Philosophical Investigations* (1953), was published after his death and criticized his earlier thoughts. His later philosophy declared that language is a "game" with many conventions, in which meaning is affected by the "context in which the words are composed" rather than by a strict and formal relationship to "reality."

Wittgenstein was diagnosed with cancer in 1949, but continued to write intensively until his death on April 29, 1951, in Cambridge, England.

Legacy

Wittgenstein energized philosophy in the twentieth century. His writing, life, and lectures had an intensity that was in many ways overwhelming. His work embodies the wrestling with words, meanings, and "reality" that absorbed most philosophical minds in the latter part of the century.

The thought of Wittgenstein's *Tractatus* helped form the Logical Positivist movement, which flourished in the 1930s. *Language, Truth and Logic*, published by A. J. Ayer in 1936, was a pivotal work of that movement. The Logical Positivists believed that traditional metaphysical ideas must be rejected in favor of scientifically verifiable facts. They sought to distinguish cognitive (factual) meaning from expressive (emotive) significance and insisted that emotive kinds of expression should not be mistaken for genuinely cognitive meanings. The need for a "genuinely cognitive" statement to be empirically verifiable played a major part in Wittgenstein's early philosophy of the *Tractatus*.

Wittgenstein's later philosophy deeply influenced the Analytic (or Linguistic) Philosophy movement, which flourished between 1945 and 1960. *The Concept of the Mind*, published by Gilbert Ryle in 1949, was a central work of this school, as was J. L. Austin's *How to Do Things with Words* (1962), which provides a theory of all uses for language. Analytic philosophers believed that traditional philosophical problems could be "solved" by focusing on the words used to discuss those problems. When that method is used, one is then able to point out "mistakes about the meaning of those words" that have "created" the problems. This idea that philosophy is a "therapy" for conceptually confused intellects was expounded in Wittgenstein's later philosophy, his post-1929 Cambridge lectures, and *Philosophical Investigations*.

Analytic Philosophy began in 1960 after W. V. Quine published *Word and Object,* a work that returned to and further developed the Logical Positivist thought of the 1930s. Similarities are currently being investigated between Wittgenstein's work and that of the French philosopher and deconstructionist, JACQUES DERRIDA (e.g., Derrida's *Of Grammatology* [1967]). Wrestling with words, meanings, and "reality" is carried on today by philosophers, psychologists, linguists, psychotherapists, cultural critics, and other thinkers. Many of the specialized elements in this broad spectrum of thought are anticipated in Wittgenstein's work.

K. T. Weidmann

WORLD EVENTS		WITTGENSTEIN'S LIFE
Germany is united	1871	
	1889	Ludwig Wittgenstein is born
Spanish American War	1898	
	1908	Wittgenstein works as engineer in England
	1911	Wittgenstein attends Cambridge University and studies with Bertrand Russell
World War I 1914–18		
	1921	*Tractatus Logico-philosophicus* is published
	1929	Wittgenstein becomes fellow at Trinity College, Cambridge
	1939	Wittgenstein is appointed to chair in philosophy at Cambridge
World War II 1939–45		
Mao Tse-tung establishes Communist rule in China	1949	
Korean War 1950–53		
	1951	Wittgenstein dies
	1953	*Philosophical Investigations* is published posthumously
Six Day War between Israel and Arabs	1967	

For Further Reading:

Malcolm, Norman. *Ludwig Wittgenstein: A Memoir*. 2nd ed. with Wittgenstein's letters to Malcolm. New York: Oxford University Press, 1984.

Monk, Ray. *Ludwig Wittgenstein: The Duty of Genius*. New York: Free Press, 1990.

Wittgenstein, Ludwig. *Tractatus Logico-philosophicus*. With introduction by Bertrand Russell. London: Routledge, 1981.

Wovoka

Native American Religious Leader;
Leader of Ghost Dance Movement
c. 1856–1932

Life and Work

Wovoka was the Paiute religious leader who became the prophet of the Ghost Dance movement of 1890.

Wovoka was born near Walker Lake in western Nevada between 1856 and 1858. His father, Tavibo, was a prophet of the first Ghost Dance of 1870, a messianic movement among the Plains Indians that preached the resurrection of the dead and the revival of traditional tribal life, which had been disrupted by white settlers streaming across the frontier. In order to hasten the promised renewal, people were instructed to perform the traditional Paiute Ghost Dance, a circle dance thought to imitate the dancing of the dead.

Following his father's death, Wovoka worked for a family named Wilson, becoming known as Jack Wilson among white settlers. His job brought him into contact with Shakers, Mormons, and Christian groups whose theme of

resurrection as well as a strict moral code influenced his evolving religious thought.

During the 1880s Wovoka returned to the Paiutes, where he acquired a reputation as a spiritual leader. By mid-decade he claimed that he had been taken into heaven in a trance and given miraculous powers. Following a serious illness in 1889, he announced that God had promised to renew the land, return the Indian dead to life, and end death and misery if the people lived upright lives, avoided war among themselves and with whites, and performed the Ghost Dance monthly.

Wovoka's message led to a major religious revival among the Western tribes, many of which sent representatives to meet the prophet. They returned to their reservations interpreting his message to meet their needs and adapting his rituals to their traditions. Among the tribes that embraced his teachings were the Arapaho, Cheyenne, Kiowa, Caddo, and Lakota Sioux.

The movement's spread, particularly among the militant Sioux, alarmed United States officials who made repeated attempts to suppress the cult. The result was the Ghost Dance Uprising that culminated in the Massacre at Wounded Knee, South Dakota, in 1890. There U.S. troops killed over 200 Lakota men, women, and children. A pacifist, Wovoka urged his people to stop dancing, and the movement gradually faded.

Wovoka worked as a shaman (holy man) and healer for the rest of his life. He died at the Yerington Indian Colony in Nevada on September 29, 1932.

Legacy

Wovoka led one of the great Native American religious revivals of the nineteenth century; it helped shape the Indian response to the incursion of white government and society.

Native Americans of the western Plains reached out to Wovoka and the Ghost Dance as an alternate to the future offered by encroaching white society. Beset by starvation, loss of ancestral land, forced relocation, religious persecution, and efforts to impose assimilation, they looked to the cult as a means of controlling their own destiny. The movement also promised to renew the traditional religion under which their society had flourished.

Although many Native Americans abandoned the Ghost Dance after Wounded Knee, it continued among some Plains tribes into the twentieth century and extended Wovoka's influence into

contemporary times. The Kiowa priest Afraid-of-bears reinterpreted the Ghost Dance for his people and served as its missionary until the federal government suppressed the tribe in 1916. At that time the Bureau of Indian Affairs forced the Kiowa to sign an agreement promising not to hold the dance in return for tribal rations and government funds. Fred Robinson continued the movement among the Dakota people in Saskatchewan, but because Canadian officials opposed the Ghost Dance, they were forced to practice it in secret. The last recorded Ghost Dances were held in the 1950s among the Dakotas and Shoshoni. Some have suggested that the movement went underground for several decades and elements of it reemerged during the Native American protest movements of the 1970s.

Wovoka's movement had a long-range impact on the Native Americans of the West. His message urging Indians to lead moral lives, work with European settlers, and end warfare helped many in the traumatic transformation of Native American life that occurred as the frontier closed and Native Americans were forced into the reservation system. The portions of his message that mirrored Christian teachings also made many receptive to Christianity. Most important, the spread of the movement among various tribes led Native Americans to perceive themselves not just as members of a specific, small group but as part of a larger Indian nation. During the late twentieth century this pan-Indian identity led to the formation of organizations such as the National Congress of American Indians and the American Indian Movement, which pushed for Native American rights.

von Dehsen

WORLD EVENTS		WOVOKA'S LIFE
Revolutions in Austria, France, Germany, and Italy	1848	
	c. 1856	Wovoka is born
United States Civil War	1861–65	
Germany is united	1871	
	1880s	Paiutes recognize Wovoka as spiritual leader
	1889	Wovoka preaches ideas of Ghost Dance movement
	1890	U.S. Army massacres 200 Lakota Sioux at Wounded Knee, S.D.; Wovoka urges end to Ghost Dancing
Spanish American War	1898	
World War I	1914–18	
	1932	Wovoka dies
World War II	1939–45	

For Further Reading:
Kehoe, Alice Beck. *The Ghost Dance: Ethnohistory and Revitalization.* New York: Holt, Rinehart and Winston, 1989.
Mooney, James. *The Ghost-Dance Religion and the Sioux Outbreak of 1890.* Chicago: Chicago University Press, 1965.

Wycliffe, John

English Church Reformer;
Forerunner of the Protestant
Reformation

c. 1330–1384

Life and Work

John Wycliffe was an English philosopher and theologian whose ideas presaged the Protestant Reformation of the sixteenth century.

Little is known of Wycliffe's early life. He was born in Yorkshire around 1330 and educated at Oxford, from which he received a doctor of divinity degree in 1372. For most of his life he taught philosophy at the university while nominally serving as a priest in various parishes.

During the mid-1370s Wycliffe became deeply embroiled in the struggle between the Crown and the ecclesiastical hierarchy over control of the English Catholic church. In a series of works including *On Divine Lordship, On Civil Leadership,* and *On the Duty of the King,* Wycliffe argued that all authority is derived directly from God and is forfeit by those in a state of mortal sin. Implying that the English Church was in such a condition, he called upon it to divest itself of worldly possessions and return to apostolic poverty and purity. He advocated that the state supervise this reform. Wycliffe's ideas earned him the support of John of Gaunt, the leader of the anti-papal faction in Parliament, who initially protected him from attempts by the Pope and English bishops to condemn him for heresy.

In 1378 Wycliffe began a systematic attack on key elements of contemporary Church doctrine and practice. He asserted that the Bible was the sole source of doctrine (*sola scriptura*) and questioned both papal authority and monasticism as not based on scripture. Most significant, he condemned the doctrine of transubstantiation (that the bread and wine used in the Mass become Christ's actual body and blood after the priest consecrates them) as philosophically unsound. Instead he asserted that they remain bread and wine after consecration but that Christ is present in the sacrament in a noncorporeal way.

Because of his emphasis on scripture, Wycliffe encouraged his followers to translate the Bible into English so that all who could read would know God's law. He also established an order of Poor Preachers to spread the biblical message.

Wycliffe's radical stand on transubstantiation cost him John of Gaunt's support. In 1382 an English ecclesiastical court denounced his teachings, and he was expelled from Oxford. He retired to a parish in Lutterworth, where he died on December 31, 1384. In 1415 the Council of Constance, a general council of the Church, condemned Wycliffe as a heretic. His remains were disinterred and burned in 1428.

Legacy

Called the "Morning Star of the Reformation" by his supporters, Wycliffe influenced early continental Church reformers and prepared the ground for the Protestant Reformation in England.

Wycliffe had a significant influence on JAN HUS, the fifteenth-century theologian who preached reform in Bohemia (part of the present-day Czech Republic). Like Wycliffe, Hus condemned clerical abuse and challenged the structure and authority of the medieval Church. Hus adopted much of Wycliffe's theology, including his emphasis on the importance of scripture as authority. Nevertheless he saw a place for conscience and tradition in determining doctrine and did not preach *sola scriptura,* the teaching that only the Bible is theologically authoritative and that all other sources of revelation—tradition, conscience—must give way to the authority of scripture. More important, he retained the doctrine of transubstantiation. In 1415 the Council of Constance, which condemned Wycliffe, sentenced Hus to be burned at the stake for refusing to recant his "Wycliffite heresies." Hus's thought spread throughout Bohemia, so that by the sixteenth-century Protestant Reformation, the Bohemian church had been reformed for over 150 years. MARTIN LUTHER (1483–1546) knew of Wycliffe through Hus's writings, but the influence of the English theologian on the German reformer is open to debate.

Following Wycliffe's death, the Lollards, as his followers became known, spread his teachings throughout England. His emphasis on scripture inspired Nicholas of Hereford and John Purvey to produce the first full English translation of the New Testament. Until the mid-fifteenth century Wycliffe's theology found supporters in academia and among the aristocracy, but the movement was gradually suppressed after 1401 when laws introduced death by burning at the stake for heresy. The Lollard Bible was banned in 1407 and the movement lost support among politically important groups after it was connected with the 1414 Oldcastle uprising against the king.

In response to the persecution, Lollardy went underground. The movement was embraced by yeomen and artisans who met secretly in homes to study scripture and other texts. These supporters revered Wycliffe but ultimately diluted the intellectual content of his theology. Yet the Lollards' emphasis on moral law, their understanding of the Eucharist, and their hatred of images were reflected in English Reformation thought. Both William Tyndale (c. 1494–1536), who produced an English translation of the Bible, and THOMAS CRANMER (1489–1556), the archbishop of Canterbury who presided over the Reformation under King Edward VI, were influenced by the movement.

von Dehsen

WORLD EVENTS		WYCLIFFE'S LIFE
Muscovite state, present-day Russia, established by Ivan I	1325	
	c. 1330	John Wycliffe born
The Plague (Black Death) in Europe	1347–53	
Hong Wo establishes Ming Dynasty in China	1368	
	1372	Wycliffe receives doctor of divinity degree from Oxford
	1376	Wycliffe begins publishing theories of authority within Church
	1378	Wycliffe begins attack on Church doctrine and practice
	1384	Wycliffe dies
	1415	Council of Constance declares Wycliffe a heretic
Beijing becomes capital of China	1421	
	1428	Wycliffe's body disinterred and burned
Ottoman Empire captures Byzantine capital, Constantinople	1453	

For Further Reading:

Hudson, Anne. *The Premature Reformation.* Oxford: Oxford University Press, 1988.

Long, John. *The Bible in English: John Wycliffe and William Tyndale.* Lanham, Md.: University Press of America, 1998.

Young, Brigham

Early Influential Mormon Leader
1801–1877

Life and Work

Brigham Young was the second president and leader of the Church of Jesus Christ of Latter-day Saints (Mormons), directed the Mormon migration to Utah, and built a vast Mormon empire in the American West. One of the most influential figures in Mormon history, he led the church during its "pioneer period."

WORLD EVENTS	YOUNG'S LIFE
French Revolution 1789	
	1801 Brigham Young is born
Napoleonic Wars 1803–15 in Europe	
Greek War of 1821–29 Independence against Turkey	
	1832 Young converts to Mormon religion
	1835 Young becomes church Apostle
	1838 Young directs move of Mormons to Nauvoo, Illinois
	1844 Young named president of church
	1847 Young leads Mormons to Utah, founds Salt Lake City
Revolutions in 1848 Austria, France, Germany, and Italy	
	1850 Young named first governor of Utah
	1852 Young endorses polygamy
	1857 Young refuses to be removed as governor
United States 1861–65 Civil War	
Germany is united 1871	
	1877 Young dies
Spanish American 1898 War	

Young was born on June 1, 1801, in Whitingham, Vermont. In 1815 he left home and worked as a carpenter, glazier, joiner, and painter. While living in Herndon, New York, Young read the *Book of Mormon* and converted to the Mormon religion in 1832. An avid missionary for the church, he was very successful at bringing in new converts and soon caught the eye of JOSEPH SMITH. In 1835 Young was appointed to the newly formed Quorum of the Twelve Apostles, a church council directly under the president. In 1838 Young organized the relocation of the Mormon community from Missouri to Nauvoo, Illinois. From 1839 to 1841 he led a successful mission in England that converted some 70,000 people and established a foothold for the church in Europe.

In 1844, after Joseph Smith, the founder of Mormonism, was shot and killed by a mob, Young became church president. To escape hostility in Illinois stemming, in part, from Smith's endorsement of polygamy, Young organized the migration of 5,000 Mormons across the Great Plains and Rocky Mountains in 1847 to the Great Salt Lake Basin. That same year he was formally made president of the church.

When Utah became a United States territory in 1850, Young was made its first governor. He came out publicly for polygamy in 1852, causing clashes between the Mormons, non-Mormons, and the federal government. Young was said to have had up to 50 wives. In 1857 President James Buchanan, responding to demands to outlaw polygamy, ordered Young to step down as governor. Young refused and federal troops were dispatched to enforce Buchanan's decision. The ensuing tensions culminated in September 1857, when Mormons and Indians killed 120 non-Mormon settlers in what became known as the Mountain Meadows Massacre. Young ultimately stepped down as governor but remained one of the most influential men in the West. He died in Salt Lake City on August 29, 1877.

Legacy

Young brought the Mormons to their "promised land" in Utah and, under his leadership, the church and its members flourished. For leading the difficult trek across the country, Young gained a reputation as the "American Moses."

Young was very influential in shaping the future of Utah. He founded Salt Lake City in July 1847 and established more than 300 Mormon settlements all over the West. Under his leadership the Mormons undertook many projects: they built large irrigation projects and formed farms and businesses; they established Brigham Young University and what is now the University of Utah; they built the Mormon Tabernacle and the Salt Lake Theater and began the Mormon Temple; they installed the telegraph and railway systems that connected many of the Mormon communities to each other and to Salt Lake City. Young gave Utah women the vote in 1870, 50 years before the 19th Amendment was passed. As forceful a leader as he was, Young was nevertheless unable to prevent the splitting of the Mormon church. In 1860 a dissenting faction founded the Reorganized Church of Jesus Christ of Latter-day Saints under the leadership of one of the sons of Joseph Smith.

Young was an autocratic and controversial leader. He legalized slavery in Utah and banned African Americans from entering the Mormon priesthood, a ban that was not lifted until 1978. While criticized for his tyranny and bigamy, Young nevertheless led the Mormons past the trauma of their founder's death and away from persecution. His organizational abilities were largely responsible for the success of the Utah colony. At his death the Mormon church claimed 150,000 members. Today there are almost 10,000,000 members worldwide.

Saltz

For Further Reading:

Arrington, Leonard J. *Brigham Young: American Moses.* Urbana: University of Illinois Press, 1986.

West, Ray Benedict. *Kingdom of the Saints: The Story of Brigham Young and the Mormons.* New York: Viking Press, 1957.

Zeno of Citium

Founder of Stoic Philosophy

c. 335–c. 263 B.C.E.

Life and Work

Zeno of Citium was the founder of Stoicism, one of the most important philosophical schools of the Hellenistic Age (323–c. 30 B.C.E.).

A Phoenician born in Cyprus, Zeno founded his own school of philosophy in Athens, in the *Stoa Poikile* (Painted Stoa, a colonnade at the northern end of the Athenian open-air marketplace), hence the name Stoicism.

All that we know of Zeno's thought comes from the writings of his students, especially his immediate successors Cleanthes and Chrysippus. Zeno developed a philosophical system that he divided into three parts: logic (the theory of knowledge), physics (the nature of the universe), and ethics (code for life).

Of these three parts, the Stoic ethical system proved most influential. To the Stoics, nature was rational, therefore perfect, so one had to live in accord with nature. In other words, what happens in life is fate, thus do not seek to control fate but instead control your emotions. Although the Stoics regarded what happened in life as preordained, individuals are, nonetheless, still responsible for their actions and conduct. Morality, then, is a rational response—virtue is the good all should seek to obtain.

Knowledge (logic), the second component of the Stoic system, was said to come through the senses alone. On the subject of nature (physics), Zeno concluded that nothing incorporeal exists; everything is material, including the soul. The basic component of the world was fire, and fire was the primordial being, Logos. Therefore, the human soul has the divine fire of Logos. The Stoic doctrine was also pantheistic; divine fire pervades the world. According to the Stoics, all events reflect the activity of divine Logos (Reason).

Stoic philosophy did not restrict itself to the *polis* (Greek city-state). During the Hellenistic period a common culture arose around the Mediterranean, and Stoicism appealed to people of every nationality and status. It did not matter if you were a king or a slave: to be a Stoic was to change oneself, not the world.

In his most famous work, the *Politeia (Republic),* Zeno posited that a society led by the truly wise needed no conventional institutions of Greek city government.

Legacy

While it is difficult to separate Zeno's ideas from those articulated by his immediate successors, it is clear that he created a new and distinct philosophical system, establishing the foundation and framework of Stoicism. Those who followed him refined and furthered his basic ideas in the three areas of Stoicism.

Zeno had a lasting influence, both among philosophers and later Jewish and Christian religious thinkers. Panaetius (c. 185–110 B.C.E.) focused more on the practical aspect of Stoic ethics, while Posidonius (c. 135–c. 50 B.C.E.) aligned Stoicism with some classical Platonic thought, such as the irrational component of the soul. The most extensive Stoic writings come from the Roman Era, where philosophers such as Seneca (c.1–65), EPICTETUS (c. 50–135) and MARCUS AURELIUS (121–180) continued the earlier focus on practical ethics.

Zeno and his followers created a philosophy—and especially an ethical code—that attracted Hebrews and Christians. Among Jewish scholars, PHILO JUDAEUS (c. 20 B.C.E.–c. 50 C.E.) adapted Stoic ideas in his defense of Judaism. Among Christian thinkers, the Stoic concepts may have influenced the author of the Gospel of John, who identifies Christ as the Divine Logos, and the later scholar ORIGEN (c. 185–c. 255). Although Stoicism became less dominant after the second century, its ideas and concepts became an essential component of later Western thought.

Renaud

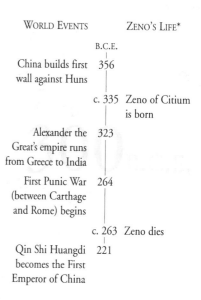

WORLD EVENTS		ZENO'S LIFE*
	B.C.E.	
China builds first wall against Huns	356	
	c. 335	Zeno of Citium is born
Alexander the Great's empire runs from Greece to India	323	
First Punic War (between Carthage and Rome) begins	264	
	c. 263	Zeno dies
Qin Shi Huangdi becomes the First Emperor of China	221	

* Scholars cannot date the specific events in Zeno's life with accuracy.

For Further Reading:

Farris, A. *Paradoxes of Zeno.* Aldershot, U.K.: Avebury Publishers, 1996.

Hunt, Harold Arthur Kinross. *A Physical Interpretation of the Universe: The Doctrines of Zeno the Stoic.* Carlton, Australia: Melbourne University Press, 1976.

McKirahan, Richard D. *Philosophy before Socrates: An Introduction with Texts.* Indianapolis, Ind.: Hackett Publishing Co., 1994.

Zoroaster

(Zarathustra)

Founder of Zoroastrianism
c. 1000 B.C.E.

Life and Work

Zoroaster, also known as Zarathustra, broke with polytheistic and ritualistic religious tradition to establish an inward-looking religion based on human dignity and choice. The core of his revolutionary religious thought was monotheism and the dualism of good and evil.

Little is known about Zoroaster's life. Scholars believe that he was born in eastern Persia (modern-day Iran) about 1000 B.C.E., although Zoroastrian tradition says he lived in

```
WORLD EVENTS        ZOROASTER'S LIFE*
                B.C.E.
                  |
Fall of Troy c. 1150
                  |
             c. 1000 Zoroaster is born,
                  |       lives, and dies
Barbarians invade  771
      China
```

* Scholars cannot date the specific events of Zoroaster's life with accuracy.

the sixth century B.C.E. By the time he was 20, he had left home in search of truth. Around age 30 he began to receive revelations from Ahura Mazda (Lord Wisdom), which he preserved in the Gathas, psalms that eventually became part of the Zoroastrian scripture known as the Avesta.

Seeking to free people from the priests of the established cults, who held power by controlling the rituals that gave access to the gods, Zoroaster developed a religious system based on inward, or personal, choices related to ethical decisions. In an attempt to address the question of evil, he introduced two revolutionary concepts: monotheism and ethical dualism that opposed "Truth" and "Lie." Zoroaster believed that there is one god, Ahura Mazda, who created all things and will judge everyone at the end of time. His twin children, Spenta Mainyu and Angra Mainyu, generated the dualistic opposing forces of good and evil, respectively. Each had chosen his own course freely, Spenta Mainyu following "Truth" and Angra Mainyu "Lie." The battle of these two forces is at the heart of Zoroaster's faith. Individuals decide which path, that of good or of evil, they will follow.

Struggling to preach his faith against priestly opposition, Zoroaster was eventually forced to flee to the protection of Kavi Vishtaspa, a powerful ruler whom he converted. Little is known about his later life or the circumstances of his death. The Avesta reports that Zoroaster was assassinated by a priest of the old religion when he was 77.

Legacy

Zoroaster's religious teachings not only served as the foundation of Zoroastrianism, but also influenced other religious and philosophical traditions.

In the fourth or fifth century C.E. many of the Zoroastrian texts were gathered into the Avesta; still others were collected into the Pahlavi books that date from the ninth century. These works contain Zoroastrian teachings on such topics as cosmology (the origin and fate of the universe), eschatology (the events of the end times), and soteriology (the nature of salvation). The Avesta anticipates the coming of a savior who was born of a virgin. It also speaks of an astral journey to heaven that

the soul must successfully complete after death. Only the just souls will be permitted to enter; the unjust will be cast into hell. Zoroastrian disciples, called magi, transmitted these beliefs from one generation to the next.

Some aspects of Zoroastrian religion are thought to have influenced other Mediterranean religions. Early Christians saw Zoroaster as a prophet who also predicted the star that would herald the Messiah's birth. In the Christian Gospel of Matthew, the magi (wise men) who visit the Christ-child are thought to be Zoroastrian astronomers. The soul's trip through the heavens is also a central feature of the highly dualistic forms of second-century Gnosticism, a religious belief that asserts that humans need special spiritual knowledge—*gnosis*—to achieve the release of their souls from their corruptible physical bodies. MANI, founder of Manichaeism, (a dualistic religious belief system asserting that there are two realms of existence, one good and one evil) saw Zoroaster as one of the three great messengers from the past. Nevertheless, because the written Zoroastrian sources are dated so late, it is often hard to establish which religion first influenced the other.

Greeks philosophers such as PLATO and ARISTOTLE saw Zoroaster as the ideal example of the virtuous wise man. His reputation declined during the Middle Ages, when he was viewed as a heretic and teacher of witchcraft but was revived during the Renaissance and Enlightenment, when he was thought to be a wise man who might link Christianity and classical Greek thought. In the late nineteenth century, German philosopher FRIEDRICH WILHELM NIETZSCHE saw Zoroaster as the first to discover that the eternal struggle between good and evil was the force behind everything. He named his hero in *Thus Spoke Zarathustra* after the prophet.

Not long after his death, Zoroaster's followers began to revert to the ritualistic and polytheistic practices he had rejected. The religion was further undermined by the Muslim conquests of Persia in the seventh century. By the tenth century the Zoroastrians had migrated to India, where they became known as the Parsis (meaning Persians). At the end of the twentieth century, over 130,000 Parsis exist worldwide. While most are found in India, some live in Iran, Pakistan, Sri Lanka, and North America.

von Dehsen

For Further Reading:
Gnoli, Gherardo. *Zoroaster's Time and Homeland: A Study of the Origins of Mazdeism and Related Problems.* Naples, Italy: Istituto Universitario Orientale, 1980.
Mehta, P. D. *Zarathushtra: The Transcendental Vision.* Longmeade, Shaftesbury, Dorset, England: Element Books, 1985.

Appendices,
Bibliography, and Index

Highlights in the History of Philosophy and Religion

B.C.E.

c. 2000 Abraham, the first biblical patriarch, is born.

c. 1367–50 Egyptian pharaoh, Akhenaton (also known as Amenhotep IV), reigns; he is the first ruler in history to advocate monolatry, the worship of one god.

c. 13th c. Moses lives; a towering figure of the Old Testament, Moses becomes known as the leader and lawgiver of the Exodus, the flight of the Jews from slavery in Egypt.

c. 1000 Upon the death of Saul and his sons in battle, David becomes king of Judah; seven years later is anointed king of Israel, thus uniting the two kingdoms.

c. 1000 Zoroaster, also known as Zarathustra, is born; he will break with polytheistic and ritualistic religious tradition to establish a religion based on human dignity and choice; he will be regarded as a prophet by other religions and sects in the Mediterranean, including the early Christians.

c. 860 Elijah, the premier Hebrew prophet of the ninth century B.C.E., plays a major role in the development of monotheism by insisting that the only true god is the God of Israel.

c. 645 Biblical prophet Jeremiah is born; he will lay the theological foundations for the Judaism of the Diaspora (Jews living outside of Palestine).

c. 624 Thales of Miletus is born; he will become the first person in Western history to explain the universe in rational rather than mythical terms; his work establishes the foundations of Greek science and philosophy.

c. 611 Anaximander is born; he will be the first known philosopher to propose a cosmology, a theory of the origin and structure of the universe.

c. 600 Buddha (Siddhartha Gautama), founder of Buddhism, is born.

c. 599 Mahavira, also known as Vardhamana, is born; he will found Jainism, a religion devoted to ascetic practices as a means of respecting all life-forms.

c. 570 Lao-tzu is born; he becomes the reputed founder of Taoism, a Chinese religious and philosophical system aimed at assisting its followers to achieve harmony within themselves and with the energy of the universe.

551 Chinese philosopher and teacher Confucius is born; he will introduce his vision of a well-ordered, harmonious society, which becomes the basis for East Asian culture.

c. 532 Pythagoras travels to Croton in southern Italy where he establishes the religious and scientific society called the Semicircle; the society focuses on the fundamental concept that all reality is mathematical in nature.

c. 484 Herodotus, often called the father of history, is born; he will set the standards and focus of historical writing for centuries.

c. 469–399 Socrates of Athens is born; he will become the first philosopher in the Western tradition to logically examine questions about moral conduct and the meaning of life.

c. 390 Shang Yang is born; he will become one of the earliest philosophers of what is later called the Chinese Legalist School of thought and, as the prime minister of Qin, build the state into a military power that will unify China during the third century B.C.E.

c. 387 Plato founds the Academy; his ideas and those of his students at the Academy, including Aristotle, form the foundation for much of Western philosophy throughout the centuries.

384 Aristotle, one of the most influential philosophers of ancient Greece, is born; his writings on various topics such as logic, natural science, ethics, aesthetics, political science, and metaphysics will become influential throughout history.

c. 371 Meng K'o, commonly known as Mencius (from the title of his major work, *Meng-tzu*), is born; the *Meng-tzu*, which is an unconnected collection of short sayings and lengthy conversations conveying a central principle that human beings are inherently good, offers one of the earliest interpretations of Confucius.

c. 335–263 Zeno of Citium is born; he will found Stoicism, one of the most important philosophical schools of the Hellenistic Age.

c. 307–306 Epicurus moves to Athens where he establishes his school known as the Garden; there he teaches the value of a pleasurable way of life unaffected by political events and promotes his ideas on *ataraxia*, freedom from disturbance and the avoidance of pain.

c. 300 Hsün-tzu, an influential Confucian moral philosopher, is born; he emphasizes the importance of ritual and education to civilize inherently self-centered human beings.

c. 280 Han-fei-tzu is born; he will synthesize and articulate Chinese legal theory in what comes to be called the Legalist School.

c. 220 Earliest possible date of Patañjali's birth; Patañjali will become the original codifier of early yogic meditation techniques and is considered to be the traditional author of the *Yoga-Sutras*, which makes possible the philosophy and practice of yoga as we know it today.

c. 60	Hillel is born; he will become the rabbi who provides the methods of interpretation that enable Judaism to adapt its historical traditions and biblical teachings to a changing world.
c. 20	Philo, the greatest Jewish philosopher of his era, is born; he will become the first religious thinker to explain and defend the Hebrew religion using the techniques of Hellenistic philosophy.
c. 5	Paul is born; after his conversion to Christianity, he conducts missionary enterprises to early Christian communities. His writings, incorporated into the New Testament, form the basis for much of Christian theology.
c. 4	Jesus is born; his preaching, actions, and life will lead to the development of the Christian religion.
c. 1st c. B.C.E. –1st c. C.E.	Mary is born and lives; she is the mother of Jesus and becomes an object of Christian inspiration as an example of God's humble, trusting servant.

C.E.

1st–2nd c.	Marcion lives; he is a Christian heretic whose challenge to traditional theology motivates the Church to define orthodox doctrine and produce the biblical canon (list of books).
c. 50	The Stoic philosopher Epictetus is born; he will claim that the universe is controlled by an overarching force called the Logos and that happiness and virtue derive from living in harmony with the Logos.
c. 95–96	Akiba ben Joseph, early interpreter of Jewish law, becomes known as the greatest scholar of the age; he is one of the most important leaders of the Jewish community.
c. 161	Roman emperor Marcus Aurelius's rule begins; a prime example of the philosopher–king in Western philosophical tradition, Aurelius writes *Meditations*, a description of his Stoic philosophy.
c. 185	Origen, one of the most important thinkers of the early Christian church, is born; he will develop the first systematic and speculative theology of Christianity and introduce patterns of thinking that become fundamental to subsequent Christian thought.
216	Mani, also known as Manes and Manichaeus, is born; he will found Manichaeism, a dualistic religious belief system that asserts that there are two realms of existence, one good and one evil.
c. 347	Jerome, one of the most significant and influential figures in the early Christian church, is born; he will translate the Hebrew and Greek scriptures into Latin.
356–362	Athanasius writes his greatest doctrinal work, *Discourses Against the Arians*, which is a defense of the orthodox teaching of the Nicene Creed and a challenge to the Arian heresy prevalent at that time.
c. 397	Augustine completes *Confessions*, a candid autobiography describing the wantonness of his youth and his conversion to Christianity.
413–426	Augustine completes *The City of God*, which offers a theological philosophy of history: God works through events to achieve his ultimate purpose, redemption.
428	Cyril denounces Bishop of Constantinople Nestorius' views in a series of letters and 12 propositions; he accuses Nestorius of separating Christ into two beings—the human and the divine—and denying the singular human–divine nature of Christ.
432	Patrick, patron saint of Ireland, is made bishop and sent to evangelize throughout Ireland.
520	Anicius Manlius Severinus Boethius addresses the question of the Trinity, using Aristotelian, rather than pure Christian, forms of reasoning to support the unity of the triune Christian deity.
c. 529	Benedict of Nursia develops his plans for reforming monasticism and writes the rule by which his monks at Monte Cassino (halfway between Rome and Naples) are governed; this rule will shape monasticism for over 1,500 years.
c. 563	Columba sails to Iona, a small island off the coast of Scotland, where he founds what will become one of the greatest monasteries in Christendom.
590	Gregory I, later known as Gregory the Great, becomes Pope; his papacy is marked by administrative and liturgical reform of the Roman Catholic church, along with increased missionary activities and even conversion by war and coercion.
c. 610	Fatimah Bint Muhammad, daughter of Muhammad, is born; she will help establish the hereditary leadership of the Shiite sect of Islam.
622	The founder of Islam, Muhammad, fearing a murder plot, flees Mecca for Yathrib (later named Medina) with his disciples; this migration comes to be known as the *hegira* ("flight" in Arabic), from which date the Muslims begin their calendar.
c. 671	Fa-tsang takes vows as a Buddhist monk; he later synthesizes the *Huayan* tradition of Chinese Buddhism.
c. 700	Shankara is born; he becomes a Hindu teacher who articulates the theory of Advaita Vedanta, the non-dualistic interpretation of the Vedas, the Hindu scriptures.
c. 717	Rabi'ah al'Adawiyah is born; she inspires a form of Islamic mysticism that synthesizes ascetic practices with theological concerns.
767	Abu 'Abd Allah ash-Shafi'i, more commonly known ash-Shafi'i, is born; an Islamic legal scholar, he writes the first treatise on jurisprudence in Islam.
c. 800	Yaqub ibn Ishaq as-Sabah al-Kindi is born; he will become one of the first Islamic scholars to preserve Greek thought and to relate the teachings of Islam to reason and science.
c. 825	Abu al-Qasim al-Junayd is born; he will become a master of Sufism and one of the first thinkers to try to relate Sufism to traditional Islam.

c. 878   Al-Farabi, the first theologian to relate Islamic theology to Greek philosophy, is born.

c. 936   Jewish Talmudic scholar Sa'adia ben Joseph completes his most important work, *The Book on Beliefs and Opinions*, in which he proposes three sources of truth: sense perception, rational intuition, and valid conclusions drawn from this data.

c. 940   Matta ibn Yunus dies; he is one of the earliest scholars to translate the works of Aristotle into Arabic and provides some of the earliest commentaries on the Greek philosopher available to Islamic theologians.

980   Sufi mystic Al-Hallaj is put on trial by Sunni authorities, because he claims that the mystical union he finds with God places him and his followers beyond the confines of religious and secular law.

c. 980   Ibn Sina (Avicenna) is born; he will become a widely respected Islamic philosopher and physician and, in his work, synthesizes Islamic theology and Greek philosophy.

c. 1017   Ramanuja is born; he will interpret the Hindu scriptures, the *Upanishads*, to allow for a distinction between the *Brahman* (God) and human beings, and, in so doing, establishes one of the principal schools of Hindu philosophy, Vishishtadvaita Vedanta, which emphasizes the importance of *bhakti*, devotion to God.

1058   Al-Ghazali is born; in his work, he will combine Islamic scholastic and mystical ideas and is thus able to bridge a serious division within Islam.

1078   Anselm of Canterbury proposes ontological argument (one based on being itself) for the existence of God.

1095   Pope Urban II preaches a passionate sermon to a large crowd at the Council of Clermont, France, and mobilizes Christian troops to the First Crusade.

1140   Bernard of Clairvaux, orthodox priest and loyal churchman, opposes theologian Peter Abelard's rationalist approach to Christianity and orchestrates Abelard's condemnation at the Council of Sens.

c. 1140   *Sic et Non* (*Yes and No*) by Peter Abelard is published; in it, he contrasts Bible passages and statements of the Church that seem to disagree and leaves judgment to the reader.

1140s   Hildegard von Bingen writes her most popular theological work, *Scivias* (*Know the Ways*); it is a collection of her early visions designed to serve as a guide to Christians living in a fallen world.

1169–95   Averroës (Ibn Rushd) completes commentaries on Aristotle's major works, including the *Organon*, *De Anima*, *Physica*, *Metaphysica*, and *Nichomachean Ethics*, and on Plato's *Republic*.

1190   Moses ben Maimon, more commonly known as Maimonides, publishes what will become his greatest and most controversial work, *Guide to the Perplexed*; it is an exposition of Jewish faith for the educated in which he tries to reconcile Aristotelian philosophical thought (using reason and logic to analyze data) with a religion based on law and tradition.

1198–1202   Ibn al-'Arabi develops his thoughts on Sufi mysticism, including his transformation of the static concept of mystical connection into a dynamic one described by the phrase "perpetual transformation."

c. 1199   Madhva, an influential Hindu teacher, is born; he will found the Dvaita (dualistic) school of Vedanta, the study of the Vedas (early Hindu scriptures).

1209   Francis of Assisi receives permission from the Pope to establish a new monastic order known as the "Lesser Brothers," which later becomes known as the Franciscans.

1265–72   Thomas Aquinas, most noted for his attempts to synthesize faith and reason, writes his greatest work, the three-part *Summa Theologica*.

c. 1375   Ibn Khaldun writes the *Muqaddimah* (*An Introduction to History*), a theoretical preparation for the writing of a universal history; in this work, he strives to establish a philosophical basis for the scientific investigation of history.

1378   John Wycliffe begins a systematic attack on key elements of contemporary Church doctrine and practice; he asserts that the Bible is the sole source of doctrine (*sola scriptura*) and questions both papal authority and monasticism as not based on scripture.

1410   Jan Hus and his followers are excommunicated from the Roman Catholic church for his aggressive reform efforts including his vigorous attacks on the moral laxity of priests.

1431   Joan of Arc is executed as a heretic following her military exploits for France during the Hundred Years' War; this war had English kings, allied with French dissidents, laying claim to the French throne.

1482   Tomás de Torquemada becomes grand inquisitor of the Spanish Inquisition, the council established by the Roman Catholic church to deal with heresy.

1494   Girolamo Savonarola establishes temporary rule in Florence after France's King Charles VIII conquers the city; a flamboyant preacher and a reformer driven by apocalyptic fervor, he bases his rule on religious authority.

1499   Nanak, founder of Sikhism, takes the first of four journeys; he preaches the holy word (*nam*) and teaches others how to pray.

1514   Niccolò Machiavelli publishes *The Prince*, wherein he presents a theory of governmental control that advocates that a ruler retain power by any means necessary.

1515–16   Thomas More writes his masterpiece, *Utopia*, which establishes him as one of the foremost proponents of humanism; in it, he imagines an ideal community whose citizens live peacefully through the rule of reason.

1517   Martin Luther issues his 95 theses against the Roman Catholic church opposing the sale of indulgences and disputing the theology that supports them; his posting of the theses launches the Protestant Reformation.

1521   Erasmus publishes *On Free Choice*, a statement of his theological position and humanistic idea that individuals have free will in all matters, including those of faith, a doctrine Martin Luther opposed.

1521   Philipp Melanchthon publishes *Loci communes theologici* (*Commonplaces of Theology*), the first systematic presentation of Lutheran theology.

1533   Thomas Cranmer, leader of the English Reformation, is consecrated Archbishop of Canterbury and publicly renounces any allegiance to the Pope.

1540   Pope Paul III approves the formation of Ignatius of Loyola's order, called the Society of Jesus (or Jesuits), which elects Ignatius as its head.

1541   Protestant reformer John Calvin returns to Geneva from exile, at the request of its citizens; he establishes a theocratic regime organized along Old Testament lines.

1562   Teresa of Ávila overcomes the opposition of her immediate superiors and establishes, at Ávila, the first community of Barefoot Carmelite nuns.

1580–88 Michel Eyquem de Montaigne publishes his major work, the *Essays*, in which he reflects on the frailty of humanity through the lens of his own experience.

1596   French mathematician and philosopher René Descartes is born; his work will set the framework for philosophy in the modern period.

1604   Sikh *guru* Arjun compiles the hymns and prayers of the previous *gurus*, together with some of his own, into the *Adi Granth* (*The First Book*); the work becomes the earliest scripture of the Sikh religion.

1620   Francis Bacon publishes *Novum Organum*, in which he outlines his new scientific methodology, including the role of inductive reasoning; this methodology has scientists collecting data through observation and experience and using them to form tentative conclusions.

1647   George Fox begins preaching his message of reliance on the "Inner Light" in each person's soul, not on the sacraments or the Bible; his beliefs lead to the formation of the Religious Society of Friends, also known as the Quakers.

1651   Thomase Hobbes's *Leviathan* is published; in it, Hobbes argues that the ideal form of government is created by people joining together under a social contract.

1662   Blaise Pascal's notes are published posthumously in *Pensees* (*Thoughts*); in it Pascal addresses the skepticism of Michel Eyquem de Montaigne and argues that reason alone is insufficient to acquire complete knowledge.

1666   Gobind Singh is born; he will become the tenth, and last, *guru* of Sikhism and the founder of Khalsa, a militaristic Sikh faction.

1670   Benedict de Spinoza publishes *Theologico-Political Treatise* anonymously; in it he proposes that humans form societies and governments to ensure their survival and defense and that reason requires such societies to be democratic.

1690   John Locke publishes *Two Treatises of Government* (1690), his most important political work; in it he attacks "the

divine right of kings," arguing that government is based on the natural rights of individuals not divine decree.

c. 1705 Influential Islamic Shiite legal scholar Aka Sayyid Muhammad Bakir Bihbihani establishes the role of the *mujtahid* as the authoritative practitioner of *ijtihad* (the rational interpretation of *Shariah*, Islamic law).

1709–34 George Berkeley publishes the theory of immaterialism in three important books: *An Essay Towards a New Theory of Vision* (1709), *A Treatise Concerning the Principles of Human Knowledge* (1710), and *The Analyst* (1734).

c. 1738 Israel ben Eliezer (Ba'al Shem Tov) preaches the ideas that were to become the precepts underlying the Jewish Hasidic movement of the nineteenth and twentieth centuries.

1740s   John Wesley begins organizing Methodist societies and in 1784 provides for the legal incorporation of the Methodism.

1748   David Hume completes *An Enquiry Concerning Human Understanding*, in which he argues that all knowledge can be reduced to impressions (sensations, passions, emotions) and ideas (faint images of the impressions).

1748   Charles Louis de Secondat, Baron de la Brède et de Montesquieu, publishes *The Spirit of Laws* (1748); in it, he addresses his primary concern about preventing abuse of power while preserving the rule of law.

1759   Voltaire publishes *Candide*, which encapsulates his philosophical ideas; in it Voltaire contends that God, if God exists at all, is either unwilling or unable to intervene in human affairs.

1762   Jean-Jacques Rousseau completes his most significant works, *Emile* and *The Social Contract*, both of which offer solutions to what he considers the pernicious effects of civilization.

1764   Thomas Reid publishes *Inquiry into the Human Mind on the Principles of Common Sense*, the first of three books that explain his philosophy of common sense; in them he argues that the mind intuitively knows certain principles, including moral principles, without the need for external stimuli.

1765   Denis Diderot completes the seventeenth and final volume of the *Encyclopédie*, one of the cornerstones of the French Enlightenment.

1766   Edmund Burke, influential political philosopher responsible for developing the foundations of modern conservative political thought, wins a seat in Parliament.

1774   Mother Ann Lee, her husband, and six other followers immigrate to the American colonies and establish the United Society of Believers in Christ's Second Appearing, commonly known as the Shakers, one of the few indigenous American religions.

1776   Thomas Jefferson drafts the Declaration of Independence, which draws on the intellectual tradition of the Enlightenment, asserting that all "men" are created equal and born with certain natural rights, which governments are formed to protect.

1776 Adam Smith writes *Wealth of Nations* in which he presents a unified theory to explain and justify the operation of commercial societies and argues that social harmony and economic progress can best be preserved in a society in which people are free to pursue their own economic interests.

1780 Johann Heinrich Pestalozzi writes *The Evening Hours of a Hermit*, the first of three books in which he explains his innovative educational philosophy—the goal of education is to guide each child individually, through participatory activities, toward independent thinking.

1781–90 Immanuel Kant publishes *The Critique of Pure Reason* (1781), *The Critique of Practical Reason* (1788), and *The Critique of Judgment* (1790); these works outline his revolutionary philosophy based upon his assertion that, instead of passively receiving objects of knowledge, the knower unconsciously organizes input from the senses.

1787 James Madison outlines a system of government including three branches joined in a shared-power system for the Constitutional Convention; the founders of the United States devise the country's new constitution at this convention.

1789 Jeremy Bentham expounds his utilitarian argument that the mind intuitively knows certain principles, including moral principles, without the need for external stimuli, in his *Introduction to the Principles of Morals and Legislation*.

1794 Johann Gottlieb Fichte publishes *On the Concept of the Theory of Science*, in which he develops the idealism of Immanuel Kant by investigating the ways in which the mind interacts with the material world.

1807 Georg Hegel writes *The Phenomenology of Spirit*, which outlines his concept of a rationally unfolding absolute Spirit or Mind (*Geist*) present, in different phases, in all aspects of reality.

1819 Arthur Schopenhauer completes his major work, *The World as Will and Idea* (revised 1844 and 1859); based on concepts drawn largely from Plato and Immanuel Kant, it attempts to distinguish between the external world and human perceptions of it.

1819 William Ellery Channing delivers his sermon, "Unitarian Christianity," in Baltimore; it articulates the liberal ideas that become the basis for early Unitarian theology and the Unitarian church.

1821 Elizabeth Ann Seton dies; known as the mother of the American parochial school system, she is the founder of the first American religious society and the first native-born American to be canonized by the Roman Catholic church.

1828 Ram Mohun Roy establishes the Brahmo Samaj (Congregation of *brahman*), the first modern Hindu reform movement, which attempts to renounce Hindu idol worship and replace it with worship of the *brahman*.

1830 Joseph Smith founds the Church of Jesus Christ, later called the Church of Jesus Christ of Latter-day Saints, or Mormons.

1833 William Lloyd Garrison helps establish the American Anti-Slavery Society (AASS) to advocate for the peaceful overthrow of slavery and racial equality.

1833–42 Auguste Comte addresses the need for a new social order in the *Course of Positive Philosophy*; his ideas establish the basis of Logical Positivism, which addresses how theoretical and abstract sciences deal with positive, observable facts; his application of Logical Positivism to human behavior results in the creation of a new discipline he calls "sociology."

1835–37 Horace Mann serves in the Massachusetts Senate from 1835 to 1837, where he helps to enact legislation establishing the first state board of education in the country; he accepts an appointment to that board as secretary in 1837.

1836–38 Ralph Waldo Emerson publishes three works—*Nature* (1836), "The American Scholar," (1837) and his "Harvard Divinity School Address" (1838)—which lead to the formation of a group of intellectuals called "Transcendentalists."

1843–49 Søren Kierkegaard completes *Either/Or* and *Fear and Trembling* (1843), *The Concept of Dread* (1844), *Concluding Unscientific Postscript* (1846), and *The Sickness unto Death* (1849), each of which represents distinct spheres of existence: the aesthetic, the ethical, and the religious.

1844 Brigham Young becomes president of the Mormon church; Young organizes the migration of 5,000 Mormons across the Great Plains and Rocky Mountains to the Great Salt Lake Basin in what will become Utah.

1848 Karl Marx, with colleague Friedrich Engels, publishes the *Communist Manifesto*; the first systematic statement of socialist thought, it describes history as a class struggle and predicts that the conflict between workers and capitalists will end with a new classless, utopian society.

1849–51 Horace Bushnell, father of American religious liberalism, publishes *God in Christ* (1849) and *Christ in Theology* (1851), in which he argues that language is symbolic and, therefore, that the text of the Bible and of traditional Christian doctrine are to be considered poetic, not literal, statements.

1851 Harriet Beecher Stowe, a fervent opponent of slavery, completes her most famous novel, *Uncle Tom's Cabin*, which helps to mobilize anti-slavery forces in the antebellum North.

1854 Henry David Thoreau, one of America's foremost Transcendentalists, publishes *Walden, or Life in the Woods*, composed of 18 essays chronicling his life at Walden Pond.

1856 David Einhorn publishes the prayer book *Olat Tamid*; the ideas expressed in it form the intellectual foundation for Reform Judaism in the United States.

1858 Bernadette of Lourdes experiences another in a series of visions in which Mary identifies herself as the "Immaculate Conception."

1861   In *Considerations on Representative Government* (1861), influential political philosopher John Stuart Mill proposes a commission, drawn from the intellectual elite, to frame legislation that would then be voted on by democratically elected assemblies.

1862–74   Phoebe Worrall Palmer, an early founder of the Holiness movement, edits the magazine *Guide to Holiness* to spread her beliefs; her message is simple and direct—that holiness is available to everyone who accepts Christ as a personal savior.

1863   Mikhail Bakunin explains and publicizes his ideas on anarchy in *The Revolutionary Catechism.*

1863   Under the leadership of Ellen Gould White, Seventh-Day Adventist congregations are formally organized with a membership of about 3,500.

mid–1870s   Ramakrishna becomes the focal point of a resurgence of Hinduism, particularly among Westernized intellectuals.

1875   Mary Baker Eddy publishes *Science and Health*, which describes her belief that only God, not the human mind, possesses the power of healing and which becomes, along with the Bible, the holy scripture of Christian Science.

1875   Helena Petrovna Blavatsky forms the Theosophical Society with Col. Henry S. Olcott.

1877–78   Charles Sanders Peirce writes a series of articles entitled "Illustrations of the Logic of Science," in which he first introduces pragmatism—his belief that the meaning of an idea can be found by observing the "practical consequences" (observable consequences).

1877–84   Baha' Allah (Mirza Hoseyn Ali Nuri), founder of the Bahai religion, completes *The Most Holy Book*, a compilation of his teachings.

1879   Jamal ad-Din al-Afghani publishes *The Refutation of the Materialists*, which denounces supporters of British rule in the Indian subcontinent.

1881   Booker T. Washington is asked to teach at Tuskegee Normal, a newly established school for blacks in Alabama. Washington later becomes president of the school and devotes the rest of his life to its expansion.

1883–85   Friedrich Nietzsche publishes *Thus Spoke Zarathustra*; in it Nietzsche portrays a wise teacher who learns how to live joyfully in spite of all life's suffering through a self-disciplined, creative acceptance of his own unique existence.

1884   Muhammad 'Abduh joins Jamal ad-Din al-Afghani in Paris to edit *The Firmest Bond*, a revolutionary journal that promotes anti-British views.

1884   Charles Taze Russell founds the Zion's Watch Tower Bible and Tract Society, later known as Jehovah's Witnesses, to spread his message rejecting the concept of the Trinity; he maintains that Jesus was not God incarnate and anticipates an apocalyptic end to the world (in 1914) that would soon usher in the kingdom of God on Earth.

1885   Josiah Strong, a proponent of the Social Gospel, publishes his most important book, *Our Country: Its Possible Future and Its Present Crisis*, in which he analyzes urban social problems and proposes solutions.

1886   Solomon Washington Gladden, who comes to lead the Social Gospel movement, publishes *Applied Christianity: Moral Aspects of Social Questions*, which explains his views on the importance of Christianity in curing social ills.

1889   Isaac Mayer Wise becomes president of the Central Conference of American Rabbis, the governing body of Reform Judaism, of which he is an early leader.

1889   Native American Paiute leader Wovoka announces that God promises to renew the land and lives of the Paiutes if they live upright lives, avoid war, and perform the Ghost Dance monthly; this marks the beginning of the Ghost Dance movement.

1890   William James publishes *The Principles of Psychology*, which becomes a landmark in the transformation of that discipline from an abstract philosophy to an experimental science.

1895   In *The Rules of Sociological Method*, Émile Durkheim establishes a scientifically rigorous methodology for sociological analysis.

1896   John Dewey opens the Laboratory School, later called the Dewey School, at the University of Chicago to test his theories on education; his theories revolve around problem solving as the method for how a child learns.

1897   Vivekananda establishes the Ramakrishna Mission in Calcutta and becomes a major force in revitalizing Hinduism in India.

c. 1900   Charles Fox Parham, founder of American Pentecostalism, interprets the account of the Pentecost in the New Testament to mean that baptism in the Holy Spirit is followed by glossolalia, speaking in tongues (recognizable foreign languages), which could be used to spread the Gospel to other regions of the world.

1901–13   Edmund Husserl publishes his first investigations into phenomenology in his books *Logical Investigations* (1901) and *Ideas: General Introduction to Phenomenology* (1913).

1907   Walter Rauschenbusch produces his most influential work, *Christianity and the Social Crisis*, often called the "bible" of the Social Gospel movement.

1909   W. E. B. Du Bois co-founds the National Association for the Advancement of Colored People (NAACP), which becomes a forum for African-American thinking and political action during the twentieth century.

1909   Maria Montessori publishes *The Montessori Method* in which she explains her educational philosophy based on the idea of individual initiative—that children learn primarily by working by themselves at their own pace.

1910–13   Bertrand Russell, in collaboration with Alfred North Whitehead, publishes the three-volume *Principia Mathematica*, which argues that mathematics can be derived from principles of logic.

1914   Aurobindo Ghose (Sri Aurobindo) founds the journal *Arya*, in which he begins to formulate and publish his concepts of Integral Yoga.

1914–16   In 1914, Marcus Garvey organizes the Universal Negro Improvement Association (UNIA) in his home country of Jamaica. The Association is designed to unify and help the black community; two years later he organizes a chapter of UNIA in Harlem, New York City.

1921   Ludwig Wittgenstein publishes his most acclaimed work, *Tractatus Logico-philosophicus*, which posits a strict relationship between language and the physical world.

1923   Martin Buber, developer of twentieth-century existential Jewish thought, publishes his important work *Ich und Du* (*I and Thou*), which examines human relations in terms of I–It and I–Thou.

1924   Mohandas Karamchand Gandhi retires as head of the Indian National Congress and withdraws from active politics. Twenty-three years later, Gandhi's ideas on nonviolent resistance help India gain independence from Britain.

1927   Martin Heidegger completes his first major and most famous work, *Being and Time*, which focuses on the relationship between human existence and what he names "Being."

1929   Jean Piaget, who will become a leader in the field of developmental child psychology, leaves the University of Neuchatel to became professor of child psychology at the University of Geneva; here he spends close to 30 years developing his ideas on the stages of cognitive development in children.

1934   An active opponent of Hitler, Karl Barth writes the draft of the Barmen Declaration, asserting the primacy of the traditional Gospel against the demands of the state.

1934   Mordecai Menaham Kaplan publishes *Judaism as a Civilization*; in it he outlines his ideas about Judaism as "the evolving religious civilization of the Jewish people," rather than only a religion.

1934   Elijah Muhammad establishes the headquarters of the Nation of Islam in Chicago following the mysterious death of Wallace D. Fard, the leader of the Nation of Islam's forerunner, the First Temple of Islam.

1935   Dion Fortune publishes *The Mystical Qabalah* in which she contends that the Kabbalah (the Jewish mystical system for interpreting scripture) can be a source of practical mysticism for Western audiences.

1935   Tenzin Gyatso is born; he will become the fourteenth Dalai Lama, the spiritual and temporal leader of the Tibetan people.

1936   John Maynard Keynes publishes *The General Theory of Employment, Interest and Money*, in which he argues that, when demand is less than supply, suppliers would cut back on production, resulting in high unemployment and economic depression.

1937   Dietrich Bonhoeffer addresses the proper role of Christians facing the Nazi regime in *The Cost of Discipleship*; in it, he presents the concept "costly grace," which compels a Christian to participate in the world's struggles without consideration of personal cost or risk.

1940   Liberal theologian and social activist Reinhold Niebuhr launches *Christianity and Crisis* to present his anti-Nazi views.

1942   Albert Camus publishes *The Stranger*, which introduces and explains his concept of "the absurd"—the contrast between human need and the unreasonable silence of the world.

1943   Jean-Paul Sartre, one of twentieth-century Europe's foremost thinkers and coiner of the term "existentialism," publishes his most significant philosophical work, *Being and Nothingness*.

1950   Menachem Mendel Schneerson assumes the leadership of the influential Orthodox Habad–Lubavitch sect upon his father-in-law's death.

1950   Mother Teresa receives the Catholic church's permission to establish a new order, the Missionary Sisters of Charity, who will minister to the poor at over 550 sites in 126 countries by the end of the twentieth century.

1951–63   Paul Tillich publishes *Systematic Theology*, the most complete expression of his thought on religious faith and its ultimate realization in Christian doctrine.

1954   L. Ron Hubbard establishes the first Church of Scientology; it is based on Dianetics, the goal of which is to erase the reactive mind, full of "engrams" (residual effects of past painful experiences) that prevent people from becoming more ethical, more aware, happier, and saner.

1954   Sun Myung Moon founds what is to become the Unification Church (Holy Spirit for the Unification of World Christianity), in South Korea.

1957   Martin Luther King, Jr., who advocates nonviolent resistance and who is to become the preeminent black civil rights leader of the United States, founds the Southern Christian Leadership Conference (SCLC).

1958   Angelo Giuseppe Roncalli is elected Pope; he takes the name John Paul XXIII and institutes the council called Vatican II, which revitalizes the Church's practices and encourages Christian unity through broader ecumenical relationships.

1959   The Maharishi Mahesh Yogi begins his first world tour during which he spreads the benefits of transcendental meditation (TM) across the world and gathers followers to the TM movement.

1960   Hans-Georg Gadamer publishes *Truth and Method*, in which he raises the question of how an individual interprets any communicative act; he argues that all interpretation is limited by our understanding of reality, which is always framed by "tradition"—that is, history and language.

1963   Hannah Arendt's *Eichmann in Jerusalem* is published; it describes her view of Nazi war criminal Adolf Eichmann and her ideas on the "banality of evil."

1964   Malcolm X ends his role as national spokesperson for the Nation of Islam following disagreements and controversy, and splits with the group.

1965   Abraham Joshua Heschel, a Jewish scholar who relates traditional Jewish teachings to the modern world, joins Martin Luther King, Jr., in the March on Selma (Alabama), one of the seminal moments in the civil rights movement.

1966–70   Michel Foucault publishes *The Order of Things* (1966), *The Archeology of Knowledge* (1969), and *Discipline and Punish* (1970); these works show his development of such concepts as "madness," "power," and "knowledge," and analyze the ways in which such concepts function within a given social order.

1967   Jacques Derrida publishes *Of Grammatology* and *Writing and Difference* that introduce his ideas on deconstructionism, which maintain that all texts embody the social, historical, cultural, and linguistic assumptions of their times.

1969   James Hal Cone's manifesto, *Black Theology and Black Power*, is published; in it, Cone analyzes the meaning of black power, the church, and the Gospel, and concludes that black power was the central message of Christ to twentieth-century America.

1971   Gustavo Gutiérrez publishes *A Theology of Liberation: History, Politics and Salvation*, which becomes the seminal book on liberation theology; the book argues that theology should be a dynamic struggle, involving the full human heart repelled by social injustice and ready to act.

1978   Feminist theologian Mary Daly publishes *Gyn/Ecology: The Metaethics of Radical Feminism*; in it she asserts that women's liberation was an ontological movement, focusing on the patterns of women's thoughts and actions, and on breaking the patriarchal manipulation of those patterns.

1978   Karol Wojtyla is elected Pope; he takes the name John Paul II and exercises influence through moral and doctrinal conservatism and through his international and political defense of traditional morality and human rights.

1978   Desmond Tutu becomes the first black general secretary of the South African Council of Churches; under his direction, the Council plays a leading role in the fight against apartheid, and Tutu becomes an internationally recognized spokesman for black South African rights.

1978–81   Leonardo Boff presents his ideas on liberation theology in *Jesus Christ, Liberator* (1978), *Liberating Grace* (1979), and *Church: Charism and Power* (1981).

1979   Ruhollah Khomeini (referred to as Ayatollah Khomeini) is named the supreme religious and political leader of Iran, ruling above the formal institutions of the state.

APPENDIX TWO:
Geographic Listing of Biographies

The listing below classifies the individuals in the book according to the place in which they conducted important work or engaged in significant activities. In most instances, this is the person's place of birth. In other cases, however, individuals left their place of origin to study and work elsewhere. In still other cases, individuals will have been prominent in more than one country or region; we have listed these under more than one heading. We have used contemporary English names for present-day countries as geographic indicators and have included parenthetical phrases to indicate the historical place name where we thought an explanation might be helpful.

Algeria

Augustine of Hippo, Saint
  Seminal Christian Theologian   354–430

Khaldun, Ibn
  Originator of the Sociological Approach to History   1332–1406

Austria

Buber, Martin
  Religious Philosopher; Developer of Jewish Existentialism   1878–1965

Wittgenstein, Ludwig
  Major Philosopher of the Twentieth Century   1889–1951

Brazil

Boff, Leonardo
  Influential Liberation Theologian   1938–

China

Confucius (K'ung Ch'iu)
  Chinese Philosopher; Founder of Confucianism   551–479 B.C.E.

Fa-tsang
  Systematizer of Huayan School of Chinese Buddhism   643–712

Han-fei-tzu
  Major Scholar of Chinese Legalist School   c. 280–c. 233 B.C.E.

Hsün-tzu
  Influential Confucian Moral Philosopher   c. 300–c. 230 B.C.E.

Lao-tzu
  Founder of Taoism   c. 570–490 B.C.E.

Mencius (Meng K'o)
  Confucian Moral Philosopher and Interpreter   c. 371–c. 289 B.C.E.

Shang Yang (Kung-sun Yang)
  Chinese Philosopher of Legalist School   c. 390–338 B.C.E.

Czech Republic

Hus, Jan
  Czech Reformer of the Christian Church   1372–1415

Denmark

Kierkegaard, Søren Aabye
  Influential Existentialist Philosopher   1813–1855

Egypt

'Abduh, Muhammad
  Architect of Islamic Modernism   1849–1905

Akhenaton (Amenhotep IV)
  Egyptian Pharaoh; Advocate of Monolatry   Reigned c. 1367–1350 B.C.E.

Athanasius, Saint
  Egyptian Bishop and Theologian;
  Developer of the New Testament Canon   c. 293–373

Cyril of Alexandria, Saint
  Architect of Early Christian Christology   c. 375–444

Moses
  First Leader and Lawgiver of the Ancient Israelites   c. 13th Century B.C.E.

Moses ben Maimon (Maimonides)
  Medieval Jewish Philosopher; Codifier of Jewish Law   1135–1204

Origen (Oregenes Adamantius)
  Synthesizer of Early Christian Theology   c. 185–c. 255

Philo Judaeus (Philo of Alexandria)
  Hellenistic Interpreter of Jewish Law   c. 20 B.C.E.–c. 50 C.E.

Sa'adia ben Joseph
  Jewish Talmudic Scholar and Synthesizer of Faith and Reason   882–942

Shafi'i, Abu 'Abd Allah, ash-
  Preeminent Islamic Legal Scholar   767–820

England

Anselm of Canterbury, Saint
  Archbishop of Canterbury; Father of Scholasticism   c. 1033–1109

Bacon, Francis
  Philosopher of Science;
  Originator of Inductive Method of Scientific Inquiry   1561–1626

Bentham, Jeremy
  English Jurist and Philosopher; Expounder of Utilitarianism   1748–1832

Berkeley, George
  Founder of Idealism   1685–1753

Blavatsky, Helena Petrovna
  Founder of the Theosophical Movement   1831–1891

Burke, Edmund
  Influential Political Philosopher   1729–1797

Cranmer, Thomas
  Leader of the English Reformation   1489–1556

Fortune, Dion
  Founder of the Society of the Inner Light   1890–1946

Fox, George
  Founder of the Quakers   1624–1691

Hobbes, Thomas
  Political Philosopher; Developer of the Social Contract Theory   1588–1679

Keynes, John Maynard
  Influential Political Economist;
  Advocate of Government Intervention in Economic Affairs   1883–1946

Lee, Ann (Mother Ann)
  Founder and Spiritual Leader of the Shakers   1736–1784

Locke, John
  Architect of Classical Political Liberalism   1632–1704

Marx, Karl
  Originator of Marxism   1818–1883

Mill, John Stuart
  Pioneer of Utilitarianism   1806–1873

More, Sir Thomas, Saint
  Author of *Utopia*; Defender of the Roman Catholic Faith   1477–1535

Russell, Bertrand
  Influential Twentieth-Century Philosopher;
  Founder of Logicism   1872–1970

Tutu, Desmond
  Anglican Archbishop of South Africa; Fighter Against Apartheid   1931–

Wesley, John
  Anglican Clergyman; Founder of Methodism   1703–1791

Wittgenstein, Ludwig
  Major Philosopher of the Twentieth Century   1889-1951

Wycliffe, John
  English Church Reformer;
  Forerunner of the Protestant Reformation   c. 1330–1384

Young, Brigham
  Early Influential Mormon Leader   1801–1877

France

Abelard, Peter
  Theologian and Philosopher;
  Proponent of the Modern University   1079–1142

Afghani, Jamal ad-Din, al-
  Influential Twentieth-Century Pan-Islamist   c. 1838–1897

Anselm of Canterbury, Saint
  Archbishop of Canterbury; Father of Scholasticism   c. 1033–1109

Bernadette of Lourdes, Saint (Marie Bernarde Soubirous)
  Roman Catholic Visionary   1844–1879

Bernard of Clairvaux, Saint
  Defender of Christianity Against Rationalism   1090–1153

Calvin, John
  Theologian; Leading Protestant Reformer   1509–1564

Camus, Albert
  Influential Existentialist Novelist   1913–1960

Comte, Auguste
  Founder of Sociology   1798–1857

Derrida, Jacques
  Postmodern French Philosopher; Proponent of Deconstructionism   1930–

Descartes, René
  Originator of the Framework of Modern Philosophy   1596–1650

Diderot, Denis
  Encyclopedist and Major Philosopher of the
  French Enlightenment   1713–1784

Durkheim, Émile
  Founder of Modern Methods of Sociology   1858–1917

Erasmus, Desiderius (traveled and worked throughout Europe)
  Humanist Theologian and Scholar;
  Christian Proponent of Free Will   c. 1469–1536

Foucault, Michel
  Wide-ranging Twentieth-Century Philosopher   1926–1984

Hobbes, Thomas
  Political Philosopher;
  Developer of the Social Contract Theory   1588–1679

Joan of Arc, Saint
  National Heroine and Patron Saint of France   c. 1412–1431

Marx, Karl
  Originator of Marxism   1818–1883

Montaigne, Michel Eyquem de
  Influential French Philosopher and Essayist   1533–1592

Montesquieu, Baron de la Brède et de (Charles Louis de Secondat)
  Originator of the Theory of the Separation of Powers   1689–1755

Pascal, Blaise
  Influential Mathematician,
  Theologian, and Philosopher of Science   1623–1662

Rousseau, Jean-Jacques
  Political Philosopher; Developer of the Social Contract Theory   1712–1778

Sartre, Jean-Paul
  Preeminent Twentieth-Century Existentialist   1905–1980

Thomas Aquinas, Saint
  Christian Theologian and Philosopher;
  Synthesizer of Faith and Reason   c. 1224–1274

Urban II, Pope (Odo of Lagery)
  Initiator of the Crusades   c. 1035–1099

Voltaire (François-Marie Arouet)
  Leading Philosopher of the French Enlightenment   1694–1778

Germany

Bakunin, Mikhail
  Russian Revolutionary; Founder of Modern Anarchy   1814–1876

Barth, Karl
  Christian Theologian and Originator of Neo-Orthodoxy;
  Active Opponent of Hitler   1886–1968

Bonhoeffer, Dietrich
  German Theologian; Influential Nazi Resister   1906–1945

Buber, Martin
  Religious Philosopher; Developer of Jewish Existentialism   1878–1965

Fichte, Johann Gottlieb
  Philosopher of Transcendental Idealism   1762–1814

Gadamer, Hans-Georg
  Philosopher of Hermeneutics   1900–

Hegel, Georg Wilhelm Friedrich
  Pioneer of Dialectical Historical Method   1770–1831

Heidegger, Martin
  Influential Twentieth-Century Existential Philosopher   1889–1976

Hildegard von Bingen, Saint
  Major Figure in Medieval Mystical Tradition   1098–1179

Husserl, Edmund
  Philosopher and Founder of Phenomenology   1859–1938

Luther, Martin
  Principal Figure in the Protestant Reformation   1483–1546

Melanchthon, Philipp
  Humanist and Reformation Theologian;
  Author of Influential Lutheran Documents   1497–1560

Nietzsche, Friedrich Wilhelm
  Influential Philosopher and Critic of Judeo–Christian Tradition   1844–1900

Schopenhauer, Arthur
  Exponent of the Metaphysical Doctrine of the Will   1788–1860

Tillich, Paul
  Theologian and Philosopher; Reconciler of Christian
  Thought with Modern Culture   1886–1965

Urban II, Pope (Odo of Lagery)
  Initiator of the Crusades   c. 1035–1099

Greece

Anaximander (in Miletus, present-day Turkey, under Greek rule)
  Philosopher–Scientist;
  Early Developer of Cosmological Theory   c. 611–c. 547 B.C.E.

Aristotle
  Influential Greek Philosopher;
  Opponent of Platonic Concept of Forms   384–322 B.C.E.

Epictetus
  Influential Stoic Philosopher   c. 50–c. 135

Epicurus
  Founder of Epicurean School of Philosophy   341–270 B.C.E.

Herodotus
  Father of European History   c. 484–c. 425 B.C.E.

Plato
  Influential Greek Philosopher   c. 428–c. 347 B.C.E.

Pythagoras
  Pre-Socratic Philosopher of Mathematical Realism   c. 580–c. 500 B.C.E.

Socrates of Athens
  First Greek Philosopher of the Western Tradition;
  Developer of Socratic Method   c. 469–399 B.C.E.

Thales of Miletus (in Miletus, present-day Turkey, under Greek rule)
  Originator of the Foundations of Greek Philosophy
  and Science   c. 624–c. 546 B.C.E.

Zeno of Citium
  Founder of Stoic Philosophy   c. 335–c. 263 B.C.E.

India

Afghani, Jamal ad-Din, al- (traveled and worked throughout South Asia, the
    Middle East, and Europe)
  Influential Twentieth-Century Pan-Islamist   c. 1838–1897

Arjun
  Fifth Sikh Guru; Compiler of the *Adi Granth*   1563–1606

Aurobindo Ghose (Sri Aurobindo)
  Founder of Integral Yoga   1872–1950

Blavatsky, Helena Petrovna
  Founder of the Theosophical Movement   1831–1891

Buddha (Siddhartha Gautama)
  Founder of Buddhism   c. 600–c. 400 B.C.E.

Dalai Lama (Tenzin Gyatso)
  Spiritual Leader of Tibetan Buddhism   1935–

Gandhi, Mohandas Karamchand (Mahatma)
  Father of Indian Independence;
  Leading Advocate of Nonviolent Protest   1869–1948

Gobind Singh
  Founder of Khalsa Sect of Sikhism   1666–1708

Madhva
  Founder of Hindu School of Dvaita Vedanta   c. 1199–c. 1278

Maharishi Mahesh Yogi
  Founder of the Transcendental Meditation Movement   1911(?)–

Mahavira (Vardhamana)
  Founder of Jainism   c. 599–c. 527 B.C.E.

Nanak
  Founder of Sikhism   1469–1539

Patañjali
  Traditional Author of the Yoga-Sutras   c. 220 B.C.E.–c. 400 C.E.

Ramakrishna (Gadadhar Chatterji)
  Hindu Mystic Reformer   c. 1835–1886

Ramanuja
  Founder of Vishishtadvaita Vedanta   c. 1017–1137 (traditionally)

Roy, Ram Mohun
  Reformer of Hinduism; Founder of Brahmo Samaj   1772–1833

Shankara
  Founder of Advaita Vedanta Hinduism   c. 700–c. 750

Teresa, Mother (Agnes Gonxha Bojaxhiu)
  Founder of the Order of the
  Missionary Sisters of Charity   1910–1997

Vivekananda (Narendranath Datta or Dutt)
  Promoter of Hinduism in Western Society   1863–1902

Iran

Avicenna (Ibn Sina)
  Islamic Philosopher; Synthesizer of Greek Thought   980–1037

Baha' Allah (Mirza Hoseyn Ali Nuri)
  Founder of Bahai Religion   1817–1892

Ghazali, al-
  Influential Islamic Theologian and Mystic   1058–1111

Hallaj, al-
Founder of the Sufi Halladjiyya Sect   c. 858–922

Khomeini, Ruhollah
Influential Twentieth-Century Islamic Leader   c. 1900–1989

Zoroaster (Zarathustra)
Founder of Zoroastrianism   c. 1000 B.C.E.

Iraq

Baha' Allah (Mirza Hoseyn Ali Nuri)
Founder of Bahai Religion   1817–1892

Bihbihani, Aka Sayyid Muhammad Bakir
Influential Shiite Legal Scholar   c. 1705–c. 1792

Farabi, al-
First Theologian to Relate Islamic Theology to Greek Philosophy   c. 878–950

Hallaj, al- (traveled and worked throughout present-day Iran, India, Turkistan,
and Saudi Arabia)
Founder of the Sufi Halladjiyya Sect   c. 858–922

Junayd, Abu al-Qasim, al-
Architect of the First Theoretical Foundations of Sufism   c. 825–c. 910

Khomeini, Ruhollah
Influential Twentieth-Century Islamic Leader   c. 1900–1989

Kindi, Yaqub ibn Ishaq as-Sabah, al-
Islamic Philosopher and Synthesizer of Greek Thought   c. 800–c. 873

Mani (Manes; Manichaeus)
Founder of Manichaeism   216–c. 274

Matta ibn Yunus
Early Arabic Commentator on Aristotle   d. 940

Rabi'ah al'Adawiyah
Architect of Sufi Asceticism   c. 717–801

Sa'adia ben Joseph
Jewish Talmudic Scholar and Synthesizer of Faith and Reason   882–942

Ireland

Columba, Saint
Founder of the Influential Christian Community at Iona   521–597

Patrick, Saint
Patron Saint and National Apostle of Ireland   c. 390–c. 461

Israel (includes Palestine)

Abraham
First Biblical Patriarch   c. 2000–1500 B.C.E.

Akiba ben Joseph (ancient Judah)
Early Interpreter of Jewish Law   c. 40–c. 135

Baha' Allah (Mirza Hoseyn Ali Nuri)
Founder of Bahai Religion   1817–1892

Buber, Martin
Religious Philosopher; Developer of Jewish Existentialism   1878–1965

David (ancient Israel)
Important Biblical Figure; Founder of Jerusalem   10th Century B.C.E.

Elijah
Hebrew Prophet; Monotheist   c. 9th Century B.C.E.

Hillel (ancient Palestine)
Influential Rabbi; Interpreter of Biblical Law   c. 60 B.C.E.–c. 20 C.E.

Jeremiah
Biblical Prophet Influential in Diaspora Judaism   c. 645–c. 570 B.C.E.

Jerome, Saint
Christian Theologian; Translator of the Bible into Latin   c. 347–419/20

Jesus
Teacher, Healer, and Savior of the Christian Tradition   c. 4 B.C.E.–c. 30 C.E

Mary
Mother of Jesus; Object of Catholic Veneration   1st Century B.C.E.–
1st Century C.E.

Origen (Oregenes Adamantius)
Synthesizer of Early Christian Theology   c. 185–c. 255

Paul (Saul of Tarsus)
(traveled and worked throughout Palestine and the northern Mediterranean)
Influential Early Christian Thinker and Missionary   c. 5 B.C.E.–c. 64 C.E.

Italy

Anselm of Canterbury, Saint
Archbishop of Canterbury; Father of Scholasticism   c. 1033–1109

Benedict of Nursia, Saint
Founder of Basic Structure of Western Monasticism   c. 480–547

Boethius, Anicius Manlius Severinus
Influential Medieval Philosopher; Architect of Scholasticism c. 480–c. 524

Francis of Assisi, Saint
Founder of the Franciscan Order of Friars   c. 1181–1226

Gregory I, Pope
Early Pope and Church Reformer   c. 540–604

Herodotus (in Thuria, under Greek rule)
Father of European History   c. 484–c. 425 B.C.E.

Ignatius of Loyola, Saint
Founder of the Society of Jesus (Jesuits)   1491–1556

Jerome, Saint
Christian Theologian; Translator of the Bible into Latin   c. 347–419/20

John XXIII, Pope (Angelo Giuseppe Roncalli)
Pope and Modern Reformer of the Roman Catholic Church   1881–1963

John Paul II, Pope (Karol Wojtyla)
Influential Roman Catholic Pope   1920–

Machiavelli, Niccolò
Founder of Modern Political Science   1469–1527

Marcion
Influential Early Christian Heretic   1st–2nd Century C.E.

Marcus Aurelius (traveled and worked throughout the Roman Empire)
Roman Emperor; Stoic "Philosopher–King"   121–180

Montessori, Maria (traveled and worked throughout Asia, Europe, and the
United States)
Educational Philosopher; Originator of the Montessori Method   1870–1952

Pythagoras (in present-day southern Italy, under Greek rule)
Pre-Socratic Philosopher of Mathematical Realism   c. 580–c. 500 B.C.E.

Savonarola, Girolamo
Italian Church Reformer; Millenarian Prophet   1452–1498

Thomas Aquinas, Saint
    Christian Theologian and Philosopher;
    Synthesizer of Faith and Reason   c. 1224–1274

Urban II, Pope (Odo of Lagery)
    Initiator of the Crusades   c. 1035–1099

Jamaica

Garvey, Marcus
    Founder and Leader of the Black Nationalist Movement   1887–1940

Japan

Moon, Sun Myung
    Evangelist and Founder of the Unification Church   1920–

Netherlands

Descartes, René
    Originator of the Framework of Modern Philosophy   1596–1650

Spinoza, Benedict de
    First Philosophical Defender of Democracy   1632–1677

Peru

Gutiérrez, Gustavo
    Originator of Latin American Liberation Theology   1928–

Poland

Israel ben Eliezer (Ba'al Shem Tov) (traveled and worked throughout Eastern Europe)
    Founder of the Jewish Hasidic Movement   c. 1700–1760

John Paul II, Pope (Karol Wojtyla)
    Influential Roman Catholic Pope   1920–

Russia

Bakunin, Mikhail
    Russian Revolutionary; Founder of Modern Anarchy   1814–1876

Kant, Immanuel
    Leading Enlightenment Philosopher   1724–1804

Saudi Arabia, Syria, and the Arabian Peninsula

'Arabi, Ibn al-
    Master of Islamic Sufi Mysticism   1165–1240

Farabi, al-
    First Theologian to Relate Islamic Theology to
    Greek Philosophy   c. 878–c. 950

Fatimah Bint Muhammad
    Daughter of Muhammad; Matriarch of the Shiite Sect   c. 610–633

Matta ibn Yunus
    Early Arabic Commentator on Aristotle   d. 940

Muhammad
    Prophet and Founder of Islam   c. 570–632

Shafi'i, Abu 'Abd Allah, ash-
    Preeminent Islamic Legal Scholar   767–820

Scotland

Columba, Saint
    Founder of the Influential Christian Community at Iona   521–597

Hume, David
    Major Enlightenment Philosopher; Critic of Empiricism   1711–1776

Reid, Thomas
    Founder of the Philosophical School of Common Sense   1710–1796

Smith, Adam
    Philosopher and Political Economist;
    Originator of Modern Liberal Economic Theory   1723–1790

South Africa

Tutu, Desmond
    Anglican Archbishop of South Africa; Fighter Against Apartheid   1931–

South Korea

Moon, Sun Myung
    Evangelist and Founder of the Unification Church   1920–

Spain

Averroës (Ibn Rushd)
    Islamic Theologian; Interpreter of Aristotle and Plato   1126–1198

Ignatius of Loyola, Saint
    Founder of the Society of Jesus (Jesuits)   1491–1556

Teresa of Ávila, Saint
    Christian Mystic;
    Founder of the Order of Barefoot Carmelites   1515–1582

Torquemada, Tomás de
    First Grand Inquisitor of Spanish Inquisition   1420–1498

Switzerland

Barth, Karl
    Christian Theologian and Originator of Neo-Orthodoxy;
    Active Opponent of Hitler   1886–1968

Calvin, John
    Theologian; Leading Protestant Reformer   1509–1564

Nietzsche, Friedrich Wilhelm
    Influential Philosopher and Critic of
    Judeo–Christian Tradition   1844–1900

Pestalozzi, Johann Heinrich
    Influential Educational Philosopher and Reformer   1746–1827

Piaget, Jean
    Pioneer of Developmental Child Psychology   1896–1980

Voltaire (François-Marie Arouet)
    Leading Philosopher of the French Enlightenment   1694–1778

Tibet

Blavatsky, Helena Petrovna
    Founder of the Theosophical Movement   1831–1891

Dalai Lama (Tenzin Gyatso)
    Spiritual Leader of Tibetan Buddhism   1935–

Tunisia

Khaldun, Ibn
    Originator of the Sociological Approach to History   1332–1406

United States

Arendt, Hannah
    Philosopher of Totalitarianism   1906–1975

Berkeley, George
    Founder of Idealism   1685–1753

Blavatsky, Helena Petrovna
    Founder of the Theosophical Movement   1831–1891

Bushnell, Horace
    Protestant Theologian; Father of American Religious Liberalism   1802–1876

Channing, William Ellery
    Early Unitarian Church Leader   1780–1842

Cone, James Hal
    Architect of Black Liberation Theology   1938–

Daly, Mary
    Influential Feminist Theologian and Philosopher   1928–

Derrida, Jacques
    Postmodern French Philosopher; Proponent of Deconstructionism   1930–

Dewey, John
    Father of Progressive Education   1859–1952

Du Bois, W. E. B.
    Black Nationalist Leader; Founder of the NAACP   1868–1963

Eddy, Mary Baker
    Founder of Christian Science   1821–1910

Einhorn, David
    Theologian of Reform Judaism   1809–1879

Emerson, Ralph Waldo
    Pioneer of Transcendentalism   1803–1882

Garrison, William Lloyd
    Leader of Abolitionist Movement   1805–1879

Garvey, Marcus
    Founder and Leader of the Black Nationalist Movement   1887–1940

Gladden, Solomon Washington
    Protestant Leader of Social Gospel Movement   1836–1918

Heschel, Abraham Joshua
    Influential Jewish Theologian and Social Activist   1907–1972

Hubbard, L. Ron
    Founder of the Church of Scientology   1911–1986

James, William
    Preeminent American Psychologist; Philosophical Pragmatist   1842–1910

Jefferson, Thomas
    Principal Author of the U. S. Declaration of Independence   1743–1826

Kaplan, Mordecai Menahem
    American–Jewish Theologian;
    Founder of Reconstructionist Judaism   1881–1983

King, Martin Luther, Jr.
    Preeminent Civil Rights Leader   1929–1968

Lee, Ann (Mother Ann)
    Founder and Spiritual Leader of the Shakers   1736–1784

Madison, James
    Principal Architect of the United States Constitution   1751–1836

Malcolm X (Malcolm Little)
    Militant Black Activist; Minister of the Nation of Islam   1925–1965

Mann, Horace
    Educational Philosopher and Reformer;
    Advocate of Free Public Schools   1796–1859

Moon, Sun Myung
    Evangelist and Founder of the Unification Church   1920–

Muhammad, Elijah (Elijah Poole)
    Leader of the Nation of Islam   1897–1975

Niebuhr, Reinhold
    Political Theologian; Advocate of Christian Political Activism   1892–1971

Palmer, Phoebe Worrall
    Founder of the Holiness Movement   1807–1874

Parham, Charles Fox
    Founder of American Pentecostalism   1873–1929

Peirce, Charles Sanders
    Founder of Pragmatism   1839–1914

Rauschenbusch, Walter
    Leader of the Social Gospel Movement   1861–1918

Russell, Charles Taze
    Founder of the Jehovah's Witnesses   1852–1916

Schneerson, Menachem Mendel
    Head of the Habad–Lubavitch Sect of Hasidic Judaism   1902–1994

Seton, Elizabeth Ann, Saint
    First American-Born Saint; Founder of the Sisters of Charity   1774–1821

Smith, Joseph
    Founder of the Mormon Church   1805–1844

Stowe, Harriet Beecher
    Prominent Abolitionist; Author of *Uncle Tom's Cabin*   1811–1896

Strong, Josiah
    Promoter of the Social Gospel;
    Leader of the Ecumenical Movement   1847–1916

Thoreau, Henry David
    Leading Transcendentalist Philosopher   1817–1862

Tillich, Paul
    Theologian and Philosopher; Reconciler of
    Christian Thought with Modern Culture   1886–1965

Vivekananda (Narendranath Datta or Dutt)
    Promoter of Hinduism in Western Society   1863–1902

Washington, Booker Taliaferro
    Influential Educator and Spokesperson for African Americans   1856–1915

White, Ellen Gould
    Founder and Spiritual Leader of the Seventh-Day Adventists   1827–1915

Wise, Isaac Mayer
    Founder of American Reform Judaism   1819–1900

Wovoka
    Native American Religious Leader;
    Leader of Ghost Dance Movement   c. 1856–1932

Young, Brigham
    Early Influential Mormon Leader   1801–1877

Chronological Listing of Biographies

Abraham	First Biblical Patriarch	c. 2000–1500 B.C.E.
Akhenaton (Amenhotep IV)	Egyptian Pharaoh; Advocate of Monolatry	Reigned c. 1367–1350 B.C.E.
Moses	First Leader and Lawgiver of the Ancient Israelites	c. 13th Century B.C.E.
Zoroaster (Zarathustra)	Founder of Zoroastrianism	c. 1000 B.C.E.
David	Important Biblical Figure; Founder of Jerusalem	10th Century B.C.E.
Elijah	Hebrew Prophet; Monotheist	c. 9th Century B.C.E.
Jeremiah	Biblical Prophet Influential in Diaspora Judaism	c. 645–c.570 B.C.E.
Thales of Miletus	Originator of the Foundations of Greek Philosophy and Science	c. 624–c. 546 B.C.E.
Anaximander	Philosopher–Scientist; Early Developer of Cosmological Theory	c. 611–c. 547 B.C.E.
Buddha (Siddhartha Gautama)	Founder of Buddhism	c. 600–c. 400 B.C.E.
Mahavira (Vardhamana)	Founder of Jainism	c. 599–c. 527 B.C.E.
Pythagoras	Pre-Socratic Philosopher of Mathematical Realism	c. 580–c. 500 B.C.E.
Lao-tzu	Founder of Taoism	c. 570–490 B.C.E.
Confucius (K'ung Ch'iu)	Chinese Philosopher; Founder of Confucianism	551–479 B.C.E.
Herodotus	Father of European History	c. 484–c. 425 B.C.E.
Socrates of Athens	First Greek Philosopher of the Western Tradition; Developer of Socratic Method	c. 469–399 B.C.E.
Plato	Influential Greek Philosopher	c. 428–c. 347 B.C.E.
Shang Yang (Kung-sun Yang)	Chinese Philosopher of Legalist School	c. 390–338 B.C.E.
Aristotle	Influential Greek Philosopher; Opponent of Platonic Concept of Forms	384–322 B.C.E.
Mencius (Meng K'o)	Confucian Moral Philosopher and Interpreter	c. 371–c. 289 B.C.E.
Epicurus	Founder of Epicurean School of Philosophy	341–270 B.C.E.
Zeno of Citium	Founder of Stoic Philosophy	c. 335–c. 263 B.C.E.
Hsün-tzu	Influential Confucian Moral Philosopher	c. 300–c. 230 B.C.E.
Han-fei-tzu	Major Scholar of Chinese Legalist School	c. 280–c. 233 B.C.E.
Patañjali	Traditional Author of the Yoga-Sutras	c. 220 B.C.E. to c. 400 C.E.
Hillel	Influential Rabbi; Interpreter of Biblical Law	c. 60 B.C.E.–c. 20 C.E.
Philo Judaeus (Philo of Alexandria)	Hellenistic Interpreter of Jewish Law	c. 20 B.C.E.–c. 50 C.E.
Paul (Saul of Tarsus)	Influential Early Christian Thinker and Missionary	c. 5 B.C.E.–c. 64 C.E.
Jesus	Teacher, Healer, and Savior of the Christian Tradition	c. 4 B.C.E.–c. 30 C.E
Mary	Mother of Jesus; Object of Catholic Veneration	1st Century B.C.E.–1st Century C.E.
Marcion	Influential Early Christian Heretic	1st–2nd Century C.E.
Akiba ben Joseph	Early Interpreter of Jewish Law	c. 40–c. 135
Epictetus	Influential Stoic Philosopher	c. 50–c. 135
Marcus Aurelius	Roman Emperor; Stoic "Philosopher–King"	121–180
Origen (Oregenes Adamantius)	Synthesizer of Early Christian Theology	c. 185–c. 255
Mani (Manes; Manichaeus)	Founder of Manichaeism	216–c. 274
Athanasius, Saint	Egyptian Bishop and Theologian; Developer of the New Testament Canon	c. 293–373
Jerome, Saint	Christian Theologian; Translator of the Bible into Latin	c. 347–419/20

Augustine of Hippo, Saint	Seminal Christian Theologian	354–430
Cyril of Alexandria, Saint	Architect of Early Christian Christology	c. 375–444
Patrick, Saint	Patron Saint and National Apostle of Ireland	c. 390–c. 461
Boethius, Anicius Manlius Severinus	Influential Medieval Philosopher; Architect of Scholasticism	c. 480–c. 524
Benedict of Nursia, Saint	Founder of Basic Structure of Western Monasticism	c. 480–547
Columba, Saint	Founder of the Influential Christian Community at Iona	521–597
Gregory I, Pope	Early Pope and Church Reformer	c. 540–604
Muhammad	Prophet and Founder of Islam	c. 570–632
Fatimah Bint Muhammad	Daughter of Muhammad; Matriarch of the Shiite Sect	c. 610–633
Fa-tsang	Systematizer of Huayan School of Chinese Buddhism	643–712
Shankara	Founder of Advaita Vedanta Hinduism	c. 700–c. 750
Rabi'ah al'Adawiyah	Architect of Sufi Asceticism	c. 717–801
Shafi'i, Abu 'Abd Allah, ash-	Preeminent Islamic Legal Scholar	767–820
Kindi, Yaqub ibn Ishaq as-Sabah, al-	Islamic Philosopher and Synthesizer of Greek Thought	c. 800–c. 873
Junayd, Abu al-Qasim, al-	Architect of the First Theoretical Foundations of Sufism	c. 825–c. 910
Hallaj, al-	Founder of the Sufi Halladjiyya Sect	c. 858–922
Farabi, al-	First Theologian to Relate Islamic Theology to Greek Philosophy	c. 878–c. 950
Sa'adia ben Joseph	Jewish Talmudic Scholar and Synthesizer of Faith and Reason	882–942
Matta ibn Yunus	Early Arabic Commentator on Aristotle	d. 940
Avicenna (Ibn Sina)	Islamic Philosopher; Synthesizer of Greek Thought	980–1037
Ramanuja	Founder of Vishishtadvaita Vedanta	c. 1017–1137 (traditionally)
Anselm of Canterbury, Saint	Archbishop of Canterbury; Father of Scholasticism	c. 1033–1109
Urban II, Pope (Odo of Lagery)	Initiator of the Crusades	c. 1035–1099
Ghazali, al-	Influential Islamic Theologian and Mystic	1058–1111
Abelard, Peter	Theologian and Philosopher; Proponent of the Modern University	1079–1142
Bernard of Clairvaux, Saint	Defender of Christianity Against Rationalism	1090–1153
Hildegard von Bingen, Saint	Major Figure in Medieval Mystical Tradition	1098–1179
Averroës (Ibn Rushd)	Islamic Theologian; Interpreter of Aristotle and Plato	1126–1198
Moses ben Maimon (Maimonides)	Medieval Jewish Philosopher; Codifier of Jewish Law	1135–1204
'Arabi, Ibn al-	Master of Islamic Sufi Mysticism	1165–1240
Francis of Assisi, Saint	Founder of the Franciscan Order of Friars	c. 1181–1226
Madhva	Founder of Hindu School of Dvaita Vedanta	c. 1199–c. 1278
Thomas Aquinas, Saint	Christian Theologian and Philosopher; Synthesizer of Faith and Reason	c. 1224–1274
Wycliffe, John	English Church Reformer; Forerunner of the Protestant Reformation	c. 1330–1384
Khaldun, Ibn	Originator of the Sociological Approach to History	1332–1406
Hus, Jan	Czech Reformer of the Christian Church	1372–1415
Joan of Arc, Saint	National Heroine and Patron Saint of France	c. 1412–1431
Torquemada, Tomás de	First Grand Inquisitor of Spanish Inquisition	1420–1498
Savonarola, Girolamo	Italian Church Reformer; Millenarian Prophet	1452–1498
Machiavelli, Niccolò	Founder of Modern Political Science	1469–1527
Erasmus, Desiderius	Humanist Theologian and Scholar; Christian Proponent of Free Will	c. 1469–1536
Nanak	Founder of Sikhism	1469–1539
More, Sir Thomas, Saint	Author of *Utopia*; Defender of the Roman Catholic Faith	1477–1535
Luther, Martin	Principal Figure in the Protestant Reformation	1483–1546
Cranmer, Thomas	Leader of the English Reformation	1489–1556

Ignatius of Loyola, Saint	Founder of the Society of Jesus (Jesuits)	1491–1556
Melanchthon, Philipp	Humanist and Reformation Theologian; Author of Influential Lutheran Documents	1497–1560
Calvin, John	Theologian; Leading Protestant Reformer	1509–1564
Teresa of Ávila, Saint	Christian Mystic; Founder of the Order of Barefoot Carmelites	1515–1582
Montaigne, Michel Eyquem de	Influential French Philosopher and Essayist	1533–1592
Bacon, Francis	Philosopher of Science; Originator of Inductive Method of Scientific Inquiry	1561–1626
Arjun	Fifth Sikh Guru; Compiler of the *Adi Granth*	1563–1606
Hobbes, Thomas	Political Philosopher; Developer of the Social Contract Theory	1588–1679
Descartes, René	Originator of the Framework of Modern Philosophy	1596–1650
Pascal, Blaise	Influential Mathematician, Theologian, and Philosopher of Science	1623–1662
Fox, George	Founder of the Quakers	1624–1691
Spinoza, Benedict de	First Philosophical Defender of Democracy	1632–1677
Locke, John	Architect of Classical Political Liberalism	1632–1704
Gobind Singh	Founder of Khalsa Sect of Sikhism	1666–1708
Berkeley, George	Founder of Idealism	1685–1753
Montesquieu, Baron de la Brède et de (Charles Louis de Secondat)	Originator of the Theory of the Separation of Powers	1689–1755
Voltaire (François-Marie Arouet)	Leading Philosopher of the French Enlightenment	1694–1778
Israel ben Eliezer (Ba'al Shem Tov)	Founder of the Jewish Hasidic Movement	c. 1700–1760
Wesley, John	Anglican Clergyman; Founder of Methodism	1703–1791
Bihbihani, Aka Sayyid Muhammad Bakir	Influential Shiite Legal Scholar	c. 1705–c. 1792
Reid, Thomas	Founder of the Philosophical School of Common Sense	1710–1796
Hume, David	Major Enlightenment Philosopher; Critic of Empiricism	1711–1776
Rousseau, Jean-Jacques	Political Philosopher; Developer of the Social Contract Theory	1712–1778
Diderot, Denis	Encyclopedist and Major Philosopher of the French Enlightenment	1713–1784
Smith, Adam	Philosopher and Political Economist; Originator of Modern Liberal Economic Theory	1723–1790
Kant, Immanuel	Leading Enlightenment Philosopher	1724–1804
Burke, Edmund	Influential Political Philosopher	1729–1797
Lee, Ann (Mother Ann)	Founder and Spiritual Leader of the Shakers	1736–1784
Jefferson, Thomas	Principal Author of the U. S. Declaration of Independence	1743–1826
Pestalozzi, Johann Heinrich	Influential Educational Philosopher and Reformer	1746–1827
Bentham, Jeremy	English Jurist and Philosopher; Expounder of Utilitarianism	1748–1832
Madison, James	Principal Architect of the United States Constitution	1751–1836
Fichte, Johann Gottlieb	Philosopher of Transcendental Idealism	1762–1814
Hegel, Georg Wilhelm Friedrich	Pioneer of Dialectical Historical Method	1770–1831
Roy, Ram Mohun	Reformer of Hinduism; Founder of Brahmo Samaj	1772–1833
Seton, Elizabeth Ann, Saint	First American-Born Saint; Founder of the Sisters of Charity	1774–1821
Channing, William Ellery	Early Unitarian Church Leader	1780–1842
Schopenhauer, Arthur	Exponent of the Metaphysical Doctrine of the Will	1788–1860
Mann, Horace	Educational Philosopher and Reformer; Advocate of Free Public Schools	1796–1859
Comte, Auguste	Founder of Sociology	1798–1857
Young, Brigham	Early Influential Mormon Leader	1801–1877
Bushnell, Horace	Protestant Theologian; Father of American Religious Liberalism	1802–1876
Emerson, Ralph Waldo	Pioneer of Transcendentalism	1803–1882
Smith, Joseph	Founder of the Mormon Church	1805–1844

Garrison, William Lloyd	Leader of Abolitionist Movement	1805–1879
Mill, John Stuart	Pioneer of Utilitarianism	1806–1873
Palmer, Phoebe Worrall	Founder of the Holiness Movement	1807–1874
Einhorn, David	Theologian of Reform Judaism	1809–1879
Stowe, Harriet Beecher	Prominent Abolitionist; Author of *Uncle Tom's Cabin*	1811–1896
Kierkegaard, Søren Aabye	Influential Existentialist Philosopher	1813–1855
Bakunin, Mikhail	Russian Revolutionary; Founder of Modern Anarchy	1814–1876
Thoreau, Henry David	Leading Transcendentalist Philosopher	1817–1862
Baha' Allah (Mirza Hoseyn Ali Nuri)	Founder of Bahai Religion	1817–1892
Marx, Karl	Originator of Marxism	1818–1883
Wise, Isaac Mayer	Founder of American Reform Judaism	1819–1900
Eddy, Mary Baker	Founder of Christian Science	1821–1910
White, Ellen Gould	Founder and Spiritual Leader of the Seventh-Day Adventists	1827–1915
Blavatsky, Helena Petrovna	Founder of the Theosophical Movement	1831–1891
Ramakrishna (Gadadhar Chatterji)	Hindu Mystic Reformer	c. 1835–1886
Gladden, Solomon Washington	Protestant Leader of Social Gospel Movement	1836–1918
Afghani, Jamal ad-Din, al-	Influential Twentieth-Century Pan-Islamist	c. 1838–1897
Peirce, Charles Sanders	Founder of Pragmatism	1839–1914
James, William	Preeminent American Psychologist; Philosophical Pragmatist	1842–1910
Bernadette of Lourdes, Saint (Marie Bernarde Soubirous)	Roman Catholic Visionary	1844–1879
Nietzsche, Friedrich Wilhelm	Influential Philosopher and Critic of Judeo–Christian Tradition	1844–1900
Strong, Josiah	Promoter of the Social Gospel; Leader of the Ecumenical Movement	1847–1916
'Abduh, Muhammad	Architect of Islamic Modernism	1849–1905
Russell, Charles Taze	Founder of the Jehovah's Witnesses	1852–1916
Washington, Booker Taliaferro	Influential Educator and Spokesperson for African Americans	1856–1915
Wovoka	Native American Religious Leader; Leader of Ghost Dance Movement	c. 1856–1932
Durkheim, Émile	Founder of Modern Methods of Sociology	1858–1917
Husserl, Edmund	Philosopher and Founder of Phenomenology	1859–1938
Dewey, John	Father of Progressive Education	1859–1952
Rauschenbusch, Walter	Leader of the Social Gospel Movement	1861–1918
Vivekananda (Narendranath Datta or Dutt)	Promoter of Hinduism in Western Society	1863–1902
Du Bois, W. E. B.	Black Nationalist Leader; Founder of the NAACP	1868–1963
Gandhi, Mohandas Karamchand (Mahatma)	Father of Indian Independence; Leading Advocate of Nonviolent Protest	1869–1948
Montessori, Maria	Educational Philosopher; Originator of the Montessori Method	1870–1952
Aurobindo Ghose (Sri Aurobindo)	Founder of Integral Yoga	1872–1950
Russell, Bertrand	Influential Twentieth-Century Philosopher; Founder of Logicism	1872–1970
Parham, Charles Fox	Founder of American Pentecostalism	1873–1929
Buber, Martin	Religious Philosopher; Developer of Jewish Existentialism	1878–1965
John XXIII, Pope (Angelo Giuseppe Roncalli)	Pope and Modern Reformer of the Roman Catholic Church	1881–1963
Kaplan, Mordecai Menahem	American–Jewish Theologian; Founder of Reconstructionist Judaism	1881–1983
Keynes, John Maynard	Influential Political Economist; Advocate of Government Intervention in Economic Affairs	1883–1946
Tillich, Paul	Theologian and Philosopher; Reconciler of Christian Thought with Modern Culture	1886–1965
Barth, Karl	Christian Theologian and Originator of Neo-Orthodoxy; Active Opponent of Hitler	1886–1968
Garvey, Marcus	Founder and Leader of the Black Nationalist Movement	1887–1940

Wittgenstein, Ludwig	Major Philosopher of the Twentieth Century	1889–1951
Heidegger, Martin	Influential Twentieth-Century Existential Philosopher	1889–1976
Fortune, Dion	Founder of the Society of the Inner Light	1890–1946
Niebuhr, Reinhold	Political Theologian; Advocate of Christian Political Activism	1892–1971
Piaget, Jean	Pioneer of Developmental Child Psychology	1896–1980
Muhammad, Elijah (Elijah Poole)	Leader of the Nation of Islam	1897–1975
Khomeini, Ruhollah	Influential Twentieth-Century Islamic Leader	c. 1900–1989
Gadamer, Hans-Georg	Philosopher of Hermeneutics	1900–
Schneerson, Menachem Mendel	Head of the Habad–Lubavitch Sect of Hasidic Judaism	1902–1994
Sartre, Jean-Paul	Preeminent Twentieth-Century Existentialist	1905–1980
Bonhoeffer, Dietrich	German Theologian; Influential Nazi Resister	1906–1945
Arendt, Hannah	Philosopher of Totalitarianism	1906–1975
Heschel, Abraham Joshua	Influential Jewish Theologian and Social Activist	1907–1972
Teresa, Mother (Agnes Gonxha Bojaxhiu)	Founder of the Order of the Missionary Sisters of Charity	1910–1997
Maharishi Mahesh Yogi	Founder of the Transcendental Meditation Movement	1911(?)–
Hubbard, L. Ron	Founder of the Church of Scientology	1911–1986
Camus, Albert	Influential Existentialist Novelist	1913–1960
John Paul II, Pope (Karol Wojtyla)	Influential Roman Catholic Pope	1920–
Moon, Sun Myung	Evangelist and Founder of the Unification Church	1920–
Malcolm X (Malcolm Little)	Militant Black Activist; Minister of the Nation of Islam	1925–1965
Foucault, Michel	Wide-ranging Twentieth-Century Philosopher	1926–1984
Daly, Mary	Influential Feminist Theologian and Philosopher	1928–
Gutiérrez, Gustavo	Originator of Latin American Liberation Theology	1928–
King, Martin Luther, Jr.	Preeminent Civil Rights Leader	1929–1968
Derrida, Jacques	Postmodern French Philosopher; Proponent of Deconstructionism	1930–
Tutu, Desmond	Anglican Archbishop of South Africa; Fighter Against Apartheid	1931–
Dalai Lama (Tenzin Gyatso)	Spiritual Leader of Tibetan Buddhism	1935–
Boff, Leonardo	Influential Liberation Theologian	1938–
Cone, James Hal	Architect of Black Liberation Theology	1938–

Alphabetical Listing of Biographies

'Abduh, Muhammad	Architect of Islamic Modernism	1849–1905
Abelard, Peter	Theologian and Philosopher; Proponent of the Modern University	1079–1142
Abraham	First Biblical Patriarch	c. 2000–1500 B.C.E.
Afghani, Jamal ad-Din, al-	Influential Twentieth-Century Pan-Islamist	c. 1838–1897
Akhenaton (Amenhotep IV)	Egyptian Pharaoh; Advocate of Monolatry	Reigned c. 1367–1350 B.C.E.
Akiba ben Joseph	Early Interpreter of Jewish Law	c. 40–c. 135
Anaximander	Philosopher–Scientist; Early Developer of Cosmological Theory	c. 611–c. 547 B.C.E.
Anselm of Canterbury, Saint	Archbishop of Canterbury; Father of Scholasticism	c. 1033–1109
'Arabi, Ibn al-	Master of Islamic Sufi Mysticism	1165–1240
Arendt, Hannah	Philosopher of Totalitarianism	1906–1975
Aristotle	Influential Greek Philosopher; Opponent of Platonic Concept of Forms	384–322 B.C.E.
Arjun	Fifth Sikh Guru; Compiler of the Adi Granth	1563–1606
Athanasius, Saint	Egyptian Bishop and Theologian; Developer of the New Testament Canon	c. 293–373
Augustine of Hippo, Saint	Seminal Christian Theologian	354–430
Aurobindo Ghose (Sri Aurobindo)	Founder of Integral Yoga	1872–1950
Averroës (Ibn Rushd)	Islamic Theologian; Interpreter of Aristotle and Plato	1126–1198
Avicenna (Ibn Sina)	Islamic Philosopher; Synthesizer of Greek Thought	980–1037
Bacon, Francis	Philosopher of Science; Originator of Inductive Method of Scientific Inquiry	1561–1626
Baha' Allah (Mirza Hoseyn Ali Nuri)	Founder of Bahai Religion	1817–1892
Bakunin, Mikhail	Russian Revolutionary; Founder of Modern Anarchy	1814–1876
Barth, Karl	Christian Theologian and Originator of Neo-Orthodoxy; Active Opponent of Hitler	1886–1968
Benedict of Nursia, Saint	Founder of Basic Structure of Western Monasticism	c. 480–547
Bentham, Jeremy	English Jurist and Philosopher; Expounder of Utilitarianism	1748–1832
Berkeley, George	Founder of Idealism	1685–1753
Bernadette of Lourdes, Saint (Marie Bernarde Soubirous)	Roman Catholic Visionary	1844–1879
Bernard of Clairvaux, Saint	Defender of Christianity Against Rationalism	1090–1153
Bihbihani, Aka Sayyid Muhammad Bakir	Influential Shiite Legal Scholar	c. 1705–c. 1792
Blavatsky, Helena Petrovna	Founder of the Theosophical Movement	1831–1891
Boethius, Anicius Manlius Severinus	Influential Medieval Philosopher; Architect of Scholasticism	c. 480–c. 524
Boff, Leonardo	Influential Liberation Theologian	1938–
Bonhoeffer, Dietrich	German Theologian; Influential Nazi Resister	1906–1945
Buber, Martin	Religious Philosopher; Developer of Jewish Existentialism	1878–1965
Buddha (Siddhartha Gautama)	Founder of Buddhism	c. 600–c. 400 B.C.E.
Burke, Edmund	Influential Political Philosopher	1729–1797
Bushnell, Horace	Protestant Theologian; Father of American Religious Liberalism	1802–1876
Calvin, John	Theologian; Leading Protestant Reformer	1509–1564
Camus, Albert	Influential Existentialist Novelist	1913–1960
Channing, William Ellery	Early Unitarian Church Leader	1780–1842

Columba, Saint	Founder of the Influential Christian Community at Iona	521–597
Comte, Auguste	Founder of Sociology	1798–1857
Cone, James Hal	Architect of Black Liberation Theology	1938–
Confucius (K'ung Ch'iu)	Chinese Philosopher; Founder of Confucianism	551–479 B.C.E.
Cranmer, Thomas	Leader of the English Reformation	1489–1556
Cyril of Alexandria, Saint	Architect of Early Christian Christology	c. 375–444
Dalai Lama (Tenzin Gyatso)	Spiritual Leader of Tibetan Buddhism	1935–
Daly, Mary	Influential Feminist Theologian and Philosopher	1928–
David	Important Biblical Figure; Founder of Jerusalem	10th Century B.C.E.
Derrida, Jacques	Postmodern French Philosopher; Proponent of Deconstructionism	1930–
Descartes, René	Originator of the Framework of Modern Philosophy	1596–1650
Dewey, John	Father of Progressive Education	1859–1952
Diderot, Denis	Encyclopedist and Major Philosopher of the French Enlightenment	1713–1784
Du Bois, W. E. B.	Black Nationalist Leader; Founder of the NAACP	1868–1963
Durkheim, Émile	Founder of Modern Methods of Sociology	1858–1917
Eddy, Mary Baker	Founder of Christian Science	1821–1910
Einhorn, David	Theologian of Reform Judaism	1809–1879
Elijah	Hebrew Prophet; Monotheist	c. 9th Century B.C.E.
Emerson, Ralph Waldo	Pioneer of Transcendentalism	1803–1882
Epictetus	Influential Stoic Philosopher	c. 50–c. 135
Epicurus	Founder of Epicurean School of Philosophy	341–270 B.C.E.
Erasmus, Desiderius	Humanist Theologian and Scholar; Christian Proponent of Free Will	c. 1469–1536
Farabi, al-	First Theologian to Relate Islamic Theology to Greek Philosophy	c. 878–c. 950
Fatimah Bint Muhammad	Daughter of Muhammad; Matriarch of the Shiite Sect	c. 610–633
Fa-tsang	Systematizer of Huayan School of Chinese Buddhism	643–712
Fichte, Johann Gottlieb	Philosopher of Transcendental Idealism	1762–1814
Fortune, Dion	Founder of the Society of the Inner Light	1890–1946
Foucault, Michel	Wide-ranging Twentieth-Century Philosopher	1926–1984
Fox, George	Founder of the Quakers	1624–1691
Francis of Assisi, Saint	Founder of the Franciscan Order of Friars	c. 1181–1226
Gadamer, Hans-Georg	Philosopher of Hermeneutics	1900–
Gandhi, Mohandas Karamchand (Mahatma)	Father of Indian Independence; Leading Advocate of Nonviolent Protest	1869–1948
Garrison, William Lloyd	Leader of Abolitionist Movement	1805–1879
Garvey, Marcus	Founder and Leader of the Black Nationalist Movement	1887–1940
Ghazali, al-	Influential Islamic Theologian and Mystic	1058–1111
Gladden, Solomon Washington	Protestant Leader of Social Gospel Movement	1836–1918
Gobind Singh	Founder of Khalsa Sect of Sikhism	1666–1708
Gregory I, Pope	Early Pope and Church Reformer	c. 540–604
Gutiérrez, Gustavo	Originator of Latin American Liberation Theology	1928–
Hallaj, al-	Founder of the Sufi Halladjiyya Sect	c. 858–922
Han-fei-tzu	Major Scholar of Chinese Legalist School	c. 280–c. 233 B.C.E.
Hegel, Georg Wilhelm Friedrich	Pioneer of Dialectical Historical Method	1770–1831
Heidegger, Martin	Influential Twentieth-Century Existential Philosopher	1889–1976
Herodotus	Father of European History	c. 484–c. 425 B.C.E.
Heschel, Abraham Joshua	Influential Jewish Theologian and Social Activist	1907–1972

Hildegard von Bingen, Saint	Major Figure in Medieval Mystical Tradition	1098–1179
Hillel	Influential Rabbi; Interpreter of Biblical Law	c. 60 B.C.E.–c. 20 C.E.
Hobbes, Thomas	Political Philosopher; Developer of the Social Contract Theory	1588–1679
Hsün-tzu	Influential Confucian Moral Philosopher	c. 300–c. 230 B.C.E.
Hubbard, L. Ron	Founder of the Church of Scientology	1911–1986
Hume, David	Major Enlightenment Philosopher; Critic of Empiricism	1711–1776
Hus, Jan	Czech Reformer of the Christian Church	1372–1415
Husserl, Edmund	Philosopher and Founder of Phenomenology	1859–1938
Ignatius of Loyola, Saint	Founder of the Society of Jesus (Jesuits)	1491–1556
Israel ben Eliezer (Ba'al Shem Tov)	Founder of the Jewish Hasidic Movement	c. 1700–1760
James, William	Preeminent American Psychologist; Philosophical Pragmatist	1842–1910
Jefferson, Thomas	Principal Author of the U. S. Declaration of Independence	1743–1826
Jeremiah	Biblical Prophet Influential in Diaspora Judaism	c. 645–c. 570 B.C.E.
Jerome, Saint	Christian Theologian; Translator of the Bible into Latin	c. 347–419/20
Jesus	Teacher, Healer, and Savior of the Christian Tradition	c. 4 B.C.E.–c. 30 C.E
Joan of Arc, Saint	National Heroine and Patron Saint of France	c. 1412–1431
John XXIII, Pope (Angelo Giuseppe Roncalli)	Pope and Modern Reformer of the Roman Catholic Church	1881–1963
John Paul II, Pope (Karol Wojtyla)	Influential Roman Catholic Pope	1920–
Junayd, Abu al-Qasim, al-	Architect of the First Theoretical Foundations of Sufism	c. 825–c. 910
Kant, Immanuel	Leading Enlightenment Philosopher	1724–1804
Kaplan, Mordecai Menahem	American–Jewish Theologian; Founder of Reconstructionist Judaism	1881–1983
Keynes, John Maynard	Influential Political Economist; Advocate of Government Intervention in Economic Affairs	1883–1946
Khaldun, Ibn	Originator of the Sociological Approach to History	1332–1406
Khomeini, Ruhollah	Influential Twentieth-Century Islamic Leader	c. 1900–1989
Kierkegaard, Søren Aabye	Influential Existentialist Philosopher	1813–1855
Kindi, Yaqub ibn Ishaq as-Sabah, al-	Islamic Philosopher and Synthesizer of Greek Thought	c. 800–c. 873
King, Martin Luther, Jr.	Preeminent Civil Rights Leader	1929–1968
Lao-tzu	Founder of Taoism	c. 570–490 B.C.E.
Lee, Ann (Mother Ann)	Founder and Spiritual Leader of the Shakers	1736–1784
Locke, John	Architect of Classical Political Liberalism	1632–1704
Luther, Martin	Principal Figure in the Protestant Reformation	1483–1546
Machiavelli, Niccolò	Founder of Modern Political Science	1469–1527
Madhva	Founder of Hindu School of Dvaita Vedanta	c. 1199–c. 1278
Madison, James	Principal Architect of the United States Constitution	1751–1836
Maharishi Mahesh Yogi	Founder of the Transcendental Meditation Movement	1911(?)–
Mahavira (Vardhamana)	Founder of Jainism	c. 599–c. 527 B.C.E.
Malcolm X (Malcolm Little)	Militant Black Activist; Minister of the Nation of Islam	1925–1965
Mani (Manes; Manichaeus)	Founder of Manichaeism	216–c. 274
Mann, Horace	Educational Philosopher and Reformer; Advocate of Free Public Schools	1796–1859
Marcion	Influential Early Christian Heretic	1st–2nd Century C.E.
Marcus Aurelius	Roman Emperor; Stoic "Philosopher–King"	121–180
Marx, Karl	Originator of Marxism	1818–1883
Mary	Mother of Jesus; Object of Catholic Veneration	1st Century B.C.E.–1st Century C.E.
Matta ibn Yunus	Early Arabic Commentator on Aristotle	d. 940
Melanchthon, Philipp	Humanist and Reformation Theologian; Author of Influential Lutheran Documents	1497–1560

Mencius (Meng K'o)	Confucian Moral Philosopher and Interpreter	c. 371–c. 289 B.C.E.
Mill, John Stuart	Pioneer of Utilitarianism	1806–1873
Montaigne, Michel Eyquem de	Influential French Philosopher and Essayist	1533–1592
Montesquieu, Baron de la Brède et de (Charles Louis de Secondat)	Originator of the Theory of the Separation of Powers	1689–1755
Montessori, Maria	Educational Philosopher; Originator of the Montessori Method	1870–1952
Moon, Sun Myung	Evangelist and Founder of the Unification Church	1920–
More, Sir Thomas, Saint	Author of *Utopia*; Defender of the Roman Catholic Faith	1477–1535
Moses	First Leader and Lawgiver of the Ancient Israelites	c. 13th Century B.C.E.
Moses ben Maimon (Maimonides)	Medieval Jewish Philosopher; Codifier of Jewish Law	1135–1204
Muhammad	Prophet and Founder of Islam	c. 570–632
Muhammad, Elijah (Elijah Poole)	Leader of the Nation of Islam	1897–1975
Nanak	Founder of Sikhism	1469–1539
Niebuhr, Reinhold	Political Theologian; Advocate of Christian Political Activism	1892–1971
Nietzsche, Friedrich Wilhelm	Influential Philosopher and Critic of Judeo–Christian Tradition	1844–1900
Origen (Oregenes Adamantius)	Synthesizer of Early Christian Theology	c. 185–c. 255
Palmer, Phoebe Worrall	Founder of the Holiness Movement	1807–1874
Parham, Charles Fox	Founder of American Pentecostalism	1873–1929
Pascal, Blaise	Influential Mathematician, Theologian, and Philosopher of Science	1623–1662
Patañjali	Traditional Author of the Yoga-Sutras	c. 220 B.C.E. to c. 400 C.E.
Patrick, Saint	Patron Saint and National Apostle of Ireland	c. 390–c. 461
Paul (Saul of Tarsus)	Influential Early Christian Thinker and Missionary	c. 5 B.C.E.–c. 64 C.E.
Peirce, Charles Sanders	Founder of Pragmatism	1839–1914
Pestalozzi, Johann Heinrich	Influential Educational Philosopher and Reformer	1746–1827
Philo Judaeus (Philo of Alexandria)	Hellenistic Interpreter of Jewish Law	c. 20 B.C.E.–c. 50 C.E.
Piaget, Jean	Pioneer of Developmental Child Psychology	1896–1980
Plato	Influential Greek Philosopher	c. 428–c. 347 B.C.E.
Pythagoras	Pre-Socratic Philosopher of Mathematical Realism	c. 580–c. 500 B.C.E.
Rabi'ah al-'Adawiyah	Architect of Sufi Asceticism	c. 717–801
Ramakrishna (Gadadhar Chatterji)	Hindu Mystic Reformer	c. 1835–1886
Ramanuja	Founder of Vishishtadvaita Vedanta	c. 1017–1137 (traditionally)
Rauschenbusch, Walter	Leader of the Social Gospel Movement	1861–1918
Reid, Thomas	Founder of the Philosophical School of Common Sense	1710–1796
Rousseau, Jean-Jacques	Political Philosopher; Developer of the Social Contract Theory	1712–1778
Roy, Ram Mohun	Reformer of Hinduism; Founder of Brahmo Samaj	1772–1833
Russell, Bertrand	Influential Twentieth-Century Philosopher; Founder of Logicism	1872–1970
Russell, Charles Taze	Founder of the Jehovah's Witnesses	1852–1916
Sa'adia ben Joseph	Jewish Talmudic Scholar and Synthesizer of Faith and Reason	882–942
Sartre, Jean-Paul	Preeminent Twentieth-Century Existentialist	1905–1980
Savonarola, Girolamo	Italian Church Reformer; Millenarian Prophet	1452–1498
Schneerson, Menachem Mendel	Head of the Habad–Lubavitch Sect of Hasidic Judaism	1902–1994
Schopenhauer, Arthur	Exponent of the Metaphysical Doctrine of the Will	1788–1860
Seton, Elizabeth Ann, Saint	First American-Born Saint; Founder of the Sisters of Charity	1774–1821
Shafi'i, Abu 'Abd Allah, ash-	Preeminent Islamic Legal Scholar	767–820
Shang Yang (Kung-sun Yang)	Chinese Philosopher of Legalist School	c. 390–338 B.C.E.

Shankara	Founder of Advaita Vedanta Hinduism	c. 700–c. 750
Smith, Adam	Philosopher and Political Economist; Originator of Modern Liberal Economic Theory	1723–1790
Smith, Joseph	Founder of the Mormon Church	1805–1844
Socrates of Athens	First Greek Philosopher of the Western Tradition; Developer of Socratic Method	c. 469–399 B.C.E.
Spinoza, Benedict de	First Philosophical Defender of Democracy	1632–1677
Stowe, Harriet Beecher	Prominent Abolitionist; Author of *Uncle Tom's Cabin*	1811–1896
Strong, Josiah	Promoter of the Social Gospel; Leader of the Ecumenical Movement	1847–1916
Teresa, Mother (Agnes Gonxha Bojaxhiu)	Founder of the Order of the Missionary Sisters of Charity	1910–1997
Teresa of Ávila, Saint	Christian Mystic; Founder of the Order of Barefoot Carmelites	1515–1582
Thales of Miletus	Originator of the Foundations of Greek Philosophy and Science	c. 624–c. 546 B.C.E.
Thomas Aquinas, Saint	Christian Theologian and Philosopher; Synthesizer of Faith and Reason	c. 1224–1274
Thoreau, Henry David	Leading Transcendentalist Philosopher	1817–1862
Tillich, Paul	Theologian and Philosopher; Reconciler of Christian Thought with Modern Culture	1886–1965
Torquemada, Tomás de	First Grand Inquisitor of Spanish Inquisition	1420–1498
Tutu, Desmond	Anglican Archbishop of South Africa; Fighter Against Apartheid	1931–
Urban II, Pope (Odo of Lagery)	Initiator of the Crusades	c. 1035–1099
Vivekananda (Narendranath Datta or Dutt)	Promoter of Hinduism in Western Society	1863–1902
Voltaire (François-Marie Arouet)	Leading Philosopher of the French Enlightenment	1694–1778
Washington, Booker Taliaferro	Influential Educator and Spokesperson for African Americans	1856–1915
Wesley, John	Anglican Clergyman; Founder of Methodism	1703–1791
White, Ellen Gould	Founder and Spiritual Leader of the Seventh-Day Adventists	1827–1915
Wise, Isaac Mayer	Founder of American Reform Judaism	1819–1900
Wittgenstein, Ludwig	Major Philosopher of the Twentieth Century	1889–1951
Wovoka	Native American Religious Leader; Leader of Ghost Dance Movement	c. 1856–1932
Wycliffe, John	English Church Reformer; Forerunner of the Protestant Reformation	c. 1330–1384
Young, Brigham	Early Influential Mormon Leader	1801–1877
Zeno of Citium	Founder of Stoic Philosophy	c. 335–c. 263 B.C.E.
Zoroaster (Zarathustra)	Founder of Zoroastrianism	c. 1000 B.C.E.

Bibliography

GENERAL HISTORICAL AND CULTURAL BACKGROUND

The following sources are included to offer the researcher information and analysis concerning the larger historical and cultural context that helped to shape the actions and thinking of individuals covered in this volume. Also, the sources can help further to elucidate aspects of these individuals' legacies, which were intimately tied to the religious and philosophical traditions they were a part of and, consequently, to the historical and cultural landscape of their time and place. Some sources cited here may also be included in other sections of the bibliography.

Appiah, Kwame Anthony and Henry Louis Gates, Jr. *The Dictionary of Global Culture*. New York: Knopf, 1997.

Avery, Peter, and Stanley I. Grossman, eds. *The Cambridge History of Iran*. Cambridge, England: Cambridge University Press, 1991.

Cahill, Thomas. *How the Irish Saved Civilization: The Untold Story of Ireland's Heroic Role from the Fall of Rome to the Rise of Medieval Europe*. New York: Doubleday, 1995.

Cannon, John, ed. *The Oxford Companion to British History*. New York and Oxford: Oxford University Press, 1997.

Gardiner, Juliet and Neil Wenborn, eds. *The Columbia Companion to British History*. New York: Columbia University Press, 1997.

Hitti, Philip Khuri. *The Arabs: A Short History*. Washington, D.C.: Regnery Publishing, 1996.

Knapp, A. Bernard. *The History and Culture of Ancient Western Asia and Egypt*. Belmont, Calif.: Wadsworth Publishing, 1988.

McGreal, Ian P., ed. *Great Thinkers of the Eastern World*. New York: HarperCollins Publishers, 1995.

McGreal, Ian P., ed. *Great Thinkers of the Western World*. New York: HarperCollins Publishers, 1992.

Perkins, Dorothy. *Encyclopedia of China*. New York: Facts On File, 1999.

Stewart, Devin J. *Law and Society in Islam*. Princeton, N.J.: Markus Wiener Publishers, 1996.

Unger, Harlow G. *Encyclopedia of American Education*. 3 vols. New York: Facts On File, 1996.

Van Creveld, Martin. *The Encyclopedia of Revolutions and Revolutionaries*. New York: Facts On File, 1996.

GENERAL RELIGION

The following sources are included to give readers a fuller context for the religious traditions covered in this volume, a context that is more complete than is possible through the individual biographies. They will provide readers with encyclopedic information on the history of and general trends in religious development across the centuries. Some sources cited here may also be included in other sections of the bibliography.

Eliade, M. *The Encyclopedia of Religion*. 16 Vols. New York: Macmillan, 1987.

Hinnells, John R. *Who's Who of Religions*. London and New York: Penguin Books, 1996.

MacGregor, Geddes. *Dictionary of Religion and Philosophy*. New York: Paragon House, 1991.

McGreal, Ian P., ed. *Great Thinkers of the Eastern World*. New York: HarperCollins Publishers, 1995.

McGreal, Ian P., ed. *Great Thinkers of the Western World*. New York: HarperCollins Publishers, 1992.

Queen, Edward L. II, Stephen R. Prothero and Gardiner H. Shattuck, Jr. *The Encyclopedia of American Religious History*. 2 vols. New York: Facts On File, 1996.

GENERAL PHILOSOPHY

The following sources are included to give readers a fuller context for the philosophical traditions and movements covered in this volume, a context that is more complete than is possible through the individual biographies. They will provide researchers with encyclopedic information on the history of and general trends in philosophy across the centuries. Some sources cited here may also be included in other sections of the bibliography.

Audi, Robert, ed. *The Cambridge Dictionary of Philosophy*. Cambridge and New York: Cambridge University Press, 1995.

Fakhry, Majid. *A History of Islamic Philosophy*. New York: Columbia University Press, 1983.

Griffiths, Morwenna, and Margaret Whiteford, eds. *Feminist Perspectives in Philosophy*. Bloomington: Indiana University Press, 1988.

Luce, John Victor. *An Introduction to Greek Philosophy*. London: Thames and Hudson, 1992.

Nasr, Sayyid Hossein, and Oliver Leaman, eds. *History of Islamic Philosophy*. New York: Routledge, 1996.

Solomon, Robert C., and Kathleen M. Higgins. *A Short History of Philosophy*. New York: Oxford University Press, 1996.

Strauss, Leo and Joseph Cropsey, eds. *History of Political Philosophy*. 3rd ed. Chicago: University of Chicago Press, 1987.

Unger, Harlow G. *Encyclopedia of American Education*. 3 vols. New York: Facts On File, 1996.

RELIGIOUS TRADITIONS

Included in this section are sources on religious traditions throughout the world. The sources might cover historical trends in those religions, the history of specialized topics within those traditions, and biographies of important people who shaped them. Some sources cited here may also be included in other sections of the bibliography.

Alger, Hamid. *Religion and State in Iran.* Berkeley: University of California Press, 1969.

Anderson, Robert Mapes. *Vision of the Disinherited: The Making of American Pentecostalism.* New York: Oxford University Press, 1989.

Andrews, Edward D. *The People Called Shakers.* New York: Oxford, 1953.

Badawi, M. A. Zaki. *The Reformers of Egypt.* London: Croom Helm, 1978.

Bakhash, Shaul. *The Reign of the Ayatollahs: Iran and the Islamic Revolution.* New York: Basic Books, 1984.

Barnes, Timothy David. *Athanasius and Constantius: Theology and Politics in the Constantinian Empire.* Cambridge, Mass.: Harvard University Press, 1993.

Berthrong, John H. *Transformations of the Confucian Way.* Boulder, Colo.: Westview Press, 1998.

Blofeld, John. *Taoism: The Road to Immortality.* Boston: Shambhala, 1985.

Boff, Leonardo and Clovodis. *Introducing Liberation Theology.* New York: Orbis Books, 1987.

Boice, James Montgomery. *Ordinary Men Called by God.* Grand Rapids, Mich.: Kregel, 1998.

Bonnechose, Emile. *Reformers Before the Reformation.* New York: AMS Press, 1980.

Bromley, David G., and Anson D. Shupe, Jr. *Moonies in America: On the Road to the Millennium.* Beverly Hills, Calif.: Sage Publications, 1979.

Burckhardt, Titus. *An Introduction to Sufism.* Wellingborough, England: Crucible, 1990.

Cahill, Thomas. *How the Irish Saved Civilization: The Untold Story of Ireland's Heroic Role from the Fall of Rome to the Rise of Medieval Europe.* New York: Doubleday, 1995.

Chadwick, Henry, *The Early Church.* New York: Penguin Books, 1967.

Chan, Wing-tsit. *Neo-Confucian Terms Explained.* New York: Columbia University Press, 1986.

Chapman, John. *St. Benedict and the Sixth Century,* 1919. Reprint. Westport, Conn: Greenwood Press, 1971.

Childs, Brevard. *The Book of Exodus: A Critical, Theological Commentary.* Philadelphia: Westminster Press, 1974.

Chopp, Rebecca. *The Praxis of Suffering: An Interpretation of Liberation and Political Theologies.* Maryknoll, N.Y.: Orbis Books, 1986.

Chryssides, George D. *The Advent of Sun Myung Moon: The Origins, Beliefs, and Practices of the Unification Church.* New York: St. Martin's Press, 1991.

Cohn-Sherbok, Dan. *Fifty Key Jewish Thinkers.* New York: Routledge, 1997.

Cone, James H. *God of the Oppressed.* New York: Seabury Press, 1975.

Cox, Harvey. *The Silencing of Leonardo Boff: The Vatican and the Future of World Christianity.* Bloomington, Ind.: Meyer-Stone Books, 1988.

Curtis, Susan. *A Consuming Faith: The Social Gospel and Modern American Culture.* Baltimore, Md.: Johns Hopkins University Press, 1991.

Damsteegt, P. Gerard. *Foundations of the Seventh-Day Adventist Message and Mission.* Grand Rapids, Mich.: Eerdmans, 1977.

De Bary, William. *The Trouble with Confucianism.* Cambridge: Harvard University Press, 1991.

Dieter, Melvin E. *The Holiness Revival of the Nineteenth Century.* Metuchen, N.J.: Scarecrow Press, 1980.

Dundas, Paul. *The Jains.* London: Routledge, 1992.

Eisemann, Moshe. *A Pearl in the Sand: Reflections on Shavuos, Megilas Ruth and The Davidic Kingship.* Baltimore, Md.: M. M. Eisemann, 1997.

Encyclopaedia Judaica. 18 vols. Jerusalem: Macmillan, 1996.

Fagan, John. *Genetic Engineering: The Hazards. Vedic Engineering: The Solutions.* Fairfield, Conn.: Maharishi International University of Management Press, 1995.

Ferguson, Everett, ed. *Encyclopedia of Early Christianity,* 2nd ed. New York: Garland, 1998.

Ferm, Donald. *Third World Liberation Theologies: A Reader.* Maryknoll, N.Y.: Orbis Books, 1986.

Frank, Richard W. *Creation and the Cosmic System: Al-Ghazali and Avicenna.* Heidelberg, Germany: Carl Winter Universitatsverlag, 1992.

Gibb, H. A., ed. *The Encyclopedia of Islam.* Leiden: Brill, 1960.

Gnoli, Gherardo. *Zoroaster's Time and Homeland: A Study of the Origins of Mazdeism and Related Problems.* Naples, Italy: Istituto Universitario Orientale, 1980.

Gorrell, Donald K. *The Age of Social Responsibility: The Social Gospel in the Progressive Era, 1900–1920.* Macon, Ga.: Mercer University Press, 1988.

Grimal, Nicholas. *A History of Ancient Egypt.* Oxford: Blackwell, 1992.

Handy, Robert T. *The Social Gospel in America, 1870–1920.* New York: Oxford University Press, 1966.

Hillerbrand, Hans. J. *The Oxford Encyclopedia of the Reformation.* 4 vols. New York and Oxford: Oxford University Press, 1996.

Hilpisch, Stephen. *Benedictinism Through Changing Centuries.* Collegeville, Minn.: St. John's Abbey Press, 1958.

Hirschfelder, Arlene and Pauline Molin. *The Encyclopedia of Native American Religions.* New York: Facts On File, 1992.

Hoffman, Edward. *Despite All Odds: The Story of Lubavitch.* New York: Simon & Schuster, 1991.

Hudson, Anne. *The Premature Reformation.* Oxford: Oxford University Press, 1988.

Isherwood, Christopher. *Ramakrishna and His Disciples.* London: Shepheard-Walwyn, 1986.

Ivanhoe, P. J. *Ethics in the Confucian Tradition: The Thought of Mencius and Wang Yang-ming.* Atlanta, Ga.: Scholar's Press, 1990.

Jackson, Carl T. *Vedanta for the West: The Ramakrishna Movement in the United States.* Bloomington and Indianapolis: The Indiana University Press, 1994.

Johnson, Paul. *A History of Christianity.* London: Weidenfeld and Nicolson, 1976.

Jospe, Raphael. *Paradigms in Jewish Philosophy.* Madison, N.J.: Fairleigh Dickinson University Press, 1997.

Kehoe, Alice Beck. *The Ghost Dance: Ethnohistory and Revitalization.* New York: Holt, Rinehart and Winston, 1989.

Kepel, Gilles. *Allah in the West: Islamic Movements in America and Europe.* Stanford, Calif.: Stanford University Press, 1997.

Kirk, John T. *The Shaker World: Art, Life, Beliefs.* New York: Harry N. Abrams, 1997.

Kolb, Robert. *Confessing the Faith: Reformers Define the Church, 1530–1580.* St. Louis, Mo.: Concordia, 1991.

Kung, Hans, and Leonard Swidler, eds. *The Church in Anguish: Has the Vatican Betrayed Vatican II?* San Francisco: Harper & Row, 1987.

Lacouture, Jean. *Jesuits: A Multibiography.* Translated by Jeremy Leggatt. Washington, D.C.: Counterpoint, 1995.

Livingstone, E.A. *The Concise Oxford Dictionary of the Christian Church.* Oxford and New York: Oxford University Press, 1996.

Maspero, Henri. *Taoism and Chinese Religion.* Amherst: University of Massachusetts Press, 1981.

Mays, James Luther, and Paul Achtemeier, eds. *Interpreting the Prophets.* Philadelphia: Fortress Press, 1987.

Mooney, James. *The Ghost-Dance Religion and the Sioux Outbreak of 1890.* Chicago: Chicago University Press, 1965.

Nadich, Judah. *Rabbi Akiba and His Contemporaries.* Northvale, N.J.: Jason Aronson, 1997.

New, Elisa. *The Regenerate Lyric: Theology and Innovation in American Poetry.* New York: Cambridge University Press, 1993.

Nicholson, Reynold Alleyene. *Studies in Islamic Mysticism.* New York: Kegan Paul International, 1998.

Paris, Erna. *The End of Days: A Story of Tolerance, Tyranny, and the Expulsion of the Jews from Spain.* Amherst, N.Y.: Prometheus Books, 1995.

Penton, M. James. *Apocalypse Delayed: The Story of Jehovah's Witnesses.* Toronto and Buffalo: University of Toronto Press, 1985.

Rahnema, Ali, ed. *Pioneers of Islamic Revival.* Atlantic Highlands, N.J.: Zed Books, 1994.

Reeves, John C. *Heralds of That Good Realm: Syro-Mesopotamian Gnosis and Jewish Traditions.* New York: E. J. Brill, 1996.

Rejwan, Nissim. *Arabs Face the Modern World: Religious, Cultural, and Political Responses to the West.* Gainesville: University of Florida Press, 1998.

Roeder, Ralph. *The Man of the Renaissance: Four Lawgivers, Savonarola, Machiavelli, Castilione, Aretino.* Cleveland, Ohio: Word Publishing Co., 1958.

Sachar, Howard M. *A History of Jews in America.* New York: Knopf, 1992.

Sells, Michael. *Mystical Languages of Unsaying.* Chicago: University of Chicago Press, 1994.

Sharma, B. N. Krishnamurti. *The History of the Dvaita School of Vedanta and Its Literature: From the Earliest Beginnings to Our Own Time.* Delhi: Motilal Banarsidass, 1981.

Silverstein, Alan. *Alternatives to Assimilation: The Response of Reform Judaism to American Culture, 1840–1930.* Hanover, N.H.: Published for Brandeis University Press by University Press of New England, 1994.

Skilton, Andrew (Dharmacari Sthiramati). *A Concise History of Buddhism.* Birmingham: Windhorse, 1994.

Tibetan Parliamentary and Policy Research Center. *The Spirit of Tibet, Vision for Human Liberation: Selected Speeches and Writings of HH the Dalai Lama.* Edited by A. A. Shiromany. New Delhi, India: Vikas Publishing House, 1996.

Tobias, Michael. *The Life Force: The World of Jainism.* Berkeley, Calif.: Asian Humanities Press, 1992.

Twain, Mark. *Christian Science.* Buffalo, N.Y.: Prometheus Books, 1986.

Van de Weyer, Robert. *Celtic Fire: The Passionate Religious Vision of Ancient Britain and Ireland.* New York: Doubleday, 1990.

von Rad, Gerhard. *Genesis: A Commentary.* Philadelphia: Westminster Press, 1976.

Wahba, Mourad, and Mona Abousenna, eds. *Averroës and the Enlightenment: The First Humanist-Muslim Dialogue.* Amherst, N.Y.: Prometheus Press, 1996.

Walker, Williston, Richard A. Norris, David W. Lotz, and Robert T. Handy. *A History of the Christian Church.* 4th ed. New York: Charles Scribner's Sons, 1985.

Wana, W. Reginald. *The Protestant Evangelical Awakening.* Cambridge: Cambridge University Press, 1992.

Weeks, Andrew. *German Mysticism from Hildegard of Bingen to Ludwig Wittgenstein: A Literary and Intellectual History.* Albany: State University of New York Press, 1993.

Wilmore, Gayraud S., and James H. Cone. *Black Theology: A Documentary History.* New York: Orbis Books, 1979.

Wright, Conrad E. *American Unitarianism, 1805–1865.* Boston: Massachusetts Historical Society, 1989.

PHILOSOPHICAL TRADITIONS AND TRENDS

Included in this section are sources on various philosophical traditions throughout the world. The sources might cover historical trends in those traditions, the history of specialized topics within those traditions, and biographies of important people who shaped them. Some sources cited here may also be included in other sections of the bibliography.

Alger, Hamid. *Religion and State in Iran.* Berkeley: University of California Press, 1969.

Anglin, W. S. *The Heritage of Thales.* New York: Springer, 1995.

Barnes, Jonathan. *Logic and the Imperial Stoa.* Leiden, Neth.: Brill, 1997.

Barnes, Jonathan. *The Presocratic Philosophers.* Boston: Routledge and Paul, 1979.

Berthrong, John H. *Transformations of the Confucian Way.* Boulder, Colo.: Westview Press, 1998.

Butterworth, Charles E. *The Political Aspects of Islamic Philosophy: Essays in Honor of Mushin S. Mahadi.* Cambridge, Mass.: Harvard University Press, 1992.

Chattin-McNichols, John. *The Montessori Controversy.* Albany, N.Y.: Delmar Publishers, 1992.

Cone, James H. *Martin & Malcolm & America: A Dream or a Nightmare.* Maryknoll, N.Y.: Orbis Books, 1991.

Curd, Patricia, ed. *A Pre-Socrates Reader.* Indianapolis, Ind.: Hackett Publishing Co., 1996.

Davidson, Herbert A. *Alfarabi, Avicenna, and Averroes: Their Cosmologies, Theories of the Active Intellect, and Theories of Human Intellect.* New York: Oxford University Press, 1992.

Dillon, Merton Lynn. *The Abolitionists: The Growth of a Dissenting Minority.* DeKalb: Northern Illinois University Press, 1974.

Evans, G. R. *Anselm and a New Generation.* New York: Oxford University Press, 1980.

Feuerstein, Georg. *The Philosophy of Classical Yoga.* Manchester, England: Manchester University Press, 1980.

Foster, John. *The Immaterial Self: A Defense of the Cartesian Dualist Conception of the Mind.* New York: Routledge, 1991.

Fu, Zhengyuan. *China's Legalists: The Earliest Totalitarians and Their Art of Ruling.* Armonk, N.Y.: M. E. Sharpe, 1996.

Gleave, R., and E. Kermelli. *Islamic Law: Theory and Practice.* New York: I. B. Tauris Publishers, 1997.

Griffiths, Morwenna, and Margaret Whiteford, eds. *Feminist Perspectives in Philosophy.* Bloomington: Indiana University Press, 1988.

Gutek, Gerald Lee. *Joseph Neef: The Americanization of Pestalozzianism.* Tuscaloosa: University of Alabama Press, 1978.

Hunsinger, George, ed. *Karl Barth and Radical Politics.* Philadelphia: Westminster, 1976.

Ivanhoe, P. J. *Ethics in the Confucian Tradition: The Thought of Mencius and Wang Yang-ming.* Atlanta, Ga.: Scholar's Press, 1990.

Jones, Howard. *The Epicurean Tradition.* New York: Routledge, 1992.

Jospe, Raphael. *Paradigms in Jewish Philosophy.* Madison, N.J.: Fairleigh Dickinson University Press, 1997.

Long, A. A. *Stoic Studies.* New York: Cambridge University Press, 1996.

Luce, John Victor. *An Introduction to Greek Philosophy.* London: Thames and Hudson, 1992.

McKirahan, Richard D. *Philosophy Before Socrates: An Introduction with Texts.* Indianapolis, Ind.: Haskett Publishing Co., 1994.

Morland, David. *Demanding the Impossible?: Human Nature and Nineteenth Century Anarchism.* Washington, D.C.: Cassell, 1997.

Nasr, Sayyid Hossein, and Oliver Leaman, eds. *History of Islamic Philosophy.* New York: Routledge, 1996.

New, Elisa. *The Regenerate Lyric: Theology and Innovation in American Poetry.* New York: Cambridge University Press, 1993.

Peerenboom, R. P. *Law and Morality in Ancient China.* Albany: State University of New York Press, 1993.

Ratcliffe, Krista. *Anglo-American Feminist Challenge to the Rhetorical Tradition: Virginia Woolf, Mary Daly, and Adrienne Rich.* Carbondale: Southern Illinois University Press, 1996.

Raymond, Diane. *Existentialism and the Philosophical Traditions.* Englewood Cliffs, N.J.: Prentice Hall, 1991.

Sarup, Madan. *An Introductory Guide to Post-structuralism and Postmodernism.* Athens: The University of Georgia Press, 1993.

Sharples, R. W. *Stoics, Epicureans, and Skeptics.* New York: Routledge, 1996.

Shun, Kwong-lui. *Mencius and Early Chinese Thought.* Stanford, Calif.: Stanford University Press, 1997.

Stewart, Devin J. *Law and Society in Islam.* Princeton, N.J.: Markus Wiener Publishers, 1996.

Trundle, Robert. *Ancient Greek Philosophy: Its Development and Relevance to Our Time.* Brookfield, Vt.: Avebury, 1994.

Wahba, Mourad, and Mona Abousenna, eds. *Averroës and the Enlightenment: The First Humanist-Muslim Dialogue.* Amherst, N.Y.: Prometheus Press, 1996.

Index

Note: Page numbers in **boldface** indicate subjects of articles.

as creator, 167
Deist concept, 91, 115
Diasporic, 98
divine pathos concept, 85
double predestination, 38
economic success as sign of favor, 38
emotional knowledge of, 95
female side, 114
goodness of, 10, 16, 40
healing power of, 56
human relationship with, 34
identity-in-difference relationship, 160
as Inner Light, 69
Jesus as, 46
male imagery of, 48
Marcionite dual, 125
Marian intercession, 103
mind as true contact point with, 154
Moses as representative, 138
as nature, 179
shema praising, 8
Unitarian oneness of, 40
See also Allah; Brahman; Trinity
God, existence of
agnosticism, 40
Cartesian dualism, 51
Hume argument against, 91
individual perceptions of, 37
moral law as faith in, 105
ontological proof, vii, 10
Pascal's wager, 148
pragmatic argument, 96
Sartre argument against, vii, 168
Thomist five-way argument for, 185
visible examples, 13
God in Christ (Bushnell), 37
God in Search of Man: A Philosophy of Judaism (Heschel), 85
"God-is-dead" theology, 144
God of the Oppressed (Cone), 43
Goethe, Johann Wolfgang von, 53, 86, 171, 179
Golden Mean in Belief, The (al-Ghazali), 75
golden plates (Mormon), 177
Golden Rule, "negative," 87
Golden Temple (Amritsar), 14, 77, 142
Goliath, 49
Goodlad, John, 155
goodness
dualistic, 123, 202
of God, 10, 40
as God's gift, 16
of humankind, 40, 81, 89, 115, 131, 163
good news (gospel), 99, 100
good works, 92
Gospels, 100. *See also* John; Luke; Mark; Matthew
Gothic War (535-53), 24
government. *See* political theory
Govinda, 175
grace, 148
Anglican emphasis, 45
"cheap" vs. "costly," 33
Hindu sects, 160
salvation through, 16
Unitarian rejection of salvation through, 40
Grant, Duncan, 107
Grant, Jaclyn, 112
Great Britain
Cambridge Platonists, 156
common sense philosophy, 162
conservatives, 36
early Christians, 41, 78, 150
empiricism, 115
Enlightenment, 192
free market economics, 176
humanism, 137
Hundred Years' War, 101
imperialism, 6, 17
Indian independence, 72, 164
Keynesian economics, 107
liberalism, 115
Methodism, 194

political philosophy, 36, 88, 134
Protestant Reformation, 45, 199
Quakers, 69
Roman Catholic reform, 199
Sikh wars, 77
utilitarianism, 25, 132
See also American Revolution; Ireland; Scotland
Great Depression (1930s), 107, 176
greatest good, 25
Greek historiography, 84
Greek philosophy
Aristotelian vs. Platonic view of reality, vi, 13
as Christian influence, vii, 19, 31, 62, 111, 145, 156, 185, 190
cosmology, 9, 61, 184
Epicurean, 61
first Islamic links to, 63, 111
Islamic commentaries, vii, 18, 19, 129
Jewish commentary, 139
mathematics, 157
Stoicism, 133, 201
view of Zoroaster, 202
See also Aristotle; Plato
Gregorian calendar, 94
Gregorian chant. *See* plainchant
Gregorian University, 94
Gregory I (the Great), Pope, 24, **78**
Gregory VII, Pope, 190
Gregory X, Pope, 185
Gregory XIII, Pope, 183
Gregory XV, Pope, 94
Gregory Nazianzus, 99
Guadalupe (Mexico), Marian vision, 27
Guattari, Felix, 68
Guide to Holiness (magazine), 146
Guide to the Perplexed (Maimonides), 139, 167
Guru Dev, 120
gurus, Sikh, 14, 77, 142
Gutiérrez, Gustavo, **79**
Gyn/Ecology: The Metaethics of Radical Feminism (Daly), 48

H

Habad-Lubavitch sect, 170
Hadewijch of Antwerp, 86
hadith, 173
hajj (pilgrimage to Mecca), 11
Halladjiyya sect (Sufi), 80
al-Hallaj, **80**, 104, 158
Hamann, Johann Georg, 91
Hamilton, Alexander, 119, 134
Hammarskjöld, Dag, 34
Hanafi-Maturidi reform movement, 80
Hanafi school, 173
Han Dynasty, 81, 89
Han-fei-tzu, **81**, 89, 174
Han Yü, 131
happiness, 25, 132
Hardenberg, Friedrich von, 66
Hargobind, 142
Hari Kishan, 142
Hari Mandir. *See* Golden Temple
Harlem Renaissance, 54
harmony, Taoist, 113
harmony of the spheres, 157
Har Rai, 142
Harrison, Beverly Wildung, 187
Hartford Female Seminary, 153
Hartshorne, Charles, 187
Harvard Center for Cognitive Studies, 155
Harvard University, 38, 96, 152, 187
Hasan, 64, 158
Hasidism, 34, 95, 170
Hatha Yoga, 149
Hawthorne, Nathaniel, 170
Head Start program, 155
healing
Christian Science, 56
Holiness movement, 146
by Jesus, 99
miracles, 27
Pentacostal, 147

See also medicine
Hebrew-Arab dictionary, 167
Hebrew Bible
Arabic translation, 167
as Church authority, 125
David, 49
early Christian scholarship, 145
Exodus, 85, 106, 138
German translation, 34
inclusions, 8
Latin translation, 99
Marcionite view of, 125
Moses, 138
patriarchs, 5
prophets, 58, 98
Torah as first five books, 138
See also Torah
Hebrews, Book of, 15, 151
Hebrew Union College, 57, 196
Hecataeus, 84
hedonic calculus, 25
hedonism, Epicureanism vs., 61
Hegel, Georg Wilhelm Friedrich, 10, 50, 66, **82**, 110, 185
critique of Kantian thought, 105
idealism, 179
as Marx and Engels influence, 127
hegira, 140
Heidegger, Martin, vi, 12, **83**, 168
Gadamer mentorship, 71
as Husserl disciple, 93
Kierkegaard as influence, 110
Nietzsche as influence, 144
as Postmodern influence, 50
Heine, Heinrich, 179
Heisenberg, Werner, 132
hell, 145
Hellenism, 154, 201
Helmholtz, Hermann von, 105
Héloise, 4
Henry I, King of England, 10
Henry IV, Holy Roman Emperor, 189
Henry VIII, King of England, 45, 62, 137
Herbart, J. F., 153
Herberg, Will, 34
Herder, Johann, 179
heresy
Albigensian, 28
Arian, 15, 99
of Averroës, 18
Donatist, 16
English Protestant, 45
of Hus, 92, 199
Inquisition against, 101, 134, 188
Islamic mystic, 80
of Joan of Arc, 101
Manichaean, 16, 123
of Marcion, 125
of Origen, 145
Pelagian, 16, 99
of Savonarola, 169
of Thomas Aquinas, 185
Vatican II liberalization, 102
of Wycliffe, 199
hermeneutics, 50, 83
definition of, 71
Hermetic Order of the Golden Dawn, 67
hermits, 15
Herod Antipas, 100
Herodotus, **84**, 184
Herschel, William, 20
Heschel, Abraham Joshua, **85**
Hesse, Herman, 144
Hexapla (Origen), 145
Hicks, John, 159, 191
Hidden Hand (of free market), 176
Hildegard von Bingen, Saint, **86**
Hillel, **87**
Hinduism
Advaita Vedanta, 175, 191
campaign against caste system, 72
Dvaita Vedanta, 118
first modern reform movement, 164
Integral Yoga, 17

Jain roots, 121
mystic reform, 159, 191
satyagaha doctrine, 112
Sikhism, 14, 77, 142
Vishishtadvaita Vedanta, 160
in Western culture, x, 30, 191
Hindu Renaissance, 159, 164
Hippo, 16
Hispanics, 32
historical materialism, 82
historiography, 84, 108, 192
history
dialectic, 82
hermeneutics, 71
Herodotus as father of, 84
sociological approach, 108, 134
History (Herodotus), 84
History of England (Hume), 91
History of Rome (Livy), 117
History of Sexuality (Foucault), 68
Hitler, Adolf, 12, 23, 33
Hobbes, Thomas, 61, **88**, 179
Locke's theory vs., 115
Machiavelli as influence, 117
"Hodgson Report" (1885), 30
Holderlin, J. C. F., 82
Holiness movement, 146, 147, 194
holistic education, 155
Holmes, Oliver Wendell, 40
Holocaust, 33, 85, 95, 170
Holy Land
Bahai, 21
birth and life of Jesus in, 100
Christian-Muslim-Jewish claims, 5
Crusades to, 13, 28, 78, 190
Judaism, 8, 188
Holy Spirit, 100, 123, 128, 146, 147
Holy Trinity. *See* Trinity
Hopkins, Gerard Manley, 94
Horace, 61
Hospitalers, 190
House of Hillel, 87
House of Shammai, 87
How Gertrude Teaches Her Children (Pestalozzi), 153
How to Do Things with Words (Austin), 197
Hsiang K'ai, 113
Hsün-tsung, Emperor of China, 65
Hsün-tzu, 81, **89**, 131
Huan, Emperor of China, 113
Huayan Buddhism, 65
Hubbard, L. Ron, **90**
Hugh of St. Victor, 10
Hugo, Victor, 53
human beings. *See* humanity
Human Condition, The (Arendt), 12
humanism, 62, 130, 137, 192
humanity
actualization of potential, 82
as basically evil, 89, 131, 143
as basically good, 40, 81, 89, 115, 131, 163
as basically selfish, 81, 89, 115, 174
as basically sinful, 23, 40, 143
Brahman relationship, 175
common sense philosophy, 162
existential choices, 110
existential condition, 39
existential relationships, 168
as God incarnate, 82
intuitive moral standards, 25
"I-Thou" relationship, 34
liberal theological view of, 37, 40
as machine, 88
perfectibility of, 20, 37, 40
perfectibility seen as illusory, 36
relationship with nature, 59, 66
Romantic view of, 179
self-actualization, 82, 110, 144
self-cultivation, 44
sociological study, 42
as unity of soul and body, 185
utilitarian motives, 25
See also individual

Human Knowledge: Its Scope and Meaning (Russell), 165
human rights, 47, 103, 181
Humbert, King of Italy, 22
Hume, David, **91**, 115, 162
Humphrey, Hubert, 143
Hundred Years' War, 101
Hus, Jan, **92**, 199
Husayn, 29, 64
Hussein, Saddam, 6
Husserl, Edmund, vi, 12, 50, 83, **93**, 96, 168
Hussite movement, 92
Hypatia, 46

I

I and Thou (Buber), 34
Iblis (fallen angel), 80
Ibn al-'Arabi. *See* 'Arabi, Ibn al-
Ibn Khaldun. *See* Khaldun
Ibn Rushd. *See* Averroës
Ibn Sina. *See* Avicenna
Ich und Du (Buber), 34
idealism
  abstract, 152
  Hegelian, 82
  Kantian, 26, 66
  metaphysical, 105
  Platonic, 156
  Spinoza's influence, 179
  transcendental, 59, 66
ideal life, 111
ideas, 91, 162
Ideas: General Introduction to Phenomenology (Husserl), 93
Igbal, Muhammad, 63
Ignatius of Loyola, Saint, **94**
"I Have a Dream" (King speech), 112
image worship, Hindu, 164, 191
imam
  immortal twelfth, 64
  as Koran interpreter, 64
  Shiite, 29, 64, 109
Immaculate Conception, 27, 128
immaterialism theory, 26
immortality, 156
imperialism, 6, 17
inalienable rights, ix, 88, 115
Incoherence of "The Incoherence" (Averroës), 18
Inconsistency of the Philosophers, The (al-Ghazali), 75
Independent, The (newspaper), 76
India
  Brahmo Samaj, 164
  British rule, 36
  Buddhism, 35
  Dvaita Vedanta, 118
  Hindu mysticism, 159
  Hindu revival, 191
  independence movement, 13, 72, 164, 186
  Islam, 140
  Jainism, 121
  Parsis, 202
  partition, 72
  Roman Catholic missions, 182
  Sikhism, 14, 77, 142
  social and political reform, 164
  Vishishtadvaita Vedanta, 160
  Yoga-Sutras, 149
Indian National Congress, 30, 72
Indian-Pakistani War (1965), 77
individual
  as basic social unit, 115
  common sense of, 162
  essence and existence, 185
  existential concerns, 110
  radical freedom of, 168
  rights of, 88, 97, 115, 119
  social role of, 12
individualism, 59
Indra's Net, 65
inductive method, 20, 132
indulgences, 116

Industrial Revolution, 55, 176
Industrial Workers of the World, 22
Industrie (periodical), 42
Inferno (Dante), 19
infinity, 9
innate principles (Platonic), 115
Inner Light. *See* Quakers; Society of the Inner Light
Inner Light Magazine, The, 67
Innocent II, Pope, 28
In Praise of Folly (Erasmus), 62
Inquisition, 101, 134, 188
Inskip, John, 146
Institutes of Christian Religion (Calvin), 38
Instrumentum (Marcion), 125
Integral Non-Dualism, 191
Integral Yoga, 17
intentionality, 93
Interior Castle, The (Teresa of Ávila), 183
International, 22
International Bonhoeffer Society, 33
International Center of Genetic Epistemology, 155
International Church of the Foursquare Gospel, 147
International College of Philosophy, 50
International Monetary Fund, 107
International War Crimes Tribunal, 165
Interpreter of Desires (al-'Arabi), 11
Introducing Liberation Theology (Boff), 79
Introduction to History, An (Ibn Khaldun), 108
Introduction to the Principles of Morals and Legislation (Bentham), 25
inventions, Shaker, 114
Iona monastery (Scotland), 41
Ionian philosophers. *See* Pre-Socratics
Iran, 3, 21, 109. *See also* Persia
Iraq, 6, 29
Ireland, 24, 36, 41, 150
Irigary, Luce, 48
Irish Church, 150
Isaac, 5, 154
Isabella, Queen of Castile, 188
Isagoge (Porphyry), 31
Isherwood, Christopher, 191
Ishmael, 5
Isis Unveiled (Blavatsky), 30
Islam
  Abraham, 5
  Bahai splinter, 21
  Crusades against, 13, 28, 78, 190
  first jurisprudence treatise, 173
  founder, 140
  14 pure souls, 64
  fundamentalists, 3, 109, 140
  Greek philosophy, vii, 13, 18, 19, 63, 75, 111, 129
  historiography, 108
  Iranian Revolution, 109
  legal interpretation. *See Shariah*
  modernism, 3
  monotheism, 140, 164
  Pan-Islamism, 6
  partition of India, 72
  Shiite-Sunni split, 64, 140
  Sikhism, 14, 142
  Spanish Christian converts, 188
  spread of, 140
  Sufi mysticism, 11, 75, 104, 158
  See also Muhammad; Nation of islam
Israel ben Eliezer (Ba'al Shem Tov), **95**
Israelites
  monotheism, 58
  Mormon beliefs, 177
  Moses leadership, 138
  unified kingdom, 49
  uprisings, 8
Israel, state of
  Arab-Jewish relations, 34
  conservative party, 36
  Lubavitchers, 170
  as promised land, 138
  Vatican relations, 103
  Zionism, 34, 57, 106

Italy
  monasteries, 24
  papal power, 78
  patron saint, 70
  Vatican City, 103

J

Jackson, Jesse, 112
Jacob, 154
Jacobi, Friedrich, 179
Jacobite church, 46
Jahangir, Emperor of India, 14
Jainism, 121
Jambu, 121
James I, King of England, 20
James II, King of England, 115
James, Henry, Jr., 96
James, Henry, Sr., 96
James, William, 51, 91, **96**, 132, 152
Jami, 19
Janowitz, Morris, 155
Jansenism, 148
Japan, 35, 65
Jaspers, Karl, 12
Jayatiirtha, Sri, 118
Jay, John, 119, 134
Jeanne d'Arc. *See* Joan of Arc
Jebusites, 49
Jefferson, Thomas, ix, 88, **97**, 115
Jehoiakim, King of Judah, 98
Jehovah's Witnesses, 166
Jeremiah, **98**
Jerome, Saint, 62, **99**, 145, 154
Jerusalem, 49, 98, 190
Jerusalem Talmud, 167
Jesse, 49
Jesuits, 94, 148
Jesus, **100**, 123
  Bahai view of, 21
  divinity controversies, 46, 99
  as God's revelation, 23
  Gospel biographies of, 100
  humanity and birth of, 125
  immaculate conception, 27
  Jewish absolution for death of, 85
  Kingdom of God, 100, 161
  Marcionite concept of, 125
  Mary as co-redemptrix, x, 103
  Mary as mother of, x, 128
  medieval heresies on, 28
  as Messiah, 49
  as Muslim prophet, 140
  nature of, 15, 23, 40, 46, 129
  new covenant concept, 98
  as personal savior, 145
  poverty and self-giving of, 32, 70, 100, 161
  Second Coming, 166, 195
  Stoic Logos, 60
  suffering by, 33
  See also Christology; Lord's Supper; Trinity
Jesus Christ, Liberator (Boff), 32
Jewish Theological Seminary, 85, 105
Jew of Malta, The (Marlowe), 117
Jews. *See* Israelites; Judaism
Jezebel, Queen, 58
Joan of Arc, Saint, x, **101**
John XXIII, Pope (Angelo Giuseppe Roncalli), **102**
John, Gospel of, 60, 128, 201
John of Capistrano, 70
John of Gaunt, 199
John of Salisbury, 4
John of the Cross, Saint, 86, 183
John Paul II, Pope (Karol Wojtyla), 70, 79, **103**, 172
Johnson, Lyndon, 107, 143
Johnson, Samuel, 26
John the Baptist, 58, 100
Joinville, Jean de, 84
Joseph, 128
Joshua, 138
Josiah, King of Judah, 98
Joyce, James, 96

Judah, kingdom of, 49, 98
Judah the Patriarch, 8
Judaism
  Abraham, 5
  Aristotelian thought, 139
  Babylonian Talmud, 167
  as chosen people, 106
  Christian split from, 49, 151
  contemporary applications, 85
  Diaspora, 98
  existentialism, 34
  faith and reason synthesis, 167
  first formulation of dogma, 139
  flexible biblical interpretation, 87
  Hasidism, 34, 95, 170
  Hebrew prophets, 58, 98
  Hellenistic, 154
  Islamic philosophers, 18
  Jesus' relationship to, 100
  Maimonist/anti-Maimonist controversy, 139
  messianism, 49, 95, 170
  mysticism, 67, 85, 95, 188
  piety linked with study, 87
  Platonic thought, 156
  Reconstructionist, 106
  Reform movement, 57, 196
  Roman Catholic relations, 85, 103
  social activism, 85
  Spanish Christian converts, 188
  Stoic ideas, 201
  Torah interpretation, 8, 87, 167
  See also Hebrew Bible; Israel, state of; Israelites
Judaism as a Civilization (Kaplan), 106
Jude, Der (journal), 34
al-Junayd, Abu al-Qasim, **104**
Jung, Carl Gustav, 155
jurisprudence. *See* law
justification doctrine, 169
Justinian, Emperor of Rome, 145
Justin Martyr, 154
Jutta von Spanheim, 86
al-Juwayni, 'Abd al-Malik-, 75

K

Kabbalah, 67, 95, 188
Kali, 159
Kant, Immanuel, 10, **105**, 115, 167
  as Hegel influence, 82
  Hume as influence on, 91
  idealism, 26, 66, 179
  as Schopenhauer influence, 171
Kapital, Das (Marx), 127
Kaplan, Mordecai Menahem, **106**
karma, 121
Karnak (Egypt), 7
Karo, Joseph, 188
Kartarpur (Punjab), 142
Käsemann, Ernst, 116
Kavi Vishtaspa, 202
Kellogg, James, 195
Kemal, Mustafa, 3
Kennedy, David M., 108
Kennedy, John F., 107, 122
kevala (perfection), 121
Keynes, John Maynard, x, **107**, 176
Key to Secrets, The (Khomeini), 109
Key to Uncle Tom's Cabin (Stowe), 180
Khadijah, 64, 140
Ibn Khaldun, 11, 63, **108**
Khalsa, 77, 142
Khomeini, Ruhollah, 3, **109**
Khusrau, Prince of India, 14
kibbutzim, 34
Kierkegaard, Søren Aabye, 23, 82, **110**
Kilpatrick, William Heard, 135
Kilwarby, Robert, Archbishop, 185
kindergarten, first, 153
al-Kindi, Yaqub ibn Ishaq as-Sabah, **111**
King, Martin Luther, Jr., viii, 43, 54, **112**
  Heschel alliance, 85
  nonviolence, 72, 73, 122, 186
King, Martin Luther, Sr., viii
Kingdom of God, 100, 161

Ratzinger, Cardinal Joseph, 32, 79
Rauschenbusch, Walter, 112, **161**, 181
al-Razi, 111
Reagan, Ronald, 176
reality
  Aristotelian vs. Platonic, vi, 13
  human interpretation of, 71
  language relationship, 197
  material vs. nonmaterial, vi
  as mathematical, 157
  as mental, 26
  Platonic, 31, 156
  sense perception of, 185
  See also knowledge
reason
  as basic moral law, 105
  as faith defense, vii, 4, 10, 13, 31, 40, 105, 129, 185
  faith synthesis with, 167
  Greek philosophy, 184
  as intellectual tool, 51
  Islamic modernism, 3
  Islamic theological, 63
  Logos, 60, 133, 201
  in nature, 66
  orthodox belief in faith over, 28
  as political order basis, 66
  revelation by, 115
  sensation vs., 91
  Stoic belief in, 126
  See also Scholasticism
Reasonableness of Christianity, The (Locke), 115
reasoning
  Aristotelian, 13
  inductive, 20, 132
Reason in the Age of Science (Gadamer), 71
Rebel, The (Camus), 39
Reconstructionist Judaism, 106
Reflections on the Revolution in France (Burke), 36
Reform Acts (G.B.), 25, 132
Reformation. *See* Protestant Reformation
Reformed churches, 23, 38
Reform Judaism, 57, 106, 196
reform movements. *See* social reform
Refutation of the Materialists, The (al-Afghani), 6
Reid, Thomas, **162**
Reign of Henry VII (Bacon), 20
reincarnation
  Dalai Lama, 47
  of Hindu Brahman, 191
  Jain, 121
  Platonic, 156
  release from cycle of, 118, 142, 175
  Scientology, 90
relativity theory, 26, 105
Religion within the Limits of Reason Alone (Kant), 105
religious communities
  first American, 172
  Gregorian reforms, 78
  Vatican II modernization, 102
  See also convents; monasticism; *specific orders*
religious experience, 96
religious freedom, 69, 97
religious pluralism, 159
religious romanticism, 37
Religious Society of Friends. *See* Quakers
religious tolerance, 69, 134
Renaissance
  historiography, 84
  humanism, 62, 137
  Machiavellian theory, 117
  Platonists, 156
  women Christian mystics, 86
renewer prediction (Islamic), 75
Reorganized Church of Jesus Christ of the Latter-day Saints, 177, 200
representative government, 36, 132
Republic (Plato), 18, 156
Republic (Zeno), 201

republicanism, 117
Republican Party (U.S.), 36
"Resistance to Civil Government" (Thoreau), 186
responsibility
  existential choices, 110, 168
  individual Jewish, 98
  political, 12
Restoring Hope: Conversations on the Future of Black America (West), 43
resurrection
  divergent Islamic beliefs, 75
  Ghost Dance, 198
revelation
  of first cause, 63, 185
  knowledge through, 148
  neo-orthodox view of, 23
  by reason, 115, 167
  Sufi mystics, 29
Revelation, Book of, 15, 100
revivalism, 146, 147, 194
revolution
  anarchist, 22
  inalienable rights underlying, ix, 88, 115
  Marxist workers, 82, 127
  theoretical opposition, 36
revolutions of 1848, 22, 82, 127
rewards and punishments, 81, 89
rhetorical criticism, 50
Ricci, Matteo, 94
Richard I, King of England, 190
Richard, Mira, 17
Rickert, Heinrich, 105
Rida, Shaykh Rashid, 173
right actions, 25
righteous ones, generational, 95
rights, individual, 97
  Bill of Rights, 119
  common sense philosophy, 162
  inalienable, ix, 88, 115
  law as source of, 36
  See also civil rights; human rights; natural rights
Rilke, Rainer Maria, 144
Ring des Nibelungen, Der (Wagner), 171
Ringsettings of Wisdom, The (al-ʿArabi), 11
Ritschl, Albrecht, 116
Ritschl, Friedrich Wilhelm, 144
ritual purification, 136
Roberts, Oral, 147
Robinson, Fred, 198
Rochester Theological Seminary, 161
Rohan, Duc de, 192
Roman Catholicism
  Anglican break from, 45, 137
  articles of faith, 128
  Augustinian thought, 16
  Barefoot Carmelites, 183
  Benedictines, 24
  Church Fathers, 28
  Counter-Reformation, 94, 183
  Daughters of Charity, 182
  as empire, 78
  in England, 137
  Erasmus critique of, 62
  faith and reason synthesis, 185
  first woman Doctor of the Church, 183
  Franciscans, 70
  Gregorian reforms, 78
  Inquisition, 101, 134, 188
  investiture controversy, 190
  Ireland, 150
  Jansenism, 148
  Jesuits, 94
  Jewish relations, 85, 103
  liberation theology, viii, 32, 79
  Marcionite challenge, 125
  Marian veneration, x, 64, 128
  medieval influential women, 86
  Missionaries of Charity, 182
  modern papal reform, 102
  parochial schools, 172
  patriarchical structure, x, 48
  reform attempts, 62, 92, 116, 169, 199
  Theotokos dispute, 46

Thomist thought, 185
  traditional teachings, 103
  Vatican II reforms, 85, 102
  visionaries, 27
  Vulgate, 99
  women's subordination, 78
  See also Christianity; monasteries, Western; papacy
Roman Empire
  barbarian threats to, 78, 126
  birth of Jesus in, 100
  European Christianization, 41
  fall of, 126, 134
  historiography, 84
  Jerusalem's fall to, 49
  Judaism under, 8, 151, 154
  Manichaeism, 123
  Marcionite churches, 125
  persecution of Christians, 126, 145
  philosopher-king, 126
  philosophical syntheses, 31
  Stoic philosophy, 60, 126, 201
Romanticism, 163, 179
Roncalli, Angelo Giuseppe. *See* John XXIII, Pope
Roosevelt, Eleanor, 143
Roosevelt, Franklin D., 176
Roosevelt, Theodore, 37, 76, 161, 170, 176, 193
Roscelin, Jean, 31
Roscelin de Compiègne, 19
Rosenzweig, Franz, 34
Rouen (France), 101
Rousseau, Jean-Jacques, 4, 61, 88, **163**
  Burke's critique of, 36
  as influence on Pestalozzi, 153
  on Montaigne's self-analysis, 133
  social contract theory refinement, 88, 163
  Spinoza's influence on, 179
Roy, Ram Mohun, **164**
Royal Society of London, 20
Rufus, Musonius, 60
Rule of Benedict, 24, 28
Rule of Columban, 24
Rules of Sociological Method, The (Durkheim), 55
Russell, Bertrand, 91, 96, 132, **165**, 197
Russell, Charles Taze, **166**
Russell, Lord John, 165
Russellites. *See* Jehovah's Witnesses
Russian revolutions, ix, 22, 127
Rutherford, Joseph Franklin, 166
Ryle, Gilbert, 197

S

Saʿadia ben Joseph, **167**
Sabbath, as Saturday, 195
Sabbathday Lake (Maine), 114
Sabbath Prayer Book (Reconstructionist), 106
Sacrifice of Isaac, 5
Sadat, Anwar, 3
Safed, 188
Saint Genet (Sartre), 168
St. Joan (Shaw), 101
St. Louis Philosophical Society, 82
Saint-Simon, Henri de, 42
Saladin, Sultan, 139, 173
Salons, Les (journal), 53
Salt Lake City, 177, 200
salvation
  by faith, 116, 130
  by good works, 92, 116
  grace vs. original sin, 16
  by individual character, 40
  personal, 146, 147
  universal, 145
  Zoroastrian, 202
Salvation Army, 146
samara. See reincarnation
Sanaʾi, 19
sanctification, 194
Sandel, Michael, 12
Sanhedrin, 87
Santayana, George, 91

Santos, Lucian, 27
al-Saqati, Sari, 104
Sarah (Sarai), 5
as-Sarakhsi, 111
Sartre, Jean-Paul, vii, 26, 39, 83, 93, 110, **168**
sati practice, 164
Saudi Arabia, 6, 11, 104
Saul, King, 49
Saul of Tarsus. *See* Paul
Savitri (Aurobindo Ghose), 17
Savonarola, Girolamo, **169**
Scandinavia, 110, 116
Schechter, Solomon, 196
Scheler, Max, 93
Schelling, Friedrich, 66, 82
Schleiermacher, Friedrich, 37
Schneerson, Menachem Mendel, **170**
scholarship
  biblical, 62, 116
  Confucian, 89
  early Christian, 99, 145
  early Jewish, 8, 87
  feminist, 48
  humanist, 62
  Islamic legal, 173
  Jesuit, 94
  Jewish piety linked with, 87
  medieval Christian, 4, 24, 70
  monastery respositories, 24
  Roman Catholic new forms, 102
  Shiite legal, 29
  Talmudic, 167
  textual criticism, 62
  See also text interpretation
Scholastica, 24
Scholasticism, 10, 19, 28, 31, 111, 139
School and Society, The (Dewey), 52
Schopenhauer, Arthur, 105, **171**
Schopenhauer Society, 171
science
  Aristotelian, 13
  collaborative research, 20
  cosmology, 9, 88
  empiricism, 51
  Greek, 184
  hypothetico-deductive method, 152
  Islamic, 19
  liberal Protestant view of, 37
  Milesian school, 184
  natural philosophy, 51
  objectivity of understanding, 105
  Pascal's Law, 148
  philosophy of, 20, 148
  positivism, 42
  pragmatic observation, 96
  Pythagorean, 157
Science and Health with Key to the Scriptures (Eddy), 56
Science of Being and Art of Living, The (Maharishi), 120
Science of Logic (Hegel), 82
scientific method, 42, 53
  for historical analysis, 108
  inductive, 20, 132
Scientology, 90
Scivias (Hildegard von Bingen), 86
Scotland
  Calvinism, 38
  common sense philosophy, 162
  Enlightenment, 91, 176
  Iona monastery, 41
  liberal economic theory, 176
Scriptures on the Transformations of Lao-Tzu, 113
Sea Priestess, The (Fortune), 67
Sebond, Raymond, 133
Secondat, Charles Louis de. *See* Montesquieu, Baron de la Brède et de
Second Coming, 166, 195
Second Crusade (1147-49), 28, 190
Second Great Awakening (1790-1830), 194
Second Sex, The (Beauvoir), 168
Second Sikh War (1849), 77
Second Vatican Council. *See* Vatican II

transubstantiation, 92, 116, 130, 199
Travolta, John, 90
Treatise Concerning the Principles of Human Knowledge, A (Berkeley), 26
Treatise of Human Nature, A (Hume), 91
Treatise on the Device for Driving Away Sorrows (al-Kindl), 111
Treatise on the Legal Precepts of the Koran (ash-Shafi`i), 173
Treatise on the Source of the Laws (ash-Sahfi`i), 173
Treatise on the Witness of Socrates (al-Kindl), 111
Trible, Phyllis, 50
Trinity, 4, 10
  Arian heresy, 15
  Aristotelian logic-based argument for, 31
  Chalcedon decree, 46
  doctrine revival, 23
  Hegelian concept, 82
  Nicene Creed, 15
  Origen concept, 145
  rational view of, 4, 10
  shamrock as symbol, 150
  Unitarian rejection of, 40
Trinity College (Dublin), 26
truth
  Bahai relativity, 21
  Buddhist, 35
  Manichaen, 123
  philosophical vs. revealed, 18
  pragmatic, 96
  Sa'adia's three sources, 167
  three kinds, 10
Truth and Method (Gadamer), 71
tsaddiq (righteous one), 95
Tuskegee Institute, 193
Tutu, Desmond, x, 32, 112, **189**
Twain, Mark, 56, 170
Twelve Shiites, 64
twelve-step programs, 96
Two Treatises of Government (Locke), 115
Tyndale, William, 199
"tyranny of the majority," 132
Tyson, Mike, 141

U

Udipi monastery, 118
Uigur kingdom, 123
Ukraine, Hasidic Judaism, 95, 170
ulama (Islamic religious scholars), 3
  Sufi mystics vs., 75
Ultimate Reality, 191
Unamuno, Miguel de, 83
uncertainty principle, 132
Uncle Tom's Cabin (Stowe), 180
unconscious (Freudian), 105
Underground Railroad, 69
Unification Church, 136
Union of American Hebrew Congregations, 196
Union Prayer Book, The, 57, 196
Union Theological Seminary, 33, 43, 143, 187
Unitarianism, 40
Unitarian Universalist Association, 40
United Methodist church, 194
United Nations, 17, 34, 47
United Society of Believers in Christ's Second Appearing. *See* Shakers
United States
  Buddhism's growth in, 35
  Calvinist influence, 38
  conservative politics, 36
  Constitution, 97, 115, 119, 134
  Declaration of Independence, 97, 115
  ecumenical movement, 181
  educational reforms, 124, 135, 153
  first American-born saint, 172
  Ghost Dance, 198
  Hasidic Judaism, 95, 170
  Hindu Vedanta Society, 191
  Holiness movement, 146
    Jehovah's Witnesses, 166
  Jesuit universities, 94

Keynesian economic approach, 107
liberal Protestantism, 37
Methodism, 194
Mormonism, 177
Pentecostalism, 147
pragmatism, 96, 152
progressive movement, 76, 161
Quaker influence, 69
Reconstructionist Judaism, 106
Reform Judaism, 196
Saint Patrick celebrations, 150
Seventh-Day Adventists, 195
Shakers, 114
Transcendentalism, 40, 59, 163, 186
Unitarianism, 40
unity of being (Sufi), 80, 158
universalism, 159
Universalist movement, 40
Universal Negro Improvement Association, 74
universals
  Aristotelian vs. Platonic, 13
  nature of, 4, 31
  Platonic, 156
  Thomist argument, 185
universe. *See* cosmology
universities
  black studies programs, 74
  eighteenth-century, 26
  humanist, 130
  Jesuit, 94
  medieval, 4, 31
  nineteenth-century, 25
University in Exile, 52
University of Paris, 4, 55
Untouchables (caste), 72
Upanishads (Hindu scriptures), 160, 164
Up from Slavery (Washington), 193
Urban II, Pope (Odo of Lagery), **190**
Usuli school, 29
Utah, 177, 200
utilitarianism, 25, 91
  common sense philosophy, 162
  Hobbesian influence on, 88
  Mill as prime theorist, 132
Utopia (More), vi, 137
utopias
  Christian Realist rejection of, 143
  classless society, 127
  Mormon, 177
  New Atlantica, 20
  Walden-influenced, 186
Utraquists, 92

V

Vaadiraaja Tiirtha, Sri, 118
Vacaspati, 175
Vadakalai, 160
Valentinus, 124
Vardhamana. *See* Mahavira
Varieties of Religious Experience, The (James), 96
Vasubandhu, 35
Vatican II, 32, 85, 102
Vdakali, 160
Vedantadeshika, 160
Vedantagrantha (Roy), 164
Vedantas, 19, 160, 164, 175
Vedanta Society, 159, 191
Vedas, 118, 120, 160
  non-dualistic interpretation, 175
vegetarianism, 121
veneration
  of Fatimah, 64
  Marian, 64, 128
Versailles agreement (1919), 107
Vietnam antiwar movement, 73, 85, 112, 165
Views of the Philosophers, The (al-Ghazali), 75
Virginia Plan, 119
Virginia Statute for Religious Freedom, 97
Virgin Mary. *See* Mary; Marian devotions

virtues, five Confucian, 44
Virtuous City, The (al-Farabi), 63
virtuous life, 60
Vishishtadvita Vedanta, 160
Vishnu, 118, 159, 160
Vivarana (commentary on Padmapada's writings), 175
Vivekananda (Narendranath Datta), x, 149, 159, 164, **191**
Voltaire (François-Marie Arouet), 20, 84, 133, 192, **192**
voting rights, 132, 200
Voting Rights Act of 1965, 112
Vulgate, 99
Vyasa, 149

W

Wagner, Richard, 171
wahdat al-shuhud (unity of being), 80, 158
Wahhabi (Islamic sect), !1, 104
Walden, or Life in the Woods (Thoreau), 186
Wallsgrove, Ruth, 48
Wang Fou, 113
Ward, Lester Frank, 42
Warner, Daniel Sidney, 146
Warrens, Barone Louise de, 163
Warring States Period (403-221 B.C.E.), 89, 174
Washington, Booker T., 53, 76, **193**
Watchtower (magazine), 166
Watchtower Society, 166
Way (*Tao*), 113
Way and Its Power, The (Lao-tzu), 113
Way of Perfection, The (Teresa of Ávila), 183
Way to Holiness, The (Palmer), 146
Way Toward the Blessed Life, The (Fichte), 66
Wealth of Nations (Smith), 91, 176
Weber, Max, 42
Webster's First New Intergalactic Wickedary of the English Language (Daly), 48
welfare programs, 107, 176
Wesley, John, 16, **194**
West, Cornel, 43
Western Female Institute, 153
Western Health Reform Institute, 195
Westminster Review (journal), 25, 132
Whewell, William, 167
Whig party, 115
White, Ellen Gould, **195**
White, James, 195
Whitehead, Alfred North, 165
White Lotus Secret Society, 123
Whitman, Walt, 49, 96
Whittaker, James, 114
Why I Am Not a Christian (Russell), 165
William II, King of England, 10
William and Mary, King and Queen of Great Britain, 115
William of Champeaux, 10
William of Ockham. *See* Ockham, William of
Williams, Delores, 112
Willich, August, 82
Will to Believe, The (James), 96
Will to Power, The (Nietzsche), 171
Wilmore, Gayraud S., 43
Wilson, Edward O., 167
Wilson, Jack (Wovoka), 198
Wilson, Woodrow, 37, 76, 170
Wise, Isaac Mayer, 57, **196**
Wissenschaftslehre, 66
Wittgenstein, Ludwig, 171, **197**
Wojtyla, Karol. *See* John Paul II, Pope
Womanist theology, 32, 112
women
  black womanist theology, 32, 112
  Christian Science leadership, 56
  education for, 153
  first Roman Catholic Doctor of the Church, 183
  medieval and Renaissance mystics, 86
  medieval monastic orders, 70
  Muslim veiling, 109

occult power of, 67
ordination of, 103, 106, 125
  Quaker leadership equality, 69
  Roman Catholic ecclesiastical subordination of, 78, 103
  Shaker equality, 114
women's rights
  Declaration of Independence as basis, 97
  early championship, 18, 25
  Hindu reform champion, 164
  nineteenth-century movement, 69, 73, 132
  Utah suffrage, 200
  See also feminism; feminist theology
Woolf, Virginia, 96, 107
Word and Object (Quine), 197
worker movements, 22, 76, 82, 127
working class, 176, 194
works righteousness, 92, 116
World as Will and Idea, The (Schopenhauer), 171
World Bank, 107
World Council of Churches, 143, 181, 189
World Parliament of Religions, 159, 191
World War I, 23, 107, 186
  Ottoman Pan-Islamism, 6
  pacifism, 165
World War II, 107
  French resistance, 39, 168
  Holocaust, 33, 85, 95, 170
  Integral Yoga, 17
  Roman Catholic rescue of Jews, 102
  theological resistance to Nazism, 23, 33, 79, 116
Wounded Knee Massacre (1890), 198
Wovoka, **198**
Wright, Frank Lloyd, 49
wu-wei (Tao concept), 113
Wuzong, Emperor of China, 123
Wycliffe, John, 92, **199**

X

Xenophanes, 9
Xiao, King of Qin, 174
Xylander, William, 126

Y

Ya'aqov Yosef of Polonnoye, 95
Yadvaprakasha, 160
Yahweh. *See* God
Yale University, 26
Yang Chu, 131
Yasodhara, Princess, 35
Yeats, William Butler, 67, 144
Yemenite Jews, 167
Yes and No (Abelard), 4
Yin Hsi, 113
yin-yang, 113
yoga, 17, 113, 149
Yoga-Sutras (Patañjali), 149
Yom Kippur, 8
Young, Andrew, 112
Young, Brigham, 177, **200**
Young Hegelians, 22
Yverdon school (Switzerland), 153

Z

al-Zahra (shining), 64
Zarathustra. *See* Zoroaster
Zen Buddhism, 35, 65
Zeno of Citium, 145, **201**
Zerubbabel, 49
Zhu Xi, 89
Zion, 49
Zionism, 34, 57, 106
Zion's Watch Tower. *See* Watchtower
Zion Watch Tower Bible and Tract Society. *See* Jehovah's Witnesses
Zoroaster (Zarathustra), 123, **202**
Zoroastrianism, 202
Zwingli, Ulrich, 15